Women in Japanese Studies

Memoirs from a
Trailblazing Generation

WOMEN IN JAPANESE STUDIES

Memoirs from a Trailblazing Generation

ALISA FREEDMAN, EDITOR

ASIA PAST & PRESENT

Published by the Association for Asian Studies.
Asia Past & Present: New Research from AAS, Number 17

The Association for Asian Studies (AAS)

Published by Association for Asian Studies, 825 Victors Way, Suite 310, Ann Arbor, MI 48108 USA.

Formed in 1941, the Association for Asian Studies (AAS)—the largest society of its kind, with over 6,000 members worldwide—is a scholarly, non-political, non-profit professional association open to all persons interested in Asia. For further information, please visit www.asianstudies.org.

©2024 by the Association for Asian Studies, Inc.

Cover Image: Iwami Reika, *Song of the Sea* C (1983), courtesy of Ms. Kato, Tolman Collection, and Jordan Schnitzer Museum of Art.

This book is dedicated to the women who came before us.

©2024 by the Association for Asian Studies, Inc.

All Rights Reserved. Written permission must be secured to use or reproduce any part of this book. Published by Association for Asian Studies, 825 Victors Way, Suite 310, Ann Arbor, MI 48108 USA.

Library of Congress Cataloging-in-Publication Data

Names: Freedman, Alisa, editor.

Title: Women in Japanese studies : memoirs from a trailblazing generation / Alisa Freedman, editor.

Description: Ann Arbor, MI : Association for Asian Studies, [2023] | Series: Asia past & present; number 17 | Includes bibliographical references. | Summary: "Women in Japanese Studies: Memoirs from a Trailblazing Generation brings together trailblazing women scholars from diverse disciplines in Japanese Studies to reflect on their careers and offer advice to colleagues. Most books present research and pedagogies. We do something different: We share lives-personal stories of how women scholars earned graduate degrees and began careers bridging Japan and North America between the 1950s and 1980 and balanced professional and personal responsibilities. We challenge the common narrative that Japanese Studies was established by men who worked for the US military after World War II or were from missionary families in Japan. This is only part of the story-the field was also created by women who took advantage of postwar opportunities for studying Japan. Women of this generation were among the first scholars to use Japanese source materials in research published in English and the first foreigners to study at Japanese universities. Their careers benefitted from fellowships, educational developments, activist movements to include the study of women and Asia in university curricula, and measures to prevent gender discrimination. Yet there were instances when, due to their gender, women received smaller salaries, faced hurdles to tenure, and were excluded from, or ignored, at conferences. Our book pioneers a genre of academic memoirs, capturing emotional and intellectual experiences omitted from institutional histories. We offer lively, engaging, thoughtful, brave, empowering stories that start larger conversations about gender and inclusion in the academy and in Japan-American educational exchange"— Provided by publisher.

Identifiers: LCCN 2023048361 | ISBN 9781952636387 (paperback)

Subjects: LCSH: Japanologists—United States. | Women scholars—United States. | Japan—Study and teaching—United States.

Classification: LCC DS834.8 .W66 2023 | DDC 952/.0099--dc23/eng/20231226

LC record available at https://lccn.loc.gov/2023048361

Contents

1. Introduction, or Blazing Trails Is Always Personal / 1
   Alisa Freedman
2. The Implausible Origins of Becoming an Asian Art Historian / 29
   Ellen P. Conant
3. An Asian Attachment / 47
   Joyce Chapman Lebra, curated by Andrew Violet
4. "In Search of Flowers Yet Unseen" / 61
   Barbara Ruch
5. Against the Odds, Persisting . . . / 85
   Marlene J. Mayo
6. Becoming a Medical Anthropologist / 111
   Margaret Lock
7. Life on Two Tracks / 115
   Takako Lento
8. A Record of Puzzlement / 129
   Phyllis I. Lyons
9. An Accidental Pioneer / 143
   Susan B. Hanley
10. "Another Girl Studying Japanese!" / 153
    Susan Matisoff
11. Becoming a Historian / 165
    Mary Elizabeth Berry
12. Serendipity and Sociology / 181
    Patricia G. Steinhoff

13.	**I Came, I Saw, I Stayed** / 203 Sumie Jones	
14.	**Mae as a Professional Scholar** / 237 Richard Smethurst	
15.	**Margins** / 243 Amy V. Heinrich	
16.	**The Presence of the Past in Life and Scholarship** / 253 Sonja Arntzen	
17.	**Two Children . . . and a PhD** / 267 Christine M. E. Guth	
18.	**Memories of Becoming a Japanese Studies Librarian** / 279 Maureen Donovan	
19.	**The Open Gate** / 289 Janine Beichman	
20.	**Confessions of a Biographer** / 303 Phyllis Birnbaum	
21.	**Backwards and in High Heels** / 309 Merry White	
22.	**Night Train to Tokyo** / 321 Susan J. Pharr	
23.	**From *Chūshingura* to Commons** / 339 Margaret McKean	
24.	**Encounters** / 353 Kate Wildman Nakai	
25.	**I Owe My Career to Men** / 359 Anne Walthall	
26.	**Embracing the Unexpected and Weaving a Life** / 369 Anne E. Imamura	
27.	**My Life in Translation** / 377 Juliet Winters Carpenter	
28.	**Still on the Way** / 383 Eleanor Kerkham	

29. **Growing Up, or How I Learned to Be a Japanese Studies Librarian** / 401
　　Kristina Kade Troost

30. **With a Lot of Help from My Friends** / 417
　　Helen Hardacre

31. **Being an Outsider-Insider** / 431
　　Barbara Sato

32. **Japanese Literature as Refuge** / 441
　　Esperanza Ramirez-Christensen

33. **Historical Periods and Major Events in Japanese Studies** / 469

Bibliography / 509

Index / 575

Discussion Questions / 603

Figures

1.1 Joyce Lebra at Kida Shrine, Fukui Prefecture, circa 1955–1957 / 2

2.1 Ginza Crossing, Tokyo, Japan, circa 1946, showing the K. Hattori Building. During the Occupation, the centrally located Matsuya Department Store was taken over by the US Army and operated as the PX / 31

2.2 Yasui Sōtarō, *Portrait of Chin Jung* (*Kin'yō*), 1934. Oil on canvas / 32

2.3 Hosokawa Moritatsu and Odagiri Mineko near the eastern slope of Mount Myōkō, Akakura, Niigata Prefecture, circa 1958 / 33

2.4 Onchi Kōshirō, *Mother and Child*, 1954. Woodblock print; ink on paper / 37

2.5 Arakawa Toyozō, Shino-style *chawan* (pottery tea bowl) / 39

2.6 Ellen Psaty with Korean artists, Seoul, 1957 / 43

2.7 *Korean Contemporary Paintings*, exhibition pamphlet, World House Galleries, 1958 / 43

3.1 Joyce Lebra, calligraphy practice, circa 1955–1957, location unknown / 55

4.1 In a small temple, Ōjōji, west of Zenkōji, a woman with a vivid pair of hanging scrolls intones the famous medieval story about the Mount Koya monk Karukaya Dōshin, which recounts his son's search for him and their reunion / 70

4.2 Okami Masao (bending), Ichiko Teiji, Matsumoto Ryūshin, and Ōba Takemitsu examine a scroll at Japan Society, New York, September 1978 / 72

4.3 Scholars surround curator Kenneth Gardner at the British Library, August 1978 / 72

4.4 Shiba Ryōtarō, Barbara Ruch, Nagai Michio, and Abe Kōbō at a press conference in Tokyo in 1985, announcing the plan to establish the Donald Keene Center of Japanese Culture / 73

4.5 The Kamakura-period portrait sculpture of Abbess Mugai Nyodai / 74

4.6   A first look at unsorted documents at Hōkyōji Imperial Convent in 1996 / 76

4.7   St. Paul's Chapel, Columbia University; (left) the opening of the service for Abbess Mugai Nyodai's 700th memorial; (right) nuns performing *sange* / 77

4.8   Restorers work on sliding door panels of Chūgūji Imperial Convent in Nara, 2008 / 78

4.9   His Majesty and Her Majesty viewing the *Imperial Convents* exhibition (2009) at Tokyo University of the Arts, University Art Museum, with University President Miyata Ryōhei, Barbara Ruch, and museum curator Kurokawa (Yokomizo) Hiroko / 79

4.10 Reigakusha orchestra members teaching Columbia *gagaku* classes, March 24, 2011 / 81

4.11 Wind professionals who trained in Tokyo on Japanese instruments in Global Artist Residencies: Rosamund Plummer (Australia, 2014), Jinny Shaw (UK, 2016), and Rolando Cantú (Mexico, 2019) / 82

7.1   Takako Lento discussing poetry with Alisa Freedman's seminar, "Women in Modern Japan," on Zoom, May 20, 2020 / 125

8.1   Nine-year-old Phyllis and her mother, Easter 1952, with the specter of Japanese Studies looming behind / 131

9.1   Susan Hanley's passport photograph, 1987 / 148

9.2   Susan Hanley with her husband, Kozo Yamamura, in Bellevue, Washington, 2016 / 149

13.1 Tsubouchi Memorial Theatre Museum, Waseda University / 207

13.2 Meeting with Howard Hibbett (left) and Adam L. Kern (right) in Hibbett's office, 2004 / 217

13.3 Giving a lecture on "Gender, Class, and Repression in Male Homoerotic Narratives of the Early Edo Period in Japan," The Ohio State University, 2017 / 223

13.4 Receiving the 2019 Lindsley and Masao Miyoshi Prize for Lifetime Achievement in Translation and Editing, Donald Keene Center of Japanese Culture, Columbia University. Pictured with Charles Shirō Inouye, Chair of the Selection Committee / 225

15.1 Donald Keene and Amy Heinrich on the grounds of Muryōji, the temple near his home in Tokyo's Kita Ward, taken on June 23, 2017, after a celebration of his ninety-fifth birthday / 249

16.1   Kataoka Shikō, from the *Sarashina Diary*, bifold screen, *Linked Lines: Japanese Women's Texts through Time* exhibition, University of Alberta, 2001 / 264

17.1   Cover of *Shinto Arts: Nature, Gods, and Man in Japan*, exhibition catalog, Japan Society, New York, 1976. Detail of seated female deity. Ninth century. Matsuno-o Shrine, Kyoto. Important Cultural Property / 275

18.1   Maureen Donovan, after winning the Tiefel Teaching Award, 2010 / 285

19.1   Janine Beichman and Donald Keene in Shizuoka, Japan, 2017 / 292

19.2   Performance of *Drifting Fires* at Zōjōji Temple, Umewaka Naohiko as *shite*, Tokyo, 1986 / 297

22.1   Susan Pharr and Margi Haas at the Tokyo Symposium on Women, July 1978 / 331

23.1   Margaret McKean with Edwin O. Reischauer, US Embassy, April 1966 / 341

24.1   Barbara Sato (left) and Kate Nakai (right), Tokyo, September 1963 / 355

25.1   Wilson J. Walthall Jr., PhD, University of Texas, 1947; Anne Walthall, PhD, University of Chicago, 1979 / 361

27.1   Juliet Winters Carpenter in James-kan at the Imadegawa Campus of Doshisha Women's College, 2019 / 380

29.1   Kristina Kade with her host grandfather, Nakatsugawa Naokazu, Hōryūji Temple, October 1970 / 402

29.2   Professor Watanabe Norifumi with Kristina Troost in his office, Hiroshima University, School of Integrated Arts and Sciences, summer of 1980 / 404

29.3   Kristina Troost with Kuramochi Shigehiro and Kuramochi Yasuko in Tokyo, June 2019 / 406

32.1   Esperanza Ramirez-Christensen with Kaneko Kinjirō, Helen McCullough, William McCullough, Tsurusaki Hiroo, Steven Carter, and Mack Horton, University of California, Berkeley, 1980 / 461

32.2   Esperanza Ramirez-Christensen, PhD graduation, Harvard University, 1983 / 464

1

Introduction, or Blazing Trails is Always Personal

Alisa Freedman

All the contributors here offered part of their lives in these memoirs not for themselves to reminisce but hoping to inspire or encourage the younger people who are on their way along or peering into a possibility of choosing the path deeper into our fields. Because of the times we happened to be born in, we groped our way into the untrodden territories of the Japan/Asian Studies field by chance, by fate, or by determination. All of us were consciously or unconsciously adventurous.
—Takako Lento[1]

I was of a generation without words for our experience.
—Barbara Ruch

The through line, Dear Reader, is that work and being can fuse.
—Mary Elizabeth Berry

ALISA FREEDMAN is a professor of Japanese literature, cultural studies, and gender at the University of Oregon. Her books include *Japan on American TV: Screaming Samurai Join Anime Clubs in the Land of the Lost* (AAS Asia Shorts book series, 2021); *Tokyo in Transit: Japanese Culture on the Rails and Road* (2010); an annotated translation of Kawabata Yasunari's *The Scarlet Gang of Asakusa* (2005); a coedited volume on *Modern Girls on the Go: Gender, Mobility, and Labor in Japan* (2013); and an edited textbook on *Introducing Japanese Popular Culture* (first edition in 2017, second edition in 2023). She served as the editor in chief of the *US–Japan Women's Journal* (2016–2022) and has published more than thirty-five articles and chapters for peer-reviewed journals and books, around twenty-five literary translations and co-translations, several guides to academic publishing, and numerous articles for general-interest publications. She is the Faculty Fellow of a university residence hall and has received a national award for her mentorship work. Alisa enjoys presenting at public events like cultural festivals, anime cons, and reading groups.

Figure 1.1: Joyce Lebra at Kida Shrine, Fukui Prefecture, circa 1955–1957. Photograph courtesy of Joyce Lebra's family and the University of Colorado Library.

Note to Reader

You are approaching a book that is personal, unconventional, spirited, brave, inspiring, thoughtful, and honest. There are different ways to read it. You might read it cover to cover, as chapters are arranged roughly chronologically to trace historical changes, while being placed in dialogue to highlight synergies and diverse viewpoints. You might turn first to chapters whose authors and titles catch your eye. Or you might seek out stories that offer particular insights into international relations, genealogies of knowledge production, the formations of jobs, women's struggles and advancements in academia, collaboration, or life-work balance—all topics covered in our book—or stories that model certain writing styles (e.g., humor or poetry). The chapters can be read in any order. To highlight the educational contexts of the United States and Canada and to reveal how notions of US hegemony have influenced the global field of Japanese Studies, all of our authors, even those born or raised outside North America, earned advanced degrees in the United States. A handy reference guide to historical events and turning points in Japanese Studies described in our chapters is appended to the back of the book. The appendix (chapter 33) provides additional context to help a broad readership understand the institutional frameworks through and against which women blazed trails that connected Japan, the United States, and Canada and made inroads toward gender equality. We have provided discussion questions to help readers reflect on and talk about the book. This introduction gives an overview of the themes and aspirations of our collaborative project and sets the scene for the chapters that follow. It explains the keywords in our title—*Women in Japanese Studies: Memoirs from a Trailblazing Generation*.

Women in Japanese Studies

Most academic books present research and pedagogies. We do something different. We share lives—stories of how female scholars earned graduate degrees, began careers related to Japan between the 1950s and 1980, and balanced professional and personal responsibilities.[2] Due to laws, social conventions, business practices, and additional factors, women have faced different choices in work and family and different access to education, jobs, and politics than people of other genders. We bring together thirty-one women whose contributions have been central to Japanese Studies to reflect on their careers and offer advice to colleagues. Included are women who came to study Japan for various reasons—personal, political, cultural, or by luck and by chance—and who have pursued different kinds of jobs, both inside and outside traditional academia, both in Japan and in North America. As Sonja Arntzen (chapter 16) explains, scholars based in Canada and the United States share similar academic organizations and presses and inhabit integrated worlds, but the differences between them provide insight into education and politics. Our contributors based in Japan also work within these American networks. Our book reflects the fact that, especially in the field's formative years, scholars of Japanese Studies were predominantly white or Japanese.

Contributors hail from diverse disciplines—including but not limited to history, art history, literature, political science, sociology, anthropology, religious studies, and library science. They established their careers during an eventful thirty years that indelibly shaped international relations, universities, academic jobs, and women's roles in the workplace and the family. They have promoted scholarly exchange through their research, teaching, mentorship, leadership, service, editing, translations, curricula, the many journals they have edited, the archives and exhibits they have curated, and the organizations and prizes they have founded.

Inevitably incomplete but as encompassing as possible, our book developed through extensive email discussions among women who, when offered the chance to do so, willingly stepped forward to tell their stories in engaging, creative, and scholarly rigorous ways. Authors volunteered to be included or were invited by members of the group who believed that their stories would disclose hidden histories, provide essential records, and encourage future generations.[3] They write in their own words about how they became graduate students, professors, translators, authors, librarians, and administrators, and what their work has meant to them. They discuss how their careers have influenced other parts of their lives: how they met partners and friends on the job, became mothers, raised families while living between countries, learned to be adaptable, stepped out of their comfort zones to gain skills and join groups, dealt with aggressions and worse, coped with losses, and put pressures on themselves to achieve. They explain how becoming bilingual and bicultural led to new opportunities, how ideas of nation had personal resonances. Their passion for their work has driven them to succeed.

This book has several audiences. As observed by a peer reviewer, the book's authors "write for people who work in or aspire to contribute to Japanese Studies, especially for the youngest among us—the students."[4] We foster a sense of academic community by telling stories that resonate with members of other fields; for example, historians of higher education in North America and of gender in the twentieth century will appreciate our discussions of these topics. While describing women's lives and experiences in academia, we also address the bigger picture of how area studies programs have developed and the roles that female academics have played in them. The book is intended to reach members of the general public interested in the cultural history of universities and to assist librarians and bibliographers in building Japanese collections by suggesting sources for acquisition. Throughout the book, we reference women who are unable to write about themselves, for example, due to other commitments, and we remember legacies left by the dearly departed. Teachers and scholars like Takagi

Kiyoko (1918-2011) and Karen Brazell (1938-2012) are prominent among them. This book is dedicated to the women who came before us. As expressed in Takako Lento's epigraph, we hope it will inspire the generations who come after.

As a result, *Women in Japanese Studies* is not an institutional history, exposé, encyclopedia, or time capsule.[5] It is not a defense of area studies, and it does not advocate for one methodology or set of theories above others. Nor is it hagiography. Instead, it is an opportunity to hear polyphonic voices of women who launched their careers during a historical moment characterized both by optimism that education could promote international peace, mutual understanding, and personal development, and by deeply embedded discrimination in the academy and other workplaces. As Sumie Jones writes, "Unlike institutional histories, in which experiences and views are bound into a unified public story that ignores the edges and borders, [personal stories] are based on the premise that any part of the human community should be heard and that each story tells of an individual experience."[6]

The authors have different backgrounds, experiences, and temperaments. They pursue different research agendas and speak different academic languages. It is impossible to fit their stories into one succinct, seamless narrative. Instead, we offer multiple perspectives on, and emotional and intellectual responses to, a constellation of changes that made it possible for women to pursue careers related to Japan in the decades after World War II. We also describe instances when women were not treated equally in job searches, when they received smaller salaries or encountered hurdles to tenure, when they were excluded from, or ignored at, conferences, and when they faced various kinds of harassment. As author Chimamanda Ngozi Adichie states in her much-cited 2009 TED talk, "The Danger of a Single Story," "Stories have been used to dispossess and to malign, but stories can also be used to empower and to humanize. Stories can break the dignity of a people, but stories can also repair that broken dignity."[7]

Gender is one important factor that comprises identity; others include age, class, and location. Some authors write frankly about gender discrimination, sexual harassment, and male-centered institutions, while others emphasize identity factors other than gender. Some discuss the role of context in how they perceived themselves or were regarded by others—for example, standing out as a foreigner while abroad or as the only woman in a seminar of men. We present different vantage points that avoid the pitfalls of subsuming diverse women under a single totalizing idea of gender. We present individual experiences in non-judgmental ways.

Thus, this book is an intervention—a feminist act (although not all contributors identify as feminists)—to provide testimonies that disrupt the dominant narratives that institutionalized power structures in education and codified stories about how fields came to be. We challenge the common view that Japanese Studies was primarily established by men who came to the United States to teach Japanese language and culture before the war (e.g., Tsunoda Ryūsaku and Serge Elisséeff),[8] who were trained at US military language and intelligence service schools during the war (e.g., Donald Keene) and who worked for the Occupation government after (e.g., Herbert Passin and Edward Seidensticker), or who came from missionary families in Japan (e.g., Edwin O. Reischauer and Donald Shively). These men were foundational figures and the professors of the contributors to this book. Yet they are part of a larger, more nuanced story.

We explain how the field was also created by women who took advantage of new opportunities for studying and teaching about Japan during the Cold War decades. Rather than being "pioneers," those who are the first to venture into uncharted territory, they were "trailblazers," people who come after pioneers and who find paths and lay trails to guide others. They followed in the footsteps of pioneering women who are no longer here to write their stories. For example, members of the Women's Army Auxiliary Corps (WAAC) and the Navy's Women Accepted for Volunteer Emergency Service (WAVES), both established in 1942, enrolled in the same military language schools as men and received similar training between 1942 and 1946. (WAAC was made a branch of the Army with active duty status and renamed the Women's Army Corps [WAC] in 1943.) Among them was Helen Craig McCullough (1918–1998), who graduated second in her class from the US Navy Japanese Language School at the University of Colorado Boulder in 1944; she worked in Japan during the Occupation, earned a PhD from the University of California, Berkeley's Department of Oriental Languages in 1955, and became a professor in the same program and an eminent translator of classical Japanese literature.[9] She married fellow Berkeley graduate student, William McCullough. While a student at Reed College in 1942, Hattie Masuko Kawahara Colton (1921–2008) and her family in Oregon were interned at Minidoka War Relocation Center in Idaho. With assistance from the American Friends Service Committee (AFSC), she was able to leave the camp and attend Mount Holyoke College and graduate with a BA (1943) and MA (1945) in political science and a minor in history. In 1949, she earned a PhD in political science from the University of Minnesota; her dissertation explored Japan-US diplomatic relations between 1931 and 1941.[10] She and her husband, Kenneth Colton, whom she met while on Fulbright and Ford Foundation Fellowships in Tokyo, worked for the US Department of State between 1958 and 1989, and she taught at its Foreign Service Institute. The names of countless female Japanese language instructors—many of them Issei (first-generation immigrants), Nisei (second-generation), and Kibei (children born in the United States but raised and educated in Japan), and non-tenured faculty members—contributed to the growth of the field, though their names have too often been lost to history.

The trailblazers profiled in our book are not the first female scholars to bridge Japan and North America, but they are members of the first cohorts of specialists trained at US universities. They are, arguably, a successful tip of a much larger iceberg. Yet citation practices and institutional histories frequently overlooked these women and their contributions to scholarship, pedagogy, and service. To summarize the context explained below, they attended graduate school during decades when Japan was transforming from a former enemy in World War II into an important but "junior" ally against the rise of communism in Asia and an exporter of new ideas and technologies, when both American and Japanese universities were expanding and opening access to more people, and when women and minorities renewed their struggles for equality.[11] Some contributors entered newly established programs in the 1950s. Many others were part of a swell in graduate enrollments at US and Japanese universities in the 1960s and 1970s.[12] They applied for their first jobs when the field was expanding and diversifying, although getting positions and rising in the ranks of academia often proved difficult for women. They established their professorial careers at a time of growing global demands for women's rights and opportunities and during an era of collective activism and widespread protest against social constrictions and political inequities. They benefited from civil rights laws of the 1960s and 1970s, including affirmative action and Title IX of the Educational Act of 1972, which changed hiring patterns and provided measures for preventing and redressing discrimination.

We use the term "trailblazing generation" as shorthand for these impactful thirty years in which the field of Japanese Studies developed and women gained a greater presence in the academy—if, by definition, a generation covers approximately twenty-five to thirty years: the time it takes for infants to become adults and then, theoretically, to have children of their own. The dates and names of generations are not standardized, and they allow room for interpretation. Generations are frequently identified by the events and zeitgeist of their decades, as in America's "Silent Generation" (1928–1945), most of whom were born before or during the Great Depression, came of age during World War II, and established the patterns of their adult lives during the Cold War of the 1950s and 1960s. Members of Japan's first "baby boom" generation, generally called "*dankai no sedai*," a term coined by economist and author Sakaiya Taichi, were born starting around 1947 and grew up during a time of national recovery and economic high growth, while the effects of the war were still vivid and visible. Contemporaneous with younger members of America's "Silent Generation" and early baby boomers (1946–1964), they entered universities in the 1960s amid rising youth attention to global issues, including mass killings and unrest, environmental pollution, and discrimination.[13] Like other generalizing keywords, "generation" risks papering over complexities and fissures for the sake of simplicity and conformity. As Barbara Ruch wrote in a group email on May 22, 2021, "Those of us from the 1950s and 1960s lived a world away, different from that of those in the 1970s and 1980s. . . . We did not (were not permitted to) dress [like they did]; our spoken and body language differed; the nature of colleagues through those decades altered radically; departmental administration was a force of another species."

Despite these limitations, generational frameworks help to explore transformations both synchronically (changes across the group) and diachronically (changes over time).[14] By extension, scholarly generations—the amount of time it takes for graduate students to complete their degrees, get their first jobs, publish their first monographs, and earn tenure or otherwise establish their careers—are useful devices for looking across academic disciplines to see historical confluences, institutional patterns, dominant discourses, and dissenting voices. The title of the book uses the preposition "from"—memoirs "from a trailblazing generation," rather than "of"—to indicate that this time frame is just a starting point and that the authors have been active long after.

A Trailblazing Generation

The memoirs included here are framed within the development of Japanese Studies, and they employ milestones in the field as reference points. Thus, it is helpful to briefly give an overview of some important changes that were instituted and trails that were blazed before 1980 to better understand the context for the personal narratives, as well as their convergences and variations.

Cultural institutions like Japan Society (established in 1907) and scholarly organizations like the Far Eastern Association (the predecessor of the Association for Asian Studies, hereafter, AAS) and its organ, *The Far Eastern Quarterly* (forerunner of *The Journal of Asian Studies*), both begun in 1941, predate the attack on Pearl Harbor on December 7 of that year. But the study of Japan in North America was largely a postwar development that reflected the cultural, political, and economic relationship between Japan and the United States, and to a certain extent Canada, along with contemporary institutional and legal changes in higher education. As analyzed by Helen Hardacre (chapter 30), a 1935 survey showed twenty-five US universities offering courses on Japan; eight of them taught Japanese language. Many faculty members teaching about Japan also taught about China. Only thirteen instructors questioned in the survey knew the Japanese language well enough to conduct research in it.[15] By 1950, there were six departments with an established curriculum on Japan: Yale University (1945), the University of Washington (1946), the University of Michigan (1947), Harvard University (1947), Columbia University (1948), and UC Berkeley (1949). Notably, these six universities were also Civil Affairs Training Schools (CATS) during World War II, programs created and operated by the United States Department of War to prepare Americans for future work in occupied areas in Asia and Europe.[16] Japan was designated as "Oriental" or "Far East" in the program names, marking it as exotic and removed from mainstream subjects.[17] Susan Hanley and Susan Matisoff (chapters 9 and 10) recall taking Edwin O. Reischauer and John K. Fairbank's "Social Science 111," the Asian Studies introductory course at Harvard, which the professors designed in 1947 and students and others involved nicknamed "Rice Paddies."[18] Mary Elizabeth Berry (chapter 11) served as a teaching assistant for a section on Japan. These names can be read as bearing traces of "modernization theory," which ranked countries according to how "developed" they seemed, with white, capitalist, democratic Europe and the United States in the lead and Asia and Africa needing to "catch up," although not all members of these programs shared these views.[19]

The study of Japan grew as a result of a confluence of factors, including faculty specialization, student interest, US Cold War policies, and the growth of universities in both Japan and the United States.[20] Ellen Conant, Joyce Lebra, Barbara Ruch, and Marlene J. Mayo (chapters 2–5) describe a time when American universities were rising in intellectual caliber and cultural influence and stood at the vanguard of emerging academic fields, despite countercurrents of anti-intellectualism and prejudice. A series of national laws supported educational advancement, for example, by making it possible for more students to earn advanced degrees (e.g., the Servicemen's Readjustment Act of 1944, commonly known as the GI Bill), by institutionalizing educational exchange as a means of cultural diplomacy (e.g., the Fulbright Program, which was established in 1946 and first signed with China and Burma in 1947 and later with Japan in 1952), and by providing fellowships for learning foreign languages and funding for area studies centers (especially the National Defense Education Act [NDEA], Title VI, 1958). The Joint Committee for Japanese Studies of the American Council of Learned Societies and the Social Science Research Council (ACLS-SSRC) calculated that a total of $19 million was spent on fostering Japanese Studies in the United States between 1958 and 1970, with more than half of that amount provided by the federal government (including the Fulbright Program).[21] Organizations like the Rockefeller and Ford Foundations also funded Japan-US cultural exchange.

The NDEA exemplified the Cold War-era use of education as a diplomatic tool and means to compete with the Soviet Union. It was inspired by the launch of Sputnik I on October 4, 1957, which initiated the Space Race with the United States, and it sought to increase the number of educated Americans to meet national security needs and to compete with the Soviet Union in science and technology. Title VI established National Defense Foreign Language (NDFL) Fellowships for studying "uncommonly taught foreign languages" like Japanese that were deemed necessary for US defense. Yet the funds came with stipulations and affidavits that raised concerns about academic freedom and complicity. For example, Phyllis Lyons (chapter 8) tells how, until the NDEA was reauthorized and amended by Congress in 1964, recipients of NDFL Fellowships were required to sign a loyalty oath stating that they would not overthrow the United States government.[22] Janine Beichman, who received this fellowship for graduate study at Columbia University between 1965 and 1969, presents a different perspective in chapter 19: "It goes without saying that the primary importance of this support was economic. However, for me and perhaps for others, it had another meaning as well: I had always felt alienated from mainstream American values, but, for the first time in my life, what I did for my private enjoyment was connected to the public good."[23]

Trailblazing women entered graduate programs at universities like Harvard, Yale, and Columbia before these institutions accepted female undergraduates.[24] Many contributors earned BAs from women's colleges, the number of which peaked in the United States in the early 1960s, or state universities that (at least theoretically) made inclusivity part of their mission.[25] At Harvard, women could attend classes alongside men and be advised by the same faculty (who were almost entirely male, assisted by female secretarial administrators), but, until 1963, they earned their degrees from Radcliffe, an associated women's university. Faculty clubs at Harvard, as well as at other schools, were limited to men and their guests. Barbara Ruch (chapter 4) describes her decision in the mid-1960s to become one of very few women to teach at Harvard.

The general view before the 1970s was that there was little economic benefit to knowing Japanese language and culture and that specialists would become academics or government workers. In 1970, the field was still young: the abovementioned ACLS-SSRC report found that five hundred people were "participating in Japanese Studies," 49 percent of whom were below age forty-one (81 percent were younger than age fifty-one).[26] At the time, more American students studied Russian than did Japanese. (Maureen Donovan [chapter 18] majored in Russian at Manhattanville College and studied abroad on a NDFL Fellowship in Leningrad [now Saint Petersburg] and Moscow in the summer of 1970.)[27] Japanese Studies experienced a growth spurt in the early 1970s. One reason described in this book is funding. The Japan Foundation (Kokusai Kōryū Kikin), established in 1972 by the Japanese government, was a major source of professorships, research fellowships, program grants, and data collection on the state of the field. The Japan-US Friendship Act (1975) created a commission to distribute a US trust fund established with the money Japan owed the United States from the reversion of Okinawa and the remaining balance in an account set up in 1962 for educational and cultural exchange.[28] Several contributors to this book won the Japan-US Friendship Commission Prize for the Translation of

Japanese Literature (first awarded in 1979) and served on the advisory councils of these and other field organizations. In addition, Japanese corporations supported Japanese Studies in the United States and Canada, as exemplified by the Nissan Motor Company's donation of $1 million to Harvard in 1973, the same year the Sumitomo Group gave $2 million to Yale.[29] The Japanese government began cost-sharing with the Fulbright Program in Japan in 1978.

The number of US universities offering Japanese Studies tripled between 1970 and 1995; in other words, the number of schools with at least one Japan specialist in 1995 was larger than the reported number of Japan specialists in 1970.[30] The contributors to this book were hired to staff these programs. Many later guided these same programs through budget cuts and changing institutional priorities and acted at the vanguard of efforts to pool resources across the field. For example, Amy Heinrich (chapter 15) was the first chair of the North American Coordinating Council on Japanese Library Resources (NCC), which devised ways to create and share Japanese collections, and she gave the group its long name. Some contributors taught in newly formed women's studies, ethnic studies, and Asian American studies programs. These programs were founded thanks, in part, to the influence of the civil rights movement, the rise of the New Left, student protests, and other activism, and by the recent inclusion of other marginalized groups, including Black and Jewish writers, into university curricula, which still focused on the experiences of white men.[31] Merry White and Susan Pharr (chapters 21 and 22) participated in the First Tokyo Symposium on Women (Kokusai Josei Gakkai) in 1978. As contributors discuss, during their graduate school days, the study of women's history and literature was regarded with skepticism. In the 1970s, Anne Walthall's dissertation advisor at the University of Chicago balked at her idea to research Hōjō Masako (1157–1225), the wife and spokesperson for the first shōgun, and called the study of women's histories a "passing fad" (chapter 25).

All the contributors studied in both Japan and the United States. They could do so thanks to fellowships, such as those from Fulbright, Fulbright-Hays, Ford Foundation, Monbushō (established by the Japanese government in 1954 and called Monbukagakushō, or MEXT, after 2001), and the Japan Foundation. Before travel was liberalized in 1964 in Japan, and while international use of yen was restricted, fellowships from the American government, universities, and private organizations were among the only means for Japanese students to study in the United States. The American contributors here were among the first foreigners to be research students at Japanese graduate programs. In 1953, Ellen Conant, then a PhD candidate at Bryn Mawr College, was part of the first cohort of around thirty Americans lecturers and research scholars sent to Japanese universities by the Fulbright Fellowship Program. She extended her study of art in Japan thanks to a Rockefeller Fellowship (chapter 2). With Fulbright Fellowships, Sumie Jones attended the University of Washington in 1962, and Takako Lento participated in the Iowa Writers' Workshop in 1965, experiences that changed their life courses and career choices (chapters 7 and 13).

In addition to financial support, fellowships provided professional networks, social connections, and other essential parts of the study-abroad experience. For example, from 1949 until it was decommissioned in 1960, the ship *Hikawa Maru* carried exchange students between Japan and the United States. Kate Wildman Nakai and Barbara Sato, then both still in high school, were roommates on the *Hikawa Maru*, an experience that marked the start of their long friendship (chapters 24 and 31). Transpacific flights became more practical in the 1960s. Even today, contributors remember the mix of emotions they felt when first arriving in Japan or the United States. They reminisce about their host families and how living with them encouraged their reflections on gender, politics, and their own places in the world. Kristina Troost (chapter 29) includes a photograph with her host grandfather taken in Nara in 1970 (figure 29.1). Contributors fondly remember staying at the International House of Japan (I-House, established in 1952 and moved to its current building in 1955), using its library (founded in 1953) with the expert guidance of librarian Naomi Fukuda (1907–2007), and meeting colleagues there. They observed their surroundings, and, by coincidence or intention, they bore witness to historical events. Sumie Jones and Esperanza Ramirez-Christensen were at Waseda University during the student strikes (chapters 13 and 32). On November 25, 1970, Joyce Lebra (chapter 3) happened upon author Mishima Yukio's speech at the headquarters of the Japan Ground Self-Defense Force moments before he committed *seppuku*, ritual disembowelment historically reserved for samurai, because she had just arrived on-site to use the library.

Our chapters explain how the study of Japan was also shaped by experiences in the United States. Contributors describe how they coped with complicated American contexts and the contradictory coexistence of intellectualism and anti-intellectualism, of liberalization and conservatism, of openness and prejudice, and with war, violence, and protest. Some trailblazing women were attracted to elements of Japanese culture that were spreading in the United States in the 1950s and 1960s because they seemed exotic and artistic: translations of Japanese literature by authors whose works reflected this image (such as Kawabata Yasunari, who won the Nobel Prize for Literature in 1968), the Japanese Exhibition House at the Museum of Modern Art (1955), forms of Zen Buddhism, judo, and samurai films. Some were deeply affected by politics and activism. Others came from Asia to study Japan in the United States because of the strength of US graduate programs that brought global students together. To many, the Vietnam War era (1964–1975) amplified generational and ideological divides in the field.

A common emotion expressed in these chapters is that of being an "outsider-insider," to borrow Barbara Sato's title of chapter 31. Figure 1.1 shows Joyce Lebra, then a Fulbright Fellow, visiting the Kida Shrine in Fukui Prefecture. As suggested by Andrew Violet, the photograph visualizes the subject positions that American female researchers embodied in 1950s Japan. Lebra, dressed in a travel suit and looking out of place, is the central focus, but the children (right) gaze at the camera, not at her. An unnamed man (left), seen only by his imposing shoulder, faces Joyce (not the camera), a potent symbol of being observed.[32] Barbara Sato writes, "A theme I held with me throughout my career: being able to be an outsider-insider who could 'manage' in circumstances where others might seem uncomfortable or overly foreign."[33] In chapter 7, Takako Lento describes giving a lecture on Japanese culture to schoolchildren in Mitchell, South Dakota, where she and her husband lived, on December 7, 1971, the thirtieth anniversary of the attack on Pearl Harbor: "In the auditorium where two hundred or so students were silently looking at me, I started speaking my heartfelt condolences to their family members and relatives who might have sacrificed their lives or been injured in the war. I wanted these young people to hear what contemporary Japan was like. This experience brought home the need for increased understanding between the two cultures."[34]

Japan specialists in the United States and Canada were expected to master their disciplines, be fluent in both Japanese and English, and be literate in Japanese culture.[35] Some contributors admit that they might not have been accepted to Japanese Studies MA programs today given their initial levels of preparation, but it was a time when programs were developing and successful students had good chances of continuing on to PhD programs or finding jobs. As Helen Hardacre explains, disciplines in Japanese Studies became more specialized, as did other areas of study in American academia: "Graduate training was lengthened, making it possible for students to receive more advanced disciplinary training as well as requiring of them increasingly higher levels of competence in Japanese language and deeper knowledge of their particular subject within Japanese Studies."[36] Many contributors attended the Inter-University Center for Japanese Language Studies (founded in 1961) and were mentored by Takagi Kiyoko, its associate director from 1961 to 1981 and a trailblazing woman in her own right.

Trailblazing women were among the first scholars to use Japanese source materials in research published in English; they filled knowledge gaps about Japan. One of the few books about Japan in the immediate postwar years was *The Chrysanthemum and the Sword* (1946) by anthropologist Ruth Benedict, often the only woman included in accounts of the origins of Japanese Studies before the 1980s. The book was written during the war at the invitation of the US Office of War Information to explain general Japanese behavior and was based on research done in the United States rather than in Japan. It was translated into Japanese in 1948 as part of Occupation efforts to make more American books available in Japanese.[37] The lack of books about Japan available in English meant that many Americans got information from the same sources, including Benedict's wartime study. The trailblazing women here did much to expand these limited cultural canons, for example, by introducing genres of art and literature to broader audiences and by translating works of living writers as well as those of historical women who had been forgotten in part due to English translations favoring men who conveyed certain images and stereotypes of Japan. Susan Hanley and Kate Wildman Nakai (chapters 9 and 24), of *The Journal of Japanese Studies* and *Monumenta Nipponica*, respectively, helped to reshape the academic discussions in the field. Margaret Lock and Margaret McKean (chapters 6 and 23) engaged in social science research that placed Japan in a comparative context. Contributors have been recognized with awards from the Japanese government and from academic organizations for their research, service, and efforts to preserve cultural heritage and increase knowledge.

Trailblazing women expanded the purview of existing disciplines and made important contributions to emerging fields, such as librarianship, modern literature, literary translation, gender studies, and popular culture studies. They participated in debates in Japanese Studies: what to prioritize when translating literature, how to conduct fieldwork, whether critical theories could be useful analytical tools, what roles scholars should play in protests and grassroots movements, and the impact of modernization theory on the study of Japan (to name a few). The field was small enough for most professors to know or know of each other. As the chapters show, the production of knowledge came both from collaboration and collusion, from inclusions and exclusions. In 1980, Barbara Sato became the first foreigner to be accepted as a regular PhD student at the University of Tokyo and one of the first scholars to study popular print media—in particular, mass-circulation women's magazines—at a time when most academic fields divided the culture of the "elite" from that of the "common people" and prioritized the former. As she writes in chapter 31, her examination committee called her research materials "commercialized trash" (*kuzu*) and dismissed her intention to write about them as otherworldly and bizarre "space talk" (*uchū banashi*). She persevered and pioneered methods for studying media representations of women in modern Japan. While engaging in scholarly activities and teaching in Japan, Barbara completed her Columbia PhD in 1994.

In general, the contributors knew they would find jobs after earning their graduate degrees, or even before, but they were less sure whether they could keep them due to systemic gender discrimination (and, in some cases, prejudice against foreigners). They doubted they would make the same salaries as men. Those who applied for jobs in the late 1960s and 1970s benefited from civil rights laws that established legal and institutional systems for promoting diversity. As Susan

Matisoff poignantly remarks in chapter 10, "I was a 'twofer': a woman in a field that had growing significance at a time when women were becoming more welcome in academia."[38] Title IX of the Education Amendments of 1972—which prohibited discrimination on the basis of sex in any educational program or activity receiving federal funding—transformed faculty-hiring practices by making job searches more transparent and equitable, and it gave all genders equal access to university facilities formerly limited to men.[39] According to Mary Elizabeth Berry, Title IX brought about a "near-revolutionary change in the recruitment process—legally mandated and institutionally enforced—at the forefront of female hiring. . . . Title IX transformed the conduct of searches: announcements of jobs had to be publicly placed and selection processes both formalized and submitted to scrutiny. Advertising. Not targeted phone calls."[40]

The number of female professors has increased, but gender gaps persist. For example, a 2018 report by the American Association of University Professors (predating the COVID-19 pandemic, which began in 2020) found that 43 percent of full-time tenured or tenure-track faculty in the United States are women. Around 50 percent of assistant professors and 45 percent of associate professors are women, but only 34 percent of full professors are—fewer women reach higher ranks. Overall, women earn only around 81 percent of what their male colleagues do; female tenured and tenure-track faculty earn 82 percent. Women of color fare worse than white women in academic retention and salaries.[41] The Japanese Ministry of Education, Culture, Sports, Science, and Technology reported that the number of women teaching fulltime at Japanese national, public, and private universities reached a historic high in 2022 of 50,975, or 26.7 percent of the total faculty, a number still well below 50 percent.[42] In general, there have been fewer academic jobs at all levels (tenure- and non-tenure-track) in the early 2020s as universities face budget cuts and the nature of teaching and advising changes (i.e., with larger class enrollments, asynchronous remote teaching, a lack of emphasis on the humanities, and less funding to support graduate students).[43]

As Susan Pharr writes in chapter 22, "All of us bear the marks of the era in which we live. . . . Dating from the early 1970s, opportunities for women were expanding exactly at the time that my career was taking shape. But a second arc is equally important: my career perfectly tracked the arc marking Japan's rise and the ebb and flow of American interest in Japan over many decades."[44] Trailblazing women did not stop after 1980 and continued to pave the way for others. As explained in these chapters, they went on to cultivate Japanese Studies in myriad ways: by writing seminal monographs, translating cultural texts, curating important research collections, editing books and journals, compiling directories, forming organizations, directing academic centers, mentoring scholars, raising awareness of Japan among the general public, and conducting extensive service to the field. In addition to fostering cross-cultural understanding and producing pathbreaking scholarship, these female scholars formed networks, collaborations, and friendships. They changed women's roles in higher education by breaking through gender barriers and setting examples for their colleagues and students. Without these women, Japanese Studies as it exists today would not have been possible. While the struggles they describe continue, their memoirs are not merely tales of discrimination. Instead, they are stories of memory and empowerment.

Scholarly Memoirs

All the contributors here have widely published in their disciplines (and some have written on the broader state of the field), but this is the first time they are publishing essays about themselves for an extensive readership. Generally speaking, a "memoir" is a first-person, nonfictional narrative told from the author's perspective and grounded in personal experiences, knowledge, and feeling.[45] Memoirists also convey their insights on people with whom they are close; in chapter 14, Richard Smethurst tells us about his wife, Mae. Written with the benefits of hindsight, memoirs are contemplations of facts as they are remembered, rather than how they were actually lived. Thus, memoirs show how the present infiltrates the past. Memoirs differ from autobiographies, which conventionally cover lifetimes and order events chronologically. Our memoirs focus on transformative interactions with people, places, and texts; they explain the significance of affective relationships in academia. Chance encounters and serendipities are key themes. The book exemplifies the importance of memoir in revealing who we are and how we want to be remembered. As a result, this collection reads more personally than most academic studies, a quality that is reflected in the conversational titles the authors chose for their chapters. Each chapter begins with the author's bio for easy reference and a quote from her text that captures a main theme of her memoir.

This book is inspired by projects like StoryCorps (begun with a recording booth in New York City's Grand Central Terminal in 2003), whose mission is to "preserve and share humanity's stories in order to build connections between people and create a just and more compassionate world."[46] In addition, this book is part of a historical moment of telling, awakening, and accountability, promoted by movements like #MeToo and Black Lives Matter that create words for discriminations, aggressions, microaggressions, and violence. Public traumas like the COVID-19 pandemic—which made us socially distant, restricted travel, and transformed how we research, teach, and collaborate—along with such personal decisions as retirement, have influenced how we recount our careers and communities. To expand on Barbara Ruch's epigraph at the start of this chapter:

> During these past long months, at a minimum, three world-shaking shifts have occurred in all our lives: the COVID-19 pandemic, the

#MeToo movement, and Black Lives Matter. Every one of these has had a profound impact on our daily lives and the very culture in which we live. The flavor of our daily diet of media, our perspectives on past and living history, have changed fundamentally. We speak now of things never before spoken. . . . In the college dormitory in a town of segregated movie theaters, elderly Black housekeepers called me Miss Barbara. When I taught at Harvard, the word "sexual harassment" had not yet been coined; I was of a generation without words for our experience. At Columbia, as at Harvard, part of the ideals of Nobility and Civility included keeping women faculty out of the Faculty House dining facility unless as a guest of a male faculty member. And in general, keeping women faculty from polluting the male culture, especially its educational philosophy, by vetoing research on Japanese women writers (unless they had died and gone to heaven or hell a thousand years ago).[47]

Megan O'Grady analyzes how memoirs are more than confessions and catharsis and instead implicate readers in larger questions about the coexistence of various "versions on things" and about who has the power to write about them:

> For many of us, writing is a solace, a method of self-sorting, and the ability to share a point of view without being shut down or condescended to has even more weight for those who haven't always been let into the conversation. This is why memoirs by women, immigrants, and minorities of all kinds are often about the effort of becoming a coherent self within larger forces—forces that are inevitably classed, gendered, and raced. For those whose perspectives are missing in the canons and histories we learned in school—who have been long ensnared in the cultural narratives of those more powerful—the memoir has served as a site of redress, a space in which to turn the tables, to make their experiences visible and their stories heard: a passage not only into literature but into a larger acceptance.[48]

To go beyond confession and catharsis, we write "scholarly memoirs": personal accounts with conversational titles and academic footnotes. We combine subgenres of "academic memoirs"—accounts structured around and legitimized by records of scholastic achievements—and "professional memoirs"—accounts of setbacks and accomplishments that chart career trajectories and locate overarching themes in one's work.[49] We look inward and delve deeper to write more than the kinds of academic narratives we prepare for tenure and promotion and outline on our CVs; we tell stories that encourage readers to reflect on their own careers, that provide mentorship, and that thank the people who helped us along the way.[50] Because the act of memoir writing is daunting, and to help our book cohere, book contributors were given guiding questions: (1) What brought you to Japanese Studies? (2) What do you see as the most important work that you have done in terms of scholarship, translation, curation, librarianship, teaching, service, and/or other fields? (3) How has your field changed? (4) What advice do you have for scholars beginning their careers? According to Cynthia G. Franklin, academic memoirs "offer crucial insights into the academy because, in offering spaces that are more musing and pliable than those afforded by theory, they can display contradictions between the personal and political without having to reconcile them."[51] The political value of memoirs comes in using them as tools to initiate change.

Authors wrote their chapters specifically for *Women in Japanese Studies* and experimented with storytelling forms. The variety of writing styles keeps readers engaged. Book chapters differ in content, style, and disposition. Some chapters are funny. Others are poignant. All are personal. Some contributors frame their memoirs within larger political events—the Occupation, the Cold War, the civil rights movement, Ampo, student protests in the Philippines, and the Vietnam War, to name a few—and broader academic developments like affirmative action, the founding of women's studies in the 1970s, and the formulation of new theories and methodologies. Some introduce an influential source text, event, achievement, or anecdote. Some reflect on their mentors and generational changes in the academic job market. Some convey what it is like to be part of two cultures at once and to be an "outsider-insider." Some, including librarians Amy Heinrich, Maureen Donovan, and Kristina Troost (chapters 15, 18, and 29), articulate how they founded collections. Some delve into more than one theme to explain how diverse experiences coalesce to form our identities. Contributors include poems inspired by their research and creative nonfiction inspired by their translations. Sonja Arntzen (chapter 16) pays homage to women's poetic diaries (*nikki*) from the Heian period, and Phyllis Lyons (chapter 8) notes the influence of Dazai Osamu. Our memoirs bear traces of the sundry personal accounts that we study, record, and teach—travelogues, tanka poems, oral histories of Americans who lived in Japan, interviews with members of Japan's radical Left, and more. We account for the different ways in which people have processed, narrated, circulated, and consumed their own and others' experiences. Most photographs are from the authors' personal collections; more than merely illustrative, they show the people and things we value.

Rather than breaking the chapters into sections or limiting their scope by confining them into categories, the memoirs are arranged roughly according to when the authors began their academic careers. This organization illustrates multiple themes and highlights synergies, while illuminating key movements in Japanese Studies and changes in higher education. Thus, *Women in Japanese Studies* speaks in multiple voices without corralling them into one overarching narrative. While grounded in the particulars of Japanese Studies, the memoirs describe events and emotions that have affected people who identify as women in other fields.

We hope that the book starts larger conversations about gender and inclusion in the academy and educational interchange and shows how intertwined the personal and professional are and can be. What we consider most meaningful about our experiences provides insight into larger issues concerning gender, nation, and education. The accomplishments and setbacks of this important scholarly generation teach us lessons about women's roles in the workplace, household, and nation. We show how individual choices—like those to study and teach abroad, master languages, translate, collaborate, become a mentor or an advisee, and create collections and records—can pay unexpected dividends for larger populations. We model new forms of scholarly memoir that capture emotional and intellectual experiences omitted from existing histories. We hope that *Women in Japanese Studies* encourages trailblazers of any gender, generation, and geography to tell their stories and to provide broader, more personal views of the histories of academic fields.

Authors refer to people by names that reflect their relationships with them, their personal levels of politeness, and their own writing styles; they use the terms that are most natural to them. Some call their advisors by their last names, sometimes with a title like "professor" or "*sensei*," while others use first names. We have decided to give full names at first mention and then not to standardize modes of address so long as people can be identified across chapters. Japanese names are given in the Japanese order of surname before given name for people who have careers primarily in Japan; the English order (given names before surnames) is used for those who work primarily in North America. Making this variety in naming visible shines a broader spotlight on the diverse experiences, personalities, and academic approaches in the book. Similarly, we have decided not to standardize English translations of the titles of texts. Authors give slightly different dates for major periods, like Heian and Edo, based on their research. We have included a list of Japanese time periods in the appended reference guide. Following the Hepburn romanization system, macrons are used to indicate long or sustained vowel sounds (for example, *rōnin*), with the exception of words commonly used in English, like "Tokyo" (not "Tōkyō") and "Kyoto" (not "Kyōtō").

Collaboration makes the book special. We are grateful to Carol Gluck, Miriam Kingsberg Kadia, Kathryn Whalen, Joan Ericson, Daniel Botsman, and Rebecca Copeland for serving as editorial advisors. The introduction and appendix benefited from feedback from Carol, Miriam, and Joan and from the book's authors. Marlene Mayo offered invaluable historical insights. Christina Laffin helped conceive the project and collaborated on an initial grant application. We are grateful for input from William Tsutsui, Jan Bardsley, David Reynolds, and two helpful, anonymous book reviewers. Kazie and Sho Sato helped complete Barbara Sato's chapter after her death in December 2021. Thanks to AAS editors David Kenley and Jon Wilson for their expertise, support, patience, and kindness. Our book is a testament to AAS's efforts to develop and archive Asia-related fields; AAS has brought together the contributors. We thank Michael Jauchen for his expert proofreading. Phyllis Birnbaum's chapter is an updated version of the introduction to her book *Modern Girls, Shining Stars, The Skies of Tokyo: Five Japanese Women* (1999). Maureen Donovan's chapter is a substantially revised, more personalized version of her article, "Those Were the Days! A Short History of the East Asian Libraries Cooperative World Wide Web," *Journal of East Asian Libraries*, no. 124 (2001): 19–22. We thank Columbia University Press and the *Journal of East Asian Libraries* for reprint permissions.

The book cover features Iwami Reika's (1927–2020) woodblock print *Song of the Sea C* (1983), comprised of geometric shapes, woodgrain textures, and gold leaf.[52] The print—created by a female artist and donated to the Jordan Schnitzer Museum of Art at the University of Oregon by Yoko Matsuoka McClain (1924–2011), a trailblazing professor of Japanese language and cross-cultural communication and an inspiration for the book—is a visual metaphor for many of our themes, including transpacific journeys, mobility, transitions, feeling in-between, navigating troubled waters, making waves, and having ripple effects by stirring up systems and initiating change.[53] We thank Ms. Kato, Iwami's niece, the Tolman Collection, and the Jordan Schnitzer Museum of Art for the use of the print; Anne Rose Kitakawa for suggesting it; and Jonathan Smith for obtaining the image rights.

Notes

[1] Takako Lento, email message, September 23, 2022.

[2] The idea of "sharing lives" is thanks to Merry White. By "North America," we mean the United States and Canada. We were unable to include scholars based in Mexico and Central America and hope that they might write a book about their experiences. For a thought-provoking discussion on race and positionality in Asian Studies, see Will Bridges, Nitasha Tamar Sharma, and Marvin D. Sterling, eds., *Who Is the Asianist?: The Politics of Representation in Asian Studies* (New York: Columbia University Press, 2022).

[3] Our project was conceived as two related panels (sponsored by the Northeast Asia Council of the Association for Asian Studies) for the 2020 Association for Asian Studies (AAS) conference, which was canceled due to the COVID-19 pandemic. After the cancellation, panel participants continued to collaborate, turned our talks into essays, and

invited additional contributors. We discussed the content of the book over thousands of emails. Book chapters went through a rigorous internal editing process, and contributors read and commented on each other's chapters. This extensive review solidified our community. We shared sample chapters with our target readership of scholars, teachers, students, and non-specialists. Their feedback helped us determine the amount of cultural context to include. For example, thanks to students' suggestions, we refer to English-language sources in our endnotes that provide additional information. Takako Lento joined my University of Oregon seminars on "Women in Modern Japan" by Zoom in 2020 and 2021 to discuss her poetry and translations (figure 7.1).

I am not a member of the generation profiled in this book but am someone who has walked in the trails they have blazed. I undertook many time-consuming, labor-intensive roles in this complex book—including project organizer, director, editor, researcher, and writer—out of my admiration for the contributors, whose works I have used in my teaching and research. I am indebted to them for cultivating the fields I have chosen and combined in my career. I look to them as role models for how to be an engaged scholar. I began this project because I wanted to preserve their stories as a valuable resource and means to understand our current moment. I have defended the book against grant reviewers and university administrators who said that compiling women's stories is not "research." Instead, every step of this book has required extensive research from the book authors and me, from deciding which stories to include and how to tell them to contextualizing the larger lessons they teach. Our book pioneers new uses of area studies education and new forms of academic writing.

I have also served as a guide. My editorial goal was to help everyone more effectively tell stories in their own voices, while drawing out synergies among chapters and making the book accessible to a wide range of readers. Simply stated, I believe editing makes a text more readable. Editors help authors convey content clearly and accurately in a well-organized manner with proper citations. Editing requires critical thinking, knowledge of the topic, judgment about what and how much to revise, writing ability, familiarity with style rules, and interpersonal communication, among other skills. (For a no-nonsense list of guidelines, see Josh Bernoff, "The 11 Qualities of Highly Paid, Ultra-Valuable Editors," *Without Bullshit*, April 12, 2017, https://withoutbullshit.com/blog/11-qualities-wickedly-valuable-editors.) I aspire to this quote by journalist David Carr: "Editors create fine stories by typing on a keyboard composed of human beings. Knowing which key to hit when and how hard to press is both an art and craft. The greats manage to be both collegial and decisive." David Carr, quoted in Insider Staff, "What Makes a Great Editor? Part 1," *Times Insider*, June 16, 2014, https://archive.nytimes.com/www.nytimes.com/times-insider/2014/06/16/what-makes-a-great-editor-part-i/#:~:text=A%20good%20editor%20is%20the,rare%2C%20but%20can%20produce%20treasure.

[4] I thank an anonymous peer reviewer for this observation.

[5] The history of Japanese Studies has been widely documented, described, and debated, as evident by these three examples. First, organizations like AAS, the Japan Foundation, the Social Science Research Council (SSRC), and the American Council of Learned Societies (ACLS) have conducted surveys and compiled directories to assess the results of funding,

needs for support, and dominant trends, and to facilitate communication among scholars. Patricia Steinhoff (chapter 12) led the data collection for the Japan Foundation's multi-year book series, *Survey of Japan Specialists and Japanese Studies Institutions in North America*. As Mary Elizabeth Berry explains in chapter 11, "There, and particularly in the analytical volumes *Japanese Studies in the United States*, Pat tells us who we are, with masterful interpretation of the information collected. An anatomist of the highest order, she underwrote most conscientious planning for the future. (Like my counterparts, I kept her surveys to hand as chair of Berkeley's Center for Japanese Studies.)" [See chapter 12, page 176.] Patricia Steinhoff, ed., *Japanese Studies in the United States: Directory of Japan Specialists and Japanese Studies Institutions in the United States and Canada*, 2 vols. (Ann Arbor: Association for Asian Studies, 1989); *Directory of Japan Specialists and Japanese Studies Institutions in the United States and Canada, Fourth Edition, 2016 Update*, 3 vols. (Honolulu: University of Hawai'i Press, 2016); *Japanese Studies in the United States in the 1990s* (Ann Arbor: Japan Foundation and Association for Asian Studies, 1996); *Directory of Japan Specialists and Japanese Studies Institutions in the United States and Canada, Third Edition*, 3 vols. (Honolulu: University of Hawai'i Press, 2006); *Japanese Studies in the United States and Canada: Continuities and Opportunities* (Honolulu: University of Hawai'i Press, 2007).

Second, scholars have reflected on genealogies of the field. Helen Hardacre wrote a useful history of Japanese Studies and invited colleagues from across the humanities and social sciences to describe key turning points in their disciplines; Helen Hardacre, ed., *The Postwar Developments of Japanese Studies in the United States* (Leiden: Brill, 1998). Paula Curtis used methods from the emerging field of digital humanities to chart hiring patterns; Paula R. Curtis, "East Asia-Related Job Market Report (2021–2022)," Paula R. Curtis, July 31, 2022, http://prcurtis.com/projects/jobs2022/. Other scholars have passionately engaged in debates—for example, over the use of critical theories, the construction of cultural canons, and legal and ethical issues. See, for example, Harry Harootunian and Naoki Sakai, "Dialogue: Japanese Studies and Cultural Studies," *positions* 7, no. 2 (1999), 593–647; John Whittier Treat, "Japan Is Interesting: Modern Japanese Literary Studies Today," *Japan Forum* 30, no. 3 (2018), 421–440; Mark McLelland, "Introduction: The End of 'Cool Japan'?," in *End of Cool Japan: Ethical, Legal, and Cultural Challenges to Japanese Popular Culture*, edited by Mark McLelland (Oxford: Routledge, 2017), 1–31.

Third, librarians have recorded the development of Japanese research collections. For example, Maureen Donovan (chapter 18) describes the impact of the growth of the internet and the globalization of manga on research libraries; Maureen Donovan, "Those Were the Days! A Short History of the East Asian Libraries Cooperative World Wide Web," *Journal of East Asian Libraries* 124 (2001), 19–22; "Challenges of Collecting Research Materials on Japanese Popular Culture: A Report on Ohio State's Manga Collection," in *In Praise of Film Studies: Essays in Honor of Mamoru Makino*, edited by Aaron Gerow and Abé Mark Nornes (Yokohama: Kinema Club and Trafford Publishing, 2001), 225–232. The North American Coordinating Council on Japanese Library Resources (NCC) has archived documents from the group's history and has interviewed trailblazing librarians, including Amy Heinrich and Kristina Troost; NCC, "Japanese

Studies Multimedia History Project: Overview," January 16, 2022, https://guides.nccjapan.org/multimediahistory; "Curated Archives: NCC Background," August 10, 2022, https://guides.nccjapan.org/archive. Frank Joseph Schulman has produced indexed bibliographies of dissertations written on Asia, including *Japan and Korea: An Annotated Bibliography of Doctoral Dissertations in Western Languages, 1877–1969* (Ann Arbor: University of Michigan Center for Japanese Studies, 1970).

[6] Sumie Jones, email message, March 4, 2020.

[7] Chimamanda Ngozi Adichie, "The Danger of a Single Story," TEDGlobal, October 7, 2009, https://www.ted.com/talks/chimamanda_ngozi_adichie_the_danger_of_a_single_story?language=en.

[8] Tsunoda (1877–1964), a graduate of Tokyo Senmon Gakkō (which became Waseda University), taught in Japan and Hawaiʻi. In 1917, he went to Columbia University at age forty to study aspects of American culture. He became a teacher of Japanese language and literature and helped to expand Columbia's Japanese library collection and, with Wm. Theodore de Bary and Donald Keene, compiled two volumes of *Sources of Japanese Tradition*, anthologies of translations of Japanese cultural texts; "Profile of Tsunoda Ryūsaku," Global Japanese Studies, Waseda University, n.d., https://www.waseda.jp/flas/gjs/en/research/profile; Tsunoda Ryūsaku, Wm. Theodore de Bary, and Donald Keene, *Sources of Japanese Tradition*, Vol. I (New York: Columbia University Press, 1958); Tsunoda Ryūsaku, Wm. Theodore de Bary, and Donald Keene, *Sources of Japanese Tradition*, Vol. II (New York: Columbia University Press, 1964).

Elisséeff (1889–1975) was the first European to graduate from Tokyo Imperial University (which became the University of Tokyo). He later served as the inaugural director of the Harvard-Yenching Institute (1934–1956); Edwin O. Reischauer, "Serge Elisséeff," *Harvard Journal of Asiatic Studies* 20, no. 1/2 (June 1957), 1–25. Marlene Mayo, Phyllis Lyons, and Susan Matisoff (chapters 5, 8, and 10) used the language textbooks Elisséeff wrote with Reischauer in the 1940s: Edwin O. Reischauer and Serge Elisséeff, *Elementary Japanese for University Students: Vocabularies, Grammars, and Notes* (Cambridge, MA: Harvard University Press, 1942); Serge Elisséeff, Edwin O. Reischauer, and Takehiko Yoshihashi, *Elementary Japanese for College Students* (Cambridge, MA: Harvard-Yenching Institute, 1944).

[9] See Mary Elizabeth Berry, et al. "Helen Craig McCullough, East Asian Languages: Berkeley," *Online Archives of California*, 1998, https://oac.cdlib.org/view?docId=hb1p30039g;NAAN=13030&doc.view=frames&chunk.id=div00035&toc.depth=1&toc.id=&brand=oac4.

[10] "Obituaries: Hattie Masuko Kawahara Colton '43," *Reed Magazine*, May 2009, https://www.reed.edu/reed-magazine/in-memoriam/obituaries/may2009/hattie-masuko-kawahara-colton-1943.html; University of Minnesota, "Commencement Program, 1949," n.d., University of Minnesota Digital Conservancy, https://hdl.handle.net/11299/57572; Hattie Masuko Kawahara, "Diplomatic Relations between the United States and Japan from 1931 to 1941," PhD Diss., University of Minnesota, 1949. Joyce Lebra (chapter 3) was also mentored by Kawahara's supervisor, political scientist Harold Quigley. Barbara Ruch (chapter 4) worked for AFSC relief efforts in 1950s Japan.

11 For more discussion on the cultivation of Japan into America's "junior" ally in the immediate postwar years, see Naoko Shibusawa, *America's Geisha Ally: Reimagining the Japanese Enemy* (Cambridge, MA: Harvard University Press, 2010).

12 SSRC-ACLS Joint Committee on Japanese Studies, *Japanese Studies in the United States: A Report on the State of the Field, Current Resources, and Future Needs* (New York: SSRC-ACLS, 1970), 13–15. For statistics and analysis, see Marius B. Jansen, "Stages of Growth," *Japanese Studies in the United States: Part 1, History and Present Condition* (Tokyo: Japan Foundation, 1988), 48–62. Reasons outside Japanese Studies include increases in student financial aid under the Higher Education Act of 1965 and changing cultural perceptions of graduate degrees.

13 For a helpful chart and topography of Japanese generations, see "Japanese Generations: Boom, Bubble, and Ice Age," *Nippon.com*, May 12, 2022, https://www.nippon.com/en/japan-data/h00535/japanese-generations-boom-bubble-and-ice-age.html. Japan's second baby boom generation started around 1971.

14 Intergenerational conversations are helpful ways to discuss changes over larger periods of time or to focus on a unifying experience. A prime example is Mari Yoshihara, ed., *Unpredictable Agents: The Making of Japan's Americanists during the Cold War and Beyond* (Honolulu: University of Hawai'i Press, 2021). Satoko Suzuki and Junko Mori edited "Our Challenges and Triumphs: Female Asian Faculty in Leadership Positions in US Colleges and Universities" as a special section of *Japanese Language and Literature* 56, no. 1 (April 2022), 209–285. Eight women born in Japan between the 1950s and 1980s explain how they became program directors and university administrators and give practical advice (for example, on professional conduct) for future academic leaders; Satoko Suzuki and Junko Mori, "Our Stories as Female Asian Leaders: Introduction," *Japanese Language and Literature* 56, no. 1 (April 2022), 211.

15 Helen Hardacre, "Japanese Studies in the United States: Present Situation and Future Prospects," *Asia Journal* 1, no. 1 (1994), 18.

16 Jansen, "Stages of Growth," 42. See "Civil Affairs Training School Records," Online Archive of California, n.d., https://oac.cdlib.org/findaid/ark:/13030/tf8t1nb33h/ (accessed July 7, 2023).

17 Examples in this book include Berkeley's Department of Oriental Languages, Harvard's Far Eastern Languages Department, the University of Washington's Far Eastern and Russian Institute, University of Iowa's Chinese and Oriental Studies Department, the University of Maryland's Oriental and Hebrew Program, and the University of Chicago's Oriental Institute (the last in the list to change its name, becoming in 2023 the Institute for the Study of Ancient Cultures, West Asia & North Africa). "Oriental Institute Changes Name to the Institute for the Study of Ancient Cultures, West Asia & North Africa," *UChicago News*, April 4, 2023, https://news.uchicago.edu/story/oriental-institute-changes-name-institute-study-ancient-cultures-west-asia-north-africa.

18 Course materials inspired books: Edwin O. Reischauer and John King Fairbank, *East Asia: The Great Tradition* (Boston: Houghton Mifflin Company, 1960); John K. Fairbank, Edwin O. Reischauer, and Albert M. Craig, *East Asia: The Modern Transformation*

(Boston: Houghton Mifflin Company, 1965); Edwin O. Reischauer and John K. Fairbank, *East Asia: Tradition and Transformation* (Boston: Houghton Mifflin Company, 1973).

[19] Shibusawa, 5. Edward Said's groundbreaking work *Orientalism* (New York, Vintage Books, 1978) analyzed how European literature (read: culture) and the academic study of the Middle East supported imperialist projects and created notions of difference between the "civilized West" and the "backward East," as well as beliefs that the East could learn from the West but not the other way around. Orientalism involves the production of knowledge, often by experts who purport to explain or represent a place that seems "faraway" to their audiences. Orientalism has been a means through which people who perceive themselves as being part of the "modern, civilized world" (read: West, the Occident) have described the so-called "East" as less developed and stuck in time; the West relies on the idea of the Orient to construct its own identity. More than being a set of knowledge about culture, Orientalism entails how the West perceives the Orient and represents it as its foil to distinguish itself from it, to lovingly celebrate it, or to exert its superiority over it. In *Women in Japanese Studies*, we consider how Orientalism influences how we view, study, and globalize culture. We expand and challenge Said's definitions by accounting for the intersection of power structures—those impacted by gender, race, class, and regional locations, in addition to nation—that have constructed Japanese Studies in North America. We question if Japanese Studies has inadvertently institutionalized Orientalism.

[20] Other books that explore how the formation of academic fields is implicated in notions of nation and hegemony include Miriam Kingsberg Kadia, *Into the Field: Human Scientists of Transwar Japan* (Stanford: Stanford University Press, 2020); Takeshi Matsuda, *Soft Power and Its Perils: U.S. Cultural Policy in Early Postwar Japan and Permanent Dependency* (Stanford: Stanford University Press, 2007).

[21] Marius B. Jansen, "History: General Survey," *Japanese Studies in the United States: Part 1, History and Present Condition* (Tokyo: Japan Foundation, 1988), 21.

[22] See, for example, "Monro Attacks Disclaimer Affidavit," *The Harvard Crimson*, October 24, 1959, https://www.thecrimson.com/article/1959/10/24/monro-attacks-disclaimer-affidavit-pa-vote/; "Congress Votes to Discontinue NDEA Disclaimer Affidavit," *The Colby Echo*, October 19, 1962, 1.

[23] See chapter 19, page 291.

[24] Harvard began awarding graduate degrees to women starting in 1963. "Women at Harvard," Harvard University Archives, October 7, 2022, https://guides.library.harvard.edu/c.php?g=1108872&p=8085578. Yale admitted female graduate students in 1892 but did not accept female undergraduates until 1969, the same year that Princeton went coed. "A Timeline of Women at Yale," Office of Public Affairs and Communications, Yale University, 2023, https://celebratewomen.yale.edu/history/timeline-women-yale#:~:text=November%201968,November%204th%2C%20Coeducation%20week%20 commences. In 1961, Sabra Follett Meservey became the first woman to be a regular graduate student at Princeton, notably in the Department of Oriental Studies. She earned a PhD in Turkish history in 1966; "History of Women at Princeton University," Princeton University Library, June 14, 2022, https://libguides.princeton.edu/c.

php?g=84581&p=543232. In 1886, astronomer Winifred Edgerton became the first woman to earn a graduate degree at Columbia University. The first Japanese woman in history to earn a PhD, Arai Tsuru (1886–1915), did so at Columbia University in psychology in 1912. On her graduation day, she married her husband, Haruguchi Takejirō, who became a professor at Waseda University. She died of tuberculosis at age twenty-nine; "Coeducation at Columbia," Columbia University Libraries, n.d., https://library.columbia.edu/libraries/cuarchives/resources/coeducation.html (January 1, 2023); Izumi Etsuko, dir., *Shinrigakusha Tsuruko Haruguchi no seishun* (The Young Days of Pyschologist Haruguchi Tsuruko) (Tokyo: Tess Planning, 2007).

Female undergraduates were permitted to attend Ivy League universities through relationships with affiliated women's colleges, for example Columbia with Barnard, Harvard with Radcliffe, and Brown with Pembroke; Marcia Synnott, "A Friendly Rivalry: Yale and Princeton Universities Pursue Parallel Paths to Coeducation," in *Going Coed: Women's Experiences in Formerly Men's Colleges and Universities, 1950–2000*, edited by Leslie Miller-Bernal and Susan L. Poulson (Nashville: Vanderbilt University Press, 2004), 111. Before affirmative action, universities could place quotas on admissions of women and minorities so that white men could remain the majority; see Genevieve Carlton, "A History of Affirmative Action in College Admissions," *Best Colleges*, December 7, 2022, https://www.bestcolleges.com/news/analysis/2020/08/10/history-affirmative-action-college/. In chapter 21, Merry White explains how she would have studied at the Sorbonne instead of traveling the world and seeing Japan had her scholarship not been revoked because she was Jewish.

[25] Leslie Miller-Bernal, "Introduction: Coeducation: An Uneven Progression," in *Going Coed: Women's Experiences in Formerly Men's Colleges and Universities, 1950–2000*, edited by Leslie Miller-Bernal and Susan L. Poulson (Nashville: Vanderbilt University Press, 2004), 3–21. In 1945, around 70 percent of American universities were coeducational, and the number rose to 75 percent in 1955 but remained around the same until 1965, twenty years later. Barbara Heyns and Joyce Adair Bird, "Recent Trends in the Higher Education of Women," in *The Undergraduate Woman: Issues in Educational Equity*, edited by Pamela Perun (Lexington, MA: Lexington Books, 1982), 66, quoted in Miller-Bernal, 7.

[26] Jansen, "Stages of Growth," 50–51.

[27] Schools in California and Hawaiʻi made up 58.3 percent of the total of Japanese language enrollments. Ibid, 51.

[28] "Public Law 94-118," Congress.gov., n.d, https://www.congress.gov/94/statute/STATUTE-89/STATUTE-89-Pg603.pdf (accessed January 1, 2023); Francis B. Tenny, "History of the Commission," Japan-US Friendship Commission, Washington, DC, 1995.

[29] Fran Schumer, "Japanese Give $1 Million to Harvard," *The Harvard Crimson*, October 13, 1973, https://www.thecrimson.com/article/1973/10/13/japanese-give-1-million-to-harvard/; "Japan Names 10 U.S. Colleges to Share Equally in $10-Million," *New York Times*, August 8, 1973, 14.

[30] Patricia Steinhoff, ed., *Japanese Studies in the United States in the 1990s*, 49, quoted in Victoria Lyon Bestor, "A Brief History of NCC," "Curated Archives: NCC Background," August 10, 2022, https://guides.nccjapan.org/archive.

31 See, for example, "Remembering the Strike," *SF State Magazine* (Fall/Winter 2008), https://magazine.sfsu.edu/archive/archive/fall_08/strike.html; "History of Asian American Studies," Princeton University, n.d., https://asamatprinceton.wordpress.com/history-of-asian-american-studies/ (accessed January 2, 2023); Alisa Freedman, "Noriko Mizuta: Biocritical Essay of a Literary Feminist and Global Scholar," *Review of Japanese Culture and Society* 30 (2018), 11–51.

32 Andrew Violet, email message, September 21, 2022.

33 See chapter 31, page 432.

34 See chapter 7, page 121.

35 Coined by E. D. Hirsch Jr., the term "cultural literacy" denotes the ability to understand and participate in a culture by being able to "read" its semiotic signs. Hirsch advocated that being culturally literate requires knowledge of the shared body of information underpinning a society. An understanding of history, beliefs, customs, arts, media, values, and idioms is also important, as spoken and written words are insufficient for social communication; E. D. Hirsch Jr., *Cultural Literacy: What Every American Needs to Know* (New York: Vintage, 1988).

36 Helen Hardacre, "Introduction," in *The Postwar Developments of Japanese Studies in the United States*, edited by Helen Hardacre (Leiden: Brill, 1998), xi.

37 "Eleven Books Reach Book Stalls," *CI&E Bulletin*, GARIOA, National Diet Library, January 19, 1949, 6.

38 See chapter 10, page 161.

39 "Title IX of the Educational Amendments of 1972," US Department of Justice, 2015, https://www.justice.gov/crt/title-ix-education-amendments-1972. See "Historical Periods and Major Events in Japanese Studies" for explanations and resources about civil rights laws.

40 Mary Elizabeth Berry, "Mary Elizabeth Berry (1978–2017)," UC Berkeley History Department, 2018, https://history.berkeley.edu/sites/default/files/150w_meb_final.pdf, 6.

41 Colleen Flaherty, "New Analysis of Faculty Pay, Representation," *Inside Higher Ed*, December 10, 2020, https://www.insidehighered.com/quicktakes/2020/12/10/new-analysis-faculty-pay-representation.

42 "Record High Number of Female University Students and Faculty Members in Japan," Nippon.com, September 12, 2022, https://www.nippon.com/en/japan-data/h01427/.

43 See, for example, Arrman Kyaw, "Report: All Faculty Types Suffer Job Losses in 2020–2021 Academic Year," April 8, 2021, *Diverse: Issues in Higher Education*, https://www.diverseeducation.com/faculty-staff/article/15108970/report-all-faculty-types-suffer-job-losses-in-2020-2021-academic-year.

44 See chapter 22, pages 336–337.

45 "Memoir," *Oxford English Dictionary*, Oxford University Press, 2022, https://www-oed-com.libproxy.uoregon.edu/view/Entry/116334?redirectedFrom=memoir#eid; Conor Monaghan, "What Exactly Is a Memoir?," *One Minute English*, 2022,

https://oneminuteenglish.org/en/memoir-meaning/; Jessica Dukes, "What Is a Memoir?," Celadon Books, n.d., https://celadonbooks.com/what-is-a-memoir/ (accessed December 1, 2022).

46 "About StoryCorps," StoryCorps, n.d., https://storycorps.org/about/ (accessed January 5, 2023). I thank Christine Yano for discussions about StoryCorps.

47 Barbara Ruch, email message, May 22, 2021.

48 Megan O'Grady, "These Literary Memoirs Take a Different Tack," *New York Times Style Magazine*, September 29, 2021, https://www.nytimes.com/2021/09/29/t-magazine/memoirs-books-nonfiction-identity.html.

49 Cynthia G. Franklin, *Academic Lives: Memoir, Cultural Theory, and the University Today* (Athens: University of Georgia Press, 2009); "A Record of Your Life," The Memoir Network, 2019, https://thememoirnetwork.com/category/professional-memoir.

50 "A Record of Your Life."

51 Franklin, 2.

52 For information about Iwami Reika and a slideshow of some of her works, see Aprile Gallant, "Remembering Iwami Reika (1927–2020)," Smith College Museum of Art, July 1, 2020, https://scma.smith.edu/blog/remembering-iwami-reika-1927-2020.

53 Yoko McClain, "My Personal Journey across the Pacific," *Modern Girls on the Go: Gender, Labor, and Mobility in Japan*, edited by Alisa Freedman, Laura Miller, and Christine Yano (Stanford: Stanford University Press, 2013), 209–225.

2

THE IMPLAUSIBLE ORIGINS OF BECOMING AN ASIAN ART HISTORIAN

Ellen P. Conant

At the present age of 101, I can still vividly recall standing, on March 7, 1947, on the bow of a boat docking in Yokohama Harbor, with the tears running down my face. How could a quirk of fate have landed me in such a calamitous situation, and how could I possibly recover my bearings? Not until long after did I realize what a critical event this proved to be in my life!

ELLEN P. CONANT was a member of the first US Fulbright contingent to Japan in 1953, where she was enrolled at Kyoto University until 1955; thereafter, she continued her studies in Tokyo until 1956 with a grant from the Rockefeller Foundation. She was a member of the College Art Association's first panel on Asian art in 1957; arranged the first international exhibition of Korean art, *Contemporary Korean Paintings*, in New York City in 1958; and directed and curated the exhibition *Nihonga: Transcending the Past: Japanese-Style Painting, 1868–1968* at the St. Louis Art Museum in 1995. Her career encompasses a plethora of symposiums, exhibitions, lectures, and publications. She is writing a reappraisal of the career of Ernest F. Fenollosa.

Discovering Japan

I was born and reared in New York City and educated in its public schools, which meant I emerged from there a confirmed urbanite. Upon my graduation from high school, my parents were opposed to my going to college because the family felt that I was needed at home to care for my ailing mother. When I was adamant about attending college, they relented, and I received my BA from Hunter College in 1942 with a major in art history and classical archaeology. Despite circumstances at home, I was determined to go to graduate school, to which my parents were implacably opposed, and I was thereafter personally and financially independent of my family. I received an MA scholarship from the University of Iowa, but found Iowa City, the program, and the faculty disappointing, and, in December, I packed my bags and returned to New York.

I went to live with a high school/college classmate at her home in New York City, found a position as secretary-assistant to the principal of Hunter High School, and began taking classes part-time for an MA in classical archaeology at the Institute of Fine Arts, New York University. Art History had only been established there in 1922, under the architect Fiske Kimball, and the current chairman of the still-developing department, Walter W. S. Cook, had managed to secure the services of some of the most eminent European art historians fleeing Nazi Germany: among them Erwin Panofsky, Walter Friedländer, Karl Lehmann-Hartleben, Richard Krautheimer, and Julius Held, as well as such able Americans as Richard Offner. Unfortunately, this arrangement took a serious toll on my health, and, by 1946, I had developed a series of minor ailments that my doctor insisted were bound to worsen.

This seemed like an ideal time to do some necessary field research in Europe, but I found it difficult to secure a visa. When I learned that the Red Cross was sending its last staff contingent to Italy early in 1947, I told them of my plight and secured their permission to join their staff. Shortly before departure, however, a Red Cross official apologetically told me that they had just been informed that the entire group was being sent to Japan and I therefore could resign with no penalty. Because I had already given up my job and apartment, I had no alternative but to leave with them, and I arrived in Yokohama in early March, deeply dejected.

The Red Cross officials in Tokyo proved most considerate and acceded to my request for an urban posting. I therefore was assigned to a Red Cross information desk located on the first floor of the Matsuya Department Store on the Ginza in Tokyo (figure 2.1). It provided all manner of vital information for military and civilian employees of the Supreme Command of Allied Powers (SCAP), which was exceedingly valuable because virtually all Japanese official and social institutions were off-limits to SCAP members.[1] The geographic, cultural, and educational information we furnished was difficult to obtain, but we were ably abetted by our

Figure 2.1: Ginza Crossing, Tokyo, Japan, circa 1946, showing the K. Hattori Building. During the Occupation, the centrally located Matsuya Department Store was taken over by the US Army and operated as the PX. Photograph courtesy of Auckland Libraries Heritage Collections, TRS-A01-15-01.

Japanese staff, mostly women whose social status, English fluency, ability, and education afforded us the means to surmount the barriers of language and military occupation. They personally enabled me to comprehend much about the country, its people, and particularly its culture that would otherwise have been impossible; through them, I first learned about the leading artists, writers, and actors and, on rare occasions, met some. The few personal and professional friends I made during this brief period lasted a lifetime, most notably Odagiri Mineko, the subject of Yasui Sōtarō's famed painting *Kin'yō* (figures 2.2 and 2.3). Furthermore, her relations to the prominent art collector Hosokawa Moritatsu, the heir of a former *daimyō* family, afforded me an opportunity to view important private collections and to interview many leading artists.[2]

By the time I was released from the Red Cross some seven months later, I had become so interested in Japan that I signed a two-year contract with the Office of Civilian Personnel and was sent to Kyoto, where I was assigned to the cultural affairs division of SCAP and authorized to liaison with Japanese officials. I was billeted at the Kyoto Hotel and soon acquired a jeep that enabled me to spend leisure hours visiting the many famous monuments in the area. I also joined the Kyoto Folk Art Association and came to know the Kansai potters and print artists, with whom I went to visit various kilns.[3] Thus I became friends with the potters

Figure 2.2: Yasui Sōtarō, *Portrait of Chin Jung* (*Kin'yō*), 1934. Oil on canvas. The National Museum of Modern Art, Tokyo.

Kawai Kanjirō and Tomimoto Kenkichi in Kyoto, and Hamada Shōji in Mashiko, and, through them, many other artists and craftsmen.[4]

European Sojourn: Wrapping up the Past

At the expiration of my two-year contract, a friend and I had saved enough money to return to the United States via China but were dismayed to find that the Chinese government had collapsed shortly before our departure. We had no alternative but to return home directly by the end of 1949. Although fascinated by Japan, I felt it imperative that I complete my MA and therefore still had to get to Europe. By early 1950, I obtained a position with the United Nations Relief and Rehabilitation Administration (UNRRA) in Germany and was sent to Nordrhein-Westfalen, where we were employed to help resettle the still-numerous European

Figure 2.3: Hosokawa Moritatsu and Odagiri Mineko near the eastern slope of Mount Myōkō, Akakura, Niigata Prefecture, circa 1958. Photograph courtesy of the author.

displaced persons. This assignment enabled me to secure a car with American license plates, and I spent my free time and holidays touring European cultural sites and institutions. Together with a fellow classmate, Jean Johnson (Young), who was en route to a Fulbright in Paris, we spent the summer of 1950 touring more distant parts of Europe, the back of the car filled with books. We headed all the way to Santiago de Compostela in Spain via Romanesque monuments, and returned to Paris via Gothic sites, including along the way all the important museums and art collections, thereby acquiring valuable research material. I returned home in time to resume my studies at the Institute, but, given my recent experience in Europe, I now decided to work with a Renaissance specialist, Professor Martin Weinberger, and wrote my thesis on the Italian Renaissance artist Andrea del Verrocchio (1435–1488). I received an MA from the Institute of Fine Arts, New York University, in June 1951.

Transitioning to Asia

Because I had already decided to pursue a career in Asian art while I was at the Institute, I managed to take courses with Professor Alfred Salmony, whose specialty was prehistoric and ancient Asian art. Because I was seeking to study the nineteenth century, it was essential that I find an institution that could better accommodate my needs. Hence, I consulted Professor Langdon Warner, the Asian specialist at Harvard, who admitted that my topic was beyond his area of expertise and that he was, moreover, soon retiring. I then sought out the eminent Japanese cultural historian at Columbia, Sir George Sansom, who said that he would have been delighted to pursue that subject with me, but he, too, was retiring. I eventually heard of Professor Alexander C. Soper, an esteemed scholar of Asian art at Bryn Mawr College, who was one of the few academics in a degree-awarding institution who was trained in Asian art and who possessed a command of both Japanese and Chinese languages. Soper had graduated as an architect during the economic crash of 1929, and he subsequently sought academic training in Western—and, ultimately, Asian—art history at Princeton. While pursuing his PhD, he spent several years in the late 1930s studying in Japan, where he acquired his command of the languages. I sought him out, and, while he was not familiar with the subject that I wanted to pursue, he agreed to serve as my supervisor and mentor. I therefore registered in September 1951 for a PhD in Asian art history at Bryn Mawr College.

Inasmuch as the college had no established courses or students in Asian art, Soper sought to train me as best he could. Given the number of courses I had already taken, it was essential by 1952 that I attempt to get to Asia to access research material, which had become possible due to the Treaty of San Francisco that legally ended the Occupation. Unfortunately, art was not a subject of immediate importance, and the few agencies and organizations that were beginning to send students to Japan informed me that art was beyond their area of interest and expertise. It seemed miraculous that, just at this time, we heard that the US government was assembling the first contingent of Fulbright scholars to be sent to Japan in the summer of 1953. I immediately applied! Given the number of American military and civilians who had been trained in Japanese language and studies during the war, and who thereafter gained experience serving with SCAP in Japan from 1945 to 1952, the likelihood of a young woman interested in Japanese art being selected was not very plausible. Imagine my astonishment when I received word that I had been accepted! I could only attribute it to the eminence of Professor Soper and to the reputation of Bryn Mawr College.

Dr. (Wilson) Leon Godshall, the executive secretary of the US Educational Commission in Japan, was insistent that the Fulbright group assemble in the early summer for orientation and then travel together to Japan, departing from Seattle on the *Hikawa Maru* on August 24 and arriving in Yokohama in September.

Because I knew that I might have to remain in Japan for an extended period, I was determined not to leave Bryn Mawr until I had taken my PhD exams and orals.[5] Although Dr. Godshall insisted it was imperative I join the rest of the group, the president of Bryn Mawr managed to secure me a reprieve. I therefore spent the summer of 1953 taking intensive Japanese language instruction at the University of Michigan, as I had the previous summer, because there was no language instruction available to me in Philadelphia. I then spent another month or so taking all my exams, which were ludicrously extensive, encompassing India, China, Korea, and Japan. Directly upon the completion of my orals, I took a plane to Los Angeles, briefly visited my sister there, and flew via Hawai'i to Japan in November 1953.

By the time I arrived in Tokyo, I found that the other Fulbright members had already dispersed throughout Japan; hence, I never had a chance to become acquainted with the group and failed to meet most of them, especially because few were stationed in Kyoto, where I was enrolled at the University of Kyoto. I fortunately became close friends with an American Nisei, Miyakawa Tetsuo, an assistant professor of sociology at Boston University who was serving as a Fulbright lecturer at Doshisha University. Because he was fluent in Japanese and likewise single, I was able to go on extremely interesting outings with him to famous sites and events. By contrast, I saw relatively little of Edward (Ted) Kidder Jr., an archaeology major with whom I had overlapped at the Institute of Fine Arts, as he was accompanied by his wife and children and was active in missionary circles.

Because there was no Fulbright headquarters in Kyoto nor staff to consult, and because no one had thought to reconfirm my housing, all that was available to me on my limited budget was the Young Women's Christian Association (YWCA), which provided only daily residence. Due to the wartime destruction of housing, the Kyoto government had levied stiff taxes on inadequately occupied private residences. I was then consulting with Takeuchi Itsuzo to write an article on his father, the noted painter Takeuchi Seihō (1864–1942), who told me of a possible rental that I should hasten to inquire about.[6] He had heard that a prominent academic family seeking to reduce housing taxes was considering accepting a tenant for the small, well-appointed house in *sukiya* style (a traditional architectural style based on an aesthetic of rustic simplicity) that they had built as an independent retirement home for their widowed mother and divorced sister. However, because the family did not wish the contentious relationship of the two women to become local gossip, they were hesitant to rent to an educated Japanese of their social milieu. Although the women were still living in a purely traditional manner and had had no contact whatsoever with foreigners or any knowledge of English, Takeuchi thought they might be willing to consider a foreign tenant. Moreover, I was so intrigued with the idea of being able to experience life in an entirely traditional setting that I disregarded the inconveniences involved: lack of heat, furniture, bedding, and bathing for a start! Because *obasan* (the widowed mother) was a devoted member of Urasenke (a school of traditional Japanese tea ceremony), the small house even had a fully appointed, attached teahouse. Still, it took them one month to agree to my putting up a pole in the *engawa* (covered corridor with wood floor) behind the main room to hang my Western clothes, an indication of their unwillingness to accept any infringement upon their traditional mode of life! As unlikely as this arrangement sounds, and, even with the efforts we took to avoid each other in the first month, the mother and her daughter soon came to care for me as fully as they would a family member.

When I attempted to register at the university, I found that the professor to whom I was assigned, Ijima Tsutomu, the head of the humanities program and a leading Kyoto academic and aesthetician who had written his doctoral dissertation on the pioneering Hellenist Johann Winkelmann (1717–1768), had not been properly consulted and thus was unwilling to accept me as a graduate student. I therefore sought out an eminent archaeologist, Arimitsu Kyōichi, who had studied and worked abroad, and persuaded him to arrange for us both to meet Professor Ijima. Feeling that my limited knowledge of Japanese was inadequate to converse with Ijima, I requested that Professor Arimitsu convey my dismay, only to be told that because Professor Ijima was his superior in age and rank, he could not possibly relay what I wished! I was so despairing that, totally forgetting my linguistic limitations, I burst forth as best I could, and, in a very few moments, Professor Ijima was overcome with laughter. He looked at me kindly and said, "I think we need coffee." Thenceforth, I could not have had a more considerate, cooperative, and competent mentor. As my interests were peripheral to his specialization and there were no art historians on the faculty, Professor Ijima arranged for me to study privately with Doi Tsugiyoshi, Minamoto Toyomune, and many other Kyoto art historians; provided introductions to all the major temples, shrines, art collections, and dealers; and took both a professional and personal interest in my well-being.[7] It would sound outrageously boastful to list the remarkable people to whom he provided introduction and access; I can never cease to be grateful and to mourn the strain he experienced as dean during the 1968 student revolt that led to his early demise.

Emerging Interests: Artists, Organizations, and Institutions

As in Tokyo, the Kyoto Folk Art Movement was extremely active, not only in pottery but also in prints, and I became close friends with one of Kyoto's leading *sōsaku-hanga* (creative print) artists, Tokuriki Tomikichirō. Through him, I came to know many of the other print artists and print dealers. This led me to seek out one of the leading print artists in Tokyo, Onchi Kōshirō, who shared my interest in German Expressionist art. Although our acquaintance was brief, I managed to secure two copies of his portrait of poet Hagiwara Sakutarō that he arranged for

Figure 2.4: Onchi Kōshirō, *Mother and Child*, 1954. Woodblock print; ink on paper. Acc. No. 2006.2029, Museum of Fine Arts, Boston.

Sekino Jun'ichirō to print for me. I told Onchi that I had greatly admired one of his early Expressionist-inspired prints, *Mother and Child* (circa 1917, figure 2.4), which I had seen at the home of the print artist and scholar Ono Tadashige, and I asked how I could secure a copy. Onchi had no prints but thought that he still had the block, which he subsequently found, and he made two prints for me, one of which I have given to the Museum of Fine Arts, Boston. I was amused when a noted dealer pronounced my copy suspect because it was printed on postwar paper!

Inasmuch as modern Japanese art had not yet received academic sanction, I soon found myself frequently traveling to Tokyo to attend exhibitions at the numerous museums and the metropolitan department stores, which alone had the funds to support extensive exhibitions of Japanese painting.[8] I also availed myself of the resources of the two newly established museums of modern art in Kamakura and Kyōbashi, Tokyo, as well as the Tokyo National Research Institute for Cultural Properties in Ueno Park. I was often in the company of Elise Grilli, who reviewed these exhibitions in her weekly art column in *The Japan Times*. I had an introduction to Frances Case (Blakemore), who oversaw exhibitions and art projects at the American Embassy, and, from there, made my way to Nishi Ginza, where I was cordially welcomed by Abe Yūji, director of the Yōseidō Gallery, which featured the work of the modern print artists.

On the recommendation of Odagiri, I secured housing for these trips at the home of a prominent diplomat, Sakamoto Tatsuki, who was likewise seeking to reduce the housing tax on his large Shinagawa home. Through Sakamoto, I met numerous other diplomats and important government officials. I also became acquainted with a circle of still-resident SCAP civilians, including Oliver Statler, who were interested in the modern creative print movement, folk art pottery, and various other crafts.[9] These civilians organized exhibitions and wrote catalogs that made many aspects of modern Japanese art familiar to Western audiences, attracting the attention and participation of so prominent a writer as James A. Michener.[10]

New Friends, New Ventures

The friends I made in Tokyo frequently directed their Western friends to visit me in Kyoto to jointly explore our mutual interest in Kyoto's remarkable sights and sounds. One such visitor was Lucy Briggs—the daughter of Ellis O. Briggs, who was then US Ambassador to Korea—who regularly stayed with me in Kyoto when visiting her parents in Seoul. A graduate of Smith College who was working for a government agency in Washington, DC, she and I had many shared interests. During the course of our outings, I evidently communicated my disappointment in not being able to study Chinese art or visit China, and, indeed, being restricted from even visiting Korea, where it was still possible to observe the influence of the great art of Tang China on Korean monuments, particularly at Kyongiu and Sokkulam.[11] She obviously relayed these woes to her father, who, after escorting Korean president Syngman Rhee to a conference in Washington, DC, decided on his return trip to provide me, in my position as a Fulbright scholar, just such an opportunity. I was vacationing with the Sakamotos in Karuizawa when, three days before Briggs's arrival, I received word of the invitation and instructions to meet him at Tachikawa air base in western Tokyo. Because my passport boldly stated that Korea was off-limits, I immediately called the Fulbright office, only to find that everyone was on summer break. Determined to go, I hastily arranged for my Kyoto family to have my passport, some clothing, and necessities shipped to me that same night. I managed to get to the air base, only to be told by the soldier in charge that I lacked the credentials to enter. They had difficulty locating the ambassador, and I was then personally escorted by the guard. I found that the ambassador was flying home as a guest of General Mark W. Clark, who was headed there for a conference, and off I went with both these men, arriving in Seoul at an airfield filled with military members and embassy staff to greet them.

Figure 2.5: Arakawa Toyozō, Shino-style *chawan* (pottery tea bowl). Photograph courtesy of the author.

There is no way that I can convey my extraordinary gratitude to Ambassador Briggs, who had me as a guest not for a few days but for over a month, and the remarkable impact this had on my life and career. During the entire visit, I stayed at the US Embassy and benefited from the assistance of his highly informed American cultural attaché, Mark Scherbacher, and his Korean staff. My knowledge of Japanese and the comparable Japanese art world—Korea having been occupied by Japan from 1905 to 1945—made it possible for me to meaningfully confer with the leading artists, art school officials, museum directors, collectors, dealers, critics, and journalists who cordially cooperated. I also met a friend of Professor Salmony, Kim Jaewon, then the director of the Seoul National Museum, and received excellent direction and assistance regarding historical sites to visit and publications to procure.[12] I could not have anticipated how soon this experience would become relevant!

My interest in modern prints and painting gradually had to compete with my mounting fascination with the work of some of the leading Japanese potters. When the associate curator of Japanese art at the Art Institute of Chicago, Margaret (Peggy) Gentles, first visited Japan in 1955, she was ably guided by Oliver Statler, who was likewise from Chicago.[13] He urged her to visit me in Kyoto, and she was so intrigued by my house and the prints and pottery I had acquired that she persuaded me to organize an exhibition of modern Japanese ceramics to be shown at the Art Institute in 1956. While it is expedient when dealing with contemporary artists to include as many as possible, we chose instead to display a dozen works by each of six leading potters who represented different ceramic traditions and modern currents, thereby showing why some of the most distinguished potters were considered ceramic *artists* who merited national honors and whose works commanded whopping prices! Because I had no institutional affiliation, Peggy handled all the mechanics while I selected works and secured information concerning the potters, which was not available in Western languages at that time. The first person I approached was my good friend Hamada Shōji, the noted Mashiko potter, who was eager to participate. However, a few days later, I received a note saying that he had to withdraw because Yanagi Sōetsu, then director of the Japanese Folk Crafts Museum in Komaba, Tokyo, objected to Hamada's participation unless he himself was in charge of the exhibition and it was strictly a folk-art exhibition. I therefore relied upon Hamada's friend and colleague, Kawai Kanjirō, to represent the Folk Art Movement. The potters chosen were Arakawa Toyozō, Tomimoto Kenkichi, Kanashige Toyo, Katō Tōkurō, Kondō Yūzō, and Taki Kazuo, and seventy-six items were displayed against a modern Japanese, hand-dyed, stenciled wall hanging by Itagaki Nenjirō (figure 2.5). Although Peggy reported that the exhibition was well-received and that the Smithsonian was considering extending it as a traveling exhibition, two of the artists were unwilling to participate.[14] Given the fragile nature of the pottery and the absence in Tokyo of the person in charge of such programs, Annemarie Henle Pope, Peggy felt it best to again rely on the art dealer Mayuyama to return the exhibits to Japan. Despite all the difficulties, we worked uncommonly well together, and Peggy and I repeatedly acknowledged our mutual indebtedness!

In early 1954, I had applied for and received the additional year of the Fulbright and hence was able to remain at Kyoto University through June 1955. I had by then become aware that Kyoto lacked a museum of modern art and the official research institutions that I needed to pursue my pioneering studies of Meiji art (1868–1912), a subject that had not yet gained academic status, even in Japan. Because the Fulbright provided only two years of funding to graduate students, I therefore was compelled to seek alternate support. Soon after I arrived in Japan in 1953, I had received a phone call from Dr. (Charles) Burton Fahs, the Director of the Humanities Division at the Rockefeller Foundation, who was seeking to broaden university programs in the humanities and to encourage Asian scholarship. I was unaware that John D. Rockefeller's wife, Blanchette, a trustee of the Museum of Modern Art in New York City, had become interested in *sōsaku-hanga*, which Dr. Fahs knew was part of my area of research. I reluctantly agreed to meet with him at the Imperial Hotel, and, well before we finished our drinks, we had become friends. I promised to assist him in any way possible, and he assured me that, if I needed additional funding, it would be forthcoming. Hence, I secured a two-year fellowship from the Rockefeller Foundation to stay in Japan from the summer of 1955 through the summer of 1957.

In the fall of 1955, I moved to Tokyo and managed to gain entry to the Tokyo National Research Institute for Cultural Properties and permission to work under the direction of Kumamoto Kenjirō, the head of Meiji traditional arts studies (*Nihonga*).[15] Here, I became close friends with one of the few female staff, his assistant Seki Chiyo, who had secured such a position during the war when all the men were absent.[16] A former Fulbright scholar helped me secure excellent housing in Kitazawa district, and I soon was comfortably established in Tokyo with a house, an institution, a professor, and a colleague. If not for the Fulbright and this subsequent grant from the Rockefeller Foundation, I could never have realized my career as a Japanese art historian.

Uprooted: Exploring Career Options

Although ideally ensconced in Tokyo, I received a letter early in 1956 from Professor Soper informing me that a rare position had opened at Smith College, and it was essential that I return home and apply for it. His adamance was partly due to feelings of guilt: shortly before, Soper had rejected Harvard's offer of the position vacated by Langdon Warner—had he accepted, I then could have taken his position at Bryn Mawr. In the spring of 1956, I reluctantly packed up my new apartment in Tokyo and returned home to New York City, found temporary lodging with friends, and went to Smith for the interview, only to realize that Smith had no intentions of hiring someone to take over the Asian art course ably taught by their professor of Chinese history. I was invited the following morning to apply for a similar position at nearby Mount Holyoke College but ultimately rejected their offer as I did not think it was a suitable environment for an urbanite like myself. I returned to Bryn Mawr, reported my experiences to Professor Soper and President Katharine McBride, and said that I was prepared to give up academia and return to Tokyo, where I was assured much more interesting and lucrative employment.

Just about this time, a former classmate at the Institute of Fine Arts, LeRoy Davidson, contacted me and said that he was leaving a position at the University of Georgia due to family difficulties and urged me to apply. Davidson, an expert in Indian art and a professor at Yale, had been among the first hired by Lamar Dodd, a very able and genial painter who had secured a major grant from the Carnegie Corporation to develop a model department of art history in the South. They had made excellent progress in this regard, but Davidson's family struggled to adapt to the Southern milieu, and he therefore accepted an excellent post as head of art studies at the Claremont Graduate University. On his recommendation, Lamar Dodd contacted me, invited me down, and offered me such an excellent position and benefits that I immediately accepted. I moved to Athens, Georgia, and began teaching courses in both Asian and Western art in September 1956.

Unanticipated Opportunities and Repercussions

At 9:30 a.m. on the morning of January 25, 1957, I was a member of the first panel on Asian art at the annual meeting of the College Art Association, held that year at the Detroit Institute of Arts. This panel was chaired by LeRoy Davidson and included Richard Edwards, Nelson I. Wu, Walter Spink, and myself. It was remarkable that I should have been chosen as the only woman and also as the only member of the panel dealing with a modern subject, namely: "Modern Japanese Painting, East versus West." I showed a stunning set of colored slides of material completely unknown to the audience and immediately thereafter was approached by Alfred R. Krakusin, the curator of the World House Galleries, which had been newly opened by Herbert Mayer in the Hotel Carlyle on Madison Avenue in New York City.[17] He was eager for me to organize an exhibition of the Japanese *Nihonga* that I had illustrated, but I assured him that, having lost the friendship of so many potters in the process of organizing the first exhibition of modern Japanese ceramics at the Art Institute in Chicago the previous year, I could not consider a Japanese painting exhibition, as this was my professional field of expertise. I had learned that it was too emotionally fraught an ordeal to make selections from among the work of living artists!

Professor Krakusin continued to pursue me so assiduously that I told him about the modern artists whose work I had been impressed by in Seoul, Korea, that was similar to what he had viewed in my College Art Association lecture. Some of these artists had studied in China, others with Japanese teachers; moreover, the annual salon in Seoul was chaired by Japanese painters. I also felt that the hardships the Koreans had endured during the Japanese occupation and the Korean War had given their work an emotional strength and poignancy that was more than a match for that of the Japanese. Because I was familiar with the contemporary art of both countries, I felt that this was an exciting opportunity to present an important body of artwork unknown outside Korea. Mayer and Krakusin readily agreed, and it was decided that I should go to Korea during the summer of 1957, make the necessary selections, and arrange for the exhibition to be shown from February 25 through March 22, 1958. Seoul's hierarchical art circles were affronted that a foreigner—and a woman at that!—should be permitted to present the first portrayal of the Korean modern art world abroad. I was even featured on the cover of *The Himang, Weekly News Magazine* in August 1957. Because this exhibition was to be shown in New York City, the thriving center of modern art, it was natural to select the younger artists who were seeking new inspiration from both their traditional past and contemporary international art currents. It is interesting to note how many of the artists featured in the exhibition have since become among the foremost modern artists of Korea (figures 2.6 and 2.7). Korean accounts of this exhibition are still based on assumptions that are far from what actually occurred.[18]

Figure 2.6: Ellen Psaty with Korean artists, Seoul, 1957. Photograph in the Lee Ungno Museum Archive, Daejeon, South Korea.

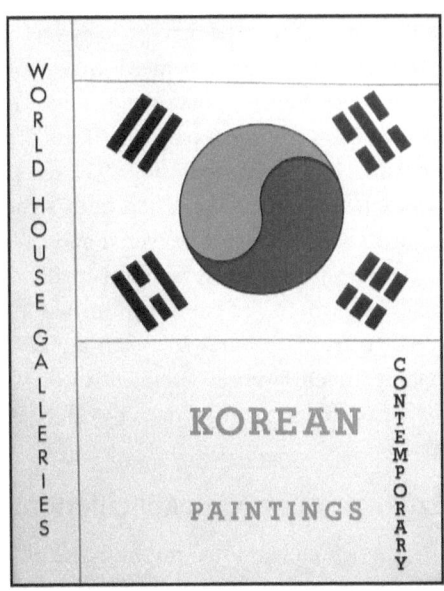

Figure 2.7: *Korean Contemporary Paintings*, exhibition pamphlet, World House Galleries, 1958. Photograph courtesy of the author.

Due to a sprained ankle, I arrived in Korea later than expected and therefore had to work quickly. Because I had additionally agreed to write a report that summer on the state of modern Asian art for the Rockefeller Foundation, it was imperative that I should have sufficient time to survey conditions in Indonesia,

Thailand, Vietnam, Cambodia, and as many other sites as I could cover, with the condition that I was back in Georgia to resume teaching in September 1957.[19] Thus, I sought to secure the assistance of a photographer in preparing artists' biographies and illustrations of each work to be exhibited at the World House Galleries. I was fortunate that Natasha Prejbiano, a friend from my time at UNRRA, was now a personnel officer for the United Nations Korean Reconstruction Agency (UNKRA), and she provided housing and introduced me to a possible photographer, Theodore R. Conant. Ted in turn recommended his close friend, the painter-film artist Lee Hyung Pyo (Hyeong-pyo Lee), and we arranged for the artists to bring their work to a central place where it could be selected and then efficiently photographed and cataloged.

Even more unforeseen than my being in Korea to organize a Korean exhibition in the first place was my marriage to Ted on August 26, 1957! We left the next day for Hong Kong, where we made the necessary arrangements for our subsequent travels to Indonesia, Thailand, Cambodia, and Vietnam, so that I might write my report to the Rockefeller Foundation.[20] In September, our travels culminated in Tokyo, from where my husband went back to his position in Seoul and I returned to the University of Georgia to fulfill my contract. As I was pregnant and expecting a child in June 1958, we decided that I would teach in Georgia until March 1958, at which time I would rejoin Ted in Seoul. We soon learned that the baby was breech and that Seoul's Severance Hospital could not accommodate me, as it had only one room for foreigners and missionaries had preference! I therefore arranged to stay with my old host family in Kyoto, and my son was born on June 10, 1958, at the Japan Baptist Hospital. By the time my daughter was born in July 1959, the United Nations, with funds from Norway, Sweden, and Denmark, had built a modern hospital in Seoul. As a result, my daughter was superbly delivered and cared for in seven languages, and I feasted on the Scandinavian cuisine of the medical staff! We resided in Seoul until September 1960, where Ted continued his work at the Ministry of Information and I agreed to teach a course in Asian art at Yonsei University. I was surprised to find that my students were still being privately tutored in Japanese and were able to use the Japanese-language archaeology publications stored in the basement of the university.

Surmounting Constraints: Expectations and Reconciliation

Upon our return to the United States in September 1960, my husband obtained a position with the Ford Foundation on a project headed by Herold C. Hunt, professor of education at Harvard University. We therefore decided to settle in the Boston area and purchased a house in Winchester, Massachusetts. Ted was engaged in challenging research as to how television could be utilized to improve elementary and secondary education throughout the United States, Canada, and the Caribbean; I accepted a temporary position at Wellesley College during their dean's sabbatical, and, despite my prior refusal, I was also engaged to teach Asian art at Mount Holyoke as part of their participation in a multi-college development of an Asian Studies program funded by the Carnegie Corporation.

Unfortunately, implicit in my marriage were certain obligations that precluded my pursuit of a full-time academic career. Moreover, a professorship might have required our living in a place where my husband was unlikely to find work and where my salary would not have covered the expenses of childcare. However, my husband's position enabled him to support our family in a location where we preferred to live and in a manner that I could not hope to match. Gender was then, as it unfortunately still is, a major issue. However, I had a remarkably compatible marriage, two bright and able children, and, in the capacity of an independent scholar, I continued to contribute to the development of Japanese art history. Even more satisfying is the fact that the Meiji era is finally receiving major critical interest and reevaluation, some seventy-five years after it first captivated me!

Notes

Ellen was assisted in writing this chapter by her research assistant and friend, Kathryn Whalen.

[1] Japan as I viewed it from the information desk is best portrayed in Lucy Herndon Crockett's memoir of her time as a Red Cross worker between 1945 and 1947: *Popcorn on the Ginza: An Informal Portrait of Postwar Japan* (New York: W. Sloane Associates, 1949). Crockett's book enjoyed wide circulation, as evidenced by the numerous reviews still available on the internet.

[2] See Ellen P. Conant, "Preserving the Past, Patronizing the Present: Hosokawa Moritatsu and Eisei Bunko," *Lords of the Samurai: Legacy of a Daimyo Family, from the Eisei Bunko, Hosokawa Collection, Tokyo*, Exhibition Symposium, Asian Art Museum, San Francisco, California, June 14, 2009.

[3] See Yoshiko Uchida, *We Do Not Work Alone: The Thoughts of Kanjiro Kawai* (Kyoto: Folk Art Society, 1953) and Bernard Leach, *Hamada: Potter* (Tokyo: Kodansha International, 1976).

[4] A graduate of the Tokyo School of Fine Arts who had studied in England between 1908 and 1910, Tomimoto Kenkichi was appointed a "Living National Treasure" in 1955. His highly personal style earned him a reputation as an innovator and consummate decorator. See Takuya Kida, Meghen Jones, and Trevor Menders, *Vessel Explored / Vessel Transformed: Tomimoto Kenkichi and His Enduring Legacy* (New York: Joan B. Mirviss, Ltd., 2019).

[5] Dr. Godshall was on a leave of absence from his post as Professor of International Relations at Lehigh University, to which he returned in 1954.

[6] See Ellen D. Psaty, "Takeuchi Seihō, A Kyoto Painter," *Japan Quarterly* 3, no. 1 (January–March 1956), 42–53, and Ellen P. Conant, "'Cut from Kyoto Cloth': Takeuchi Seihō and His Artistic Milieu," *Impressions* 33 (Spring 2012), 71–93.

[7] See Tsugiyoshi Doi, *Momoyama Decorative Painting*, translated by Edna B. Crawford (New York: Weatherhill, 1977), and Toyomune Minamoto, *Illustrated History of Japanese Art*, translated by Harold G. Henderson (Kyoto: K. Hoshino, 1935).

[8] See Hugo Munsterberg, "Art Study in Japan," *College Art Journal* 13, no. 2 (Winter 1954), 132–134.

[9] Oliver Statler, *Modern Japanese Prints: An Art Reborn* (Rutland, VT: Charles E. Tuttle Company, 1956).

[10] James A. Michener, *The Floating World: The Story of Japanese Prints* (New York: Random House, 1954), and *Japanese Prints: From the Early Masters to the Modern* (Rutland, VT: Charles E. Tuttle Company, 1959).

[11] The self-designated founder of the Japanese Folk Art Movement, Yanagi Soetsu, and his close colleague, the British potter Bernard Leach, drew many of their ideas from their travels in Korea while that country was under Japanese occupation. See Ellen P. Conant, "Leach, Hamada, Yanagi: Myth and Reality," *Studio Potter* 21, no. 1 (December 1992), 6–9, and "Bernard Leach, Frank Brangwyn, and Japan," *Studio Potter* 27, no. 2 (June 1999), 15–20.

[12] Furthermore, Professor Arimitsu, who had been working in Korea since 1931, had been asked to remain and assist Kim Jaewon in organizing the National Museum in Seoul, which reopened in 1948.

[13] Employed originally as a secretary, Gentles became one of the first female curators of Asian art in the United States by cataloging the Clarence Buckingham Collection of Japanese Prints.

[14] See Edith Weigle, "Pottery Made by Japanese Is Fascinating," *Chicago Daily Tribune* (September 8, 1956), 23.

[15] Kumamoto Kenjirō, "Ōyatoi gaikokujin" (Foreign Employees of the Meiji Government), *Bijutsu* (Art) 16 (Tokyo: Kajima kenkyūjo shuppankai, 1976).

[16] Seki Chiyo, "Kōkyo sugido-e ni tsuite" (Cedar Door Paintings of the Meiji Palace), *Bijutsu Kenkyū* (Art Research) 264 (July 1969), 1–32.

[17] "Historical Note: World House Galleries Records, 1927–1991, Bulk 1953–1980," *Archives of American Art, Smithsonian Institution*, accessed March 2, 2022, https://www.aaa.si.edu/collections/world-house-galleries-records-6036/historical-note.

[18] Chung, Moojeong. "Korean Art Represented in the United States in the 1950s," *Korean Modern & Contemporary Art History* 14 (2005), 7–41. Existing texts suggest that Korean scholars are still unaware of the unconventional manner in which this exhibition originated.

[19] A copy of this unpublished report, submitted to Dr. Fahs in 1957, remains in the author's possession.

[20] At this time, I also arranged an exhibition on the work of the Indonesian painter Affandi, which was shown at the World House Galleries from July 1 to July 26, 1958.

3

AN ASIAN ATTACHMENT

Joyce Chapman Lebra, curated by Andrew Violet[1]

> *During the mid-1950s, I was an anomaly as an American woman researching Japanese history. I was the first woman PhD in Japanese history in the United States, so I was uniquely placed at the time. Because the Japanese had no category in which to place me, I had a kind of freedom not enjoyed by Japanese counterparts.*

JOYCE CHAPMAN LEBRA (1925–2021) was a historian of Japan and India at the University of Colorado Boulder. She was the first American woman to earn a PhD in Japanese history (Radcliffe, 1958). Her books include *Jungle Alliance: Japan and the Indian National Army* (1971), *Ōkuma Shigenobu: Statesman of Meiji Japan* (1973), *Japanese-Trained Armies in Southeast Asia: Independence and Volunteer Forces in World War II* (1977), *The Indian National Army and Japan* (2008), and an edited collection, *Japan's Greater East Asia Co-Prosperity Sphere in World War II: Selected Readings and Documents* (1975). She published four historical novels inspired by her experiences in and research about Hawai'i, Japan, and India, and coedited three books on women and work in Asia: *Women in Changing Japan* (coedited with Joy Paulson and Elizabeth Powers, 1978), *Chinese Women in Southeast Asia* (coedited with Joy Paulson, 1980), and *Women and Work in India: Continuity and Change* (coedited with Joy Paulson and Jena Matson, 1984). She was awarded the Order of the Rising Sun, Gold Rays with Neck Ribbon by the Japanese government (2021).

ANDREW VIOLET is a painter, writer, and graphic designer who works at the Libraries of the University of Colorado Boulder. He was good friends with Joyce Lebra and leads the "CU Legend Series" that features her. He is broadly interested in all things spiritual, with a present emphasis on Buddhist Madhyamaka philosophy, and hopes one day to pursue a PhD on the subject.

Childhood in Hawai'i

Think of it as the beginning, then—the birth of an infant, a girl child, in the coldest state in the nation, at the coldest time of year, and on the shortest day of the year, the winter solstice of 1925, just four days shy of Christmas. What would an Indian astrologer, or any astrologer for that matter, foretell for this baby's future, born in such frigid, forbidding Minnesota surroundings? No doubt her parents greeted her with warmth and joy, though it was not always easy to tell, for they seemed more often to point her in a direction they deemed proper childhood behavior than to enfold her in a soft embrace. My mother was a woman who entertained no doubt whatsoever about what was right and what was wrong, what was black and what was white. My father, though of a gentler nature, was often away from home pursuing his professorial duties and research at the University of Minnesota.

For some months during my first year, we lived in a town on the southern coast of France while my father did research in North Africa. I have no infant's memory of an experience that must have enchanted my mother and older sister. During my third year, when I was still a toddler not allowed outside on my own, my landscape altered dramatically. My personal geography now lay in Honolulu, where the ocean pours on to infinity or until the eye meets the horizon, where doves greet first light with gentle murmurs, where red earth grows good pineapples, where the air holds the morning dew, and where flowers bloom whatever the time of year. This is where bent old Chinese women, barely able to walk, hobbled on bound feet, where Filipinos shouted encouragement to favorite feisty cocks fighting, where my father showed us small marine creatures in tidal pools, and where sand seeped up between our toes. This was the map etched on my heart; this was home, my personal geography. Our first home in this tropical island was happily right on Waikiki Beach, in an apartment building of Royal Hawaiian pink, just steps from the sea. By this age, I had a baby brother, Kent, and we became barefoot childhood playmates. I discovered quite soon the pleasures of swimming, or at least dog-paddling, which I did one day following my older sister, Frances, into the ocean. This was where I belonged, clearly, and perhaps I was a marine creature in some previous life. As soon as I was able to make my own way around, I recall spending each Saturday at the beach, each week eating the same lunch, a peanut butter sandwich and a chocolate soda. I count this a happy childhood. Ever since my early ventures into the sea, I never feel totally at home far from the ocean.

Honolulu, in the Territory of Hawai'i, remained home for the next several years while my father was dean of the College of Tropical Agriculture and Human Resources, founded in 1907 and the first college at the University of Hawai'i. Here was where my consciousness was birthed, where I spent my growing childhood years, growing so tall, in fact, that I was often the tallest girl in class, told to stand in the back row with the boys when we had class photos taken at Punahou School, the same school attended by Barack Obama decades later. In later years, I would have been happy to stand with the boys, though at the time I disliked having to stand behind the class.

The first primary school I attended was a Montessori-style private school where pupils were encouraged to proceed at their own pace. The problem was that I did not progress; I did not learn to read for two years. My parents must have wondered if I suffered from some unknown genetic flaw. I remember going for testing, test after test after test. It was not until third grade that a diagnosis revealed that I was dyslexic, trying to read backward and transposing numbers consistently. My parents transferred me to Punahou School and breathed a sigh of relief when at last I began to read. I have never stopped since.

At Punahou my friends were Chinese, Japanese, Portuguese, and Hawaiian, a mixed ethnic tapestry that marked my psyche, my sense of what was normal. And it was a predominantly Asian mixture, since the largest ethnic group in the islands was Japanese, around 40 percent of the population.[2] I learned decades later that Punahou at the time had ethnic quotas.

After perhaps a year, the family moved from our Waikiki apartment to a large house in Manoa Valley, closer to the university and my father's work there. This house sat in a large compound owned by agriculture professor Frederick George Krauss, and three or four other houses were inhabited by members of the Krauss family. One of the children, a young man, lived in a small house in the backyard, or perhaps it was his studio. I remember that he had hundreds of spider specimens in boxes, and even at an early age, I suffered from acute arachnophobia. I could not stand to look at these creatures, nor can I to this day.

I sometimes played with Japanese children in the neighborhood, and we also had for many years a wonderful Japanese housekeeper, Kiyome. She had been sent to Japan as a girl "to learn nice Japanese ways." From her and from playmates, I learned some Japanese words and was proud that I could count to one hundred in

Japanese. My interest in things Japanese was spawned during this childhood. We were surrounded by evidence of Japanese culture—festivals, celebrations, temples, all part of our familiar environment. These Hawaiian years also meant that I was removed from mainstream American culture and society.

I recall my father taking Kent and me to the harbor to see a young man from Japan who had sailed across the Pacific alone in an eighteen-foot boat. Amazing. Even more dramatic to me was when he took us to the Honolulu Airport to see Amelia Earhart's plane. I never forgot this inspiration, and it returned to me decades later when I wanted to learn to fly. It seemed our father was showing us that a person could do whatever he or she could dream. It was he who also took us to explore tidal pools at the shore. These powerful lessons my father taught returned to memory many times in my later life.

During our last two years in Honolulu, we lived in a lovely home in Makiki Heights, above Punchbowl, which is now a military cemetery. From this aerie, we had a 180-degree vista from Diamond Head to beyond Pearl Harbor and the Ewa Mountains. We could see Navy vessels and passenger ships leaving the harbor and passing Diamond Head. From there, we could see sugarcane fields burning in the night sky when cane was cut, and smell the pungent cane smoke that spread over the land. Below our home, a family of Hawaiians lived in a small wooden house, apparently on land my father had purchased. In the house lived a girl my own age named Esther, whom I once visited with the idea of making friends. My parents, however, regarded them as squatters on our property and forced them to move. I have no idea where this Hawaiian family moved. Could this be right? I wondered. I mourned what this must have meant for Esther, and many times during my long life, I have remembered her and wondered what became of her. I never forgot her and am sure that my sense of justice was born from that day, seeing Hawaiians pushed from their land, their culture suppressed under the onslaught of missionaries and the pineapple and sugar-plantation economy. My father, as the director of the Hawai'i Agricultural Experiment Station at the university, was linked to this plantation economy, controlled by the Big Five families, four of them descended from missionary forebears. (The Big Five began as sugarcane processing companies and wielded political power; they included C. Brewer & Co., Theo H. Davies & Co., Amfac, Castle & Cooke, and Alexander & Baldwin.) Pineapples were a daily food for our family during our Hawaiian years; to me they were also a daily reminder of injustice.

Minnesota Years

When I was thirteen, my father made what I felt was a seriously bad decision. He decided to return to the University of Minnesota as the dean of the graduate school, scheduled to become the university president. I agonized at the thought of leaving my island home and friends. I would lose all I loved: the smell of salt air, the waves gentle on my skin, the silvering of the sea when the sunset blaze dims, the wide night sky, the deafening blast of a myna convention at dusk, the fragrance of plumeria and star jasmine, and the sweet juiciness of mangoes and pineapples. Worst of all, my father passed away unexpectedly, just four months after leaving Hawai'i, and my mother was left to provide for my brother, Kent, and me. My sister, Frances, had graduated from Punahou and was given a year to study art in Italy before enrolling at Radcliffe. I felt a huge rupture in my heart.

Kent and I both attended the University of Minnesota, he in physics and me in Asian Studies and political science. These were the years following Pearl Harbor, which horrified me because the attack was made on my Hawaiian home. I debated whether or not to continue my interest in Japan, the nation that bombarded Hawai'i. My conclusion was that I should try to learn what had motivated Japan to undertake such a disastrous course. The professor who most included me was political scientist Harold Quigley, who was in the postwar Occupation of Japan.

I decided to continue on for an MA. I also began studying the Japanese language in the remnants of the Army Specialized Training Program (offered at state universities to supply the military with technically trained soldiers). Our teacher was an exotic Japanese German woman married to a general in the tsar's army. He shot himself in Russia while we were in her class. In later years, when I was studying in Japan, she and I became friends. She was then selling tobacco from Kentucky fields to the Japanese government tobacco monopoly, an occupation at which she was far more suited than language teacher. She confided in me that it was very easy for her to make money in this role. While in Tokyo, she stayed at Frank Lloyd Wright's iconic Imperial Hotel, and I always enjoyed visiting her there.

While studying for my MA, I met Bill, a fellow graduate student, with whom I shared some classes. We started dating, and, because he was also focused on Japan, we had similar interests, his in anthropology and mine in history. We went on a canoe trip to some of Minnesota's ten thousand lakes, my mother as chaperone! When he proposed, I hesitated. I was considering a different intriguing offer. A recent graduate of the law school was planning to travel in a kind of homemade boat with his wife and dog, first south along the Mississippi River and then eventually through the Panama Canal and up to Alaska, where a job awaited him. They were looking for a crew member, and I thought it would be a thrilling adventure. I debated but finally decided to marry Bill. In retrospect, I might have been better off taking the boat trip, but it certainly would have meant a very different life trajectory. My mother was anxious to see me married, fearing that if I didn't decide soon, I would become an "old maid."

Harvard Years

Bill and I married during Christmas vacation and took off in a very old car with all our belongings crammed into it for Bill's PhD program in anthropology at Harvard. Hardly an ideal honeymoon. We lived in a tiny two-story house attached to a repair garage in Brookline and ate forty-two pounds of peanut butter that first year. I wrote the peanut butter company, hoping for a carton, but did not even get a letter back. For the next two years, I worked at various menial jobs in Cambridge and Boston. There seemed to be no way to use my education in this rarefied, highly educated environment, and these were not good years for me. After three years, I was accepted at Harvard, and I embarked on my own PhD program in Japanese history, with a second field in Indian history. This also meant studying the Japanese language, a forbidding challenge unless one has a photographic memory needed to memorize the 1,800 characters required to read even a newspaper. Professor Edwin O. Reischauer, later US ambassador to Japan from 1961 to 1966, did not teach history; he taught us beginning Japanese. The section language teacher was a tough taskmaster, a Japanese American woman we hated, though she and I later became friends. Meanwhile, Bill took off for Okinawa to do anthropological research for his dissertation. This was effectively the end of a marriage that was a mistake almost from the start. But I have to admit that the marriage had one advantage—it got me to Harvard on the way to my PhD and an avenue for a productive life.

Research in 1950s Japan

In 1955, I received a Fulbright Fellowship for my own dissertation research in Japan. Reischauer was my dissertation advisor. I had wanted to research the Indian National Army for my dissertation, which would have enabled me to combine my two fields of Japan and India. I first learned of the Indian National Army from Professor Daniel Ingalls Sr., with whom I took several individual readings in Indian history. Reischauer, however, insisted that I do an exclusively Japanese topic. So I chose Ōkuma Shigenobu (1838–1922), a statesman of the Meiji era and the founder of Waseda University and a major political party (Kenseitō).[3] I was fortunate to have my fellowship renewed for a second year. Travel to Japan in those early years was by the *Hikawa Maru*. Arriving in Japan for the first time was a culture shock. Few foreign faces were to be seen in Tokyo then, unlike now, when foreigners fluent in Japanese are common in the city. Black markets still flourished in the alleys, and coffee, rice, and sugar were rationed. Farm women carrying huge loads of rice on their backs were a common sight on city trains. The government had no program for returning vets, and bedraggled white-clad men on crutches and with missing limbs hung out in train stations, where they slept in cardboard boxes. The country had been devastated, every major city pulverized except for Kyoto, a museum in itself.

I know I was often frustrated in a store or post office when a clerk took one look at my foreign face and decided that there was no way to understand this strange manifestation, even when I spoke my politest Japanese. It wasn't only my Japanese that was the problem. In the mid-1950s, soon after the end of the American Occupation, the Japanese had little experience with Japanese-speaking foreigners, the *gaijin* others.

The Fulbright commission in Japan housed me with the Tamiyas, the family of Tamiya Hiroshi, a biochemist and microbiologist who was a professor at the University of Tokyo, and I became intimately familiar with the lifestyle of a middle-class family in the 1950s. There was no indoor plumbing and no electric refrigerator, so the iceman came. The bath was a wooden *ofuro* heated for the whole family, including me, so I made an appointment on the days when the bath was heated. You washed and rinsed before entering the tub to soak, in proper order for family members—women and children last—but, apparently, as a guest, I had first soak. The loo was a hole in a wooden floor, and on Fridays when the honey bucket man came to empty the accumulation, it was wise to be away from the house.

Mrs. Tamiya taught French cooking, and I always enjoyed the mouthwatering sample she gave me of the week's lesson. The daughter, Takako, was a piano student who assiduously practiced the scales each morning at eight-thirty. The son, Hajime, was a sensitive boy who was unaccountably ignored by his father. The family tragedy was Hajime's death by suicide, which devastated his mother. Takako later became professor at the prestigious Tokyo University of the Arts.[4] Professor Tamiya told me years later that they regarded me as "their American daughter." He had the habit of asking for my opinion on various aspects of Japanese society and culture.

I spent my days in libraries at Waseda University and the University of Tokyo on the trail of Ōkuma Shigenobu. I made friends mostly with men because there were few if any women academicians then, and many men became close friends over the years. University libraries were notoriously cold in the winter, and I carried pocket warmers in my coat pockets and ate noodles for lunch along with other students and staff members. Because there was no ladies' room on the University of Tokyo campus, we had to take our chances in the men's rooms.

My response to Japan morphed through several stages, beginning with my early culture shock, and, after I made friends and lived with the Tamiyas, I went through a romantic phase, during which I visited Ōkuma's birthplace in Saga, Kyushu. On the same trip, I stopped in Nagasaki and took a bus trip. The bus conductress sang "*Un bel di, vedremo*" from Giacomo Puccini's opera *Madama Butterfly* at the house overlooking the promontory where lived the woman who had inspired Pierre Loti's novel *Madame Chrysanthème*, on which the opera is based. One evening, strolling through the city, a young passing gentleman greeted me—"Good evening"—in perfect English. The moment resonated with the history of Nagasaki, where a tiny island off the coast was the only place in Japan where foreigners were allowed to live during the more than 250 years of the feudal Tokugawa era. This was the avenue through which "Dutch learning" entered this otherwise isolated nation.

Another such moment came sometime later as I sat at the entrance to the shrine to General Nogi Maresuke, hero of the Russo-Japanese War (1904–1905) who committed *seppuku* with his wife following the death of the Emperor Meiji in 1912. As I sat there reading, an elderly farmer in leggings, faded jacket, and cap approached and said to me in Japanese, "Is it alright if I enter?" Startled, I nodded, assuring him it was. He, after all, had more right to be there than I. At the entrance to the shrine was a bamboo dipper and a concrete water trough incised with the words, "cleanse the spirit."

I also studied calligraphy during these two Fulbright years, both Japanese and Chinese styles (figure 3.1). My teacher was a calligraphy master, and my fellow student was art critic for *The Japan Times*. I appeared on a television program of foreigners doing Japanese things. I had several of my calligraphy scrolls beautifully mounted and later had a show of them in an art gallery in Boulder. I remember that on the program was also a little blond boy holding a tray of stacked noodle bowls balanced on his shoulder as he bicycled to deliver them.

One fortuitous advantage I had in researching Japanese history, especially in the 1950s, was that if a Japanese person was convinced of your seriousness of purpose, he would take it almost as a duty to go out of his way to give you every possible assistance. I benefited from this more times than I can mention. When I was researching military history, I worked many times in a setting where there were no women, Japanese or foreign. I was able, for example, to gain access to the National Institute for Defense Studies, Military Archival Library (commonly called the War History Library) through a fortuitous introduction, whereas Japanese scholars and journalists had difficulty. As an American woman scholar in those days, there was no category I fit, and I'm sure gatekeepers shrugged their shoulders, thinking an American woman was just an oddity, no doubt harmless—just let her in. I had other advantages.

My Harvard PhD was a great advantage in Japan, because not only do the Japanese regard Harvard as the premier American university, but also they hold Reischauer in high esteem.[5] In addition, during the mid-1950s, I was an anomaly as an American woman researching Japanese history. I was the first woman PhD in Japanese history in the United States, so I was uniquely placed at the time. Because the Japanese had no category in which to place me, I had a kind of freedom not enjoyed by Japanese counterparts. Titles and statuses are definitive in Japan, so, in

Figure 3.1: Joyce Lebra, calligraphy practice, circa 1955–1957, location unknown. Photograph courtesy of Joyce Lebra's family and the University of Colorado Library.

a way, I enjoyed a triple advantage: my association with Harvard, my association with Ambassador Reischauer, and my status as an American woman in Japan.

The University of Colorado Boulder

During my year as a visiting professor at the University of Texas, I was approached by the University of Colorado for a job interview. I had visited Boulder once and knew it was a small town. Having lived in Tokyo, I thought of myself as a big-city girl and wondered how I could survive in such a tiny place. Instead of going to Boulder, I accepted a job at the Newark campus of Rutgers University. But at both the University of Texas and Rutgers University, I taught Western civilization rather than Japanese or Asian history. When Colorado approached me a second time, I relented and went to Boulder. My most vivid memory of the job interview was seeing a friend, anthropology professor Gordon Hewes, walking a large chimpanzee on a leash across campus.

I arrived in Boulder in time to teach in the fall of 1962. For fifteen years, I was the only woman in the History Department, and salary discrimination was the order of the day. This was before the second phase of the American women's movement began. No one spoke yet of "sexual harassment." You can imagine. Power in the department was in the hands of a poker-playing, cigar-smoking, "good old boys" cabal. Department meetings were held in a small room with one tiny window and several members smoking cigars.

But at last I was able to teach the history of Japan and India. Another advantage in these early years was that the Dean of Arts and Sciences was receptive to innovative ways to teach, and, over the years, I probably taught Japanese history in twenty-five different courses. Later deans liked to wield their red pencil on any new course proposal. Another advantage of teaching at Colorado was that, whenever I received a fellowship for research support in Japan or India, the university was willing to grant me leave so long as I published results of my research.

I was still perplexed about how I would survive in what seemed after Tokyo and Newark to be a very small town. An idea came to me during my first Boulder Thanksgiving dinner at the home of my History Department colleague, Bob Athearn. The other guest there was Dan Grace, an undergraduate who taught flying lessons. Strange as it may seem, though I'm afraid of heights, I decided to give it a try. Flying became my great diversion during my first two years in Boulder, and it helped me adjust to life so far from the sea. After soloing, my longest flight was to an Association of Asian Studies regional meeting in Lawrence, Kansas.

Research in 1960s India and Japan

My first opportunity for a research trip after I began teaching at Colorado came with another Fulbright Fellowship (1965–1966) to India to research the Indian National Army (INA), the topic I had wanted to pursue for my PhD dissertation. I was finally able to begin researching this military force that fought for Indian independence in World War II with Japanese military help. I was excited that I would be able to combine my two interests, Japan and India. The results of my research on the INA were published first in Japanese translation in 1968, then in Singapore in 1971 under the title *Jungle Alliance: Japan and the Indian National Army*. The book was republished decades later, also in Singapore, titled *The Indian National Army and Japan*, and was basically the same book with a new title.[6]

On my flight from Delhi to Tokyo after the close of a year full of study, social events, and illnesses, I sat next to a Japanese gentleman, Toshio. When I spoke to him in Japanese, he must have been startled. He told me that he had been a pilot in World War II. The next day, Sunday, as I was dining in the hotel, he appeared, and I invited him to join me. This was the beginning of a friendship that spanned several continents and proved most valuable to my INA research. I then spent my summer of 1966 researching the INA in Tokyo.

My new friend generously offered me the use of his office and introductions to any military men I wished to meet. He took me to the War History Library at the headquarters of the Japan Ground Self-Defense Force at Ichigaya (Japan's Pentagon), housed in buildings of prewar concrete. There, I met the director, a critical meeting in a country where personal introductions pave the way for any endeavor. Without this introduction, I would have had no means to access this highly restricted library, where I wanted to research Japan's wartime policy toward India. I met several INA-related individuals, both military and civilian, in Tokyo. By the end of the summer, I had met and interviewed many generals. These interviews were especially valuable, as these men were near the end of the lives. I met Fujiwara Iwaichi, founder of the INA and now a general. He spoke of his memoir, which Toshio had been helping to translate, and during our conversation, he compared himself to Lawrence of Arabia.[7] He became emotional when speaking of the INA, and it was obvious that his fostering of Indian independence was based on a deep commitment, not simply a propaganda ploy for Japan. When he campaigned for a seat in the National Diet, he lost by a narrow margin. Someone quipped that had he run in India, he would have been elected. A Japanese proverb, "A defeated general doesn't talk," worked against him, I suspect. Despite losing twenty pounds in India and suffering subsequent health issues in Tokyo, I managed to gather a lot of research data during this summer stay. I am fortunate to have had many more opportunities to continue research in Japan and India since then, not only on the INA but also on other topics. For example, I received a fellowship from the National Endowment for the Humanities (1970–1971) for research in Japan, and again I was fortunate that the university granted me leave. I was able to extend it to two years with a half-year grant from the Australian National University in Canberra and a half-year teaching appointment at Macquarie University in Sydney. This meant I could spend a whole year in Australia, sandwiched in between two half years in Tokyo. During these two years, I also spent a few weeks conducting interviews in Singapore, Kuala Lumpur, and Djakarta.

November 25, 1970

In the fall of 1970, I researched Japan's wartime policies and activities in Southeast Asia, a big project that resulted in two books.[8] This meant going at least once a week to the War History Library. The fateful day—Wednesday, November 25, 1970—began for me like any other: going through the security check and walking up the hill to the library with Keiko, the young woman assisting me. We went into the reading room and sat down at a table assigned to us and began reading the documents I had requested about the Japanese 15th Army operations in Burma. The persistent screech of police sirens jarred my consciousness. I glanced out the window and saw several police cars in front of the headquarters building. People began pouring into the area in front of the administration building. Curious to know what was going on, I went out and joined the growing throng of soldiers and civilians. Suddenly, on the balcony appeared a face I recognized from the dust jackets of many novels: author Mishima Yukio, dressed in a uniform designed after a World War II Amy issue, with a white sweatband around his head. Four young, uniformed men joined him, and they unfurled a long white banner over the balcony wall and exhorted everyone to listen. Mishima's harangue continued for twelve minutes, during which he glanced at his watch from time to time. Incredulous soldiers responded, "Fool!" and "Go take a cold shower!" When I realized that I, a tall foreigner and the only foreigner on the scene, was standing directly in Mishima's line of vision, I became uncomfortable and moved to one side. At the same time, I thought, this is a historic event, and I'm standing here. Mishima and his cohorts then disappeared from the balcony into the office of the commanding general behind the balcony.

The whole headquarters compound was in chaos: helicopters circling overhead, newsmen swarming everywhere, soldiers gesticulating and shouting. I saw a few soldiers pointing at me, so I decided to head back into the library. Before I entered the door, I saw three police cars leaving the compound, each with a young man uniformed like Mishima. A few minutes later, we heard what Mishima had done: before a horrified bound-and-tied commanding general, Mishima had committed *seppuku*, disemboweling himself, after which one of his lieutenants lopped off his head with a samurai sword in a feudal military ritual. We learned later that the first lieutenant had missed and struck Mishima's back, and the job was left to another of the young soldiers, so that two of them were beheaded. For three hours, I hesitated to leave the compound, knowing that it would be surrounded by right-wing sympathizers who supported the crazed agenda. When I finally left, I hurried past the guards to the subway and the safety of the International House where I was staying. My adrenaline was working overtime and continued to do so through the night. I went straight to the I-House library and checked out Mishima's book *Sun and Steel*, in which he theorized about death on nearly every page. Unable to sleep, I read about his idealization of the suicides of early historical figures for a noble cause. Sleep still eluded me, so I got up and jotted down my impressions of the incredible events of the day.

Mishima's act electrified Japan and made headlines around the world. At the urging of my friend Perpetua, I took my impressions to the newspapers, and *The New York Times* and *Mainichi Daily News Tokyo* both bought my story, my first venture into journalism.[9] For weeks, I was besieged by media people wanting to interview me, as though I had some special insight into the psychology of this unimaginable event. In a letter to my mother in December 1970, I wrote that I had worn calluses on the soles of my feet, running from one appointment to the next, trying to fit in everything before I left for Southeast Asia. The same month, I traveled to Kyushu to lecture at the university and to meet more generals. In my last letter from Tokyo, I wrote that I had five appointments in one day, including hearing the defense minister speak, going to the Burmese Embassy, and attending a seven-course wedding dinner and reception.

Women in Asia

In 1975, the first international year of women, I decided to turn my attention away from the political and military history that had so far preoccupied me and to write about women's history. I discussed the possibility of a research project on Japanese women in the workforce with Joy Paulson, my graduate student, and we decided to organize a team project in which each individual was responsible for researching an occupation: a graduate student researching bar hostesses, a nun studying suicide, Gail Bernstein from the University of Arizona investigating farm women, a Tokyo resident looking at dentists, and an editor looking at women in sports. I selected the category of women in the service industries. Our research resulted in *Women in Changing Japan*.[10] A better title would have been simply *Japanese Women in the Workforce*. Following the success of this venture, two years later, Joy and I decided to try a second similar project in Southeast Asia, focusing on women of the Chinese diaspora in Singapore, Kuala Lumpur, and Bangkok.[11] Heartened by this second successful outcome, Joy and I decided to try yet a third team-research project, this time in India, where we selected the cities of Delhi, Mumbai, and Trivandrum, Kerala.[12]

Postscript

An Asian attachment I must mention, speaking of good luck, is that I have recently learned that in May 2021, I shall be decorated by the government of Japan with the Order of the Rising Sun, Gold Rays with Neck Ribbon. Who could have imagined such an ending to my long, fortunate life? So, clearly, I must remain alive and ambulatory until May. Actually, it's only the announcement that will arrive in May. The award will not be given until September, so I must remain alive until September, quite a challenge at age ninety-five.

Notes

[1] These excerpts come from Joyce Lebra's unpublished memoir by the same title, written soon before her death in 2021 and housed at the University of Colorado Boulder. They are included here with permission from her family and from the University of Colorado Library. They illustrate how, to Joyce, history was always a living presence inseparable from a place and people. From her PhD thesis research in Japan to her groundbreaking work on the Indian National Army and its implications for emergent postwar nationalism in Southeast Asia, Joyce followed the threads of relationship across cultures and languages that arose in response to Western colonialism and told *their* stories.

[2] Editorial note: see, for example, Eleanor C. Nordyke and Y. Scott Matsumoto, "The Japanese in Hawai'i: A Historical and Demographic Perspective," *Hawaiian Journal of History* 11 (1977), 165.

[3] See Joyce Lebra, *Ōkuma Shigenobu: Statesman of Meiji Japan* (Canberra: Australian National University Press, 1973).

⁴ Editorial note: we have been unable to confirm Takako Tamiya's position at the Tokyo University of the Arts. Any leads would be appreciated.

⁵ Editorial note: Harvard officially awarded PhD diplomas to women in arts and sciences starting in 1963. Before then, women registered and received degrees through Radcliffe College but could take classes at Harvard and be advised by Harvard professors. The Radcliffe Graduate School closed in 1963 after the Harvard Graduate School of Arts and Sciences began accepting women. Harvard University Archives, "Who Was the First Woman to Earn a Doctoral Degree at Harvard University?," Harvard University Library, December 14, 2021, https://askarc.hul.harvard.edu/faq/326845#:~:text=In%20 1963%2C%20more%20than%20twenty,women%20candidates%20for%20the%20Ph.

⁶ Joyce Lebra, *Chandora Bōse to Nihon* (Chandra Bose and Japan) (Tokyo: Hara shobō, 1968); *Jungle Alliance: Japan and the Indian National Army* (Singapore: Asia Pacific Press, 1971); *The Indian National Army and Japan* (Singapore: ISEAS, 2008).

⁷ Fujiwara Iwaichi, *F. Kikan: Japanese Army Intelligence Operations in Southeast Asia during World War II*. Translated by Akashi Yoji. Hong Kong: Heinemann Asia, 1983.

⁸ Joyce Lebra, ed., *Japan's Greater East Asia Co-Prosperity Sphere in World War II: Selected Readings and Documents* (London: Oxford University Press, 1975); *Japanese-Trained Armies in Southeast Asia: Independence and Volunteer Forces in World War II* (Hong Kong: Heinemann Educational Books, 1977).

⁹ Joyce Lebra, "Eyewitness: Mishima," *The New York Times*, November 28, 1970, 26; "Last Speech on Balcony Witnessed," *Mainichi Daily News Tokyo*, November 28, 1970.

¹⁰ Joyce Lebra, Joy Paulson, and Elizabeth Powers, eds., *Women in Changing Japan* (Stanford: Stanford University Press, 1978).

¹¹ Joyce Lebra and Joy Paulson, eds., *Chinese Women in Southeast Asia* (Singapore: Times Books International, 1980).

¹² Joyce Lebra, Joy Paulson, and Jena Matson, eds., *Women and Work in India: Continuity and Change* (New Delhi: Promilla, 1984).

4

"In Search of Flowers Yet Unseen"

Barbara Ruch

Have things changed? Yes, radically in a multitude of ways. In short, I was not (and could not be) as you are able to be now. We have now at our disposal tools not dreamed of yesterday, and we can speak about experiences in words not then yet coined.

BARBARA RUCH (pronounced "Roosh") is a professor emerita at Columbia University and was the founder (1968) of the IMJS: Institute for Japanese Cultural Heritage Initiatives, where she also still serves as director. She was founding and initial director (1986–1990) of Columbia University's Donald Keene Center of Japanese Culture. Initiating the Imperial Buddhist Convent Research and Restoration Project (1989), she spearheads their ongoing conservation efforts, exhibitions, and publications. For her pioneering work on Japanese culture, she received the inaugural Minakata Kumagusu Prize (1991), the Aoyama Nao Prize for Women's History (1992, first non-Japanese recipient), the 42nd Bukkyō Dendō Kyōkai (BDK) Award (2008, first female and non-Japanese recipient), the Kyoto Governor's Culture Award (2011), and other honors. She is the only academic awarded the Imperial Decoration, Order of the Precious Crown, with Butterfly Crest (1999). Since 2006, she has directed the Columbia/Barnard/Juilliard Gagaku-Hōgaku heritage instrumental music performance program.

First Encounter

The year was 1954. Early morning fog halted our antiquated freighter outside Tokyo Bay. After three weeks over turbulent February seas that were anything but "pacific," we were at last in sight of land. In the sudden stillness of waiting, the only sound was the clamoring of seabirds soaring above, adding to our feeling of impatience.

Seven that evening, we finally made our way into the Yokohama Harbor. The structures that lined the pier were no different than those we left behind in San Francisco, but the stevedores scurrying below wore straw rain capes with thin white towels tied around their foreheads. Japan at last.

Representatives of the American Friends Service Committee (AFSC) and the Society of Friends (Quakers) greeted us while we waited for the passage of baggage through customs. I was stunned to look down and see that on this, my mission of peace and reconciliation, I had traveled on a ship the hold of which also contained US military tanks and trucks.

The car ride to Tokyo through an endlessly dark landscape revealed nothing of this unfamiliar land. My new "home," Friends Center, the residence of Esther Rhoads, of Friends Girls School and an English tutor to members of the imperial family, was also the headquarters for virtually all Quaker postwar relief activity. Tucked away high among temples and wooden houses on the top of Mitadai-machi hill, it had been miraculously spared from the disastrous firebombing.

Day of Infamy

Going back more than a decade, December 7, 1941, was the notorious "Day of Infamy," the day of the Japanese naval attack on Pearl Harbor. Ironically, it also marked the day when Japanese Studies in the United States, as we have come to know it, was inseminated.

To say that Japanese Studies was conceived in 1941 is not exactly accurate. Affluent elites who had the leisure and the means to satisfy their interests had, since the early nineteenth century, begun their great archaeologies and ownership-assemblage of objects of beauty from Egypt to Japan.

Until bombs and torpedoes did their work, however, Japanese Studies was not a recognized program of academic pursuit in the universities of the world. The fact of the matter is that, without the huge investment of American military money and personnel, it is doubtful that Japanese Studies would exist as it does today in our universities.

The role of the US military as father to Japanese Studies presented me with a dilemma. As an anti-war Quaker, I had gotten into trouble with my peers in high school for refusing to compete for sales of war bonds and stamps, competitions that, after all, were not about selling cookies but were to raise funds to buy bullets, bayonets, and bombs to kill not only enemy soldiers and but also millions of innocent civilians living in their way. With the war over, however, I was forced to view the role of the US military also as a revelation when I realized they had organized, funded, and educated in Japanese language almost every graduate school professor under whom I was to study or whose books I was assigned to read, including Wm. Theodore de Bary, Howard Hibbett, Donald Keene, Ivan Morris, E. Dale Saunders, and Edward Seidensticker.

The 1930s and 1940s

There is no doubt in my current nonagenarian's mind, therefore, that a defining factor of my encounter with Japan was my exposure to the Quakers of Philadelphia, my parents, each separately, having converted to the Society of Friends in spite of an ancestry of Alsatian/German Catholicism on the paternal side and Scottish atheism and Pennsylvanian Dutch Lutheranism on the maternal side. Philadelphia was and is the center of America's Quaker anti-war influences and "all-humans-are-equal" anti-segregation activities.

At Abington Friends School (for girls), from which I graduated in 1950, I had studied Latin and biology, hoping to facilitate my entrance into medicine, but my high school advisor made it clear that only a miniscule number of girls were admitted to pre-med colleges. (Years later, I learned that, indeed, Yale, for example, did not admit girls as freshmen in pre-med until 1973.) The well-known Quaker institution, Earlham College, on the other hand, offered me a four-year merit scholarship, which greatly relieved my teenage angst.

Going to the Midwest from Philadelphia for the first time, it was a great shock to discover that Richmond, Indiana, in 1950 was racially a strictly segregated city. Fortunately, Earlham was open to students of all races, as was the freshman women's dormitory where I was to live. The encapsulation, however (no discrimination, no alcohol, no drugs, no crime), was not a preparation for postgraduate life in the 1950s.

Then, too, Japan meant nothing to me except a remote island nation, a recent Asian enemy now suffering the miseries of defeat. Japan was absent from all curricula. Earlham's current fame as a Japan-focused undergraduate college is due to Jackson Bailey's efforts there a decade after he ceased to be my AFSC colleague in Tokyo.

A Quaker in Tokyo

As innocent as one could be in those days in one's first job out of college, I was now in a country about which I knew next to nothing and could not speak its language. A country distrusted, even widely hated around the world. I gradually came to realize, however, that I was in another kind of protective bubble of sorts, in that most Japanese I met were introduced to me through Quaker postwar relief and restoration work. The anti-war stance and historic emergency relief work by the Society of Friends among victims on both sides of multiple wars on several continents had been recognized in 1947 with the Nobel Peace Prize. Further, I had attended the same Philadelphia Quaker meeting as Elizabeth Vining, tutor of the then Crown Prince (Akihito), and I was now living with her successor, Esther Rhoads.

Despite my parents' and friends' fears, and in spite of desolate conditions and unaccustomed relief work, all my experiences were positive ones. I suffered only from the loneliness of language deprivation. Anyone is quick to learn to greet, to thank, to purchase, to ask directions. But heart-to-heart talk was impossible. One's very body language betrayed one's inability to grasp the significance of the moment.

For me, loneliness always led to books, and I felt a burst of joy when I discovered a small bookstore in Tokyo where some English-language books were available. The pickings were small, but among the most prominent representations of fiction on those meager shelves was Arthur Waley's translation (1925–1933) of *The Tale of Genji*. I later learned of the enormous gaps and misunderstandings that had marred Waley's solitary labors, but Lady Murasaki Shikibu's work (as read through Waley) nonetheless stunned me. I had the arrogance of youth—a young college graduate who had double-majored in the early literature of England and America and social psychology, and I believed I *knew* what defined a novel and various forms of poetry. How could Lady Murasaki, however, break all those rules and produce a masterpiece? It must be Waley's sleight of hand. I would not, could not, let it go. I vowed to myself that, when I got back to the States, I would go to graduate school and learn how to read classical Japanese, which then, to me, constituted dumbfoundingly bewildering genre-defying marvels—Rubik's-Cube masterpieces—in their original language.

Home to Philadelphia and on to New York

I lived a lifetime of unforgettable days and years in Japan about which I'll write one day but not here; it was then AFSC work to repair destroyed lives, not academic.

In Philadelphia in 1958, however, I was lucky, probably beyond anything imaginable today. The University of Pennsylvania's Oriental Studies Department, world-famous for Ancient Near Eastern and Indian Studies, had recently added Japanese language and literature. They admitted me easily and awarded me a work-study fellowship.

Those were happy days among gentlemanly professors who treated me seriously and shared freely their own excitement about their respective fields. That atmosphere bred in me the desire to continue. How could I stop halfway? I even spent a long sweaty "no-AC" summer in a dorm at Columbia University studying more advanced Japanese language with the kind, severe, magnificent teacher Ichiro Shirato; he gave me a true sense of confidence in the language for the first time and made me comfortable at Columbia. I targeted Columbia doctoral study because of him and the presence of a young assistant professor, Donald Keene, and his awe-inspiring mentor, Tsunoda Ryūsaku. The Ford Foundation was then generously supporting "area studies," and, after I was vetted by Robert Scalapino, they committed to funding my entire four-year doctoral program at Columbia.

Nowhere in those late-1950s days in Japan and studying in Philadelphia had there been any hint that being a female was a hindrance. Those joyful, carefree days, however, came to an end when I entered my doctoral courses at Columbia, the only woman among a dozen men. Most have now vanished from the scene, but some who became prominent in the field were blatant in their disapproval of me among them: "What are you doing here?" "What do you want?" "You should be at home having babies and not toying with graduate study and usurping grants that are intended for serious men like us." It was all so adolescent that it did not make me waver; it was just unpleasantly annoying, like flies in summer.

There would be times much later, however, when, with obtuse but I'm sure the best of intentions, women colleagues would tell me how lucky I was not to have had to juggle motherhood with an academic life, as they did, not knowing that the deaths of my two daughters, Laura and Sarah, who had not lived into their childhoods, were never to me a fortunate roll of the dice.

It was premature to expect Japanese Studies-related graduate work to be a well-mapped, well-paved road in the 1950s and 1960s. There were certainly unexpected potholes and jolts.

Enamored as I was of what little I then knew of Japanese literature, it was a total shock when I encountered in Donald Keene's *Anthology of Japanese Literature* the medieval short story "The Three Priests" (*Sannin hōshi*), one of the most disturbing pieces of misogyny I had ever read—despicable men who robbed and murdered women, now monks, chatting on top of Mount Koya, forgiving each other and bonding as monks and fellow males. Without comment on the misogyny, Keene wrote that this work is "the finest of these stories."[1]

I knew that not to be true, having poured myself into *The Story of Yokobue* (*Yokobue no sōshi*) for my Penn MA.[2] And by then I knew for a fact that the genre called *otogi zōshi* (companion books) was neither "nursery tales," as Keene described, nor was the male-bonding story the best of the lot.³ He was writing, after all, when no one in the West yet knew a thing about Japanese medieval short stories, so instead of being the fearless cant of the securely seated, this was probably just evidence of the general ignorance shared by all of us.

Looking back, "The Three Priests," rather than driving me from the field, reinforced my determination to pursue the whole medieval short story genre for my doctorate. I had dipped into the genre enough to know it spoke to the heart and was a repository for essential aspects of medieval Japanese cultural life.

There were those like me who, with a little trowel, barely scraped the surface of this unturned field. Those who came after—Maggie Childs, for instance—got into substance. Then Keller Kimbrough produced numerous excellent translations despite the exotic book titles that obfuscate the quality between their covers. Laura Moretti's 2020 book, *Pleasure in Profit: Popular Prose in Seventeenth-Century Japan*, provides a deep cultural plowing that opens up the field for whole new crops and reveals how these works of medieval and early modern fiction were eagerly sought, and how, despite deep medieval roots, they educated a wide variety of Edo citizens as well.

Kyoto, Home of My Heart

The two years in the 1960s when I was sent to Kyoto University as a requirement for my Columbia doctorate were the most important years of my life. Classrooms were leftover wooden barracks—no glass in the windows, no heat, taking notes with gloves on, muffler impeding my view, some lecturers slipping into casual Kyoto dialect. But the city and my homestay family became mine forever. That city, as it was then, the family, my mentors, and my beloved friends are all long gone now, but, years later, when Barack Obama was elected president, it was to my favorite tree on the west bank of the Kamo River that I retreated to be alone so that I could shed tears of joy.

Back to New York

I should not leave my Columbia graduate school years without a word about Ivan Morris. He had done his dissertation with Arthur Waley on *The Tale of Genji*, and so I had sent for it and read it before I took his class. We were, therefore, colleagues in *Genji*. He gave me many lunchtimes and coffee times, however, in which he stretched my mind to areas I would never have nurtured on my own, persuading me to translate a chapter, "From Carnal Literature to Carnal Politics" (*Nikutai bungaku kara nikutai seiji made*), by the famed political theorist Maruyama Masao (1914–1996) and giving me the courage to be active outside my medieval world.

The widely voiced lament that there are not enough women mentors cannot be denied. In my graduate school days, however, there simply were no women professionals on the department faculty at all. One woman, however, stands out in my mind. Miwa Kai (1913–2011), the multitalented, bilingually well-read, and profoundly knowledgeable then librarian of the Chinese-Japanese collection, was someone I deeply admired. Her very existence rendered an authenticity to our environment. She was indispensable. I could see clear as day, however, that she was viewed by most professors and students as a servant or "staff." They were gentlemanly and thanked her for her yeoman labors in finding and decoding things for them. But truth be told, the effortless thank-yous over time grew to ring like an empty bell. I cannot get rid of the echo of entitlement in those words or their ironic resonance.

The Real World

I felt both lucky and rewarded for my hard work to be offered a faculty position at both the University of Michigan and Harvard University, even before I had defended my dissertation. At the time, Michigan had been designated by the US government as *the* Center of Japanese Studies in the United States in multiple disciplines. Harvard, not so, for multiple reasons.

"I don't know what to do," I said to Professor Keene. To my surprise he said, "You may be swayed to accept the position at Harvard for a variety of reasons, but I advise you not to." Startled, I asked why not. He replied, "I'm thinking of your career in the long run, and, to be frank, Harvard does not tenure women. To my knowledge, they have never tenured a woman." I was convinced he must be out of date and countered, "Surely now in the 1960s, they can't still be cloistering the men." Good counselor that he was, he said, "You have to make up your own mind."

For some centuries, the emperor had been couture-wrapped in magnetic garb, and I now was like iron filings. In the "I know best" delusion of youth, turning a deaf ear, I chose Harvard. I remember that sense of euphoria riding my bicycle through Harvard Square to my new apartment after seeing off in their car my proud visiting parents.

Ten years later, in 1974, the late Rulan Chao Pian became the first tenured woman in the Harvard-Yenching Institute and the Department of Far Eastern Languages (which was not yet an official department). Her doctoral dissertation on Song Dynasty music had been completed fourteen years earlier in 1960. The first woman to be tenured at Harvard itself was not until 1978.

Cambridge

Euphoria is but a brief moment in time.

In Cambridge there was the true joy of getting to know people in other departments who were there at the same time: Ben Schwartz, Ezra Vogel, Victor Mair. Inside my department as a member of the faculty, however, I was made to question my very self-identity. Invited to lunch at the faculty club by an eminent male (of course) colleague, I tasted the humiliating fact that women could enter only as "guests"; male faculty only could become members, and only members could use the "faculty" club. This added to my growing realization that women at that time and place were measured on some unseeable scale whereby their worth was inevitably some unknowable but considerable fraction less than males.

I cringe with mortification when I remember that Tamako Niwa (1922–2015) was introduced to me as "Miss Niwa, the language assistant." Not until many years later did I discover that "Miss Niwa" was Dr. Niwa, with a 1956 PhD from Radcliffe (women then could not get a Harvard PhD), and that her doctoral dissertation had been on the medieval diary of Lady Nakatsukasa no Naishi. The patronizing way she was introduced to me and my acceptance of it all at face value fill me to this day with remorse.

At that time and place at Harvard, women academics had no agency.

The existence of "language assistants" notwithstanding, Harvard at that time, still under the influence of Latin and Greek traditions, chided me if I gave equal value to students being able to speak fluently with their prospective colleagues in Japan as I did to decoding and translating texts.

There was also something unsettling and tone-deaf about the popular name by which these elite male faculty, and by now coed students, referred to their entry-level Asia survey class as the "Rice Paddies" course.[4]

Some reality history may never be told; yet why are we skirting around it—the way we used to see and hear "no evil" in the dehumanization of "Colored Only" signs in many states in America or in the alienating adolescence of "male only faculty clubs." Then, too, in my day, the term "sexual harassment" had not yet been coined; I was of a generation without words for our experience.

As time passed, there were experiences not appropriate to this essay that led to my commitment to leaving Harvard. I began negotiations to relocate, and one place outshone them all.

Penn and the Founding of the Institute for Medieval Japanese Studies

In just the six or seven years since my Penn MA, the University of Pennsylvania had been organizationally and physically transformed. The Oriental Studies Department now had three clear administrative subdivisions, one called "East Asian Studies." The humanities had a new building all its own. My office was to be next to that of a man, young like me, named Noam Chomsky; the faculty club, they assured me, would welcome my membership without a sex change.

The definitive ingredient, in addition to my professorial post, was their commitment to supporting my dream of establishing an international, interuniversity Institute for Medieval Japanese Studies (IMJS). Its first nest, "a room of its own," would be in the Van Pelt Library—a floor-space no larger than a queen-size mattress, but it had a door that locked, bookshelves, and a filing cabinet—indispensable tools at that ancient time when "the computer" was still in utero down in the Electrical Engineering School, being incubated in a refrigerated space the size of a long-distance bus.

My new "real" life, then, began in 1968. My mission, apart from teaching, was to encourage research on all aspects of Japanese culture during those more than four medieval centuries (1185–1600) out of which prior, all-male literary scholars had selected the exclusively male repertory theater of Noh and Kyōgen, and the primarily male world of *renga* poetry and battle tales (*gunki*), as their canon. Historians were in the thrall of fiefs, power politics, and battles, all universally the rumbles of male leaders. In the multiple rolling meadows of medieval Japanese cultural heritage, subject matter lay wide open, ripe with untouched fruit.

Etoki: Venturing into Fieldwork

Medieval paintings of Japanese daily life are filled with depictions of the era's "media," women and men engaged in *etoki*, "the telling of pictures" (figure 4.1). Every Japanese academic I spoke to in the 1970s, however, assumed the art had died out in the face of modern entertainments like cinema and television. On the theory that *etoki* was far more than entertainment, however, and must still involve deeply entrenched religio-secular cultural rituals and experiences, I began my first ventures to look for it. One after the other, as I traveled around to temples in Kyoto, Nara, Wakayama, Hyogo, Toyama, and so on, the "telling of pictures" of historical events, the lives of saints, and the afterlife of heavens and hells emerged as a living part of community temple activity to this day.

Ultimately, to my deep satisfaction, *etoki* rose to academic consciousness. An *etoki* academic association was formed; its journal, *Etoki kenkyū* (*Etoki Research*), ran from 1983 to 2011. Akai Tatsurō published a definitive book, *A Genealogy of Etoki* (*Etoki no keifu*) in 1989. At last, in 2006, Ikumi Kaminishi published a full English-language study, *Explaining Pictures: Buddhist Propaganda and Etoki Storytelling in Japan*.

You will be interested to note, in the 1970s, the era of my ventures in fieldwork, the Japan Travel Bureau and other agencies refused to handle reservations for a woman traveling alone, a taboo apparently formed from traditional mores that women did not travel alone and that Japanese women who did were usually

Figure 4.1: In a small temple, Ōjōji, west of Zenkōji, a woman with a vivid pair of hanging scrolls intones the famous medieval story about the Mount Koya monk Karukaya Dōshin, which recounts his son's search for him and their reunion. Photograph by the author, courtesy of the IMJS Archives.

intending suicide. My fieldwork method, therefore, involved just showing up at an inn's door and requesting a night's stay. I was never refused, but once, in Nara, I ended up in a kitchen storeroom; in Ishikawa, it was a luxury suite at a golf club, where I had to pay as if I were two.

Not a Mentor but a Fairy Godfather

I cannot remember (if I ever knew) how he learned of me, then newly settled and teaching at Penn, but John Whitney Hall of Michigan, later Yale, although never my mentor, was my fairy godfather. He reached out to me in 1972 and invited me to join the otherwise all-senior male scholars, thirteen from the United States, twenty from Japan, to participate in the "Conference on the Muromachi Age: Its Society and Culture" to be held in 1973 in Kyoto. I was not to be a gofer nor an auditor but a presenter of whatever I was researching that was most meaningful to me in the conference context.

Jack Hall's magic wand was a first for me. I felt it shed from me, by then almost forty, the artificial shell that marked me "woman." There, I was seated like all others around the table, just another scholar among already famous men: Akiyama Terukazu, John Rosenfield, Hayashiya Tatsusaburō, Marius Jansen, Stanley Weinstein, Donald Keene, Toyoda Takeshi, and others. My presentation there, "Medieval Jongleurs and the Making of a National Literature," rocked a boat or two but was one of the most important products of my early scholarship; still today, I meet those influenced by it. Our resulting Japanese book (1976) retained the original conference title (see above), but when the English version came out (1977), the title lost those essential words "society and culture." It became simply *Japan in the Muromachi Age*, another example, in my view, of Western academia's aversion to "culture" and the long-standing effort to escape the Japaneseness of area studies and gain approval as a Western historical discipline.

The *Nara Ehon* Resurrection

My serendipitous discovery of a hoard of cardboard boxes containing a cornucopia of magnificent Japanese hand-painted and calligraphed religio-secular story books and scrolls in a storage closet in the Chester Beatty Library in Dublin on a trip home from Japan inspired my next major initiative. Many books and scrolls dating from the fifteenth through eighteenth centuries had poured out of Japan during the nineteenth and early twentieth centuries, purchased by wealthy collectors. Scattered around the world unknown to today's scholars, they needed first to be relocated. Step two was to provide access by organizing what ultimately became the "First International Research Conference on *Nara Ehon*," whereby Japanese scholars could be brought to the sites of the largest collections (August 16–17, 1978, in London; August 18–24, 1978, in Dublin; and August 28–31, 1978, in New York) to study these lost manuscripts. I invited eighteen Japanese scholars, plus European and American non-Japanese with related expertise—roughly forty in all.

Organizationally and financially, the conference was a nightmare. Everything was unprecedented. I found that the Japanese government would fund Japanese scholars going abroad to *teach* about Japan but not to *study* about Japan. All "policies" had to be negotiated back to blank slates and then recreated into unfamiliar international and interdisciplinary configurations. Finally, with a support letter from the Japan Business Federation (Keidanren) in hand, I was authorized to go to their fifty-some corporate members, tell my story, and essentially beg. It took months. Some were supportive and generous. One gave me a brown paper bag out of his desk drawer (the petty cash?).

In the 1970s, interdisciplinary study was frowned upon; those attempting it were considered dilettantes. Occupying quite separate and highly guarded fiefs, specialists in painting, calligraphy, literary texts, religious anthropology, and medieval book and scroll antiquities did not collaborate. These eminent invitees had never before sat together around a table to examine and share knowledge about the same work. Even Kantō and Kansai area scholars in the same field had never before collaborated; some had never even met in person (figures 4.2 and 4.3).

Our collaborations led to the first-ever exhibitions of foreign-owned *Nara ehon*, first at Japan Society (September 1–17, 1978, New York), then the next year

Figure 4.2 (left): Okami Masao (bending), Ichiko Teiji, Matsumoto Ryūshin, and Ōba Takemitsu examine a scroll at Japan Society, New York, September 1978.

Figure 4.3 (right): Scholars surround curator Kenneth Gardner at the British Library, August 1978. Photographs courtesy of Kadokawa shoten and the IMJS Archives.

at the Suntory Art Museum (August 14–26, 1979, Tokyo), and Gallery Shibunkaku (August 30–September 11, 1979, Kyoto). We also worked together to publish several books, including *Nara Ehon Abroad: Illustrated Literature from Medieval and Early-Modern Japan* (*Zaigai Nara ehon—chūsei kinsei emaki ezōshi*), published by Kadokawa shoten. An important but critical part of my negotiations with Kadokawa resulted in their in-house editors and photographers accompanying us to London, Dublin, New York, Tokyo, and Kyoto, donating all their team's time and travel costs in exchange for publication rights. They also supplied free use of their photographs and microfilm to all participants.

Since then, *Nara ehon* (as art, popular literature, religious teachings, and manuscript books) has become a standard and unified subject of research in Japan; conferences are held, and new publications (photographic reproduction, analyses, and translations into modern Japanese and several foreign languages) appear. The price of *Nara ehon* on the market, however, skyrocketed (*désolé!*).

In the early 1980s, Joshua Mostow, then a graduate student at Penn, led the next generation in perceiving Japanese illuminated literary works as inseparable *visual and audio* amalgams. The most recent and most brilliant expansion of efforts to resurrect Japanese pictorial narrative scrolls and books located outside Japan has been *Love, Fight, Feast: The World of Japanese Narrative Art*, the project and exhibition (2021) at the Museum of Rietberg (Zurich).[5]

Founding the Donald Keene Center of Japanese Culture

In the 1970s, Donald Keene asked me to take on one semester of his Columbia courses every year so that he could spend that term yearly in Japan. In the late

1970s, therefore, I commuted to Columbia one day a week. In 1984, I moved full-time to the faculty of my doctoral alma mater, and Columbia agreed to house the IMJS as well.

Despite his worldwide renown, word had come down from on high in 1985 that, when Donald Keene retired one mandatory day not too far off, Columbia would likely not replace him. University needs had higher priority than teaching "the exotic subject" of Japanese literature. Clearly, endowment was the only guarantee of survival and continuity. All agreed, but no one stirred. Others, without their name already crowning something similar, vociferously opposed the founding of a Keene Center. If the IMJS was anything, I thought, it was an engine for cultural rescue. I went around to colleagues' offices to gather ideas and support.

One prefers to forget the laborious, pitted, and rock-filled road to successful actualization. A certain senior professor knocked the wind out of me with unforgettable words: "You women have too much time on your hands," he said. "You will fail and you will bring shame to our university."

This was not male students throwing verbal-harassment spitballs at females. Not annoying flies in summer. This was full artillery from a general. I still have the holes in my heart.

But tenacity is a necessary quality. As is flexibility. So on my own I went to Japan. Major Japanese literary figures, Japanese friends of Donald Keene, some of whom I, too, knew well, joined me in Tokyo to plead the case to the Japanese public (figure 4.4).

Figure 4.4: Shiba Ryōtarō, Barbara Ruch, Nagai Michio, and Abe Kōbō at a press conference in Tokyo in 1985, announcing the plan to establish the Donald Keene Center of Japanese Culture. Photograph courtesy of the IMJS archives.

Figure 4.5: The Kamakura-period portrait sculpture of Abbess Mugai Nyodai. Photograph courtesy of Nishikawa Kyōtarō and the IMJS Archives.

A year later, with hard work, we successfully raised the several million dollars needed to create an endowed chair, the Shinchō Chair of Japanese Literature for Donald Keene, the anchor for the new (1986) Donald Keene Center of Japanese Culture (DKC). Everyone then wanted ownership of the newborn, however. For four years, I served as its director, and after getting programs started, I was able to pass the directorship over to another colleague in 1990. Happily, the DKC has been preserving Japanese literature at Columbia for more than thirty years now.

A Korean nun once said to me, "When you hit an obstacle, become as water and flow around it."

Abbess Mugai Nyodai

Casually leafing through a book containing photographs of Kamakura-period (1185–1333) portrait statues of eminent Buddhist clergy one day in the early 1980s, I was struck by one that, to my eye, seemed somehow matronly. Indeed, it turned out to be the startlingly lifelike statue of a Japanese Rinzai Zen abbess,

Mugai Nyodai (1223–1298), made shortly after her death by a superb but unnamed sculptor (figure 4.5).

Already deep into my career and having taught for years, I was more than shocked; I was angry. In not a single book or course had I ever encountered the word "abbess." Whenever the word "nun" appeared in literature, it usually referred to a grief-stricken woman with seemingly no alternative but the tonsure. The whole female side of Buddhist culture, ignored by male scholars, had thus been absent from my consciousness as well. I chastised myself for failing to realize that all these years I had simply swallowed what I was served.

Nishikawa Kyōtarō, then head of the Nara National Museum and one of the original scholars to study Abbess Nyodai's statue and designate it a cultural treasure, gave me superb photographs of her, one of which has hung beside my desk all these years. She and I have bonded as collaborators ever since. I look at her. She looks at me, and says, "Well now, what are you going to do about it?"

And so, in 1989 at Columbia, we launched the first American "Workshop on Women and Buddhism in Premodern Japan: Research Strategies for a Newly Developing Field."

Not until then had I encountered malice in misogyny. At the opening of this first workshop for American scholars, with guests invited from Japan, an eminent colleague, whom I had invited to give a few opening words, stood and said, "I fail to see the relevance of this workshop. We here at this university have always historically taught about nuns. Women are always becoming nuns in *The Tale of Genji* and throughout Japanese history. I wish you well, but I feel there is just an unnecessary redundancy here."

I could not believe what my ears were hearing. The power to intimidate was being exercised boldly and in public, but it created an atmosphere he did not expect. Three participants in the audience stood up and walked out on him. I deemed it best to just "ignore and proceed." Throughout the workshop, both men and women seemed liberated. I was deeply moved when a senior male scholar from elsewhere said our workshop had validated a research subject that had long been explicitly taboo in many religion departments, including his. He had tears in his eyes, which brought them to mine.

In Kyoto in 1993, seeking entrée to the highest-ranking convent that traced its history back to Abbess Nyodai, I asked advice of everyone in my network of professors and friends. The unanimous responses were: "Give it up." "They won't let you in." "They turn all of us away." One night a familiar voice in my head said, "What are you going to do about it?" The next morning, emboldened by the challenge but with deep trepidation as if plunging off a cliff, I picked up the phone and dialed. A cheerful young nun said good morning, and my tension vanished.

Figure 4.6: A first look at unsorted documents at Hōkyōji Imperial Convent in 1996. Photograph courtesy of the IMJS Archives.

Introducing myself, I told her I had recently published a book in Japanese that referenced Abbess Nyodai and asked if they would allow me to place a copy on their altar as an offering to her memory.[6] "When would you like to come?" she asked.

The next afternoon began my thirteen-year friendship with Abbess Kasanoin Jikun, which lasted until her death at age ninety-two in 2006.[7] Through her, I gained entrée to many other convents; she made our research and restoration work a joyful, living reality. We discovered a whole world of unknown treasures and documents, research that continues to be led superbly by Monica Bethe and Patricia Fister in Kyoto (figure 4.6).

With support from the Mainichi Broadcasting System, Inc. (Osaka), I invited nine imperial nuns to New York to conduct a service commemorating the 700th death anniversary of Abbess Nyodai in 1998 (figure 4.7). This greatly raised interest in Japan in the long history of aristocratic women and their influence on the nature of Japanese Buddhism and court culture. It also opened new programs in women and Buddhism in both Japanese and foreign academia. Conjointly, we held the first "International Symposium on the Culture of Convents in Japanese History," ultimately inspiring the publication of *Engendering Faith* (2001) by scholars from many disciplines, which highlighted women's impact on the cultural development of Buddhism in Japan.

Figure 4.7: St. Paul's Chapel, Columbia University; (left) the opening of the service for Abbess Mugai Nyodai's 700th memorial in 1998; (right) nuns performing *sange*. Photographs by Lynn Saville, courtesy of the IMJS Archives.

My approach to the World Monuments Fund (WMF), which assists in architectural restoration of important historic buildings worldwide, was hindered by their confusion about what is Japanese architecture and what is artwork (which they do not support). Are the painted and calligraphed sliding panels that separate rooms to be defined as "interior walls" or just "interior décor"? It took a trip to Japan by the WMF president to see firsthand and for the first time just what comprised Japanese architecture (!) before they agreed in 2002 to collaborate on the restoration of convents. To start, WMF raised more than $1.6 million from US philanthropists to match Nara City and Nara Prefectural support for on-site conservation work in Nara imperial convents (figure 4.8).

I learned much from just drinking tea with Abbess Kasanoin Jikun as our friendship deepened. Chuckling, the nuns confessed to having an "allergy to scholars" (with "present company excepted") because of the patronizing stance of the grand male professors from universities who felt "entitled" to come in and research the storehouses of "ignorant" nuns. "We just say, 'It's not convenient today,' and keep the gate shut." A Japanese woman scholar had once gained entrée, but the undercurrent of her subtle prejudice against the continuing existence of the aristocracy in Japan did not go well for the objectivity of her work.

Figure 4.8: Restorers work on sliding door panels of Chūgūji Imperial Convent in Nara, 2008. Photograph courtesy of the Oka Bokkōdō restoration studio and the IMJS Archives.

That there remain only thirteen imperial convents in Kyoto and Nara (when once there had been many) is due to one of the great unstudied attacks on Japanese culture activated by the Meiji government when it set its crowbar into the center of the nation's sacred places of worship, pried the shrines from the temples, and severed the gods from the buddhas. Buddhist nuns were ordered to be defrocked and to become Shinto maidens or else desacralize and go "home." For the first time in history, imperial women were forbidden to become abbesses of Buddhist temples.[8]

Her Majesty Empress Michiko (now Empress Emerita) has been graciously and enthusiastically since 1999 giving personal support. For how many centuries had pre-Meiji imperial women, ancestors of His Majesty, and Her Majesty's predecessors, become abbesses and spent their lives honing the heritage of high-court arts and praying for the health and safety of the realm?

In culmination of mutual trust and scholarship, for the first time in history, more than two hundred treasures from all thirteen Japanese imperial convents were shown publicly in an exhibition at Tokyo University of the Arts, University Art Museum (April 14–June 14, 2009, figure 4.9). Whole rooms, and altars, too, were reconstructed in the galleries and proved to be a revelation to the viewing crowds. The bilingual catalog, *Amamonzeki: A Hidden Heritage: Treasures of the Japanese Imperial Convents* (*Amamonzeki jiin no sekai: Kōjo-tachi no shinkō to gosho bunka*), was named among that year's best publications worldwide by Holland Cotter (*The New York Times*).[9]

Figure 4.9: His Majesty and Her Majesty viewing the *Imperial Convents* exhibition (2009) at Tokyo University of the Arts, University Art Museum, with University President Miyata Ryōhei, Barbara Ruch, and museum curator Kurokawa (Yokomizo) Hiroko. Photograph courtesy of the IMJS Archives.

A Rose Is Not Always a Rose

My personal identification as a cultural historian of premodern Japan confuses a number of colleagues. "I thought you were an art historian," is a remark I hear often—no doubt because of my early work first on *etoki*, then *Nara ehon* and *emaki*. Then, due to my ongoing work in the Imperial Buddhist Convents, there are those who assumed my field is Buddhism or women's studies. Those who list me as a premodern Japanese literature specialist do so because of the genre of my PhD dissertation. All this has sadly excluded me from surveys of premodern historians.

This widespread misleading phenomenon of mislabeling has its roots not just in antiquated academic departmentalization but in the foundational conflict that arose during the 1940s and 1950s between the sudden emergence of "area studies" in conflict with the old Europe-born "disciplines" on which the university structure has been built. Upstarts like Japanese Studies or Korean Studies were viewed as devoid of the well-established foundational Eurocentric "theories" and lacking "methodologies."

A person in Japanese Studies needed to be accepted by the standards of, for example, a Eurocentric history of art and archaeology department or a history department to gain acceptance in Western academia. Japanese literature specialists especially were stranded; there was no disciplinary department (Romance Languages, for example) in which to seek academic salvation. Some then gravitated to the new field of comparative literature.

The Cultural Language of Music

Few are aware that Japanese musical instruments were totally removed from Japanese schools in the late nineteenth century by government policy and replaced by Western musical instruments. Viewed as "modern machines" due to having keys and levers, they were therefore seen as part of the Industrial Revolution and adopted as essential ingredients to "modernization" and "Westernization." From then on, music education in Japan has been Western music—a kind of self-imposed colonization. (Of course, look at the many Japanese piano and violin stars of Western music that now shine on Euro-American stages!) For 150 years or so, generations of Japanese, however, have lost all familiarity with their own musical heritage.

The twenty-first century now, thankfully, is a different world. Young Japanese and non-Japanese composers and musicians have created a renaissance of Japanese-heritage instrumental music, both traditional and in new music genres. Further, they have completely ended the male-centric tradition; all genders now play together in their secular *gagaku* (classical court music) ensembles (except at the palace itself and at certain shrines), and all heritage instrumental groups otherwise do not discriminate by genres.

At Columbia, a flame was lit one night by the students. I had invited on a shoestring Nakamura Kakujō, the eminent biwa singer, to perform. The hall was vast; in the middle of the stage, in a single spotlight, he sat alone, black-robed, on a maroon *zabuton* floor cushion. The audience comprised New Yorkers and lots of Columbia students.

Out of the silence, he began slowly to intone the opening phrases of the "Sea Battle at Dan-no-ura" from the medieval *Tales of the Heike* (*Heike monogatari*) that sang of the tragic encounter of men and ships that spelled the end of the Heike clan. He sang in Japanese, his biwa magically sounding the whiz of arrows, the thud against armor. Pulsating, the performance seemed to elicit, from the floor, walls, and ceiling, the cries of long dead men, the crash of waves, and the moan of ships.

In the sudden silence at the end came involuntary cries of "Bravo!" from the back of the hall, even from those who did not understand Japanese. Music students swarmed the stage like birds to grain. Moved by instrumental and vocal sounds they had never heard before, they pressed him: "How do you do that? Show me!" It is this kind of moment when the language of music commands changes and breaks through rusted academic barriers.

For years, I taught *Tales of the Heike* from texts, playing last-leg Heike singers on 78 rpm records, being chastised by colleagues for "playing around" with literary texts, yet knowing in my heart how far the texts were from the authentic passion

Figure 4.10: Reigakusha orchestra members teaching Columbia *gagaku* classes, March 24, 2011. Photograph by George Hirose, courtesy of the IMJS Archives.

of the performed work. Donald Richie once wrote that "it is not impossible to read the Noh as literature, but it is difficult."[10] He equated reading Noh plays as literature to someone who sits in silence and reads a music score. I experienced this truth with *Tales of the Heike*.

That evening, students hungered for the language of Japanese music.

For many reasons, we could not start with the biwa. But I could deliver better. In 2005, Kawai Hayao, my longtime friend, Jungian psychologist (and Western flutist!), and then head of the Agency for Cultural Affairs, enthusiastically endorsed our proposal to launch not a lecture course but a hands-on, falling-in-love-with-the-instrument heritage instrumental training program of *gagaku* (Japanese sacred and court music) and *hōgaku* (Japanese art music) for credit in the Music Performance Program that trains the ensembles in the Department of Music at Columbia (figure 4.10).

Every year, we have eminent musicians as mentors and have even succeeded in certifying some students as now professional players and composers! Our student-musicians, from many fields and departments, include American and foreign students (figure 4.11). Perhaps it is the Quaker influence in me, but, while the world's nations are attacking each other with weapons and words, when I see students of those same warring nationalities playing together the *gagaku* melody *Music of the Divine Heavens (Etenraku)* with all their hearts, as one, in the *gagaku* ensemble, I think this is the way the world should be.

 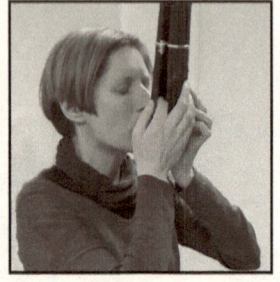 

Figure 4.11: Wind professionals who trained in Tokyo on Japanese instruments in Global Artist Residencies: Rosamund Plummer (Australia, 2014), Jinny Shaw (UK, 2016), and Rolando Cantú (Mexico, 2019). Photographs courtesy of the IMJS Archives.

Looking Back

If my memories here have come down pretty hard on the male academics who created the parameters and substance of Japanese Studies, that is clearly because I lived through these very early years and was too blind to understand the later ramifications. Looking back, I can see now the impact. But today, just spreading female icing on the cakes already baked by those men is not the answer.

About to retire from teaching, I sought the one colleague I thought most likely to assure that deep reading of women writers would not vanish from the curriculum. I called on her to discuss the possibility of some sort of continuity to my two-semester survey course on major women writers (premodern and modern). Her immediate and discussion-ending reply still rings in my ears: "I do theory. I don't do women." I wondered afterward what she thought of, say, Sumie Jones, one of our influential theorists and specialists on women writers (see chapter 13). What is theory? It is not an abstract tool. You cannot come to theory without knowledge of the internal consciousness and external pressures of writers *you have read*.

To say we need more women faculty can go nowhere if intimidated by the career-endangering "area studies" versus the required "disciplinary theory" conflict. Yes, we need more women simply because it is an affront and immoral to bar women. All humans should at least have equal access. But "more women faculty" can be a "straw horse." It can never leave the stable without heart, mission, and vision.

Nor dare we overlook the men whose work made crucial advancements. To pluck out a random example or two, James Dobbins's work on the nun Eshin-ni (1182–1268) should have stimulated an outpouring of scholarly reexaminations of this dynamic female religious leader and turned over a lot of pronouncements about her husband, Shinran. But the vested interests of huge political and religious institutions, entwined with academic ones, may make this impossible for some time, if ever. Hank Glassman, on the bodhisattva Jizō, singlehandedly transformed our understanding of this central figure in Japanese Buddhism, brought him home, and showed him in the context of women's rituals, deeply engaged with humans, not a tool of intimidating priests.

Conclusion

Have things changed? Yes, radically in a multitude of ways. In short, I was not (and could not be) as you are able to be now. We have now at our disposal tools not dreamed of yesterday, and we can speak about experiences in words not then yet coined. Columbia claims 47 percent of its new tenured and tenure-track faculty in 2022 were women.[11] Yet, that same year, the tenured faculty makeup of my present departmental affiliation, for example, had not changed in the twenty-some years *since I retired from teaching*: all men, one woman. The curriculum has perhaps worsened as foundational premodern cultural primary source exploration has shrunk while a new focus on modern entertainments (both secular and political) attracts. Sadly, there are still old gaping holes. A current doctoral student in the Department of Art History and Archaeology studying Zen calligraphy expressed astonishment last year when I urged her to look at Zen abbesses' calligraphy as well. "Nuns did calligraphy!? I had no idea!"

Despite the difficult, painful even, sorting through the good and bad of a long academic life, I am nonetheless grateful to have been asked to reflect on my life in Japanese Studies. It has instilled in me an urgency to tell you things that may stir you, the reader, to realize, in the context of your own life, how far we have already come and yet to see some of the exciting possibilities the future holds that only you can accomplish. Scholarship is full of discovery and excitement and joy.[12] One must find one's place where neither status quo nor complacency sucks the oxygen out of the air.

We are living in a time when all our cultures are being rewritten. The United States has changed. Japan has changed. Past history, however, is over and unchangeable. It is our vantage points that can and must change. With that shift, perspectives deepen, meanings change. I cannot envision an academic life devoted to training the next custodians of a canon selected by nineteenth-century male Japanese scholars and replicated by Euro-Americans in the twentieth. Japanese Studies is an endless field that extends beyond the horizon of what you are able to see from your current vantage point. As the wayfaring poet-monk Saigyō observed at Yoshinoyama: "From last year's known path / I'll take another route now / to view flowers yet unseen."[13]

Notes

I could not have completed this "*solicited*-tale" of memories without the collaboration of two superb administrators at the IMJS: Institute for Japanese Cultural Heritage Initiatives, Executive Director Ken Aoki, and Assistant Director Akemi Yoneyama, who prepared my photographs electronically and flew me, as it were, on that well-known medieval white horse, safely over the marshes and quicksand of today's high tech. I am deeply grateful.

[1] Donald Keene, *Anthology of Japanese Literature: From the Earliest Era to the Mid-Nineteenth Century* (New York: Grove Press, 1955), 322.

[2] Later reexamined at Donald Keene's retirement; see Barbara Ruch, "Transformations of a Heroine: Yokobue in Literature and History," in *Currents in Japanese Literature: Translations and Transformations* (New York: Columbia University Press, 1997).

[3] Sometimes translated "bedtime stories." There is no evidence Japanese architecture had designated "nurseries" as in the West nor the custom of reading to children at "bedtime."

[4] "Rice Paddies" was the nickname given by those involved with the course "Social Science 111." See chapter 1.

[5] Collaboration by collectors, curators, and scholars brought together a huge array of works from Moscow to Stockholm in a magnificent exhibition and catalog of Museum Rietberg (Zurich), September 10–December 5, 2021.

[6] Barbara Ruch, *Mō hitotsu no chūsei zō* (Another Perspective on Medieval Japan) (Kyoto: Shibunkaku Publishers, 1991), winner of the Minakata Kumagusu Prize and the Aoyama Nao Prize.

[7] See Barbara Ruch, "A Wreath of Memories," in *In Iris Fields* (Ayamegusa Nikki), edited by Barbara Ruch and Michiyo Katsura (Kyoto: Tankōsha, 2009, bilingual book), 14–18.

[8] Abbess Rokujō Shōzui of Dōmyōji Temple southeast of Osaka has recorded the traumatic events experienced by her predecessor, Abbess Shōkei Kajūji (1845–1899), on a CD-ROM, *Sasa no shizuku* (Dewdrop on a Bamboo Leaf). See "Dōmyōji CD-ROM," *IMJS Reports* 13 (December 2003), 37, https://www.imjs-jchi.org/vol-13-december-2003/.

[9] Holland Cotter, "The Art of the Book, the Book of the Art," *New York Times*, November 27, 2009, https://archive.nytimes.com/query.nytimes.com/gst/fullpage-9C0CE1DF163EF9 34A15752C1A96F9C8B63.html.

[10] Donald Richie, *A Lateral View: Essays on Culture and Style in Contemporary Japan* (Berkeley: Stone Bridge Press, 1992), 113.

[11] Lee Bollinger, "Our Accelerated Faculty Diversity Efforts," Office of the President, October 29, 2021, https://president.columbia.edu/news/our-accelerated-faculty-diversity-efforts.

[12] See my "Preface" in Karen M. Gerhart, ed., *Women, Rites, and Ritual Objects in Premodern Japan* (Leiden: Brill, 2018), vii–xvii.

[13] Saigyō's (1118–1190) poem reads: Yoshinoyama / kozo no shiori no / michi kaete / mada minu kata no hana wo tazunemu. For full bibliography and details about my present activities and those of the Institute which I still direct, see the homepage of the IMJS, www.imjs-jchi.org and chusei-nihon.net.

5

AGAINST THE ODDS, PERSISTING . . .

Marlene J. Mayo

> These are many ways to contribute to Japanese Studies, all of them important: scholarship, curriculum transformation, exhibitions, conferences, student exchange programs, library and archival collections, translations, editing, centers, and institutes, but one must be prepared to overcome hurdles that stand in the way.

MARLENE J. MAYO is an associate professor emerita at the University of Maryland. She edited *The Emergence of Imperial Japan: Self-Defense or Calculated Aggression?* (1970), coedited *War, Occupation, and Creativity: Japan and East Asia, 1920–1960* (2001), and authored over twenty articles and book chapters. Her many leadership positions include serving as chair of the Northeast Asia Council of the Association for Asian Studies, president of the Mid-Atlantic Region of the Association for Asian Studies (MAR-AAS), chair of the Columbia University Seminar on Modern Japan, and founder and chair of the Washington and Southeast Regional Seminar on Japan. At the University of Maryland, she cofounded the Committee on East Asian Studies (now a center) and served several times as chair, and she established the Undergraduate Certificate Program in East Asian Studies. She initiated the 20th Century Japan Research Awards for use of Maryland's Gordon W. Prange and East Asia Collections, and the Marlene Mayo Graduate Paper Prize for MAR-AAS. She has curated and compiled important archival resources, including the *Marlene J. Mayo Oral Histories with Americans Who Served in Allied Occupied Japan* (University of Maryland Libraries).

Growing Up in Detroit

My path to becoming a Japan historian had nothing to do with family missionaries, diplomats, or military service. It was a combination of childhood and academic experiences that coalesced in college. I was the only child of Southern rural parents who met and married in Detroit, and of the Great Depression and World War II. I grew up, a Baptist fundamentalist, in the Detroit public school system from kindergarten through university. Pride of place was instilled during primary school: Detroit was the fourth-largest city in the United States and known as the country's "Arsenal of Democracy," as so named by President Franklin D. Roosevelt in one of his 1940 Fireside Chats. Everything came together by my senior year in college. I was a history major and determined, somehow, to go to graduate school and become a Japan historian.

For my ninth birthday in July 1941, my parents gave me a small radio for entertainment. Although I read a lot as a child and cycled to the local library, I soon became a fan of radio programs and loved to distinguish the voices of radio personalities. After church on Sunday morning, December 7, my afternoon program was suddenly interrupted by the Pearl Harbor announcement. The memory is vivid. This was the first event to thrust me from the comfort of family and friends into the outside world—I had not been aware of World War II in Europe, certainly not of total war in China. It must have been a mild winter day because I remember running out to the backyard to tell my parents. I recall my mother's fear that my father, a police officer, might be drafted. I remember the naming of Captain Colin P. Kelly (1915–1941) as the first American air casualty of the Pacific War. In grade school, we followed war news in *Junior Scholastic Magazine* and had occasional blackout practice. Although I had cousins fighting on both fronts, I mainly recall the Asia-Pacific War. This memory was probably reinforced by a newspaper comic strip, *Guadalcanal Diary*, based on a 1943 book by reporter Richard Tregaskis.[1] About this time, a classmate circulated small black-and-white photos of dead Japanese soldiers that her older brother had taken in battle. I spotted propaganda posters and billboards depicting Hitler, Mussolini, and, instead of Hirohito, a generic Japanese man with round glasses and buck teeth. The last shock to a thirteen-year-old who had been safe in the United States were visual images of the atomic bomb, a huge awesome cloud and the debris of a whole city—not yet of human bodies, photographs of which were published much later.

From Cass Tech High to Wayne University

In tenth grade, I transferred to a select high school, Cass Tech, as a music major but discovered greater talents in history and literature. By graduation, religious and racial hypocrisy had begun to provoke serious questioning of my early beliefs. With a tuition fellowship and a book subsidy from the Detroit Board of Education, I felt grateful and lucky to reach the apex of the Detroit public education system, Wayne University (now Wayne State University), a large urban institution. Although the school was majority white in the early 1950s, it was ethnically diverse and enrolled foreign students, principally from India and the Caribbean. Many of us, if not most, were probably the first in our families to finish high school. My father, from a family of seven, made it to the tenth grade in a Mississippi country school. In the Appalachians of southwest Virginia, my mother, one of twelve children, made it to the sixth or seventh grade but was sent to work at age thirteen as a tutor and housemaid. I have lovely memories before kindergarten of sitting in her lap while she read from children's books. She was enthusiastic about my academic dreams and sympathetic to my growing interest in the outside world; my father, although puzzled, was not opposed.

In the early 1950s, I commuted to Wayne by bus as I had to high school. Our professors, primarily white men, knew who we were, our class and backgrounds, and did extremely well by us. I had only two courses with women faculty—biology and gym. With little grass, surrounded by concrete and busy streets, Wayne was indeed "a place of light," as the title of its anniversary book in 1968 proclaims.[2] Increasingly, East Asian and Japanese Americans came into my consciousness. In first semester English, S. I. Hayakawa's *Language in Thought and Action* made a huge impression. Published in 1949 and based on an earlier edition titled *Language in Action* (1939), it tackled propaganda and prejudice, using the concept of shades of gray—exciting to me as I learned to question assumptions and binary assertions.[3] However, years later, I was disappointed in Hayakawa's stance against student activists while a professor and president (1955–1973) at San Francisco State College (now a university). I loved history, enjoyed a variety of courses as a major, and, in my junior year, I took a class on the "Far East," the term used in those days. Our textbook was Kenneth Scott Latourette's *A Short History of the Far East*, and the professor was Thomas Frank Mayer-Oakes, who I was surprised to learn, after his death, was among the Pacific War veterans who became postwar Japan Asianists.[4] As an undergraduate student at the University of Chicago, Mayer-Oakes had joined the first Japan-America Student Conference (a summer cultural and educational exchange program started by and for university students) in 1934 and toured Japan and Manchuria for three months. A wartime graduate of the US Navy Japanese Language School at Boulder, Colorado, in 1943, he had been assigned to the Allied Translation and Interpreter Section (ATIS) in Australia. He was the successor in 1947 to Sinologist Earl Pritchard, one of the founders of the Far East Association (forerunner of the Association for Asian Studies [AAS]) and its bibliographical series. As it turned out, I would become the youngest of five students taught by Mayer-Oakes in the early 1950s who went on to earn doctoral degrees in East Asian history. The others were Harry Harootunian, Bernard

(Bernie) Silberman, and Eugene Soviet in modern Japan and Allen Linden in modern China. Arthur P. Dudden and Hayden White were other history majors of note in that era.[5]

Another powerful memory from Wayne was a special lecture on the United States Bill of Rights for a joint assembly of political science classes. The speaker was Hattie Masuko Kawahara, a recent PhD (1949) from the University of Minnesota. How ironic to hear such a lecture by a Japanese American whose rights, and those of her family, had been denied during the war. She had been permitted to relocate from an assembly center in 1942 to finish her college degree at Mount Holyoke and was the author of an article for *Mademoiselle* in August 1944, "I Am an American."[6] But, suddenly, she was no longer at Wayne. Years later, I caught up with her when she asked me to lecture on Japan at the Foreign Service Institute. I learned that she had won a Ford Foundation Fellowship in 1952 for research in Tokyo on Japan's National Diet and, while there, had met and married an American intelligence officer, Kenneth Colton. After they moved to Washington, DC, in the late 1950s, Hattie joined the Foreign Service Institute, US Department of State, where she had an important role in developing the foreign area language and training program and became a dean.

Senator Joseph McCarthy of Wisconsin was a malign presence during my undergraduate years. Famed journalist Edward R. Murrow had delivered a searing television expose of Senator McCarthy's communist name-calling tactics in March 1954, and the Senate would censure him formally at the end of the year. Moreover, in the spring of 1954, my college friends and I were absorbed by the Army-McCarthy Hearings, which were displayed for our enlightenment on a small black-and-white television set in a dismal but convivial cafeteria.[7] The 1950s were scarcely a bland period in domestic and international politics. The Korean War was uppermost, too, during most of my college years. For my generation, who were children of the Great Depression and World War II, the Korean War was never "a forgotten war." It erupted in the month of my graduation from high school, sent young men of my age off to battle, and revived fears of the atomic bomb. It did not end until a truce in the summer of 1953. Alas, it would be a while before the scholarly study of Korea itself entered the East Asia curriculum on some semblance of equality.

Fulbright Year in London

As I was becoming more Japan-conscious at Wayne, another opportunity opened up. I worked part-time in the scholarship office, which was run by a dynamic woman, Virginia Brodel. In my junior year, she told me about a new category of Fulbright Fellowships for recent college graduates. I was already pondering how and where to continue as a history graduate student. I had taken four courses in

English history with Goldwin Smith, another formative professor, and decided I had sufficient background to apply for study of the British Commonwealth of Nations at the London School of Economics. By the time the acceptance letter arrived, I had taken a second course with Mayer-Oakes and made a firm shift to Japan. American and European history would never lack coverage, I thought, but Japan should also have a prominent place in the pantheon. Worried about accepting the fellowship under false pretenses, I wrote to my assigned tutor, William N. Medlicott, a distinguished economic historian. He promptly sent back a reassuring letter. "Come along," he urged, "I would like to know more about mid-nineteenth-century Anglo-Japanese relations." With relief, I went to England and enjoyed the best year of my life (1954–1955), an academic and cultural feast. As a send-off, Mayer-Oakes invited me and my parents to his home for a dinner of roast beef and Yorkshire pudding. The ocean voyage was exciting. One of my cabin mates was Mary Maples (Dunn), future dean at Bryn Mawr and president of Smith College. Another, who was headed for Oxford University, was an organizer for the International Ladies' Garment Workers' Union.

At our first formal meeting in London, Professor Medlicott's advice was to do what I could not do in the United States: forget classes, go to the archives to learn how to use primary sources, and present a seminar paper at the end of the year. My future path and methodology were set. I have continued to love archives—the content, detail, quotidian, analysis, and resulting narrative of storytelling. Off I went, early morning every day, to the Public Record Office (now the National Archives in Kew) on Chancery Lane. Since the search room was cold, heated only by a fireplace, we wore winter coats and wrote notes by pencil, taking our gloves off and on. I began with the 1860s because British documents were open only seventy years back. I soon came across the records of an early Meiji statesman named Iwakura Tomomi (1825–1883), a former court noble and canny politician who led the Iwakura Mission to the United States and Europe (1871–1873). In a larger context, I wondered to what extent the Mission's agenda and the observations of its members—"Ministers of Modernization," to appropriate Silberman's title for his 1964 book—might help explain the Meiji Restoration (some scholars preferred the term "Meiji Renovation") and commitment to nation-building.[8] When I learned that the School of Oriental and African Studies (SOAS), University of London, had appointed a modern Japan historian, Professor William Beasley, to an endowed chair, I signed up for his first seminar. It was of enormous value because Western scholarship on Japan was sparse at the time. I read and reread Professor Beasley's 1951 book, *Great Britain and the Opening of Japan, 1834–1858*, which necessitated a reevaluation of the first American diplomatic overtures.[9] To take breaks from research, I went to see ballet, opera, theater, and film, and on long vacations with fellow students on the Continent, getting as far as Greece, former Yugoslavia, and Turkey (most East European countries were closed to us). My friend Carol Elder (later Bauman), a Marshall Scholar who later earned a PhD at the London School of Economics and had a great academic and political career, was determined to reach Asia Minor, and so we took a ferry from Istanbul across the Bosporus Strait.

I hesitated to renew my Fulbright Fellowship. Medlicott's advice was to return to the United States where, he said, language training and area studies were superior to anything offered in Britain. It was the first time I heard the expression "area studies," a construct later criticized for lack of theory or for being a cover for intelligence operations but maintained today in universities as a multidisciplinary field. I decided to apply to Columbia University and Radcliffe College, requesting financial aid. Again, I met good fortune. William T. R. Fox, head of Columbia's Institute of War and Peace Studies, happened to be in London with his wife, the recipient of a research fellowship, and he offered to interview me. Our meeting went well, and Columbia's subsequent acceptance letter included the offer of a Ford Foundation Foreign Area Training Fellowship. Radcliffe accepted me but without financial aid. I felt partial to Columbia, anyway, thanks to listening to a radio broadcast during its bicentennial year (1953–1954) and reading Columbia professor Jacques Barzun's *Teacher in America*.[10] Besides, it was in New York City, which I had visited with a tour group from Wayne in 1953.

Graduate Years at Columbia University

I entered Columbia University in the fall of 1955 on what turned out to be five years of financial support in Japanese and East Asian History—from the abovementioned Ford Foundation Foreign Area Training Fellowship—that included a year of doctoral research in Japan. Within Japan, then unknown to me, 1955 was a pivotal year: "Ban the Bomb" protests and fallout from the *Lucky Dragon 5* incident (in which a Japanese fishing boat was contaminated by nuclear fallout from US H-bomb testing at the Bikini Atoll in 1954); the founding of the Liberal Democratic Party (LDP); the first Five-Year Economic Plan; the Housewives' Debate in the magazine *Fujin kōron* (*Women's Review*); the Eisenhower administration's authorization of covert CIA activity in Japan; and the murder of Emmett Till. 1955 also marked the arrival in New York of the Hiroshima Maidens for reconstructive surgery. Back in New York, Harold Strauss and Knopf were gearing up to publish modern Japanese fiction in English translation. The exhibit of a traditional Japanese house at the Museum of Modern Art in New York City was continuing to attract record numbers of visitors. The craze for foreign films and the fixation on auteurs, including Japanese films and directors, was underway. This was the beginning of large-scale American cultural interest in Japan, and D. T. Suzuki taught at Columbia University from 1952 to 1957.

In this context, East Asian Studies was beginning to take off at Columbia University, although the fear of McCarthyism was still lingering over academe.

Columbia's East Asian Institute had been set up in 1948 on the fourth floor of a stately old mansion, the Casa Italiana, by Sir George Sansom and Hugh Borton (the first American to earn a PhD in Japanese history). Columbia generously awarded me nine credits for my Fulbright year. I majored in East Asian history with a focus on Japan and lived in the graduate women's dormitory. Early on, I met two impressive women graduate students, both supportive, who had preceded me in Japanese Studies: Marleigh Grayer Ryan in literature and Ann Rasmussen in economics. Allen Linden, a fellow Mayer-Oakes student, and his wife, Adina, were gracious dinner hosts. I took almost as many courses on China as Japan and am indebted to China historians L. Carrington Goodrich and C. Martin Wilbur. A young Donald Keene taught early Japan, visibly unhappy in the role, but shined in two magical courses on Japanese literature. Professor Borton, who had lived in Japan twice during the 1930s, first as a Quaker humanitarian and then as a doctoral candidate, argued that Japan should not be lumped together with Germany and Italy as fascist, an approach contrary to recent scholarship. I did not know that he had an important wartime role in shaping American policy for Occupied Japan. Many refugee students and scholars from China were around but hardly any from Japan. For the first time, I had Asian teachers—Franklin Ho for an enjoyable geography course, and Ichiro Shirato, a devoted and skilled instructor, for Japanese. Our language textbook was a partly revised wartime primer, *Spoken Japanese* (1945) by Bernard Bloch and Eleanor Jorden (an improvement, older classmates told me, over the more esoteric approach of Elisséeff-Reischauer-Yoshihashi's *Elementary Japanese for College Students* [1944]).[11] If there was a language laboratory, there were no assignments. Miwa Kai, a magnificent librarian, was the head of the Japanese holdings. There were no women professors in the history department or in East Asian Studies, with the exception of a course in art history at Barnard College taught by China specialist Jane Gaston Mahler, which I foolishly did not take. (The first Japanese art historian arrived in 1961, the year I defended my dissertation.) I was fascinated by the visit in 1956 of famous Japanese philosopher and critic Hasegawa Nyōzekan but understood little of his talk. A more controversial Japanese visitor, given the atmosphere, was economist Tsuru Shigeto, who spoke in impeccable English about Japanese trade with Communist China. As an academic role model, I looked up to Mary Clabaugh Wright, Yale's historian of modern China, but did not have the chance to meet her.

Otherwise, the cultural feast that had begun in London continued in New York; whenever my friends and I could afford them, we got tickets to the New York City Ballet, New York City Opera, "the old Met" on Thirty-Ninth Street, and Broadway plays and musicals. (Museums did not require tickets in those days.) The only Japanese restaurant nearby, or should I say the only one with a Japanese name, was Aki's on 119th Street (the closest item on the menu to Japanese food was butterfly shrimp). Near City Center, a frequent haunt of my grad pals, there was

Miyako, an authentic Japanese restaurant, which had managed to survive during the war years and had tablecloths. The radio habit stayed with me, and I was able to listen to classical music in my dorm room late at night after studying, a glorious privilege, I thought, since I had been a music major in high school.

I managed to finish my PhD in five years, which was probably too fast. Midway through, I had a scare: suddenly, the Ford Foundation ended my fellowship. I heard the rationale was that women married, left the field, and were a financial risk. This seemed ignorant, even in the mid-1950s. Marleigh was already married and obviously devoted to her field. Although Ann did leave for marriage in 1959, she completed her dissertation in 1962 on Japanese investment in Manchurian industries and later was the main author of a book on Southeast Asian religious art.[12] Coming to my rescue, Borton tapped into a small campus fund and helped me put together part-time jobs. Then, somehow, he got the fellowship restored, but he left in 1957 to become president of his alma mater, Haverford College. Suddenly, the advanced language professor departed for a senior position at the Library of Congress just as I was beginning his course. Shirato came to my aid and, to my great fortune, arranged for me to continue Japanese language training for two summers at the University of Michigan with Dr. Hide Shohara. A prewar overseas student and a graduate of elite women's schools in Japan, Shohara had earned a doctorate in linguistics at Michigan and had been on the language staff of the university's wartime US Army's Intensive Japanese Language School for enlisted men. After passing the written doctoral exams, I settled into intense preparation for the orals. The required coverage was broad: all of Japanese and Chinese history for my major; all of American history for my minor. Filled with anxiety, I became a hermit in my dorm room. At this point, Herschel Webb, a translator for ATIS during the Occupation, returned from doctoral research in Japan to become Borton's successor and was one of my examiners. Because Webb had already finished but not yet defended his dissertation, Wilbur was technically my official advisor. The orals went extremely well, although one of the Japan examiners failed to turn up. A hasty telephone call produced a substitute, a former journalist and China expert who asked all the right questions. The American historian led a reverential conversation on his hero, Thomas Jefferson (without mention of slaveholding). The orals were the highlight of my young academic life and led to a good relationship with Webb, who was soon simply "Herschel" to me. Lunch followed at the faculty club with Wilbur, who did the same for all of his graduate students. (Only men could be members of the faculty club.) I accepted his offer of a glass of sherry, putting aside my waning Baptist scruples.

Doctoral Research Year in Japan

The next step was a year of doctoral research in Japan (1958–1959). I sailed from Los Angeles, third class, on one of the passenger ships of the American

President Lines (SS *President Hoover* and SS *President Wilson*), sharing a cabin with missionaries and practicing with chopsticks at dinner. It took us twelve days, with a short stop in Honolulu. During the voyage, I became close friends with Noriko Kogishi (later Yamaguchi), who had earned an MA in education from the University of Buffalo. The first stop in Tokyo was the recently opened International House (I-House) for orientation. The well-stocked I-House library, presided over by Fukuda Naomi, would become a sanctuary. She had earned a library degree at the University of Michigan in 1939, where she held one of the last prewar Barbour Scholarships for women students from Asia and the Middle East. With help from the Fulbright office, I rented a mixed Japanese-Western-style apartment in a house in the Ogikubo neighborhood in west Tokyo, about forty minutes by subway and train from central Tokyo. There were many signs of a recovering economy after the Korean War: black-and-white television sets on the shelves of neighborhood restaurants, dazzling displays of electrical appliances, and a multiplicity of small taxicabs. But still the occasional sight of a horribly maimed veteran soliciting on a street corner or in a railway station.

For the last three months in Japan, Noriko insisted that I live with her family. Her grandmother, a Christian born in Hokkaido, gave tea ceremony lessons in a special tatami room. Her mother ran a small furniture workshop nearby, and her father worked at the National Diet Library. Her two brothers looked forward to business careers. I saw firsthand how a busy white-collar father, away on weekdays, relaxed with his family on Sundays. To ensure that I learned about traditional Japanese culture, he paid for Noriko and me to spend a week in Kyoto and joined us for a party with *maiko* (geisha in training). Noriko had already stimulated a love of Japanese art and aesthetics, new subjects to me, by organizing a tour of the town of Mashiko in Tochigi Prefecture to see potters at work. An unexpected result of the year was a greatly increased interest in Western art after attending a traveling Van Gogh exhibition at the new Museum of Modern Art in Tokyo in 1959. The Japanese crowds were so huge that I got only glimpses of the paintings, but this was sufficient to spur many future visits to art museums back home.

In Japan that year, our small group of grad students was not unaware of the CIA. One of our pastimes was to guess who among ourselves or other academics might be an agent. My main purpose was to complete my dissertation research on the Iwakura Mission to America and Europe. I had narrowed my topic to Japan's unequal treaties with Western countries and their significance in early Meiji international relations and cultural nationalism. I had no university affiliation, and it was probably through Miss Fukuda's numerous connections that I met Professor Shimomura Fujio of the University of Tokyo, a well-known diplomatic historian. I loaned him a microfilm copy from the National Archives of the Mission's negotiations in Washington, DC, and he, in turn, introduced me to the university's Historiographical Institute. I was honored to meet another diplomatic historian, Ōkubo Toshiaki, the grandson of a major member of the Iwakura Mission. Absorbed in diplomatic records, I wondered how to make the story of treaty negotiations compelling and not just a recitation of "he said" then "he said." I wanted to show how diplomacy had been a skill to carry out policy and find peaceful solutions. For later study, I set aside the contribution of the Mission to Meiji enlightenment. During a visit to the Kanda used-bookstore neighborhood, I found an original copy at an affordable price (for only 2,500 yen, equivalent to $4.30) of the five-volume diary of the Mission, compiled by Ambassador Iwakura's private secretary, Kume Kunitake (1839–1931), and published in 1878. It was a primer on Western institutions, and it was intended, I speculated, to promote the agenda of the early Meiji government—to foster a particular perspective of modernity and its benefits to Japan. I also met Haga Tōru, a young professor who had an equal obsession with the Mission. Our mutual quest for greater knowledge of its travels, observations, and legacy would last for decades, and he included me in a Japanese-language collection of essays on the Mission in 2003, as had Ōkubo Toshiaki in 1976.[13]

At I-House, I often met fellow graduate students for discussions of research. One of the friendliest was Nakamura Sadako (later Ogata), who earned a PhD in political science at Berkeley in 1963 and published a classic on Japan's invasion of Manchuria. Among the American graduate students, my closest friend was a Fulbright Scholar. We frequented an amazing range of old and new coffee shops in Tokyo, browsed in Kanda bookstores, and met every Sunday at the I-House library to catch up on new publications. Back in the United States, he asked to join my new project, a translation of the Kume diary. The friendship was severely tested when he later presented a paper at a major conference on the modernization of Japan without mentioning me as a collaborator or project originator (my version came later in *Monumenta Nipponica*, 1973).[14] As a reminder of the era, only one woman, the British scholar Carmen Blacker, was invited to participate in the conference. The conference was one of five on studies of the modernization of Japan; it resulted in five prestigious books and was important to budding careers (see chapter 11). Why not invite Joyce Chapman Lebra and Barbara J. Teters, whose careers were established in the 1960s? Joyce Lebra, much admired for having finished her history PhD (Radcliffe, 1958) with a dissertation on a Meiji statesman, Ōkuma Shigenobu, was also frequently around I-House and great fun to be with.[15] She told me that I was right to choose Columbia but never explained why. We would share the same fate in our first job searches, finding positions at good institutions but with limited opportunities to teach about Japan. Marleigh, who was then in Kyoto to continue her doctoral research, became seriously ill. Although restored to good health by a Japanese doctor, her degree was delayed until 1965. I admired her for sticking with her dissertation topic on Japan's first modern novel, *Ukigumo* (*Floating Cloud* by Futabatei Shimei [1887]), against her advisor's wishes.[16]

Job Odyssey

Back at Columbia (1959-1960), I began to search for academic jobs while finishing my dissertation. I sat in on Herschel's class on modern Japan, although I had already passed my orals. It was the best class I had ever taken and was of enormous help in preparing my first lectures. I frequently spotted Herschel and Marleigh in deep discussion at lunchtime in my dorm cafeteria. They were involved in founding the Association of Teachers of Japanese (ATJ) and editing its first newsletters. Marleigh also assisted Herschel in compiling *Research in Japanese Sources; A Guide* (1965).[17] Her legacy is extensive and includes publications on early Meiji authors; the development of a Japanese major while chair of the Department of Asian Languages and Literatures, University of Iowa (1972-1981); and serving as Dean of Liberal Arts and Coordinator of Asian Studies at the State University of New York at New Paltz (1982-1996). In tribute to her scholarship and in remembrance of her devotion to the field, the New York Conference on Asian Studies offers two annual college-student writing prizes in her name.

I experienced a feminist epiphany in those last days at Columbia. Wilbur took me aside. After praising me for finishing my PhD work so quickly, he warned that I might have difficulty in finding a job because I was a woman. Maybe I could at a lesser college or if I would accept a lower salary than a man. I was startled. Male professors had not been condescending; male graduate students had been collegial. However, I spotted an ad for a tenure-track position in East Asian history at Hunter College at a salary that seemed like a fortune ($6,400) and with a subsidy ($800) to purchase library books on East Asia. I was selected but soon disappointed. I was of value because of my minor in American history, not as an East Asianist. I taught four courses a semester (standard for everyone at that time), but three of them were on American history, including the European background of Colonial America; only one, alas, was devoted to East Asia—none specifically to Japan. I alternated semesters between Hunter downtown—all women—and Hunter uptown, a new coed branch in the Bronx (renamed Lehman College). Commuting by subway and bus was time-consuming, but I managed to finish and defend my dissertation in April 1961. One of my most vivid memories from my time at Hunter is of an encounter uptown during the early civil rights movement. A Black male student stopped me in the hall and asked why Black names were not in the textbook. Who would he recommend? Frederick Douglass. It was a powerful lesson in persons and events that had been overlooked, slighted, or lost in history, and it was a lesson equally applicable to Japan. When I learned that the Library of Congress had copies of the newspaper Douglass published in DC in the early 1870s, I wondered whether he had noticed the visit of the Japanese Mission. Briefly, in a few lines, but he had.

Although the Hunter position provided security and outstanding students (also, my chair was female), my wish was to be a full-time Japan historian. With reluctance, I left after three years and continued my odyssey. Next was Sarah Lawrence College in 1963. Although the idea of an expensive women's college did not appeal to me, it offered the opportunity to be an East Asianist, if not a Japan specialist. The university president participated in my job interview. There were no ranks, and we were simply designated as faculty members. My first assignment, based on the assumption that I knew all about all of Asia, was to prepare the entire college for a visit by Madame Ngo Dinh Nhu (the powerful wife of the chief advisor and brother of the South Vietnamese president), part of an American lecture tour. I did my best, and I learned a lot about Southeast Asia and postwar decolonization, but the students deserved an outside expert. Within days of the lecture, the South Vietnamese president and Madame Nhu's husband were assassinated. Then came a period of intense grief following President Kennedy's assassination on November 22. After returning to a semblance of normality, we heard Betty Friedan lecture on her recent book, *The Feminine Mystique* (1963). Preparation for a regular four-day schedule of individual meetings and one weekly class with challenging students, however, was so exhausting that I had little time for research and feared a further loss of skills. One day in my office, I detected that some of my letters had been opened. One was from Columbia, wondering why I hadn't responded to an offer to teach Herschel's graduate course during his leave. Aware of my situation, Herschel was giving me a chance to be a Japan historian. There was an investigation, and, although I never received a formal report, friends on the committee told me that the culprit was a senior administrator who had ordered the campus postmistress to forward my letters to him. Whatever the truth was, he was gone the following year.

I accepted a promising position as an untenured associate professor at Bucknell, a private coed liberal arts university in Pennsylvania, and taught courses on Japan and East Asia to responsive students and supervised my first master's thesis. The small history department was collegial. Having mollified Columbia, I commuted to New York by bus once a week to teach Herschel's course and to supervise his master's candidates. Although it was dispiriting to learn that I had been grossly misled about a huge award to expand East Asian Studies at Bucknell, I was resigned to staying. Herschel, ever helpful, encouraged me to submit, successfully, two essays to *The Journal of Asian Studies*.[18] He sent my file to Northwestern University for a job opening, but it was returned immediately with the rebuke that the history department did not hire women. At a job interview at the AAS conference, the interviewer for Indiana University walked out when he saw I was a woman. However, I had support through my ties at Columbia to publish essays, thanks to Professors Arthur Tiedemann of the City College of New York and James Morley, a political scientist at Columbia. Tiedemann solicited a chapter for a textbook and Morley arranged for publication of my first paper for the American Historical Association.[19] He later invited me to become a member of the Columbia University Seminar on Modern Japan, an intellectual lifeline to the present day. Bernie and Harry included me in their 1966 book on *Modern Japanese Leadership: Transition and Change*.[20]

Arriving at the University of Maryland

Then came a miracle, or so it seemed. In spring of 1966, an ad appeared in *The Chronicle of Higher Education* for a tenure-track position in Japanese history at the University of Maryland. My interview at an AAS conference with the chair, David A. Shannon, went extremely well. He offered to back me for promotion and tenure if I would enter as an assistant rather than associate professor. Another responsibility, in his words, was to put the university's Japanese Language Collection "on the map." I felt at home when I visited Maryland—a large, public, coed institution and, later, the flagship campus of the University of Maryland system. Finally, after six years, I was a full-time Japan historian—with two courses on Japan, occasional special courses or a seminar, and shared responsibility every other semester with the China historian for courses on East Asian civilization. Although the schedule was heavy at nine credits each semester, I envisioned greater opportunity for research and publication. My specialized courses ranged from US-Japan relations, the Asia-Pacific War, and Japanese empire to the Japanese diaspora, postwar Japan through film and fiction (co-taught), and women in modern Japanese history. I enjoyed the 1970s, a golden age of master's theses and the supervision of my first dissertation. Undergraduates were eager to learn about Japan and East Asia. In the 1980s, their focus was on economic relations; in the 1990s, popular culture. Then, gender and sexuality held sway.

Although I was expected to help publicize the Japanese Language Collection, I knew very little about it—only that it was massive and had arrived in Maryland as the Occupation was ending in 1952. It had been packed in over fifty wooden crates and sent to the university at the expense of Gordon W. Prange, a member of the Civil Intelligence Section and a historian of prewar European history (on leave from the University of Maryland). His job during the Occupation had been to compile an official record of General MacArthur's campaigns in the Southwest Pacific. A naval officer during the war, he had become obsessed with the Pearl Harbor attack and privately conducted interviews in Tokyo with former high-ranking admirals and generals. His hope on returning to College Park was to inspire an institute for military history. The materials, however, were met with indifference and neglect for many years, and the crates were housed, unopened, in several campus locations, including basements.

Finally, in 1964, a Japanese librarian, Hideo Kaneko, and a small staff were recruited to begin the huge task of unpacking, organizing, cataloging, and shelving the collection in the basement of the main library. After four years of work in a dreary, damp space, Kaneko returned to his former position at Yale. I learned more about the collection from his successors. In addition to monographs and novels, it included virtually all Japanese-language publications—monographs, books, magazines, newspapers, and news releases—evaluated by Occupation censors between 1945 and 1949, along with documentation of the censors' decisions. In short, it was a treasure to be preserved and shared. Progress, however, would depend on future collaboration with a like-minded group of colleagues.

My over forty-five years at Maryland were also spent in curriculum transformation and community outreach; to do so, I and like-minded colleagues needed to overcome many hurdles. The gains and setbacks, particularly at the beginning of the 1960s and 1970s, reflected a larger pattern of resistance to second-wave feminism in academe and an initial indifference to non-Western studies.

Fulbright Year in Japan

During my second year at the University of Maryland (1967–1968), I received a second Fulbright Fellowship for research in Japan during the centennial of the Meiji Restoration. It was fascinating, even overwhelming, to be back after eight years. I was stunned by the changes in the post-Olympics Tokyo landscape: highways cutting through the city, roads crowded with shiny new automobiles, the speed of the *shinkansen* bullet train, new and higher buildings. Old haunts were gone, but the shops and offices in the central Marunouchi district were much the same, and the restored Meiji Shrine and garden were a place of repose. Also gone were vestiges of the "little Americas," former housing settlements for Occupation military and civilian officials and their families. In contrast were protests against the Vietnam War. The husband of a new Japanese friend was among the professors assaulted by students and beaten with a pot over his head. In early January 1968, during an interlude at a conference in Fukuoka, several of the participants and I witnessed a large and highly agitated crowd at the nearby Sasebo in protest against the arrival of an American nuclear carrier. Japanese friends shared our grief over the assassinations of Martin Luther King Jr. on April 4, and Robert F. Kennedy on June 6. I vividly remember a student's question when I returned, "Do the Japanese have telephones?" I was so startled that I worked up a long list of the numerous things in which Japan was already first and second, including transistor radios, color televisions, chinaware, sewing machines, guitars, pianos, and the international audience and prizes for films by Kurosawa Akira and Ozu Yasujirō. Toyota was still on the way—plus the 1968 Nobel Prize in Literature for Kawabata—and, oh yes, telephones.

I lived at I-House, where I came to know and admire several American women scholars of Japan who are now gone: Barbara J. Teters, Hazel J. Jones, Mae Smethurst (who was there with her husband, Richard, a Japan historian and contributor to our book, see chapter 14), and Sharon Minichiello. Barbara Teters, a former teacher at the University of the Sacred Heart and a political scientist on leave from Iowa State University, had earned a PhD in 1955 (University of Washington) and published a series of well-received articles on Meiji topics.[21] She was exceedingly helpful with tips about bookstores, cafes, and underground shops and coffee houses, and how to get through the turnstiles of the National Diet Library. She later became president of the Midwest Conference on Asian Affairs in 1973 and chair of the political science department at Mississippi State University from 1973 to 1978. During a family visit to Mississippi, I caught up with her and sensed deep unhappiness. I later heard, by her account, that a famous alumnus, a US senator, had run her out as "that Northern liberal woman." Barbara disappeared, or so it seemed to her friends. But she resurfaced in higher administrative positions: vice-chancellor for fiscal affairs at the University of Arkansas (1979–1981) and vice-chancellor and provost at Southern Illinois University (1982–1987), then perhaps one of the highest administrative ranks attained by a woman scholar of Japan. Hazel Jones was an ambulance driver in the Korean War and later became the third American woman to earn a PhD in Japanese history (University of Michigan, 1967). She taught Japanese history over fourteen years at the University of Alberta, was a key figure in developing its East Asian Studies Program, and produced a significant body of scholarship. She then departed for Japan, apparently with the hope, as she once told me, of becoming a Japanese citizen. Mae Smethurst (PhD, University of Michigan, 1968) was a classics scholar at the University of Pittsburgh, where she was highly regarded for comparative studies of the Noh theater and Greek drama.[22] She introduced me, a devoted fan of kabuki, to the pleasures of Noh and classical Japanese drama. Sharon Minichiello, a graduate student, earned a PhD (University of Hawai'i at Manoa, 1975), published books, won awards, and for many years served as the director of her university's Center for Japanese Studies.[23] The struggles and successes of these women should not be forgotten.

Founding the Committee on East Asian Studies

I returned to the University of Maryland in 1969 to find a changed climate in the history department. The predominantly white male faculty were not as welcoming or as interested in Japan as Shannon had been before. From my perspective, the department's attitude toward Japan ranged from toxic to myopic. Hiring faculty to teach about China was acceptable but not beyond one professor. Even the outside experts who reviewed the department every five years had little concern for Asia, dismissing half the world with the comment that the department "couldn't cover everything," further implying, as my colleague in Chinese history and I commiserated, that it must teach every twenty-five years of American history in depth while we had to cover all of Japan and China. These attitudes had considerable bearing on efforts to promote East Asian Studies, but there were many bright spots, several sympathetic colleagues, and enough encouragement at crucial moments to fortify my decision to persist. Our growing band of East Asianists collaborated as best we could in dealing with department chairs, deans, provosts, presidents, and regents. Along the way, undergraduate and graduate students and librarians were crucial to successful outcomes. And I managed to publish long articles and present conference papers, edit two books, and undertake the oral history project described below, although it was not a preferred course for a monograph-centered history department.[24]

The first hurdle in 1969 was creating a vehicle for expanding the curriculum beyond North America and Europe and for community outreach. To borrow a phrase, "First, there was a committee." I was happy to learn that Kaneko's successor in the library was the legendary Fukuda Naomi. Her presence, though only for one year, was pivotal both for the Japanese Collection and East Asian Studies. We met frequently, wondering why so little had been done by the male faculty—no lobbying, no fundraising, no event planning. A separate department was not possible for administrative and financial reasons, but most of us preferred to remain in our disciplines. The answer was an interdisciplinary committee. Because we knew a woman couldn't be seen as the originator or head, we planted the idea with one of the senior professors who quickly made it his own. Our first meeting, ad hoc and only including six people, was in October 1969. We reported to two deans, Arts and Humanities and Behavioral and Social Sciences. We decided on a name, the Committee on East Asian Studies (CEAS), elected a chair, and set priorities. Our first achievements included upgrading Chinese language courses, introducing Japanese language courses, and replacing the terms "Orient" and "Far East" with "East Asia." Fukuda's successor in the 1970s, and the committee's new member, was Jack Siggins. Trained in library science and East Asian Studies at the University of Chicago, he was devoted to CEAS and the Japanese Collection before leaving in 1979 to join Kaneko at Yale. His replacement, Frank Joseph Shulman, was indefatigable in circulating information about the Japanese Collection, furthering the cataloging, and pleading for preservation of fragile documents.

A Turning Point at Stanford University

Meanwhile, at the recommendation of my new Africanist colleague, I received an award (1972–1973) to use the Stanford University Hoover Institution's archival collections on US-Japan relations. It began as a great year, although my office windows were still broken from student protests against the Vietnam War, and I was uncomfortable with the politics of the institution. I felt more at ease after meeting John K. Emmerson, a senior fellow and former Japan diplomat, and another wonderful librarian, Emiko Moffitt, the head of Hoover's Japanese holdings. Out of the blue, I was approached to apply for a position in Japanese history. I wasn't responsive; I had ended my job pursuit at Maryland and wasn't sure if I was Stanford material. The history department pressed for acceptance and sent an elaborate itinerary: a cocktail reception, seminar presentation, and interview. Then, just as suddenly, it was reduced to a talk. Hoping for feedback, I spoke on the topic I was scheduled to present at the annual conference of the American Historical Association. It went well, and I probably would have dismissed the incident as just another sexist slight. But during the flight to the conference, I overheard two senior Stanford history professors in the seats directly ahead, laughing and saying much too loudly, "The answer to affirmative action, women and African Americans, is to interview them but not hire them." I discussed the episode with Emiko and decided to file a complaint. Although the young woman assigned to interview me did not seem to take the issue seriously, apparently a dean did. Perhaps others had complained. The next year, Stanford recruited its first woman historian. Emiko would later file and win a sexual harassment complaint. In 1991, she became one of the original members of the North American Coordinating Council for Japanese Library Resources (NCC). (For additional information on the founding of NCC, see chapter 15.)

A benefit of the Hoover award and an unexpected influence on my feminist consciousness was a paid six-week research trip to Japan in the spring of 1973. It was probably at this time that I saw Joyce again at I-House, happy to hear that she was teaching courses on Japan and India at the University of Colorado Boulder. I joined her lead in signing a letter of protest to the head of I-House for banning women from a luncheon seminar with an important visiting guest scholar. He permitted only one woman to attend, the abovementioned Ogata Sadako, a former student of the guest and a professor at International Christian University, and explained with a smile that his model was the prestigious Council on Foreign Relations. In fact, the Council, under heavy criticism, was on the verge of admitting women. In a later I-House episode, I signed a joint letter initiated by Joyce to keep the beautiful Japanese garden intact. When one of my former Black history colleagues at Maryland became chancellor of the University of Colorado in 1976, I sent her a letter at Joyce's request in support of salary equity. As a protest against discrimination, Joyce had refused to accept a university honor.

Overcoming Hurdles

After I returned to Maryland in 1973, I worked again with CEAS to overcome administrative hurdles, departmental politics, and systemic problems at the university to create a new position in Japanese language and literature. During this unrest, I took my first steps into fundraising with a successful application to the Japan Foundation for a staff-expansion grant in art history, and we hired a recent PhD from Michigan. A wonderful new colleague, she first had to overcome the same obstacle that Joyce and I had faced. In violation of the terms of the grant, the department chair attempted to assign most of her time to courses on Western art history. When we protested, the chair claimed interference but backed down at the threat of a lost position. Although tested by turnover, the line became permanent and is held today by a prominent Japan art historian.

In addition, CEAS was able to create a new position in Japanese language and literature in 1976. The search committee recommended Eleanor Kerkham, who had earned a doctorate from Indiana in 1974 and had taught at Colby College, where she created the school's Japanese Studies major (chapter 28). Because she was teaching at Tenri University (Nara, Japan), two members of CEAS who were about to go on research leave had stopped in Tokyo to interview her. Soon after Eleanor's arrival in Maryland, she was told by the dean that a more formal search needed to be conducted for a tenure-track hire. An elaborate search committee of eight was appointed. The chair offered to trade a sexual encounter with Eleanor for his vote. To Maryland's credit, he was replaced after an investigation revealing multiple offenses. Eleanor won appointment again. She developed Maryland's Japanese language and literature curriculum and, with the help of a team, created a Japanese-language business course. However, rancor in the program had continued to such an extent that the dean turned to an outside reviewer, who singled out Eleanor as "brilliant" but otherwise recommended a thorough housecleaning. The dean canceled culture courses that were seen as not having academic merit, created three tenure-track lines, and instituted a search for an established scholar to create a department with full language majors. The oversight role of CEAS ended as the Department of East European and East Asian Languages and Literatures emerged in the 1980s, and Eleanor gained tenure. Harassment, primarily on the Japanese language side, finally ended with the arrival of Thomas Rimer as department chair and as the second Japanese literature professor (1987–1992). Fair and judicious, he brought new money and prestige to CEAS. He encouraged research and publication, inviting me to a 1988 conference at the Woodrow Wilson Center, Smithsonian Institution, DC, on postwar fiction and culture in West Germany and Japan, and including my essay on literary censorship (thanks also to Carol Gluck) in his coedited book (1991).[25] A 1992 CEAS conference on war, reconstruction, and creativity in East Asia produced a book (2001), which Tom and I coedited with Eleanor.[26] In the 1990s, Japanese became the second-most popular foreign language major. Continued growth of the faculty and another name change led to the present Department of East Asian Languages and Cultures. Eleanor played a primary role in creating the foundation of a viable department, drafting the proposal for the Japanese major, lobbying for a tenured Japanese linguist and two full-time language teachers, backing student petitions for courses on Korean language, chairing CEAS, and raising outside funds to hold conferences.

In the midst of Eleanor's ordeal in 1976, I, too, had come under attack. I was elected the chair of CEAS in the spring of 1976 while I was away on a semester leave.

I did not vote and was surprised by the outcome. The vice-chancellor confirmed the appointment. At the CEAS meeting the following fall, I presented a vision for future growth but faced ugly backlash. Apparently, it was an offense for a woman to head CEAS. Five men—two senior professors, a demoted professor, and two newly hired assistant professors who did not know me—launched a public and widespread campaign to shame me, extending, as I was to learn later, well beyond the campus. It was a shock, demoralizing as intended, and led to self-doubt and reflection. While senior male administrators said they had never seen anything like it, didn't understand the motivation, and failed at mediation, Jack Siggins, the librarian, organized an effective counterpetition. The two assistant professors paid the greatest cost and lost their contracts. In addition to chairing CEAS, I was appointed to two additional high-level university committees, far beyond my rank and expertise, to help fend off, I surmised, a possible lawsuit. In fact, I consulted the lawyer of a linguist who had won his case but decided a lawsuit would be counterproductive.

I was grateful that the women who knew me from the early campus women's movement came to my defense. Instead of becoming a well-organized movement, we first existed in several clusters with different priorities: equity in recruitment, salaries, and promotions; increased opportunities for women in law, medicine, science, and engineering; and the establishment of a women's studies program. My group embraced all three goals. When we coalesced into a caucus, three of us took a petition for a women's studies program to the vice-chancellor, who, although lukewarm, passed it on as he had for programs in African American Studies and Jewish Studies. The proposal was accepted, and a search committee was formed to recruit a one-year interim director to conduct a national search for a permanent director. I was selected, but my chair refused to meet the condition of a single course release. The English Department, under its first woman chair, came to the rescue and permitted one of our activists to take the position. The search led to a magnificent find, Carol S. Pearson, who, in three years, was able to establish a viable interdisciplinary women's studies program that soon became a department. I benefited twenty years later, in 1993, from its first summer workshop in curriculum transformation as I began a shift in teaching and research to the gendering of modern Japanese history. I signed up for another seminar a few years later and became intrigued by the little-known story of Eleanor Roosevelt's trip to Japan in 1953 and her encounters with students, housewives, and women workers.

Another boost to my morale at that difficult time was my election to the AAS Northeast Asia Council (NEAC), first as a member and later as the chair (1975–1978). There, I met John Oh, a Korean political scientist, and his wife, Bonnie Oh, a historian. Their work inspired me to incorporate the study of Korea into East Asia Civilization courses at Maryland and to create courses on Korean history. The

AAS regional committees take turns nominating the candidates for AAS president; when it was NEAC's turn, we selected linguist Eleanor Harz Jorden, who became the first woman scholar of Japan to hold that position (1980). NEAC fundraised to create small research grants and sponsor lectures by distinguished scholars. Susan Pharr wrote a winning proposal to the Japan-US Friendship Commission, the origin of the present-day NEAC outreach activities.

Grateful for such strong signs of campus and outside support, I continued as head of CEAS, ultimately serving four times (until the 1990s). With the help of a publicity-savvy undergraduate student, we launched a yearlong series of events in 1976 and 1977. Edward Seidensticker, who had won the National Book Award in 1971 for his translation of *The Tale of Genji*, was one of our speakers and attracted a crowd of more than two hundred. One of the deans was so impressed that he became our biggest advocate. In 1979, at the initiative of CEAS and the Maryland libraries and with the blessing of the Board of Regents, the Japanese Collection was divided into (1) Japanese primary sources, named the Gordon W. Prange Collection, and (2) secondary materials, named the East Asia Collection. A dedication ceremony was held in the spring of 1979; Prange, his family, and university officials were present, and Japan's new representative to the United Nations, Dr. Ogata, my friend from I-House, was the keynote speaker. From 1991 to 2000, she become the first woman and the first Japanese national to hold the position of United Nations High Commissioner for Refugees.

One of the first visitors to the newly named Prange Collection in 1979 was Japanese scholar and literary critic Etō Jun, then a fellow at the Woodrow Wilson Center, Smithsonian Institution, DC. Although we held different political views, our conversations would deepen my interest in media control and civil censorship during the Occupation. In addition, my involvement with questions of naming, preservation, and access to the Prange Collection had already reinforced a shift in research focus from Meiji Japan to the twentieth century and transwar Japan. In May 1977, I accepted an invitation to participate in a two-day conference on "Americans as Proconsuls" at the National Museum of History and Technology (now the National Museum of American History) and was asked by the editor of the subsequent book to submit two chapters: one about the planning for post-defeat Japan and one on the rationale for imposing civil censorship.[27] My former Columbia professor, Hugh Borton, one of the planners, also participated in the conference and book.

CEAS continued to grow and ran a full program of lectures, seminars, conferences, film screenings, music and dance performances, and art exhibits. To our delight, the president and provost of the university attended our twentieth anniversary celebration in 1989. Our budget was small, but we found cohosts and partners. There were many highlights on the Japan side. In the era before iPhones, YouTube, and streaming services, our audiences were enthralled by 16 mm films. When a projector broke down during a showing of Kurosawa Akira's *Seven Samurai* in 1978, the audience waited patiently for a repair. A choir of young Japanese on tour of the United States sang in the chapel. A new CEAS member, a professional kotoist, organized several recitals by Japanese musicians and lecture-demonstrations of Noh. In 1987, we observed the fortieth anniversary of Japan's postwar Constitution, featuring Carol Gluck as the keynote speaker and a panel of several surviving members of the secret committee that had written the first draft in February 1946. In 1993, two Japanese American actors came from New York to read excerpts from oral histories on Japan at war. A huge event in 1995 was a two-day conference on "Violent Endings, New Beginnings," commemorating the fiftieth anniversary of the end of World War II, cohosted by the Prange Collection and Archives II (College Park). The Japan Information and Cultural Center, DC, invited participants to a reception at the old residence of the Japanese ambassador. In 2000, with several campus partners, CEAS ran a workshop on "Intersections: Class, Race, and Gender in Occupied Japan," a significant event on a personal level in furthering my knowledge of gender studies and interacting with new and older scholars in the field. CEAS did not always succeed. We lost several excellent scholars to parochial tenure decisions and were unable to persuade the economics department to recruit an East Asianist. Keeping busy, CEAS hosted two annual conferences of the Mid-Atlantic Region Association for Asian Studies (MAR-AAS, 1982 and 2007). I later served several years on the MAR-AAS advisory council and one term as president (2006–2013). MAR-AAS has been an unending source of learning, friendship, and uplift—evidence of the value of regional conferences for the continued growth of Asian Studies at the grassroots level.

Washington and Southeast Regional Seminar on Japan

In addition, in 1972, I helped inaugurate a regional Japan seminar. Robert Ward, chair of the Japan Committee, Social Science Research Council-American Council of Learned Societies (SSRC-ACLS), asked me (as he did others throughout the country) to organize interdisciplinary Japan seminars to bring together both local and isolated scholars. This was the origin of the Washington and Southeast Regional Seminar on Japan. We had a subsidy to reimburse travel expenses and to print and mail papers to participants in advance (no email attachments in those days). We met twice a semester on Saturday afternoons, alternating between Maryland and Georgetown. A large turnout in the early 1980s was amused when the representative of the Ford Motor Company drove up in a Toyota for a discussion of Japanese car sales in the United States. Meetings usually attracted thirty to thirty-five participants. For example, Penny Mason drove from Florida; Ann Waswo brought a carload of colleagues from Virginia; Sharon Nolte came from Appalachian State University. Eleanor Hadley of the General Services

Administration was a local member. Of special note is Sandra T. W. Davis, the fourth woman by my count to earn a PhD in Japanese history (University of Pennsylvania, 1968). A productive historian and the author of a book and articles, she left academe owing to unattractive job opportunities.[28] In the mid-1990s, new leaders took over as interest in the seminar began to wane, owing partly to the loss of our subsidy but more importantly to the arrival of the internet. Scholars no longer felt so isolated.

The regional seminar deepened my interest in Occupied Japan. Several local members had served in the Occupation and had many friends and acquaintance from those years. In addition, Martha J. Ross's MA thesis on the teaching of history at Maryland from the mid-nineteenth century through the 1960s, which included oral histories for the latter period, reinforced my respect for oral history as a primary source.[29] (In 1976, Ross cofounded the Oral History Association of the Mid-Atlantic Region and served as its president [1978–1979]). She was president of the Oral History Association (1984–1985). It began to seem almost an obligation to conduct an oral history project on Americans in Occupied Japan. I applied for a Japan Foundation grant in 1978, naming Richard and Dallas Finn as primary consultants. They had lived in Japan from 1948 to 1954—Dick, a graduate of the US Navy Japanese Language School, as a Foreign Service Officer, and Dallas as an educator and architecture expert.[30] I doubt that I would have been successful without the support of John Whitney Hall and Marius Jansen, who were then serving on the American Advisory Council of the Japan Foundation. The award was enough to get started. I spent two days with Martha to get her advice. She said, "Don't think of the process in the style of TV's *60 Minutes*." Oral history was not a matter of cornering a person, prying for secrets, or eliciting confessions. Instead, it involved simply letting interviewees tell their stories with as little interruption as possible, for as long as they wished, and without others present. The goal was not polished interviews but stories, unvarnished, perhaps with rough edges, for later use by scholars. The bulk of funds were used to hire a typist and a graduate assistant, Kay Dove, who conducted several of the interviews. The fellowship was renewed but without administrative funds. As a result, the transcripts of over one hundred oral histories sat in a filing cabinet outside of my office for several years and were used mainly to introduce seminar students to primary sources. After discussions with the manager of the Prange Collection, Amy Wasserstrom, and the curator, Eiko Sakaguchi, I decided in 2010 to donate the tapes and transcripts to their care, which has continued today with a new curator, Kana Jenkins. The libraries named it the Marlene J. Mayo Oral Histories Collection, and Eiko organized a surprise reception. By then, the Prange Collection was housed in spacious quarters, including a conference room adorned with two beautiful screens donated by the Japan Information and Culture Center, Washington, DC. Since 2001, the University of Maryland Libraries and the Center for Historical

Studies have jointly financed annual 20th Century Japan Research Awards to doctoral candidates and established scholars for use of the Prange Collection. Users, in turn, have produced an excellent body of scholarship.

In the last years before retirement, Eleanor Kerkham and I collaborated with CEAS to draft a successful proposal to the Freemen Foundation for a four-year, $2-million grant. The foundation was offering a rare opportunity for colleges and universities, museums, and art institutes to expand their East Asian programs. Our proposal called for curriculum transformation seminars, faculty expansion, library resources, and special events. The amount seemed to overwhelm administrators, who decided to create a hybrid and somewhat awkward executive committee with CEAS representation and chaired by an associate dean of the College of Arts and Humanities. Nevertheless, the grant helped us reach a larger campus community, including people who were in business, science, and technology. Two permanent tenure-track positions were created, And, finally, we became a center in 2005, with Carol Gluck's return as keynoter to join in celebration.

In Retirement

CEAS events were varied, interdisciplinary, extracurricular, and community-centered. In retrospect, although often ephemeral, they linger in happy memory and enhanced knowledge. Our permanent achievements include the Department of East Asian Languages and Cultures; an expanded and more diverse East Asian curriculum and faculty; a twenty-four-credit Undergraduate Certificate Program in East Asian Studies; and broader access to the rich resources of the Gordon W. Prange Collection. These are many ways to contribute to Japanese Studies, all of them important: scholarship, curriculum transformation, exhibitions, conferences, student exchange programs, library and archival collections, translations, editing, centers, and institutes, but one must be prepared to overcome hurdles that stand in the way. In retirement, I have been able to catch up with the work of younger scholars, here and abroad, and to continue with my great love of archival research. I have the good fortune to enjoy the company of such icons as housewives' activist Oku Mumeo, human rights advocate Eleanor Roosevelt, and humanitarian Esther B. Rhoads. I end on a happy note with a list of positive changes at my university: the arrival of a new dean, a renewal of concern, and a restoration of tenure lines in modern Chinese history, modern Japanese history, and Asian American history.

Notes

[1] Richard Tregaskis, *Guadalcanal Diary* (New York: Random House, 1943).

[2] Leslie Hanawalt, *A Place of Light: The History of Wayne State University* (Detroit: Wayne State University, 1968).

[3] S. I. Hayakawa, *Language in Action* (Madison: College Typing Company, 1939); S. I. Hayakawa, *Language in Thought and Action* (New York: Houghton Mifflin, 1949).

[4] Kenneth Scott Latourette, *A Short History of the Far East*, revised edition (New York: Macmillan, 1951).

[5] Arthur Dudden, father of Japan historian Alexis Dudden, served in the Navy during the war and earned an MA and PhD at the University of Michigan afterward. A distinguished historian who spent most of his career at Bryn Mawr, he was the founding president of the Fulbright Association (1976). Hayden White, an influential historical and literary theorist, as well as a Fulbright Scholar, served in the Navy at the end of the war and entered Wayne on the GI Bill. His MA and PhD were from the University of Michigan, and his primary academic positions were at Stanford University and the University of California, Santa Cruz.

[6] Hattie Masuko Kawahara, "I Am an American," *Mademoiselle* 19 (1944), 258, 276, 301.

[7] My first important encounter with daytime news on the new medium of television was in a drab coffee shop in 1951, my sophomore year. Because we did not have a television at home, memory of this comes back quite clearly. I watched the Kefauver Senate Hearings on organized crime in America. Although daytime, it attracted a huge TV audience. The televised Army-McCarthy Hearings were in late spring 1954, just before my graduation. By then, my family had a television. (I got up early for the coronation of Elizabeth II in 1953). While home, I watched Edward R. Murrow's nighttime show, *See it Now*, including the March 1954 shaming of McCarthy, but I also saw daytime hearings at Wayne at lunch or between classes.

[8] Bernard Silberman, *Ministers of Modernization: Elite Mobility in the Meiji Restoration, 1868–1873* (Tucson: University of Arizona Press, 1964).

[9] William Beasley, *Great Britain and the Opening of Japan, 1834–1858* (London: Luzac and Company, 1951).

[10] Jacques Barzun, *Teacher in America* (Boston: Little, Brown, and Company, 1945).

[11] Bernard Bloch and Eleanor Harz Jorden, *Spoken Japanese: Book One* (New York: Henry Holt and Company, 1945); Serge Elisséeff, Edwin O. Reischauer, and Takehiko Yoshihashi, *Elementary Japanese for College Students* (Cambridge, MA: Harvard-Yenching Institute, 1944).

[12] Ann Rasmussen Kinney, *Japanese Investment in Manchurian Manufacturing, Mining, Transportation, and Communications, 1931–1945* (New York: Garland Publishing, 1982); Ann R. Kinney, Lydia Kieven, and Marijke J. Klokke, *Worshipping Siva and the Buddha: The Temple Art of East Java* (Honolulu: University of Hawai'i Press, 2003).

[13] Marlene Mayo, "The Western Education of Kume Kunitake, 1871–1876," *Monumenta Nippponica*, 28, no. 1 (1973), 3–67; "Kume Kunitake no *Bei-Ō kairan jikki* o tōshite" (On Kume Kunitake's *True Record of Travels in America and Europe*), *Iwakura shisetsu no kenkyū* (Research on the Iwakura Mission), edited by Ōkubo Toshiaki, (Tokyo: Munetaka shobō, 1976), 263–326; "Philadelphia Monogatari: Hida Hamagorō no kōjō shisatsu" (The Philadephia Story: Hida Hamagorō's Factory Tour, 1872), *Iwakura shisetsudan no hikaku bunka shiteki kenkyū* (Comparative Cultural Studies on the Iwakura Embassy), edited by Haga Tōru (Kyoto: Shibunkaku Publishing Company, 2003), 47–89.

[14] Marlene Mayo, "The Western Education of Kume Kunitake, 1871–1876."

[15] Joyce Lebra, *Ōkuma Shigenobu: Statesman of Meiji Japan* (Canberra: Australian National University Press, 1973).

[16] Marleigh Grayer Ryan, *Japan's First Modern Novel: Ukigumo by Futabatei Shimei* (New York: Columbia University Press, 1972).

[17] Herschel Webb, *Research in Japanese Sources: A Guide* (New York: Columbia University, 1965).

[18] Marlene Mayo, "A Catechism of Western Diplomacy," *Journal of Asian Studies*, 26, no. 3 (1967), 389–410; "The Korean Crisis of 1873 and Early Meiji Foreign Policy," *Journal of Asian Studies*, 31, no.4 (1972), 793–818.

[19] Marlene Mayo, "Attitudes toward Asia and the Beginnings of Japanese Empire," *Occasional Papers of the East Asian Institute* (New York: Columbia University, 1967), 16–31; "Bakumatsu-Early Meiji Japan," *An Introduction to Japanese Civilization*, edited by Arthur Tiedemann (New York: Columbia University Press, 1974), 132–180.

[20] Marlene Mayo, "Rationality in the Meiji Restoration: The Iwakura Mission," in *Modern Japanese Leadership: Transition and Change*, edited by Bernard Silberman and Harry Harutoonian (Tucson: University of Arizona Press, 1966), 323–369.

[21] For example, Barbara J. Teters, "Press Freedom and the 26th-Century Affair in Meiji Japan," *Modern Asian Studies* 6, no. 3 (1972), 337–351.

[22] For example, Mae Smethurst, *Dramatic Action in Greek Tragedy and Noh: Reading with and beyond Aristotle* (Washington, DC: Lexington Books, 2013).

[23] For example, Sharon Minichiello, *Retreat from Reform: Patterns of Political Behavior in Interwar Japan* (Honolulu: University of Hawai'i Press, 1984).

[24] See the book's bibliography for a list of works published during this period.

[25] Marlene Mayo, "Literary Reorientation in Occupied Japan: Incidents of Civil Censorship," in *Legacies and Ambiguities: Postwar Fiction and Culture in West Germany and Japan*, edited by Ernestine Schlant and J. Thomas Rimer (Washington, DC: Woodrow Wilson Center Press and Baltimore: Johns Hopkins University Press, 1991), 135–161.

[26] Marlene J. Mayo, "To Be or Not to Be: Kabuki and Cultural Politics in Occupied Japan," in *War, Occupation, and Creativity: Japan and East Asia, 1920–1960*, edited by Marlene J. Mayo and J. Thomas Rimer with Eleanor Kerkham (Honolulu: University of Hawai'i, 2001), 269–309.

[27] Marlene J. Mayo. "American Planning for Occupied Japan: The Role of the Experts," in *Americans as Proconsuls: United States Military Government in Germany and Japan, 1944–1952*, edited by Robert Wolfe (Carbondale: Southern Illinois University Press, 1984), 263–320 and 498–515; "Civil Censorship and Media Control in Early Occupied Japan: From Minimum to Stringent Surveillance," in *Americans as Proconsuls: United States Military Government in Germany and Japan, 1945–1952*, edited by Robert Wolfe (Carbondale: Southern Illinois University Press, 1984), 263–320 and 498–515.

[28] Sandra T. W. Davis, *Intellectual Change and Political Development in Early Modern Japan: Ono Azusa, A Case Study* (Cranbury, NJ: Associated University Press, 1980).

[29] Martha J. Ross, "Clio at College Park: The Teaching of History at the University of Maryland, 1859–1968," MA Thesis, University of Maryland, 1978.

[30] They later published books about Japan: Richard Finn, *Winners in Peace: MacArthur, Yoshida, and Postwar Japan* (Berkeley: University of California Press, 1995); Dallas Finn, *Meiji Revisited: The Sites of Victorian Japan* (New York: Weatherhill, 1995).

6

BECOMING A MEDICAL ANTHROPOLOGIST

Margaret Lock

We married ourselves in a Shinto shrine in front of ten thousand invisible deities but later formalized matters at the British Consulate. It was at that juncture that I realized that I wanted to get out of laboratory work for good and become an anthropologist, whose area of specialty would be Japan.

MARGARET LOCK is the Marjorie Bronfman Professor Emerita at McGill University. Her research focuses on embodiment, comparative epistemologies of medical knowledge, and the global impact of biomedical technologies. She is the author and/or coeditor of eighteen books and 220 articles. Her five monographs have won major awards. She is a Fellow of the Royal Society of Canada, Officier de L'Ordre National du Québec, Officer of the Order of Canada, and an elected member of the American Academy of Arts and Sciences. She has been awarded the Canada Council for the Arts Molson Prize, the Canada Council for the Arts Killam Prize, a Trudeau Foundation Fellowship, a Gold Medal for Research by the Social Sciences and Humanities Research Council of Canada, a Career Achievement Award from the Society for Medical Anthropology, and the McGill University Medal for Exceptional Academic Achievement.

I am approaching eighty-seven years of age and was born in England at a time when the majority of girls were expected to leave school at fifteen and possibly work at a menial job for a few years before marriage, after which time they spent their lives as housewives. In my case, I was employed by a local hospital laboratory, where I was trained to be a technician, and spent my days calibrating and testing blood and urine samples. The senior technician, a male, decided that it was not appropriate for me to undertake tests on fecal samples, and he opted to do them himself.

After a couple of years, I decided to leave my family home in Kent in order to live in London, where I worked as a technician at the Royal London Hospital. But the lure of "exotic" travel captured my imagination, and Canada was currently advertising in England for individuals to emigrate. I landed a position in a Toronto laboratory, but, after a year or two, decided to team up with my close Australian friend of the day, Palma Berger, to pick up a drive-away car that needed to be taken out West. We drove for the most part on unpaved, dirt roads for over 2,500 miles, meeting many large, fearsome bears en route who would bang on the windows of parked cars. Eventually, we ran out of money and stopped in Banff, where we found work as waitresses in a restaurant whose customers were primarily working cowboys. We then drove way up north to Dawson City in the Yukon Territory, where Palma met the man whom she shortly thereafter married. I drove south to Vancouver, where I once again worked in a hospital laboratory, but I came to the conclusion that the Bay Area in California was where I wanted to live and work. I caught a bus from Vancouver to San Francisco, where I obtained a position in the UCSF Medical Center on Parnassus Avenue.

My future husband, Richard, was also working there, and people encouraged us to meet each other, but we independently responded that we hadn't come all that way to end up spending time with someone from the UK. However, we eventually met when Richard came to visit the women I was living with at the time. We soon became close, but Richard, a former captain of the judo team at Cambridge University, announced that he was off to Tokyo to see the 1964 Olympic Games and planned to stay in Japan indefinitely.

One version of this history is that I ran after him to Japan, while the other is that he wrote and begged me to join him there. We married ourselves in a Shinto shrine in front of ten thousand invisible deities but later formalized matters at the British Consulate. It was at that juncture that I realized that I wanted to get out of laboratory work for good and become an anthropologist, whose area of specialty would be Japan.

In 1965, we were living in a six-mat tatami room in Shinjuku, Tokyo, and found well-paid work teaching English to businessmen employed by Showa Shell Sekiyu (Shell Oil Company). In 1966, we left Japan, traveled overland through

Afghanistan, Turkey, and Greece, among other countries, to England to visit family, and then went on to Berkeley, California, where we had both been accepted to do graduate work—Richard in comparative literature and myself in anthropology, which involved ethnographic research based in Japan. This, of course, entailed learning Japanese. I was accepted at the Inter-University Center for Japanese Language Studies, by which time, 1972, we had two small children. Japanese was our youngest child's first language.

During the second year, I did fieldwork, primarily in Kyoto, when much time was spent observing patient care in clinics where the practitioners were using acupuncture and massage as their primary treatment modalities. This culminated in the writing of my first book, *East Asian Medicine in Urban Japan: Varieties of Medical Experience*.[1]

I then had two additional visits to Japan in the 1980s and 1990s, for two years each time, to do further research that resulted in numerous articles and two more books: *Encounters with Aging: Mythologies of Menopause in Japan and North America* and *Twice Dead: Organ Transplants and the Reinvention of Death*.[2] More recently, my research has focused on Alzheimer's disease, but this has not had a Japanese component, although one of my past doctoral students, Junko Kitanaka, now a professor at Keio University, is carrying out in-depth research into this matter, having already completed extensive research into depression.

I was a Japan-Canada Bilateral Exchange Fellow in 1982 and delivered a series of lectures in Tokyo in 1983 and 1984 as the St. John's Professor at St. Luke's International Hospital. During this time, I was a resident in Kyoto, where I was a visiting professor of anthropology at Kyoto University, sponsored by Professor Yoneyama Toshinao, and I traveled to Tokyo regularly on the *shinkansen* bullet train to deliver the lectures. In 1993, I delivered the World Federation for Mental Health Margaret Mead Memorial Lecture in Tokyo. Over the years, I received numerous grants to undertake research in Japan; most significant among these was one that enabled me to carry out, with superb research assistance, one segment of a large comparative project on the experience of menopause, which was conducted in Manitoba, Boston, and in several places in Japan, both urban and rural. The resultant book, published in 1995 by the University of California Press, is titled *Encounters with Aging: Mythologies of Menopause in Japan and North America*. The Japanese component has a sample size of over 1,100 women, and the book remains in print. The statistically significant findings show definitively that Japanese women report a significantly lower rate of hot flashes as they go through menopause than do American or Canadian women. In-depth research at the biological level has shown that the use of soy in the Japanese diet is responsible for this. It has also been shown that when women of Japanese origin living in the United States tend to increasingly eat a Western-style diet, their experience of hot flashes increases.

On reflection, I am very satisfied that I have devoted so much time over the years to research in Japan. At a talk I gave three years ago at Keio University, a member of the audience stood up and said that he wanted to thank me for having taught him, and no doubt his friends and colleagues, so much about living in Japan that they themselves simply took for granted in their everyday lives. At that juncture, I fully understood just how important and powerful carefully documented ethnography can be.

Notes

[1] Margaret Lock, *East Asian Medicine in Urban Japan: Varieties of Medical Experience* (Berkeley: University of California Press, 1980).

[2] Margaret Lock, *Encounters with Aging: Mythologies of Menopause in Japan and North America* (Berkeley: University of California Press, 1995); Margaret Lock, *Twice Dead: Organ Transplants and the Reinvention of Death* (Berkeley: University of California Press, 2001).

7

LIFE ON TWO TRACKS

Takako Lento

My parents and teachers agreed that I should study English, as English was widely viewed as a helpful skill for a future professional career. As to my interest in Japanese literature, my mother said I could always study that on the side: "After all, it's in your own language." I liked the idea of maintaining a double-track mode, and that stuck with me throughout my life.

TAKAKO LENTO is a prizewinning literary translator, author, and poet who has taught at universities in Japan and the United States. After graduating from Tsuda College (Tokyo), she earned an MFA from the Iowa Writers' Workshop (with assistance from a Fulbright Fellowship) and an MA from Kyushu University. As a faculty member at the University of Iowa, she initiated the teaching of Japanese culture and literature within the Chinese and Oriental Studies Department. Her publications include more than twelve books of translations of Japanese poetry, Japanese translations of two books by Nikki Giovanni and James Baldwin, and three books on improving English communication skills for Japanese speakers. She received the Japan-US Friendship Commission Prize for the Translation of Japanese Literature for *Collected Haiku of Yosa Buson* (with W. S. Merwin, 2013) in 2014 and for *Pioneers of Modern Japanese Poetry* in 2019. Her own poetry is included in *A Book of Women Poets from Antiquity to Now* (1980).

In the Beginning

When I was in fifth grade, my teacher, Mrs. Nonaka, asked the class to write poems for homework. She told us to carefully observe things and write what we discovered about them. One late afternoon it started to snow, which was a rare event in Kyushu where I grew up. I went outside and was fascinated to see gray flakes flying about against the dark gray sky and dusting the hedges white. I wrote a three-liner:

> **Snow**
> *Snow is coming down*
> *When I look up into the sky*
> *It looks like gray dust dancing*

In class, we read our own poems out loud. Mrs. Nonaka commented kindly on each. She said she liked my poem, particularly because I carefully observed the falling snowflakes. That made me happy. She opened my eyes to poetry, the world of poetry that has grown so much larger for me since. She was my very first mentor.

I grew up to be a bookworm. Naturally, I wanted to study Japanese literature in college. But my mother, in particular, firmly believed that girls should be educated so they could support themselves if needed. She had watched single and widowed women struggle to survive during the postwar era. She saw them as casualties of a prewar system that had failed to educate them properly. My parents and teachers agreed that I should study English, as English was widely viewed as a helpful skill for a future professional career. They recommended that I attend Tsuda College, founded in 1900 by Tsuda Umeko, a pioneer in women's higher education.[1] As to my interest in Japanese literature, my mother said I could always study that on the side: "After all, it's in your own language." I liked the idea of maintaining a double-track mode, and that stuck with me throughout my life.

A Creative Writing Course

At the start of my junior year at Tsuda College, I applied for a creative writing course offered by Professor Thomas Fitzsimmons, a poet, writer, and Fulbrighter.[2] I wrote a short story in English about a young boy aspiring to be an artist and submitted it for screening for the class. I was admitted to this class along with a dozen juniors and seniors. I started writing poems in English. Professor F. encouraged me to keep writing. His mentorship had a decisive impact on my future. Much later (he must have told me back then, but I probably did not understand its full import), I found that he had contacted Paul Engle, the renowned director of the Iowa Writers' Workshop, about me. Engle replied that he would accept me tuition-free if travel and accommodations were secured. So some papers were forwarded to the Fulbright office in Tokyo. I was invited for an interview and, after some time, received a request for my poems in Japanese, which I supplied. At midcourse in my graduate studies at Kyushu University, I received a Fulbright Fellowship to attend the Iowa Writers' Workshop. A new world was about to open for me.

Iowa Writers' Workshop

In early September 1965, I arrived at the Iowa City Municipal Airport, after having changed flights in Honolulu, Los Angeles, and Chicago. The US Department of State personnel who welcomed me in Honolulu had put me on a plane to Los Angeles, assuring me that someone would meet me at the Iowa City Municipal Airport. But no one was waiting for me. I tried calling Engle but got no answer. Two university hospital nurses, who were waiting for a friend whose flight had been delayed, noticed me—tired, puzzled, and dismayed—and asked what had happened. Then a tall young man arrived to meet his friend. The three of them started talking so fast that I only caught the gist of their plan: this young man would take me home and then drive back to pick up his friend, whose plane was also delayed! I must have looked scared. René Chevray, the young man, told me that his wife was Japanese and phoned to let me speak with her. It so happened that Keiko Chevray taught Japanese, and René was a PhD candidate in engineering at the university.[3] They took me in and showed me around the town. Because I still couldn't reach Engle, on Monday, René took me to the registrar's office. I was registered, assigned to the Burge Hall dormitory, and told to find Engle at the Writers' Workshop.

That was how I met my next mentor. Engle came to the door, stuck his big hand out with his eyes wide, and boomed, "Welcome! You've been missing for three days!" I'd been given his old home phone number. Keiko and René treated me like their little sister throughout my stay, and I felt safe living in this college town in the middle of cornfields. I was grateful for all the confusion and mishaps at my arrival because if I had not been stranded at the airport, Keiko and René might have been polite strangers for the two years I was there.

The fall semester started shortly afterward. Poetry workshop classes were held in a Quonset hut, a remnant of wartime temporary buildings, which looked like a semicylinder lying on the grassy bank by the Iowa River. It was stuffy in warm weather and cold in winter, but aspiring poets were happy to have a cocoon-like place of their own. In a poetry workshop, a group of two dozen would heatedly discuss the mimeographed poems of the day, selected from the group's work. My teachers included poets Donald Justice, George Starbuck, and Marvin Bell, who have attained lasting reputations.

Engle told me that I was actually in a pilot for the International Writing Program (IWP, officially inaugurated in the fall of 1967). His idea was to establish a colony of writers from all over the world to experience genuine US culture, share their own cultures with their fellow writers, and focus on writing. He organized parties and trips to celebrate various occasions and to visit the program's supporters. These events included members' readings of their own work and fascinating talks by American writers, such as popular novelists Kurt Vonnegut and Nelson Algren, who taught at or visited the Writers' Workshop. Over two years, I made friends with poets and novelists from China, the Philippines, Bangladesh, England, Japan, and the United States. My exposure to cross-cultural communication had begun.

Views of the Broader World

In the summer of 1966, the PEN Congress (the annual meeting of the illustrious PEN International society of writers) was held in New York City. Engle took us, the international group, to New York and housed us at a New York University dormitory. We were invited to observe PEN programs and events. Engle even accompanied us to a play at the Lyceum Theater and a preview of *Annie Get Your Gun* at the brand-new Lincoln Center. We had a fabulously immersive New York City experience.

During this visit, I had the good fortune to meet the Japanese PEN delegation led by Tateno Nobuyuki, chair of the Japan PEN Club, and the former chair, Itō Sei.[4] To my surprise, Itō made kind and perceptive remarks about my poems and explained that he had read them during the selection process for my Fulbright Fellowship. The delegation adopted me into the group, and we attended various special functions. I helped Tateno greet Arthur Miller, chair of PEN America, at a United Nations reception—my first interpreting experience. I met Donald Keene at a private dinner party for the Japanese delegation at the Fifth Avenue residence of Ivan Morris, another renowned translator and scholar of Japanese literature. These events opened my eyes to an international network of people interested in Japanese literature in a context so much broader than I ever could have imagined. (Twenty-five years later, I visited Donald Keene at Columbia University, and he encouraged and helped me in my literary translation activities.)

When the Japanese delegation decided to leave New York for Europe one day early, they suggested that I should fill in for Itō in a panel discussion on the current state of poetry in the world, which was held at a New Jersey college in conjunction with the PEN Congress. I told them that I was not at all qualified to do so. But they said that they wanted to have a Japanese voice represented there and would help me to prepare. Itō briefed me on the development of modern poetry in Japan and suggested some brief remarks I should make on contemporary Japanese poetry.

He also told me that I would receive an honorarium of fifty dollars, which was a considerable amount at the exchange rate of 360 yen to a dollar. It sounded like an added scholarship. I took a deep breath and decided to help out. The well-attended panel discussion by representatives from several countries ended with enthusiastic applause. As nervous as I was, I only remember participating in the discussion, sitting next to a feisty scholar from Scotland who scoffed at "formless" free verse, which he compared to "chopped-up spaghetti."

Over time, I realized what a once-in-a-lifetime opportunity this had been. This amazing experience helped dispel any fears of the new in my subsequent journey in the United States. More importantly, Itō's perspective on modern Japanese poetry stayed with me as an incomparable guide for many years to come.

Back in Iowa, I wrote poems in the poetry workshop and translated modern Japanese poetry in the newly established translation workshop while I took courses in American and English literature. I completed my MFA with a thesis made up of my poems, translations of modern Japanese poets, and an introductory essay on modern Japanese poetry. Part of this thesis was later published in the *Texas Quarterly* (spring 1968).[5] In the early summer of 1967, I returned to Japan, as per the Fulbright Program's requirement of a two-year stay in one's home country.

Teaching in Iowa

But a year later, when the Fulbright office changed my status to that of a teacher, I was back at the University of Iowa as a full-time instructor in what was then called the Chinese and Oriental Studies Department. The department, chaired by Professor Y. P. Mei, was expanding its Japanese program. Because the department already had a full-time linguist to teach language classes, my role was to teach one Japanese culture course and to create the university's first offerings in Japanese literature (two courses), for which I was free to choose the contents. I decided to teach modern Japanese poetry in one course and contemporary novels in the other.

Teaching Japanese culture opened my eyes to the students' limited understanding of Japan, its people, and its history. I wanted to provide, at the very least, a sound and unbiased introduction to Japan. Fortunately, the university library had a good collection of Japanese books in history, sociology, and anthropology. I took notes from those books to prepare for class and lectured in English from my notes in Japanese. (This experience proved to be foundational training for consecutive interpreting at conferences and in lectures.) In addition, I gratefully used the resources of the Consulate-General of Japan in Chicago. It offered a lending library of materials, including well-produced introductory films on Noh and kabuki, available at no cost for educational purposes. Those 8 mm and 16 mm films were precious and exceptional teaching materials in the days when there were no videos, internet access, or search engines at our fingertips. I used them for my class and also shared them with faculty members, particularly those in theater, and other interested friends, before returning them.

Novels by Kawabata Yasunari, Mishima Yukio, and Ōe Kenzaburō, among others, were already available in English translation. Kawabata's Nobel Prize in Literature in 1968 stimulated additional literary translations. This aroused curiosity about Japanese fiction among students from other departments, including graduate students in comparative literature.

Modern Japanese poetry was another story—English translations were few. So I used some translations from my MFA thesis and translated additional poetry to supplement them. In class, I used those translations for "in-depth study." We discussed each poem: what is happening, who is speaking, why, in what cultural confines, and what is its relevance to us? Students were engaged, and the lack of published translations did not hinder us. But I wished students would have had access to a broader range of poetry that they could have read on their own. Something like a *Norton*-type anthology of modern Japanese poetry . . .

I stayed closely connected with Engle and the IWP during those years. Engle encouraged me to talk with the resident writers and invited me to their gatherings and events. When they welcomed new poets in residence, he made sure that we met. Gōzō Yoshimasu, the poet in residence in 1970 and 1971, was one of them. Gōzō was at the early phase of his spectacular career as a poet and multimedia artist. He has been kind and generous in advising, guiding, and providing resources for me for various projects. I owe him a debt for his mental mapping of the contemporary Japanese poetry scene, which has become a guidepost for my translation activities.

In the spring of 1971, the Academy of American Poets held a conference on poetry and translation in New York City. They invited three distinguished Japanese poets—Tamura Ryūichi, Tanikawa Shuntarō, and Katagiri Yuzuru—to read their poetry and participate in panel discussions on translating poetry, for which I was asked to interpret. The conference was well attended by poets, translators, and academics. I was happy to see that Japanese poetry was featured and that the importance of translating it was being recognized.

After the conference, the three poets traveled across the country, giving readings at universities along the way, including at the IWP, where Gōzō was still in residence. Tamura had been a young modernist poet when the Pacific War started, barely old enough to be mobilized to serve in the Japanese military toward its end. Tanikawa was in elementary school, where he was subjected to a military-mandated education. Gōzō's schooling started during the postwar democracy. There was barely sixteen years' age difference from the oldest to the youngest, but they represented three different generations of great postwar poets. To have them all in Iowa City at once was an unusual and fortunate occasion.

Tamura had been the poet in residence for the IWP's inaugural year (1967–1968). In honor of his return to Iowa City, Engle presented him with a book hot off the press, *World without Words*, a selection of his poems in my translation.[6] This was the first book-length selection of Tamura's poetry in English and probably one of the earliest book-length translations of any postwar Japanese poet.

One afternoon, Tanikawa visited with students from the Japanese and Chinese Studies classes. Their lively question and answer session made me realize how curious each side was about the other, and how eager to learn. Having a casual but serious chat with a Japanese poet was a new experience for our students. Their enthusiasm assured me that their interest in Japanese poetry was genuine and that the Japan program would grow. Tamura, Tanikawa, and Gōzō have been my great friends and mentors in poetry ever since.

Pearl Harbor Day in South Dakota

After three years of teaching at the University of Iowa, I moved to Mitchell, South Dakota, in 1971, when my husband took a teaching position at Dakota Wesleyan University. Generally, the people I came across in this small conservative town were welcoming and kind. That fall, I was asked to give a lecture on Japanese culture to students in a core program. I was happy to oblige. I picked December 7 from among the few dates offered, without giving much thought to its significance in US-Japan relations. On the morning of the lecture, I opened the *Mitchell Daily Republic*, the local newspaper, and froze. A huge five-inch banner across the top of two center pages screamed, "Remember Pearl Harbor," commemorating the thirtieth anniversary of the start of the Pacific War. I realized what the day meant to the community. Most likely these students' families had been directly affected by the event that galvanized the entire nation against Japan for four years. I had no choice but to stand in front of them and simply be honest. In the auditorium where two hundred or so students were silently looking at me, I started speaking my heartfelt condolences to their family members and relatives who might have sacrificed their lives or been injured in the war. I wanted these young people to hear what contemporary Japan was like. This experience brought home the need for increased understanding between the two cultures.

Temporary Stay in Japan / Transition to the Next Phase

In 1974, we relocated to Japan when the Kyushu Institute of Technology invited my husband to be advisor and teacher under a Ministry of Education grant. He was responsible for helping technical faculty members prepare their research papers for presentation at international academic conferences. He enjoyed his work, but at home, he was frustrated seeing Colombo speak Japanese on television. As yet, there was no satellite broadcasting to feed bilingual versions of foreign shows and movies to the home. I started translating the dialogue into English for him. When I stumbled over short interjections, he would give me the original words through lipreading. Without realizing it, I was taking lessons on colloquial English usage and training for simultaneous interpreting.

I kept myself busy as an adjunct, teaching English at Kyushu University, Kyushu Institute of Technology, and municipal and private universities in the region. At a woman's junior college, I taught American poetry. I ordered about thirty copies of *The Norton Anthology of Modern Poetry* for the class through a bookstore in Iowa City. The students were thrilled to have their own weighty collection. They even initiated a poetry writing activity to produce a class anthology of their own poems. (Decades later, one of the students found me on Facebook and wrote that she still treasures the *Norton* and refers to it for her creative activities. I was moved. How I wish I'd had a big anthology of Japanese poetry like that back in Iowa!)

I published academic papers, poems, and translations as a member of the Kyushu branch of the American Literature Society, and my translations of poetry by Tamura and Osada Hiroshi appeared in *TriQuarterly 31: Contemporary Asian Literature* (1974).[7] I also interpreted for US State Department guests when they gave lectures on art and literature at the Fukuoka American Cultural Center, including Robert Creeley, William Gaddis, and Edward Albee. At home, I continued to translate Japanese poetry into English, write essays on contemporary American poets for literary journals such as *Waseda bungaku* (Waseda Literature), and translate American authors. My translations of *A Dialogue* by James Baldwin and Nikki Giovanni and Nikki Giovanni's *Gemini* were published in Tokyo in 1977 and 1978, respectively.[8] These two books were originally suggested to the publisher by Osada, who had been the poet in residence at the IWP (1971–1972). He enlisted me as the translator.

In 1977, we moved back to the United States and settled down in Clifton, New Jersey, thirteen miles from the middle of Manhattan. I attended literary conferences in New York City, such as the Academy of American Poets' conference on translation, while translating modern Japanese poets. One day, I received a call about an event on haiku at Japan Society. They needed an interpreter for their distinguished guest speakers, haiku poet Mori Sumio and literary critic Yamamoto Kenkichi. There was a sizable audience in the handsome auditorium, and the guests' speeches, as well as the discussions after, were well received. I felt happy helping people cross the linguistic and cultural divide. Before the end of that year, I received inquiries about interpreting services from several members of the audience. *OCS News*, a Japanese-language community paper, gave me a weekly column on English usage. I wrote about miscommunication caused by the careless use of simple words, drawing from my own daily life. These columns became the basis for my three books on English usage published later in Tokyo.

Boom Years

The late 1970s through the 1980s were a dynamic and fluid period in US-Japan relations. Japan's prowess in the manufacturing, technological, and economic spheres was undeniable, and Americans, willingly or not, found they had to reassess their position with respect to their Japanese counterparts. A flood of articles and books, such as Ezra Vogel's *Japan as Number One: Lessons for America* (1979), provided concerned readers with analyses of the source and the potential consequences of Japan's success.

The recognition of Japan as an economic power accompanied the realization of a pressing need for deeper understanding and better communication between the two countries across all fields of endeavor. American institutions, corporations, and governmental organizations put considerable effort into learning more about Japan, its people, their mindsets, and Japanese social and business protocols. I began to see new faces on negotiating teams in conference rooms and boardrooms, including Japanese Americans, Americans who had lived in Japan, and those educated in Japan Studies. More and more, young American corporate employees and professionals spoke fluent Japanese. But few of them were trained to facilitate communication between their principals. In this environment, the demand for strong interpreters and cross-cultural consultants grew rapidly, not only in the business world but also in specialized fields such as technology and law.[9]

Around this time, I happened to meet Anafu Kaiser, a true trailblazer among Japanese interpreters. With her commanding personality, strong organizational skills, and exceptional language ability, she was building a network of freelance interpreters based on a clear vision of the mission and discipline of interpreting. She referred me to engagements for consecutive interpreting in several different fields, including finance, technology, and litigation. She also placed me as a simultaneous interpreter at large academic and corporate conferences in medicine, politics, finance, electronics, and software engineering.

Such assignments, plus my work with my own portfolio of clients, brought home the variety and range of business connections between the United States and Japan. In working with companies as varied as AT&T, NTT, NHK, Japan Tobacco, IBM, and Merck, I saw how deep the links were between the two countries, not just in business and the sciences but also in academic and cultural fields.

In the course of traveling around the United States, Europe, and Japan, I had many opportunities to meet other Japanese interpreters. The overwhelming majority were women. The women's movement of the 1970s had opened the door to management roles for women in the United States, but the glass ceiling still kept them from leadership positions. The situation was even more discouraging for women in Japan. That was likely a major reason why so many highly educated and linguistically talented women with leadership qualities chose to work on their own as interpreters. They could control their destinies, contribute to progress and cross-cultural understanding, and earn a handsome living all at the same time.

I was happy to be associated with these women. For my part, though, poetry was just as important. During work with one of my high-tech clients, I received word that one of my English poems, found in the files of the IWP, had been included in *A Book of Women Poets from Antiquity to Now* (1980).[10] The engineer I was working with was amused at my interest in poetry, and how pleased I was. "Well, I guess that's exciting," he said.

Cross-Cultural Considerations

While interpreting in meetings and conferences, I often saw cases of miscommunication between the parties in spite of the accuracy of the translation. Misunderstandings and awkward situations could arise from basic cultural assumptions on either side. In 1983, I started a consulting practice called Interculture Communications. Under this entity, I offered cross-cultural seminars, executive briefings, and interpreting services. Management seminars and cross-cultural training were popular on both sides of the Pacific at that time, but few included hands-on interpreting. Eventually, I offered this comprehensive service to divisions of companies, such as Bristol Myers Squibb, Sony, and Johnson & Johnson, and I also began a twenty-year affiliation with MIT's School of Architecture + Planning to assist with its professional seminars. This approach made communication go much more smoothly. In business negotiations, for example, once executives were briefed on cultural matters, they did not need lengthy explanations of the reasons for confusion or misunderstanding. I could simply direct their attention to the epicenter of the problem at hand, and they would come up with a solution on their own, which generally led to satisfying results.

W. S. Merwin, Mentor in Poetry Translation

Poetry was not forgotten in the bustle of business obligations. For years, I translated poetry or did some writing on planes and trains on my way to providing cross-cultural consulting and interpreting services to corporations and institutions. My translations appeared in *A Play of Mirrors: Eight Major Poets of Modern Japan* (1987), edited by prominent poet and critic Ōoka Makoto and my Tsuda College mentor, Thomas Fitzsimmons.[11] This led to working with Ōoka on a translation of his *The Colors of Poetry: Essays on Classic Japanese Verse* (1991), with a preface by Donald Keene.[12] Ōoka's encyclopedic knowledge of modern Japanese poetry was a formative influence on my later work.

Another fulfilling long-term project was providing translations of and critical essays about several modern Japanese poets for Poetry International Web (PIW, poetryinternational.org), a global resource created by the Poetry International Festival Rotterdam. Tanikawa, founder and funder of the organization's Japan domain, had referred me to Yotsumoto Yasuhiro, the founding editor of PIW's Japanese domain. Yotsumoto made selections from a poet's work, asked me to

Figure 7.1: Takako Lento discussing poetry with Alisa Freedman's seminar, "Women in Modern Japan," on Zoom, May 20, 2020. Photograph courtesy of Alisa Freedman.

translate them, and wrote a cogent introduction. I learned much from working with him. He is yet another mentor and colleague in introducing Japanese poets to the world.

Then came a truly hectic period of literary endeavors. First, based on the Tamura translations on PIW, Wayne Miller contacted me about Tamura, which led to us coediting what became *Tamura Ryūichi: On the Life and Work of a 20th Century Master*, the second volume in the *Unsung Masters* series from Pleiades Press.[13] I was also working on the translations and introduction for Tanikawa's *The Art of Being Alone: Poems 1952–2009* from Cornell University Press' Cornell East Asia Series (CEAS).[14] These books gave two major poets the presence in academia that their work deserved—and both came out in 2011.

In that same year, I had the honor of assisting Tanikawa in establishing the Tanikawa Shuntarō Fund at Cornell University, a permanent fund to support the publication of translations of modern Japanese poetry and criticism. He set up this fund to materialize his long-held vision of making modern Japanese poetry available to the world. The first book published with the assistance of the fund was *Pioneers of Modern Japanese Poetry*, a bilingual volume containing selected poems and my translations from four twentieth-century innovators, with a critical introduction.[15] Kaneko Mitsuharu's poems in the book won the Japan-US Friendship Commission Prize for the Translation of Japanese Literature (2018–2019). Hopefully, many other translators will take advantage of this opportunity to further Tanikawa's vision.

In 2013, I retired from business to focus on poetry. W. S. Merwin and I had been co-translating the haiku of Yosa Buson off and on since the late 1990s, and it had reached the point where the manuscript needed concentrated attention.

Merwin was perhaps the most honored poet and translator of his generation, a two-time winner of the Pulitzer Prize for Poetry, a recipient of the National Book Award, and a former US Poet Laureate. Because it had been my dream to bring Buson into the English-speaking world through Merwin's art of translation, I did not want to miss this opportunity.

Merwin made it clear from the outset that he wanted to present Buson as a poet in English, not just produce a seventeen-syllable haiku transcription. I wanted to help him meet Buson as a person and poet. For this purpose, we agreed on a method: for each of the 868 haiku in *Buson kushū* (Buson Collection), I prepared a worksheet with five elements: the sound pattern, each word with its meaning(s) and function, a basic translation, scholarly annotations, and comments by haiku practitioners. I would mail a bunch of worksheets to Merwin in Maui, where he lived, and he would mail them back to me with his version, comments, and questions written on each sheet. I typed all his handwritten haiku, comments, and questions in blue (which was his color) and my answers in brown (my color) and sent it all back to him. We traded these shipments multiple times as we revised the translations.

Through this exercise, I was reeducated by witnessing Merwin's art of translation at work. Typing out the evolving versions opened my eyes to how Merwin brought poetic force and focus to a haiku. I realized how a *shosei*, an apprentice writer, must have learned his skill from *sensei*, the master writer, in olden times by acting as an assistant to produce clean copies.

Collected Haiku of Yosa Buson contains English translations of all 868 haiku of *Buson kushū* and his three existing *haishi* (free verse).[16] Published in 2013, it was a finalist for the PEN Translation Prize that year, and it received the Japan-US Friendship Commission Prize for the Translation of Japanese Literature (2013–2014). Gōzō, a Buson aficionado, provided invaluable help in this endeavor, collecting source material and reference books and guiding our publisher, Copper Canyon Press, through a grant application to the Japan Foundation, including writing an enthusiastic letter of recommendation. Donald Keene's encouragement to Merwin and his advice on Romanizing protocols were invaluable.

Although retired from business, I still led a double-track life. I started volunteering for the Princeton Festival, a performing arts summer festival. As a member of its guild, I helped build and expand outreach programs to share the love of opera and musicals with the larger community, especially young students. I often thought of Mrs. Nonaka and how I got hooked on poetry in elementary school.

In 2018, when the festival produced *Madama Butterfly*, I asked Kashiwagi Mari, whom I had met through Yotsumoto and PIW, if she had a few butterfly poems for our publicity. It turned out she had thousands. We decided to produce a poetry reading for her in conjunction with the performance. It was such a success that the festival has had a poetry reading every year since. Paradoxically, the pandemic provided the stimulus to make the readings truly international through virtual stagings in 2020 and 2021.

Mari decided to publish her butterfly poems, and we collaborated on the English version and published it in a pair with the original in Tokyo as a two-volume boxed set, an unusual format, in 2020.[17] The *Butterfly* poems have been exceptionally well received worldwide through virtual readings in which Mari participates, and the "Rainbow" poem in the collection received the silver prize at the Mini-Poetry Conference 2021 in China. In 2021, my translation of Tanikawa's *Ordinary People* also appeared from Vagabond Press, along with *Selected Poems of Shinkawa Kazue* in translation by Yotsumoto and myself.[18] These two poets are of the same generation, but their works are dramatically different.

After the Buson book was published, I worked with Merwin to select his poems for Japanese translation. Merwin, as per his usual practice, did not provide any comments on his poetry but helped me create a representative collection of his later work. The resulting book was published in 2022, his third memorial year.[19]

Looking back, I realize how fortunate I have been, meeting these amazing people who had their sights fixed on something bigger than the ordinary and their vision open to the world. They have taught, guided, assisted, and encouraged me through all these decades. Their good grace still guides me even though some of them have passed away. I thank them all from the bottom of my heart and ask them to keep me in their hearts as well. A big anthology, like the *Norton*, of modern Japanese poetry in English translation is still in my hopeful dreams.

Notes

[1] Tsuda Umeko (1864–1929) was the youngest (at age six) of five girls sent to the United States in 1871 on the Meiji government's Iwakura Mission in the hope of educating them to lead efforts to improve education for women. Tsuda stayed in the United States for eleven years and graduated from Bryn Mawr College. She established Joshi Eigaku Juku (Women's English School) in 1900. The name was changed several times, including to Tsuda College (Tsuda Juku Daigaku) in 1948. The English name was changed to Tsuda University (consisting of two colleges) in April 2017.

[2] Thomas Fitzsimmons was a professor at Oakland University. He founded Katydid Books to publish books of modern Japanese poetry in English translations.

[3] Keiko Uesawa Chevray is director emerita of the Japanese Language Program at Columbia University, coauthor of *Schaum's Outline of Japanese Grammar*, and namesake for the Keiko Chevray Award for Japanese Language at Columbia. In the 1980s, I was reunited with Keiko in New York City, when she was teaching in Columbia's Japanese Language Program. She referred me to The New School to teach accelerated English to Japanese corporate employees in the financial field. René was also teaching at Columbia.

[4] Itō Sei (1905–1969) was a prolific poet, novelist, translator, literary critic, theorist, and activist. He introduced translations of contemporary novelists, such as James Joyce and Virginia Woolf, to Japanese readers in the 1930s, and put forth literary theories associated with stream of consciousness, which in turn influenced writers like 1968 Nobel Prize Laureate Kawabata Yasunari.

[5] Takako Uchino, "Western Influence on Modern Japanese Poetry," *Texas Quarterly* (spring 1968), 128–138.

[6] Tamura, Ryūichi, *World without Words*, translated and edited by Takako Uchino Lento (Champaign, IL: Ceres Press, 1971).

[7] Osada, Hiroshi and Tamura Ryūichi, "Poems," *TriQuarterly 31: Contemporary Asian Literature*, translated by Takako Uchino Lento (Evanston: Northwestern University, 1974): 86–89, 199.

[8] James Baldwin and Nikki Giovanni, *Wareware no kakei* (A Dialogue), translated by Takako Lento (Tokyo: Shōbunsha, 1977); Nikki Giovanni, *Futagoza no on'na* (Gemini), translated by Takako Lento (Tokyo: Shōbunsha, 1978).

[9] Takako Lento, *Dame! Sono eigo. Bijinesu hen* (No, That Does Not Work in English: For Business Situations) (Tokyo: Kodansha International, 1999); Takako Lento, *Dame! Sono eigo. Nichijō seikatsu hen* (No, That Does Not Work in English: For Everyday Life) (Tokyo: Kodansha International, 2002); Takako Lento, *Chigai ga wakaru, Amerika eigo renshū-chō* (Learn the Differences: American Usage) (Tokyo: DHC, 2002).

[10] Aliki Barnstone and Willis Barnstone, eds., *A Book of Women Poets from Antiquity to Now* (New York: Schocken, 1980), 180.

[11] Ōoka, Makoto and Thomas Fitzsimmons, eds., *A Play of Mirrors: Eight Major Poets of Modern Japan* (Rochester, MI: Katydid Books, 1987).

[12] Ōoka, Makoto, *The Colors of Poetry: Essays on Classic Japanese Verse*, translated by Takako U. Lento and Thomas V. Lento (Rochester, MI: Katydid Books, 1991).

[13] Takako Lento and Wayne Miller, eds., *Tamura Ryūichi: On the Life and Work of a 20th Century Master* (Warrensburg, MO: Pleiades Press, 2011).

[14] Tanikawa, Shuntarō, *The Art of Being Alone: Poems 1952–2009*, translated and edited by Takako Lento (Ithaca: Cornell East Asia Series, 2011).

[15] Takako Lento, ed. and trans., *Pioneers of Modern Japanese Poetry* (Ithaca: Cornell East Asia Series, 2019).

[16] Yosa Buson, *Collected Haiku of Yosa Buson*, translated by W. S. Merwin and Takako Lento (Port Washington: Copper Canyon Press, 2013).

[17] Kashiwagi, Mari, *Butterfly*, translated by Takako Lento (Tokyo: Shichōsha, 2020).

[18] Tanikawa, Shuntarō, *Ordinary People*, translated by Takako Lento (Sydney: Vagabond Press, 2021); Shinkawa, Kazue, *Selected Poems of Shinkawa Kazue*, translated and edited by Takako Lento and Yotsumoto Yasuhiro (Sydney: Vagabond Press, 2021). The Tanikawa book was short-listed for the 2022 Lucien Stryk Asian Translation Prize.

[19] W. S. Merwin, *W. S. Merwin senshishū 1983-2014* (W. S. Merwin Poems, 1983-2014), translated by Takako Lento (Tokyo: Shichōsha, 2022).

8

A Record of Puzzlement

Phyllis I. Lyons

With gratitude to Dazai Osamu for providing a template

> *People who teach history are called "historians." People who teach anthropology are called "anthropologists." But what about people who teach literature? Many of my peers have been happily untroubled about nomenclature, but it remains strange to me, looking back over a long career of teaching Japanese literature and finding myself still wondering—I know what I've been doing, but why can't I name it?*

PHYLLIS I. LYONS is an associate professor emerita at Northwestern University. She created Northwestern's Japanese Language and Literature Program and guided it for thirty-eight years, from a tiny entry in the Program of African and Asian Languages into a central member of one of the newest departments at Northwestern, Asian Languages and Cultures. Her publications include *The Saga of Dazai Osamu: A Critical Study with Translations* (1985), winner of the Japan-US Friendship Commission Prize for the Translation of Japanese Literature (1985), and a translation with author's afterword of Tanizaki Jun'ichirō's *Kokubyaku*, as *In Black and White: A Novel* (Columbia University Press, 2018). She was awarded the Order of the Rising Sun, Gold Rays with Rosette by the Japanese government (2018).

This is the not-fictional truth: I never intended to become a college professor. I did not intend *not* to be one either, but neither did I have any notion to be something else. I never had the enviable sort of committed trajectory that my peers and colleagues always seemed to have. I became an English major in college because I liked to read novels; and, while I was standing around waiting for someone or something to tap me on the shoulder and give me a hint about what to do next, forty years went by, and it came out that I had had a career in Japanese Studies.

What had happened in that time? I had started and nurtured for decades a Japanese language and literature program at a major university that astonishingly hadn't had one. I had directed for years an international studies program that I'd been roped into helping design. I had taught hundreds (thousands?) of students: some of whom thought I digressed too much and bored them to tears; some of whom thought my classes had transformed their lives and taught them more about life and the human spirit than they had ever expected from "Japanese literature;" and the rest were fairly satisfied. I had listened carefully and helped young people who knew what they wanted to do after this stage of life was over but not necessarily how to do it; and I listened sympathetically to those who, like me, didn't really know what they wanted to do or who they wanted to be. I had had experiences here and there that brought amazing joy and grinding grief, sometimes both at the same time. I had traced out some ideas that somehow popped up unexpectedly in my head, which I was able to wrestle into a transmissable form that some other people seemed to have enjoyed reading. I had helped design a new department. Hmm...

After all this time, though, I am still puzzled about what I did and how I managed to do it. One measure of how old one is is that so many people who significantly traveled with you are gone. Some have simply vanished, and you wonder what they are doing, or if they even *are*. You know that others no longer *are*. The ongoing mystery, however, is that what was and what is are still inextricably intertwined and continue to be for as long as I am present to answer the question, "So, how did you get here?" What follow are some experiences that brought me to be implicated in Japanese Studies, many of which are as alive to me today as they were seventy years ago, and which sometimes seem even more vibrant than what happened yesterday.

Japanese Studies

How did you get into Japanese Studies? Probably all Japanese Studies professionals are asked that. There was an easy, if unenlightening, answer that seemed to satisfy most people without requiring bothersome detail: "Well, I lived in Japan as a child ..." (figure 8.1).

Figure 8.1: Nine-year-old Phyllis and her mother, Easter 1952, with the specter of Japanese Studies looming behind. Photograph courtesy of the author.

Coming back to the United States at the age of fifteen, after six years of growing up in Japan, had not been good. My new high school classmates were not interested in what I'd seen, what I'd done; the life I'd lived only made me strange. I learned quickly not to talk about it. That life fit nowhere. I buried it.

As a confused college senior, I had already decided graduate school was not for me. They let you read novels as an undergraduate English major. English, American, French, Russian, German . . . I read hundreds of novels. But I already knew that in graduate school, you didn't read novels—you read what other people said about novels. (Years later, I got a letter from a former student who was doing a graduate program in Japanese literature. Sadly, she was quitting the program. "They don't seem to be interested in Japanese literature. They only want to talk about Derrida." See?)

Had I been five years or so younger, maybe I'd have gone to law school. That's what confused English majors seemed to be doing by that time. And besides, what can you do with an English major if, instead of immersing yourself in the alternate lives reading novels lets you do, you have to teach students what other people have said about the novels? That's the part of the English major I'd already found boring. Then chance stepped in.

My undergraduate university did not seem to have anything Japanese going on in the early 1960s. But there was a new professor, and I read his course description in the catalog: modern Japanese history. Hmm, I once lived in Japan; maybe I could learn something about it. On the first day of class, he came into the classroom, passed out the syllabus, and then told us: "We are going to work on modern Japanese history, but you'll never understand anything about Japan unless you read some Japanese novels. So here's a list of some important ones to read. Read them."

Japanese wrote novels? It had never occurred to me that Japanese wrote novels. I was astonished. I suddenly wanted to read more novels and go back to this place I used to think I knew.

How to get back? There was no JET Program at the time; if there had been, I guess I would have been a JET and would never have gotten into Japanese Studies at all. But my professor told me, "If you want to go to Japan, go to graduate school, and they'll send you to do research work." Dutifully, I followed Harry Harootunian's advice and entered Japanese Studies.

It turned out that you had to be able to read Japanese to read Japanese novels. Too bad I had not learned to read—or even to speak—Japanese while I was there as a child. A couple of years into my graduate program, I was attending summer school after two years of Japanese language study at a university that was not my own graduate university. This summer program was in part teaching how to speak Japanese, but there was also much competition in naming how many kanji characters you knew. My home program didn't teach you to speak. Reading was the only essential skill. But I had never had to keep track of how much I was capable of.

During that summer, I also learned that, magically, there was a secret society spread throughout the globe. Educational sociologists had a name for it: "third-culture kids." These were children who had spent significant time growing up in a culture that was not their own but had returned to the home culture, for better or worse. I was not alone. My dislocations and puzzlement had been noted by researchers. I learned that Japanese Studies is filled with such people—"So get on with it" seemed to be the message.

One day, I was lined up with other graduate students to sign for my summer stipend. It was a National Defense Foreign Language Fellowship, and the stipulation for getting it was that you had to agree to work for the US government—or at least teach the language and culture you were learning. (It turned out that American universities ever after were populated by faculty like me who took the money and ran—to teaching.) Some of the languages included were Chinese, Japanese, Korean, Russian, and some unexpected ones: Thai, Vietnamese . . . Why those strange ones? In the mid-1960s, we didn't know it yet, but Washington knew Vietnamese was soon going to be important in the national defense game. I was probably in the last year of students who had to sign a loyalty oath to get the government money, a kind of pledge of allegiance to the United States. Some graduate students were much exercised about this government interference in their education, but I figured that, if I were a threat to national security, domestic intelligence agencies already knew it, and I blithely signed it. Standing in front of me in line to get his stipend was a tall young man, and we got to talking. He was in anthropology and had lived in Japan with his father, who was a professor at a famous American university. He asked what I was doing. I said, "Japanese." He smiled strangely, and said, "So you didn't escape" (there may have been an "either" at the end, but I don't remember now). I looked over his shoulder as he bent to sign his name. It was Reischauer. It turned out that, in fact, his sister had been in my class at St. Maur in Yokohama. Oh, Joan. St. Maur in Yokohama . . .

Language

In time, I became a professor of Japanese literature, but I've always been puzzled that there seemed not to be a name for what what I have been professing for half a century. People who teach history are called "historians." People who teach anthropology are called "anthropologists." But what about people who teach literature? Many of my peers have been happily untroubled about nomenclature, but it remains strange to me, looking back over a long career of teaching Japanese literature and finding myself still wondering—I know what I've been doing, but why can't I name it?

But language learning: that is something we can sink our teeth into. My graduate university was a major one, but the Japanese program was just fledgling, although Chinese already had a solid presence there. The department was located in an Oriental Institute—you know, Sumerian, Akkadian, ancient Hebrew . . . Chinese and Japanese were taught in an environment of dead languages— languages to be read, not spoken. (Given today's political climate, that "Oriental Institute" has recently become the Institute for the Study of Ancient Cultures, West Asia and North Africa [ISAC]. Yes, it is prosaically more accurate and less "colonial," but it betrays its history. Isn't historical clarity one responsibility of academic institutions? *Teach* what "oriental" means, then and now, don't erase history. Sigh.) Our first-year Japanese textbook was the Elisséeff-Reischauer-Yoshihashi *Elementary Japanese for College Students* (1944); the vocabulary words in the final lesson are: Lieutenant-General/Vice-Admiral (*chūjō*); Major-General/Rear-Admiral (*shōshō*); etc. Clearly, there were particular objectives for learning Japanese in 1944.[1] (Roy Andrew Miller told me once, when I asked how they had managed to learn so much Japanese in such a short time during the war, "The military language schools had the best incentive plan: if you *didn't* do well, they handed you a rifle and put you on a troop ship!")

In time, I learned the reality of a joke I'd heard: Students from my university were famous (notorious?) for being able to get off the plane and go straight to the library to start doing research but were in danger of starving to death because they didn't know how to ask, "Where is a restaurant?"

There were the mistakes. The Inter-University Center for Japanese Language Studies in Tokyo worked hard to make me conversationable, but there was the day I tried out my nascent spoken Japanese at the local *yaoya-san* (greengrocer). Instead of just pointing, I confidently asked for "that mountain of potatoes, please." I knew the word for potatoes—*bareisho*—because I had read a famous Kunikida Doppo story, "Meat and Potatoes" (*Gyūniku to bareisho*).[2] There was a titter from the housewives standing around. I didn't know that there had been a significant vocabulary change between 1901 and 1967, and the word for "potato" had long been *jagaimo*. (You can see what a trauma it was—I blush to this day.)

A fellow graduate student, who later became the executive director of a major Japan-related funding agency, had his trials, too. As a man, he spent some of his time in the company of the men at the neighborhood bars and, naturally, learned some of their particular vocabulary. He became a fan of the offerings in his local sweets shop, particularly *manjū* (little steamed cakes) filled with *anko* (sweet red bean paste). His brain freeze one day, mixing syllables of the two words, provoked more of a sharp intake of breath than a titter from the housewives buying after-school treats for their children: *man-ko*. Not a word for polite sweets-shop company, although perfectly cromulent among men—the lower part of the female anatomy.

(A cautionary, and perhaps apocryphal, story that was told to students at that summer school I attended about a crucial element of spoken Japanese: When General Douglas MacArthur was heading the Occupation in Japan, he went to many social functions accompanied by, among others, an officious officer who was proud of his facility with the Japanese language and went around introducing himself to Japanese guests as "MacArthur's advisor." He did not know the difference between short syllables and long syllables. He wanted to say "advisor." The word in Japanese is *komon*—short syllable. Instead he'd say *kōmon*—long syllable. That meant, "nether end of the alimentary canal." Maybe he was MacArthur's *kōmon*, after all.)

And yet I did learn it. When later students in my own first-year Japanese classes asked me how long it would take to learn Japanese, I answered with what must be the standard not-so-cheery joke: the rest of your life.

My Father

My father was a storyteller. Many of his stories referred to his experiences as a petroleum refining engineer in Japan. In 1948, with no knowledge of Japan, and, only three years after the end of the war, he was sent by his oil company to travel all around Japan from Hokkaido to Kyushu for a number of months to investigate if there was anything left of Japanese refineries that could be salvaged to get the economy going again or if they would have to build from the ground up. Donald Keene has told charming stories of his early experiences in Japan right after the war. My father had a similar store of experiences, of going to places that had never seen a foreigner, of *ryokan* (inns) that had no idea of what foreigners ate—and, besides, there was very little to eat in those days anyway—of teaching *ryokan* staff that lighting three hibachi to keep the foreigner warm and then closing the *amado* (wooden sliding doors closing out rain or cold) tightly was not a kindness but something that led to the splitting headache that is a sign of carbon monoxide poisoning. He loved Japan. His memories became mine, and many of them have been passed on to my students whenever it seemed appropriate.

The Melody Lingers On

In the 1950s, when my father had the family with him for his next work assignment in Japan, entertainment for American business partners of Japanese companies often included geisha parties. My father happily attended them. American company wives had deep suspicions about what went on at these geisha parties, but my father insisted that most husbands got the message: the ladies were to be treated with respect (although some boors did force private arrangements for after the party). They were professional entertainers, not free for the picking. My father described the parties as being like sophisticated children's birthday parties, with the geisha, like mothers, keeping track of the games and songs and dancing. If the guests seemed to be getting bored, well, time for intervention and the introduction of a different game. There was, of course, a great deal of drinking, with the prize for winning a drinking game being much laughter and more drinking to assure goodwill, and there was a great deal of singing of Japanese folk songs and learning Japanese folk dancing—a practice perhaps democratized into today's karaoke. My father would later teach my brother and me what he could remember of the games and songs he learned at the parties. Many of the songs he learned turned out to be classics of Japanese children's culture. Unusual for an American businessman, my father took language lessons and learned some Japanese; his voice was not very melodic, but he used it with great enthusiasm. His children did not share his linguistic gifts or incentives and went to international schools; we learned the songs phonetically from him but quickly forgot even his little summaries of what they meant. But unbeknownst to me, one remained hidden away.

Years went by, and the songs faded from my memory. One day I was reading a Dazai Osamu story,[3] and, suddenly, my eyes stopped on one line: *ima wa yamanaka / ima wa hama / ima wa tekkyō . . .* I'd heard these words and remembered a melody and words echoing in my memory, and now as I read it, I knew what the words meant: "Now we're in the mountains / Now we're by the sea / Now there's a railroad bridge . . ." He'd learned it, and I'd memorized it perfectly, and it had remained imprinted on my brain! Later, I learned that this song had been written in the early 1900s to celebrate the opening of a new train line connecting the Tohoku (northeastern) hinterlands to the capital, and everyone knew it. But that first moment of shocked recognition remains in my heart.

More years went by. I was now a university professor. A man already well regarded in the Foreign Ministry (who became even more distinguished in government and international circles when his tour of duty was completed and he returned to Japan) was dispatched to our city as consul-general. One night, my husband and I invited him to our apartment for a low-key "American home supper." Also present was my father, now in his nineties. As the evening wore on, the consul-general and my father hit it off, and they began singing songs together, many of them the same ones my father had learned at geisha parties. And wouldn't you know it? Suddenly I was singing with them: "*ima wa yamanaka / ima wa hama / ima wa tekkyō . . .*" Forty years later, my father still remembered it, and now I knew what it meant as I joined in. Thus, the fruit of many years of commitment to Japanese Studies.

Earthquakes

I came from New York originally. It is a place without earthquakes. It was a shock to encounter earthquakes, such frequent earthquakes. Nine-year-old me would lie in bed and feel the bed shake and wonder if it was an earthquake or just my heart beating in fear. But there was a big one in 1952 that even made cracks in the walls. The family story is that when it hit, my mother leapt out of bed, yelled to my father to get me, and raced down the hall to get my younger brother. The shaking had awakened me, and I stumbled on my own into the second-floor hallway, joining my mother and brother who were clinging together. No father. My mother shouted out to my father, "Where are you?" From the bedroom came a groggy voice, "I can't find my slippers."

Many years later, I began to work on the writer Tanizaki Jun'ichirō. He wrote that he had an earthquake phobia. His elderly nursemaid had often told him in his childhood about the Great Ansei Earthquake of 1855, which she had experienced as a young girl, and he wrote about wondering when the next Big One would come for him. Earthquakes appear in his stories from well before the September 1, 1923, Great Kantō Earthquake, but it is a commonplace for students of Tanizaki to note that, although he was an Edokko ("son of Old Tokyo") born and bred, after the Great Kantō Earthquake, he left Tokyo and lived most of the remaining forty years of his life near Osaka in Kansai (Western Japan). In one of his pre-Great Kantō Earthquake stories, a man is lying in bed, feverish and suffering the pain of a massive toothache, and he begins to hallucinate that there is a strong earthquake shaking his room. As I read my childhood fear revived, I felt myself almost moaning with him.[4]

Then, of course, came the terrible March 11 Great Tohoku Earthquake and tsunami in 2011. I sat on the other side of the ocean watching television with the same footage repeated over and over and taken from a townside perspective, of the tsunami looming up from outside the harbor of Miyako and then racing into the harbor, breaching the concrete retaining walls and then smashing into and over the fishing boat docks and then into buildings and then spreading through the streets of the town, and I remembered the friends I had made in that town so many years ago, who had taken me to the now drowned fish market to get fish straight from the boats.

I don't exactly have a phobia, but earthquakes loom larger in my consciousness than I like to think, even though I no longer live in an earthquake zone.

Synchronicities

I seem to have been immune to some very important technological and intellectual world changes. My uncle was one of founders of Silicon Valley, but my computer skills remain rudimentary. Among my undergraduate teachers were Harry Harootunian and Hayden White, and I should have been in on the ground floor of the enormous paradigm shift that produced critical theory as the vocabulary of cultural analysis in many academic disciplines; but I managed to evade that, too.

Standing at my third-culture viewing spot, being in "the field" has often seemed mysterious to me. There is this place, Japan, with its culture, but what to say about it? You can speak in the language of "history" or "economics" or "literature," but what do those disciplines—systems of vocabulary—have to do to explain what the effect of an encounter with the enormity of what "Japan" is? When I think of my experience of being in the field, my attachment to it seems both larger and smaller than an academic discipline, more like discrete frames of a film, not a running filmstrip narrating a career. The frames seem to contain people, not ideas, and they seem to exist clearly today, even as they happened long ago.

In one frame in 1970, I join a crowd of people standing in front of a bookstore, all engaged in *tachi-yomi* (standing and reading, often without buying), all leafing through a special photo edition of a news magazine that has just appeared on the newstands: after twenty-five years, censored photos taken of terribly damaged people and hellish destruction on the streets on the day of, and the few days after, the bombing of Hiroshima, have just been released. I feel no sense of menace from the crowd, but I am horrified. I am American. I am ashamed, and I leave.

A fairy-tale moment: we children crawl through a hole we've found in a high concrete wall surrounding a whole block in our neighborhood and find ourselves in a deserted, large, silent, old Japanese garden, but we hesitate to approach the sprawling Japanese house in the distance and quickly flee. We do not even tell the maids what we have done, so we never learn what this mysterious place is. Many years later, when I read Tanizaki's novella, "The Bridge of Dreams" (*Yume no ukihashi*), this is the scene I see.[5]

There are also deliciously scary images that fill other frames. The cutaway model of a man's chest and belly in the local pharmacy window I often stopped and stared at, showing all the different kinds of parasites that could be crawling through your innards (de-wormings were an annual medical event, whether you had any symptoms or not). Or the stand in front of a little restaurant across from the train station, where a chef presided over a big chopping board beside the charcoal grill, and we often stood watching him dip his hand into a water-filled barrel, come up with a wriggling little eel-like thing (*dojō*), and, in one continuous motion, ram a spike through the creature's head, gut it, stretch it on bamboo skewers, and put it on the grill for a 1950s Japanese-foresighted version of a fast-food dinner. And indescribably nasty-looking, dark, squirmy blobs (*namako* [sea cucumber]) that occupied little pans in the fish store right next to real fishes lying beside them. (To me, they looked like the mysterious greeny-black stuff waving back and forth in the water of the open sewers that ran beside local streets everywhere. Once, we joined in neighborhood excitement when a large snake was found swimming in one of them, and one brave man pulled it out to great applause.)

In another frame, I'm with friends in the late 1960s on the Rikuchū Kaigan (the seacoast so devastated forty years later in the March 11 earthquake and tsunami), holding our breaths and diving for *uni* (sea urchin) to be cracked open, scooped out, and eaten raw, while our more long-breathed friends scraped *awabi* (abalone) off the underwater rock walls and roasted them on the beach for us all to share.

There are frames where the spotty memory is overlain with things I learned later as I filled it in with Japanese history I didn't know at the time: only a few short years earlier, Japanese schoolchildren were running down the streets following American jeeps, crying, "*Chokorēto, chokorēto!*" (Chocolate, chocolate!) at the American soldiers. Now (in 1952), there were few Americans where we lived in Ōmori, and so as my brother and I passed the local elementary school on our way to the train to our school, at first we were objects of curiosity. The Japanese children in the schoolyard came running to the fence of the school and waved to us, yelling, "*Harō, harō!*" (Hello, hello!). But soon they got used to us and mostly ignored us as they got ready to go in for the start of their classes. Until winter came—and for the first time, my brother wore his knit stocking cap. Suddenly, shouts of joy met us as they raced over to the fence and cried, "*Santa kurosu, santa kurosu!*" (Santa Claus, Santa Claus!). We were too late for chocolate to be a special American thing but were right on time for Santa Claus to have entered into the evolving children's culture.

What I further did not know until over half a century later, nor probably did our little Japanese friends then, was that Ōmori had by 1944 become the site of an American prisoner-of-war camp at the ocean's edge just a couple of miles away, so the memory must have been in the minds of some adults who saw us going to school. We didn't even know the shore was so close. How grateful I am now that at least we and Japanese schoolchildren both knew Santa Claus—although my brother resisted the next time our mother tried to put the cap on him.

In another frame, I am nine years old, and my parents have just told me the Occupation is over. I am walking in the neighborhood right after a rain. Toward me comes an elderly couple. There is a line of paving stones down the center of the narrow alley to raise pedestrians above the unpaved surface so they don't have to walk in the mud. We are both walking on the paving stones, from opposite directions. I was brought up to know that young people defer to their elders, so I would have stood aside to let the couple pass anyway. But the thought runs through my head: This is their country again, whatever that means. And I step into the mud to let them pass. My first political thought?

In another, I am planting rice in 1968 in Tsugaru, Aomori. The farm folk invited me to join them while I was staying in their town doing dissertation research, and there is much gentle joshing as I discover, barefoot, how soft and deep the mud is for the seedlings to start their transplant transition from the crowded seedbed to be spaced out in a real paddy, which will be drained before long so they can grow to strong maturity. I look behind me and see that there are a couple women planting their straight rows on either side of me, and as they go by, they are quietly straightening out the meandering line of seedlings I have planted.

Yet again, I am ten years old. It is the first day I am responsible for getting my brother and myself from Ōmori to school in Yokohama all by myself. I get us on the streetcar at Sakuragichō, the end of the train line, to head for the tunnel through the hill above Motomachi, where our schools are. After a few minutes, I realize there is no tunnel ahead: we are heading out into vegetable fields. In parts of Yokohama, there is still farmland close in, left after the destruction of the war and not yet built up again. I start to cry. I don't speak the language, there are all strangers around me, we are lost. My seven-year-old brother tugs at my sleeve: "It's all right, it's all right, we're okay." A Japanese man comes over and somehow figures out what the problem is. Seven years after a horrible war, a man—who knows what his story is?—gets us off the streetcar, waits with us for a returning streetcar, takes us back to Sakuragichō, and gets two lost American children onto the right path.

And yet not so long before, in the same year, 1952, we see that American cars are still burning the next day outside the Palace moat in Tokyo, in the aftermath of Japan's first May Day observance since the end of the Occupation, when it had been forbidden. The day before, the English-language FEN radio station (the Far East Network of the Americans-used-to-be-Occupiers) had urged Americans not to go outdoors because there was no way to project what would happen when Japanese workers joined workers of the world in celebration.

And I am in Tokyo again in 1970 when the US-Japan Security Treaty is up for renewal and tens of thousands of students take to the streets in protest. And American graduate students dress up nicely and march with banners to the US Embassy, the men with ties and the women in high heels, to protest the American war in Vitenam.

But another frame: I am following the trail of one of Tanizaki's characters in the novel I am translating, *In Black and White* (*Kokubyaku*), as he wanders through the ruins of Yokohama, still evident some years after the city's destruction in the 1923 earthquake.[6] Trying to get a sense of the time and place, I find a book called *The Death of Old Yokohama in the Great Japanese Earthquake of September 1, 1923* (1968).[7] It is a recollection decades later by an American businessman, Otis Manchester Poole, who married into the commercial aristocracy of the Yokohama expatriate community that had grown up from the 1870s opening of Japan to foreign trade. It uses his journals and memories of the September 1, 1923 earthquake and the following days to give a startlingly moving view of those who lived through the firestorms spawned by the quake and those who did not make it. Motomachi, an elegant shopping street when I knew it in the 1950s: in 1923, it was only a little Japanese "town" (*machi*) at the "foot" (*moto*) of that hill with the tunnel that in 1952 my streetcar used to pass through on my way to school. In 1923, the Western community was at the top of the hill, the Bluff—oh, that's where my school was. And the terror at the end, as the Americans and British residents and the Japanese servants living nearby, are cut off on the Bluff from escape with the fires pushing them from behind, and to the brink of the cliff two hundred feet above Motomachi. The foreign residents fashion ropes, lower women and children first and then men. And the Japanese come after, trying to get away, too. Too many too late. Poole echoes the screams and dull thumps as bodies hit the ground. I feel a synchronicity of horror: Yokohama in 1923, recreated in 1968, and still alive in my memories of the sounds and sights conveyed on television as I sat and watched all day in 2001 the catastrophe of 9/11. The thud of bodies hitting the ground.

This is clearly a solipsistic view of my place in the field. But it is what my decades before, during, and after being in the field are to me. I have no special lessons from it, no guidance to give, no arguments to make. I construct no politics, no theories. For sure, I was there, and I am here. And Japan colors most of what I know. The past is as contemporaneously alive within me as any event happening "today." That is my experience of the field of Japanese Studies.

Notes

[1] Serge Elisséeff, Edwin O. Reischauer, and Takehiko Yoshihashi, *Elementary Japanese for College Students* (Cambridge, MA: Harvard-Yenching Institute, 1944).

[2] Kunikida Doppo, "Meat and Potatoes," in *River Mist and Other Stories*, translated by David Chibbett (New York: Kodansha International, 1983), 136–151.

[3] It is in the story "The Seagull" (*Kamome*). Dazai Osamu, "Kamome," *Dazai Osamu zenshū* (Collected Works of Dazai Osamu) vol. 3 (Tokyo: Chikuma shobō, 1967), 84–99. In 1940, with more stability in his life, Dazai was looking back on a disastrous period five years earlier. The childhood song evoked an image of a train going anywhere—and nowhere—while he was "standing all alone in the middle of a burned-out field." Phyllis Lyons, *The Saga of Dazai Osamu: A Critical Study with Translations* (Stanford: Stanford University Press, 1985), 118. But my memories of the song were all warm.

[4] Tanizaki Jun'ichirō, *Byōjoku no gensō* (Sickbed Fantasies), in *Tanizaki Jun'ichirō zenshū* (Collected Works of Tanizaki Jun'ichirō), vol. 4 (Tokyo: Chūō kōronsha, 1983), 155–183; "Tanizaki Jun'ichirō, Sickbed Fantasies" (*Byōjoku no gensō*), translated by Phyllis I. Lyons, unpublished.

[5] Tanizaki Jun'ichirō, "The Bridge of Dreams," in *Seven Japanese Tales*, translated by Howard Hibbett (New York: Berkley Publishing Group, 1965), 67–106.

[6] Tanizaki Jun'ichirō, *In Black and White: A Novel*, translated by Phyllis I. Lyons (New York: Columbia University Press, 2018).

[7] Otis Manchester Poole, *The Death of Old Yokohama in the Great Japanese Earthquake of September 1, 1923* (New South Wales, Australia: Allen & Unwin, 1968).

9

An Accidental Pioneer

Susan B. Hanley

*One mentor at Harvard bluntly told me that it didn't matter
where I studied; I would only end up getting married and
dropping out to have children. I stopped consulting him.*

SUSAN B. HANLEY is a professor emerita at the University of Washington. She was involved with *The Journal of Japanese Studies* for thirty years, from its start, serving as the managing editor (1973–1986), editor (1986–1998), and coeditor (1998 until her retirement in 2003). Her publications include articles in *Chūō kōron*, *The Journal of Interdisciplinary History*, and *The Cambridge History of Japan*. She coedited *Family and Population in East Asian History* with Arthur P. Wolf (1985). Her favorite project is *Everyday Things in Premodern Japan: The Hidden Legacy of Material Culture* (1997), which was first published in Japanese as *Edo jidai no isan* (1990). This book won the Joseph Roggendorf Prize in Japan and the John W. Hall Book Prize from the Association for Asian Studies. She and her husband, Kozo Yamamura, published four novels under the pen name Michael S. Koyama.

I am amused every time I think of myself as a "pioneer woman" in Japanese Studies. It was only through coincidence that I became a professor of Japanese history. I loved to travel and see how other people lived, even before I went to school. I was fascinated by the history of the Pilgrims when my brother was into dinosaurs. I assigned ages to the members of my paper doll families, so it was natural that I would study the population of villages. I loved to read. But Japan? When I was a tween, I refused to read a story about Asian twins on the grounds that it was too far removed from my own life. I liked stories about Americans and the British.

When I was about twelve, I discovered ballet, and it was ballet that got me through my teen years. The highlight of my dance "career" was at age eighteen when I danced in the corps in a performance of *Aurora's Wedding* with the Minneapolis Symphony Orchestra before an audience of five thousand. But I always knew my talents were academic, and, after two years at Macalester College, I gave up trying to combine ballet with college.

The first Sputnik was launched in 1957, my freshman year. I decided that Americans had to know more about the Soviet Union, and so I took Russian, intending to major in Russian history. But Macalester was not a very challenging college in the 1950s; I liked the students but not most of my classes. I became friends with a dorm mate, Ann Reischauer, the daughter of Edwin O. Reischauer, who was then a professor of Japanese history at Harvard. When Ann suggested I go home with her for the summer, I was delighted. My aunt, Susan Haskins, head of the Catalog Department at Widener, got me a job in the bowels of the library. After a summer in Cambridge, my dream became to transfer to Radcliffe. With great luck and much joy, I was admitted for my junior year.

I had planned to continue with Russian Studies at Radcliffe, but the requirements would entail a fifth year of college, which I could not afford, so I changed to a general history major. I took the "Rice Paddies" course (the nickname for the introductory East Asian history course) taught by Reischauer and John K. Fairbank and loved it.[1] Then I wrote an honors thesis based on archived missionary letters that would reveal a "small window on Meiji Japan." But still I was not committed to Japan and had not studied the language.

I needed to make career plans. I thought it would be exciting to become a Foreign Service Officer. A male officer gleefully proclaimed to a group of Radcliffe students that they loved to have women enter the Foreign Service because they would marry a fellow officer, the wife would quit, and they would get two trained officers but only pay a salary to one. I immediately scratched the Foreign Service off my list of possible careers.

I decided to pursue graduate studies and sought advice. One mentor at Harvard bluntly told me that it didn't matter where I studied; I would only end up getting married and dropping out to have children. I stopped consulting him. I thought it would be best to visit Asia before I started graduate school. Through a legacy and savings from gifts, plus a generous gift from my Aunt Susan, I had enough money for a year abroad if I was very careful. I applied to five universities in five Asian nations, but the only university that wrote back was the International

Christian University (ICU) in Tokyo. And that's how I ended up in Japan and in Japanese Studies.

Life in Japan during the 1960s was completely different from what today's American students face. ICU placed me in a doctor's home in 1961, and, although the owner was a middle-class professional with a large home in Kunitachi on the outskirts of Tokyo, the house had no flush toilet, no telephone, and no water heater. Heat was provided in most rooms by *hori-gotatsu* (a charcoal brazier under a table), portable kerosene stoves, and charcoal-filled warmers to take to bed. I wasn't permitted a kerosene stove, and I froze. Contact with home was by single-sheet blue aerogram letters, so it would take two weeks to get a reply to a query. I was truly alone in a foreign country with no Skype, Zoom, email, or any of the current ways to maintain contact with family and friends and a psychological tether to the United States. I was immersed in Japanese life but almost clueless as to how to behave and, at first, with little ability to speak Japanese. But I fell in love with the country, and, at the end of my year's stay, I wept as my plane took off from Haneda Airport.

Very little was available in English on Japan in the early 1960s. The Reischauers, particularly Haru, were very helpful and encouraging, but, when I look back at how little I knew about Japan, I still grimace at all the mistakes I made during my first year there. The only book in English that touched on Japanese society was Ruth Benedict's *The Chrysanthemum and the Sword*.[2] The teaching of the Japanese language was in the early stages of development, and my instructor at ICU couldn't explain grammar. A couple of us used to guess at it and then try to explain it to the other students while the young instructor stood by. When I entered Yale after a year in Japan, I was put into a more advanced class than my knowledge warranted because of a scheduling conflict, and, as a result, I have never properly studied or grasped Japanese grammar.

I was the only student in the Japanese MA program at Yale in 1962 who had been to Japan. There was such a small body of academic work in English on Japan that we could be expected to read almost all of it. I found Yale to be a much friendlier place than Harvard and particularly enjoyed my classes with John (Jack) W. Hall and Hugh T. Patrick. I received an MA in Japanese Studies in 1964, but I still had not settled on a career; my immediate goal was to go back to Japan. I managed to get myself hired part-time at the Nosei Chosa Iinkai, a research organization connected to the Ministry of Agriculture and Forestry, and, thanks to Professor Roy Andrew Miller at Yale, to study at the same time at the Inter-University Center for Japanese Language Studies. This combination worked because I was one of only two students at the Center who were so "advanced" that there were no classes suited for us. How amazed I am today at the level of students at the Center compared to back in the mid-1960s!

After my year at the Inter-University Center, I spent a second year working at the Nosei Chosa Iinkai. I found life in Japan very congenial. Keeping house was very different from in the United States—very basic, with no central heat, no refrigerator at first, public baths for bathing, and shopping in tiny shops—and I found it fun. Japan suited me socially as well because women, even married women, socialized with other women and not as couples. I felt like a misfit in the United States with all my friends paired off and many with babies, but when I began to read *Time* as if I were reading about a foreign country, I decided it was time to return home. With Professor Hall's encouragement, I entered the PhD program in History at Yale. It's hard to believe today, but he convinced me by saying that I would certainly be offered an academic position when I had completed the degree. There were also generous fellowships, such as the National Defense Foreign Language (NDFL) Fellowships and Social Science Research Council (SSRC) Fellowships, so I completed my degrees without going into debt.

As an MA student, I had written a long paper on population in the Tokugawa period, and, after I was fortuitously introduced to Professor Akira Hayami, who was doing seminal work in historical demography at Keio University, I decided to write my dissertation on Tokugawa village population using documents in Okayama, where Hall had connections. I wanted to study ordinary people, not politics, government, or leaders, but my choice of research was unusual, not only for the study of Japan but also for historians in the 1960s. Professor Hall was horrified when he read my research proposal for an SSRC grant, but I reassured him that it was not the prospectus I intended to submit to Yale's History Department.

I soon discovered how tedious population research could be. I hired a Japanese student to transfer to my forms the information in the *shumon-aratame-cho* (population registers) for the village of Fujito in Okayama Prefecture, and then I had to transfer all the information, minus names, to forms that could be used for the punch cards that would generate data for a computer analysis. And much of the analysis I had to do by hand. I ended up doing most of the work in the United States, as by then I had met Kozo Yamamura and married him.

And that's another part of the history of Japanese Studies in the United States. In the 1960s there were so few scholars interested in the Japanese economy that Henry Rosovsky (Harvard) and Hugh Patrick (Yale) decided in 1966 to bring them together at what they named the Japan Economic Seminar. It would meet monthly during the academic year, rotating among Harvard, Yale, and Columbia, which were all within easy driving distance from one another. I learned that one of Hugh's students was attending, and I had the temerity to ask if I could, too. He very kindly told me I could, and it changed my life. I showed up at the Harvard meeting in September 1967 as one of two women in a group of perhaps a dozen men—American scholars and visitors from Japan. It was at this Japan Economic

Seminar that I met Kozo, whom I married in June 1969. He always said he had no choice because of the paucity of women at these meetings.

Marrying Kozo rather narrowed my job opportunities. Although he was only five years older than me, Kozo had been quickly promoted during the 1960s and was already a professor at Boston College. There were no positions open for me in the Boston area. The grapevine must have been working well because we were offered jobs at the University of Washington (UW), Kozo as a professor and me as a research associate (because I had yet to complete my dissertation). We went as visitors to the Far Eastern and Russian Institute, which was rapidly developing its Asian Studies programs. I was to become the fourth Japanese historian at UW, although one became Provost and so was not active in the field. The History Department was alarmed by what I was told they called "Yellow Peril," and I was never welcome in that department during my three decades at UW, except for teaching classes with a History designation. Nor did the senior professors consider historical demography and the study of material culture suitable subjects for historians.

During our year as visitors in Seattle, we received offers out of the blue to spend a year doing research at the Population Institute at the East-West Center in Honolulu. We were delighted and accepted immediately. It was here that we accomplished most of the research for the book we wrote together, *Economic and Demographic Change in Preindustrial Japan, 1600-1868*.[3] Kozo convinced me that a combination of his research on the Japanese economy and mine on population would result in a stronger book than either of us writing separately. He proved to be right, but it could have been a bad mistake on my part, as I had to convince my tenure committee that I had written half of the book, and which half was mine.

Living up in the rainy hills of Honolulu—where we were subject to cockroaches, rats in the washing machine, and a wild pig in the garden, and where we had an office in a World War II-era, jerry-built building without AC—didn't suit us. Likewise, the East-West Center was dependent on grants for survival, so it was an easy decision to return to the University of Washington, Kozo as a tenured professor and me as a "visiting assistant professor." There was no such thing as a "spousal hire" in the 1970s, but I realized that was what I was. After a few years, the administration said I could no longer be a visitor, and I was hired as an assistant professor. I have never had a job interview, and I knew that I had been hired because the university wanted Kozo, so I did my best to earn my keep. I taught the courses no one else wanted to teach, but I liked teaching the large survey course in Japanese history and the various required seminars for graduating seniors and incoming MA students in Japanese Studies.

From 1970 until 2003, with the exception of my year in Honolulu (1971-1972), I had an office on the fourth floor of Thomson Hall, but, during those same

Figure 9.1: Susan Hanley's passport photograph, 1987. Photograph courtesy of the author.

decades, I had a position first at the Institute, then in the School of International Studies, and finally in the Jackson School of International Studies. I was always in the same university department; only the name changed. I felt very much at home during the period when the focus was on area studies but much less so when the shift was made toward politics and policy.

During our first year in Seattle, the university received the news that it had been granted one of the million-dollar grants the Japanese government gave to ten American universities.[4] What a windfall! The Japan faculty had to decide how to use it. At the end of the academic year in 1971, Kozo and I spent a week house- and puppy-sitting for Doug North, who later received the 1993 Nobel Prize in Economics. We decided to host a dinner party for our Japan colleagues at his house overlooking Puget Sound, and it was here that *The Journal of Japanese Studies* was conceived.

The various editorial positions were parceled out among the UW faculty, and, because I wasn't a regular faculty member and was the most junior, I was made the managing editor, a half-time position. Because I was the only one paid to do any work, I ended up designing the *Journal*, handling all the correspondence, overseeing the printing (hot type in the 1970s), copyediting, and proofreading. It was enormous fun to be at the birth of what turned out to be a major publication in the field, and to deal with the Japan specialists who wrote and reviewed for the publication.

Figure 9.2: Susan Hanley with her husband, Kozo Yamamura, in Bellevue, Washington, 2016. Photograph taken by Jay Rubin and courtesy of the author.

I edited thirty volumes of the *Journal*, which comes to sixty issues. From managing editor, I became editor, and then, as we had increasing submissions in the humanities, I asked for a coeditor. John Treat coedited with me until I retired and remained on the board after that, providing stability in the transition. I loved the work, but it was never-ending, even when I was on vacation and away from Seattle. My only regret is that, when I was a full-time professor, editing the *Journal* slowed down my research time, and I never did finish projects I had planned.

Kozo and I were hired not long after a nepotism rule preventing spouses from serving together on the faculty had been terminated. There were pluses and minuses to working in the same program three doors down the hall from my husband. Together, we covered the required courses for the BA and MA degrees in Japanese Studies, and so we were under subtle pressure not to take a long sabbatical away from the university. When we did spend time in Tübingen in 1984, it was after we had completed teaching our full quota of courses in Seattle. Three years later, we spent several months in Duisburg, also in Germany, and I went on two-month research trips to Japan as well. What made up for the lack of sabbaticals away from Seattle was the funding available for yearly trips—and sometimes more than one—to Japan.

Nevertheless, I managed to publish articles and to coedit, with Arthur P. Wolf, *Family and Population in East Asian History*.[5] My favorite research project was *Everyday Things in Premodern Japan: The Hidden Legacy of Material Culture*.[6] A shorter version was published in Japanese.[7] Both versions won prizes: the Joseph Roggendorf Prize from Sophia University for the Japanese version, and the John W. Hall Prize for the one in English. I enjoyed working on this book so much that I was actually sad when I sent the final draft to the press.

When my husband turned sixty-eight, he decided he wanted to slow down. When he retired, so did I, and we left Seattle in 2003 to satisfy our wanderlust. We spent several months in Montpellier in the south of France. I was a Canterbury Teaching Fellow in Christchurch, New Zealand (thankfully before the earthquakes), and I held a research position at the Institute for Research in Humanities at Kyoto University. Eventually, we settled down to rotating residence in Honolulu in the winter and the village of Grindelwald, Switzerland, in summer. They were twelve time zones apart, and the cheapest way to travel was on a round-the-world fare. I am still amazed that I have flown round the world more than a dozen times. After Kozo's death in 2017, I moved back to Seattle, and the COVID-19 pandemic ended my peripatetic lifestyle.

In retirement, Kozo started writing thrillers in the hopes of getting economic messages to a wider readership beyond just other economists. I joined him in the writing of three thrillers published under the pen name Michael S. Koyama. We also published Kozo's life story as fiction, *The Boy Who Defied His Karma*, under the same pen name.[8] His autobiography had to be fictionalized because Kozo had served in military intelligence in the US Army, but he said the book was 90 percent true, just with changes in names and locations. I initially thought fiction would be easier than academic writing because there are no footnotes, but it turned out to be like trying to remember the lies you've told.

How would I assess my career in the early years of Japanese Studies in the postwar era? I feel I was extremely fortunate to be a part of this. It was very exciting to be involved in the growth of the field when Japan was considered so important that money for study, research, and conferences was plentiful. We worked on important issues never tackled before, and I was involved in every aspect of the field, both because of my editing work and because I taught a survey course in Japanese history for three decades.

It was not so much fun being a woman in academia during those years. The departments I was involved in were dominated by senior white men. There were only two women in the History Department when I arrived. The chair made it very clear when I was taken to be introduced to him that I was not welcome in the department, although I was expected to teach history courses. For some years, I saw no female faces at the faculty meetings in my own department. The faculty were men, and the administrative staff were women. The female staff didn't consider me one of them and made it clear they didn't want to socialize with me. Nor did the men. My colleagues would gather to go to the faculty club for lunch, but never did they knock on my door, which was ajar, to ask me to join them. I would wait a few minutes and then pluck up the courage to go to the faculty table. Because I worked, I didn't fit in and didn't have time to meet the women in my neighborhood, so, for the first dozen years I lived in Seattle, I had no friends here.

Then, in the 1980s, something changed. More women were hired, and both teaching staff and administrative staff no longer had an invisible line dividing them. The younger men had working wives, and, with these colleagues, I no longer felt I was merely tolerated. But senior men were in control, and, although I received regular merit increases, these were so low that I eventually needed to be given two affirmative action raises. However, I never applied for these, and it was male colleagues who requested them for me.

I felt discriminated against as a woman from my high school years through my academic career, but, oddly enough, my husband, who was both Asian and an immigrant, claimed he never felt the kind of discrimination I faced. However, from my college years on, it was men who encouraged me to pursue an academic career, and I had a husband who fully supported me. I had no female mentors in my career. I will be ever grateful to my aunt, who not only paid for half of my first year in Japan but also, as the first woman officer of the Harvard College Library, showed me what a woman can accomplish.

I must also pay tribute to my mother, Frances Hanley, for her quiet support of my career choices. Her family forced her to become a teacher rather than a nurse. When I was about thirteen, she sat me down and told me that I was to follow any future I wanted, and I was certainly not to feel that I had to give up a career to live with her. My father had died when I was not yet five, and my mother had a hard time supporting my brother and me, but never did it occur to any of us that I wouldn't go to college. I know she was very nervous about my going off to Japan at age twenty-two, but she never said anything. What she said to me as a young teen freed me of familial obligations, but it was also scary in that I knew from an early age my future was up to me. I have learned that I was very lucky not to have been constrained as some of my friends were.

When I look at women in academia now, the situation seems reversed from when I entered the field. There are lots of women; the UW History Department and the Jackson School are full of them, and both departments currently have female chairs. Women are no longer alone in a sea of men, many of whom thought women still belonged in the kitchen or at least in subservient roles. But the money and the positions have dried up, which makes a career studying Japan a lot harder than it used to be. And so much research has been done on Japan that studies have become ever narrower, which I saw in my last years as an editor. I was so lucky to be in Japan in the pre-1964 Tokyo Olympics years when so much of prewar life was still there to be experienced. I'm very glad I was in at the beginning of serious Japanese Studies and wouldn't trade places with anyone. My accidental career as a "pioneer" was indeed serendipitous.

Notes

[1] "Rice Paddies" was the student nickname for Social Science 111. See chapter 1.

[2] Ruth Benedict, *The Chrysanthemum and the Sword* (London: Secker and Warburg, 1947).

[3] Susan B. Hanley and Kozo Yamamura, *Economic and Demographic Change in Preindustrial Japan, 1600–1868* (Princeton: Princeton University Press, 1977).

[4] "Japan Names 10 U.S. Colleges to Share Equally in $10-Million," *New York Times*, August 8, 1973, 14.

[5] Susan B. Hanley and Arthur P. Wolf, eds., *Family and Population in East Asian History* (Stanford: Stanford University Press, 1985).

[6] Susan B. Hanley, *Everyday Things in Premodern Japan: The Hidden Legacy of Material Culture* (Berkeley: University of California Press, 1997).

[7] Susan B. Hanley, *Edo jidai no isan* (The legacy of the Tokugawa Period) (Tokyo: Chūō Kōronsha, 1990).

[8] Michael S. Koyama, *The Boy Who Defied His Karma* (Honolulu: Mutual Publishing, 2011).

10

"Another Girl Studying Japanese!"

Susan Matisoff

I recognized a particular corner, turned left, and arrived, a quarter century later, at the door of my 1959 homestay, filled with memories of that time and place where I had been another girl just beginning to study Japanese.

SUSAN MATISOFF is a professor emerita at the University of California, Berkeley. She joined the Berkeley faculty in 1999 after teaching for nearly three decades at Stanford University, where she also holds emerita status. She is the author of *The Legend of Semimaru, Blind Musician of Japan* (Columbia University Press, 1978). Her articles and book chapters include "*Kintōsho*, Zeami's Song of Exile" (*Monumenta Nipponica*, 1977); "Images of Exile and Pilgrimage, Zeami's *Kintōsho*" (*Monumenta Nipponica*, 1979); "Lord Tamekane's Notes on Poetry: *Tamekanekyō Wakashō*" (coauthored with Robert N. Huey, *Monumenta Nipponica*, 1985); "Reflections of Terute: Searching for a Hidden Shaman-Entertainer" (*Women and Performance: A Journal of Feminist Theory*, 2002); "Barred from Paradise? Mount Kōya and the Karukaya Legend" (in *Engendering Faith: Women and Buddhism in Premodern Japan*, edited by Barbara Ruch, 2002); "The Log Cabin Emperor: Marginality and the Legend of Oguri Hangan" (*Cahiers d'Extrême-Asie*, 2002-2003); and "*Oguri*: An Early Edo Tale of Suffering, Resurrection, Revenge and Deification" (*Monumenta Nipponica*, 2011).

Two years of high school German proved to be the unlikely first step in a chain of connections leading me to Japanese Studies. Established in 1932 and still in operation today, the Experiment in International Living (hereafter, "the Experiment") is a cultural exchange program for young people that has undergone some changes over the years. In its current form, it "offers high school summer abroad programs on five continents that empower young people to step off the beaten path, experience the world as a classroom, immerse themselves fully in another culture, and build the knowledge and skills needed to confront critical global issues."[1] But back in the 1950s, its scope was much narrower, sending American youth (including high school and young college students) only to a number of countries in Europe. Through this program, I spent the summer of 1957 living in the household of a doctor in Höxter-am-Weser, Germany.

Two years later, when the Experiment was starting to expand beyond Europe, my parents were willing and able to support me for another such summer, and I was eager to see a different part of the world. The Experiment had obvious trepidation about sending young Americans to what was seen as a challenging country. The group I joined was selected for the second year of the Experiment's existence in Japan, and our orientation materials were enthusiastic but full of caveats. "All of your simplest assumptions will fail to serve you in Japan." "Let it be your major premise that you cannot make judgments about any aspect of Japanese life in Western terms and do anything but confuse yourself." "The facial characteristics and the skin color of the Japanese may give you a strong reaction of foreignness and difference." (The obvious assumption here was that all the US participants would be white.) "Their language is far too difficult to be learned in a short time. Your objective, as far as language learning goes, will be to pronounce like an educated person the Japanese names and expressions of courtesy that you will use." "You will have so much to learn that spending a lot of time on the intricacies of the language will be a waste of time."

In any event, full of enthusiasm from my German experience, I met up in Seattle with my cohort of ten young Americans—most, like me, were just through their freshman year of college. After a prop plane flight with a fuel stop in Anchorage, we arrived at Haneda Airport and were immediately bussed to an old *ryokan* in Hakone, where we enjoyed a few days of orientation and minimal language instruction. It was here that I learned I had been singled out for a special "experiment." The expectation had been that each of the ten of us would live with a family in the city of Nagano. In each household, there would be a high school or college student with some knowledge of English. But there was a problem. Nine such families had volunteered to host, but in the tenth household, the oldest child was a girl of twelve. No English speaker. And here the German connection came in. The father in the family was a medical doctor familiar with German textbooks, as they were generally used for prewar medical training in Japan. He spoke some German. So did I! Moreover, I was a chemistry major with an interest in medicine. Obviously, they had their match. So I found myself again in the household of a doctor with a small attached private hospital, a pattern already familiar to me. This time, though, my host family's home was close to the vast Zenkōji complex, which I could then only assume was a typical Buddhist temple.

We sputtered along as best we could with German, sign language, a few words of English, and a lot of goodwill. I was challenged for sure, and, because the German-speaking father was in his office practice most of the day, I felt I must start learning Japanese as quickly as possible, even though "spending a lot of time on the intricacies of the language" had been deemed to be "a waste of time."

Fortunately, the Experiment was a program intended for serious-minded students, and we had been encouraged to read as much as possible before the trip. The reading list I still retain is a reminder of how little had been published concerning Japanese culture by 1959. As preparation, I had read Ruth Benedict's *The Chrysanthemum and the Sword* (1946), D. T. Suzuki's *Zen Buddhism* (1956), Edwin O. Reischauer's *The United States and Japan* (1950), and a few more.[2] Although there were no language-teaching materials on our list, I knew I enjoyed learning new languages, and I had brought with me a small dictionary and a copy of Samuel Martin's *Essential Japanese: An Introduction to the Standard Colloquial Language* (1954).[3] Whenever I had free time, if not off on the nearly daily local excursions arranged for our group of ten, I immersed myself in Martin's text. I learned as much as I could, both language and culture, and was quite happily fascinated by what I observed and experienced that summer.

Our program included a week in Tokyo. Much of my memory is blurred after all these years, but I do recall that I had an English-language map that showed Occupation-era alphabetical street names. Harumi-dori, for example, was then Avenue Z. While in Tokyo, we students had a meeting that would be unimaginable today. We were invited to the US Embassy to meet the ambassador. The gentleman in question was Douglas MacArthur II, the general's nephew. He explained to us that the reason for his invitation was that we, young as we were, had unusual knowledge. He told us that not one member of the embassy staff had ever been invited to a Japanese home, and then he spent quite a bit of time asking us about what life in a Japanese household was like! The very concept of a "homestay" was unprecedented. I came away a bit startled, realizing that my scant knowledge *was* unusual and that there were real limits on Americans' awareness of Japan. I knew I had only scratched the surface, but that scratch had awakened an itch to learn more.

I returned to the United States in late August, this time via a stop in Hawai'i, only days after it was granted statehood. I went back to begin my sophomore year as a chemistry major at Radcliffe College, then the women's partner college to Harvard, with shared classes. Organic chemistry in a class of about two hundred men and a handful of women students was an enormous challenge. I survived it, but I was rapidly losing confidence in my abilities as a budding scientist, and my memories from Japan kept pulling at me. I had an opportunity available only at the few US colleges where the study of Japanese was possible at that time, and, by the end of fall semester, I declared a change of major. Henceforth, it was to be Far Eastern Languages.

I began taking the courses relating to Japan that were open to undergraduate students. The first of these was the yearlong survey course on East Asian history (or perhaps it was called "Far Eastern history"), colloquially known to all as "Rice Paddies," taught by Edwin Reischauer and John Fairbank.[4] Because it was now into the second semester, the course began in the Tokugawa period. I don't remember how far along in Chinese history we were. I would be able to circle back to the beginning in the following fall semester. At that point, too, I would finally begin formal instruction in Japanese.

At that time, my older brother happened to be living in Ann Arbor. He told me he had noticed that the University of Michigan was offering a summer introductory course in Japanese. Deciding that such a class might give me a real head start, I enrolled in what proved to be a pleasant, slow-paced course in conversational Japanese. I'm sorry that I don't remember the name of the instructor, a visitor from the University of Arizona, I think, who had recently served in the Occupation. But I certainly remember the name of the teaching assistant: Kimie Tōjō, the youngest daughter of General Hideki Tōjō. I imagine that there were then very few native speakers of Japanese at the university. Ms. Tōjō had been quietly studying at the University of Michigan for the past year, supported by an anonymously funded scholarship.[5] I don't recall how we class members knew of her parentage. It wasn't an issue in class, and she was a cheerful model as a native speaker. While I was in Ann Arbor, at a party given by a mutual friend, I met someone whose immediate response to me was, "Another girl studying Japanese!" I didn't run across her again until seven years later, but her influence on me, eventually, was significant.

Back at Harvard, I enrolled in the oddly numbered course "Japanese Aab." This year-long intensive course was intended to provide two years of instruction, forming half of a normal load of four courses per semester. There were daunting aspects to this new path. Graduate students could enter the field at that time without significant previous language training. I recall a class of twenty or so students. Four of us were undergraduates: Bill Sibley (who became a professor at the University of Chicago), Peter Grilli (who later became the President of Japan Society of Boston), another Radcliffe student whose name I don't remember, and myself. Most were graduate students in Chinese or Japanese. And at the opposite extreme, one was a postgraduate. John Rosenfield was just beginning Japanese and would go on to his distinguished career teaching Japanese art history on the Harvard faculty.

In the first semester, our class was taught by Howard Hibbett and Itasaka Gen. The textbook, published in 1942, was authored by Reischauer and Serge Elisséeff: *Elementary Japanese for University Students*.[6] The need for something newer, with less emphasis on military Japanese, was evident. Hibbett and Itasaka were at work creating a replacement, using some of these materials for our instruction as well. In the second semester (Japanese Bab), Reischauer replaced Hibbett as the primary instructor. Sometime in mid-semester, there was an unusual interruption of the class. A department secretary came into the room, and I could hear her quietly tell him, "Mr. Reischauer, Washington is on the phone." After ten minutes or so, he returned to the classroom, apologized for the delay, said nothing else, and resumed the class. The next day, his appointment as ambassador to Japan was announced. Recalling my meeting with his immediate predecessor, I knew this was going to bring an enormous change in the level of ambassadorial knowledge of Japan, although I was sad to lose him as a teacher. I cannot imagine that anyone else ever went directly from teaching a second-year language class to holding an ambassadorship!

As the year was ending, assured that I had two years' worth of Japanese under my belt, I decided I ought to be able to read a Japanese novel and would spend the summer doing so. I do not think I ran this plan past Professor Hibbett, although it surely would have been wise to ask his advice. In any event, back in Ann Arbor for another summer, I spent many hours nearly every day in the library with the text of Natsume Sōseki's novel *Kusamakura*. I'm sure I picked it because it was relatively short and because I had already read *Kokoro* in translation. Painstakingly, I worked my way through, paragraph by paragraph. After figuring out as much as I could, I would check a page or so at a time against a translation I had found, by Takahashi Kazutomo, published in 1927.[7]

All of this led to Professor Hibbett's decision that I should "skip" third-year Japanese. That decision proved to have an enormous effect on my future. In the small fourth-year class, I met Jim Matisoff, newly returned from Japan where he had studied in the highly intensive Japanese class for foreigners at International Christian University. Three months after meeting, we returned to the next semester's class wearing our matching wedding rings.

Before our lives and plans began to merge, I had decided that I wanted to go on to graduate school and thought it would be wise for me to go elsewhere because I'd already taken so many of the classes available at Harvard. I applied to Columbia and Berkeley, and, not long after our marriage, I learned I'd been accepted at both schools. Jim was in linguistics, not entirely happy with Harvard's department, and ready for a change himself. Berkeley had a strong linguistics department and offered him admission as well. In June 1962, after my graduation, we headed west. But I was soon unhappy. I had expected to be studying with Donald Shively, but he had left Berkeley for Stanford, on what may have been rather short notice. I arrived to find that the graduate classes in Japanese literature that year were being taught by an advanced grad student or by a visiting lecturer, a Japanese national whose training was in English literature. This was a thudding comedown after my undergraduate years. Jim thrived in the linguistics department, and I profited from excellent classes in classical Chinese, Chinese history, and Korean language. But after three semesters, although in good standing in the department, I dropped out.

A few months later, our first daughter was born, and, in January 1965, we headed off to Northern Thailand, where Jim would do his dissertation research. At that point, I was a happy full-time mother, and living in Chiang Mai then was a bit like being in paradise. I'm sure, if anyone thought about it, I just looked like another woman student who had "wasted" her education. These were still the days of academic employment through the "old boy's network." Before the end of our eighteen-month stay, without any interviews or other in-person vetting, Jim received a job offer from Columbia. We moved from "paradise" to gritty New York City, and, soon after our arrival, our second daughter was born. I spent one semester cooped up in a small Columbia faculty apartment with a toddler and an infant. Our apartment was a block from the campus and thus close to Kent Hall, where Donald Keene was teaching. The opportunity to study with him and other luminaries was irresistible. I applied again for admission and was again accepted, to begin the following fall.

In the process of applying, I stopped by the department to ask whether there was someone I should talk with. I was directed to the office of Marleigh Grayer Ryan, an assistant professor who was serving as the graduate advisor in Japanese. The meeting was memorable because she assured me that I would be admitted and laughingly said that they needn't worry that I'd get pregnant and drop out since I'd already done that. She herself was visibly pregnant. Eventually, she shifted the conversation to ask me for advice about nursing! As I was walking the short block back home, it occurred to me that she was the first woman professor I had ever met. There were precisely two women with professorial appointments at Harvard in my undergrad years, Cora Du Bois in anthropology and Cecilia Payne-Gaposchkin in astronomy, but I had never laid eyes on either of them. I think that Miyeko Murase was already on the Columbia art history faculty at the time, but I did not meet her until many years later.

Three years had gone by since I had left Berkeley, and I hadn't been reading or speaking Japanese. To prepare for my return, I spent two hours every weeknight, after the babies were asleep, relearning kanji and vocabulary. Somehow the grammar had stuck with me. Then we spent another summer in Ann Arbor as Jim attended a Summer Linguistics Institute run by the Linguistics Society of America. The University of Michigan summer school classes provided just the rehabilitation I needed. Back in New York, I took out a loan that allowed me to hire a housekeeper-nanny, and, in fall 1967, I entered the Columbia department as a full-time student.

At Columbia, I found a wonderful group of peers. My first class with Donald Keene was a seminar on Noh. I was one of five students. Since four of us were women, I had no reason to think that I was in a place unwelcoming to us. But one day, as I was waiting for the English department class before our seminar to end, a woman burst out the door. "Try getting an academic job as a woman!" she said in a loud, sarcastic voice. "Not a problem in my field," I thought.

I was in residence at Columbia for five semesters. It was a joy to encounter so many rich classes, particularly the four seminars offered by Donald Keene. My timing was fortunate because, in the following year, he began a permanent arrangement with Columbia that had him teaching just one semester each year so he could otherwise be in Japan. Other than the students in my own cohort, including Janine Beichman (chapter 19), I got to know well some of the more advanced graduate students. One was Karen Brazell, the other "girl" who had exclaimed over our common interest in Japanese when we first met at a mutual friend's party in Ann Arbor. We became close lifelong friends.

As the years passed, Karen's many accomplishments marked her as one of the most important women in our field. If she were still with us, her own memoir would surely belong in this volume. Lacking that, I wish to pay tribute to her memory by pointing out how some of her experiences were benchmarks in the developing field of Japanese humanities. I remember Karen as being a visionary leader in the field whose many academic contributions deserve acknowledgment, in addition to being an extremely giving friend and colleague.

When we re-met, Karen was writing her dissertation, a study and partial translation of the then recently discovered medieval diary, *Towazugatari*. It would lead to her first book, *The Confessions of Lady Nijō* (1973).[8] The book made a real splash by winning that year's National Book Award for Translated Literature. Karen completed her PhD in 1969 with Donald Keene as her advisor. I recall hearing about how she was hired for her first teaching position, although I am not sure whether it was she or Keene who later told me the story. What I learned was that Princeton was looking to appoint an assistant professor in Japanese just around the time that Karen was finishing up. With the "old boy" network still in full swing, the search committee chair at Princeton contacted Keene to ask for a recommendation. He recommended Karen, but Princeton was taken aback. I don't recall who it would have been on the phone from Princeton, but Keene told them that Karen was his best student at the time, that they should interview her, and that he wouldn't give them any other name unless they did that first.

Princeton did interview and hire Karen, but, when tenure time came, she was turned down. As a woman academic fifty-plus years ago, Karen was perhaps a bit too unfamiliar a species for Princeton to appreciate. Cornell set things right. At the time of her hiring, Cornell's program in Japanese was in its infancy compared to its strength in other areas of East Asian and Southeast Asian Studies. Karen became the chair of the Department of Asian Studies (1977–1982). She founded the Japanese Studies doctoral program, served as director of the East Asia Program (1987–1991), and established the Cornell East Asia Series of scholarly books. A vivid presence on campus, she helped to raise the profile of the humanities at the university, including serving a term on the Cornell Board of Trustees (1979–1983).

In the mid-1970s, the Social Science Research Council (SSRC) teamed up with the American Council of Learned Societies to encourage the formation of a small group conference in the Japanese humanities along the lines of previous conferences in the social sciences. They turned to Karen to execute the plan. Eschewing typical formats, Karen organized a series of three meetings at six-month intervals on the intentionally broad topic "Time and Space in Japanese Studies." There were roughly fifteen participants at the first meeting in January 1976, with just a couple of changes of personnel at later sessions. When Ron Aqua, the SSRC liaison for the third conference, mentioned how surprising it was to have a conference where roughly half the participants were women, Karen's response was, "They're there when you know to look for them!"

Karen thought creatively about the conference sessions. The first two were held in relatively spartan accommodations at Yale and Cornell, respectively. The third met at the Sheraton Maui, where we assembled punctually at 7:00 a.m., got started while eating breakfast, worked intensely until 1:00 or 2:00 p.m., and then broke for beach time. Quite intentionally, Karen did not try to mold the outcome of these meetings into a unified "conference volume." Rather, she encouraged the various participants to pursue the individual threads of research we had been developing and refining in our conference presentations. For me, the result was a translation and analysis of the temporal and spatial imagery in *Kintōsho*, Zeami's poem-diary of his exile to the island of Sado late in life.[9]

In 1998 Karen founded and became the first director of Global Performing Arts Consortium, a multilingual digital archive for global performance traditions. She was a true early innovator in digital humanities. This ongoing project first arose from her long-standing interest in performance studies. Her second book (with Monica Bethe), *Nō as Performance* (1978), a seemingly modest Cornell East Asia Series monograph, marks a true turning point in the study of Noh theater.[10]

Several other books and many articles, plus a group of fine scholars who were her doctoral advisees, are left as part of her legacy.

Japanese Studies was in a period of rapid growth and expansion when Cornell hired Karen. There was as yet no organized "job market" with orderly postings of open positions. My own hiring experience was decidedly different from hers. In 1972, I was living in Berkeley, just finishing my dissertation, and realizing that there appeared to be zero academic positions available anywhere nearby. I was not prepared to look for a teaching post that would require long-distance commuting or keep me from being home in time for dinner with my family. Trying any approach I could think of to find a job, I drove down to Stanford and met with Albert Dien, a historian of China whom I had gotten to know when he was a visiting professor at Columbia. I told him, "I'm almost done with my dissertation. I know there are no jobs at Stanford, but if you hear of anything in the Bay Area, administrative or whatever, you know, think of me." I gave him my CV. Two months later, he called me, mentioning that he was then the acting chair of the Asian Languages Department. The call was very sudden and rushed. The gist was to ask, "Could you come down here? I'm sorry this is such a rush. The Chinese ping-pong team is coming." (This was the very first break in US-China relations.) And he said, "I've only got a minute, but can you be down here next week to give a talk? We have a new position open in the department." When I told him that I had never given a talk and could only speak about my dissertation, he assured me that was fine. I prepared my first-ever presentation on a week's notice. And, to my shock, I was soon offered an assistant professor appointment. Sometime later, I learned about the scheme that had brought this about. Stanford had decided that they should take steps to add more women to the faculty. The provost at the time established a pool of money and told departments that they could get an incremental position in their department if they could show that they had a fully qualified woman candidate. So that's how I began my career at Stanford. It was essentially a pure affirmative action hire. I was a "twofer": a woman in a field that had growing significance at a time when women were becoming more welcome in academia.

In my earliest years of teaching, all my classes, like those of my departmental colleagues, had small enrollments. Because I had absolutely no teaching experience, the first years were challenging until I gradually found my feet in front of the classroom. Students who chose to take my lecture classes came with genuine interest. There were then no "breadth" requirements bringing in undergraduates merely intent on clicking off the "other cultures" box on the list of required course types. I discovered that I particularly enjoyed enabling students to read texts in the classical language. In classes with readings in modern Japanese, I focused on fine-grained issues of translation. Most students had completed three years of modern

Japanese instruction taught entirely by native speakers, and many commented to me that this inverted focus made them realize what was truly involved if, for instance, they needed to translate passages of academic Japanese to cite in a paper or article. I was at first intimidated by the idea of teaching graduate students, but, before long, these became my favorite teaching experiences. Working one-on-one with those who were writing their dissertations was the highest joy.

After twenty-seven years at Stanford, I moved, academically speaking, to Berkeley. The East Asian Languages and Cultures Department had advertised to hire a new department chair from outside. For me, the move meant the end to what had been a brutal, nearly one-hundred-mile round-trip commute between home and campus. Becoming chair of the very department I had dropped out of many years before was certainly an unexpected twist, and it did strongly suggest that I had not put my early education to waste.

The path of my research had its beginnings in the first class I took from Donald Keene, the abovementioned 1967 Noh seminar. In the initial class meeting, he announced that we would each have to translate a Noh play as our semester project. Since none of us had read even a single Noh in Japanese, he had come prepared with a list of titles of untranslated plays. As it happened, he assigned me *Semimaru*. I found the poetic language a huge linguistic challenge and an equally great pleasure; and the plot was certainly intriguing since it involved two imperial children, the offspring of Emperor Daigo, and, unlike other Noh, had two central characters, not just one dominant role.

In the following semester, Keene's seminar topic was *jōruri* (Edo-period puppet theater texts). This time, the assignment was to translate one act of what are typically five-act dramas. Again, the assignments were largely arbitrary, but mine was not, and I was very lucky. Keene told me he had noticed that there was an early play by Chikamatsu Monzaemon (1653–1725) also called *Semimaru*. It was little mentioned in Japanese scholarship, and my task would be to translate the third act, an act drawn closely from the Noh. Before long, the spring 1968 student "uprising" at Columbia erupted.[11] Classroom buildings and libraries were closed. The seminar continued to meet, now in Professor Keene's living room. Because I lived near campus, the medieval history course I was taking at the time met in *our* living room.

These were strange times, and all five of us in the seminar were told to take "incomplete" grades and finish our work during the summer. Again, I was fortunate. With regular tutorials from Takagi Kiyoko (scholar of Japanese history and religion, associate director of the Inter-University Center for Japanese Language Studies, and poet) who was then visiting as a lecturer, I worked on my translation. Takagi-sensei, who was respected and beloved by generations of students at the Inter-University Center for Japanese Language Studies, seemed to enjoy the challenges of deciphering Chikamatsu's play. Thanks to her, by the time the summer was over, I had a finished draft of the whole text, not just the third act. As I remember our conversation, Keene later encouraged me to use these two seminar projects as the beginnings of a dissertation. As he recalled matters, he had doubted that a dissertation should try to cover more than one period or genre and had tried to dissuade me. One of us remembered that wrong, but, in any case, the history of the legend of Semimaru became the subject of my dissertation and, with extensive revision and reorganization, my book.[12]

As part of the research for the book, I became interested in the texts of a type of performance known as *sekkyō-bushi*, or "sermon ballads." *Sekkyō-bushi* had a relatively brief heyday as popular entertainment in seventeenth-century urban centers, but it was soon outstripped in popularity by *jōruri*. The most popular of these "ballads" are in the form of a life story of extreme suffering leading to the sufferer's reincarnation, or reidentification, as a deity. This relatively obscure genre fascinated me in part because the texts retain a strong oral flavor. Exploring the circumstances of their creation, I encountered evidence of the significant role of women narrators whose importance in the history of *sekkyō-bushi* had essentially been forgotten. My research on the *sekkyō-bushi* texts generally focuses both on textual issues and on the hints these narratives offer concerning the lives of the socially marginalized medieval itinerant preacher-entertainers whose voices carried the earliest performances. One of these narratives, *Karukaya*, concerns the misery of a father and son after the father, Karukaya, abandoned his family for a life devoted to Buddhist study. Most versions of the narrative relate how the two were unknowingly reunited, with the son never recognizing the father's identity.

Karukayasan Saikōji is a sub-temple of Zenkōji, the huge temple complex in Nagano that was my first introduction to Buddhist architecture and iconography. This little temple is housed in a compound tucked behind storefronts along the historical pilgrimage route, now the main shopping street, approaching the main gate of Zenkōji. I did not notice the place in 1959, but, in 1985, my Karukaya research brought me there. In the compound stand two *jizō* statues identified as representing Karukaya and his son, Ishidōmaru. After enjoying hearing the wife of the priest of this temple tell me the local version of the Karukaya narrative, I walked a few blocks along the shopping street toward Zenkōji. I recognized a particular corner, turned left, and arrived, a quarter century later, at the door of my 1959 homestay, filled with memories of that time and place where I had been another girl just beginning to study Japanese.

Notes

[1] The Experiment in International Living, "History & Mission," https://www.experiment.org/about-history-mission/ (accessed January 11, 2022).

[2] Ruth Benedict, *The Chrysanthemum and the Sword* (London: Secker and Warburg, 1947); D. T. Suzuki, *Zen Buddhism: Selected Writings of D. T. Suzuki* (New York: Doubleday, 1956); Edwin O. Reischauer, *The United States and Japan* (Cambridge, MA: Harvard University Press, 1950).

[3] Samuel Martin, *Essential Japanese: An Introduction to the Standard Colloquial Language* (Rutland, VT: C. E. Tuttle Company, 1954).

[4] "Rice Paddies" was the nickname for Social Science 111. See chapter 1.

[5] See "Tojo's Daughter in U.S. to Study," *New York Times*, June 16, 1959, 26.

[6] Edwin O. Reischauer and Serge Elisséeff: *Elementary Japanese for University Students: Vocabularies, Grammars, and Notes* (Cambridge, MA: Harvard University Press, 1942).

[7] Natsume Soseki, *Unhuman Tour*, translated by Takahashi Kazutomo (Tokyo: The Japan Times, 1927).

[8] Karen Brazell, *The Confessions of Lady Nijō* (New York: Doubleday, 1973).

[9] Susan Matisoff, "*Kintōsho*, Zeami's Song of Exile," *Monumenta Nipponica* 32, no. 4 (Winter 1977), 441–458; "Images of Exile and Pilgrimage, Zeami's *Kintōsho*," *Monumenta Nipponica* 34, no. 4 (Winter 1979), 449–465.

[10] Karen Brazell and Monica Bethe, *Nō as Performance: An Analysis of the Kuse Scene of Yamamba* (Ithaca: Cornell East Asia Series, 1978).

[11] Initially, students protested plans to erect a new gymnasium on nearby parkland, seeing the location and planned usage as racist. Broader issues, including opposition to the Vietnam War, were also motivations for action. The demonstrations and building occupations were quashed by heavy police action on April 30, 1968.

[12] Susan Matisoff, *The Legend of Semimaru, Blind Musician of Japan* (New York: Columbia University Press, 1978).

11

BECOMING A HISTORIAN

Mary Elizabeth Berry

The Berkeley history department appointed only one woman to the faculty in the 1950s and none in the 1960s, despite significant size and heady hiring: forty-five men were recruited in the 1960s.

MARY ELIZABETH BERRY is the author of *Hideyoshi* (1982), *The Culture of Civil War in Kyoto* (1994), and *Japan in Print: Information and Nation in the Early Modern Period* (2006). She is an elected fellow of the American Academy of Arts and Sciences, a past president of the Association for Asian Studies, and a recipient of the Award for Scholarly Distinction from the American Historical Association. Her current research concerns the economic culture of the seventeenth century.

I met Thomas Carlyle Smith (named after a baseball player, not the Scottish writer) when I joined the Berkeley faculty in 1979. He was sixty-two. I was thirty-two. From the start, and for over twenty years, we met regularly (sometimes weekly) to discuss whatever I was writing at the time. Almost always, we talked while walking through the theatrically beautiful campus, which had been laid out for botanical research. A serious gardener, Tom loved the landscape and many particular trees: the Italian stone pines near Tolman Hall, the live oaks near the Faculty Club, the cherries near California Hall, the redwoods and Hollywood junipers everywhere.

A man of few words, Tom also loved the pace of conversations interrupted or halted by close looks at leaves and needles, bark and cones and flowers.

He marked up my drafts with specific thoughts, leaving to walks the large, hard matters of plot and voice—the decisions about what sense to make of the sources and how to write the story for readers. His own work turns on fiercely clear arguments, often counterintuitive ones informed by comparisons with European history, that he develops with ruthless control of evidence. No stray leads. The prose is quiet, the tempo brisk, the focus unwavering. I learned a great deal from these choices, although not because Tom—so modest a scholar that he shrugged off his near-deity status in the field as a failure of judgment—ever pressed them. He led me, rather, to ceaseless review of the value of my own, largely different choices. Was I writing history that deserved a chance to last?

This kind of question, and the confidence that collegial critique would produce positive answers, defined the culture of the Berkeley history department. Members read one another's work—across the boundaries of time and space—with religious ardor. Teaching, too, was often shared. Among my best readers and closest partners in the classroom were Robert Brentano (medieval Italy) and Lynn Hunt (early modern France). But it was chiefly Tom Smith's astonishing gifts of time and respect, especially when I was revising a very flawed dissertation into a better book (*Hideyoshi*), that helped me think of myself as a historian.[1] This was new.

I spent my first two years of high school, when my father was stationed at Misawa Air Force Base, boarding at the International School of the Sacred Heart in Tokyo (1960–1962).[2] There, I learned the rudiments of French and Latin grammar, memorized startling loads of Middle English poetry, and joyously entered the ritual life of a Sacred Heart convent. (The order was founded in Paris in 1800. Had much changed, other than the English curriculum, by 1960? Certainly not the gloves.) Japan was more real to me as a setting for the school than a place of independent interest. Still, I was taken enough by Tokyo neighborhoods to begin coursework on Asia at Manhattanville College of the Sacred Heart (my mother's alma mater) and, eventually, to major in Asian Studies.

The program there had begun to take shape around the time I entered in 1964. With funding through Title VI of the National Defense Education Act, Manhattanville appointed Kwan Ha Yim to teach East Asian history and brought in members of the Columbia faculty— Wm. Theodore de Bary and Paul Varley among them—to offer both evening lecture series and mini-courses. Regular instruction in Japanese language and literature began when Columbia's Fumiko Fujikawa joined the faculty in my sophomore year. Chinese would follow. And the curriculum expanded as several professors of Western philosophy (David Dilworth, Mother Adele Fiske, and Robert A. McDermott) undertook research and teaching on South and East Asian subjects.

My major was a stew of anything Asian on offer, regardless of discipline or other focus, although I did pursue a misnamed honors project, based entirely on secondary sources, concerning the Meiji Restoration. (I asked why, against the odds, it had succeeded. I remember that France figured significantly.) At the dean's invitation, Marius Jansen drove from Princeton to "examine" me on my work—surely the most genially gentle examination on record—and to share a lunch, accompanied by decent wine and good tableware. The visit typified a remarkable program fashioned of administrative ambition with the support of new funds, excellent friends on nearby campuses, a local faculty open to challenge, and students ready to act on curiosity. If the program at this very small college founded in 1841 to educate Catholic women always remained modest (and diffuse), the attention to students was so serious that five of us from early cohorts went on to careers in the field. The others in this group are Maureen Donovan, for decades the Japanese Studies librarian at The Ohio State University (chapter 18); Anne Feldhaus, Distinguished Foundation Professor of (South Asian) Religious Studies at Arizona State University and a president of the Association for Asian Studies; Barbara Brennan Ford, a former curator of the Japanese collection at the Metropolitan Museum of Art in New York City; and Theresa Kelleher, a specialist in Chinese thought who joined the Manhattanville faculty and chaired the Department of Asian Studies. (Dr. Kelleher is my cousin. An uncle, Father Thomas Berry, and an aunt, [once Sister] Margaret Berry, were also professors of Asian Studies.)

I knew early on that I wanted a job "when I grow up." I assumed it would be in a school (the only place where I had seen more than a handful of women professionals) and probably as a nun (the calling of three aunts and most of my models who, I believe, had also looked to the convent, whatever its other pulls, for the promise of work). I had chilled on the convent during college but not the priority of a job. So I applied to graduate school in search of credentials that might land me employment, optimally in a small college like Manhattanville. The subject was oddly unimportant to me. I had been brainy and hardworking enough throughout my education to do well across the board (although Professor Moriarty's "A" in physics was a stunner) and expected that, once focused and trained, I could teach almost anything pretty well.

My carelessness about a specialty sprang less from a magpie virtuosity, however, than a taste for authority, for a job that might start in the classroom but lead to administration. Raised in the hierarchical institutions of the United States Air Force and the Roman Catholic Church, I combined a distrust of power (nurtured by the socialist strains of the Gospels, which were paramount for my family) with a deference to the powerful people whom I (and my conflicted family) looked to for virtuous leadership. (Matthew Arnold's *Culture and Anarchy* was a favorite text.)[3] The Sacred Heart superiors in high school and college—Mothers Elizabeth Britt, Bridget Keogh, Catherine Maher, Elizabeth McCormack, Anne Stoepel—were so brilliant to my young eyes that I hoped for a career, emulating theirs, in guiding a school. And, indeed, I spent most of my time away from the library. I sought the stage, both in theater productions and extemporaneous speaking competitions. I ran student councils and campus newspapers. Particular issues were important to me, from local policies on sex and drugs and discipline to national struggles over race and war. (I came to oppose the Vietnam War only in 1968, long influenced by my father's role in the military. We both changed course that spring. He elected retirement to begin counseling conscientious objectors at Fort Bragg.) Just as important to my vision of myself, nonetheless, was the eerie conceit that I could rise to the administrative wisdom of a Bridget Keogh.

So, a subject for graduate school applications? What I knew best was English literature. Philosophy was a close second. Still, my college major was Asian Studies. I ran with it.

In 1968, I entered the master's program at Harvard in Regional Studies—East Asia. Our group was large (too large for any close counsel) and almost comically incoherent in preparation. We barely sorted ourselves by national focus, not at all by discipline or period of interest or anything like professional purpose (obscure for many of us). We just took the courses on offer (as I had in college), auditing or enrolling in as many as a week could hold. History, literature, art, religion, sociology, anthropology. Such breadth was a hallmark of East Asian training in general. The paradigmatic surveys, known as "Rice Paddies," moved across East (and parts of Southeast) Asia, the disciplinary spectrum (if discipline was remarked at all), and the longest *durée*.[4] Graduate seminars, too, moved promiscuously across a still-thin bibliography in English (from George Sansom and Ruth Benedict to Herschel Webb and Robert Bellah). And when it came to writing MA theses, most of the Japan cohort assembled under the oversight of a forbidding trio—Edwin O. Reischauer, Donald H. Shively, and Albert M. Craig—to explore a random collection of topics chosen, in my case, impulsively and with little grounding. (I wrote on the Confucian philosopher Ogyū Sorai [1666–1728].)

Study of an area, often solitary and never in a formal group of any size, had been the rule for our teachers. Almost all the specialists on Japan were formed by typically early and substantial experience there (in missionary families, military service, or chance employment), by rare graduate mentors in a handful of language departments, and by generative connections to the Japanese scholars who welcomed them for the protracted periods of doctoral research that underlay their careers. Cultural fluency came to define them in a "field" made of space. (Ed Reischauer had an unrivaled knowledge of Nara sculpture. Al Craig knew everything to be known about classical and medieval horse raising.) Yet even as academic programs expanded in the 1950s and 1960s, the focus on area persisted at Harvard and a number of other Ivies. The reasons were partly structural. Study of the premodern histories of non-Western countries, for example, was centered in language and literature departments where presumptively arcane philological standards could be enforced. Some good sense here was troubled by not a little ideological sensibility. And it merged with inertia and expedience—in managing budgets, securing appointments, funding students, policing boundaries—to preserve area emphases in MA programs as well as the joint PhD programs (such as History and East Asian Languages and Civilizations) that tended to be weak on joints.

At least in my own time, however, the area emphasis primarily reflected the intellectual investment of the faculty in integral learning: historical study of Japan, say, was impoverished without attention to literature and religion and art (and more, inexhaustibly). There was little flaccid or romantic about these men or their mission. They had too much immediate knowledge of wartime and postwar Japan to indulge in sentimentality on the one hand or condescension on the other. Nor did they lean on any easy cultural fluency. In research and teaching, they struggled rigorously with the sources they used, the questions they asked, and, to a lesser extent, the comparative scholarship they needed to engage.

But yes, and occasioning profound controversy, they also ventured into Cold War politics and ideologies of development as participants in the "Conference on Modern Japan" (held in Hakone in 1960) and contributors to the (empirically revelatory if conceptually vexed) *Studies in the Modernization of Japan*.[5] More roiling was the silence of senior Asianists in all fields, and across the country, about the Vietnam War. The Committee of Concerned Asian Scholars was founded in 1968 by graduate students and young faculty to protest that war unequivocally and to denounce the perceived complicity of a profession that should have used its authority to speak out. I was there, although in an outer circle. And while a convert, I was unsettled by a sometime stridency that made the world monochrome.

So, among my many Harvards were the hot arenas of political meetings (often in Memorial Hall) and the cool, alternative-universe rooms for seminars (always at 2 Divinity Avenue). Most seminars, especially after I was admitted into the PhD program in History and East Asian Languages and Civilizations, focused on the real dogma of the area studies creed: first (and second and third), you must read the documents competently. Following some introductory work at Manhattanville (the "Naganuma system" of language education) and a summer at the University of Hawai'i (Title VI support in action again), I thrashed through merciless courses with Edwin Cranston, Gen Itasaka, and Yori Oda before even more grueling courses with Howard Hibbett and Donald Shively, which focused on primary sources. They taught with humility and certainly instilled it, even while tethering academic accomplishment to textual immersion and optimum knowledge of Japanese bibliography.

I absorbed the lessons, beginning to imagine myself as more than a fringe scholar aimed at administration. They were reenforced by the peerless Takagi Kiyoko at the Inter-University Center for Japanese Language Studies, then in Tokyo's Kioi-chō neighborhood, and by the wonderful Kubota Fuyuhiko, a graduate student recruited by Hayashida Tatsusaburō to read documents with me at Kyoto University while I worked on my dissertation. In many ways, that dissertation was a misadventure. An old appetite for literature and philosophy had led me originally to Hayashi Razan (1583–1657), almost as soul-chilling a challenge as Ogyū Sorai and just as wrong for someone barely literate in his texts. But a year in Kyoto, and weekly walks with Karen Brazell and Henry Smith through the places of its past, turned my sights to the history of the city. Karen and Henry were mighty influences. And our club—the Rakuhoku Kōkō-mae Kokenchiku Kenkyū-kai, named after Karen's bus stop—led me to a dissertation on "Hideyoshi in Kyoto: The Arts of Peace" about the person who decisively shaped the city we know today.

But I ran recklessly through both the research and the writing, composing the better part of the draft in about six months (with a quota of two to three pages a day) back in Cambridge. I was dying to get out of graduate school—out of the prolonged adolescence, out of the student storms over fellowship decisions and the like. Above all, I wanted distance from an emerging love affair with Shively that, mutually deep, was as fraught then as it would be now. (He removed himself early from my orals and dissertation committees, replaced by Mr. Reischauer.)

I went on the job market with an unfinished, still primitive dissertation in 1973. I received an offer and assumed an appointment at the University of Michigan in the history department in 1974 (salary: $12,000). Shively and I married in 1980.

The Equal Pay Act was enacted by the US legislature in 1963 and the Civil Rights Act in 1964. The law that transformed faculty hiring, however, was Title IX of the Education Amendments of 1972: "No person in the United States shall, on the basis of sex, be excluded from participation in, be denied the benefits of, or be subjected to discrimination under any education program or activity receiving federal financial assistance."[7] Before that, what we baldly but not badly called the "old boys' network" held traction. The Berkeley history department appointed only one woman to the faculty in the 1950s and none in the 1960s, despite significant size and heady hiring: forty-five men were recruited in the 1960s. The oral histories of my colleagues help reveal the hiring strategies. Delmer Brown, a champion of women faculty later in life, describes a characteristic approach when he was departmental chair in the 1960s: he identified the contenders for a China appointment as Joseph Levinson and Benjamin Schwartz following a phone conversation about the available talent with John King Fairbank at Harvard.[8]

Women had long made up a meaningful fraction of PhD recipients in Tier 1 institutions (for example, 12 percent of the Berkeley history department cohort in the 1960s and 20 percent in the 1970s).[9] But consequential entry into faculties, if spurred by agitation on individual campuses, depended on Title IX, which effectively required that announcements of jobs be publicly placed and that selection procedures be both formalized and submitted to official scrutiny. (In time, public universities would require that search plans be certified, candidate pools quantified, short lists approved, "de-selection" criteria specified for each rejected candidate, and full reports on completed searches filed.)

Like many contributors to this volume, I was part of the 1960s and 1970s swell in female graduate enrollment. And I was a job applicant under the new Title IX regime. For the University of Michigan, I responded to an ad, submitted copious materials, requested recommendations, went through a preliminary interview at a convention (proverbially conducted by three men in a hotel bedroom), and visited the campus to meet the senior faculty and make the rounds of receptions. This near-revolutionary change in process went largely over my head (what did I know of phone calls between barons?). And the effects were slowly felt.

I joined the Michigan faculty in 1974 with four other assistant professors, all male, in what would prove a late stage in once hectic hiring throughout the profession. There were two women already on the faculty, both assistant professors in US history. The departmental chair, David Bien, welcomed me as a third by rejoicing that "women have now reached critical mass" (in a department numbering around fifty). Natalie Davis had earlier served on the faculty, as had Sylvia Thrupp, who held a chair reserved for a woman. Elizabeth Eisenstein would succeed Thrupp, and Louise Tilly would be appointed to the faculty as well. Five of us by 1978.

I was the youngest recruit in my cohort, utterly raw, and—with that unfinished dissertation and several strong male competitors (who let me know that I was a surprise choice)—a logically suspect beneficiary of affirmative action. I take the point. Still, I felt thoroughly welcomed, at both the formal dinners of seniors and the potlucks of juniors, usually following home games. (My father marveled, when I told him about the Michigan offer, that the biggest college football stadium in the country was there.) I lived across the street from the main campus, a place—given the eternal winters—strangely sparse in warming conifers but thrilling in early spring with the horse chestnuts, in late spring with every apple varietal. Around the corner was the Center for Japanese Studies, often my base. Michigan was not Harvard. Discipline prevailed over area. The center was nonetheless a sparkling place of intellectual energy and—with Dick Beardsley, Bill Sibley, Bob Cole, Ed Seidensticker, and Cal French—an oasis of common culture.

There was the rub. My fate depended not on that great center (where my linguistic and area competence might matter) but the great history department. And I knew so little of that discipline. My principal encounter with mainstream academic practice had been a single graduate seminar with H. Stuart Hughes on nineteenth-century European intellectual history (I wrote on Hippolyte Taine, France again) and preparation for his part of my doctoral orals (during which I referred to John Stuart Mill's *The Subjection of Women* as the "subjugation" of women, a moment Hughes managed with class).

So, I spent many waking moments at Michigan trying to figure out what historians do. Essential to my education were the questions raised at job talks and departmental reviews of graduate progress. (Just what were my colleagues looking for? Charles Tilly—with his search for seminal questions—seemed to me a weathervane.) I also inhaled lectures from visitors (Emmanuel Le Roy Ladurie left me as puzzled as edified) and shared long dinners with those marooned in utility apartments (night after night with Charles Boxer and Vlado Dedejir). And I listened to students—never hesitant in undergraduate courses but mesmerizing in graduate debate. In seminars and other fora, I was taught by Robert Borgen, Karen Gottschang, Robert Innes, Louis Perez, Mark Ramseyer, and others.

I tried to apply the lessons to revisions of my dissertation, which was becoming a political biography of Hideyoshi, and thought the result encouraging. But my midcareer review at Michigan, meant to predict chances for tenure, was bad. There was little written and no oral feedback from colleagues. Just "no" (amplified by the devastating scuttlebutt that I seemed to be writing for something like *Smithsonian Magazine*). It was a relief to learn that the focus was the dissertation. The revision did merit a positive word, although one so brief that the emphasis remained on the negative.

Receiving tenure at Michigan was notoriously tough. Among the casualties close to my time were the two young women in the department when I arrived. A presumption prevailed, I think, that survival was exceptional, which may help account for the hands-off conduct of senior faculty members, who engaged sparingly in counsel and manuscript critique of juniors. This seemed normal enough to me. I had written my dissertation in solitude. Although, to be fair, I plowed through most of it at a wild pace, determined to be done and out, and finished it during my first months in Ann Arbor without sending drafts to mentors in Cambridge.

Maybe madly, I did hold out hope for tenure at Michigan and applied to Berkeley as what I assumed was an ill-fated plan B. When I was offered the job there, I dithered over the decision, not least because, to my shock, Michigan surpassed the offer and urged me to stay put. In the end, I resigned from Michigan as of 1978 and, following a year of leave in Japan, began life in Berkeley in 1979.

There, too, the application process had been transformed by Title IX. There, too, the results were felt slowly. Adrienne Koch, the sole woman appointed to the history department before 1970, had long before left for another job and died relatively young. Natalie Davis, appointed in 1971, had also departed (like Koch, for family reasons). Three women were appointed subsequently: Diane Clemens (1972), Paula Fass (1974), and Lynn Hunt (1974). When I joined them, women numbered four in a faculty of fifty-three. (Nine more women were recruited in the 1980s and four more in the 1990s. Not until 2020 did women represent 50 percent of the history department faculty.)[10]

I was welcomed with the warmth I had known at Michigan. But I was also welcomed with the hands-on counsel of colleagues who believed they had hired me for life and expected the Hideyoshi manuscript to become a book as good as their own. This faith, exemplified by Tom Smith, helped inspire foundational revisions that made and defended an argument (concerning the conciliation and alliance of a Toyotomi regime that, breaking with Oda precedents, enabled a federal form of union). I think my work, reflecting my formation, has always been a hybrid. It comes at history from an angle—perhaps a literary one responsive to unruly sources I tame tentatively—that disturbs the clear paths cut, for example, by Tom. I do it, however, as a card-carrying member of a guild Tom taught me to think of as my own.

Will I continue to do it? I've been battling the manuscript of a fourth monograph for over a decade, delayed in part by the mounting administrative labor I once saw as a calling and then embraced as an avocation. Let me recommend it. It's been precious, since service to good institutions remains to me a life-giving responsibility. (Back to Matthew Arnold.)[11] But another angle on the book battle. It dates from the time I was roughly the same age as Tom when we met. Remember that our walks focused on my drafts, not his. He had plenty of them, old and new, piling up in the right-hand drawers of his desk. Yet while he would prepare a collection of his essays during our time together (as I would prepare a coedited volume on Edo-period families), he neither circulated nor published something original. I don't know the reason. I now suspect it. The work remains hard and gets harder. The standards—one's own in the past, those of young colleagues in the present—weigh heavy. And rhythms change. Now seventy-six, clearing out my office in Dwinelle Hall, entwined in the lives of two daughters and three grandchildren, Zooming with three siblings I never knew as well before, and keeping order in everything from the roof to the paperwork, I no longer write with the daily quota that was long a spine. Still, the book calls on most days. The through line, Dear Reader, is that work and being can fuse.

A word about the gender issues intimated above. The powerful men of my youth were priests and the senior officers who joined my father for rounds of golf and cocktails. (I learned to handle a five iron and mix martinis.) In the schools that were my center, women alone controlled decisions and organized all activity (from basketball to music) until I graduated from college. A few were near-sadists in their skill at humiliation. Several others found their mission in instilling obedience. But most were fervent pedagogues, and some were intellectuals, both at Sacred Heart and Saint Francis Convent School in Honolulu, where I completed high school. Stern on themselves, they were sterner on us, with gritty assignments and punishing criticism. I've kept my papers, from ninth grade ("first academic") through college. The comments? "Get to the point." "Don't be silly. Cut the flowery prose." "How much time did you spend on this essay?"

Women largely vanished from authority from the time I entered graduate school in 1968 until the 1990s, when, at Berkeley, more of us became full professors and a small number served in administrative posts. (Carol Christ, Berkeley's chancellor since 2017, was a chair and a dean before appointment in 1994 as executive vice-chancellor and provost.) At Harvard, the only woman on the East Asian faculty was Rulan Chao Pian, who, after decades as a lecturer, was promoted to professor of music in 1974. (Note the proximity to the Title IX legislation.) At Michigan, I knew no women in leadership positions.

Life in a mostly male world was expected, once beyond the walls of female education. It felt familiar, since my early models, more formidable than their successors, had readied me for the work. And it was courteous. A general decorum in all the faculties I knew was amplified by a scholarly avidity for good students (more often women than men at Harvard, I suspect) and for strong young colleagues.

There was occasional misbehavior. Without consent, I was hugged and kissed after rides home, groped when I accepted tickets to concerts, and asked—early on a Saturday morning—to welcome an unexpected visitor armed with coffee and pastry. All of this was reasonably easy to manage. But there was real danger on our horizons as well. My experience of violence (a random rape in Harvard Yard, an anonymous stalking at Berkeley) was surely not singular. It was isolating and unshared, however, in a world suffused in silence. We did not discuss trials presumed to be personal. They are not, which we are coming to understand.

The gender conversations that did occur, led by male colleagues, turned on disquiet over how a landmark law was changing departmental cultures. Nomenclature ("Ms." and gender-neutral nouns) caused minor friction. Surveillance of hiring procedures provoked some fury. Multiple fears—that "affirmative action" might undermine rankings, feminize the profession, and compromise male breadwinners—surfaced on the edges of recruitment conversations. In the offing were the profound changes to old cultures that proved lasting rather than spectral: two-career households and faculty pregnancies. In the background were the many consequences of the "sexual revolution" that further unsettled understandings of family and departmental sociability: increasing divorce, partnerships outside of marriage, greater numbers of singles, and a general severing of private from professional imperatives.

Time would calm some alarms and provide recourse for others. Not all. I mention two. One emerged from the expectation (shared by several nuns) that I would defer to my seniors on contentious matters. The problem was not the expectation (are powerful people ever comfortable with dissent?) but the slide among a few critics toward judgment (dissent was "bad behavior") and the conflation of bad behavior with gender (I was a "disruptive woman"). If diminishing, the problem persists. And the second is related. I was asked (five times and without success) to apply for jobs at the Ivies. Fair fights all, I think, in predictably complex circumstances. Yet it bears mention that academic combat can go low. During one endgame I was described (according to trustworthy insiders) as "a noncollegial bitch" and "a department destroyer." Gender again got mixed into conflict. The invective probably didn't matter. (I had a record of outspokenness, readily available to critics.) The point is that barriers are resilient. Gratuitous injury happens. And collective intolerance of venality will always matter.

I hasten to add that unfairness cuts in many directions and is hardly unique to women. Not least, men have hazed other men in tests of masculinity. And with the contraction in many of our disciplines, most younger academics face a new cycle of turmoil in hiring and professional opportunity.

I close with a short litany of the women who entered the earlier turmoil with transformative energy, easing it for me on a personal level and sustaining the profession for all of us. Experts in their fields, they also belong to a Japan Studies sorority forged by the area emphases in much of our training as well as the complex connections of gender and affinity in what long felt like intimate circles of common calling. I have no comparable circles in the discipline of history. We have been fortunate in the gift of community.

First, three contributors to this volume who deserve remark as exceptional field builders.

The creation of the Japan Foundation in 1972 was undoubtedly the most important institutional development in my lifetime. With its generous and multifaceted support (of individual scholars, programs, faculty appointments, libraries, and much more), the Japan Foundation became core to all our work. Many members of the American Advisory Committee, mixed in gender from its inception, helped guide the mission. The towering presence was the eminent sociologist Patricia Steinhoff, who led the data collection for multiple iterations of the Japan Foundation's *Survey of Japan Specialists and Japanese Studies Institutions in North America* (chapter 12). There, and particularly in the analytical volumes *Japanese Studies in the United States*, Pat tells us who we are, with masterful interpretation of the information collected. An anatomist of the highest order, she underwrote most conscientious planning for the future. (Like my counterparts, I kept her surveys to hand as chair of Berkeley's Center for Japanese Studies.)[12]

Another boon arrived in 1973, when the Japanese government made grants of $1 million to each of ten leading Japan programs in North America (the "Tanaka Ten").[13] Alone among the ten, the University of Washington faculty invested in the collective good by founding *The Journal of Japanese Studies* (first number in 1974), a boundless gift to the field. Susan Hanley (chapter 9), a pathbreaking social scientist, was influential in the decision and served as editor for over twenty-five years. Spartan frugality personified (hence, the duration of the journal), she was also a prescient host of lectures and colloquia, a resourceful encourager of talent, and a judicious arbiter of (not infrequent) scholarly rows. Hats off, too, to Martha Lane Walsh, the uncannily adroit managing editor who has held the enterprise together.

A similar salute to Kate Nakai (chapter 24), another major historian who did not invent a journal but surpassed the standards of a fabled predecessor (Michael Cooper) when she served as editor of *Monumenta Nipponica* from 1997 to 2010. *Monumenta Nipponica* has been our DNA—home, beyond seminal essays, to crucial translations and extended book reviews that are unrivaled in the field.

(A shout-out here to Joanna Handlin Smith, a China scholar who long served as editor of *The Harvard Journal of Asiatic Studies* and guaranteed the quality of another of our essential publications. I nominate her as an honorary member of our sorority.)

Next, two librarians among the early field builders whose contributions, like those of several successors represented in this volume, rank toward the top in historical bearing.

Naomi Fukuda (1907–2007), a graduate in English from Tokyo Women's Christian College, served as librarian at many organizations, including Tokyo Imperial University (later, the University of Tokyo), the Ministry of Foreign Affairs of Japan, and the General Headquarters of the Supreme Command of the Allied Powers.[14] She was the founding librarian at the International House of Japan (1953–1970) and, following "retirement," became the Asian Studies Librarian at the University of Michigan (1970–1978), where I knew her. Famously remembered as tutor and research assistant to Robert K. Reischauer, she was better known to myriad students and colleagues as an inexhaustible engine of help and hilarity. Well under five feet tall (she had chairs custom-made to prevent her legs from dangling), she commanded every room she was in with a steel will and a wicked wit. When problems arose (from politics to funding), she was on the phone with her invariable opener: "*Undō shiyō!*" (Maybe, let's agitate!) Her many publications include *A Guide to Japanese Reference Books* (a revision and translation of *Nihon no sankō tosho*).[15] In 1984 she received the Order of the Precious Crown, Wistaria, from the Japanese government.

I did not know Elizabeth Huff (1912–1988), "Miss Huff" to everyone who did know her, a Harvard PhD in Chinese literature, who, unable as a woman to find a faculty appointment, came to Berkeley in 1947 as founding curator and head of the East Asian Library. She had spent most of the previous seven years in China, including thirty months of internment by the Japanese army in Shantung. Once at Berkeley, she doubled and then redoubled the library's holdings by 1950. As boldly, she gained approval in that year from the president and regents of the University of California to make the richest acquisition in our collection: one hundred thousand items from the Mitsui Bunko in Tokyo, the archive of the great commercial and banking house founded in the seventeenth century. (Other university libraries had passed on the opportunity.) Donald Shively concludes his obituary by quoting her final annual report: "Rest you merry, books and loyal staff who shaped a treasure-house."[16]

Many scholar-pedagogues in Japanese language programs left everlasting marks on the field. Among those deserving great recognition are Eleanor Jorden (1920–2009), Michiko Kwok (dates unknown to me), and Yori Oda (1935–2018). I confine remarks here to Takagi Kiyoko (1918–2011). For all of us who studied at the Inter-University Center for Japanese Language Studies during her time there (1961–1981), I suspect she looms largest as an inspiration. She somehow broke through our often-juvenile Japanese conversation to convey fellow respect for us as academics, to grapple with our ideas, to make us believe we could do this.

An elegant and—given her ascetic demeanor—surprisingly emotional poet (with several published collections), she was also a scholar of religion who wrote on Saigyō (1118–1190), Higuchi Ichiyō (1872–1896), and the eight female emperors of Japan.[17] After leaving IUC, she served as a professor of religion at Ochanomizu and Tōyō Universities.

As something close to a census-keeper of our people, I would like to go on with numerous profiles.[18] Again, constraint. The incomparable Karen Brazell (1938–2012) will live in many of our essays. As will several others. So, I conclude with just one final toast. To Helen Craig McCullough (1918–1998).

Born in Hollywood (yes, really), she graduated from Berkeley in 1939 with a BA in political science (yes, really), then worked as a census clerk and "junior administrative technician" in the Civil Service Commission.[19] Following sixteen months at the Navy Japanese Language School in Boulder (1943–1944), she spent over five years as a government translator, first for the Chief of Naval Operations in Washington, DC, and subsequently for the Allied Occupation in Tokyo. Next, graduate school at Berkeley (PhD, 1955). Although consistently at work on important translations and commentaries (the earliest were the *Taiheiki* and *Yoshitsune*), what she calls "regular employment" began only in 1964, when she was appointed as a lecturer at Stanford, where her husband, William H. McCullough (1928–1997), held a professorial position. Helen accompanied Bill to Berkeley in 1969, again with an appointment as a lecturer. In 1975, at the age of fifty-seven, she was made a professor. (Once more, note the proximity to the Title IX legislation.) Helen would eventually publish eleven major translations of Japanese classics, in multiple genres spanning a millennium, as well as many essays.[20] The magnitude of the accomplishment is unparalleled. Occasional honors came to her late in life, including a medal of honor (*kunshō*) from the Japanese government in 1996. Yet what mattered to her—Bill and their son, Dundas, above all; baseball, Mozart operas, high-season crabmeat, and her brilliant California take on a Japanese garden lower on the list—was the daily work of guiding graduate students in a calling, and in a department, that she venerated. Frighteningly austere and unbending in standards, Helen McCullough taught all of us close to her that lives well lived require work embraced scrupulously.

Notes

[1] Mary Elizabeth Berry, *Hideyoshi* (Cambridge, MA: Harvard University Asia Center, 1982).

[2] During the second year, after the school ceased taking boarders on campus, my father settled my younger sister and me at the Study House in Tokyo of the School Sisters of Notre Dame, about a mile's walk from the school.

[3] Matthew Arnold, *Culture and Anarchy: An Essay in Political and Social Criticism* (New Haven: Yale University Press, 1994).

⁴ "Rice Paddies" was the nickname for Social Science 111. See chapter 1.

⁵ Princeton published three volumes (edited by Jansen, Shively, and Ward) under this series title (1965–1971). The Hakone conference, funded by the Ford Foundation and conducted in Japanese, brought together thirty-one scholars (mainly from Japan and the United States) to explore, in the Japanese context, the universalistic paradigm of historical progress, derived from the work of Max Weber, known as "modernization theory." Subsequent conferences on the same subject generated the essays collected in the *Studies in the Modernization of Japan* volumes. The conference and series remain political flashpoints in the Japan field. See Marius B. Jansen, ed., *Changing Japanese Attitudes toward Modernization* (Princeton: Princeton University Press, 1965); Robert Ward, ed., *Political Development in Modern Japan* (Princeton: Princeton University Press, 1968); Donald H. Shively, ed., *Tradition and Modernization in Japanese Culture* (Princeton: Princeton University Press, 1971).

⁶ Mary Elizabeth Berry, "Hideyoshi in Kyoto: The Arts of Peace," PhD diss., Harvard University, 1975.

⁷ Education Amendments Act of 1972, 20 U.S.C. §§1681–1688 (2018).

⁸ I assembled extensive material concerning female faculty and PhD recipients in the history department for a campus-wide endeavor to mark the 150th anniversary of the decision by the University of California regents in 1870 to admit young women "on equal terms in all respects as young men." See Mary Elizabeth Berry, "Mary Elizabeth Berry," Department of History, University of California Berkeley, 2020 and 2021, https://wayback.archive-it.org/16283/20211216050814/https://history.berkeley.edu/sites/default/files/150w_meb_final.pdf; and "Women in the Department of History," Department of History, University of California, Berkeley, 2020 and 2021, https://wayback.archive-it.org/16283/20210913182815/https://history.berkeley.edu/women-department-history.

⁹ Ibid.

¹⁰ Ibid.

¹¹ I've performed many jobs in many settings. The bigger ones included chairing Berkeley's Center for Japanese Studies; four departments (history, my home, as well as anthropology, demography, and South and Southeast Asian Studies); the American Advisory Committee of the Japan Foundation; and the Humanities Class of the American Academy of Arts and Sciences. I also served as president of the Association for Asian Studies. All the smaller jobs (starting with setting up and breaking down event rooms) taught me most of what I know and made at least as much difference.

¹² See, for example, Patricia Steinhoff, ed. *Japanese Studies in the United States: Directory of Japan Specialists and Japanese Studies Institutions in the United States and Canada*, 2 vols.; *Directory of Japan Specialists and Japanese Studies Institutions in the United States and Canada, Fourth Edition, 2016 Update*, 3 vols.; *Japanese Studies in the United States in the 1990s; Directory of Japan Specialists and Japanese Studies Institutions in the United States and Canada, Third Edition*, 3 vols.; and *Japanese Studies in the United States and Canada: Continuities and Opportunities*. Another invaluable resource for understanding the development of Asian Studies, from its inception, is Peter Zhou, ed., *Collecting Asia: East*

Asian Libraries in North America, 1868–2008 (Ann Arbor: Association for Asian Studies, 2010).

[13] The "Tanaka Ten" were Columbia, Harvard, Princeton, Stanford, University of California, Berkeley, University of Chicago, University of Hawai'i, University of Michigan, University of Washington, and Yale.

[14] Much of this paragraph relies on Izumi Koide, "Chronological Biography of Naomi Fukuda," *Journal of East Asian Libraries* 145 (2008), https://scholarsarchive.byu.edu/cgi/viewcontent.cgi?article=2596&context=jeal; Yasuko Makino, "Eulogy of Ms. Naomi Fukuda," *Journal of East Asian Libraries* 145 (2008), https://scholarsarchive.byu.edu/cgi/viewcontent.cgi?article=2588&context=jeal.

[15] Fukuda Naomi, *Nihon no sankō tosho* (Tokyo: Nihon no Sankō Tosho Henshū Iinkai, 1962); *A Guide to Japanese Reference Books* (Chicago: American Library Association, 1966).

[16] See Donald H. Shively, "Elizabeth Huff and the East Asiatic Library at the University of California, Berkeley," *Journal of East Asian Libraries* 79 (1986), https://scholarsarchive.byu.edu/cgi/viewcontent.cgi?article=1373&context=jeal.

[17] Takagi Kiyoko, "Religion in the Life of Higuchi Ichiyō," *Japanese Journal of Religious Studies* 10/2–3 (1983), 123–147; *Sakura: Sono sei to zoku* (Cherry Blossoms: Sacred and Profane) (Tokyo: Chūō Kōronsha, 1996); *Hachinin no jotei* (The Eight Female Emperors of Japan) (Tokyo: Taimeidō, 2002).

[18] I hope appropriate acknowledgement can be made, among others, of Felicia Bock, Elise Grilli, Eleanor Hadley, Joyce Lebra, Takie Sugiyama Lebra, Miriam Silverberg, Patricia Tsurumi, Marian Ury, and Carolyn Wheelwright.

[19] See Mary Elizabeth Berry et al., "Helen Craig McCullough, East Asian Languages: Berkeley," *Online Archives of California*, 1998, https://oac.cdlib.org/view?docId=hb1p30039g;NAAN=13030&doc.view=frames&chunk.id=div00035&toc.depth=1&toc.id=&brand=oac4.

[20] Helen's books include an annotated translation of the *Kokin Wakashū: The First Imperial Anthology of Japanese Poetry* (Stanford: Stanford University Press, 1985), with a companion volume, *Brocade by Night: "Kokin Wakashū" and the Court Style in Japanese Classical Poetry* (Stanford: Stanford University Press, 1985); *The Tales of Ise: Lyrical Episodes from Tenth-Century Japan* (Stanford: Stanford University Press, 1968); *A Tale of Flowering Fortunes: Annals of Japanese Aristocratic Life in the Heian Period*, vols. 1 and 2 (Stanford: Stanford University Press, 1980), which was produced together with William McCullough; *Okagami, The Great Mirror: Fujiwara Michinaga (966–1027) and His Times* (Princeton: Princeton University Press, 1980); *Taiheiki: A Chronicle of Medieval Japan* (New York: Columbia University Press, 1956); *Yoshitsune: A Fifteenth-Century Japanese Chronicle* (Stanford: Stanford University Press, 1966); *The Tale of the Heike* (Stanford: Stanford University Press, 1988); and *Classical Japanese Prose: An Anthology* (Stanford: Stanford University Press, 1990).

12

SERENDIPITY AND SOCIOLOGY

Patricia G. Steinhoff

> *My own life has been enriched both by favorable social circumstances and serendipity, which together have led to unexpected opportunities.*

PATRICIA G. STEINHOFF is a professor emerita at the University of Hawai'i, where she was the founding director of the Center for Japanese Studies and continues to serve as curator of the Kōji Takazawa Collection of Japanese Social Movement Materials. Her books include *Tenkō: Ideology and Societal Integration in Prewar Japan* (1991); *Nihon sekigunha: Sono shakaigakuteki monogatari* (*Japan Red Army Factions: A Sociological Tale*, 1991, 1993; republished as *Shi eno ideologi: Nihon sekigunha* [*Deadly Ideology: The Japanese Red Army Factions*], 2003); and *Rengō sekigun to Aum shinrikyō: Nihon shakai o kataru* (*Rengō Sekigun and Aum Shinrikyō: Talking about Japanese Society*, coauthored with Ito Yoshinori and Takahashi Mayumi, 1996). She has published over a hundred articles and book chapters. In addition, she compiled and published the *Directory of Japan Specialists and Japanese Studies Institutions in the United States and Canada* for the Japan Foundation (1989, 1995, 2006, 2013, and 2016), along with three monographs analyzing the state of Japanese Studies in the United States (1996, 2007, and 2013). She is editor or coeditor of several essay collections on Japan, including *Conflict in Japan* (coedited with Ellis Krauss and Thomas Rohlen, 1984), *Doing Fieldwork in Japan* (coedited with Theodore and Vickey Bestor, 2003), and *Going to Court to Change Japan: Social Movements and the Law* (2014). She is editor of *Destiny: The*

Secret Operations of the Yodogō Exiles by Kōji Takazawa (2017), and *Alternative Politics in Contemporary Japan: New Directions in Social Movements* (with David Slater, forthcoming in 2024).

Introduction

I have taken this opportunity to apply my sociological perspective to my lifetime as an early female academic in Japanese Studies, incorporating both why I studied what I did and how my academic career meshed with my personal life. I consider myself a symbolic interactionist, which means that I look holistically at the social structure, social interactions, and other factors that come together in any social situation. I also view social situations dynamically, as changing and developing over time. Those elements and conditions shape the decisions that people make to navigate through their lives. Just as often, they carry people along effortlessly so that they find themselves in another situation without having made any conscious decisions at all. My own life has been enriched both by favorable social circumstances and serendipity, which together have led to unexpected opportunities.

I was born two days after Pearl Harbor in December 1941 and raised in Highland Park, Michigan, as the only child of two professional parents from quite different backgrounds. Both of my grandmothers had run small businesses, one in Michigan and the other in Riga, Latvia. We lived upstairs from my paternal grandparents, who took care of me while my parents worked fulltime, my father as a lawyer and my mother as a high school English teacher. We moved to our own house just before I entered fourth grade, and I became a latchkey child. Both parents were active in community organizations, and, soon, my father was elected municipal court judge in Highland Park. Both parents supported and encouraged me in everything I did but also expected me to be independent, to excel academically, and to behave responsibly as a judge's daughter.

When I was growing up, Highland Park was an integrated, multiethnic community with a large working class of unionized blue-collar workers in the automobile industry, an array of shopkeepers and small entrepreneurs, plus an educated middle class that my parents were a part of. My mother taught in predominantly Black Detroit high schools, and her friends and fellow teachers, both Black and white, visited our home. My father often performed civil weddings in our living room. Highland Park's award-winning school system provided a broad, comprehensive education that included strong vocational training plus college preparatory education. Only about a quarter of the graduates went on to college. I took Latin, French, and advanced English classes, but I also learned to cook and sew in home economics from fourth grade through high school. In my senior year, I edited the high school newspaper and won some academic awards but also was named a Betty Crocker Homemaker of Tomorrow.[1] I grew up believing that I could do anything I wanted with my life. After all, I was both the daughter and the granddaughter of independent, resourceful working women. Nobody ever told me there were limits.

Generational Time Context

I only applied to the University of Michigan and was invited into the Honors College for the fall of 1959. That summer, I pored through the fat college catalog, amazed at all the languages they taught. I decided to learn Japanese, which resonated with books I had read in high school: *The Tale of Genji* and *The Chrysanthemum and the Sword*. After meeting my language requirement with French, I took intensive Japanese for a year and became a Japanese language and literature major. This was before the modern textbooks for Japanese were written, and my first-year intensive Japanese course began with a semester of spoken Japanese using a World War II Army language school textbook. Few undergraduates took Japanese. Most of my classmates were graduate students on National Defense Foreign Language (NDFL, now Foreign Language and Area Studies, FLAS) Fellowships who had previously been in the military in Japan.

I was part of a new generation of young Americans just starting to study Japanese, who had no prior experience with Japan and were intrigued by the challenge of learning to read characters and speak an Asian language. In 1960, that was not a job qualification for anything, but I simply wanted to major in something that would *not* qualify me to teach high school. My mother wanted me to be economically independent but only knew high school teaching, so this was one of my few acts of adolescent rebellion. Neither parent ever questioned what I was taking at the University of Michigan or what I planned to do with it. My father only gave me one firm warning when I left for Ann Arbor: "Whatever you do, don't join anything." Just a few years earlier, the anti-communist purges of the McCarthy era had destroyed many careers.

The time period when I grew up in the early 1960s was a particularly important factor in my subsequent academic trajectory. In addition to studying Japanese out of sheer intellectual curiosity, as a high school newspaper editor, I gravitated naturally to the student newspaper, *The Michigan Daily*. As a dutiful daughter, I didn't join anything, but the *Daily* was close to the center of the political activity swirling around the campus, which focused initially on the civil rights movement. Because Ann Arbor was beyond the range of the Detroit newspapers, the *Daily* saw itself not only as a campus newspaper but also as the daily paper presenting the news of the world to U of M students.

By my second year at Michigan, the *Daily* was my home base, and I rotated as a night editor responsible for the next morning's paper, which was printed downstairs from the editorial offices by union typesetters. The editor in chief that year was Tom Hayden, who became an active participant in the civil rights movement after graduating from Michigan, and, a few years later, was one of the Chicago Seven activists who were tried for their involvement in anti-Vietnam War protests during the 1968 Democratic National Convention. The *Daily* not only reported on local civil rights activities by students; those events were often planned and discussed in the *Daily* offices by activists involved in student government or a local student political party called Voice, which subsequently became a chapter of Students for a Democratic Society (SDS).[2]

During that year under Hayden's leadership, the *Daily* editors submitted a formal complaint to the university with information its editors had been collecting for years about serious invasions of privacy by the dean of women. As a cub reporter, I had covered a small story that became part of this collection, about the dean sending a letter to the parents of a coed to report that she was dating someone of another race, which the dean said was "not acceptable in the Ann Arbor community." That led to a three-month official investigation by a faculty committee, the first time in history that such an inquiry had been prompted by student complaints. During that time, the *Daily* faced heavy criticism from the student government council for its alleged "irresponsibility," which the paper also reported. When the faculty committee validated the students' concerns and recommended sweeping changes in the Office of Student Affairs, on May 30, 1961, the *Daily* published a front-page story and an editorial signed by all the senior editors encouraging open discussion of the issues raised, which attracted national attention. The dean was soon forced out.[3] The *Daily*'s exposé challenged the prevailing view that the university acted *in loco parentis* and should oversee the private behavior of students under twenty-one. It was an early indication of new attitudes and challenges by students in the 1960s.

Through the *Daily*, I learned about a summer 1961 trip to Japan sponsored by the US National Student Association. That trip changed my life.[4] There were eight or nine American students on the trip, and I was the only participant who was studying Japanese. Half the trip was spent in Tokyo, where we stayed at the International House of Japan, and our guides were two young men who had been active in the 1960 Ampo protests the previous year. We were treated as an official delegation from the US National Student Association, even though we had simply paid to take the trip. We met members of the National Diet and even had an audience with the Crown Prince and Princess, which the Imperial Household Agency skillfully maneuvered so that we met separately by gender. The Crown Princess, later Empress Michiko, had been a student leader at her university, and she began asking the women in English about student government in the United States, so I ended up discussing student government at American universities with her. For the other three weeks, we traveled around Western Japan with students from the Wakayama University English Speaking Society and their American professor. I returned from the trip with a deepened commitment to the study of Japan, and much-improved spoken Japanese. I am still in email contact with two of the Wakayama students, who later had international business careers.

Sliding into Academia in Japanese Studies

Having avoided becoming a high school teacher, as I neared the end of my undergraduate studies, the only viable alternative was to go to graduate school. By then, I knew that I wanted to use Japanese language as a tool but not as my academic focus. I chose sociology as a broad field that would help me make sense of Japanese society. In my junior year, I had also been invited to take the required graduate seminar for the interdisciplinary MA in Japanese Studies and subsequently began working part-time at the Center for Japanese Studies for the two faculty members who taught the course. Through them, I learned about the new Stanford Center for Japanese Studies in Tokyo (now the Inter-University Center for Japanese Language Studies) that was administered by Stanford University. I applied to Stanford's MA program in Japanese Studies, thinking that after a year, they might send me to the center. Instead, they awarded me an NDFL Fellowship to attend the center for the first year. That bit of serendipity set the course of my life in more ways than one.

The center was housed that year on the campus of International Christian University (ICU). The intensive program pushed my language skills to a functional level, but there were additional benefits. When the first housing arrangement that I had made before going to Japan did not work out, the ICU housing office helped me arrange to live with the family of a Japanese management consultant.[5] I learned a tremendous amount from the wife's beautiful Japanese as well as from long conversations with the husband about Japanese management, and I have remained in touch with four generations of that family. Finally, there was the biggest serendipity of all. There were five students from the University of Michigan at the Stanford Center that year. Besides me, three were graduate students whom I knew already from my classes, and the fourth was an older undergraduate who had been in the military. Our first meeting at the center was inauspicious because he made a disparaging comment about the *Daily*, but, later, I got to know him better; Bill Steinhoff and I have been married for over fifty years.

Our Japanese society class was held at the home of the Japanese professor, Nagai Michio. One day after that class, Bill lent me a manuscript he had received from a friend. It was written by David Riesman, coauthor of *The Lonely Crowd*, and described the people he had met during a VIP tour of Japan.[6] Riesman was a sociologist in the Department of Social Relations at Harvard, which also had two established Japan sociologists and seemed to be an ideal place for me to continue my graduate studies. I was surprised to learn that Riesman had a Japan connection, but I knew he subscribed to several student newspapers as a way of keeping tabs on the pulse of student life. During the *Daily*'s troubles two years earlier, Riesman had written a letter supporting the newspaper, which we had published.[7] After reading the manuscript, I wrote him a letter telling him how much, as a *Daily* staffer, we had appreciated his letter. I explained my background in Japanese and my desire to do further graduate work in sociology and asked whether, if I learned some more sociology, I might become his student at Harvard in the future. He wrote back saying that, if I had worked at the *Daily*, I already had an education in sociology! He said he did not teach graduate students, but he would pass my letter on to the Japan specialists who did. That serendipitous sequence of events led to my admission to the doctoral program in sociology at Harvard in the fall of 1964.

After my year of language study in Japan, I abandoned the Stanford MA program and went straight to Harvard to begin my doctoral studies. The time period is particularly relevant here because my experience is quite inconceivable for graduate students today. It has much more to do with when I was in graduate school than my personal qualifications. By 1964, the Vietnam War was heating up, and male students were subject to the draft unless they had a student deferment. At the same time, higher education in the United States was expanding rapidly to meet the growing demand for a college-educated workforce. Universities were hiring faculty to meet the demand, and graduate programs were pushing out PhD candidates to fill those positions. Harvard's sociology graduate program addressed the situation by accepting students with a BA directly into a PhD program, in which students took their comprehensive exams at the end of the second year. If they passed their comps, they immediately began doing dissertation research. If they failed, they left the program with an MA.

Harvard's program was unusual in another way. It was part of a multidisciplinary unit called the Department of Social Relations that combined sociology, social anthropology, clinical psychology, and social psychology. The department had been formed several years earlier by dissidents who left anthropology and psychology departments that were less interested in the social aspects of behavior to join the sociologists. I knew none of that before I got there, just as I knew little about the formal discipline of sociology. There were nine students in my sociology cohort; I was the only woman, although there were plenty of female graduate students in the other parts of the department. The nine of us studied together amicably, and I experienced no discrimination from either students or faculty in the department.

The Harvard sociology program was dominated by Talcott Parsons and his complex structural-functional model. While most American sociology departments at the time were functionalist, Parsons's particular theory permeated the air at Harvard. Moreover, the only statistics course required for the PhD was a seminar in nonparametric statistics and Bayesian inference. The real statistics course was an elective that I did not take. The course that profoundly shaped my understanding of sociology was a seminar on symbolic interaction, whose readings have shaped my approach to sociology ever since. The department was also unusual in having not one but two Japan sociologists. Robert Bellah was the senior faculty member; he became my advisor and gave me an office next door to his. The other was Ezra Vogel, who had just joined the department. I had met him earlier when he gave a talk at Michigan. Vogel contacted me soon after I arrived and invited me to participate in a group that met together weekly to report on our reading in Japanese. I did not take any classes from either Bellah or Vogel but worked informally with both.

During the second year, while my classmates and I were preparing for comps, Bellah asked my thoughts about a dissertation topic. I offered two possibilities: politeness levels in Japanese and *tenkō*, or ideological conversion. I had read an article by psychiatrist Robert Jay Lifton, who had interviewed young Japanese participants in the 1960 Ampo protests and reported that many of them had made a *tenkō*.[8] I already knew two Japanese veterans of the Ampo protests from my summer in Japan, and the topic of protest resonated with my experiences at the *Daily*. Bellah ignored the politeness topic and pounced on *tenkō*. However, he said I needed to study the *real tenkō* problem, the mass *tenkō* of Japanese who had renounced their commitment to the illegal prewar Japanese communist movement under pressure from the authorities.[9] Bellah had done historical research for his sociology dissertation at Harvard, so I wrote a grant proposal to do research on prewar *tenkō* in Tokyo. This was another instance of serendipity that has profoundly shaped my subsequent research on Japan. It also reflected the atmosphere of the Harvard sociology doctoral program. They did not teach a lot of sociology, although we studied with some of the biggest names in the field. Instead, the program instilled the confidence that we could figure out how to do whatever our research required.

I received a fellowship to spend the next year in Tokyo studying *tenkō*. Bellah had arranged my affiliation with the Institute of Social Science at the University of Tokyo, which has been my academic home in Japan ever since. My advisor there was his friend, the political scientist Ishida Takeshi, who had a broad historical perspective. *Tenkō* was a major phenomenon in Japanese history of the 1920s and 1930s and was understood as history of thought (*shisōshi*). The major three-volume research study on the topic, which had come out a few years earlier, was a series of chapters by individual authors who had each studied the transitions in one individual's thinking over time.[10] I knew I did not want to take that approach.

Instead, I wanted to understand how mass *tenkō* had been organized by the government, how all the participants understood what they were doing, and how they interacted. That meant I also needed to understand as background how the underground communist movement arose and who participated in it. I discovered that after the war ended, a lot of previously classified administrative documents turned up in the used bookstores of Tokyo. The librarian at the institute had been collecting such documents from the Thought Section in the Criminal Affairs Bureau of the Ministry of Justice (Shihōsho Keijikyoku Shisōbu), the government agency that had prosecuted violators of the law under which members and associates of the illegal Communist Party had been prosecuted. In addition to detailed information about how the Thought Section carried out its mission, I found many formal *tenkō* statements of individuals and also collected writers' fictionalized accounts of their *tenkō* experiences. At the time I was doing my research in the mid-1960s, many people who had been involved in *tenkō* in the late 1920s and 1930s were still alive, so I was able to round out my library research with interviews of several participants. I learned to "see" institutions and social structure and to "hear" how people experienced *tenkō* pressure.

After a year and a half of fieldwork in Tokyo, I returned to Harvard in January 1968, where I was invited to become a teaching assistant for Riesman's special Harvard College course, which was an amazing experience. There were half a dozen teaching assistants, all of whom except me were already working professionals. We met for weekly dinners at the Riesman home, followed by a presentation on the next week's topic by one of the TAs. Bellah had moved to Berkeley by then, so Vogel took me under his wing. That spring, before I had finished my dissertation, I was hired to become the first woman faculty member in the University of Hawaiʻi's sociology department.

My job search would be unimaginable today. That year, there were three academic positions in the United States for a Japan specialist sociologist or anthropologist. Aside from the Hawaiʻi position, one was at the University of California, Santa Cruz, which had hired anthropologist Tom Rohlen, and the other was at Yale. Vogel, who had taught at Yale before returning to Harvard, warned me not to apply to Yale unless I really wanted to go there. Because I was about to get married that summer and my husband-to-be had said he would go anywhere west of the Rockies, I did not apply to Yale. However, on my way home from Japan in January, I had stopped for a few days in Honolulu, where Michael Weinstein, who was a year ahead of me in the Harvard sociology program, had just started teaching at the University of Hawaiʻi. When I visited him on campus, he said the department was hiring and the department chair wanted to meet me. I was embarrassed because I had come from the beach and was wearing rubber flip-flops, so Mike took off his shoes and went in barefoot! It turned out that the department was particularly interested in hiring a Japan specialist because over half the undergraduates at the University of Hawai'i were second- or third-generation Japanese Americans and the department offered a course on Japanese society. It had also just started a PhD program. I applied for the position, and, later in the spring, the chair of the search committee invited me to attend a conference of the Law and Society Association at Northwestern University. That was the full extent of my job search. No formal site visit or job talk, no PhD in hand.

Bill and I were married that summer in Michigan and moved to Hawai'i in August, where I began teaching a three-three course load. Bill found work as an urban lumberjack, a skill he had learned working summers for the Forestry Department in Flint, Michigan, cutting down trees dying of Dutch elm disease, which had paid for his education at the University of Michigan. I had no time during the first semester to do much more on the dissertation. On the day after Christmas, my husband announced that the dissertation needed to get finished, and I would have no newspapers, no television, no phone chats, and no beach outings until it was finished. I set to work under his watchful eye, and, six weeks later, the dissertation was completed. Following Harvard's practice at the time, if my three readers thought it was satisfactory, I did not have to do an oral defense. I received my degree that June without having returned for a defense.

As I began teaching, I also realized that I was walking away from Parsonian functionalist sociology. I set the dissertation aside and began thinking about my next project, which would return to my interest in postwar social movements in Japan. I had learned from the *tenkō* study how vulnerable prewar Japanese were to external social pressure when they were isolated in jail and subjected to pressure to change their ideas. Most of the people who made a *tenkō* had been unable to maintain their commitment to political ideas when they were isolated from other members of the group and subjected to severe pressure in a criminal justice system that was heavily tilted toward confession and contrition. The end of World War II and the subsequent Allied Occupation of Japan had led to a new Constitution that gave people more individual rights and shifted the balance in the criminal justice system. It had also transformed the educational system in ways that initially encouraged more individual thinking and independence. I thought this might constitute a natural experiment for comparison. Once the dissertation was finished, I began looking for such a situation in postwar Japan. While I had been doing library research in Tokyo, a major period of political protest was beginning to erupt on the streets outside. I had not paid much attention to it while I was there, and I left Japan before it reached its peak.

An Unexpected Diversion

Meanwhile, developments in Hawai'i drew my attention away from Japan. In our first year in Hawai'i, Bill, who had been interested in the legalization of abortion for some time, attended a public forum where he learned that a key Hawai'i legislator was seriously considering legislation that would remove all the penalties for abortion. When the state legislature held hearings a few months later, he encouraged me to testify. The hearings at the Capitol spread over two evenings and were covered by all the national news media. I met two other UH professors who were also testifying: Roy Smith, a pediatrician in the School of Public Health, and Mickey Diamond, a sexual behavior researcher in the Anatomy Department of the new medical school.[11] When we gathered at the legislature to watch the final passage of the legislation in 1970, the three of us realized it was now our responsibility to do research in the first state to legalize abortion.

For the main study, Smith and Diamond secured initial support to begin studying who was getting legal abortions and what kinds of medical issues there were. We added to our team Jay Palmore, a demographer with the Sociology Department and the East-West Center. Through Smith, we secured the cooperation of the major hospitals where all abortions would be performed. We obtained federal funding, and the study expanded. Much of it was basic survey research, which needed to be analyzed quantitatively. I had learned virtually no statistics at Harvard, but Palmore patiently taught me what I needed to know.

Meanwhile, Diamond negotiated with the Population Council to fund a book about how the law had passed, which enabled me to collect the materials from the legal process. I wrote the book during my first sabbatical, and Diamond wrote the chapter on the opposition.[12] In today's terms, it was a social movement study, but, at the time, there was no field of social movement studies, so I simply applied some of the tools I had used in my dissertation to try to understand how Hawai'i's abortion law came to be passed.

The abortion research came about by serendipity, in the sense that it happened to occur in a place where I was living, my husband encouraged me to get involved, and I ended up as part of a research group that had the unique opportunity to study it. Because of our federal funding, these studies also supported a fair number of graduate students. Although I was by far the most junior member of the team, I was treated as an equal member. Our papers were all coauthored, listing authors in order of participation, so I was first author on several of them.[13] I learned more traditional forms of sociological research through participating in this study for a decade, but my perspective remained symbolic interactionist.

In my fifth year at the University of Hawai'i, I was tenured and promoted to associate professor. I was teaching regularly about Japan, along with other sociology courses, and was able to develop some new courses that reflected my interests. I published an article from my dissertation and presented papers at conferences, but my publications primarily reflected my non-Japan research.[14] My time in graduate school preceded second-wave feminism, and, when it developed in the 1970s, I resisted the notion that I ought to study women and claim rights or preference because I was a woman. In retrospect, however, my decade of abortion research was an early contribution to women's studies.

While I was busy with this research in Hawai'i, Japan was experiencing a major protest cycle from the late 1960s to the early 1970s. I tried to keep abreast of what was happening, but the situation was too sensitive for the kind of research I hoped to do. Once again, serendipity opened the door. On May 30, 1972, Bill and I were watching the late-night news on television. In those days, the local news in Honolulu was broadcast at 6:00 p.m., but the national news was taped in California, put on a plane, and broadcast at 11:00 p.m. Sometimes you would stay up until then only to be informed that the news had not arrived. On this night, the news reported on a terrorist attack at Lod Airport (now Ben Gurion Airport) in Tel Aviv, Israel, that had been carried out by three young Japanese men from a radical group. Two had died in the attack, but one had survived and was in custody.

Bill immediately said, "You should interview him! Isn't that just what you've been looking for?" Three young Japanese men had carried out an extreme act out of political conviction, and now the one survivor was arrested and would be tested by isolation in a prison. But the prison was in Israel, not Japan. How was I going to interview him? Once again, my resourceful husband came to the rescue, reminding me that the Prime Minister of Israel at the time was Golda Meier, who had once been a Milwaukee schoolteacher. He encouraged me to write her a letter and simply ask if I could interview the Japanese prisoner, which I did. I also followed the military trial through the news media and tried to find out what I could about the situation over the course of the summer. Right after the trial ended, I received an air letter from the Attorney General of Israel, giving me permission to interview the survivor, Okamoto Kōzō. With an introduction from my former professor in Japan, Nagai Michio, who by then was affiliated with the Asahi newspaper company and doing research at the East-West Center on the UH campus, I was able to meet the Okamoto family in Kyushu on my way to Israel and take his textbooks to him. Traveling to Israel to interview the survivor was just the beginning. I needed to know about the group that had carried out this attack, how they related to other groups, and how the Japanese social control agencies had dealt with the protests, but I was too busy with other things.

Like most female foreigners studying in Japan, I had realized early on that we were treated as a non-gendered category and enjoyed many otherwise male privileges. My honors advisor at Michigan (Professor Hide Shohara) had been a woman, as had been my first sociology instructor there, and I also had good role models as the child of two working parents. I always assumed I could do everything: have a career, marry, and have children. I did have it all, thanks to finding a supportive husband and landing in Hawai'i, which already by the 1960s had a very high proportion of married women in the labor force. Even though there was no institutional support such as maternity leave, there were plenty of dual-income families around me, and it seemed that the wives who were not working outside the home were running home-based childcare for others. In the 1970s, we had two children, four years apart, the first born during a sabbatical and the second during a research grant. Both went to a home-based childcare in our neighborhood until they were old enough to go to preschool. Later, our children walked two blocks after school with many of their classmates to attend the local Japanese school. Our son had been born prematurely due to a medical error and had special needs that he later overcame, but I was able to keep working the whole time thanks to research support from the abortion project that had reduced my teaching load.

Back to Japanese Studies

A decade later, I was free to concentrate on Japan again and was awarded a Fulbright Fellowship for my next sabbatical (1982–1983). With my husband and two young children in tow, I went back to the Institute of Social Science at the University of Tokyo. Once again, there was an important element of serendipity in how my research developed. My sponsor was again Ishida, who asked what help I needed. I said I wanted to find a female research assistant who was close enough to the recent protests to help me make the necessary contacts. Within hours, his activist wife had found the perfect assistant: an older graduate student whose husband had been imprisoned during the protests. She took me to the office of Kyūen Renraku Sentā (Support Contact Center), the organization that had been created to provide social and legal support to New Left students who had been arrested. The Kyūen staff told me that a major trial had recently ended, and, while the cases were being appealed, I would be able to visit the defendants in prison using the regular visiting procedures. My assistant guided me through the process because she had done it herself. I could have used Fulbright contacts to get permission to do a single set of interviews, but using the ordinary visiting system has allowed me to continue prison interviews for this research with new prisoners for forty years. It took me a while to recognize that Kyūen itself embodied exactly the sort of capacity to resist the state that I was looking for.

Initially, I wanted to learn about the origins of the original Red Army Faction and trace its development.[15] I was soon introduced to Takazawa Kōji, an independent journalist with ties to the Red Army Faction, who had become a recognized authority on the Japanese New Left and had published several reliable books about it.[16] He lent me early Red Army publications to copy and introduced me to members to interview. I traced the Red Army Faction's subsequent offshoots, the Yodogō group that had hijacked a plane to North Korea in 1970 and remained there, the Japanese Red Army based in the Middle East, and the United Red Army, which had formed in Japan when remnants of the Red Army Faction merged with another group in 1971.[17] It was the trial of the latter group's leaders, the main United Red Army trial, that had just concluded and whose participants I was interviewing at Tokyo Detention House.[18] I was beginning to attend other trial sessions and observe the activities of support groups associated with specific trials. Takazawa introduced me to Mosakusha, the underground bookstore in Shinjuku that was also a creation of the late 1960s protest cycle. After that first year of intensive fieldwork, I began returning to Japan every summer to touch base and collect new materials. I always made the rounds of the Kyūen office, Mosakusha, and Takazawa's office near Mosakusha.

When we returned from our family year in Japan, Bill said I could go to Japan whenever I wanted, but he would stay home with the children. During those years, we usually also had a younger relative or family friend from Michigan living with us. When I first knew him in Japan, Bill had spent time in South Vietnam with some old friends who were US Army Special Forces advisors to the South Vietnamese military. Later, when I was doing dissertation research, he went back to Vietnam with press credentials to delve more deeply into the impact of the Vietnam War on the young Americans who participated in it. After we moved to Hawai'i, he continued to meet and interview people. He soon realized that what he wanted to write could be better done in fiction rather than journalism, so he took creative writing classes at the University of Hawai'i and later earned an MFA at the Iowa Writers' Workshop while I stayed in Hawai'i with the children. Thereafter, I provided the stable income so he could stay at home to write.

By the mid-1980s, I was ready to start writing a book about the Red Army Faction and its offshoots. The United Red Army trial that I had dropped into by chance in 1982 was a key puzzle, so I started there. It involved a terrible internal purge in the winter of 1970, when remnants of the Red Army Faction and another group had joined forces and retreated into the mountains, only to end up killing a dozen of their own members. Knowledge of the purge had sent shock waves through the Japanese New Left from which it never recovered; the movement participants could not understand how it had happened because they were trying to analyze it from within a Marxist framework. As a total outsider, I used what had become my standard analytical approach to examine the purge as a group process, trying to reconstruct what had happened from the various firsthand accounts that had been written plus my prison interviews with some of the surviving participants. On one of my annual short trips, Takazawa encouraged me to give him a manuscript that he could arrange to publish in Japan. On my next trip, I brought him the book manuscript draft, which opened with my interview in Israel, then traced the emergence of the Red Army Faction and its offshoots, concluding with very brief accounts of the Yodogō group in North Korea and the Japanese Red Army in the Middle East. I had written it as a straightforward analytical account of the movement, not as an academic work of sociology. He read it, approved, and made the arrangements with a Japanese publisher, who lent me the company's in-house translator.

Meanwhile, although I had tried to stay involved in Japanese Studies while concentrating on abortion research, word spread in the 1980s that I had "returned to Japanese Studies." I was soon involved in national committees concerned with Japanese Studies and a collaborative project that produced a coedited volume on *Conflict in Japan*.[19] Locally, I was also involved in creating the Center for Japanese Studies at the University of Hawai'i and became its founding director. Through my involvement with the Association for Asian Studies and my service on the Japan Foundation's American Advisory Committee, I volunteered to produce a directory of Japan specialists and Japanese Studies in the United States and Canada. I knew many of the people in the small field of Japanese Studies and understood how it was organized through area studies centers. I also knew how to do survey research and was able to base the project initially at the AAS offices in Ann Arbor. They lent me their programmer, who introduced me to the magical power of relational databases. I ended up doing four successive directory studies and writing three monographs analyzing the current state of Japanese Studies in the United States for the Japan Foundation (1988–2016).[20]

Midcareer as a Juggling Act

The first directory study concluded just before my next sabbatical (1989–1990), when another Fulbright Fellowship paid for one semester at the American School in Japan for our daughter, who was then in high school and comfortable in Japanese. Our son stayed in Honolulu with Bill and the young man from Michigan who lived with us. After the whole family was together in Japan for the Christmas break, Bill took the children back to Honolulu while I stayed in Japan for a few more months. My research topic that year was anti-emperor protest, which Takazawa had brought to my attention. Surrounding the death of the Shōwa emperor and the ceremonies for his successor's accession, there was a yearlong cycle of small, politically sensitive protests about these ceremonies. During that year, the translator and I worked on the Japanese translation of my manuscript on the Red Army groups, one chapter a month. Near the end of my time in Japan, Takazawa arranged to take the translator, Shiomi Takaya (the theorist of the original Red Army Faction who had just been released from prison), and me to see the sites in the mountains where the United Red Army purge had taken place. My write-up of that experience became the final chapter of the book. It was published the following year and was in print in Japan through two publishers for more than a decade.[21]

During the 1990s, my position as a tenured faculty member at the University of Hawai'i was an anchor of stability as our family dealt with the ups and downs of life. In the early 1990s, my widowed father developed Alzheimer's disease and became my responsibility. We moved him from Florida, and he lived with us until he died. It was a stressful time that led to open heart surgery for me, but we survived it and sent both children off to college on the mainland and successful lives and careers.

I had intended to revise the original English manuscript for a more academic American audience when I returned to Hawai'i in 1990, adding more about the two offshoots of the Red Army in exile in North Korea and the Middle East. However, just at that point, people who had returned from exile and been arrested began to go on trial in Japan. There was an enormous amount of new material that changed my understanding of many aspects of the movement. I spent the next two decades following those trials and their trial support groups, doing more prison interviews, and trying to understand what had really happened, particularly inside the two exile groups in North Korea and the Middle East. As I continued to follow events in real time, I began to realize that the trial support groups I had been following constituted an interesting social movement and were a small part of a much broader network. I expanded my focus from trial support groups to encompass the wide range of small, informal groups that constitute what I came to call Japan's invisible civil society. Later, I was able to do fieldwork on them during a short stint as a visiting researcher at the Institute of Social Science at the University of Tokyo. Eventually, that fell into place as the long-term impact on its former participants of the repression of the New Left protest cycle.

In 1993, Takazawa Kōji donated his extensive archive of Japanese social movement materials to the University of Hawai'i, which I facilitated as director of the Center for Japanese Studies. I became the de facto curator of the collection, responsible for overseeing and finding funding to catalog it. With advice from library staff, I used my knowledge of relational databases to set up a system for bilingual cataloging of the materials into an independent database, secured funding, and hired Japanese graduate students to do the cataloging. With a federal grant, we finished cataloging the original donation and produced a searchable bilingual bibliographic website that made the materials more accessible.[22] We have received several additional installments of materials that will keep us busy for the next few years. Visitors have come from all over the world to visit the collection as part of their research, and my own research has been enriched immeasurably by having the Takazawa Collection materials readily available.

While we were cataloging the Takazawa Collection in the 1990s, Takazawa was visiting the Yodogō group in North Korea regularly. He became suspicious about what they had been doing during their years of exile and began tracking the clues down all over the world. In 1998, he published a book that exposed the Yodogō group members in North Korea not as the lonely, trapped survivors of the 1970 hijacking that took them to North Korea but instead as converts to North Korea's national ideology of Juche. They had made a *tenkō* and had been working as North Korean operatives, luring several young Japanese to North Korea. I shared the book with the students working in the Takazawa Collection, who decided we should translate it into English. It was published in 2017 as *Destiny: The Secret Operations of the Yodogō Exiles*.[23]

New Directions and Reflections

In the same time period, through some comparative work with two other social scientists who had studied similar radical groups in the United States, Italy, and Germany, I began to understand the deep parallels between the Japanese protest cycle and the concurrent New Left protest cycles in other countries, which put into different perspective some features I had thought were characteristically Japanese. That led me to begin participating in the European Consortium for Political Research (ECPR), which has a lively section on political violence. My colleague Gilda Zwerman and I have shared our comparative studies of the US and Japanese protest movements with a European audience and gained new insights from their work.[24]

All this research on the Japanese New Left has appeared piecemeal in dozens of journal articles and book chapters, often as the response to invitations to contribute them, when I realized I had relevant material that could be analyzed to fit the topic.[25] Eventually, I have come to see the Japanese New Left protest cycle itself from a new perspective. My effort to understand the social context and dynamics of these movements from the perspective of their participants was both a strength and a weakness of my sociological approach. While I knew that the repression of the protest cycle had stifled and delegitimized protest activity for several decades, and while I understood the role of both the state social control agencies and Japanese mass media in perpetuating fear of protest throughout the society, it took me much longer to appreciate that the New Left protest cycle itself had produced an unprocessed cultural trauma that overwhelmed mainstream Japanese society and left traces that are still visible half a century later. Along the way, I have also coedited several books that provided an opportunity to promote the work of younger scholars in Japanese Studies.[26]

As I struggle to bring closure to my seemingly endless research project on the Japanese New Left and the Red Army groups, my original plan of adding a couple of chapters to the book I had published in Japanese to cover the groups in North Korea and the Middle East has turned into a trilogy, with my translation of Takazawa's *Destiny: The Secret Operations of the Yodogō Exiles* of *Destiny*, as one volume. I am nearly finished updating my original Japanese book to brings the events to the present and to reflect on their long-term impact on Japanese society, and I am starting work on the final volume on the Japanese Red Army in the Middle East.

When examining a life course retrospectively, it is very easy to trace a line that seems to lead in a clear direction and to ignore all the paths not taken. The 2022 war in Ukraine has reminded me that, when I left the Stanford Center in 1964, I came home via what was then the cheap way to get to Europe: the Japan-Soviet Friendship Society's ship from Yokohama to Nakhodka in the Soviet Far East, a short train ride to Vladivostok, and then an Aeroflot flight to Moscow (because the train across Russia was closed to outsiders due to conflict with China). Bill had taken that same route about a month earlier.

I was joined by a Stanford Center student who spoke Russian. I had learned some baby Russian as a toddler when we lived with my grandparents. We had learned in planning the trip that the one cheap way to travel in the Soviet Union without the required guide and expensive hotel room was to go car camping. I spent one day in Riga, Latvia (then part of the Soviet Union), finding my father's birthplace, while my friend went on to Finland. We met in Helsinki, rented a car, and went car camping from Leningrad to Moscow and then to Western Europe through Poland and East Germany before flying back to the United States.

By the time Bill and I moved to Hawai'i in 1968, I had a grand plan to extend my work on *tenkō* in Japan with comparative research on *samizdat* (self-published) underground literature in the Soviet Union and thought control in China. Following Ezra Vogel's practice, I began studying Russian in Honolulu with a tutor, a Russian grandmother from Saint Petersburg who had left during the 1918 revolution and eventually ended up in Hawai'i with her professor son and Japanese daughter-in-law. Bill and I took a modern Russian literature class together at the University of Hawai'i. We took two more summer car camping trips in Russia and Eastern Europe over the next few years, buying a car in Europe and then shipping it back to Hawai'i. I learned enough Russian to manage on those trips and even published a little article on abortion in the USSR that I translated with my tutor's help, but the *samizdat* literature had all been translated into English before I could read it in Russian.[27] I kept studying Russian for several years because my persistent tutor simply would not let me quit, while my grand comparative research plans were forgotten.

When Bill and I went to Hawai'i, we thought we were there on a lark and would move back to the "real world" in a couple of years. During our second winter, I was invited to a site visit at a mainland university with a Japanese Studies program. I came back feeling that we were already in a beautiful place with no winter, where I could do all the things I wanted to do and live without a lot of external academic pressure. Having sailed through life up to that point as an exciting adventure that took me where I wanted to go without even knowing it, settling into a life in Hawai'i seemed to be another fortuitous opportunity, and I never looked back.

In using the tools of sociology to analyze my academic life as a woman in Japanese Studies, I have emphasized the role that serendipity has played and how I have combined career with family. When I began to study Japanese in 1960, I never imagined where it would take me. When I finished my dissertation on prewar *tenkō* and thought about finding a postwar Japanese comparison, I never dreamed that the group I happened to latch onto would have offshoots that persisted into the twenty-first century and that I would still be writing about them even after I retired. At each juncture in my life, serendipity led to developments I could not have anticipated. My entire adult life has been woven out of following where those bits of serendipity led. I am grateful for all the opportunities I have been given. It has been a glorious ride.

Notes

[1] See "Remembering Betty Crocker Homemakers of Tomorrow," General Mills, April 9, 2013, https://www.generalmills.com/news/stories/remembering-betty-crocker-homemakers-of-tomorrow. I am in good company, as Senator Elizabeth Warren also was a Betty Crocker Homemaker of Tomorrow.

[2] Students for a Democratic Society (SDS, 1960–1974) was the student affiliate of the League for Industrial Democracy (founded in 1921). Its first president was Tom Hayden, who worked with the Student Nonviolent Coordinating Committee in the South in 1962, the year after his graduation from the University of Michigan. He wrote the basic draft of the Port Huron Statement, which was produced at the SDS convention held June 11 to 15, 1962, at a United Auto Workers (UAW) retreat outside Port Huron, Michigan. My roommate at the time was Sharon Jeffries, the daughter of a UAW staff member. She was one of several University of Michigan students who attended the convention and helped write the statement. The Port Huron Statement guided SDS and the New Left movement for the next few years, until SDS gave birth to the underground organization the Weathermen (1969–1977). "Resistance and Revolution: The Anti-Vietnam War Movement at the University of Michigan, 1965–1972," *Michigan in the World,* University of Michigan, 2015, www.michiganintheworld.history.lsa.umich.edu/antivietnamwar/; Tom Hayden, *Reunion: A Memoir* (New York: Macmillan Publishing Company, 1988).

[3] Senior Editors 1960–61, 1961–62, "An Editorial. . . " *The Michigan Daily*, May 30, 1961, Bentley Historical Library, University of Michigan. The *Daily* covered aspects of the story on several occasions in 1960 and 1961. The dean's resignation received similar treatment when it was announced on September 30, 1961. Robert Farrell, "Bacon Quits Post: To Remain Dean during Semester," *The Michigan Daily*, September 30, 1961, 1, 2. Archives of *The Michigan Daily* from 1890 to 2014 are held at the Bentley Historical Library at the University of Michigan. Searchable facsimile pages are available online and downloadable

in pdf format at https://digital.bentley.umich.edu/midaily. See also Linda Robinson Walker, "The Last Dean of Women," *Michigan Today*, Summer 2002, 6–9.

[4] The National Student Association was a confederation of student government organizations at American colleges and universities, founded in 1947 and active until it merged with another organization in 1978. It helped educate student leaders on a variety of issues, housed the United States National Student Press Association and its College Press Service, and supported connections between American students and their counterparts in other countries through various programs and services. During the 1950s and 1960s, it received covert financial support from the CIA, which was revealed in 1967, but it survived the scandal. See Louis Menand, "A Friend of the Devil," *The New Yorker*, March 16, 2015, https://www.newyorker.com/magazine/2015/03/23/a-friend-of-the-devil.

[5] Hatakeyama Yoshio was a director of the Japan Management Association and the author of several management bestsellers. Yoshio Hatakeyama, *Kaisha wa naze tsubureru ka* (Why Do Companies Fail?) (Tokyo: Manajimento raiburarī, 1958); Yoshio Hatakeyama, *Manager Revolution!: A Guide to Survival in Today's Changing Workplace* (Stanford, CT: Productivity Press, 1985).

[6] David Riesman, Nathan Glazer, and Reuel Denney, *The Lonely Crowd: A Study of the Changing American Character* (New Haven: Yale University Press, 1961).

[7] The letter begins: "During the past year I have become a one man Gideon Society for *The Michigan Daily* which seems to me one of the most alert, outspoken, and altogether interesting student dailies published anywhere in this country. Its coverage both of educational issues and of the world scene appear to me admirable—a model which I wish other student papers, more devoted to the trivial, the fraternal and the gossipy, might emulate." David Riesman, "Letters to the Editor: The Daily and the Nation," *The Michigan Daily*, May 10, 1961, 1.

[8] Robert Jay Lifton, "Youth and History: Individual Change in Postwar Japan," in *The Challenge of Youth*, edited by Erik H. Erikson (Garden City, NJ: Doubleday & Company, 1961), 260–290.

[9] Years later, I learned from a letter he wrote to *The New York Review of Books* that, as a student at Harvard, Bellah had belonged to the Communist Party and then had made a *tenkō*. Robert Bellah et al., "'Veritas' at Harvard: Another Exchange," *The New York Review of Books*, July 14, 1977, https://www.nybooks.com/articles/1977/07/14/veritas-at-harvard-another-exchange/.

[10] Shisō no Kagaku Kenkyūkai, *Tenkō*, 3 vols. (Tokyo: Heibonsha, 1959–1962).

[11] My testimony offered a sociological analysis of when women were most likely to seek abortions and why: if they became pregnant before they were married and ready to start families, particularly if they had ambitions beyond marriage and wanted to protect their futures; if they wanted to space their pregnancies between children; and if they experienced unwanted pregnancies when they already had all the children they could afford and could provide for. It was sheer speculation when I testified, but our later research demonstrated that it had been a very accurate prediction, with premarital pregnancy as the most common situation.

[12] Patricia G. Steinhoff and Milton Diamond, *Abortion Politics: The Hawaii Experience*. (Honolulu: University of Hawai'i Press, 1977).

[13] Articles include Patricia G. Steinhoff, "Pregnancy Decisions: Locating the Psychological Factors," *Pacific Health* 4 (1971), 11–15; Patricia G. Steinhoff, Roy G. Smith, and Milton Diamond, "The Characteristics and Motivations of Women Receiving Abortions," *Sociological Symposium* 8 (1972), 83–89; Roy Smith, Patricia G. Steinhoff, James A. Palmore, and Milton Diamond, "Abortion in Hawaii, 1970–71," *Hawaii Medical Journal* 32, no. 4 (1973), 213–220; Patricia G. Steinhoff, James A. Palmore, Roy G. Smith, Donald E. Morisky, and Ronald Pion, "Pregnancy Planning in Hawaii," *Family Planning Perspectives* 7, no. 3 (1975), 138–142; Patricia G. Steinhoff, "Premarital Pregnancy and the First Birth," in *The First Child and Family Formation*, edited by W. B. Miller and L. Newman (Chapel Hill, Carolina Population Center, 1977), 180–208.

[14] The advice I received when I left Harvard was either to write a book or publish chapters from my dissertation as articles. Because I wanted to publish a book, I did not publish articles from the core of the dissertation and instead presented my research in conference papers. I never did write a book based on my dissertation, but, two decades after the dissertation was submitted, Vogel arranged for it to be included in a series of unpublished Harvard Department of Social Relations dissertations that were published by Garland Press. Patricia G. Steinhoff, *Tenkō: Ideology and Societal Integration in Prewar Japan* (New York: Garland Publishing Company, 1991). Today, I encourage students to publish both articles and a book from their dissertation.

[15] For more explanation on the Red Army Faction (Sekigunha), see "Historical Periods and Major Events in Japanese Studies," pages 492–493.

[16] See, for example, Takazawa Kōji, *Destiny: The Secret Operations of the Yodogō Exiles*, edited and translated by Patricia G. Steinhoff, et al. (Honolulu: University of Hawai'i Press, 2017); *Heishitachi no yami* (The Soldiers' Darkness) (Tokyo: Marujusha, 1982); *Frēmu appu* (Frame-Up) (Tokyo: Shinchōsha, 1983); *Zenkyoto Graffiti* (Tokyo: Shinchōsha, 1984); *Shukumei* (Tokyo: Shinchōsha, 1998).

[17] For information on the United Red Army, see "Historical Periods and Major Events in Japanese Studies," page 493.

[18] Most trials in Japan are not continuous but instead meet several times a month, and the rare contested trial can go on for years. The seven United Red Army defendants facing the most serious charges, three from the Red Army side and four from Nagata Hiroko's group (see page 493), were initially supposed to be tried as one group in Tokyo District Court. Just as the trial was set to begin, Red Army leader Mori committed suicide in his cell at the Tokyo Detention House on New Year's Eve, 1971. The six remaining defendants, who faced long prison terms or the death penalty, were following the Kyūen strategy of mounting a strong defense to drag out the trial process (including appeals) for as long as possible, because even though they remain in solitary cells, persons in unconvicted detention have more privileges than regular prisoners serving sentences. (Ironically, persons awaiting the death sentence are also held in Tokyo Detention House because they are technically in unconvicted detention until the death sentence is carried out.) Then, in 1975, the Japanese Red Army in the Middle East carried out a hostage-taking

incident in Kuala Lumpur to free some of their colleagues in custody in Japan, and two of the United Red Army defendants were on the release list. Bandō Kunio from the Red Army Faction was released and joined the JRA in the Middle East, while Sakaguchi Hiroshi from Nagata's group (who had led the Asama Sansō siege, during which two policemen and a bystander were killed) declined and remained on trial in Tokyo. Two years later, the JRA staged an airline hijacking in Bangladesh to demand the release of a list of prisoners in Japan. Uegaki Yasuhiro, the lone remaining Red Army member in the trial was on the list for release, but he also chose not to go. A few years later, two more defendants from Nagata's group split off into a separate trial because they no longer agreed with the collective defense position. That left Nagata, Sakaguchi, and Uegaki when the initial trial finally ended in 1982. Nagata and Sakaguchi received death sentences, while Uegaki received a twenty-year sentence. It was those three whom I interviewed multiple times at Tokyo Detention House while they appealed their convictions, which were finally confirmed by the Supreme Court in 1993. Uegaki completed his sentence (which included time in unconvicted detention) and runs a bar in Shizuoka. Nagata died in prison of complications from a brain tumor in 2011, and, as of this writing, Sakaguchi remains on death row at Tokyo Detention House. For discussion of how I conducted prison interviews, see Patricia G. Steinhoff, "New Notes from the Underground: Doing Fieldwork without a Site," in *Doing Fieldwork in Japan*, edited by Theodore Bestor, Patricia G. Steinhoff and Victoria Lyon-Bestor (Honolulu: University of Hawai'i Press, 2003), 36–54. "Doing the Defendant's Laundry: Support Groups as Social Movement Organizations in Contemporary Japan," *Japanstudien* 11 (1999), 55–78, includes an explanation of unconvicted detention in the Japanese criminal justice system.

[19] Ellis S. Krauss, Thomas P. Rohlen, and Patricia G. Steinhoff, eds., *Conflict in Japan* (Honolulu: University of Hawai'i Press, 1984).

[20] See chapter 11, note 12, 179–180.

[21] *Nihon no Sekigunha* was later republished as *Shi eno ideologi: Nihon Sekigunha* (Tokyo: Iwanami bunko, 2003). A shorter analysis of the United Red Army purge was published in English as "Death by Defeatism and Other Fables: The Social Dynamics of the Rengo Sekigun Purge," in *Japanese Social Organization*, edited by Takie Sugiyama Lebra (Honolulu: University of Hawai'i Press, 1992), 195–224.

[22] University of Hawai'i, "The Takazawa Collection of Social Movement Materials at the University of Hawai'i," June 14, 2001, http://www.takazawa.hawaii.edu.

[23] The original Japanese book, Takazawa Kōji, *Shukumei*, won the Kodansha Prize for nonfiction in 1998. The English translation by my students, and with translator's notes, an introduction, and a short follow-up chapter by me, was published as Takazawa Kōji, *Destiny: The Secret Operations of the Yodogō Exiles*.

[24] See, for example, Gilda Zwerman, Patricia G. Steinhoff, and Donatella della Porta, "Disappearing Social Movements: Clandestinity in the Cycle of New Left Protest in the United States, Japan, Germany, and Italy," *Mobilization* 5, no. 1 (2000): 85–104; Gilda Zwerman and Patricia G. Steinhoff, "When Activists Ask for Trouble: State-Dissident Interactions and the New Left Cycle of Resistance in the United States and Japan," *Repression and Mobilization*, edited by Christian Davenport et al. (Minneapolis: University

of Minnesota Press, 2005), 85–107; "The Remains of the Movement: The Role of Legal Support Networks in Leaving Violence while Sustaining Movement Identity," *Mobilization: An International Journal* 17, no. 1 (2012), 67–84.

[25] See, for example, Patricia G. Steinhoff, "Hijackers, Bombers and Bank Robbers: Managerial Style in the Japanese Red Army," *Journal of Asian Studies* 48, no. 4 (1989), 724–740; "Death by Defeatism"; "Three Women Who Loved the Left: Radical Women Leaders in the Japanese Red Army Movement," in *Re-Imaging Japanese Women*, edited by Anne Imamura (Berkeley: University of California Press, 1996), 301–323; "Mass Arrests, Sensational Crimes, and Stranded Children: Three Crises for Japanese New Left Activists' Families," in *Imagined Families, Lived Families: Culture and Kinship in Contemporary Japan*, edited by Akiko Hashimoto and John Traphagan (Albany, NY: State University of New York Press, 2008), 77–110; "No Helmets in Court, No T Shirts on Death Row: New Left Trial Support Groups," in *Going to Court to Change Japan: Social Movements and the Law in Contemporary Japan*, edited by Patricia G. Steinhoff (Ann Arbor: University of Michigan Center for Japanese Studies, 2014), 17–44.

[26] My most recent coedited book is David H. Slater and Patricia G. Steinhoff, *Alternative Politics in Contemporary Japan: New Directions in Social Movements* (Honolulu: University of Hawai'i Press, forthcoming in 2024).

[27] Patricia G. Steinhoff, "Abortion Data from the Soviet Union (Summary Report of "Statistical Analysis of Outcomes of Pregnancies,' by N. S. Sokolova)," *Abortion Research Notes* 1, no. 3, November (1972).

13

I Came, I Saw, I Stayed

Sumie Jones

This essay is my way of rereading and critiquing my life meandering into new paths at the periphery of the discursive development of comparative literature and Japanese Studies in my new homeland since the 1960s. I will narrate the course of my career not chronologically but according to ten thematic rubrics.

SUMIE JONES is professor emerita at Indiana University Bloomington, where she taught from 1978 to 2006. Specializing in eighteenth-century comparative literature and arts, with a focus on Japan's Edo and Meiji periods, Jones is known for her unique interpretation of literary, visual, and dramatic texts from the perspectives of psychoanalysis, semiotics, and theories of gender and sexuality. Her books include *Retorikku to shite no Edo* (*The Rhetoric of Edoism*, 1992). She is the editor in chief and featured translator of a three-volume anthology of early modern Japanese urban literature: *A Kamigata Anthology: Literature from Japan's Metropolitan Centers, 1600–1750* (2020), *An Edo Anthology: Literature from Japan's Mega City, 1750–1850* (2013), and *A Tokyo Anthology: Literature from Japan's Modern Metropolis, 1850–1920* (2017). She received the Indiana University Trustees Teaching Award (2002) and the Lindsley and Masao Miyoshi Prize for Lifetime Achievement in Translation and Editing (Donald Keene Center of Japanese Culture, Columbia University, 2017).

I arrived at Japanese Studies late and from the outside. The end of the war removed the cultural blindfolds from the eyes of the Japanese, who began to voraciously take in anything foreign. Having studied English and French in college, I came to the United States as a graduate student. Once away from Japan, like many other foreign students, I began to see my homeland in a new light and to acquire insight into Japan's culture and society. This gave me a comparative perspective on what I saw and experienced while living in the United States for decades.

An ongoing experience defies understanding; it can be interpreted only retrospectively through layered films of accumulated perspectives gained from other experiences. The process will never reach a definitive conclusion about the meaning of the experience but will reveal impressions of the experience that were not visible before. This essay is my way of rereading and critiquing my life meandering into new paths at the periphery of the discursive development of comparative literature and Japanese Studies in my new homeland since the 1960s. I will narrate the course of my career not chronologically but according to ten thematic rubrics.

Close Reading

I was born into a clan of wholesale tea merchants in the city of Kōfu, west of Tokyo, at the time when nationalism was rapidly rising. Years before my birth, the authorities, threatened by the rise of communism and anarchism among the young, took to censoring leftist publications and imprisoning the offenders. As teenagers, my uncles and their friends were by no means behind the time in their private study of progressive ideas. I later heard a few household employees recalling the method they had invented for concealing vulnerable books during police raids. Together with some of the family's female members, they ran out of the house, hiding the vulnerable items under their aprons to later find better hiding places for them. Under the circumstances, new books were rarely published, and my childhood reading was limited to the classics held in our family house.

Lovers of literature and the arts were conspicuous in my parents' branch of the clan. Three generations of family, household employees, and friends living in the same, albeit spacious, house meant that parental care could not always reach me and my younger brothers. A precocious and sickly child, I was often left to the care of my uncles and their friends, who taught me to read, write, and sing. My father, who had studied the *Man'yōshū* (*The Collection of Ten Thousand Leaves*) with master poet-scholar Saitō Mokichi, sat with me before dinner each day to listen to my recitation of one long poem or another from Japan's first poetic anthology.

The devastating last stages of the war put a stop to the idyllic course of my private education. My youngest uncle, at age fourteen, had been chosen to enter the National Army Cadet School, and the rest of my uncles and their friends, including those who had just entered college, were drafted by the time I was five. I read and reread the sixteen volumes of *An Anthology for Young Citizens of Japan* (*Nihon shōkokumin bunko*) and other books left behind by my uncles, as little else was available.[1] The city library offered only children's books promoting war. My paternal grandmother was lauded in the local newspaper as the "Mother of Soldiers": her youngest son had volunteered to join the air force, later to be part of the kamikaze team, and her five older sons had been drafted, two of them to die before they reached any battlefield. My grandmother kept a folded clipping of the article in the bottom drawer of her comb box, locking up her grief along with her bejeweled hair ornaments, which she never wore for the rest of her life.

After the war, one of my aunts, an avid reader and book collector, became my guide. I read with her Meiji and Taishō period renditions of Stendhal and Dumas *fils* as well as novels by Ozaki Kōyō, Kuroiwa Ruikō, and other nineteenth-century writers. Her penchant for the romantic and weird rendered my repertory necessarily lopsided, but I was, in all likelihood, the best-read third and fourth grader in the prefecture. For forty years after the end of the war, my aunt hosted at her house monthly group reading sessions on *The Tale of Genji* (*Genji monogatari*) and group rehearsals on the Noh performance. Several women participated in both series, my mother and I attending occasionally. It is hard to tell how many times they went through *The Tale of Genji* from the beginning to the end over the decades. The repetition of reading aloud in both groups allowed me to taste the physical character of the text. The Noh group had a shorter life; it disintegrated itself after a production at a hotel of *The Angel's Robe* (*Hagoromo*), the standard number for beginners.

While in middle school, I took to typing in English several plays by George Bernard Shaw and Oscar Wilde word for word on onionskin paper with a hand-me-down Remington typewriter. Typing them letter by letter made me obsessively interested in how written works were put together. Both playwrights were in rebellion against the established system and often played against both sides of any argument, which evoked my sympathy, and the sharp irony with which they wrote glued my eyes to the pages. I did not copy prose narratives, which would have taken too long to type. Instead, I devoured European novels in Japanese translation. My renditions of what I had read the night before kept several classmates entertained on our commutes home during our middle school and high school years. In retelling a novel daily in a short space of time to a small and regular audience, my instinctive approach was the so-called "*explication de texte*," a primitive representation of a work as a matter of literal contents, form, and rhetorical figures. My version excluded any consideration of the author or the work's social and political background. I was thus amenable to the logic of New Criticism when I grew up to be a graduate student in the United States.[2]

Theater

I have always been a frustrated actor. After a few productions of children's plays in the neighborhood, I brought to the director Alfred Lord Tennyson's *Enoch Arden*, probably translated and illustrated by Nakahara Jun'ichi, a popular illustrator, designer, publisher, and entrepreneur who invented the sensitive aesthetics for the rising girls' culture in postwar Japan.[3] I proposed to convert the poem into a stage script for the next production, with myself playing the role of the tragic hero, the sailor who loses his wife to his best friend. The director told me gently that the poem was too difficult and its theme inappropriate for middle schoolers. I was bringing Tennyson to a troupe whose repertoire consisted of *Little Red Riding Hood* and *Snow White*. Besides, she, a high school student, would have been appalled by my male chauvinistic heroism. Looking back, I turn red: what an unbearably insensitive smart aleck I must have been!

Ever since I was in grade school, my ambition was to major in English literature at the University of Tokyo, where I expected to join the likes of the creative group of students who had surrounded Natsume Sōseki (1867–1916) at the turn of the century. I ignored the fact that the state of postwar Japan could not bring about a second coming of Sōseki or a set of students with the leisure needed for the pseudo-scholastic conversations that I envied them for. Intending to realize my ill-informed ambition, I prepared to take the University of Tokyo's entrance examinations in eight subject areas. At the time of application for admission, my dream was crushed by my oldest aunt's declaration that girls in the clan were not allowed to go to coeducational universities. I was startled to be categorized out of the blue as a girl. Being the eldest of the girls, I was told to be a model for my female cousins by going to a woman's junior college.

Neither my obnoxious literariness nor my interest in theater found an outlet at the junior college division of Tokyo Women's Christian University—until I stumbled into a session of the Shakespeare Study Society, of which all the members were juniors and seniors from the university division. They studied one of the master's plays throughout the academic year and performed it, in the original language, on stage at the end. This time, it was *Hamlet*. I, a freshman, was given a few minor roles, including the sailor who delivers Hamlet's letter to Horatio. Mrs. McAlpine, our acting coach, dismissed my idea of wearing a black eye patch and carrying a telescope (what ludicrous stereotyping I did with the role!). A talented actor herself, she showed me how a sailor looked and moved, giving me my first training in acting. All day long, I practiced my sailor walk, with my bottom dropped low and knees wide apart, a posture I could not shake off long after the production.

For my junior year, dodging my relatives' watchful eyes, I enrolled myself in the evening division of the Faculty of Letters (Bungakubu) at Waseda University,

Figure 13.1: Tsubouchi Memorial Theatre Museum, Waseda University. Photograph courtesy of Waseda University.

the leading institution for the study of literature and a hotbed for student acting. Tsubouchi Memorial Theatre Museum, built in honor of Tsubouchi Shōyō, the first Japanese translator of Shakespeare's entire oeuvre, and modeled on the Elizabethan Fortune Playhouse, symbolized Waseda University's authority in theater research (figure 13.1). My three brothers, then in college and in high school, contributed their allowances to cover my admission fees, and the university's dean of academic programs gave me a part-time job in his office, completing my excuse for staying in Tokyo for a few years of experience, which at that time was commendable for a woman before marriage.

Acting, not being part of Waseda's curriculum, was left to student groups, who trained themselves to present their art on campus and at theaters in the vicinity. My attempt, however, to associate myself with student theater failed dismally. What turned them off was my critique of Konstantin Stanislavski's system (called "method" in American theater and film industries) and my disdain for plays superficially portraying the downtrodden with rags on their backs and pots and pans dangling from their waists.[4] They were all "angry young men" in the fashion of John Osborne's *Look Back in Anger*.[5] Was I aiming at enlightening the theater enthusiasts by demonstrating how Mrs. McAlpine would direct a Shakespeare production or how Comédie Française would handle Racine? My hubris, based on my knowledge of established plays and dramaturgy, did not go unpunished: the postwar tide of socially conscious theatricality passed by me without even a nod.

As my second choice, I knocked on the door of the popular *Rakugo* Study Group, wishing to learn the Edo-style staged narratives. My hopes were dashed again on the grounds that *rakugo* was an exclusively men's art. Much later, at Indiana University, I learned that Elizabeth Armstrong, one of my students, had found a crack through which to slip into the male fortress of comic narration.[6] She was the first woman, as well as one of the very few non-Japanese, who performed in public in Tokyo. While in Bloomington, she delivered, in her crisp Edo-style Japanese, two classics with an entertaining introduction in English. Much to my surprise, Armstrong was entirely self-taught: she repeatedly imitated each master's performance on sound tapes. A disciple learns by imitating his master sitting in front of him. She did the same in front of a tape recorder.

Kabuki, a familiar form of entertainment from childhood, turned into a subject of study while I was at Waseda thanks to Gunji Masakatsu, who asked me to act as interpreter for his seminar on kabuki. He assigned dance an equal importance as drama in kabuki's aesthetic, psychological structure, history, and anthropological context.[7] To me, dance scenes had seemed a necessary evil: a boring portion that the audience had to put up with while waiting for the next dramatic moments. While acting as an interpreter in Gunji's seminar for an American scholar of dance, Margaret Erlanger, I learned much about kabuki and acquired some skill in representing this theatrical form in English. Harboring no interest in each other's work, Erlanger and I never met outside the seminar, but I learned later that she founded dance education as a subject for college curriculum.

Two decades later, I taught my dream course, "History of Kabuki," at Indiana University. We concluded with a campus production of a play in English, *The Love Suicides at Jordan River* (set on the bridge over a little stream on campus). It was an all-student production, written in English by Vince Amlin based on my outline that combined a seventeenth-century *jōruri* puppet play and a mid-nineteenth-century kabuki play, directed by Vanessa Nolan, with stage and prop design by Joannah Peterson, and acted by the rest of the class. Tsutsumi Harue, one of my dissertation advisees at the time, helped me advise the student actors for this first production on campus. Tsutsumi had already debuted as a playwright in Japan with her *Kanadehon Hamlet* (*Kanadehon Hamuretto*), a tragicomic play depicting a rehearsal for an imagined first production in Japan of Shakespeare's *Hamlet* by kabuki actors under the direction of Morita Kan'ya XII (1846–1897), the leader in reforming kabuki for the modern age.[8] The reputation of the campus production of *The Love Suicides at Jordan River* was such that our troupe was invited to put it on for an audience of hundreds at the third annual "Asia in the Curriculum" Symposium in Indianapolis. Over the years, Tsutsumi and I have become theater-hopping comrades, with her as my coach in my pursuit of current productions of kabuki and modern Japanese plays.

Having practiced Noh chanting and acting with my aunt's group, I came to read and chant the texts more seriously under the influence of my maternal uncle, a businessman who took daily lessons after work with a Hōshō School master.[9] By the time I was in graduate school, he was called upon to be part of the chorus for the *shite*, or the lead actor. For years, the chances I had to attend a Noh performance came in the form of tickets sent by this uncle when he was scheduled to be on stage at Suidobashi Noh Theater (currently known as Hōshō Nōgakudō) in Tokyo.

I taught Noh plays in translations by Royall Tyler[10] in "Drama," one of the required genre courses in comparative literature, and in a seminar on premodern Japanese culture, extensively using performances on VHS and DVD. A graduate student, Shelley Fenno Quinn, who had studied for six years with great masters of the Kanze School, was a guide for my seminar as she demonstrated instrumental and dance performance for us. For my translation anthology described below, Quinn contributed translations of anonymous Edo-period parodies of Noh plays—homoerotic comedies that stay brilliantly close to the original—juxtaposing each classical Noh play and the parody side by side and line by line, both done in her English rendition, which, in turn, adheres in wording and rhythm closely to the original and its parody.[11] I suspect that Quinn is the first legitimate Noh scholar who has dared to present bawdy parodies in translation.

Political Movements

Waseda University turned out to be not only a garden of literary learning but also a fortress for radical student movements. Loud shouts from demonstrations no longer seemed discordant to the silent austerity of the surrounding buildings. When Zengakuren (All Japan Student Federation) mounted an all-campus strike, I successfully broke the scrum formed by a dozen or so of those leftist students in front of the Faculty of Letters building by arguing with them. Inside, Suzuki Yukio, professor of English, and I had a one-on-one session on Laurence Sterne's *The Life and Opinions of Tristram Shandy, Gentleman*.[12] Its peculiar narrative strategy shunned any simple-minded meaning-seeking reading, running ahead of the poststructuralist theories that captured my interest later.

The pressing issue for the student protesters in 1960 was the proposed revision of the US-Japan Security Treaty that warranted the United States to occupy Japan. The treaty required renewal that year, and President Dwight D. Eisenhower was expected to visit Japan to sign it. With slogans like "No more security pact!" and "Eisenhower go home!," some impassioned protesters rose in insurrection, and the police turned to violence. The riotous groups were only a small part of the three hundred thousand citizens that formed a packed demonstration in front of the National Diet Building on one day in June that year and swarmed into the building on another, attempting to prevent the signing of the treaty. The treaty was forcefully signed by Prime Minister Kishi Nobusuke (in office 1957–1960), who was compelled to resign and to resolve his cabinet and the National Diet. President Eisenhower did not land in Japan.

My most-admired professor was Kurahashi Ken, specialist of American literature and activist for peace. Because American literature was considered beneath the distinction of the Faculty of Letters and good only for the likes of the Faculty of Education (Kyōiku gakubu), I had to wait until I entered graduate school before I could study with him. As a member of his first seminar, I took part in the group's barhopping, dinners at his house, and visits to theaters where he directed performances, but I declined to come to walks in protest of the US occupation of Okinawa.[13] I had the cynical view that every revolution led not to a world of equality but only to another oppressive power. To me, Marxian "superstructure" constituted the entire world, rendering the "base" meaningless, whether or not a revolution took place there. Kurahashi always took the remaining five students on long marches around the Hibiya Park. Excluding my bookish self from activism, I entirely missed out on the historically significant moments, which became lodged deeply into the foundation of my friends' intellectual and ethical principles.

Even a political ingénue, however, acquires some sense of awareness once she crosses the Pacific Ocean, as I did in the mid-1960s. My kind host family proposed to call me "Suzie," a name "anyone could pronounce and remember." I protested and asked them to call me "Sumie." I later heard frequently the proud remark about the United States being "a melting pot," which represented the ideology of embracing other peoples to assimilate them into a unified utopia that was America. In contrast, Japan showed its true colors as a closed culture of "Japanese uniqueness" that did not welcome others. Japan accepted immigrant workers and gave them national health benefits but did nothing to let them settle comfortably as Japanese. People who did not look or behave Japanese in the expected ways were packed in the "*gaijin*" (foreigner) category forever. In opposite ways, both cultures suppressed the individual.

Gender and race prejudices were not on my radar for a long time. When I came to Indiana after completing my study in Seattle, I saw nothing wrong in finding only three women among thirty-some members of the faculty of the Department of Comparative Literature. One was a lecturer, who left after a while, and the other two were associate professors who retired years later without being promoted to full professorship. By the time I became a full professor, women faculty members had increased to a respectable number. A colleague in the Department of East Asian Languages and Cultures, Kyeong-Hee Choi, who was writing her dissertation on postcolonial and maternal narratives in Toni Morrison and others, asked me to find out if I had been the first Asian woman in our university to be promoted to the rank.[14] Her question to me sounded odd, but, to satisfy her curiosity, I called the faculty records office and learned that I was, in fact, the first in the College of Arts and Sciences, but someone in the School of Optometry had been promoted before me.[15] The two of us turned out to be the only Asian women promoted on the entire campus of more than ten schools. This pointed to a racial and gender problem at the School of Arts and Sciences and the University as a whole and shocked some political consciousness into me.

Gender and Feminism

In our chats over lengthy dinners, Choi taught me lessons on politically critical thinking. I was a poor student interested only in literary art and theories as independent from the real world around me. Very likely due to my earliest education by teenage boys, the authors such as Yosano Akiko, Hayashi Fumiko, and others came to attract my attention much later. At Waseda, where many women were being admitted to the English Department at the time, Charlotte and Emily Brontë, and particularly Virginia Woolf, were the popular topics for graduation theses. I admired these women writers but disliked the discourse of women appropriately writing solely about women. My thesis was on Charles Dickens in light of the Industrial Revolution.

At the University of Washington, I was mistaken for a promoter of the women's liberation movement because I decorated my office with a nude photograph of the suicidal bodybuilding author Mishima Yukio trying to look like a samurai at the moment of disembowelment that I had cut out of *Life* magazine. Roger Sale, a charismatic member of the English department and a spokesperson for progressive ideas in *The New York Review of Books*, took the framed photograph as my way of objectifying men to challenge the patriarchy. By his recommendation, I was taken to be a leading member of the "women's lib" on campus for a short while.

While an assistant professor at Indiana University, I was appointed a Bunting Fellow at the Mary Ingraham Bunting Institute, Harvard University. Not only did I have limited knowledge of feminism but I was also the only fellow who was writing about male authors. I objected to early feminism for endeavoring to knock down the phallus while at the same time raising women's power into something erect and high—a phallic matriarchy. My fellow fellows at the Bunting Institute, however, were not so militant and engaged me in their debates on theory.

Among the fellows, Barbara Johnson, already one of the leading figures of the Yale school of poststructuralist theory, met with three or four of us at her office from time to time. I remember her demonstration of the method of deconstruction using a story by Zola Neale Hurston.[16] Unfamiliarity with the author or the work's context effectively isolated it for me as a pure text, as it was in the case of a successful New Critical analysis. Diane Middlebrook reported on her findings on poet Anne Sexton, of whom she later published a controversial biography.[17] At a few of those sessions, I demonstrated methods of semiotics in reading verbal texts and images. Discussions at those meetings and conversations at occasional dinners at Cambridge restaurants were stimulating but did not leave a distinct mark on my own writing.

Ellen Bassuk, a member of the Department of Psychiatry at Harvard Medical School, attended my lecture at Radcliffe College on reading William Hogarth's lithographs and corrected my use of Freudian theory of transference in my analysis of the act of reading images. The materials she left on my lap taught me much about feminist revisionism of Freudian theory. I was not convinced that Freudian transference could not be metaphorically applicable to the act of reading images, but I removed the idea from an article I later published on the verbal and pictorial art of Hogarth in comparison with book illustrations by Kitao Masanobu (alias of the fiction writer Santō Kyōden, 1761–1816).[18]

In my criticism of feminism as a way of erecting another system to replace patriarchy, I was looking for a theory that would be androgynous: emphasizing the sameness and interchangeability of the power of signification between the sexes that came with a sign that was horizontal instead of vertical, liquid instead of solid.

Feminist awareness of this semiological difficulty in existing concepts, and feminists' struggle to discover more flexible ways for talking about gender, inspired a conference, "Feminism Beside Itself," which was held in Bloomington. It critiqued the excited and confused state feminism had reached and at the same time explored ways in which an alternative feminism, outside and yet close by, could be discovered. The conference was in preparation for a book edited by Diane Elam and Robyn Wiegman.[19] Judith Allen and I were invited as general discussants on the themes of the project. The intention, it turned out, was not a confrontation of perspectives between a feminist and an anti-feminist: the two of us were not diametrically opposed to each other in many ways. The project, we found, was to critique, rather than affirm, the history and goals of feminism. It was an attempt at decentering feminism and opening it up to more fluid thinking. Elam's own deconstructive analyses certainly brought feminism close to my theory of reading.

My tardiness in approaching feminism was chiefly caused by my focus on the eighteenth century. I was studying Diderot, Boileau, Voltaire, Swift, Pope, and Fielding, as well as their Chinese and Japanese counterparts—all male writers whose wonderfully witty and ironic works did not include a woman's subjective consciousness. No wonder I seldom found a woman sitting with me in a seminar! Whether in Chinese, Japanese, English, or French, eighteenth-century literature was full of scholasticism, satire, comedy, scatology, and pornography, and that, I gathered, made the eighteenth-century offensive or uninteresting to women. In Japan, women who specialized in Edo-period literature were rare, indeed. This meant that I would be collaborating with men mostly in my writing, editing, and organizing projects for years to come.

Two feminists captured my attention very early. One was Camille Paglia, a controversial social and cultural critic often appearing on television and journals, who was dubbed an "anti-feminist feminist." Her *Sexual Personae: Art and*

Decadence from Nefertiti to Emily Dickinson, by dividing Western civilization into the orthodox strand represented by Rousseau and the rebellious half represented by de Sade, assigned value and power to writings of dissention through her analyses of literature ancient and modern.[20] She wrote and spoke "to offend," which struck me as a brilliant rhetorical strategy. The book never failed to cause heated debates in my seminars like "Sexuality and the Arts, East and West" and "Premodern Japanese Literature."

The other is novelist and essayist Matsuura Rieko, whose writings I have followed since I read her *Natural Woman* (*Nachuraru ūman*) before its publication.[21] It was the first blatantly lesbian novel I had encountered. Her "gentle castration" (to borrow from the title of her essay) in all her works appealed to me.[22] She removes the phallus from the male, or female, sexual organ and decentralizes coitus within human relationships while highlighting writing and reading as sources of both pleasure and difficulty in relationships. Her pursuit of narrative as an exploration of her deconstructive theory culminated in the two-volume *Oyayubi P no shugyōjidai* (*The Apprenticeship of Big Toe P* by Michael Emmerich's rendition).[23] In *The Reverse Version* (*Ura vājon*), she explores interactions between writing and reading/critiquing through the nonsexual cohabitation of two women who never see each other, one writing fiction, the other reading and criticizing its daily segments.[24] The author sets up a pure, or blank, setting untainted by sexuality or concrete details of quotidian life in order to pursue her exploration into the relationship between writing and reading.

I failed to persuade any of my theory-minded graduate students to choose Matsuura as her dissertation topic or to translate the two-volume novel until Joanne Quimby proposed to include Matsuura in her dissertation. I remember a long chat with her, standing outside the building in which the Department of East Asian Languages and Cultures was housed. According to Quimby's later recollection, I was "gushing" about *The Apprenticeship of Big Toe P* and lamented my own "boring heterosexual life." Indeed, Matsuura reduced heterosexuality to nothing, or rather erased any distinction between the subject and object, as well as between heterosexuality, homosexuality, bisexuality, and transsexuality. Quimby proceeded to interview Matsuura in Japan and successfully completed her dissertation with my colleague Edith Sarra, whose expertise in the study of women in literature far exceeded my half-baked knowledge.[25] Books by Sarra impressed me with her analyses of courtly living and storytelling on the part of women in *The Tale of Genji* and other writings by women of ancient Japan.[26]

My Theory of Overtext

When I entered an MA program at the University of Washington, the discipline of comparative literature was graduating from the narrow study of influence relationships. René Wellek and other founding fathers of comparative literature at Yale University organized into "periods" and "-isms" the literature of the entire "world," which for them was Europe.[27] The newly fashionable discipline excluded Asia so that Asianists were obliged to manipulate accepted geographical and literary historical categories by treating, say, Tang Dynasty poetry as a variation of Romanticism.

Structuralism, a theory of anthropological and linguistic systems of human culture and communication proposed by Claude Lévi-Strauss and others, soon liberated us from the confines of national languages, separate cultures, and historical periods. The concepts of mythology and kinship made it easy to discuss literature across cultures and disciplines. We departed from the notion of "work" that New Criticism had taught us earlier and began to talk about "text." I discovered poststructuralism after I began teaching, which led me to my study of the semiotics of reading and writing.

I learned to think of Japanese literature in the light of theory as I attended an NEH Summer Institute entitled "Curricular Models for Japanese Literature and Criticism," codirected by Masao Miyoshi and Earl Miner and held on Princeton's campus. Miyoshi, a long-established critic of British Victorian literature, had just turned to modern Japanese fiction.[28] "So, you are Sumie," Miyoshi said, extending his hand for a handshake at the first party for the institute, "Your Tanizaki article is brilliant and so wrongheaded." "What a coincidence!" I shot back, "Your *Accomplices of Silence* is brilliant and soooo wrongheaded." He replied, with a smile, "I love women who talk back." Irked by this male-chauvinistic declaration but not finding a quick retort, I proceeded to attack his book for its English-speaking perspective and Aristotelian logocentrism. He and I argued all summer on the rare occasions when we found ourselves face-to-face. He did not share the sort of precocious literary upbringing and canonical Japanese legacy that Yoshiyuki Nakai (discussed in more detail below) and I did, but arguing with Miyoshi gave me a different sort of inspiration.[29] After that summer, Miyoshi and I involved each other in our collaborative work. We continued to argue about literature and criticism on the phone far into his old age.

Miner's name had been familiar to me as editor and coeditor of two of the twenty-volume anthology of John Dryden's collected works.[30] In addition, he had been writing on and translating Japanese linked poetry from Sōgi to Matsuo Bashō.[31] At the time, Miner and I seemed to be the only early modern East-West comparatists in the United States. I included him in *The Tale of Genji* conference (described below) and collaborated with him on a book project as well as in panels at the International Comparative Literature Association (ICLA) congresses.

It was an intense eight-week seminar, during which the participants lost sleep debating matters of theory and Japanese literature. On weekends, I typed my dissertation poolside while the others swam and partied. On nights when most fellows had dates, Chieko Ariga and I, left alone in the dorm, would sit in the kitchen, she drinking sake and I a yogurt drink, and talk about mismatched subjects, she on the gender problem of Japan's education and communication and I on my interpretation of the assigned texts of the day. At wee hours, Ariga often broke into singing *enka* popular songs in her alluring voice.[32]

Yoshiyuki Nakai was the outspoken critic of the two directors' interpretations of the literary text for each session. He and I later worked on collaborative projects and exchanged lengthy fax messages, particularly on his prescient plans for an online book on the history of Western arts (at a time when even Google had not thought of digitized publication). I came to know his spouse, Kate Nakai, as she occasionally joined her husband and me at meals or events in Tokyo (see chapter 24). After Yoshiyuki's death, I sent Kate Xerox copies of my correspondence with him, which led to our direct communication with each other on our work. She enjoyed the first volume of my three-part anthology of literary translations, and I admired the extraordinary approach she and her co-translators took in presenting the case of executed Christian sorcerers during the early nineteenth century.[33]

Shortly after my return to Indiana University, my colleague Ingeborg Hoesterey began a theory reading group.[34] For each session at her house, we read one chapter of a representative book. Jacques Lacan, who extended Freud on anthropological and philosophical grounds, offered to me the most challenging and engaging texts.[35] His notion of the "mirror stage" in the formation of the ego helped me as it did feminist theorists. The group flourished for a few years until the theory of autobiography dominated our readings and the group disintegrated. But it was a wonderfully inspiring group of like souls who enjoyed the difficulty of the texts we tried to decipher each time. It was an early 1980s phenomenon, when academics also formed study groups to learn how to use word processors. Both were part of a new tide in academe of stepping into the new and impenetrable by joining hands.

About that time, I was assigned to teach an introductory graduate course on theory and criticism. Unlike my colleagues in other departments, I took an evenhanded approach, favoring or focusing on no singular school of thought. Along with each week's selection from theory, I chose one appropriate literary text in English translation from any language, including Japanese, to test the theory. Writing comments on each student's analytical report on the weekly reading in relation to earlier readings in class, and endlessly chatting with them in my office, kept me sleepless for the entire semester.

In my seminar on modern Japanese literature, Eiji Sekine stood out as someone with a solid foundation in theory, having been trained at the University of New Sorbonne Paris III—the home of theory.[36] We shared an interest in those of the period's literature and arts that invited poststructuralist readings. Sekine taught me some of the concepts of Gilles Deleuze, who until then had been only a name to me. Although I lacked the knowledge of the history of European philosophy, I, as a Freudian critic, sympathized with Deleuze. It was his ideas of self, difference, and the real that led me to semiological theories of reading.[37]

Because of my interest in jokes, satire, and sexuality, I had been earlier baptized into theories on the relationship between the text and the reader. Wolfgang Iser, in his theories of the "gap" and the "implied reader," acknowledged the part the reader plays in the formation of meaning.[38] In the type of writings I dealt with, however, the text did not remain as stable as Iser assumed because the power of the reader, I believed, rendered it mobile and changeable. It was my close reading of eighteenth-century texts that led me to Umberto Eco, who acknowledged the role of the reader in "activating" the text.[39] I turned into a semiotician of early modern literatures.

A fashionable approach in Japanese Studies in the United States was subtextual criticism, inspired by Paul Ricoeur's suspicion of overt meaning.[40] It seemed to promote reading the hidden, usually political meaning in spite of the text—pulling the rug from under its feet, so to speak. Harry Harootunian's New Historicist reading of the backside of Japan's intellectual and social history had a strong influence on literary criticism; it took ten years before subtextual reading rediscovered words, images, rhythms, and other familiar elements of literary art.[41] Julia Kristeva's notion of "intertext," which brought the attention back to word and writing by claiming the multiplicity and interrelatedness of a text and between texts, nicely accommodated the sort of literature I had in mind.[42] Indeed, I could agree that all texts are interrelated, and every text is intertext, but her scheme is enclosed in the world of written texts. In order to add the reader as the supreme power, I devised a theory of what I called "overtext."

My idea was that the act of reading adds a layer of interpretation on top of the text since each reader brings in her understanding of literature through which to read any text. I described this general idea in a graduate seminar. Among its members was Margaret Key, scholar of Abe Kōbō's literature.[43] When I tried out some ideas for my overtext theory in this seminar, Key successfully articulated some of the aspects about which I myself was still a bit hazy. I explained that a literary work, through a mixture of references, perspectives, and tones, consists of layers of possibilities for comprehension, and the reader adds on top multiple layers of overtexts formed by her previous readings and life experiences. In short, the text she reads is tailored to her. Key pointed out that the overtextual layers existed around the text, in front of the reader in the forms of an introduction, critical study, and even advertisements. Key suggested that my book ought to concretely demonstrate this idea by appending a bunch of translucent films on a

Figure 13.2: Meeting with Howard Hibbett (left) and Adam L. Kern (right) in Hibbett's office, 2004. Photograph by Hiromi Yampol, courtesy of the author.

ring, like those color samples paint shops use. Thus, the reader of my book may see my point by combining different shades through which the text is read. I wrote several articles and conference papers in Japanese and English, partially applying the concept to early modern Japanese literature; one of these articles argues for literary translation as an act of overtext.[44]

Japanese Studies

There was an ulterior motive for choosing Japanese literature as a chief part of my professional future. My advisors—Frank J. Warnke (seventeenth-century European poetry), Glenn Hatfield (eighteenth-century British literature), and Constantine Christofides (classical European arts)—advised me to add my own native literature to my field of study. They pointed out that I, "being and looking Japanese," would not find a job teaching European comparative literature. Indeed, Ching-hsien Wang, with whom I studied classical Chinese literature and with whom I worked as a research assistant, had written his dissertation on ancient Chinese poetry for a PhD in comparative literature at Berkeley.[45] I duly followed their advice and added Japanese literature to my graduate study by taking a course on the Noh and its comical interlude *kyōgen* with Richard McKinnon, one of the early translators of plays in the genre.[46]

I proposed a dissertation on Natsume Sōseki's literature theory (*Bungakuron*), as the breadth of his reference to European, Japanese, and Chinese literatures made my project comparative, and the book's reputation for reconditeness posed an inviting challenge for me.[47] Although the entire body of his works had been familiar to me since childhood, I set out to examine them closely. Rereading them as a grown-up comparatist, Sōseki's works revealed their roots in Edo-period mentality and artistry. But my reading repertory in Japanese had not yet included many of the popular late-Edo books. Turning to that period, I discovered *gesaku*, the comical and satirical writings of the literati.[48] *Gesaku* works, often combining verbal and pictorial texts on the same page, struck me as perfectly suited for an approach much freer and broader than New Criticism. My adored Sōseki was instantaneously replaced by Hiraga Gennai (alias Fūrai Sanjin, 1728–1779), arguably the most famous *rōnin* (masterless samurai) of the period as well as a legitimate botanist and mineralogist, controversial mechanical inventor, and suspicious industrial projectionist in addition to being the author of books of comical lectures (*dangi*) that satirized religion, philosophy, and world history in sexual and scatological terms. His parody of the traditional love-suicides' journey (*michiyuki*) as the creeping of a couple of lice on the poet's back is a quintessential example of Gennai's writing, which is rendered into "Gennaiesque English" by Timon Screech.[49] I wished to analyze the works of Gennai and other wits of his time as well as those of later followers of *gesaku* writing.[50]

Gesaku had been generally excluded from the Japanese literary canon. Iwanami shoten publishers had made the daring step of including some in its anthology, *Nihon koten bungaku taikei* (*Anthology of Japanese Classical Literature*, 102 volumes), which encouraged scholars and general readers in Japan to pay as much attention to *gesaku* as to canonical works. In the English-speaking world, recognition of *gesaku* was slower in coming. Even Donald Keene, the best-known authority on Japanese literature and theater, whose books were arguably the most widely read and trusted English-language source of information on Japan's culture, hardly discussed *gesaku* in his anthology of early modern literature.[51]

Thus, I discovered the type of writing in Japanese to which my critical approach was best suited, but it was hard to imagine the existence of an informed audience, especially in English. When Haruko Iwasaki, a student at Harvard at the time, was asked by her advisor, Howard Hibbett, how many people she thought would read her dissertation on such an esoteric subject as literati friends' circles during the mid-eighteenth century, she replied that there were six: Hibbett himself, her fellow student Robert Campbell, me, Nakano Sanbin (her most admired authority on Edo literature), and two others.[52] Witty and sharp-tongued, Iwasaki, by making an esoterica out of *gesaku* and excluding the common crowd, embodied the eccentricity of *gesaku* camaraderie.

It was Hibbett who rescued me from my distress about the inaccessibility of *gesaku* literature for scholars and students. Coincidentally, Hibbett's interest was moving from early to late Edo literature.[53] Soon after I took a position as lecturer at Indiana University, he invited me to give a lecture at Harvard. Embarrassed, I told him that I had finished only one chapter of my dissertation. In response, he praised it as the best piece of writing he had seen on late-Edo literature. Hibbett's request to discuss my next chapter, which was to be on the aforementioned author Santō Kyōden, obliged me to write that chapter very quickly. While at the Bunting Institute, I attended Hibbett's seminars on Edo literature and served as a commentator for the students' discussions and presentations. This congenial group of scholars soon grew into a *gesaku* study group led by Hibbett, which led to decades of collaborative projects (figure 13.2).

Another lucky encounter was with Haga Tōru, a specialist of early modern poetry and painting in Europe and Japan. Because he was the author of the best book on Hiraga Gennai and was stepping into comparative readings of poetry and painting, we found ourselves thinking along the same lines.[54] By the request of Henry Remak, Director of the Institute for Advanced Study at Indiana University, I organized an eight-week faculty seminar on reading pictures centered around Haga's work.[55] He was an imaginative narrator of the way images echoed global assortments of art and poetry and an encouraging listener for the seminar members, who took turns giving presentations. He and I gave a joint colloquium on dwellings in Edo arts and literature, which led us to further collaborations in international projects.

A visiting position at the University of Tokyo provided me with the opportunity to take part in planning a Tokyo congress of the International Comparative Literature Association and to coedit one of its mammoth volumes of proceedings.[56] Even after this position ended, I continued to participate in meetings of Kawamoto Kōji's monthly literary theory seminar, conducted mostly for the benefit of graduates from the comparative literature program. Some years later, I was a visiting professor at the International Research Center for Japanese Studies (Nichibunken) in Kyoto and participated in Komatsu Kazuhiko's seminar on *yōkai* (the weird) and Hayakawa Monta's reading group on *shunga* (erotic art), which buttressed my limited knowledge of both subjects.[57] Inoue Shōichi's books were most impressively original, and Inaga Shigemi's writings on Orientalism in the arts and other subjects hit a sympathetic chord in me.[58]

I stayed on in Japan for an extra year by working with Watanabe Kenji at Rikkyō University on preliminary research for my anthology on Edo-period literature.[59] Watanabe and I met with groups of prospective translators, coeditors, and advisors who resided in Tokyo. Being an expert of Edo pleasure quarters, Watanabe gave me guided tours of Yoshiwara and its vicinity.[60] He also assigned his student Gotō Ryūki to help me get around the campus. Gotō later became part of the anthology team and helped apply to libraries and museums in Tokyo for copies of materials in their holdings and reprint rights. Because Rikkyō's library collection was too small for my purposes, I frequently took cabs to Waseda University, where I was aided by Tan-o Yasunori, professor of art history, in obtaining rare materials. Under his influence, I stepped deep into the study of *nanshoku* (male homoeroticism) in early modern literature (figure 13.3).

The "Death" of Literature

For four decades after the war, comparative literature reigned over all methods of literary studies. Any "golden age," however, seems to carry an inborn schedule for its death. As soon as I arrived as a member of the thriving department at Indiana University, I was told that the discipline was already dead. "God Himself died during the fifties," I quipped, but I soon began to observe a drastic decline in our discipline. Many comparative literature departments in the United States closed or merged with English departments or foreign language programs. Foreign language programs tended to be funded either by national governments or endowments, while comparative literature programs lacked clear-cut affiliations for attracting funding.

More importantly, it was the focus on literature that reduced our discipline to irrelevance. Yale University was rumored to have eliminated canonical texts from the classroom altogether, and Duke University's English Department unapologetically announced that its curriculum consisted solely of theory. Roland Barthes's semiology of all things turned our eyes to music, photography, fashion, and gesture, even down to the geography of Japan's imperial castle, so that literature came to occupy only a tiny space as one of many subjects of signification.[61] In addition, Michel Foucault's anthropological approach to culture and society diminished the supremacy of literature, and British New Historicists deconstructed the orthodox borders between high and low language, culture, race, and gender, wiping away the privileged territory of canonical literature.[62] The "great books" were now defended only by the likes of William F. Buckley Jr., the ultraconservative host of PBS's *Firing Line* (1966–1999), a public affairs television program.[63] We were deep into the age of cultural studies.

Commissioned to write an article on the fate of English literature in the US academy, I interviewed students and faculty in Indiana University's Department of English.[64] I was shocked to learn that all the new hires had been cultural studies specialists and that British classics were no longer in the curriculum. Neither literary critics nor literary masterpieces existed any longer. I found it was not comparative literature but literature itself that had passed away. Fortunately, our Department of Comparative Literature survived without sacrificing its emphasis on literature. From the start, the department was known for courses that crossed the boundaries of white European and canonical literary inquiries, embracing film, opera, ballet, fine arts, and architecture, along with translation and East-West studies. This sort of inclusiveness made it easy for our program to embrace the theory and practice of cultural studies rather than being absorbed into it.

Historians did better with anthropological and sociological thinking than close-reading literary textual types like me. Mary Elizabeth Berry (chapter 11), for example, held a conference on "*asobi*" (play), featuring papers on high and low life in Japan from ancient times to now, in which she herself presented a paper on bathing and other amusements among the imperial nobility "while Kyoto burned."[65] The conference's perspective was not New Historicist, but it certainly highlighted the material culture of each period of Japan's history.

New Historicists defeated the orthodox direction of the historiographical gaze from the above to below and from the geographically central to the remote; stories were to be told from below and from the periphery. Susan Hanley's reading of things and systems during the Edo and Meiji periods in the context of consumers' well-being was narrated from the point of view of the governed and was detailed and informative—very much like Mitamura Engyo's encyclopedic writings and Ishikawa Eisuke's essays and novels about life in Edo (chapter 9).[66]

I had believed that obsessive curiosity about objects belonged to the most primitive stage in one's intellectual growth, and it was soon bound to be overtaken by a desire for words. This way of thinking, I now realize, is no different from the logocentric prejudice against images and performance that had always irked me. A happy union of thing and word, however, is possible, as in the case of Michiko Suzuki's study of kimono.[67] She pairs readings of Kōda Aya's writing about her kimono with readings of the kimono themselves, resulting in a piece of writing about writing, in which the subject and the object come together as writers.

When I met Junko Habu, an archeologist, I told her that I had never come anywhere near archeology except that I used to frequent the Minato Ward Museum of Folk Materials (Minato Kuritsu Minato Kyōdo Shiryōkan). The curator, Matsumoto Takeshi, showed me great "archeological" finds from the Edo period and taught me how to "read" the skeletons unearthed by recent construction projects. I had believed that archeology was defined by unearthing prehistoric bones and shells, as exemplified by research at the Ōmori Shell Mounds (Ōmori Kaizuka) archeological site in Tokyo. I learned that digging up pots, pans, and umbrellas sitting only meters below the surface also deserves the same name.

At this time, Japan was at the height of the bubble economy (1985–1991), and the Minato Ward, the highest-priced district in Tokyo, was being targeted by venturesome investors, resulting in quick changes of ownership and the construction of new buildings. At the same time, major additions to subway lines were being made surrounding the ward. All this digging yielded daily harvests of archeological finds. Amused by my story, Habu told me that, during my visits at the museum, I was actually looking at some of the items she had dug up with Matsumoto. She then sent me the table of contents of a book on which she and Matsumoto had collaborated.[68] I kick myself now for having taken my newly acquired knowledge as a skill no more meaningful than my famous gift wrapping and for having missed the significance of skeletons and umbrella bones as material culture. I am delighted, however, to have found a coincidental tie between myself and a colleague in another discipline through the accidental meeting of our stories.

Teaching

Hibbett's approach to teaching, which I observed in his seminars, inspired me to change mine. He distributed neither syllabus nor bibliography. In fact, there was no lecture. He would serve green tea in teacups of a tasteful design along with Japanese *sobamanjū* sweets made by his wife. The opening of the session was formulaic: he would ask the students, "Have any of you found anything interesting lately?" One of them, most frequently the aforementioned Campbell, would do a show-and-tell with an Edo-period *gesaku* book he had purchased at an old bookstore in Boston. The featured member of the session would read a draft of his term paper, and the rest of the class would ask questions about it, followed by my comments. Finally, Hibbett would conclude the session with a short witty remark.

The students were elated describing the materials they found or commenting on the paper presented, as they probably imagined their contributions seeping into their master's inner archives of knowledge and taste. Their discussions were always lively in the same way my classmates and I at the University of Washington had happily conducted our seminar whenever our instructor was away from campus. Hibbett, however, was far from absent: his quiet presence was pedagogically and almost spiritually meaningful. Upon returning to Indiana, I imitated Hibbett's non-teaching method (figure 13.3). Sitting on top of the desk, I would open the session by saying, "Good morning! You've read *Northanger Abbey* over the past four days. Who among you loved it? Who hated its guts?" I no longer lectured. The students were divided between Jane Austen lovers and haters, arguing with one another, asking me questions occasionally, and one or two coming to the whiteboard to sum up the arguments from opposing camps. My new approach yielded far better papers than before: the students were no longer training themselves to parrot the teacher.

To propagate the charm of Japanese literature and arts, I brought to Bloomington experts, such as Kishi Tetsuo of Kyoto University and Takahashi Tōru of Nagoya University, to coteach with me, and I took advantage of my research collaborators who stayed for a semester or longer, such as Ohsawa, Haga, Kawamoto, and Watanabe: they voluntarily met with groups of students to help their research in Japanese Studies. Associating with distinguished specialists from the source of the objects of their study had immense benefits for the students: they not only acquired confidence as future specialists but also connections by which they could later study in Japan.

I cotaught "Love in Literature East and West" with my colleague Clifford Flanigan. As I experimented with teaching *waka* without translation according to poet Stanley Burnshaw's method, Flanigan exclaimed that he now understood why the English translations he had read of *waka* and haiku had never moved him.[69] The students enjoyed proposing possible "translations" using the word-

Figure 13.3: Giving a lecture on "Gender, Class, and Repression in Male Homoerotic Narratives of the Early Edo Period in Japan," The Ohio State University, 2017. Photograph courtesy of Cordelia Driusssi.

to-word equivalents I showed. The students and I were fascinated by Flanigan's presentation of eroticism in medieval hymns. For our discussion of eros and religion in St. Augustine's *Confessions*, Flanigan acted as the saint, circling around inside the circle of students like an animal in cage, tearing out his hair, and crying, "Why, God, do you give me sexual desire that torments me so?"

My course on Kurosawa Akira's films, cotaught with my colleagues Jurgis Elisonas and David Neumeyer and involving film and theory experts from Indiana University and other schools and organizations, inspired an all-day workshop on the filmmaker's work for the Tokyo congress of the International Comparative Literature Association, in which our teaching team, some of the speakers, and a few of our students made presentations. David Medine's paper, which demonstrated law as Kurosawa's theme and language, and Lewis Dibble's, which pointed to the signifying power of sounds of all sorts in his films, stirred the large audience into lively discussion.[70] Kurosawa himself was scheduled to take part in the workshop as well as to give a keynote lecture for the entire congress but canceled both because he had begun filming *Rhapsody in August* (*Hachigatsu no rapusodī*) sooner than planned. Nogami Teruyo, scriptwriter and producer as well as the manager of Kurosawa Productions, participated in the workshop in his place.[71] Following my correspondence with Kurosawa surrounding the event, I received many useful materials from Kurosawa Productions, including a set of laser discs of the entire collected works of Kurosawa, making Indiana University's Herman B. Wells Library the only holder of the set in the United States. (An agreement with US distributors stipulated that the sets were not to be sold outside Japan).

Teaching gives us a certified raison d'être and the pleasure of being part of young people's intellectual progress, which makes teaching addictive. Once you are drawn into it, it occupies all of your attention and life. You plan big events in order to stimulate your students, win grants to help their finances and give them training, and stay up all night writing recommendations. Eventually, you find that you have no time to work on your book projects that have been ongoing for decades. Looking back, I now know that my perpetual procrastination in finishing my book manuscripts was, in fact, by choice: it's teaching that has made my life meaningful.[72]

Translation

In the late 1950s and 1960s, great translations of Japanese literature emerged, many of them ably executed by scholars who had been trained in Japanese during the war in military language programs and who had participated in war intelligence efforts, including Hibbett, Keene, Edward Seidensticker, Helen Craig McCullough, and William McCullough. The Kyoto-born Donald Shively, who served as a Japanese Language Officer in the US Marine Corps, also became a scholar and translator of Japanese literature.[73] Unexpectedly, it was one of America's military schemes that opened up a wide road for the study and translation of Japanese literature.

The general readership must have found the literature "inscrutable," as Japanese people were called in those days, and that very inscrutability of the works may have tickled their taste for the exotic. Kabuki's first postwar American tour received similar responses, with critics thoroughly exoticizing it by claiming no comprehension of its contents but appreciation of its stylization. Americans' Aristotelean assumptions got in the way when they confronted non-Western art. I felt called upon to guide Americans to the interior of Japan's people and culture.

Translation would be the primary bridge between cultures. My serious interest was nurtured during my thirteen-year marriage to Frank W. Jones, a multilingual comparatist and translator of Greek, French, German, and Franco-African literatures. I came to acknowledge translation as an art form while watching him grope for words, rhymes, speech styles, and the flow of sentences, and I occasionally enjoyed chances to read his drafts and offer ideas.[74]

Indiana University's Department of Comparative Literature was extraordinary in making translation, where the faculty were most productive, one of the central strands in its curriculum. Thirteen years of cochairing a faculty seminar on translation with Breon Mitchell carried me deeper into translation in theory and practice, which formed a foundation for my ambitious work in preparing an

Figure 13.4: Receiving the 2019 Lindsley and Masao Miyoshi Prize for Lifetime Achievement in Translation and Editing, Donald Keene Center of Japanese Culture, Columbia University. Pictured with Charles Shirō Inouye, Chair of the Selection Committee. Photograph courtesy of Cordelia Driusssi.

anthology of Japan's early modern urban literature.[75] Some of the invited speakers for the seminar joined the team of translators of my three-volume anthology.

Classical and modern Japanese literature was well represented in English translations. The early modern literature, in contrast, constituted a gaping gap in the canon for teaching Japanese literature. To commemorate Hibbett's retirement, John Solt began compiling a set of pocket-size volumes of individual translations from Edo-period books.[76] Around 2000, Haruo Shirane and I exchanged ideas for the anthologies we were separately planning. Published in 2002, his anthology was the first large-scale compilation in English of writings of the period, a welcome addition to available translations. He includes a broad range of representative works, from intellectual thought to popular fiction and theater, organized according to chronology and genres of writing; as such, it stands as a reliable and orthodox storehouse of materials for research and teaching.[77] Our anthology took a different approach and instead aimed at establishing equal status for canonical and non-canonical texts, emphasizing hitherto untranslated texts. In order to recreate the pleasure of reading close to what the original readers in premodern Japan experienced, we chose to arrange texts according to themes.

Shirane's anthology follows the standard presentation format used in Japan, the written text almost fully occupying the printed page, while the original picture-text combination is treated as an illustration to the page. We, however, included graphic books in the same format as their originals. We brought a revolution in embedding translated text into each pictorial page. For those heterodox aspects, Michael Emmerich called ours "a quirky anthology" in his review for *The Journal of Japanese Studies*.[78] Shirane's and my anthologies have been used widely in graduate and undergraduate courses on popular culture and on Japanese Studies.

Each of our three volumes is dedicated to the urban area that led the others as centers of civilization. The focus of production and consumption shifted neatly into three urban areas: Kamigata, chiefly Kyoto and Osaka, took the lead for the first one hundred years of the Edo period, appealing to the rising bourgeoisie.[79] Our *Kamigata Anthology: Literature from Japan's Metropolitan Centers, 1600–1750*, presents this period. The center then shifted to Edo, the seat of the shōgun's government, where inventions by samurai and merchant elites inspired a broader and profitable enterprise, as represented in our *An Edo Anthology: Literature from Japan's Mega-City, 1750–1850*.[80] The start of the Meiji parliamentary monarchy did not cause a rupture in literary and artistic outputs, but the arrival of Europe as a new model civilization to emulate, and the trend of an ambitious younger generation leaving home for education and career, created a West-friendly and Tokyo-centric landscape, as shown in our *Tokyo Anthology: Literature from Japan's Modern Metropolis, 1850–1920*.[81] The cover of each volume depicts nameless persons doing jobs common to these cities and their times, and it features artistic media popular in these historical moments: dumpling sellers outside a kabuki theater in a gilded handscroll for the Kamigata volume, women working in the kitchen in a *ukiyoe* print for the Edo volume, and waitresses and other workers at a beef restaurant in oil paints for the Tokyo volume.

Collaboration

Collaboration, I have found, takes much more time, labor, and mental involvement than work done alone because, by its very nature, it draws together separate perspectives. In directing a project, I aim at presenting it, be it a book or a conference, not as a cohesive whole but as a polyphonic gathering of difference and sameness. The process requires much discussion and rethinking between the participants, rendering each project complex and slow-moving. My chief collaborative projects have been: (1) a conference on *The Tale of Genji*, (2) a conference on sexuality in Edo culture, and (3) the abovementioned anthology of literary translations.

First, to cultivate confidence and ambition among the dispirited East Asian graduate students at Indiana University, I aimed to increase the program's fame and the students' income. I thought a well-funded international conference on Japan's best-known classic, *The Tale of Genji*, would do the job. A preliminary draft for an elaborate description of my plans was met with mixed responses from funding agencies. They found the contents remarkable, but why did a mere lecturer want to organize a project of this scale? To counter their objection, Eugene Chen Eoyang, a senior colleague, offered to codirect the project; we spent two years preparing grant proposals. I conceived topics and engaged prospective participants, and he planned logistics and budget. In conjunction with the conference, I wanted to offer the world's first exhibition of the twelfth-century picture-scroll of *The Tale Genji*. Japan's Agency for Cultural Affairs approved the idea and offered to finance and manage the shipping of the national treasure. The Gotoh Museum, one of the two holders of the scroll, eagerly agreed, but the Tokugawa Art Museum, the other holder, did not. As an alternative, I turned to major US museums and private collectors that held important works of premodern art based on *The Tale of Genji*. Eoyang and I left the exhibition to the staff of the university's museum of art.

My second conference resulted from a four-year collaborative research project, titled "Sexuality and Edo Culture," conducted with Haga, Mathias Forrer, Kobayashi Tadashi, Henry Smith, James Ulak, and Timothy Clark and spanning several locations. I conducted a workshop at the Art Institute of Chicago (hosted by Ulak), a theory workshop and study of works at the British Museum (hosted by Clark), with study visits at the Victoria and Albert Museum (London) and the National Museum of Scotland (Edinburgh), both led by Clark. The project concluded with a conference, workshops, and exhibitions in Bloomington. *Imaging/Reading Eros: Proceedings for the Conference, Sexuality and Edo Culture, 1750–1850* was published by Indiana University's East Asian Studies Center.[82] Revised papers were expected to be published in English and in Japanese, but unfortunate circumstances blocked the process of my editing the two versions. I have disappointed some of the participants who submitted their thoroughly revised manuscripts in English and in Japanese translation.

Our three-volume anthology, engaging some seventy scholar-translators, is the most extensive collaborative work I have ever done. The editorial board consisted of Hibbett and Nobuhiro Shinji, dubbed the "walking dictionary of Edo-Meiji books."[83] Hibbett combed through the manuscripts after the coeditors did for stylistic improvements, while Nobuhiro answered questions regarding nebulous expressions and other obscure matters in the original texts. Campbell, who would have been the best possible choice for the role of coeditor for the Edo volume, proved to be much too busy as the host of the Japanese literature program on television on the NHK, and in his many other media appearances while teaching at the University of Tokyo. Having submitted drafts for his translations of *gesaku* and edited manuscripts by several others, he could no longer respond to email messages from us. Neither Hibbett nor I could imagine a replacement.

With much regret, I proceeded as the sole editor of the volume. Watanabe served as my specialist proxy for negotiating with museums and libraries in Japan, chiefly overseeing Gōtō's footwork in obtaining images and permissions for printing on my behalf. In addition, I often asked Watanabe's opinion on certain terms and issues when the group could not reach consensus. The staff at the University of Hawai'i Press pointed out that because he did not edit, he could not be treated as a coeditor, recommending instead that he be called "Japan advisor."

Unlike the Kamigata volume, the Tokyo volume readily attracted funding. Inclined to philosophy, coeditor Charles Inouye sought logic and meaning in literary works while I found value in their heterodoxy, ambiguity, and nonsense.[84] We occasionally struggled to compromise while going over the translation drafts—a good exercise for both of us. We shared an admiration for Noguchi Takehiko, a sharp-tongued cultural critic who, for example, wrote a book on Edo's devastating earthquake of 1885 as an indication of the failure of the lengthy Tokugawa shōgunate rule. Writing the book shortly after the great earthquake in the Kobe area in 1995, he argued that the calamity was a sign of the failure of the lengthy domination of the corrupt Liberal Democratic Party.[85] I had known Noguchi as the leader of student protests at Waseda, and Inouye had studied with him at Kobe University after Noguchi became a prolific author of prizewinning books. Noguchi's writings had a strong impact on our understanding of the problematic modernity of Meiji history and culture.

Working with Adam L. Kern on the Kamigata volume was a very different experience. Because he and I shared knowledge of the vast repertory of early Edo literature, we occasionally argued with each other, as specialists in Japan would, about certain "facts" regarding Edo customs, the consensus of modern scholarly interpretation, and the meaning of individual words. Kern's celebrated wit certainly added color to *gesaku* translations. I sometimes had to ask him to tone down his puns when they seemed to be excessive. That, I must admit, was akin to trying to tame a spirited *gesaku* writer of Edo. Kern was the first follower of my close-to-the-original approach to translating *kibyōshi*, as demonstrated in his translations of three works by Masanobu-Kyōden in his book on Edo's "mangacomic culture," as he called it.[86]

The above is a meandering story of my meandering life, with goofy errors and unexpected successes. At each stage, I was unwillingly and unwittingly drawn into a specialty. My career is made up of collaborators, assistants, students, and friends who have given me the sense of pleasure in work that has kept me going. Museum curators and librarians have helped me with complicated searches and requests for reprint permissions, while the authors of reviews and evaluations of my work put my ideas in perspective and encouraged my efforts. Material support was provided by the National Endowment for the Humanities, American Council of Learned Societies, Social Science Research Council, Japan Foundation, Toshiba International Foundation, Suntory Foundation, Lilly Endowment, and Indiana University. Representing the team of my collaborators, I thank all of those supporters for their patience and generosity. I am also grateful to the Donald Keene Center of Japanese Culture at Columbia University for honoring me with the Lindsley and Masao Miyoshi Prize for my lifetime achievement "as a translator and especially for her work as a translator and editor of *A Kamigata Anthology: Literature from Japan's Metropolitan Centers, 1600–1750; An Edo Anthology: Literature from Japan's Mega City, 1750–1850; A Tokyo Anthology: Literature from Japan's Modern Metropolis, 1850–1920*" (figure 13.4).[87]

My advice for younger scholars is not to heed advice from us seniors. By the virtue of our age, we tend to form a consensus (*teisetsu*) on every issue and turn into "mentors." Make use of your seniors' praise, support, and encouragement but do not obediently follow their *teisetsu*. It is beginners whose restless minds question orthodox premises and grope for discovery in unique ways. Listen to your younger colleagues and students. Belong to academic organizations through which to meet new people and new perspectives.

Notes

[1] Yamamoto Yūzō, ed., *Nihon shōkokumin bunko* (An Anthology for Young Citizens of Japan) (Tokyo: Shinchōsha, 1935–1937). For a list of volumes, see "Nihon shōkokumin bunko," *The Showa Bookshelf*, November 5, 2009, https://theshowabookshelf.wordpress.com/2009/11/05/nihon-shokokumin-bunko-library-of-books-for-the-younger-generation/.

[2] Generally speaking, theories of New Criticism advance that texts include within them all that is needed to understand them, and, thus, readers do not need to know authors' biographies, historical contexts, and other extratextual information. Practitioners engage in close reading and consider the relationship between literary content and form. For a concise definition, see "New Criticism," *Glossary of Poetic Terms*, Poetry Foundation, 2022, https://www.poetryfoundation.org/learn/glossary-terms/new-criticism; M.H. Abrams and Geoffrey Galt Harpham, *A Glossary of Literary Terms*, 11th edition (Thomson Wadsworth, Belmont, CA, 2014).

[3] Nakahara Jun'ichi, *Inokku Āden Tenisun* (Enoch Arden, Tennyson), *Himawari* (Sunflower) 4, no. 5 (June 1950), n.p.

[4] Konstantin Stranislavski's *An Actor Prepares* (New York: Theatre Arts, Inc., 1936) was among the revered textbooks for young and aspiring actors. See also Konstantin Stanislavski, *Stanislavsky on the Art of the Stage*, translated by David Magarshack (London: Faber, 2002).

[5] John Osborne, *Look Back in Anger* (New York: Penguin Books, 1982).

[6] Armstrong later translated Terayama Shūji's works into English: Terayama Shūji, *The Crimson Thread of Abandon: Stories*, translated by Elizabeth L. Armstrong (Honolulu: University of Hawai'i Press, 2014); *When I Was a Wolf*, translated by Elizabeth L. Armstrong (Kumamoto: Kurodahan Press, 2018).

[7] Gunji Masakatsu, *Odori no bigaku* (Aesthetic of Dance) (Tokyo: Engeki Shuppansha, 1957).

[8] Tsutsumi Harue, *Kanadehon Hamuretto* (Hamlet without Tears) (Tokyo: Bungei Shunjusha, 1993). "Kanadehon Hamlet" was translated by Faubian Bowers with David W. Griffith and Hori Mariko, *Asian Theatre Journal* 15, no. 2 (1998), 181–229.

[9] Noh plays are performed in the manner handed down in five schools specializing in the style of *shite* (the role of protagonist): Kanze, Hōshō, Kita, Kongō, and Komparu. All schools except Kita were founded in the Nara period, six centuries ago. Kanze, Hōshō, and Kita (derived from Kongō during the early modern period) are mainly based in Tokyo. Kanze, the largest, and Hōshō, the second in size, perform at the National Noh Theatre in Tokyo, but the plays are staged in many cities in Japan not only in established Noh theaters. Noh is also performed on stages set up at other venues, including at the Imperial Palace, old *daimyō* houses, and shrine and temple grounds, often at night with torches lit around the stage. For a definition of the Hōshō School, see "Noh Terminology," *The Noh.com*, 2022, https://db2.the-noh.com/edic/2010/05/hosho_school.html.

[10] Royall Tyler, *Japanese No Drama* (New York: Penguin Classics, 1993).

[11] See, for example, Shelley Fenno Quinn, "The Back Side of Noh Chant: A Yatsushi 'Takasago,'" in *Imaging/Reading Eros: Proceedings for the Conference, Sexuality and Edo Culture, 1750–1850*, edited by Sumie Jones (Bloomington: Indiana University East Asian Studies Center, 1996), 135–138; republished as "The Back Side of Noh Chant," in *A Kamigata Anthology: Literature from Japan's Metropolitan Centers, 1600–1750*, edited by Sumie Jones, et al. (Honolulu: University of Hawai'i Press, 2020), 392–398. Her other works include *Developing Zeami: The Noh Actor's Attunement in Practice* (Honolulu: University of Hawai'i Press, 2005).

[12] Laurence Sterne, *The Life and Opinions of Tristram Shandy, Gentleman*, edited by Judith Hawley (New York: Norton, 2018).

[13] In the Japanese academic structure, each graduate student belongs to the seminar of a faculty member from their admission to the completion of a degree. The seminar's instructor advises the student on choices of graduate courses, possible thesis topics, and strategies for the job search. The relationship often becomes personal and continues far beyond the completion of a degree.

[14] Kyeong-Hee Choi, "When the Colonized Mother Speaks: Post-Colonial and Maternal Narratives of Toni Morrison, Park Wanso, and Buchi Emecheta," PhD diss., Indiana University Bloomington, 1996.

[15] For information about early female professors in Indiana University's School of Optometry, see Ellie Kaverman, "Ingeborg Schmidt: 'The First Lady of Visual Science,'" *Voices from the IU Bicentenial*, May 19, 2020, https://blogs.iu.edu/bicentennialblogs/2020/05/19/ingeborg-schmidt-the-first-lady-of-visual-

science/#:~:text=Once%20such%20story%20is%20that,the%20IU%20School%20of%20 Optometry.&text=Ingeborg%20Schmidt%20was%20born%20on,%2C%201899%20 near%20Tartu%2C%20Estonia. Andrea Walton, *Women at Indiana University: 150 Years of Experiences and Contributions* (Bloomington, Indiana: Indiana University Press, 2022).

[16] Barbara Johnson, *A World of Difference* (Baltimore: Johns Hopkins University Press, 1988); Zora Neale Hurston, *Their Eyes Were Watching God* (New York: Chelsea House Publishers, 1998).

[17] Diane Middlebrook, *Anne Sexton: A Biography* (New York: Vintage, 1991).

[18] Sumie Jones, "William Hogarth and Kitao Masanobu: Reading Eighteenth-Century Pictorial Narratives," *Yearbook of Comparative and General Literature* 34 (1985), 37–73.

[19] Diane Elam and Robyn Wiegman, *Feminism beside Itself* (London: Routledge, 1993).

[20] Camile Paglia, *Sexual Personae: Art and Decadence from Nefertiti to Emily Dickinson* (New York: Vintage, 1991).

[21] Matsuura Rieko, *Nachuraru ūman* (Natural Woman) (Tokyo: Chikuma shobō, 2000).

[22] Matsuura Rieko, *Yasashii kyosei no tame ni* (Tokyo: Chikuna shobō, 1994); Matsuura Rieko, "For a Gentle Castration," translated by Amanda Seaman, in *Woman Critiqued: Translated Essays on Japanese Women's Writing*, edited by Rebecca Copeland (Honolulu: University of Hawai'i Press, 2006), 194–205.

[23] Matsuura Rieko, *Oyayubi P no shugyōjidai* (Tokyo: Kawade shobō shinsha, 1992); Matsuura Rieko, *The Apprenticeship of Big Toe P*, translated by Michael Emmerich (New York: Kodansha International, 2010).

[24] Matsuura Rieko, *Ura vājon* (The Reverse Version) (Tokyo: Chikuma shobō, 2000).

[25] See Joanne Quimby, "Performative Citation and Allusion in Matsuura Rieko's *Oyayubi P no shugyōjidai*," *Publications of the Association for Japanese Literary Studies* 20 (2019), 87–95.

[26] Edith Sarra, *Unreal Houses: Character, Gender, and Genealogy in The Tale of Genji* (Cambridge, MA: Harvard East Asian Monographs, 2020).

[27] René Wellek inaugurated comparative literature as a theoretical discipline that encompassed the generality of history, philosophy and literature by authoring, with Austen Warren, *Theory of Literature* (New York: Harcourt, Brace, and Company, 1948). The book opened up literary criticism to deconstruction, which became the mark of Yale University's comparative literary study. See also René Wellek, *A History of Modern Criticism: 1750–1950: American Criticism: 1900–1950* (New Haven: Yale University Press, 1986).

[28] See Masao Miyoshi, *Accomplices of Silence: The Modern Japanese Novel* (Berkeley: University of California Press, 1975); *As We Saw Them: The First Japanese Embassy to the United States (1860)* (Berkeley: University of California Press, 1979). Earl Miner, *Japanese Linked Poetry* (Princeton: Princeton University Press, 1979).

[29] Nakai Yoshiyuki, *Ōgai ryūgaku shimatsu* (Circumstances of Ōgai's Study Abroad) (Tokyo: Iwanami shoten, 1999).

[30] See Earl Miner, ed. *The Works of John Dryden*, Volume III: *Poems 1685-1692* (Berkeley: University of California Press, 1969); Volume XV: *Plays* (Berkeley: University of California Press, 1976).

[31] See, for example, Earl Miner and Hiroko Odagiri, *The Monkey's Straw Raincoat and Other Poetry of the Bashō School* (Princeton: Princeton University Press, 1981).

[32] See, for example, Chieko M. Ariga, "Dephallicizing Women in Ryūkyō Shinshi: A Critique of Gender Ideology in Japanese Literature," *Journal of Asian Studies* 51, no. 5 (August 1992), 565–586.

[33] Fumiko Miyazaki, Kate Wildman Nakai, and Mark Teeuwen, translators, *Christian Sorcerers on Trial: Records of the 1827 Osaka Incident* (New York: Columbia University Press, 2020).

[34] See Ingeborg Hoesterey, *Pastiche: Cultural Memory in Art, Film, Literature* (Bloomington: Indiana University Press, 2001).

[35] See, for example, Jacques Lacan, Alan Sheridan, and Malcolm Bowie, *Écrits: A Selection* (London: Routledge, 1977).

[36] See, for example, Sekine Eiji. *"Tasha" no syōkyo: Yoshiyuki Jun'nosuke to kindai bungaku* (Erasure of the "Other": Yoshiyuki Junnosuke and Modern Literature) (Tokyo: Keiso shobō, 1993).

[37] For example, see Giles Deleuze, *The Deleuze Reader*, translated by Constantin Boundas (New York: Columbia University Press, 1993); Giles Deleuze and Félix Guattari, *Anti-Oedipus: Capitalism and Schizophrenia*, translated by Robert Hurley (New York: Penguin Classics, 2009).

[38] Wolfgang Iser, *The Implied Reader: Patterns of Communication in Prose Fiction from Bunyan to Beckett* (Baltimore: Johns Hopkins University Press, 1974).

[39] See Umberto Eco, *The Role of the Reader: Explorations in the Semiotics of Texts* (Bloomington: Indiana University Press, 1979).

[40] Paul Ricoeur, *Freud and Philosophy: An Essay on Interpretation*, translated by Denis Savage (New Haven: Yale University Press, 1970).

[41] See, for example, Harry D. Harootunian, *Things Seen and Unseen: Discourse and Ideology in Tokugawa Nativism* (Chicago: University of Chicago Press, 1988).

[42] See Julia Kristeva, "Word, Dialogue, and Novel" and "The Bounded Text" in *Desire in Language: A Semiotic Approach to Literature and Art*, translated by Thomas Gora, Alice Jardine, and Leon S. Roudiez (New York: Columbia University Press, 1980), 36–91.

[43] See, for example, Margaret Key, *Truth from a Lie: Documentary, Detection, and Reflexivity in Abe Kobō's Realist Project* (Lanham, MD: Lexington Books, 2011).

[44] See, for example, Sumie Jones, "Overtext: A Theory of Reading and Writing in Early Modern Literature and Arts," *Poetica* 52 (1999), 19–36; "Edo bungaku no ōvā tekusuto: *gesaku*-shinron ni mukete." (Overtext in Edo Literature: Toward a New Theory of Playful Writing), *Edo Bungaku* 20 (1999), 98–114; "Translation as Overtextual Reading: or, How to Compose a Japanese Rap in English," *Translation Review* 93 (2015), 99–116.

45 Ching-hsien Wang, *The Bell and the Drum: Shih Ching as Formulaic Poetry in an Oral Tradition* (Berkeley: University of California Press, 1974).

46 Richard McKinnon, *Selected Plays of Kyōgen* (Tokyo: Uniprint, 1968).

47 Natsume Sōseki, *Bungakuron* (Literature Theory), 2 Volumes (Tokyo: Iwanami bunko, 2007).

48 *Gesaku*, or "playful composition," was an Edo product, created and enjoyed by samurai-class literati during the mid-eighteenth century and spread to the merchant class. It includes: *dangibon* (lecture books), *sharebon* (books of manners), *kibyōshi*, or "yellow covers," an intellectual and satirical version of *akahon*, or "red books" for children, and *kurohon*, or "black books" consisting of stories taken from kabuki plays.

49 Hiraga Gennai, "A Lousy Journey of Love: Two Sweethearts Won't Back Down," translated by Timon Screech, in *An Edo Anthology: Literature from Japan's Mega-City, 1750–1850*, edited by Sumie Jones (Honolulu: University of Hawaiʻi Press, 2013), 60–64.

50 Sumie Jones, "Comic Fiction in Japan during the Later Edo Period," PhD diss., University of Washington, 1979.

51 See Donald Keene, *World within Walls: Japanese Literature of the Premodern Era, 1600–1867* (New York: Columbia University Press, 1976).

52 Haruko Iwasaki, "The World of Gesaku: Playful Writers of Late Eighteenth-Century Japan," PhD diss., Harvard University, 1987; Robert Campbell, ed. *Yomu koto no chikara* (The Power of Reading) (Tokyo: Kōdansha, 2004); Robert Campbell, ed. *Nihon koten to kansenshō* (Japanese Classics and Epidemics) (Tokyo: Kadokawa shoten, 2021); Nakano Sanbin, *Kinsei shin kijinden* (New Biographies of Eccentrics of Early Modern Japan) (Tokyo: Iwanami shoten, 2004).

53 See, for example, Howard Hibbett, *The Floating World in Japanese Fiction* (London: Oxford University Press, 1959); *The Chrysanthemum and the Fish: Japanese Humor since the Age of the Shoguns* (Tokyo: Kodansha International, 2002).

54 Haga Tōru, *Hiraga Gennai* (Tokyo: Asahi Shimbunsha, 1981).

55 Haga Tōru, *Kaiga no ryōbun: kindai Nihon hikakubunkashi kenkyū* (The Realm of Painting: A Study in Comparative Cultural History of Modern Japan) (Tokyo: Asahi Shimbunsha, 1990); *Tōgen no suimyaku: Higashi Ajia shiga no hikaku bunkashi* (Water Current from the Peach Blossom Spring: A Comparative History of East Asian Poetry and Painting) (Nagoya: Nagoya University Press, 2019).

56 Margaret R. Higonnet and Sumie Jones, eds. *The Force of Vision 2: Proceedings of the XIIIth Congress of the International Comparative Literature Association* (Tokyo: ICLA Executive Committee, 1995).

57 See Komatsu Kazuhiko, *An Introduction to Yōkai Culture: Monsters, Ghosts, and Outsiders in Japanese History*, translated by Hiroko Yoda (Tokyo: Japan Publishing Industry Foundation for Culture, 2018); Hayakawa Monta, *Shunga: Japanese Erotic Art* (Tokyo: PIE books, 2010).

58 Inoue Shōichi, *Tsukurareta Katsura-Rikyū* (The Myth of Katsura Princely Villa) (Tokyo: Kobundo, 1986); Inaga Shigemi, *Kaiga no Tōhō: Orientarizumu kara postomodanizumu e*

(*The East in Painting: From Orientalism to Postmodernism*) (Nagoya: Nagoya University Press, 1999).

[59] Sumie Jones ed., with Kenji Watanabe, *An Edo Anthology: Literature from Japan's Mega-City, 1750–1850* (Honolulu: University of Hawai'i Press, 2013).

[60] Yoshiwara is the name of an enclosed district outside Edo's city limits dedicated chiefly to sexual entertainment and authorized by the shōgunal administration in 1617. Being the only government-sanctioned district in all Japan, Yoshiwara boasted its scale, the quality of its prostitutes, and its formal regulations imposed on the clients. During the day, men and women went sightseeing and shopping there. At night, men would hold poetic competitions, and boys would be taken there for sex education.

[61] Roland Barthes, *Empire of Signs*, translated by Richard Howard (New York: Hill and Wang, 1983).

[62] See, for example, Michel Foucault, *The Foucault Reader*, edited by Paul Rabinow (New York: Pantheon, 1984). For a concise definition of "New Historicism," see *Glossary of Poetic Terms*. Poetry Foundation, 2022. https://www.poetryfoundation.org/learn/glossary-terms/new-historicism. Also see M.H. Abrams and Geoffrey Galt Harpham.

[63] I recall an episode of *Firing Line* in the early 1990s in which Buckley interviewed three or four young professionals who had recently graduated from elite universities. They all lamented the absence of English literature in their college curricula. Multicultural education had become so widespread that there were student demonstrations against literary classics. Buckley's belief in established literature, music, and arts ran through the thirty decades of *Firing Line*.

[64] Sumie Jones, "Samayoeru bungaku: Amerika no eibungakkai no jijō" (Literature in Exile: The Status of Literature in US Academia) *Bungaku* 1, no. 3 (2000), 33–39.

[65] Mary Elizabeth Berry, *The Culture of Civil War in Kyoto* (Berkeley: University of California Press, 1994).

[66] Susan Hanley, *Everyday Things in Premodern Japan: The Hidden Legacy of Material Culture* (Berkeley: University of California Press, 1997); Mitamura Engyo, *Mitamura Engyo zenshū* (Collected Works of Mitamura Engyo), 28 vols. (Tokyo: Chūō kōronsha, 1975–1977); Ishikawa Eisuke, *Ōedo risaikuru jijō* (The State of Recycling in Great Edo) (Tokyo: Kōdansha, 1994).

[67] Michiko Suzuki, "Reading and Writing Material: Kōda Aya's Kimono and Its Afterlife," *Journal of Asian Studies* 76, no. 2 (2017): 333–361.

[68] Junko Habu, "Rekishi kōkogaku to senshi kōkogaku: Kita Amerika no rei o chūshin to shite" (Historical Archeology and Prehistorical Archeology: Surrounding Examples from America), in *Kinsei kingendai kōkogaku nyūmon* (Introduction to Early Modern and Modern Archeology), edited by Suzuki Kimio (Tokyo: Keio University Press, 2007), 264–271; Matsumoto Takeshi, "Edo no Bosei: haka ni komerareta mibun chitsujo" (Burial Rules in Edo: Social Class Order Hidden in Tombs), in *Kinsei kingendai kōkogaku nyūmon* (Introduction to Early Modern and Modern Archeology), edited by Suzuki Kimio, (Tokyo: Keio University Press, 2007), 179–193.

[69] Stanley Burnshaw, *The Poem Itself* (New York: Holt, Rinehart, and Winston, 1960).

[70] Lewis Dibble, "Crimes of Meaning: Kurosawa and Allegory," *The Force of Vision 6: Inter-Asian Comparative Literature*, edited by Kawamoto Kōji, et al. (Tokyo: International Comparative Literature Association, 1995), 501–507; David Medine, "Law and Kurosawa's *Rashomon*," *The Force of Vision 6: Inter-Asian Comparative Literature*, edited by Kawamoto Kōji, et al. (Tokyo: International Comparative Literature Association, 1995), 470–476.

[71] See, for example, Nogami Teruyo, *Tenkimachi: Kantoku Kurosawa Akira to tomoni* (Waiting for the Weather to Turn: Working with Director Kurosawa Akira) (Tokyo: Bungei Shunju, 2001).

[72] My graduate students and assistants have been my colleagues and comrades in study. Throughout this chapter, I give examples of their ideas and what they have done with them to illuminate new directions for Japan Studies or comparative literature. To name a few additional examples: Roger Thomas, who was a cataloger at our university library before becoming a graduate student, published two books inspired by his PhD research: *The Way of Shikishima: Waka Theory and Practice in Early Modern Japan* (Lenham, MD: University Press of America, 2007) and *Counting Dreams: The Life and Writings of the Loyalist Nun Nomura Bōtō* (Ithaca: Cornell East Asia Series, 2021). Jon LaCure, one of the first word processor wizards on our campus, designed a means of statistical inquiry that could reveal what made *waka* poetry tick. He analyzed the rhetorical features of the poems in *Kokinwakashū* (*Poems Old and New*), Japan's earliest imperial anthology dating from around 905. It was the first example of an IT approach to Japanese poetry I have encountered. See Jon W. LaCure, *Rhetorical Devices of the Kokinshū: A Structural Analysis of Japanese Waka Poetry* (Lewiston, NY: Edwin Mellen Press, 1997). William J. Farge, a Jesuit Father, wrote an MA thesis on sixteenth-century Jesuits who translated Christian texts to convert Japanese without allowing them to acquire any theological knowledge. This sharply critical thesis became the basis of his book, *The Japanese Translations of the Jesuit Mission Press, 1590–1614: De Imitatione Christi and Guia De Pecadores* (Lewiston, NY: Edwin Mellen Press, 2003). He wrote a PhD dissertation on Baba Bunkō's (1718–1759) fiercely satirical performed *dangi*, in which he likened persons in power to monsters of one kind or other. Bunkō was the only writer-performer to be executed during the entire Edo period of rampant censorship. Farge took Bunkō to be a hero who sacrificed his life to speak against the hypocrisy of the governing power. I protested by saying that Bunkō was, after all, an entertainer who kept testing waters with increasingly dangerous materials and higher fees until he was arrested red-handed. There was no middle point at which we could meet. Farge held on to his idealistic image of Bunkō and published his dissertation as a book: *A Christian Samurai: The Trials of Baba Bunko* (Washington, DC: The Catholic University of America Press, 2016). This is proof that your instructor's advice may not always be practical.

[73] See, for example, Donald Shively, *The Love Suicide at Amijima (Shinjū ten no Amijima): A Study of Japanese Domestic Tragedy* (Harvard: Harvard-Yenching Institute, 1953).

[74] See, for example, Bertolt Brecht, *Saint Joan of the Stockyards*, translated by Frank W. Jones (Bloomington: Indiana University Press, 1970), which won the National Book Award in 1971.

[75] See Sumie Jones, "Vanishing Boundaries: Translation in a Multilingual World," *Yearbook of Comparative and General Literature* 54 (2008), 121–134.

[76] John Solt, ed., *An Episodic Festschrift for Howard Hibbett*, 26 vols. (Los Angeles: highmoonoon, 2000–2010). My contribution is *The Shirokoya Scandal: Two Ways of Looking at the Case Judged by Magistrate Ōoka Tadasuke*. vol. 23 (2010).

[77] Haruo Shirane, ed. *Early Modern Japanese Literature: An Anthology, 1600–1900* (New York: Columbia University Press, 2002).

[78] Michael Emmerich, "*A Tokyo Anthology: Literature from Japan's Modern Metropolis, 1850–1920*, ed. by Sumie Jones and Charles Shirō Inouye," *Journal of Japanese Studies* 44, no. 2 (2018), 445.

[79] "Kamigata," or "the upper regions," referred to the imperial city of Kyoto and its vicinity, including Osaka. "Going up to Kyoto" and "traveling down to Edo" were common expressions based on the superiority of Kyoto and Osaka's culture to that of Edo, the new center of government.

[80] Edo, in the province of Musashi, remote from the civilized cities of Kyoto and Osaka, was designated by Tokugawa Ieyasu (1543–1616) as the seat of government for the Tokugawa shōgunate. The city needed to be built from scratch, while the transportation and other systems were created to establish the shōgun as the virtual ruler of Japan. In terms of arts and crafts, Edo remained consumers of Kamigata products for one and a half centuries.

[81] Tokyo, meaning "Eastern Capital," was the new appellation for Edo after the Tokugawa shōgunate submitted its governance to the emperor, who moved from his palace in Kyoto into the Edo castle. Under the Meiji emperor, Tokyo became a showcase of modernity, inspiring new kinds of literature and arts.

[82] Sumie Jones, ed. *Imagining/Reading Eros: Proceedings for the Conference, Sexuality, and Edo Culture, 1750–1850* (Bloomington: Indiana University East Asian Studies Center, 1996).

[83] Shinji Nobuhiro, *Rakugo wa ikanishite keisei saretaka* (How Did *Rakugo* Originate?) (Tokyo: Heibonsha, 1987).

[84] See, for example, Charles Shirō Inouye, "Pictocentrism," *Yearbook of Comparative and General Literature* 40 (1992), 23–39; *Evanescence and Form: An Introduction to Japanese Culture* (New York: Palgrave Macmillan, 2008).

[85] Noguchi Takehiko, *Ansei Edo jishin* (The Ansei Earthquake of Edo) (Tokyo: Chikuma shobō, 1997).

[86] Adam L. Kern, *Manga from the Floating World: Comicbook Culture and the Kibyōshi of Edo Japan* (Cambridge, MA: Harvard East Asian Monographs, 2006); *The Penguin Book of Haiku*. New York: Penguin Classics, 2018.

[87] "Japan-US Friendship Commission Prize for the Translation of Japanese Literature and the Lindsley and Masao Miyoshi Prizes," Donald Keene Center of Japanese Culture, 2022, https://www.keenecenter.org/translation_prize.html. The Lindsley and Masao Miyoshi Prize for Lifetime Achievement in Translation and Editing is listed with the Japan-US Friendship Commission Prizes (for book-length translations) but is a separate award that has been given only a few times in the past.

14

Mae as a Professional Scholar

Richard Smethurst

> *The bottom line is that Mae paid a price for having come into her field as a woman at the time that she did, but she overcame that disadvantage and had a very productive, pathbreaking career.*

MAE J. SMETHURST (1935–2019) was a professor of classics and East Asian literature at the University of Pittsburgh and a pioneer of comparative studies of Noh and Greek drama. Her books include *The Artistry of Aeschylus and Zeami: A Comparative Study of Greek Tragedy and Nō* (1989), winner of the Hitomi Arisawa Prize, and *Dramatic Representations of Filial Piety, Five Noh in Translation* (1998), winner of the 2001 Japan-US Friendship Commission Prize for an outstanding translation of premodern Japanese literature.

RICHARD SMETHURST is a professor emeritus at the University of Pittsburgh. His books include *A Social Basis for Prewar Japanese Militarism* (1974), *Agricultural Development and Tenancy Disputes in Japan, 1870–1940* (1986), and *From Foot Soldier to Finance Minister: Takahashi Korekiyo, Japan's Keynes* (2007).

Mae graduated from Dickinson College in June 1957, summa cum laude with a major in Latin and French. (I graduated cum laude, lower down in the pecking order, with a major in European history, in 1955.) We were married in December

1956, and we spent most of the first six months of our marriage apart—I in Tokyo, Mae in college. Mae joined me in late June 1957, and we started our married life together in Japan. I served as a first lieutenant in Army "intelligence," Mae as a Latin, French, and English teacher at an international high school (private school, not Army school) in Japan. During that year, we saw our first Noh play, *Dōjōji*, at a "Noh for Foreigners" presentation. In the summer of 1958, we were transferred to Baltimore, where I spent one more Army year doing security clearance investigations, and Mae taught fourth grade at the Roland Park Country School, a fancy private girls' school in Bal'more. By the way, the mayor of Baltimore in 1958 and 1959 was Thomas D'Alesandro Jr., father of Nancy Pelosi.

In the fall of 1959, we went to the University of Michigan for graduate school. Mae was admitted provisionally because she knew Latin but not ancient Greek. But over the summer that year, she taught herself ancient Greek, often while we watched Cary Grant and Myrna Loy in *The Bachelor and the Bobby-Soxer* on late-night television. (Mae wrote her PhD thesis on Aeschylus's Greek tragedy trilogy, the *Oresteia*, by the way. She was smart and a fast learner.) In the spring of 1960, her mentor and the chair of the Michigan classics department called her into his office and told Mae, "You are the best first-year graduate student we have ever had in our program. But we are not going to give you a fellowship because you are a woman and will have babies and drop out of the profession." In 1961, largely because he was outraged when the same thing happened to his daughter, the chair changed his tune, gave Mae a fellowship, and strongly supported her from then on. In fact, I would say that Gerald Else had a very powerful influence on Mae's development, not only as her teacher but also by inviting her to take part in cross-cultural conferences and workshops he organized. In some ways, she also taught him by introducing him to non-Western productions of Greek tragedies.

Mae and I both got jobs at the University of Pittsburgh in 1967, I in the tenure stream, Mae as a one-year appointment. Arthur Hansen, one of her Michigan professors, but who by that time had moved to Princeton, wrote to Walter Evert, then the dean of humanities at Pitt, and told him that he would be foolish to miss the chance to hire Mae. And so he offered her a job. A year later, the new chair of the classics department gave Mae an appointment as an assistant professor in the tenure stream. In 1973, both Mae and I were promoted to the rank of associate professor with tenure. Although both Mae and I had job offers from other universities in the 1970s and 1980s, we stayed at Pitt for two reasons. First, we never got job offers from the same place at the same time. Second, from the 1970s on, major Japanese corporations supported Japanese Studies at Pitt, partly because of Mae. In fact, Mae and Keiko MacDonald sat at our dining room table and wrote a successful long-term proposal to the Toshiba International Foundation, which brought Mae and others who studied the Japanese performing and graphic arts money both to bring theater troupes and film festivals to Pitt and to fund their research. (Did you know that Keiko wrote a dissertation about Japan's and Noh's influence on William Butler Yeats?[1] The impact of Japan on Western modernism hooked Mae and me from our first trips to Japan.) Although many Japanese scholars (including women scholars) called me Smethurst-sensei and her Mae-sensei, they took her as a major player in Noh studies. In fact, when Mae quizzed one of her female colleagues on this difference in what we were called, she answered, we call you by your first name, not your family name, because we like you so much. Touché!

In 1979 and 1980, Mae, now an associate professor, received a fellowship from Dumbarton Oaks, a Harvard University research center on Hellenic studies located in Washington, DC, to do research there on her comparison of Greek tragedy and Noh. She was not stigmatized there as a woman, except once, when she could not go in the front door of the Cosmos Club when she was invited there for lunch. And at the center, she met the second of her mentors, the late Bernard Knox, and also another young scholar, Susan Cole, who went on to a long career as a professor of classics at SUNY Buffalo. Both became lifelong friends.

In the mid-to-late 1980s, Mae and I both were promoted to the rank of professor. But I was promoted before Mae, not I think because I deserved it more but for other reasons. First, my next book came out in 1985, Mae's in 1989.[2] Her book came out after mine because, in the late 1970s and early 1980s, Mae retooled herself as a scholar of comparative theater, comparing Greek tragedy and Japanese Noh drama and writing about productions of Greek tragedy in Japan. This required Mae to learn Japanese, which she did with her own requisite speed and ability. For a year (1961–1962), we lived with the Yasubas, a Japanese family in Tokyo, and Mae learned spoken Japanese by talking to family members, not, as I had done, in the classroom. I once asked Yasuba Sachiko, a senior member of our family, "Whose Japanese is better, Mae's or mine?" She answered, "Mae's. She sounds Japanese. You sound like a textbook." In the 1970s, Mae collaborated with Matsudaira Chiaki, Kyoto University professor of Western classical studies (*seiyō kotengaku*); his protégé Kiso Akiko; and the professional translator Shimazaki Chifumi, and learned to read medieval Noh texts.

When her book, *The Artistry of Aeschylus and Zeami: A Comparative Study of Greek Tragedy and Nō*, came out from Princeton in 1989, it revolutionized the medieval Japanese field. In 1989, it won the Hiromi Arisawa Memorial Award for best English-language book on Japan. But the book should have been published, and the promotion should have taken place at least as early as mine—some Pitt professors seem to have resisted her promotion to the rank of professor on the grounds that comparative theater was not what classicists should do, and only the intervention of Karen Brazell, a senior scholar of Noh at Cornell University, brought about Mae's promotion. Altogether, Mae wrote or edited four comparative books on Noh and Greek tragedy, and her book *Dramatic Representations of Filial Piety: Five Noh in Translation*, published in the Cornell East Asia Series in 1998, won the 2001 Japan-US Friendship Commission Prize for the Translation of Japanese Literature, given at the Donald Keene Center of Japanese Culture at Columbia University.[3] She played a major role in bringing Noh into the comparative theater world. And this is true in Japan, too; Kiso, mentioned above, translated both of Mae's major comparative works into Japanese.[4] Mae thus had a major influence on broadening both the fields of Western classics and Noh studies in Japan. Ask Kiso or Yamanaka Reiko, director of the Hōsei University Nogami Memorial Noh Theatre Research Institute, whose own successful battles as academic women make Mae's look mild.

At the end of her career, Mae wrote about productions of Greek tragedy in Japan. In a series of articles, Mae demonstrated how the Greek Tragedy Study Circle at the University of Tokyo (Girisha Higeki Kenkyūkai) in the 1960s (of which she was a member, 1961–1962), and then the directors Suzuki Tadashi, Ninagawa Yukio, and Miyagi Satoshi, used an imported theater form to make important points about the ultranationalism, anti-immigration, and sexism of postwar Japanese society.[5] This organization and these directors focused on *Philoctetes, Antigone, Medea,* and *The Trojan Women* to make these points. As we can attest because we saw it on stage, in Miyagi's production of *The Trojan Women*, the three gods who decide at the beginning of the play on the fates of Troy and Greece speak English and are not the Olympian gods but are instead Roosevelt, Churchill, and MacArthur, complete with a cigarette in cigarette holder, cigar, and corncob pipe, respectively. And we saw Miyagi's *Antigone* in front of the Tokyo National Museum, a building created in the 1930s in the tradition of "imperial art"; King Creon and his soldiers appeared "on stage" from inside the building, associated in the audiences' mind with World War II militarism, to sentence Antigone to being buried alive. Mae's last publication, "Euripides in Japan," published in 2020 after her death, discusses productions of Greek tragedies by these groups and directors.[6]

Let me add two more dimensions to Mae's career. First, from 1987 until 1994, Mae served as chair of Pitt's Department of Classics. I served as chair of the Department of History at the same time. For reasons I cannot explain, neither of us was more or less successful as chairs. Both of us were able to persuade the dean of the Faculty of Arts and Sciences to create new positions for our departments to hire outstanding young (then) scholars: in my case, Marcus Rediker, who has written extensively about merchant seamen, the Amistad Rebellion, and abolitionism; in Mae's case, Mary-Louise Gill, who now holds a chaired position in classics and philosophy at Brown University.

In the 1990s, Anne Weis, then chair of the fine arts department, told Mae about a five-volume set of Noh prints in the basement of the Frick Fine Arts

Library. Apparently (although we have found no paper trail), around 250 prints in five bound volumes had been bought in the 1920s by Frederick Mortimer Clapp, department chair at the time, using money provided by the heiress Helen Clay Frick, and the prints sat uncataloged in the library for around seventy years. Mae and I persuaded Rush Miller, then the head of the Pitt library system, to digitally scan the prints and put them online. Mae and I set about writing essays and descriptions for the website, and she raised money from the Toshiba International Foundation to help defray the expenses. The prints on the website, *Tsukioka Kōgyo, the Art of Noh, 1869–1927*, have grown to four multivolume sets (over six hundred separate prints).[7] Without Mae, this project would not have taken place. I have inherited her part of our role in working on it. Mae is my mentor in Noh studies.

The bottom line is that Mae paid a price for having come into her field as a woman at the time that she did, but she overcame that disadvantage and had a very productive, pathbreaking career. She was the first woman in the Department of Classics at Pitt to become an assistant, associate, and then full professor, and the first to be department chair. She won the Pitt College of Arts and Sciences Outstanding Teaching Prize in 1969, early in her career. But she never received an accolade as a University Professor or received any other such honor.

Notes

[1] Keiko MacDonald, "In Search of the Orient: W. B. Yeats and Japanese Tradition," PhD diss., University of Oregon, 1974.

[2] Richard Smethurst, *Agricultural Development and Tenancy Disputes in Japan, 1870–1940* (Princeton: Princeton University Press, 1986); Mae Smethurst, *The Artistry of Aeschylus and Zeami: A Comparative Study of Greek Tragedy and Nō* (Princeton: Princeton University Press, 1989).

[3] See, for example, Mae Smethurst, *Dramatic Representations of Filial Piety: Five Noh in Translation* (Ithaca: Cornell East Asia Series, 1998); Mae Smethurst, *Dramatic Action in Greek Tragedy and Noh: Reading with and beyond Aristotle* (Washington, DC: Lexington Books, 2013).

[4] See, for example, Mae Smethurst, "Aisukyurosu to Zeami no doramatourugi—Girisha higeki to nō no hikaku kenkyū" (Aeschylus and Zeami's Dramatology: A Comparative Study of Greek Tragedy and Noh), translated by Kiso Akiko, *Geinōshi kenkyū* (Research on the History of Performing Arts) 127 (1994), 57–60; *Aisukyurosu to Zeami no doramatourugi—Girisha higeki to nō no hikaku kenkyū* (Aeschylus and Zeami's Dramatology: A Comparative Study of Greek Tragedy and Noh), translated by Kiso Akiko (Tokyo: Hosei daigaku shippankai, 1994); *Girishia higeki to nō ni okeru 'geki tenkai': Arisutoterēsu o tebiki ni, soshite kare o koete* ("Theatrical Development" in Greek Tragedy and Noh: From Aristotle and Beyond), translated by Watanabe Kōji and Kiso Akiko (Tokyo: Nogami kinen Hōsei daigaku nōgaku kenkyūjo: 2014).

[5] See, for example, Mae Smethurst, "Ninagawa's Production of Euripides' Medea," *American Journal of Philology* 123, no. 1 (2002), 1–34; "Interview with Miyagi Satoshi,"

PMLA 129, no. 4 (2014), 843-846.

[6] Mae Smethurst, "Euripides in Japan." *Brill's Companion to Euripides*, Vol. 2, edited by Andreas Markantonatos (Brill: Leiden, 2020), 1088-1108.

[7] *Tsukioka Kōgyo, the Art of Noh, 1869-1927* (University of Pittsburgh. 2011-2022), https://exhibit.library.pitt.edu/kogyo.

15

MARGINS

Amy V. Heinrich

*But I began to suspect that what interested me was not
so much mainstream scholarship. My interests
were instead a bit marginal.*

AMY V. HEINRICH received her PhD at Columbia University in 1980 and taught modern Japanese literature for seven years. She joined the C. V. Starr East Asian Library at Columbia in 1987, where she worked for twenty-one years—eighteen as its director—until her retirement in 2009. She is the author of *Fragments of Rainbows: The Life and Poetry of Saitō Mokichi, 1882–1953* (Columbia University Press, 1983) and editor of *Currents in Japanese Culture: Translations and Transformations* (Columbia University Press, 1997), essays in honor of Donald Keene. She was a member of the Tokyo-based tanka poetry group Uchūfū for many years. In 1991, she became the founding director of the North American Coordinating Council on Japanese Library Resources (NCC). Her leadership positions in the field include serving as vice-chair of the Japan-US Friendship Commission.

When I transferred to Barnard College in 1965 to begin my junior year, my older brother, who had recently graduated from Columbia College and was then in med school, said to me, "You can't consider yourself educated in the second half of the twentieth century if you know nothing about Asia." He went on to tell me about the many courses at Columbia on Asia that I could take, and he recommended the year-long "Oriental Humanities" course to start. "I'll give you my books," he added. I still have many of them. Because the course covered the "Orient" from the Bosporus to the Pacific, it didn't reach Japan until the middle of the second semester. I also have the fresh memory of reading some poems in Donald Keene's *Anthology of Japanese Literature* that spring. These poems from the *Hitomaro Collection* (featuring poems by Kakinomoto no Hitomaro, the most important poet of the *Man'yōshū*), in particular, gave me chills then and still do now:

Dialogue poems

If the thunder rolls for a while
And the sky is clouded, bringing rain,
Then you will stay beside me.

Even when no thunder sounds
And no rain falls, if you but ask me,
Then I will stay beside you. [1]

I decided to start studying Japanese after I finished college. First I worked for a while. Then my husband and I spent a year and a half in Japan while I thought about applying to graduate school to study Japanese poetry. In 1973, my second application was successful, and I finally started graduate school in the fall of that year.

In my first year, I took courses in both classical and modern Japanese. By the end of the year and after finishing the classical Japanese final, I realized that I could, with effort, actually read classical tanka. I was so filled with joy at reaching my original goal that I bought myself a present. I continued my studies, supported by fellowships and enthusiasm. I wanted to work on modern tanka, thinking it would maybe be easier than classical. Donald Keene lent me his chapter on modern tanka poets from the second volume of *Dawn to the West*, then still in manuscript form. He thought I might find a poet I wanted to work on for my master's essay. I found Saitō Mokichi, who was deeply influenced by the *Man'yōshū* and was therefore somewhat hard to read and translate; the "pillow words" (*makurakotoba*, or epithets) and classical grammar were apparent in his poems. Nonetheless, I translated and discussed his sequence "My Mother is Dying" (*Shinitamau haha*) to earn my MA.[2] I continued into the PhD program.

Four years later and eight months pregnant, I took my orals and did miserably. I had trouble concentrating and could not focus properly. Donald Keene told me not to worry about it; nobody asks how well you did, only if you passed. Nonetheless, I cried for days. A few weeks later, my first son was born. A few days later, I received notification that I was awarded a Fulbright Fellowship to research my dissertation in Japan. My husband wanted to put off a second baby until I finished my dissertation, and I agreed.

We went back to Japan in 1977 with our four-month-old son. It was not easy getting settled with an infant. During the first month there, while staying with generous friends, our baby had a high fever, and I had not yet located a pediatrician. But talking to my friends' pediatrician on the phone was the first, maybe the only, time I felt I was speaking Japanese fluently. She became our son's pediatrician for the next eighteen months.

In the spring of 1978, I followed Donald Keene's advice and entered into the heart of my tanka education. He believed that trying to write tanka was an important step in learning how to read them, and, at his repeated suggestion, I joined his friend Takagi Kiyoko's *tankakai* (poetry group), Uchūfū, the name referring to poetry of the cosmos or universe.[3] The group, nearly all women, met once a month, and participants were expected to submit their poems to Takagi-sensei before the meeting. She wrote them in brush and ink on sheets of newsprint paper, leaving them anonymous; numbered them in random order; and taped them on the wall. (In later years, she typed the poems on her word processor and had copies made for all participants.)

One of the members read each poem out loud twice. Then participants chose the ones they were most interested in discussing and wrote their numbers on slips of paper. The numbers were tallied, and the poems were discussed in order of their popularity. The poets remained anonymous during the discussion except to the discussion leader. People felt free to express their opinions openly without worrying about the status of the poet but were expected to be polite. I felt glad when I had chosen one of Takagi-sensei's poems. I felt elated the rare times when anyone chose one of mine. I was also thrilled to see my poems published in the group's journal, *Uchūfū*.

Uchūfū members were mostly a generation older than me; many had been educated before the war. The standard was to use *kyūkanazukai* (historical *kana* orthography) and classical language; I solidified my knowledge of what I had learned in classical Japanese by reading Mokichi's poems. Twenty-five or so years later, the median age of the group was younger, and members no longer used classical language. The group also was no longer nearly entirely female.

In the spring of 1979, my husband and I moved back to New York City, and I tried to keep writing tanka, although I had trouble doing so when not hearing Japanese all day. But I continued writing my dissertation, "The Life and Poetry of Saitō Mokichi, 1882–1953." I wanted to defend it while Donald Keene was in New York and before he returned to Japan in June. (At the time, Donald Keene lived half the year in New York and half in Japan.) My son and I went to live with my mother in the country for about four months, while my husband, Richard, a steel sculptor, built an entire apartment in one half of an otherwise empty loft in Tribeca we had bought before going to Japan. The other half of the loft is his studio. We are still in both halves of the loft.

As I wrote my dissertation, Donald Keene read it chapter by chapter, writing corrections and suggestions in light pencil between the typed lines; in the earliest chapters, he wrote between *all* the typed lines.[4] He later told me he could distinguish by how well the sections were written when I was writing on a topic that interested me and when I was writing merely what I felt I had to address. I wanted to write about Mokichi's poems and how they were made; I was much less interested in writing about his life. I thought my experiences writing tanka and listening to Uchūfū critiques helped me learn to read tanka.

I finished my dissertation, passed the defense, and was awarded a PhD in 1980.[5] My first academic presentation was the following year, in a panel on modern tanka at the annual conference of the Association for Asian Studies. Having waited to have another child until I finished my PhD, I was then pregnant with my second son. The paper was on the process of learning how to read tanka by trying to write them. I asked Takagi-sensei to read my paper and comment on it; she thought it made good sense. The discussant for the panel, however, did not. He left my presentation for comment until last and then critiqued it severely, thinking I was claiming that one cannot read tanka well without writing them. I politely responded to his misreading, and the panel ended. I left to go to the ladies' room. Two women followed to tell me that they both thought the discussant had indeed misread the paper and that they agreed with me. They were both highly regarded scholars of Japanese literature and became my lifelong friends: Susan Matisoff (chapter 10) and Karen Brazell.[6] But I began to suspect that what interested me was not so much mainstream scholarship. My interests were instead a bit marginal.

Nonetheless, I started to look for teaching jobs. My husband—having finally found a studio that was close to perfect, with high ceilings in a concrete and steel building and therefore legal to weld in—did not want to leave New York. At the time, his request to stay seemed reasonable to me; after all, he had left New York for extended periods to come with me when I wanted to go to Japan. Later on, it occurred to me that, if I had been earnest in following a usual academic path, I would at least have insisted on discussing it. I taught briefly at Columbia, New York University, and St. John's University, and a year at Princeton. I discovered that I did not enjoy teaching, although I was pretty good at it. Many of my colleagues found it enriching and learned new things as they taught and exchanged ideas with students and colleagues. I found it exhausting.

I had taught a bibliography course at Columbia for PhD students shortly after getting my PhD, after the unexpected death of the instructor, Professor Herschel Webb. My main qualification was that I was available. Professor Gari Ledyard, who was then chair of the Department of East Asian Languages and Cultures, said, "You took the course, and you got an A." He offered to lend me all of Professor Webb's course notes. Still, I needed a great deal of help and received it weekly from Miwa Kai, a familiar and helpful face to generations of students and faculty. This was an early start of the integration of my scholarly training and my later library work.

The traditional path for a humanities PhD was academic, but, when a job came up at Columbia's C. V. Starr East Asian Library, I went for it. Research library work was well within the academic world but in a way I found enriching. I drew on my experiences teaching the bibliography course and learned from my librarian colleagues, who always answered my questions. I felt I was getting an education in librarianship as I went along and that the work was both congenial and important.

The East Asian library world was changing, however. The Japan-US Friendship Commission (JUSFC) and the Japan Foundation, the two organizations most responsible for funding East Asian libraries (essentially the oldest and largest East Asian libraries) no longer had the funds to do so. As the field of Japanese Studies expanded, many professors found themselves at institutions without libraries to support their research. The answer seemed to be to create a national collection, in function if not in fact.

I was asked in 1991 to be the founding director of a new national organization to address this goal. At the time, I was the acting director of the Starr East Asian Library and only four years into librarianship. The administration work of both roles involved steep learning curves. I had organizational help from Eric Gangloff, then JUSFC executive director, and Isao Tsujimoto, then executive director of the New York Office of the Japan Foundation. But I had to do the rest myself: write a mission statement, select participants, organize meetings, keep records, and more. I also gave it the clunky name of National Coordinating Committee on Japanese Library Resources (NCC), for which I have felt apologetic for thirty years. It is now the North American Coordinating Council instead of the National Coordinating Committee, but it is still referred to as NCC.

Perhaps the most difficult task was to establish NCC as a nonprofit independent organization so it would be able to raise money. I worked with an IRS agent who helped me enormously and made me laugh in the process. He told me the IRS manual was two inches thick, and he had read and understood every word in it. He went on to say there were no words he didn't understand; there were sentences, paragraphs, even whole chapters he didn't understand, but he understood every word. We were successful in the end.

But not everyone in the field, especially among librarians, was happy. There was dissatisfaction with me as the first director and with the inclusion of academics on the committee. Librarian colleagues were dissatisfied with me because they thought that I wasn't a "real" librarian. Some thought the first director should have been Japanese. Others said librarians didn't need faculty to tell them how to do their jobs. And some faculty at first could not understand why they needed to meet with librarians. Here was another place where I found my interests and perceptions to be a little marginal. And that was not a bad thing: getting librarians and academics to work together was a valuable learning experience for us all.

NCC first undertook the Multi-Volume Sets Project. Libraries could apply for large sets of materials that fit their own collections; these materials also would be resources for the nation. Applicants had to commit to lending materials from any set that was awarded through the program. This required some libraries to adjust their lending rules (for example, to lend microfilm, which was usually only used on-site). The project provided many valuable materials and created a small step toward a national collection. In fact, I recently looked up the haiku journal *So'un* and found four records in WorldCat (an international union catalog of tens of thousands of libraries). One was from a library in Japan. One of the three in North America had this notation:

> *Edited by: Ogiwara Seisensui.*
>
> *NCC-funded title; to be lent free of charge locally and nationally through ILL.*
>
> *Originally published monthly: Tōkyō; Kamakura: Sōunsha, 1911–1992.*

I was pleased to see that record. The Multi-Volume Sets Project is part of library history. But after thirty years, NCC has grown and diversified dramatically. The NCC website shows projects and partnerships unimaginable thirty years ago.

I learned a great deal from both my administrative positions and enjoyed them both, although the learning process was sometimes difficult. I was happy to share what I was learning. I served on multiple committees and in a number of positions, many at Columbia; the external ones related to Japan and Japanese Studies were where the margins meet, and they were the most satisfying. Two of the most important positions were in the organizations that helped found the NCC. I was a member of the American Advisory Committee to the Japan Foundation (1996–2002) and served on its committee on Institutional Program Support. I was a member, temporary vice-chair, and executive committee member of JUSFC (2001–2007). From 1998 to 2000, I was a member of the Binational Information Access Working Group of the US-Japan Conference on Cultural and Education Interchange (CULCON) and a member of CULCON itself from 2001 to 2007.

Figure 15.1: Donald Keene and Amy Heinrich on the grounds of Muryōji, the temple near his home in Tokyo's Kita Ward, taken on June 23, 2017, after a celebration of his ninety-fifth birthday. Photograph courtesy of Seiki Keene.

I continued working with poetry. In 1999, I presented a paper, "Cosmic Tanka: Recreating Universes," to the University Seminar on East Asia: Modern Japan, about our tanka society. It was about the meetings of the group, and the title refers to the name Uchūfū. The unpublished paper contains my translations of tanka from Takagi's five poetry books, some of her only poems in English.[7] In addition, the editor of *The Tanka Journal* asked me to translate five or so poems from the contemporary poetry collections he periodically sent me from 2001 through 2007. My final translations were from the collection *Bagdad Is Burning* (*Bagudaddo moyu*) by Okano Hirohiko. One poem that remains with me most closely since then follows:

the one I lost
track of
in the heat of battle
sixty years gone
and he's still so young[8]

In 2009, Hotta Mitsuo, the founder of the antiquarian book company Yushodo (which merged with Maruzen in 2016), visited Starr, and I showed him some of the library's rare books. He was especially taken by an illustrated book of tanka, *Miyakowasure no ki* by Tanizaki Jun'ichirō, describing the hardships of living in a war-torn country as he experienced them with his family. Mr. Hotta said he would like to produce a facsimile edition, if I agreed to translate it and Donald Keene, who had donated the book (a gift to him from Tanizaki) to the library, agreed to write a preface. We both agreed, and he produced a beautiful book, *Memoir of Forgetting the Capital*.[9]

The other poems that most stay with me were written following the triple disaster of earthquake, tsunami, and nuclear meltdown on March 11, 2011. Mr. Tsujimoto had returned to Japan that March after retiring from the Japan Foundation and continued his long habit of reading the poetry columns in the *Asahi* newspaper. He was deeply moved by poems about these disasters and wanted to make them more widely known in Japan and abroad. Laurel Rasplica Rodd volunteered to do the translations, and, as the number of poems Mr. Tsujimoto selected increased, she sought collaborators. She consulted with Mr. Tsujimoto and then asked Joan Ericson and me to work with her.[10] The three of us decided not to be listed by name as the translators and instead to list only the names of the poets. We divided the poems, read and annotated each other's drafts, and agreed upon the final versions. It was liberating to cooperate on translations; one could take risks and be sure the results would be carefully reviewed. This wonderful experience widened my approach to translating tanka. And we were glad to help make the voices of those poets available. A poem from Ishijima Takako from the project reads:

> *A large shoe and a small shoe, one each*
> *lined up, still muddy*[11]

Mr. Tsujimoto and his wife Kyoko created the nonprofit Studio for Cultural Exchange (Bunka Kōryū Kōbō), which, along with other organizations, supported the project (originally called *Voices from Japan*). To make the work public, an exhibition of calligraphic versions of the poems were displayed at the Cathedral of Saint John the Divine in New York (June 15–August 8, 2012) and poets and translators were invited to give readings of the poems when the exhibition opened. Similar events were held at Colorado College (March 25–April 6, 2013) and at the American School in Japan (March 2013). Students and faculty traveled to Tōhoku to meet with and interview many of the poets. The resulting interviews, poems, and translations were published in 2014 in *The Sky Unchanged: Tears and Smiles* (*Kawaranai sora: nakinagara warainagara*). I believe Joan, Laurel, and I were all sorry when our part of the project ended.

The overlapping margins of my academic and my librarian lives enhanced each other. I loved working in and for the Starr Library, where I did nearly all of my dissertation research. My experiences researching and teaching helped me to understand and articulate what was needed for the communities of undergraduates, graduate students, local faculty, and scholars from around the world who use this beautiful library. It was significant work that broadened my life and expanded my mind. I am proud of what I accomplished. I have helped the library develop collections and expand its staffing in the Korean and Tibetan collections to address growing academic needs. Staff members I hired during my tenure became colleagues who themselves are being recognized for their contributions to libraries.

But now, in my retirement, I most often return to the poetry.

> *as aftershocks continued*
> *they fled their islands—*
> *black tailed gulls*
> *seem to sleep each night*
> *rocked by the waves*
> — Yamamura Yoichi[12]

> *still, after all,*
> *spring has come again—*
> *dimly shrouded*
> *blossoms of Fukushima:*
> *plum, peach, cherry*
> — Mihara Toko[13]

Notes

[1] Quoted in Donald Keene, ed. *Anthology of Japan Literature: From the Earliest Era to the Mid-Nineteenth Century* (New York: Grove Press, 1955), 40. The original is found in Nippon Gakujutsu Shinkōkai, *The Manyōshū: The Nippon Gakujutsu Shinkōkai Translation of One Thousand Poems* (New York: Columbia University Press, 1969), 58.

[2] I later published a version of my MA essay. Amy Vladeck Heinrich, "'My Mother is Dying': Saitō Mokichi's *Shinitamau haha*," *Monumenta Nipponica* 33, no. 4 (Winter 1978), 407–439.

[3] Associate director of the Inter-University Center for Japanese Language Study from 1961 to 1981, Takagi Kiyoko published five volumes of tanka, as well as works in history, poetics, and philosophy. All her tanka books refer to cherry blossoms in their titles— starting with her first book, *Hana akari* (The Light of the Cherry Blossoms, 1978) to her last book, *Sakura no shizuku* (Cherry Tree Droplets, 2006). After retiring from the center, she taught at Ochanomizu University and Tōyō University before earning her PhD in philosophy at the University of Tokyo in 1991. Janine Beichman was also a Uchūfū member but at a different time (see chapter 19).

[4] While editing the collection of essays in honor of Donald Keene, I learned that nearly all of his students had learned to write well. See Amy Heinrich, ed., *Currents in Japanese Culture: Translations and Transformations* (New York: Columbia University Press, 1997).

[5] Amy Vladeck Heinrich, *Fragments of Rainbows: The Life and Poetry of Saitō Mokichi, 1882–1953* (New York: Columbia University Press, 1983).

[6] As Susan Matisoff describes in chapter 10, she and Karen Brazell met in college, and they both earned PhDs in medieval Japanese literature from Columbia University. Susan's first major publication was *The Legend of Semimaru, Blind Musician of Japan* (New York: Columbia University Press, 1978). Karen was at Cornell for the bulk of her career. She received the National Book Award for her first book, *The Confessions of Lady Nijō* by Nakanoin Masatada no Musume (New York: Doubleday, 1973).

[7] The other ten tanka are found in "Last Chance: Tanka by Takagi Kiyoko, translated and introduced by Amy V. Heinrich," in *IUC Gold: Celebrating Fifty Years of Excellence,* edited by Indra A. Levy (Yokohama: Inter-University Center for Japanese Language Studies, 2013), 84.

[8] Okano Hirohiko, "Bagdad Is Burning," translated by Amy V. Heinrich, *The Tanka Journal* 30 (2007), 1.

[9] Tanizaki Jun'ichirō, *Memoir of Forgetting the Capital*, translated by Amy V. Heinrich (New York: Yushodo and Columbia University Press, 2010).

[10] Laurel Rasplica Rodd received her PhD from the University of Michigan and taught Japanese language and literature at the University of Colorado Boulder for most of her career. She translated the *Kokinshū*—Laural Rasplica Rodd with Mary Catherine Henkenius, *Kokinshū: A Collection of Poems Ancient and Modern* (Princeton: Princeton University Press, 1984)—and the *Shinkokinshū: A New Collection of Poems Ancient and Modern* (Leiden: Brill, 2015). Among her other work are studies of Buddhism and modern poets. Joan Ericson received her PhD from Columbia University and teaches at Colorado College. Her publications include *Be a Woman: Hayashi Fumiko and Modern Japanese Women's Literature* (Honolulu: University of Hawai'i Press, 1997).

[11] Tsujimoto Isao, ed., *Kawaranai sora: nakinagara warainagara* (The Sky Unchanged: Tears and Smiles) (Tokyo: Kōdansha, 2014), 76.

[12] Ibid., 40.

[13] Ibid., 78.

16

The Presence of the Past in Life and Scholarship

Sonja Arntzen

Only later did I learn the Japanese proverb, "mekura hebi ni ojizu": "The blind do not fear snakes." It sums up my naiveté, but I have no regrets. Ikkyū's poetry became the unifying thread upon which I slowly added beads of knowledge.

SONJA ARNTZEN taught at the University of Alberta and the University of Toronto. Now living on Gabriola Island in British Columbia, she continues her research in Japanese literature of the Heian and medieval eras and her experiments with poetry writing. Her books include *Ikkyū and the Crazy Cloud Anthology: A Zen Monk of Medieval Japan* (2022), *The Kagerō Diary: A Woman's Autobiographical Text from Tenth-Century Japan* (1997), and *The Sarashina Diary: A Woman's Life in Eleventh-Century Japan* (Columbia University Press, 2014; Reader's Edition, 2018).

Given this chance to look back over a lifetime, I find myself wondering at the vagaries of chance that lead us in one direction or another. How did I end up devoting my life to the study of premodern Japanese literature?

Foundation Stones

Raised in a Vancouver suburb, the child of a Norwegian immigrant fisherman and second-generation Norwegian mother, both of whom only had an elementary school education, there was nothing in my upbringing that augured such a future. But there were small nudges. My sister married a banker whose first post was in Vancouver's Chinatown. After my brother-in-law learned from his Chinese clients how to order Chinese food, our family dinners were always in Chinese restaurants. Still a young child, walking through the streets of Chinatown, I was fascinated by the Chinese script everywhere. "What kind of writing is that?" I asked and was told, "Those are pictures." I could not see the pictures, but that early encounter with Chinese sowed a seed.

My sixth-grade teacher, Mr. Copeland, sowed another seed. He was a classicist who expanded our history curriculum to include ancient Greece and Rome. He told us about Heinrich Schliemann's excavation of Troy digging through four thousand years of history with teaspoons. I know now that he gave us a highly romanticized version of Schliemann's project, but the story inspired me to want to become an archaeologist. Instead, I became a kind of textual archaeologist, working to excavate meaning from layers of historical change in language. Mr. Copeland addressed us students as "scholars," investing that word with such dignity. And although I took it completely for granted at the time, he treated us equally, boys and girls alike. The humanistic ideal of the scholar, often traditionally thought of as a male domain, was not so for Mr. Copeland.

I credit my father, too, for making me feel that any career was open to me. Although economic circumstances had denied him much of an education, he was a natural thinker interested in new ideas and science. His dream was that I become a nuclear physicist. Although it turned out that I was not gifted in that direction at all, he never held it against me. I cannot remember anyone discouraging me from any path because I was a girl.

I think one aspect of my childhood formation that predisposed me to like classical Japanese literature was an innate feeling of affinity for the natural world. In recent years, I have been writing long poems and tanka in English. The traditional Japanese literary strategy of mixing poetry and prose in autobiographical writing has always attracted me because I think the combining of registers, especially given the open-ended meaning of poetry, produces a complex, more relatable picture of a person. Therefore, I take the liberty of including a few of my own poems in this chapter. This poem sums up moments of awareness in my childhood:

> *dust motes shining gold*
> *in the rays of spring sunshine*
> *as my mother sweeps and sings*

a clear stream candled with saffron skunk cabbage
barely leafed branches above
weaving with a soft breeze

our garden always full of flowers
spring to summer, primula, japonica, iris, gladioli
ripe in the fall with apples, plums, pears
not a one forbidden to me

the warm steady chug of
an Easthope engine[1]
under my sleeping pallet
as our little troller[2]
heads through the early morning rain
to the fishing ground

such were the stones laid
in the foundation of my being

University in the 1960s

I started university in 1962 at the University of British Columbia (UBC) with no clear idea of what I wanted to study. I was just excited by the freedom of university life. My first two years were not distinguished academically. In the "Old Caf," a cafeteria under the university auditorium, there was a long table that served as a gathering place for students of a bohemian predilection. I spent a lot of time there and often paid more attention to the books recommended there than to those assigned in my courses. One such recommendation was the Daoist classic, *Lao Tzu: Tao Te Ching* (*The Classic of the Way and Virtue*). It was not only my introduction to Chinese philosophy but also seemed to express my own latent thoughts. It was one of the nudges that led me in the direction of East Asia.

Nonetheless, I first majored in French literature because of the thrill of discovering, during my first year, that a bit of extra study beyond high school French allowed me to read works of French literature without needing a dictionary for every page. I also majored in fine arts because I liked art and, like so many students in the 1960s, felt no need to be practical about my studies. In my third year, I took Asian art and found myself enthralled by calligraphy even though I had no access to its meaning. I thought, "Wouldn't it be far out to be able to read a language that could be written that beautifully?" I resolved to study Chinese or Japanese before I left university. My ignorance was so profound at that point that I assumed there was little difference between the two languages. I would have taken Chinese as my first choice, but the Cultural Revolution raging in China was eradicating the classical culture to which I felt drawn. I also wanted to study the language of a country I might be able to visit one day, so in autumn of 1965, I enrolled in first-year Japanese.

In addition, I signed up for a course in Japanese literature in translation that was taught by Shūichi Katō. Originally trained as a doctor, Katō left medicine to become a professional writer and published essays in major Japanese journals and newspapers. A polyglot equally at home in French, German, and English, by the late 1950s, he was recognized as a leading spokesperson for the postwar generation in Japan. Of his reputation and influence in Japan, I knew nothing at the time. Nor was I aware that the program in Asian Studies at UBC was only four years old. Katō was new to the university and to teaching Japanese literature. As I learned in recent years, he was discovering, and in a sense, making, classical Japanese literature his own as he taught it to us.[3] Perhaps that is why his lectures were so fresh and stimulating. With each class, I felt a highway opening up before me. The past was alive for Katō. His ability to draw striking and insightful analogies between Japanese and European literature created a vast context for all he taught us. Moreover, as I also realized much later, his selection of subjects was not at all aligned with standard *kokubungaku* (study of the national literature).[4]

A case in point was Katō's devotion of two whole classes to the medieval Zen monk Ikkyū Sōjun (1394–1481), even though Ikkyū's medium of expression was *kanshi* (poems in Chinese). Moreover, there were very few translations of Ikkyū's poetry available in English. Katō himself was working with a German scholar on translations of Ikkyū's poetry into German. I was enthralled by what Katō told us about the man and his poetry. Up to that point in the course, I had been charmed by *waka* poetry. I loved its seemingly infinite play with seasonal imagery, but my untrained appreciation could discern no differences in personality between the poets, and the restraint of its expression in both form and topic seemed limiting. Ikkyū, by contrast, was a poet of bold expression and powerful emotion, someone who loved passionately, got angry, and protested the ills of his time. In the 1960s, these characteristics made Ikkyū seem relatable and almost contemporary. I told myself, "Someone has to translate this poet and let his voice be heard too as an authentic part of Japanese literature." After the second class, I went up to Katō and asked, "If I worked very hard, might I be able to translate Ikkyū's poetry?" After all, even though I had just started studying Japanese, Katō had already allowed me to audit a graduate course in which they were reading *waka* of the *Kokinshū*, a tenth-century poetry anthology. How much harder could *kanshi* be? He smiled and said, "It will take you a while." With that reply, the course of the next twenty years of my life was set, and I ended up becoming a university professor.

Graduate Study at UBC and in Japan

Those twenty years began with one year of self-study in Japan, after which I was accepted into the master's program at UBC. I would never be admitted into a graduate program now with so little preparation, but it was pioneering days for the program at UBC and for the field in general. There was almost no secondary literature on Ikkyū's poetry in Japanese, let alone in English or French. At a point when my study of modern Japanese had barely begun, I needed to tackle literary Chinese as well as the specialized language of Chinese Buddhist texts. Only later did I learn the Japanese proverb, *"mekura hebi ni ojizu"*: "The blind do not fear snakes." It sums up my naiveté, but I have no regrets. Ikkyū's poetry became the unifying thread upon which I slowly added beads of knowledge.

Katō left UBC at the end of my first year in the master's program to take up a post at the Free University of Berlin. Shotaro Iida, a scholar of Indian Buddhism, took over supervision of my work. Iida was a passionate, rigorous scholar to whom I will always be grateful for curing me of a lackadaisical attitude toward punctuality. I completed my MA in 1970, took a year away from studies to work at the Canadian Pavilion at Expo '70 in Osaka, and was admitted to the PhD program at UBC with a new supervisor, Leon Hurvitz, a scholar of early Chinese Buddhism, who had left the University of Washington to come and collaborate with Arthur Link, another scholar of Chinese Buddhism at UBC, and also as a personal protest against the Vietnam War. In fact, the graduate program in Asian Studies at UBC was full of young American men avoiding the draft. Presenting a prickly personality at our first meeting, Hurvitz turned out to be the most supportive advisor a student could wish for. A philologist to the core, Hurvitz had devoted himself to the study of the languages he needed to trace Buddhism's transmission to China. From Hurvitz, I learned to be wary of what one wanted the text to say and to never shirk the painstaking work necessary to make sure what the words could say within their own historical context. A doctoral fellowship from the Japan Foundation (1976–1978) allowed me to work with Yanagida Seizan at Kyoto University's Jinbun Kagaku Kenkyūjo (Institute for Research in the Humanities) and with Hirano Sōjō of Hanazono University. Again, I was blessed with wonderful mentorship. Yanagida was a model for reading texts of the past with empathy as well as for having a rigorous sense of historical linguistics; Hirano, as an ordained monk within Ikkyū's own Daitokuji monastic lineage, offered a deep knowledge of the understanding of Zen texts that had been transmitted within that lineage. As I look back, I see that I did not have any women scholarly mentors, but I can say with deep gratitude that all my teachers treated me with respect as a partner in learning. In fact, for the first part of my university life, I can say I lived with little awareness of being a woman.

Mothers, Motherhood, and Research

The reality of being a woman was brought rather forcibly to my attention by becoming pregnant in the first year of my PhD program, mere months after the head of the department had warned me, "Now, don't go and get pregnant." I took a break from classes after the birth of my child, but I was able to keep making progress with my research because of childcare support from my mother. Throughout my daughter's childhood, my mother was always there, freeing me time and time again to work. The firm foundation of love and stability she gave both of us has borne us through many difficulties. Naturally open-minded, my mother also had an instinctive, down-to-earth sense of what women's liberation was about. Once, my mother took a guided tour of the University of Hawai'i campus. When they got to the sunken garden, the guide remarked, "Before women's liberation, beauty pageants used to be held here." A disgruntled gentleman complained, "What the hell has women's liberation got to do with beauty contests?" My mother quickly informed him, "Oh, don't you know? We are all beautiful now."

During the two years of graduate work in Japan, when I was essentially a single mother, it was the other mothers in Kyoto's Ichijōji neighborhood who became a vital support. Being a mother in Japan enabled me for the first time to participate in Japanese women's society. I saw how much women contribute to the strength of community in neighborhoods. The trajectories of the lives of the other mothers were fascinating to me. They were all housewives despite having university educations, but their eyes were on the future because they were all planning that their daughters would have careers of their own. Their wisdom and humor brought delight to daily life, and their generosity in sharing my tasks of motherhood was an enormous contribution. The appreciation for mothers, both my own and mothers in Japan, laid the groundwork for my later embrace of feminism. I should add that Yanagida and Hirano also accommodated the constraints on my time—Yanagida by never minding if my daughter played in the courtyard at the Jinbun while we met, and Hirano by inviting me to his temple in Katada so that my daughter could play with his children during our consultations.

> *the remains*
> *of the temple's old*
> *stone and sand garden*
> *ringing with the laughter*
> *of children on tricycles*

First Academic Position: University of Alberta

There were three openings in the field of Japanese literature in North America when I completed my PhD in 1979. One was at The Ohio State University, and the other two, thanks to Japan Foundation staff-expansion grants, were at the University of Alberta. I was hired at the fledgling East Asian Studies program at the University of Alberta. This was before the Japan "boom" in the 1980s (see chapter 22). Alberta is the "Texas" of Canada; not noted for looking outward, but flush with profits from oil in those days, the provincial government was pouring money into the universities. Those funds, however, were tied to tangible results like enrollments. The East Asian Studies program was still the "love child" of the History Department and directed by the redoubtable Hazel Jones. Her partner, Yukie Miyakawa, a master language teacher, was building the Japanese language program. She had created a Japanese calligraphy course to protect the enrollment numbers for Japanese language. Two large sections of the course could be filled every term thanks to exchange students from Hong Kong seeking "easy credits" on the strength of their childhood training with the brush. Jones and Miyakawa wanted to increase the intellectual content of this course, and, needing Miyakawa for nurturing the serious students in Japanese language, assigned the calligraphy course to me because, although I had no certificate in calligraphy, I had been practicing the art since my first year in Japan with a couple of Japanese teachers and, more recently, with Yim Tse, a Chinese librarian at UBC and an accomplished calligrapher.

While keeping the calligraphy component, I transformed the course into a history of the Japanese writing system, which proved to be an illuminating perspective from which to view Japanese history and culture. Because most of the students were of Chinese background, they entered the course with an antipathy toward Japan, learned from their elders and education, combined with a guilty attraction to Japanese popular culture, which was just then beguiling the youth of former Asian adversaries with anime and "trendy dramas" (television series focused on youthful romance). Gaining an appreciation for the 1,200 years during which the Japanese had revered and productively absorbed Chinese literary culture provided a balance for the unhappy history of the last hundred years and nurtured a recognition of kinship. It was satisfying to see the insights expressed in their answers to the essay questions on exams and to listen to the one or two students who would invariably come up at the end of each term and say things like, "I had always been taught to hate Japan, but now I see there is more to its culture than I knew."

Meanwhile, there were only three students in the first class I offered in Japanese literature.[5] The enrollments gradually increased but were seldom more than fifteen. I worked hard to make the study of premodern literature attractive by incorporating creative writing assignments, such as holding *uta-awase* poetry contests and *renga* (linked verse) writing sessions in English.[6] Expressing themselves in early writing modes created empathy in the students for literature of the past.

The economic boom of Japan in the mid to late 1980s swelled our enrollments in Japanese language courses. The passion for anime that was sweeping through youth culture around the world by that time also brought us more students. Moreover, Japan's wealth translated into support for many kinds of cultural exchange. I dedicated much of my time in those years to community outreach, organizing visits of tea masters and Noh troupes and assisting fundraising for a Japanese garden and pavilion at the University of Alberta Botanic Garden. At a UBC conference in 1984, I met the calligrapher Kataoka Shikō. Based in the Osaka area, Kataoka had a large number of students both there and in Tokyo. A gifted teacher who inspired creativity in all her students, she had a missionary zeal to communicate the wonders of calligraphy to an audience outside of Japan, despite her limited English language skills. I became her student and friend. We collaborated on several touring exhibitions over the next twenty years, starting with a joint venture between her and my former teacher Yim Tse.

Publication of My First Book

But Ikkyū was still with me, and my research on him culminated in the publication of *Ikkyū and the Crazy Cloud Anthology* in 1986. What to do next? I made a tentative start on a project I called the "China of the Mind" in medieval Japanese writers. It was based on the realization that Ikkyū had lived his whole life in a China of his imagination, just as I had lived the last twenty years of my life in an imagined medieval Japan centered around Ikkyū's textual world. I was interested in that kind of idiosyncratic relationship with the past through texts.[7]

However, I attended a conference, "The Effect of the Feminist Approach on Research Methodology," at the University of Calgary in 1985. It included not only presenters in the humanities but also in the social sciences and pure sciences. What a revelation that conference was to me! It was as though I had only ever observed my hand from the back, and now I had turned it over and gazed at the palm. The conference also exposed me to new schools of literary theory. I became interested in questions of female voice and agency, questions that can reveal many kinds of insights precisely because they can have no definitive answers. At the same time, a wave of gratitude welled up in me for all the women writers and activists who had opened up the social world for more than a century so that I could live my life virtually unhampered by the traditional constrictions on women. Not being used to thinking in terms of masculine and feminine, from this new perspective, I realized that I had devoted the last twenty years to researching one of the most "masculine" topics in Japanese literature, the *kanshi* of Japanese Zen monks.

> *Even as a girl child,*
> *somewhere inside*
> *I felt like an old man.*
>
> *And as an adolescent*
> *somewhere inside*
> *a little old man*
> *laughed at my youthful folly.*

Once I gave my old dad
a statue of a wizened Chinese sage
for his birthday,
but I might have been giving him me.

Later,
after studying the culture
of the wise old men of China
and realizing the depth
of its misogyny,
I thought...
how fitting a lesson
it would be
for an old guy
who never gave a thought
about women
to be born
into a woman's body
and learn to appreciate it.

Suddenly, too, the presence of so many women writers at the foundation of the vernacular literary tradition in Japan stood out as an extraordinary phenomenon. Reading Virginia Woolf's *A Room of One's Own* (1929), I had the uncanny impression that her literary voice and style had much in common with those of Heian women writers, particularly in the way her sinuous sentences captured sensual perceptions and how her narrative moved by associative connections rather than logical thought. Because I had read almost none of the Heian authors in the original up to this point, I tested this impression by starting with the *Kagerō Diary* (*Kagerō nikki*), written circa 974 by a woman known as Michitsuna's mother, which gives an intimate account of twenty years of the author's troubled marriage. I read it side by side with Edward Seidensticker's translation, *The Gossamer Years* (1964). I felt that my observations were validated, but I discovered that, while Seidensticker's translation served the content of the diary well enough, it transmitted very little of the author's style. Her voice was one with her style, and I was smitten with it. The thought occurred, "someone has to do a translation that conveys her style," and thus was set my next ten years' work. A Japan Foundation Fellowship supported a year's research at Tokyo Women's Christian University (Tokyo Joshi Daigaku) to consult with Akiyama Ken, a scholar on *The Tale of Genji* and another generous mentor. Moreover, I benefited enormously from regular meetings at a coffee shop with Shinozuka Sumiko, an independent scholar who researched premodern literature and criticism as part of her own practice as a tanka poet, uniting *kokoro* (heart-mind) and *kotoba* (words) in the time-honored tradition.[8] She shared photocopies of a long series of articles she had written for a tanka journal, which were essentially *Kagerō Diary* reading notes that formed the basis for her magnum opus, *The Kagerō Diary: Heart-Mind and Expressions* (*Kagerō nikki no kokoro to hyōge*). My translation of the *Kagerō Diary* was published in 1996, the same year that the University of Alberta was able to establish a master's program in East Asian Studies, thus opening up for me the joy of working with graduate students.

Collaborations

My next major research project was decided at the Pacific Ancient and Modern Language Association Conference at Claremont in 1998, where I had two days of stimulating conversation with Itō Moriyuki, who has dedicated his life to researching the *Sarashina Diary* (*Sarashina nikki*), written circa 1060 by Sugawara no Takasue no Musume, an account of forty years of a woman's life constructed around the relationship between fiction and life. Itō is comparatively rare in his generation of Heian specialists for being interested in literary criticism in English about Japanese literature. While a graduate student, he read Ivan Morris's translation, *As I Crossed a Bridge of Dreams*, and he had wanted for years to have someone translate and interpret the *Sarashina Diary* in a way that would reveal all that Morris's introduction left out or, in his opinion, distorted. He enrolled me in this project that took longer than expected—sixteen years—during which I moved from the University of Alberta to the University of Toronto (2000–2005) and then retired to Gabriola Island in the Salish Sea to pursue a *"han nō han gaku"* (half-farming, half-scholarship) lifestyle. It was never a full-time project for either of us; our most intensive work was done together in person. Itō and his wife came many times to Gabriola Island, and I had the opportunity to visit Tokyo for a few extended stays.

I will share two anecdotes from our work together. Once, Itō came to Gabriola in May and stayed at our family cabin that is graced with a few old apple trees. The moon was full and the blossoms full, too. He phoned me the next morning in some excitement to report, "I have seen *asa midori* (lucent green)," which is the opening line of the poem from the *Sarashina Diary* that was selected for the *Shinkokinshū* imperial *waka* anthology. The poem goes:

> *Lucent green—*
> *misting over, becoming one*
> *with the blossoms too;*
> *dimly it may be seen,*
> *the moon on a night in spring*

(asa midori
hana mo hitotsu ni
kasumitsutsu
oboro ni miyuru
*hana no yo no tsuki)*⁹

Itō had written an entire article about the originality and evocative power of this one phrase. He continued, "In my youth, I saw night skies without the contamination of electric illumination, but it is so long since I have been able to experience a naturally radiant sky like that." It was a moment that deepened the understanding of that phrase for us both.

The other episode took place in Tokyo in Itō's office at Gakushūin Women's College (Gakushūin Joshi Daigaku). We were wrestling with how to express the way Takasue no Musume creates an overall pattern of light and dark in her work, and how darkness in particular is both negative and positive depending on the context. Itō looked over to me and cited the line from Simon and Garfunkel's song "Sound of Silence": "Hello darkness, my old friend." Allusion has always played a strong role in classical Japanese writing. The citation of phrases from famous poems could be used like pictures to convey "a thousand words" and unite the speaker and addressee through a shared understanding. Itō's allusion to that popular song had the same power and united us in an ineffable way.

Roughly the same period of time was enlivened by a productive academic collaboration with my colleague at the University of Alberta, Janice Brown, a specialist in modern Japanese literature. We were successful in getting grants from the SSHRC (Social Sciences and Humanities Research Council of Canada) for a long-term project (2000–2006) on premodern and modern Japanese women's writing. These funds supported a major conference at the University of Alberta in 2001 titled "Across Time and Genre: Reading and Writing Japanese Women's Texts" (resulting in the publication of conference proceedings), a focused workshop in 2006, and the work of a number of graduate students at both the University of Alberta and the University of Toronto. For the 2001 conference, Kataoka put together a solo exhibition of calligraphy works based on excerpts of Japanese women's writing from the premodern to the modern period. The exhibition, *Linked Lines: Japanese Women's Texts through Time* (August 16–September 7, 2001), complemented the academic papers perfectly (figure 16.1).

Quirin Press published a revised and expanded reprint of my *Ikkyū the Crazy Cloud Anthology* in 2022. Since it had been out of print for more than twenty years, it was a pleasure to see this work of my youth take on a new life. In 1999, I married Richard John Lynn, a scholar of classical Chinese literature whose work ranges from the *Zhuangzi* to that of the literati poet Huang Zunxian (1848–

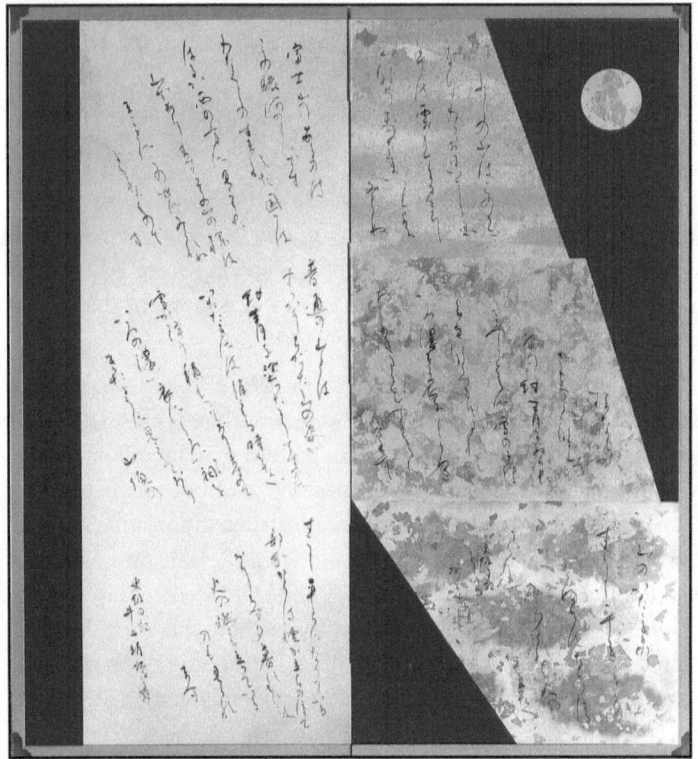

Figure 16.1: Kataoka Shikō, from the *Sarashina Diary*, bifold screen, *Linked Lines: Japanese Women's Texts through Time* exhibition, University of Alberta, 2001. Photograph courtesy of Kataoka Shikō's estate.

1905), secretary in the first Chinese diplomatic legation in Japan (1877–1882). Working again intensively with Chinese texts to prepare the revised Ikkyū book, I felt fortunate to have a resident Sinologist on hand to advise on interpretations of troublesome lines, to search out digital resources, and, of course, to provide camaraderie, particularly during the pandemic isolation of 2020 to 2021. I help him with Japanese texts, too, so one aspect of our marriage has been collaboration.

My current project is the product of another chance encounter, this time with a young girl who swam briefly into the orbit of our family. She loved poetry and Japanese culture; I thought she was just the right age to enjoy *The Tale of Lady Ochikubo* (*Ochikubo monogatari*), which is a "Cinderella" romance, the story of a persecuted stepdaughter rescued by a handsome noble. But it is no fairy tale; almost half this anonymous novel is devoted to a nitty-gritty account of the hero's revenge on the stepmother. I gave the young girl a copy of the Whitehouse-Yanagisawa translation (1971). Despite her literary bent, she could not get past the first few pages. Rereading it myself, I understood why. The familiar voice in my head said, "Someone has to translate this tale in a way that reveals the genius of its storytelling." This project has brought about a complete revision of my translation strategies and style. I had to be much freer, getting shockingly close to adaptation, pushed that way by what I see as the special needs of a work of "popular" literature. My translation is tentatively titled *Tale of the Lady of the Low Chamber*, and the work brings hours of joy as well as challenge.

Coda

Mine has been a life in service to premodern texts with the goal of communicating them to as wide an audience as possible. I have been indebted to theoretical writing for shifting my research perspectives and choices of texts to translate and for providing ways of opening up the texts for readers, but my primary contributions have been as a scholar-translator.[10] Working across language and culture, I have sought to create empathy with modes of being in the past, some of which are very different from contemporary modes and some that seem similar. What is the value of connecting with human experience in the past? I think that any expansion in what we can identify with encourages tolerance. And why the past? On the one hand, the last century or more of scientific investigation in fields like paleontology, anthropology, and genetics has deepened our intellectual awareness of connection with our earliest ancestors, but, on the other hand, developments in communications technologies seem to have promoted a sense of modern uniqueness and an excessive concern for whatever is "trending." Apparently, the term "terminal uniqueness" is used in Alcoholics Anonymous programs of recovery to denote the psychological trap of feeling one's own suffering is utterly different from that of everyone else and thus impossible to alleviate. Sometimes I wonder if our modern age is not subject to a similar mental state. Ultimately, however, I find my own attraction to the past inexplicable. All I do know is that I have found such consolation in a sense of kinship with voices of the past, and I have rejoiced to see students find wonder and seeds for personal growth in those voices.

Notes

[1] Over several decades, the Easthope company in Vancouver produced the most reliable and durable marine engines ever made. Their steady "ka chug, ka chug" was the music of the BC coast.

[2] Trolling is a form of fishing unique to the Pacific Northwest adapted from the fishing techniques of the Indigenous peoples. Weighted lines are slowly towed from which other lines with lures and bait are streamed.

[3] See Shūichi Katō, *A History of Japanese Literature, Volume 1: The First Thousand Years*, translated by David Chibbett (London: Macmillian Press, 1979), a translation of Katō

Shūichi, *Nihon bungakushi josetsu* (An Introduction to the History of Japanese Literature) (Tokyo: Chikuma shobō, 1975).

[4] I wrote about Katō's research and teaching style in "Katō Shūichi no nihon koten bungaku kenkyū—sono kokusaiteki eikyō no kansuru shiken" (Katō Shūichi's Research on Classical Japanese Literature: A Personal View of Its International Influence), in *Katō Shūichi o nijūisseki ni hikitsugu tame ni* (To Have Katō Shūichi Carry On into the Twenty-First Century), edited by Miura Nobutaka and Washizu Tsutomu, (Tokyo: Suiseisha, 2020), 111-126.

[5] One of those students was Sharon Domier, who, as a librarian of Japanese materials, has gone on to make so many and varied contributions to her field.

[6] See Sonja Arntzen and Janice Brown, "Old Pond, Students Leap In, Sound of Laughter: Creative Projects in the Teaching of Classical Japanese," *Japanese Language and Literature* 35, no. 1 (April 2001): 17–36.

[7] Belatedly, I published an article that distilled my thoughts on this topic, at least so far as Ikkyū is concerned: "Chinese Community of the Imagination for the Japanese Zen Monk Ikkyū Sōjun," *Rethinking the Sinosphere Volume 2; Poetics, Aesthetics, and Identity Formation*, eds. Nanxiu Qian et al. (Amherst: Cambria Press, 2020), 67–94.

[8] Shinozuka Sumiko, *Kagerō nikki no kokoro to hyōgen* (The Kagerō Diary: Heart-Mind and Expressions) (Tokyo: Benseisha 1995). I discuss this tradition in "In Defense of Kokoro: The Study of Classical Japanese Literature in North America within the Context of the Debate over a World System of Anthropology," *Ritsumeikan Journal of Asia Pacific Studies* 6 (December 2000), 81–83.

[9] Sugawara no Takasue no Musume, *The Sarashina Diary*, translated with an introduction by Sonja Arntzen and Itō Moriyuki (New York: Columbia University Press, 2014), 174.

[10] Michael Emmerich gives an eloquent exposition of the role and importance of the "scholar-translator" in our field in *Tale of Genji: Translation, Canonization, and World Literature* (New York: Columbia University Press, 2013), 383–403.

17

TWO CHILDREN ... AND A PHD

Christine M. E. Guth

Childbirth and motherhood in the United States and Japan as a graduate student and young academic defined the trajectory of my career as a historian of Japanese art in the patriarchal world of 1970s academia and beyond.

CHRISTINE M. E. GUTH has taught at Princeton University, Harvard University, the University of Pennsylvania, and the University of California, Berkeley, among other institutions. She led the Asian specialism in the Victoria and Albert Museum and Royal College of Art's Postgraduate History of Design Program (2007–2016). Her publications include *Art, Tea, and Industry: Masuda Takashi and the Mitsui Circle* (1993); *Longfellow's Tattoos: Tourism, Collecting, and Japan* (2004); *Hokusai's Great Wave: Biography of a Global Icon* (2015); and *Craft Culture in Early Modern Japan: Materials, Makers, and Mastery* (2021). She is currently researching culinary relations between Japan and the United States (1854–1920).

"Christine, hello! I think this is the first time I have seen you not pregnant!" The speaker was Maryell Semal, the right-hand woman behind Rand Castile's successful directorship of the Japan House Gallery in New York (1971–1985). She was welcoming me to the gallery, where preparations were underway for the opening in September 1976 of the exhibition *Shinto Arts: Nature, Gods, and Man in Japan*, of which I was cocurator with Kageyama Haruki.

Her observation was intended as a friendly tease, but it was nonetheless an indication of the singularity of and the ambivalent attitudes at the time toward those who sought to combine motherhood with scholarship, even among women. I began my studies toward a PhD in Harvard's Department of Fine Arts (today the Department of History of Art and Architecture) in 1970, directly after graduating from the Catholic University of Louvain, in Belgium, where I had studied with the renowned Buddhologist Étienne Lamotte. After receiving my undergraduate degree in Oriental Languages and History, I wanted to continue my studies, but dissertation work with Lamotte would have meant translating a Buddhist text of his choosing, and my interests lay in the material expressions of Buddhism as it had traveled from India across Asia. With his blessing (literally, as he was a Monseigneur), I applied to Harvard and was accepted, despite the fact that I had no formal art historical training. I had my first child, a daughter, two years later in Tokyo, and my son three years later in Boston, the day after completing a draft of my dissertation. I carried a breast pump with me the following spring when I flew from Cambridge to Chicago for my first job interview. Childbirth and motherhood in the United States and Japan as a graduate student and young academic defined the trajectory of my career as a historian of Japanese art in the patriarchal world of 1970s academia and beyond.

When I entered graduate school in 1970, there were only five programs awarding PhDs in Japanese art history: Harvard, Princeton, the Institute of Fine Arts of New York University, the University of Michigan, and Columbia. Miyeko Murase, who taught at Columbia, was the sole woman teaching Japanese art history at the time. Like John Rosenfield at Harvard, whose dissertation was on Indian art of the Kushan era (30–375), Murase had not initially planned to study Japanese art but switched at her advisor's recommendation.

The 1970s saw dramatic growth of the field as a steady stream of new women scholars began their studies, completed their dissertations, and assumed positions in institutions and museums across the country.[1] In 1969, Louise Cort, a specialist in Japanese ceramics, was appointed Assistant Curator of Asian Art at the Fogg Art Museum (now part of the Harvard Art Museums). She later broke new ground in a remarkable study of Shigaraki pottery and its makers.[2] In 1973, Julia Meech, Rosenfield's first graduate student, became Assistant Curator of Japanese Art at the Metropolitan Museum of Art. A scholar of exceptional range, she went on to publish a study of Meiji prints based on a collection donated to the Met and an award-winning study of Frank Lloyd Wright as a collector of Japanese prints.[3] The late Carolyn Wheelwright, a student of Shimada Shūjirō at Princeton, coedited with Shimizu Yoshiaki, *Japanese Ink Paintings from American Collections*, a major exhibition whose scholarly catalog established a new standard for the field.[4] Five years later, in 1981, after completing her dissertation, she was hired to teach Japanese art history at Yale. Other rising scholars included Willa Tanabe, Laura Kaufman, and Melinda Takeuchi studying at Columbia, NYU, and Michigan, respectively.[5]

The visibility and intellectual abilities of these and other women challenged the monopoly of male scholars. Their areas of research, approaches, and interpretations brought new heterogeneity to the field. They also questioned norms in ways that were not always welcome. Male faculty members in Harvard's Department of Fine Arts openly expressed dismay about teaching women who they believed would only go home and have babies. An applicant with impressive credentials in European art history, who had put her career plans on hold while her children were young, though armed with a prestigious Danforth Graduate Fellowship for Women, was turned down because she had four children. She persisted, was later accepted, and became a pioneer in the study of Japan's modern print movement (*sōsaku-hanga*). In a world of male entitlement, the idea that a woman could make a rational choice about balancing the personal and professional was inconceivable.

During this decade, the number of institutions offering undergraduate and graduate courses in Japanese art grew with financial support from the US and Japanese governments and private foundations. There were also generous corporate sponsorships of loan exhibitions from Japan. The appreciation and study of Japanese art have always been bellwethers of prevailing international political and economic relations. The Japanese government was adept in using art to influence how Americans saw Japan, having practiced this form of soft power since the nineteenth century. In the years following World War II, the promotion of Japanese aesthetics—woodblock prints, tea ceremony, flower arranging, and Zen painting—helped to diffuse the image of Japan as a militaristic nation. In the 1970s, when many Americans viewed Japan's economic growth as a threat to the United States, investment in culture was mobilized to promote greater understanding between the two nations.

I did not intend to specialize in Japanese art, having studied the language for only a year. I was fascinated by the hybrid forms of material culture in Central Asia and by the Buddhist art of China, but neither region was open to American travel yet. Japan became an attractive option not only because it was accessible but because Buddhism was a living religion there. Its religious arts also raised fascinating questions about cultural assimilation. Buddhist art in Japan had developed its own distinctive artistic language, grammar, and vocabulary, but how did the process of translation work? John Rosenfield's seminars did little to address such complex questions, since most classes were dedicated to the study and preparation of catalogs of American collections of Japanese art. These provided students with opportunities for working with original works of art but left it up to them to address larger intellectual issues on their own.

Beyond the required mastery of Japanese, Chinese, and two European languages, the study of Japanese art history was a serious challenge since there were still few scholarly English-language publications in the field. Even those new to the discipline of European and American art were already familiar with the conceptual framework that informed it and could dare to challenge it. This was not true for those studying Japanese art history, where a publication like Linda Nochlin's 1971 landmark article, "Why Have There Been No Great Women Artists?," was beyond the realm of possibility.[6] It would be decades before scholars like Chino Kaori would bring a gendered perspective to the study of Japanese narrative handscrolls.[7]

I struggled to grasp what constituted the canon of Japanese art and how it had come to be, a topic that continued to be an intellectual concern long afterward, resurfacing in my second book, *Art, Tea, and Industry: Masuda Takashi and the Mitsui Circle* (1993). My first go-to source on this question was a six-volume bilingual compendium compiled by Japan's Cultural Properties Commission (Bunkazai Hōgo Iinkai) between 1963 and 1967.[8] It features high quality color photographs of all the works then designated National Treasures (*kokuhō*). If I was to understand Japanese art, I thought, knowing what was considered important in the cultural context of the country that had produced and consumed it was critical. The selection of works designated as National Treasures was heavily weighted toward the religious arts of the Nara (710–784) through the Muromachi (1336–1568) periods, and there were no works dating from the Meiji period (1868–1912) or later. Unlike the modern canon of European or American art, which was shaped largely by the considerations of connoisseurs, the designation of *kokuhō* was determined by government officials and heavily inflected by nineteenth- and early twentieth-century geopolitics. The descriptive entries in the compendium, like much of the Japanese scholarship at the time, were empirical, narrowly focused, and filled with technical, descriptive, and historical detail. Useful as they were as a starting point, each of these oversize publications, in its teal-blue, cloth-covered case, weighed about twenty pounds. They were too heavy to lift off the shelves when I became pregnant.

As my language skills improved, to gain a grounding in the field, I increasingly turned my attention to *Nihon no Bijutsu, The Arts of Japan*, a series of generously illustrated monthly publications, each focusing on a particular topic and written by a leading scholar in the field. Although small in scale and relatively short in length, they reflected current Japanese scholarship in a way that satisfied experts but was also accessible to non-specialists. Since 1966, when the publisher Shibundō launched the series, volumes had appeared on a wide range of topics, including Japanese design motifs, Kyoto ceramics, tea ceremony utensils, the arts of Shinto, narrative picture scrolls, Meiji Western painting, ink painting, and *haniwa* (terracotta clay figures). These were the first books translated and adapted as part of a project supervised by John Rosenfield and Louise Cort. They were among the 111 works on Japanese art and architecture translated between 1970 and 1974, more than in any other field of Japanese Studies.[9]

Believing that the translation of selected volumes from the series would provide a scholarly foundation and help gain visibility and credibility for the field of Japanese art in the United States, Rosenfield enlisted colleagues and graduate students at Harvard to take on books whose focus meshed with their research interests. Elizabeth ten Grotenhuis, for instance, translated a volume on Pure Land Buddhist painting and later wrote the definitive English-language study on Japanese Mandala paintings.[10] Translation and adaption by specialists set the volumes published under Rosenfield's auspices apart from others carried out by professional translators.

The project was controversial (shouldn't graduate students be carrying out their own original research rather than translating the work of others?), but for me it was hugely beneficial. In effect, it launched my professional career. By translating *The Arts of Shinto* (*Shinto no bijutsu*), I familiarized myself with the thinking of Kageyama Haruki, a scholar who, to a large extent, had created this field of study.[11] Grateful that his book was made available to an audience outside Japan, he became a valuable contact when I began my dissertation research on Shinto sculpture.

In the fall of 1972, my husband was awarded a Monbushō scholarship (now the Japanese government's MEXT Scholarship Program) to study Japanese legal history at the University of Tokyo, and I was able to arrange an affiliation at a conservative university where I hoped to be mentored by a scholar who had written a number of interesting articles about Shinto arts. I had not, however, informed the university that I was pregnant. Eager to start work before my baby was born, I made an appointment to meet my would-be mentor, but after politely greeting me, he left the room. University authorities were equally nonplussed. Concerned that it would not be safe for me to work in the library in my condition, they urged me to work at home.

The first weeks after our arrival in Tokyo were consumed with finding an obstetrician. No one wanted to assume responsibility for a woman in her sixth month of pregnancy sight unseen. Eventually, a young Taiwanese doctor who was training at the Tokyo Hitachi company hospital agreed to take me as his patient. I didn't know what to expect when I went for my first checkup, but I was nonetheless surprised to find that there were no private changing rooms. In the large communal space where I joined four or five other young women to undress before my examination, I quickly became the object of intense scrutiny and questions. While they were all wearing special belly wraps (*haramaki*), some with additional protection for their unborn child in the form of talismans from Shinto shrines tucked into the folds, I had none. Wasn't I concerned for my baby's health, they asked? I had never felt so alien.

The doctor examined me and then called in my husband. Although the doctor did not speak English, he could read it, and he had carefully gone over the records I had provided from Harvard's health services. After many apologies, he informed us that Harvard had made an error in calculating my due date. I would deliver two weeks earlier than they had indicated. On December 12, we rushed to the hospital when contractions were about five minutes apart only to be told that it was too early to be there. Since we lived at some distance, however, I was allowed to stay overnight, but my husband went home. My doctor was not present when I delivered my first child, a daughter, only few hours later. More apologies followed.

At Hitachi company hospital, I experienced firsthand the collective socialization in Japan that I had only read about. In the United States at the time, it was standard practice to administer epidurals and other medications to alleviate pain during childbirth unless one requested otherwise. In Japan, however, "natural childbirth," which I wanted, was the norm. My delivery was quick, but, when I cried out during especially painful contractions, the nurse asked me to quiet down so as not to disturb other patients. The sense that the hospital was a shared public space was further reinforced the day after my daughter was born, when the fifteen or so women in my ward were presented their infants and asked to carry them to a classroom with a circular wooden bench where we were told to be seated. Instruction in how to hold, and especially nurse, our babies followed, with a nurse going around the room to check if each infant had latched onto her mother's breast.

Japanese women remained in hospital for ten days following delivery, but I was ready to leave before the first week was out. There was no television or other distraction, and we were discouraged from reading. Childbirth, I was told, put a strain on the eyes, so it was important to hold off until fully recovered. I only learned later that most Japanese women welcomed the long hospital stay because they were expected to resume full family responsibilities as soon as they returned home. The trade-off was that they could count on help with childcare from their extended family. Unable to find a reliable babysitter, I spent the next six months at home translating *The Arts of Shinto* with my daughter sleeping nearby.

The field of art history has changed in many ways, but one constant is the need to study works of art firsthand and to secure quality photographs and the permission to publish them. Seeing works in private collections in Japan was virtually impossible in the 1970s. Close study of devotional icons in temples and shrines was challenging. Even gaining access to those in museums—unless they were on display—required introductions from established scholars. When I had settled on Shinto sculpture as the topic of my dissertation and planned to travel to Japan, Rosenfield provided me with an introduction to Kurata Bunsaku, a sculpture specialist and director of the Nara National Museum. He received me cordially enough but asked why I wanted to study Shinto sculpture since this would prove difficult for a woman. This was a question that could be read in many ways, but I took it to refer to the conservative world of Shinto scholarship and problems of accessing images that were still in shrines. Many of the works I proposed to study were *hibutsu*, secret icons, revealed to the public, if at all, only on ritual occasions and rarely, if ever, displayed in public exhibitions. As a young woman, and a foreigner to boot, I feared I would not be taken seriously enough to be permitted to study works that were part of the national patrimony.

Female scholars were rare in Japan at the time, and the few who were active in the field of art history, such as Yanagisawa Taka, a specialist of Buddhist painting, had to overcome obstacles in order to achieve professional recognition.[12] Yanagisawa became a mentor to a number of Rosenfield's graduate students, both men and women, and in so doing did much to advance the study of Japanese art in the United States. Elizabeth ten Grotenhuis, who became the first tenured professor in Japanese art history at Boston University, and Anne Nishimura Morse, the first female curator of Japanese art at the Museum of Fine Arts, Boston, benefited from her intellectual generosity.[13] Both successfully combined family and career.

I was not able to see all the works I wanted to write about, but I was nevertheless exceptionally fortunate in having the support of several scholars with the power to open the doors to museum and temple collections. Through Kurata, I was able to study a triad representing the deity Hachiman and two female attendants originally from the tutelary shrine attached to Yakushiji temple in Nara. Because it was designated a National Treasure and the temple did not have suitable facilities to care for it, it was stored at Nara National Museum. Hubert Durt, a fellow Lamotte student and distinguished Buddhologist who had worked in Kyoto for many years, introduced me to Manabe Shunshō, a scholar of Buddhist art who was then at the Tōji temple museum. He allowed me into the temple storerooms, where another Hachiman triad, also National Treasures, were kept in a special humidity-controlled vault. The hour I spent locked in the vault with these three, life-size polychrome statues was one of the most memorable of my career. The analysis of these two Hachiman triads formed the core of my dissertation. In retrospect, it is clear that I did not bring sufficient criticality to many thorny questions surrounding Shinto arts in my thesis (and later, my book), but my argument that the selection of wood and method of carving were central to the meaning of *shinzō*, statues of *kami* (deities), predisposed me to think about the organic and transformative nature of materials in a wider context.[14] In 2007, when I began teaching in London, I developed a course on the material cultures of Asia that examined objects on the basis of their physical properties and materials. My book, *Craft Culture in Early Modern Japan: Materials, Makers, and Mastery* (2021), grew out of this course and the many stimulating exchanges with colleagues in the design history program at the Royal College of Art and Victoria and Albert Museum who shared an interest in materials and materiality.

The publication of *The Arts of Shinto* in 1973 opened up an aspect of Japanese art that was largely unknown to the Anglophone world. There were statues of *kami*, paintings associated with the Kasuga and Kumano Shrines as well as illustrated handscrolls recounting the histories of many Shinto shrines in Western collections, but they were generally classified as Buddhist art. Kageyama's book alerted viewers to the features, functions, and contexts that distinguished these from orthodox Buddhist icons, spurring interest among collectors, scholars, and curators. Rand Castile, recognizing the compelling visual qualities of this material, contacted the Agency for Cultural Affairs (Bunkachō), about holding an exhibition devoted to Shinto Arts, the first ever outside of Japan.

The 1970s was a golden age for international exhibitions of Japanese art organized with the support of the Agency for Cultural Affairs.[15] In addition to *Shinto Arts*, during this remarkable decade, Japan Society hosted *Namban Art: The Art of the Southern Barbarians during the Momoyama Period*; *Art Treasures from the Imperial Collections*; *Tagasode: Whose Sleeves . . . Kimono from the Kanebo Collection*; *The Tokugawa Collection: No Robes and Masks*; *Genre Screens from the Suntory Museum of Art*; and *Chanoyu: Japanese Tea Ceremony*. Such events made Japan Society *the* place to see the finest works of art from Japanese collections in New York. (Dedicated galleries at the Metropolitan Museum of Art would not open until 1987.) Displayed under conditions that often made the works easier to study than in Japan, and accompanied by well-written and illustrated catalogs, these exhibitions fostered growing enthusiasm for and interest in forms of Japanese cultural expression that were previously known only to specialists in the field. Many included works designated as National Treasures and Important Cultural Properties (*jūyō bunkazai*), such as the ninth-century statue of a female *kami* featured on the cover of the *Shinto Arts* catalog, that probably would not now be allowed out of the country given the more stringent loan regulations today (figure

Figure 17.1: Cover of *Shinto Arts: Nature, Gods, and Man in Japan*, exhibition catalog, Japan Society, New York, 1976. Detail of seated female deity. Ninth century. Matsuno-o Shrine, Kyoto. Important Cultural Property. Photograph courtesy of Japan Society.

17.1). Lacking any grounding in Japanese art, those who reviewed these shows for *The New York Times* and other newspapers often signaled their importance by listing the number of nationally registered works on display.[16]

When plans for the Shinto show got underway, Peter Grilli, then Director of Education at Japan Society, proposed a film introducing Shinto as "a culturally unifying force throughout Japanese history."[17] At Harvard at the time, Professors James Ackerman and Oleg Grabar were engaged in the production of documentary films intended to contextualize the study of architectural history. At Rosenfield's recommendation, Fogg Fine Art Films, the producer, also took on the film on Shinto for which I became co-scriptwriter with Grilli.[18] The film was so over budget after the initial trip to Japan, however, that Harvard disassociated itself from it, but Grilli successfully found grants to support its production. Although it was intended to complement the *Shinto Arts* exhibition, it was only released in 1978. The visually stunning film later came to be widely used to enrich undergraduate teaching on Japanese culture and was aired on many PBS stations across the United States.

I joined the film crew on their first research trip to Japan in the summer of 1975, when I was pregnant with my son. Although Rosenfield had recommended me for the project, he was concerned that he would be held responsible if something untoward happened during our travels. I assured him that I was in good health and that my husband, who had just completed his dissertation but didn't have a job, would look after our daughter for the few weeks that I was away.

We were welcomed at all major shrine complexes we visited: Ise, Kasuga, the Kamo and Kitano Tenjin Shrines in Kyoto, and Nachi and the Kumano shrines on the Kii Peninsula. My pregnancy was never a problem, although at one inn where we shared a twelve-mat room, there was some puzzlement about the fact that none of the three men I was traveling with was my husband. At one shrine, on a sweltering hot day, the shrine priest, looking at me, said "*medetai tokoro*" (such a joyous thing), then appointed an assistant to lead me away to drink refreshingly cool water drawn from a sacred well said to help with easy childbirth. None of my male colleagues were offered anything to drink.

When I flew to New York City in the fall of 1976 to present a paper at the symposium that accompanied the *Shinto Arts* exhibition, I had just started teaching Japanese art history at the University of Kansas in Lawrence. My husband and I had driven there together with our two children during the summer, but he soon returned to Cambridge, where he had a postdoctoral fellowship at the Harvard Law School. The auditorium at Japan Society was packed, and I was nervous. Unbeknownst to me, the audience included Professors Wen Fong and Marius Jansen, who were scouting for someone to teach Japanese art at Princeton following Shimada Shūjirō's retirement. After my lecture, they introduced themselves and unexpectedly invited me to visit Princeton. I had not submitted a formal application, but much to my surprise, three months later, Fong called and offered me the post. In the summer of 1977, the four of us piled back into our now well-traveled station wagon and drove to Princeton. Six years later, after many a tussle with Fong, who had definite ideas about what and how to teach Japanese art that did not match mine, I was denied tenure. It was a painful experience, but one that provoked me to push even harder against the then narrow boundaries of the field.

After leaving Princeton in 1983, I did not hold a tenure-track position again until 2007, when I was invited to teach in London, where I remained for nearly a decade. Before going to London, I taught at many institutions, often filling in for colleagues on sabbatical. These short-term posts kept me informed of developments in the field while also giving me the freedom to explore methodologies and topics that challenged disciplinary norms—from tattooing among nineteenth-century globetrotters and the use of rayskin in early modern Japanese crafts to the ritual disposal of sewing needles (*hari kuyō*) in Japan.[19] They also brought me into contact with female graduate students often seeking advice on how to manage family and career. With so many contingencies and individual particularities at play, I was sometimes hesitant to offer counsel but could always say honestly, "It's not easy, but it's possible."

Notes

[1] For wide-ranging perspectives on the state of the field, see Mimi Yiengpruksawan, "Japanese Art History 2001: The State and Stakes of Research," *The Art Bulletin* 83, no. 1 (March 2001): 105–122; John M. Rosenfield, "Japanese Art Studies in America since 1945," in *The Postwar Development of Japanese Studies in the United States*, 161-194, edited by Helen Hardacre (Leiden: Brill, 1998).

[2] Louise Cort, *Shigaraki, Potter's Valley* (Tokyo: Kodansha, 1979).

[3] Julia Meech-Pekarik, *The World of the Meiji Print: Impressions of a New Civilization* (Tokyo: Weatherhill, 1986); Julia Meech, *Frank Lloyd Wright and the Art of Japan: The Architect's Other Passion* (New York: Harry N. Abrams, 2001).

[4] Shimizu Yoshiaki and Carolyn Wheelwright, *Japanese Ink Paintings from American Collections, the Muromachi Period. An Exhibition in Honor of Shūjirō Shimada* (Princeton: Princeton University Art Museum, 1976).

[5] See, for example, Willa Tanabe, *Paintings of the Lotus Sutra* (Tokyo: Weatherhill, 1988); Melinda Takeuchi, *Taiga's True Views: The Language of Landscape Painting in Eighteenth-Century Japan* (Stanford: Stanford University Press, 1992). Additional works are listed in the book's bibliography.

[6] Linda Nochlin, "Why Have There Been No Great Women Artists?," *ARTnews* (January 1971), 22–39, 67–71.

[7] On her career, see Melissa McCormick, "On the Scholarship of Chino Kaori," *Review of Japanese Culture and Society* (December 2003): 1–24.

[8] Bunkazai Hōgo Iinkai (Japan's Cultural Properties Commission), *Kokuhō* (National Treasures), 6 vols. (Tokyo: Mainichi Shimbunsha, 1963–1967).

[9] This figure is cited in a numerical table of "publications of serious works" on Japan translated in America or by Americans in Elizabeth Massey and Joseph Massey, *CULCON Report on Japanese Studies at Colleges and Universities in the United States in the Mid-70s* (New York: Japan Society, 1977), 132. See, for example, Saburo Mizoguchi, *Design Motifs* (*Monyō*), translated and adapted by Louise Allison Cort (Tokyo: Weatherhill,

1973); Ryōichi Fujioka, *Tea Ceremony Utensils*, translated by Louise Allison Cort (Tokyo: Weatherhill, 1973).

[10] Okazaki Jōji, *Pure Land Buddhist Painting*, translated and adapted by Elizabeth ten Grotenhuis (Tokyo: Kodansha, 1977); Elizabeth ten Grotenhuis, *Japanese Mandalas: Representations of Sacred Geography* (Honolulu: University of Hawai'i, 1999).

[11] Kageyama Haruki, *The Arts of Shinto* (*Shinto no bijutsu*), translated and adapted by Christine Guth-Kanda (Tokyo: Weatherhill, 1973).

[12] On her career, see John M. Rosenfield, "Yanagisawa Taka (1926–2003)," *Archives of Asian Art 54* (2004): 99–100.

[13] See, for example, Anne Nishimura Morse, ed., *Drama and Desire: Japanese Paintings from the Floating World* (Boston: Boston Museum of Fine Arts, 2007).

[14] Christine Guth-Kanda, "Shinzō: Hachiman Imagery and Its Development," PhD Diss. Harvard University, 1976; *Shinzō: Hachiman Imagery and Its Development* (Cambridge, MA: Harvard University Press, 1985).

[15] For a complete listing of the exhibitions held during this period, compiled on the seventy-fifth anniversary of Japan Society, see the catalog of the show curated by Kurata Bunsaku, *Hōryūji: Temple of the Exalted Law: Early Buddhist Art from Japan*, translated by W. Chie Ishibashi (New York: Japan Society, 1981).

[16] See, for example, John Russell, "Art Treasures of Shinto," *New York Times,* September 10, 1976, 62.

[17] Email exchange with Peter Grilli, September 25, 2021.

[18] Peter Grilli and David Westphal, dirs. *Shinto: Nature, Gods, and Man in Japan* (Cambridge, MA: Fogg Fine Arts Films, 1978).

[19] These projects include Christine Guth, *Longfellow's Tattoos: Tourism, Collecting, and Japan* (Seattle: University of Washington Press, 2004); "Theorizing the *Hari Kuyō*: The Ritual Disposal of Needles in Early Modern Japan," in *Encountering Things: Design and Theories of Things*, edited by Leslie Atzmon and Prasad Boradkar (London: Bloomsbury, 2017), 65–80; *Craft Culture in Early Modern Japan: Materials, Makers, and Mastery* (Berkeley: University of California Press, 2021).

18

MEMORIES OF BECOMING A JAPANESE STUDIES LIBRARIAN

Maureen Donovan

I learned that building a good research library was predicated on librarians becoming futurologists in a sense, thinking about what future researchers would want from sources that could be collected now.

MAUREEN DONOVAN, professor emerita at The Ohio State University, retired in 2015 after thirty-seven years as Japanese Studies librarian at The Ohio State University (1978–2015), preceded by four years as East Asian reference librarian at Princeton University (1974–1978). During a career that coincided with the creation of the World Wide Web, the expansion of globalization, and the widespread popularity of Japanese popular culture, she undertook many pioneering initiatives at those libraries and with colleagues nationally. With her African Studies Librarian colleague at The Ohio State University, she developed and taught a course, "Understanding the Global Information Society," that became a requirement for international studies and globalization majors.

My first foray into the stacks of Columbia University's East Asian Library when I arrived as a graduate student in 1970 was terrifying. Thousands of books in

East Asian languages, crammed onto metal shelves, with the heat turned up oppressively high throughout the year. Pages turning into "corn flakes," crumbling to the floor. I could not find my bearings at all. For one thing, I was inadequately prepared for the graduate program I was entering and could hardly read the books. Nonetheless, those stacks, and the reference books shelved in the reading room, commanded my attention, and I did not turn back. Being stubborn by nature, I was determined to pursue access. From the very beginning, my motivation for continuing with East Asian Studies focused on books, libraries, and information.

For as long as I can remember, I have been fascinated with how books open connections and overcome boundaries of time and space. This passion motivated my choice of Russian as my modern language in high school, during the post-Sputnik era when an "iron curtain" reduced our awareness of life and culture in the Soviet Union. While American news sources offered boring, sterile images of daily life there, I was using my dictionary to read stories and jokes in the humor magazine *Krokodil* (Crocodile, 1922–2008) and other publications that Russians themselves were reading. I continued those studies with a Russian major at Manhattanville College, and I studied abroad on a National Defense Foreign Language Fellowship in Leningrad (now Saint Petersburg) and Moscow in the summer of 1970. The insights gained in undergraduate Russian Studies gave me confidence later in my career when I set about, starting from the mid-1980s, to collect the kinds of manga that millions of Japanese people were enjoying, an effort that continued until my retirement in 2015, by which time the manga collection that I built had become a special feature of Ohio State's Billy Ireland Cartoon Library and Museum (BICLM).

In an advanced Russian summer course at Middlebury College in 1968, I expanded my international interests from the USSR toward East Asia following conversations with two classmates who were already working professionally in that area, one as an interpreter at the United Nations and the other as a diplomat with the Japanese Ministry of Foreign Affairs. During that Vietnam War era, I began to reflect on how much stronger my knowledge of the Soviet Union became with studying the Russian language. I was determined to achieve a deeper understanding of East Asia through language study. But which language? Since my interest was in the cultures of East Asia, my classmates both advised me to study Chinese—as the foundation of East Asian cultures—on my return to Manhattanville for my junior year, which I did.

Because I could not achieve enough Chinese language in my two remaining years of undergraduate study to fulfill my goals, I continued with graduate study in East Asian Languages and Cultures at Columbia University (EALAC). Amazingly, it was still possible in those days (when American interest in foreign cultures was still uncommon) to enter that graduate program with such weak preparation! It was challenging, but I persevered and achieved enough proficiency for an MA degree, with a focus on modern Chinese literature, working under Professor C. T. Hsia. Among the requirements was reading knowledge of Japanese, which I obtained through a special course on "Japanese for Chinese Majors." I also took some courses in modern Japanese history. Thus began the preparation for what became a career as a Japanese Studies librarian.

My first academic library job was not in an East Asian library. As a graduate student, I applied for a student position in Columbia's East Asian Library but was turned down in favor of a candidate who was a native speaker. Instead, I took a job in the acquisitions department of Columbia's Law Library. My supervisor was an inspiring librarian named Meira G. Pimsleur. Among other duties, she put me in charge of managing the receipt and filing of African legal gazettes. Whenever a coup d'état occurred in an African nation, I wrote to the new government, requesting continuation of our subscription to their legal publications. I found this very exciting! It taught me that librarians play a critical role in information access and exchange, something that seems obvious but that had not occurred to me previously. I learned that building a good research library was predicated on librarians becoming futurologists in a sense, thinking about what future researchers would want from sources that could be collected now, an outlook I maintained while building Ohio State's Japanese Collections.

Mrs. Pimsleur was one of my references when I was admitted to Columbia's School of Library Service (SLS) after completing the EALAC MA in 1973. During that one-year program, I was also enrolled in Columbia's International Fellows Program (IFP). On the one hand, I was exposed to a curriculum in SLS that emphasized a librarian's role in library user education and research support. Fortunately, I was able to take Professor David G. Johnson's EALAC course, "Chinese Bibliography and Research Methods," as an elective. Combined with what I was learning at SLS, it opened my eyes to possibilities for improving user education and engagement services in an East Asian Library.

On the other hand, participation in the IFP included two trips to Washington, DC. On the second trip, our assignment was to meet with someone working in our field. On April 4, 1974, I spent three hours talking with K. T. Wu, Head of Chinese Collections at the Library of Congress. He suggested that I contact James S. K. Tung, Head of the Gest Library and East Asian Collections at Princeton University for further discussions of library services for East Asian Studies.

Because it was getting close to my graduation from SLS, I was looking for a position, casting a wide net to law firms, businesses, and colleges in a difficult economy following the oil shock of 1973 and 1974 and deep government cutbacks, but, being intrigued with the idea of a conversation with Mr. Tung as a fitting capstone to my academic studies of East Asia, I went to see him. After a short conversation and tour of the library with its famous rare book holdings, Mr. Tung asked me to translate a text engraved on a marble slab on his desk from classical Chinese to English, without using a dictionary. I was puzzled by this request but, thanks to my training for the MA degree, I was able to do it. A few days later, I received a call from Princeton's personnel office asking if I would be interested in applying for a brand-new (unadvertised, grant-funded) opening for an East Asian reference librarian. Of course, I applied and was appointed.

When I arrived at Princeton, Mr. Tung was just finishing his term as chairperson of the Committee on East Asian Libraries (now the Council on East Asian Libraries, or CEAL), where discussions about the future of the field, and especially the need to rethink recruitment for East Asian Studies librarians, were taking place. By coincidence, my meeting with K. T. Wu took place just after the annual CEAL meeting, where this was on the agenda. One of the most important lessons I gained under Mr. Tung's tutelage was the value of participating in CEAL to stay abreast of trends and receive support from colleagues. During the 1980s, I took minutes for the annual meetings and was the first woman elected as the chairperson. During my term (1991–1994), I led the effort to change CEAL's name and expand member participation by creating additional officer positions. At the time, many wondered if CEAL could ever change, but I had confidence in my colleagues and was able to rally their support to make it happen. It has been a more vibrant organization ever since. I also quickly learned about CEAL's global role, with members from all over Europe, Australia, and Asia facing the same challenges we did. This drew me into international discussions, meetings, and conferences on issues of access to Japanese information and the management of East Asian libraries that continued beyond my term as CEAL chair. I trace all that involvement back to inspiration received while I worked under Mr. Tung.

During the four years (1974–1978) that I was East Asian reference librarian at Princeton, I quickly became more comfortable working with Chinese materials and then turned my focus to improving my Japanese skills by auditing classes and exchanging conversation with Japanese students. I pestered visiting scholars, especially Tsurumi Kazuko, who was in residence for a full academic year, to teach me about Japanese academic publishing, research resources, reference books, and whatever else I needed to know.[1] Carol Gluck was running a monthly seminar at Columbia on Japanese publishing history at that time, which I joined occasionally. Princeton Professors Marius B. Jansen and Martin Collcutt taught a proseminar in research methods and resources for Japanese Studies for their graduate students, in which I participated as an auditor, still doing all the assignments. Gradually, I began to navigate Princeton's Japanese research resources with confidence and started teaching undergraduates and beginning graduate students how to find their way as well. Teaching continued to be an important part of my work throughout my career. At Ohio State, in addition to collaborating with Richard Torrance in teaching Japanese bibliography, I also taught about manga and the global information society.

What was access to Japanese information like in the mid-1970s? Japanese newspapers and magazines were collected in Tokyo for a couple of months and then spent weeks being transported to Princeton by sea mail. Word would get out when those boxes arrived, and anyone interested would come to read "news" that was already months old! "International" reference books had very little inclusion of Japanese names or organizations, and, even when they did, surnames and given names were often mixed up, impeding access. Furthermore, there was a widespread assumption that Japan, having lost the war and then having experienced the oil shock, was no longer going to be a target of much academic interest in the United States. The large investment needed to build a Japanese research collection for such a small number of projected users certainly discouraged the growth and spread of Japanese Studies at that time.

At Princeton, I met Jim Bartholomew, already a tenured Associate Professor of Japanese History at The Ohio State University. We married in 1978 and moved to Columbus, Ohio, where I became a half-time Japanese cataloger at Ohio State's library and also enrolled as a graduate student in Asian—especially Buddhist—art history, working under John C. Huntington. Although I never completed that degree, I continued to be active in the field, advising art history students and even serving on some dissertation committees. Before leaving Princeton, I gathered words of advice from colleagues. Among other things, I heard this: avoid purchasing works of living authors because those would be duplicated in collected works after they died. It did not make sense to me! Furthermore, it did not fit with the goals of the Japanese faculty at Ohio State, where Japan—its contemporary culture as well as its history—was seen as quite dynamic and very much alive. After all, Honda was already building its first factory in neighboring Marysville, Ohio (it opened in 1979).

The stacks at Princeton in those days (as well as at other major centers of Japanese Studies) were filled with comprehensive multivolume research resources, giving an impression of a codified culture. At that point, I had yet to visit Japan, but, when I did go later and experienced bright and attractive Japanese bookstores, I felt a sharp contrast with those stacks. I began thinking about how to make a library appear to its users as something that is alive, not dead. I wanted Ohio State's collection to appeal and beckon to students and researchers alike, with essential reference and research resources but also more popular and accessible materials.

The process of developing such a collection started as soon as I arrived at Ohio State, when I realized that the library did not have the reference books needed for cataloging Japanese books. I applied to the Japan Foundation for a grant, which was successful, and set about cataloging the backlog. When bibliographer duties were added and my position expanded to full-time beginning in 1981, William J. Studer, the library director, hired Shizue Matsuda, who was then a Japanese Studies Librarian at the Indiana University Library, as a consultant to teach me the ropes and support my early efforts in selecting and acquiring Japanese materials.[2] A highly committed professional, Matsuda-san was also well known for questioning assumptions. In particular, she was bothered with a tendency for libraries to copy each other in book selection. She lobbied colleagues to strive for less duplication across Japanese libraries nationally, with a goal of more comprehensive access to Japanese research resources (through interlibrary loan). She was a wonderfully supportive mentor whose vision of thinking nationally about Japanese holdings I fully embraced, pursuing it throughout my career.

After several short trips to Japan supported by The Ohio State University, I spent 1995 and 1996 in Tokyo on a Japan Foundation research fellowship at Keio University, sponsored by Harada Takashi, who spent his own sabbatical two years later working with me at Ohio State as a visiting scholar. The year in Tokyo was a key turning point for me. I was astonished by the widespread extent of manga and anime, which were everywhere I looked. After returning to Ohio State, I discussed this with Lucy Shelton Caswell, founder of the BICLM, and we decided to collaborate on a systematic collection of Japanese manga, something that has continued even after my retirement. It was also during that sabbatical at Keio that I fully internalized my role as a professional working in Japanese Studies and gained the confidence needed to find my own path forward. Prior to that, I thought of myself as someone who was continuing to learn, broadening my horizon. I became fully committed during that year in Tokyo. Furthermore, both Jim and our son, Thomas, were in Tokyo with me. Jim pursued his own research on a Fulbright Fellowship at the University of Tokyo, while Thomas spent a formative sixth-grade year developing a deep love for Japan and its culture. As I fully embraced my role in Japanese Studies, my family's interest and support were essential. During 2003 and 2004, I spent another sabbatical as research fellow at the International Research Center for Japanese Studies (Nichibunken) in Kyoto, where I expanded my familiarity with Japanese academic research culture and infrastructure and did research on manga history.

At Ohio State, as a librarian charged with a budget, my priority was meeting the needs of the university's researchers—namely, finding specialized materials not then available at existing centers of Japanese Studies, which included, for example, biographies of Meiji-era scientists, local election data, contemporary poetry, documents on rice farming practices, soil maps, and language pedagogy journals, as well as manga. By bringing those research needs to the attention of funding agencies, such as the Japan Foundation and the Japan-US Friendship Commission, I obtained funding for Ohio State's collection growth and contributed to a wider

Figure 18.1: Maureen Donovan, after winning the Tiefel Teaching Award, 2010. Photograph courtesy of Pam McClung.

understanding of the increasingly diverse needs of Japanese Studies researchers, whose interests reflected an expanding engagement between the United States and Japan.

I also collected Japanese company histories. These self-published primary sources were not widely held then, but it was especially appropriate that they be collected in Ohio, where so many Japanese companies were setting up business in cooperation with Honda's expansion. The initial idea came from Professor Bradley M. Richardson, who had browsed through these books at used bookstores in Japan and recognized their research potential. Gradually, collecting company histories became a cooperative effort, with many universities working together to acquire these valuable sources. The labor-intensive effort of writing to companies to request their histories provided a stimulus to deepen connections with librarians in Japan, as well as with colleagues in the United States, especially Hiroyuki Good (a Japanese Studies librarian, University of Pittsburgh). Koide Izumi (a librarian at the International House of Japan and later at the Shibusawa Eiichi Memorial

Foundation) was an enthusiastic supporter. She introduced me to Murahashi Katsuko (who was then librarian at the Keidanren Japanese Business Federation), the foremost authority on these sources. I arranged for Murahashi-san to visit Ohio State and give a talk at the Japanese Company Histories Interest Group meeting at the Association for Asian Studies. She reciprocated by inviting me to Japan for visits to several strong collections of company histories and to give a talk at the Special Libraries section of the Japan Library Association (Nihon Toshokan Kyōkai). In this regard, I also met Takagi Toshiro (Japan External Trade Organization) and Takagi Kazuko (former head librarian at the International University of Japan), who both came to Ohio State as visiting scholars from 2002 to 2004.

My experiences during the early years of my career gave me a foundation that prepared me for many later challenges locally, regionally, and nationally. One thing kept leading to another. At meetings of the Midwest Japanese Library Collections in the 1980s (sponsored by the Japan Foundation and the Japan-US Friendship Commission), the idea of sharing tables of contents of journals to promote resource sharing came up. This led me to undertake research into the use of scanners and "image processing" for transfer via emerging information technologies, leading to several grants. Through one of those projects, the East Asian Libraries Cooperative World Wide Web, I began working with Kinema Club, at that time a group of graduate students sharing tables of contents of film journals held at various libraries. Ohio State became the host for their website and its highly intellectual discussion listserv (KineJapan) for many years. Through Markus Nornes and Aaron Gerow, founders of Kinema Club, I met Makino Mamoru (whose Japanese film studies collection is now at Columbia University); he inspired me to develop the manga collection into a research collection comprising resources related to manga in addition to the works themselves. Over the rest of my career, I pursued various approaches, including databases, blogs, wikis, videos, and Twitter, as well as presentations and workshops, to bring Ohio State's distinctive Japanese holdings to wider attention, and, in turn, make them more dynamic and responsive to the needs of potential users.

I realize that I came into the field of Japanese Studies librarianship at a moment before the older generation had retired so that I could learn from them. At the same time, I enjoyed learning from younger colleagues as they entered the field and watching them grow professionally to assume leadership roles. I bonded with Tokiko Bazzell (Japan Specialist Librarian, University of Hawai'i), who asked me to be her mentor as she was studying library science while working for a Japanese corporation. We continued as close colleagues and collaborators. I hired Yukari Sugiyama as an undergraduate student assistant at Ohio State. She became inspired to pursue a career in my footsteps and is now working at Yale University in metadata services related to Japanese Studies. Over the years, many young librarians coming into East Asian Studies librarianship found their first jobs at Ohio State or at the Online Computer Library Center (OCLC, also located in Columbus). They helped me keep abreast of new ideas.

Now in retirement for several years, I look back on my career and appreciate that I was very lucky, coming into the field when I did, having a career that coincided with increasing US engagement with Japan and the expansion of the internet. It was a lot of work, though! Many people in the United States and in Japan helped and supported me along the way, including wise administrators at Princeton and Ohio State, wonderful colleagues locally, nationally, and internationally, and, especially, dedicated assistants without whom little would have materialized. I had opportunities to undertake pioneering initiatives, such as various web projects and the manga collection. The growing importance of East Asian libraries meant that, sooner or later, someone would lead the transformation of CEAL that happened during my term as the last chairperson of CEAL, with subsequent leaders being called "president." Looking back at what I accomplished, much of it almost seems inevitable. I am so impressed with how "alive" Japanese library collections seem today! As a pioneer, who had the privilege of sometimes being a step or two ahead of others, I had many exciting and wonderful experiences along the way.

Notes

This chapter is a substantially revised and a more personal version of "Those Were the Days! A Short History of the East Asian Libraries Cooperative World Wide Web," *Journal of East Asian Libraries* 124 (2001), 19–22. We are grateful to the journal editors for reprint permissions.

[1] Tsurumi Kazuko was professor of sociology at Sophia University. The daughter of Tsurumi Yūsuke and sister of Tsurumi Shunsuke, both prominent intellectuals, as well as granddaughter of the major political figure Gotō Shinpei, she was a popular opinion leader in her own right. She graduated from Tsuda University, studied at Vassar College, and received a PhD in sociology at Princeton University in 1966. Her book, *Social Change and the Individual: Japan before and after Defeat in World War II* (Princeton: Princeton University Press, 1970) drew on a wide range of primary sources, such as autobiographical essays written by participants in local writing circles in rural areas of Japan. Her research explored the writings of Minakata Kumagusu and Yanagita Kunio in the indigenous development of sociology in Japan. She also explored connections between modernity and animism in Japan. She served as a mentor to many foreign researchers.

[2] Shizue Matsuda was born in Honolulu and educated in Japan, graduating with an undergraduate degree in library science from Keio University. She served as librarian for the Atomic Bomb Casualty Commission in Hiroshima. With fluency in English, Chinese, and Japanese, she received a PhD in Chinese literature from Columbia University in 1978 and was East Asian Studies Librarian at Indiana University from 1972 until her retirement in 1986.

19

THE OPEN GATE

Janine Beichman

For me, living in a time with far fewer barriers to female self-realization, the opened gate made it easy to enter the field of Japanese Studies.

JANINE BEICHMAN is a professor emerita of Daitō Bunka University (Tokyo) and translator of Japanese poetry. Her books include *Masaoka Shiki: His Life and Works* (2002); translations of Ōoka Makoto's criticism, as well as *Beneath the Sleepless Tossing of the Planets: Selected Poems, 1972–1989* (2019), translations of Ōoka's own poetry, for which she received the Japan-US Friendship Commission Prize for the Translation of Japanese Literature (2019–2020); and translations of Ozawa Minoru's *Well-Versed: Exploring Modern Japanese Haiku* (2021) and Ishigaki Rin's *This Overflowing Light: Rin Ishigaki, Selected Poems* (2022). She is the author of the Noh play *Drifting Fires* (1985).

A Sudden Pivot

One day late in my senior year of college, still undecided about what to do after graduation, I ran into my good friend and confidant Henry Tylbor. Warsaw-born and a brilliant polyglot a decade older than me, Henry had more experience and a larger imagination of the world, which is to say he could imagine intellectual adventures and byroads that might never occur to me. I had been dipping into old Irish folk tales, thinking I might go on to graduate school and specialize in them, but, after I shared a few over coffee, Henry bluntly said they sounded pretty childish. Then he added:

"Why don't you choose something more interesting?"

"Like what?" I asked.

"Well, you could try Japanese," came the swift reply.

Inspired by Henry's suggestion, the next day found me browsing the paperback rack of my corner bookstore, where I came across Donald Keene's *Modern Japanese Literature: An Anthology*. Far removed as I am from those days, I still recall reading the excerpt from Mishima Yukio's *Confessions of a Mask* (translated by Meredith Weatherby) included in Keene's anthology—the image of the fourteen-year-old hero and his friend Omi confronting each other on a log in Mishima's novel has never left me.[1] Its combination of purity and sensuality was like nothing I had ever read before.

I can see now that the young woman I was then was eager for a gate that opened onto a new world, even a different civilization. Almost overnight, I decided to apply to graduate school in Japanese literature.

I later discovered that Keene's anthologies inspired many others to go into Japanese Studies. But my sudden pivot grew from my life more organically than it might seem. My mother was an artist and studied with the well-known Japanese woodblock printmaker Munakata Shikō in New York City. Thanks to her taste in design, the centerpiece of our living room was Isamu Noguchi's coffee table, now iconic but then the badge of being avant-garde, a triangle of glass with rounded corners that seemed to float atop two wooden wedges of wood, all held together without glue or screws. My mother's aesthetic was part of a broader current of Asian-inflected design in 1950s America, epitomized by the Japanese Exhibition House at New York's Museum of Modern Art. Brought in separate pieces from Japan and meticulously reconstructed in the museum's garden, this structure, which I saw with my parents, was on exhibit from June 1954 to October 1955.[2] The building's four-mat tea ceremony room made a strong impression on me. It seemed to express a microcosmic image of the universe and became the inspiration for my first-ever research paper in high school.

Unaware as I was of the connections, in aesthetic terms it was but a small step from the graceful minimalist lines of the Noguchi table to the sharp, clean beauty of Mishima's prose. Looking back, I see that my mother's sensibility made it possible for me to swiftly change the direction of my life. And what seemed to be a change of direction was, in a sense, a homecoming.

Walking through the Gate

I entered the world of Japanese Studies at an auspicious time. In 1964, Columbia University was one of the few American universities with an East Asian Languages and Cultures (EALAC) program. Bizarre as it may seem now, it was then common for a student to enter graduate school in East Asian Studies without ever having studied an East Asian language. You simply took graduate courses in content subjects while doing undergraduate intensive courses in the language. I was able to pack the equivalent of three years of language study into one summer (taught by Marleigh Grayer Ryan) and two academic terms (taught by Fumiko Fujikawa).

Another stroke of luck was the availability of funding. A few years before I entered graduate school, the launch of Sputnik 1 on October 4, 1957, which triggered the Space Race between the United States and the Soviet Union, had inspired the National Defense Education Act (1958). For the first time, fellowships were offered by the United States government to study "unusual" languages like Japanese that were considered necessary for America's defense. I supported most of my four years of graduate coursework (1965–1969) at Columbia with National Defense Foreign Language (NDFL) Fellowships (called Foreign Language and Area Studies [FLAS] Fellowships after the 1970s). It goes without saying that the primary importance of this support was economic. However, for me and perhaps for others, it had another meaning as well: I had always felt alienated from mainstream American values, but, for the first time in my life, what I did for my private enjoyment was connected to the public good.

My third stroke of luck was that Donald Keene was on the faculty. Keene's long-term project was to make Japanese literature a respected and important part of world literature. He was a kind of missionary, enlightening the West about what he once called "this wonderful literary tradition."[3] His ideal was Arthur Waley, whose translation of *The Tale of Genji* (1921–1933) had deeply impressed such literary giants as Virginia Woolf. In fact, he dedicated his *Anthology of Japanese Literature from the Earliest Era to the Mid-Nineteenth Century* to Waley.

In his fourth-year classical Japanese class and in his graduate seminars, all of which were dedicated to translating classical texts, Keene was a strict but supportive teacher. His usual method was to go around the table, asking each student to translate a few lines. Many years later, I compared notes with others who had been his students, and all agreed that he never paused to correct a student who made a mistake. Instead, he simply translated the same passage aloud himself. When I brought this up with Keene (we were both living in Tokyo then and often spoke), he told me it was important to never embarrass a student by pointing out a mistake. I suddenly realized that I had been the beneficiary of this policy without knowing it; it was one of the reasons why he had been able to instill me with

Figure 19.1: Janine Beichman and Donald Keene in Shizuoka, Japan, 2017. Photograph courtesy of Suzuki Nobuyuki.

confidence. I felt a little like a medieval poet being initiated into one of the secret teachings (*hiden*) of their master (figure 19.1).

Noh

My first encounter with Noh on stage took place during my second summer of Japanese study (1966), when I traveled (with generous support from my parents) to Japan. It was at a small theater in Kyoto, where the audience sat on tatami. The play was *Izutsu* (*The Well-Curb*), a tale of heart-piercing nostalgia for young love.[4] The story itself was intensely human and warm, but there was a mysterious and otherworldly quality to the formal style in which it was told. The shapes of the actors in their stiff silk costumes were faintly reflected in the luster of the polished cypress stage, and their spotless white *tabi* as they moved across the boards suggested a fantastic sea creature gliding slowly and surely over the surface of the ocean. I felt a strong and mysterious attraction, familiar and alien at the same time. It was almost like falling in love. The thought came: You would have to marry into this culture to understand it.

Back at Columbia, I was ready for fourth-year (non-intensive) language courses, the first of which was classical Japanese. I had Ivan Morris for one term and Donald Keene for the other. The next year, I was ready for Keene's graduate seminars, which were devoted to reading the many yet untranslated masterpieces of classical Japanese literature. Twice a week, half a dozen or so students gathered under our sensei's tutelage, focusing on a single genre or author each term.

In the Noh seminar, the term papers were translations of Noh plays, chosen for us by Keene. In the late 1960s, Keene's Noh seminar students produced enough translations to make a book, *20 Plays of the Nō Theatre*, which included my translation of *Yugyō yanagi* (*The Priest and the Willow*) by Kanze Kojirō Nobumitsu (circa 1435–1516). (Now, Noh is more commonly used than Nō in English-language discourses.) In his review of the book for *The New York Times Book Review*, the distinguished poet Kenneth Rexroth wrote: "It is a little as though someone had turned up a thousand lines lost from Homer or Isaiah."[5]

A Family Story

Matsukaze (*Pining Wind*), a play about the love of two fisher girls for a court noble, was a particular favorite of Keene's because of its poetic beauty. Twenty-five years after I studied the play with Keene, my younger daughter, Miyabi (Abbie) Yamamoto, then an undergraduate at Barnard College, received permission to take the same graduate seminar that I had. *Matsukaze* was again one of the texts. Abbie reported that when they had done the very last lines, Keene looked up, and said with a quiet smile, "It doesn't get much better than this, does it?' Tears made his eyes shine.

My daughter confided that this was the moment when she decided to make Japanese literature her major.

Masaoka Shiki

By December 1969, I had passed my orals and been awarded a Fulbright-Hays Fellowship for doctoral research in Japan. I was also getting ready for my late December wedding in Tokyo to Takeo Yamamoto, whom I had met while he was a postdoc at the University of North Carolina at Chapel Hill.

No sooner were we back from the honeymoon than I went to the Jimbochō bookstore district of Tokyo to buy the fifteen-volume complete works of Masaoka Shiki (1867–1902) (*Masaoka Shiki zenshū*, 1924–1927), whose life and works were to be the topic of my dissertation. It seemed an extravagance to me, but Takeo insisted that I needed it, and I was glad to follow his advice. Our Tokyo apartment was so small that the nearby library of the University of Tokyo, where I was allowed auditor status, became perforce my base of operations.

Shiki is a canonical writer and considered to be the father of the modern haiku, but, at that time, he was almost unknown outside Japan except for a small number of poems that appeared in anthologies. My master's thesis had been, at Keene's suggestion, a partial translation of Shiki's sickbed diary, *A Drop of Ink* (*Bokujū itteki*, 1901). When it came time to decide on the topic for the doctoral dissertation, Keene went against the prevailing pattern of changing to a new topic for the doctorate by urging me to continue my work on Shiki and to enlarge the project to include both his biography and his literary works, from his haiku and tanka to his diaries and criticism. For four years, while I lived in Japan, Keene and I worked entirely by postal mail, except for the dissertation defense, for which I had to fly to New York. I traveled with my infant daughter (the first of my two daughters) and stayed with my mother in Connecticut. For the defense, we drove into New York, and my mother babysat for my daughter at the home of an old friend on the Upper West Side while I went up to Columbia for a few hours, then rushed back so I could make my daughter's breastfeeding time. I had expressed milk for her, but she was not interested in the bottle. To have passed the defense and to have a newborn baby was paradise. But I am getting ahead of my story, so let me retrace my steps to the period during which I was writing my dissertation in Tokyo.

Takagi Kiyoko

During this period, I was also a member of the Wind of the Universe tanka society (Uchūfū), which involved participating in the group's monthly tanka-writing workshop and publishing tanka in its eponymous magazine.[6] I joined the group at the behest of Dr. Takagi Kiyoko (1918–2011), one of its senior members and a tanka poet herself, who stressed that if I wished to write about Shiki's tanka in my dissertation, I should practice the form myself.

I had first come to know Takagi-sensei in New York in 1968, when she was a lecturer at EALAC, on sabbatical from her post as associate director of the Inter-University Center for Japanese Language Studies (IUC, located in Tokyo before it moved to Yokohama). At that stage of my studies, I did not know enough Japanese language to read *A Drop of Ink* on my own, and, unlike Noh and other classical texts, there were no annotated editions to aid me. It was only thanks to the months Takagi-sensei spent reading Shiki with me every week that I was able to translate the diary and write my master's thesis.

At a time when women in Japanese academe were as rare as snow in summer, Takagi-sensei earned a doctorate from the University of Tokyo, Japan's most prestigious university. I once asked her if she had been discriminated against as a woman. In response, she related two anecdotes. First, as a teaching assistant during her graduate studies, she once overheard two professors talking in the office next door about the marks they planned to give their students that term. Takagi, said one, deserved the highest grade, but, because she was a woman, if he gave it to her, she would get conceited, and so he planned to mark her down a grade. Second, she said that, at one point, IUC had asked her to be the director, but she decided to be associate director instead because she knew that the center would not be taken seriously in Japan if it were run by a woman. She told me these anecdotes in a calm voice, with no apparent sense of indignation, but by then I knew her well enough to realize that she did not waste energy on expressing anger, as angry as she must have been. Sexual discrimination was among the givens of her life, but, instead of overtly fighting it, which she knew would have been a losing battle, she worked around it.

Some years after her retirement from IUC, in the 1990s, Ōoka Makoto (1931–2017), arguably the most influential poet and critic of his generation, featured one of Takagi-sensei's tanka in his long-running and tremendously popular *Asahi shimbun* newspaper column, "A Poet's Notebook" (Oriori no uta, 1979–2007). Thanks to this, a small part of her poetic oeuvre became known to millions of Japanese readers.

Donald Keene and Masaoka Shiki

In 1973, the dissertation was almost done, and I was pregnant with my first child. At this juncture, many teachers, both now and then, would have mentally written me off, assuming that, after I became a mother, I would give up scholarship out of necessity or choice. But Keene was different. Looking ahead to my forthcoming defense in New York, he welcomed the baby. "Congratulations on your forthcoming baby," he wrote in a letter, "I can imagine that its arrival will make it difficult for you to travel, etc. I will try to help."

Not having experienced any form of sexism during my studies (or nothing I perceived as sexism), I took Keene's accepting attitude for granted. It was only later that I realized how unusual his support was. This must be one of the primary reasons why Keene had so many female students who went on to professional careers in Japanese Studies. For example, of the five students in the Noh seminar the year I took it, four were women—Susan Matisoff (chapter 10), Carol Hochstedler, Felice Fischer, and me—and all progressed to professional careers in Japanese Studies. Paul Novograd, the only man, went into the family business as owner of the iconic Claremont Stables in New York.

My work on Shiki served me well years later when I was asked to translate Ozawa Minoru's *Well-Versed: Exploring Modern Japanese Haiku* (*Meiku no yuen: Kingendai haiku jikkuri wo yomu*, 2018). Aside from Shiki himself, many of the poets represented in the book were familiar to me already because they had been influenced by Shiki either during his lifetime or after it. I mention this because it shows how valuable Keene's advice on choosing a topic for my master's and doctoral dissertation was. He was a mentor whose advice I felt I could trust completely.

Testing the Waters of Academe

After successfully defending my dissertation in 1974, I began teaching Japanese literature (Noh, classical poetry, medieval linked verse, the haiku of Yosa Buson, and modern Japanese short stories) as an adjunct instructor in what was then the international division of Sophia University in Tokyo. As at Columbia, the language of instruction was English, and class was devoted to translating and discussing the texts we read. In the Noh seminar, however, I asked the students to write their own Noh plays in English for their term papers rather than translating plays. Preoccupied though I was with the project of reconciling motherhood and work, somehow I found the willpower and time to keep up with my classes and to publish the first edition of my biography of Masaoka Shiki, which was later republished twice.

In the autumn of 1980, I was invited to take my first full-time academic post. It was at a newly established national university in Tsukuba, Ibaraki Prefecture, then about two hours from Tokyo. Before the Tsukuba Express train, which opened in 2005, the time from Tokyo to Tsukuba was twice as long as it is now. For six and a half years, I worked at the University of Library and Information Science (ULIS), which in 2002 merged with Tsukuba University and is now a university department. My working conditions were ideal. I was asked to teach one course in English literature and, for the rest, was free to teach Japanese and comparative literature in whatever way I wanted to. Starting from this point in my academic career, all my classes were conducted in Japanese. I had my own office, and the university was a mere fifteen-minute bike ride from our new home.

The university was unable to give me a permanent position because it was a national university and I was not a Japanese citizen. The workaround for this, which was the rule at national universities at that time, was the position of "foreign faculty" (*gaikokujin kyōshi*). Lack of job security was not a major concern because I was verbally assured that the university meant to renew the contract every year. As Ivan P. Hall explains, this turned out to be an empty promise for me and others later on.[7]

However, there was an upside, at least as far as I was concerned. As a noncitizen, not only was I barred from holding a permanent position, but I was also ineligible for anything relating to the governance and administration of the university. I could not even attend faculty meetings. This was perfect for me since my own research, which at that time focused on Noh theater and was beginning to gravitate toward the great poet Yosano Akiko as well, demanded all the time left after teaching and family life.

Drifting Fires

During my years at ULIS, I published and presented on the relationship of Noh to ritual and on the history of New Noh in Japan and other countries. ("New Noh" is a translation of the Japanese "*shinsaku Nō*," a term for plays made from the twentieth century onward to distinguish them from the classical Noh canon.) I also continued to study Noh singing (*utai*) and dancing (*shimai*) with a professional Noh master.

Figure 19.2: Performance of *Drifting Fires* at Zōjōji Temple, Umewaka Naohiko as *shite*, Tokyo, 1986. Photograph courtesy of Maejima Yoshihiro.

The culmination of my involvement with Noh was the English-language New Noh, *Drifting Fires*, which was performed in traditional Noh style in Tsukuba and Tokyo and later in other styles in the United States. The plot concerned space travelers (the *waki*, or "sidemen") from the Veil Nebula visiting the place which was once the planet Earth and meeting the spirit of the last human being (the *shite*, or lead role, in the play).[8]

The genesis of the play was a dream I had for years of recreating my favorite Noh plays in an English-language idiom, not merely translating the words but transplanting the form itself into another culture. Much as the sonnet had wended its way from Italy to France to England, I believed that this should be possible for Noh as well.

My earliest inspiration was probably the music drama *Curlew River*, which I saw in the late 1960s in New York. This beautiful "parable for church performance," as the subtitle goes, composed by Benjamin Britten to text by William Plomer, was based on the early fifteenth-century Noh play *The Sumida River* (*Sumidagawa* by Kanze Motomasa Jurō [circa 1394–1432]), which tells the tragic story of a mother gone mad from grief as she searches for her young son, who has been kidnapped by slave traders.

To realize my dream, I needed a detailed blueprint of the musical and performance patterns of Noh. This was provided in the early 1970s, when Yokomichi Mario's pioneering analysis of the structure of Noh was translated and recontextualized for an English-speaking audience in Frank Hoff and Willi

Flindt's *The Life Structure of Noh*.[9] When my Noh teacher, Umewaka Naohiko, spontaneously suggested that I write a New Noh and offered to perform the *shite*, the central role, the idea became reality.

At Expo '85 in Tsukuba in August 1985, *Drifting Fires* was first performed in Japan in orthodox Noh style, with choreography by Umewaka Naohiko, who, as he had promised, also performed the role of the *shite*, and music by Richard Emmert. In 1986, the play was performed at Zōjōji Temple in Tokyo (figure 19.2). In May 1993, Yuriko Doi's Theatre of Yūgen in San Francisco produced it in a different style, with original music, choreography, and costumes. Separately, students at New College of Florida performed it in their own way. All these productions used the original English script. Later, a version in traditional Japanese dance style (*Nihon buyō*), using Ōoka Makoto's beautiful translation, was performed at the National Engei Hall. This variety of performance styles was what I had hoped for. I was not trying to reproduce Noh in English but to help the evolution of American Noh. I later found out that the poet Gary Snyder had had the same idea the first time he saw Noh.[10]

Daitō Bunka University

In 1987, I moved to Daitō Bunka University (DBU), a large university with three campuses in Tokyo and neighboring Saitama Prefecture. There, I became the only non-Japanese full-time tenured professor of Japanese literature on the faculty. I continued to teach in Japanese and had the same freedom to decide the titles, contents, and organization of my courses as I had at ULIS.

Because DBU is a private university, there were no constraints on a foreign citizen participating in administration. With full membership in the university community came additional responsibilities. Faithfully attending faculty meetings and serving on various committees was imperative. Furthermore, the faculty duties of preparing, proctoring, and grading multiple entrance exams became more and more onerous and time-consuming over the years.

Then there was the grueling commute to the Saitama campus where I taught, almost three hours each way from our home in Tsukuba. I sometimes wonder how I survived it for twenty-five years. One motivation was the generous salary and research budget. But the deepest motivation was the joy I got from helping young people find beauty and meaning in the classical and modern Japanese poetry that I loved. Burnout was something I never experienced.

Even now, I sometimes find myself missing the feeling of sitting around a table with a group of young people, talking about wonderful poems that they may be meeting for the first time in their lives.

Ōoka Makoto

When the planning for the debut performance of *Drifting Fires* began, I thought a translation should be available to the audience and brashly sent the script to Ōoka Makoto, whom I had never met, asking if he could suggest a translator. Because several people had assured me that Ōoka, arguably the best-known poet and critic in Japan at the time, might not even answer my letter, I was excited when he not only replied but also invited me to his home to talk about the play. Then, to my surprise and delight, he offered to translate *Drifting Fires* himself. Thus began a close working relationship that influences me even now.

Ōoka and I met face to face only two or three times a year, but we worked on a number of projects together. A few years after he translated *Drifting Fires*, the *Asahi Evening News* (the English-language edition of the *Asahi shimbun*), on Ōoka's recommendation, asked me to do a weekly translation of his poetry column, *Oriori no uta* (see page 295). In this long-running daily column on the front page, Ōoka introduced Japanese poems of all styles and periods and provided pithy commentary. For around twelve years, I translated over five hundred columns, titled "A Poet's Notebook." Each one was carefully vetted by Ōoka, and we exchanged faxes at least once a week. Email existed at the time, but Ōoka did not use it; he preferred to write by hand. Thanks to that, I have a folder full of our exchanges, with his spirited handwriting (some English, some Japanese) twining like sturdy branches among my typewritten words.

Because Ōoka knew English well, he was able to point out problems in my drafts, and, if I was unsure which version of a translation was best stylistically, I could solicit his opinion. It was a mentor-student relationship, as I had had with Takagi and Keene. The difference was that, in contrast to my work on Shiki's writings, in this case, the author was alive, which was thrilling. The translations were ultimately compiled into three books, each with a slightly different selection of poems.[11]

Ōoka called on me again when Katydid Press (run by Thomas Fitzsimmons) invited him to publish a second collection of his own poems. This became *Beneath the Sleepless Tossing of the Planets: Selected Poems by Makoto Ōoka*, which in its revised edition, won the Japan-US Friendship Commission Prize for the Translation of Japanese Literature (2019–2020).

Ōoka also introduced me to the poetry of three contemporary Japanese women poets, suggesting that I might like to translate them. Gravitating immediately to Ishigaki Rin (1920–2004), I began publishing translations and interpretations of her work while Ōoka was still alive, a project which culminated in *This Overflowing Light: Rin Ishigaki, Selected Poems* (2022).

Yosano Akiko

In the late 1970s, the women's liberation movement and second-wave feminism inspired me to study women writers. At this time, Yosano Akiko (1878–1942), the premier female poet of modern Japan, was one of only two women with a secure place in the canon of modern Japanese literature. The other was Higuchi Ichiyō (1872–1896), best known for her fiction. Akiko attracted me because, first and foremost, she was a poet.

My research on Akiko began with a mystery. Her inclusion in the canon was based on a single work, *Tangled Hair* (*Midaregami*, 1901), published in the late summer of her twenty-second year. To be fair, two of her modern-style poems, "Thou Shalt Not Die" (Kimi shinitamou koto nakare, 1904), which denounced the Russo-Japanese War (1904–1905), and "The Day the Mountains Move" (Yama no ugoku hi kitaru, 1911), which celebrates female power, were also treasured. The jewel, however, was *Tangled Hair*.

That intrigued me because Akiko published prodigiously in a variety of genres for over forty years. Was it possible that the mostly male arbiters of literary reputations were unable to appreciate her later poetry because it did not meet their expectations of what a woman should write? The more I read of Akiko's later poems (and there were thousands), the more convinced I became that the answer to my question was yes. Ōoka helped me again because he was one of the few critics who recognized the worth of her later works. When I wrote my first article about Akiko, which attacked the conventional view that she had written nothing of note after the age of thirty, he published it in his own magazine.[12]

To help Akiko gain the place she deserved in the canon of world literature, I became her biographer. In 2002, with support from the National Endowment for the Humanities, I published *Embracing the Firebird: Yosano Akiko and the Rebirth of the Female Voice in Modern Japanese Poetry*, which covered Akiko's life and works through *Tangled Hair*. It was the fruit of over twenty years of research and translation. I later earned grants from the National Endowment for the Arts and the PEN/Heim Translation Fund to produce a second volume and a comprehensive book of translations of Akiko's poetry to spotlight the later works.

Akiko wrote a number of abstract poems. For example, in *Princess Saho* (*Sahohime*, 1909), she writes:

> *As it opened*
> *I walked through*
> *the enormous gate*
> *It hasn't closed behind me*
> *O this enormous gate!*

(*Hirakarete*
ware wa
iritaru daimon yo
ushiro tojizaru
kono daimon yo)

This poem can be read as a coded description of Akiko's own life, with "the enormous gate" acting as a metaphor for the many barriers to female self-realization that existed in Akiko's youth at the turn of the twentieth century. The gate opens mysteriously, and the poet, seizing the moment, walks through. Then she turns back and, looking up at "this enormous gate," exclaims again at its size and the fact that it has not closed behind her. The implication is that there will be time and space if others choose to follow. This is a poem that suggests its own future.

An abstract poem, like an abstract painting, can (and should) have different meanings for different readers. For me, living in a time with far fewer barriers to female self-realization, the opened gate made it easy to enter the field of Japanese Studies. I like to imagine myself as one of the women who followed Akiko through the open gate, and to think of the many others still to follow.

Notes

My deepest thanks to Phyllis Birnbaum, Meredith McKinney, and Nancy Ross for their feedback and comments, and to Columbia University Archivist Jocelyn K. Wilk for information on Kiyoko Takagi's time at Columbia.

[1] Mishima Yukio, *Confessions of a Mask*, translated by Meredith Weatherby, in *Modern Japanese Literature: An Anthology*, edited by Donald Keene (New York: Grove Press, 1960), 429–438.

[2] MoMA, "Japanese Exhibition House, June 16, 1954–October 15, 1955," *MoMA*, n.d., www.moma.org/calendar/exhibitions/2711 (April 22, 2022).

[3] Quoted in Eriko Arita, "Donald Keene: A Life Lived True to the Words," *The Japan Times*, September 6, 2009. https://www.japantimes.co.jp/life/2009/09/06/people/donald-keene-a-life-lived-true-to-the-words.

[4] "Izutsu," in *The Noh Drama: Ten Plays from the Japanese*, edited by Nippon Gakujutsu Shinkōkai (Rutland, VT: Charles E. Tuttle Company, 1960), 91–105.

[5] Janine Beichman, translator, "The Priest and the Willow," *20 Plays of the Nō Theatre*, edited by Donald Keene and Royall Tyler (New York: Columbia University Press, 1970), 219–236; Kenneth Rexroth, "No Action, No Climax, But Realization," *The New York Times Review of Books*, January 10, 1971, Section BR, 8.

[6] As she describes in chapter 15, Amy Heinrich was also a Uchūfū member but at a different time.

[7] The situation for Tsukuba University foreign faculty was even worse than mine because they were given no notice at all, while I was given several months' notice. See Ivan P. Hall, "Academic Apartheid at Japan's National Universities," *JPRI Working Paper*, Japan Policy Research Institute, October 1994, 7. For information regarding verbal promises for permanent employment, see JPRI Staff, "Foreign Teachers in Japanese Universities: An Update," *JPRI Working Paper No. 24,* September 1996, 1.

[8] My publications about the play include: "*Drifting Fires*: An American Nō," *Asian Theatre Journal* 3, no. 2 (Autumn 1986), 233–260; "Eigo no shinsaku Nō hyōen: 27 nen no kaiko" (The English New Noh *Drifting Fires*: 27 Years Later), *Hikaku Nihongaku kenkyū sentā kenkyū nenpō* (Comparative Japanese Studies Annual Bulletin) 9 (2013), 45–67; "Noh in English: Encounters Near and Far," *Japan Quarterly* 33, no. 1 (January–March 1986), 88–92.

[9] Frank Hoff and Willi Flindt, *The Life Structure of Noh: An English Version of Yokomichi Mario's Analysis of the Structure of Nō* (Tokyo: Concerned Theatre Japan, 1973). First published in *Concerned Theatre Japan* 2, nos. 3 and 4 (Spring 1973): 209–256.

[10] Snyder has not published an American Noh, but I believe his long poem cycle *Mountains and Rivers without End* (1996) is based on the three-part *jo-ha-kyū* (slow introduction, development, fast conclusion) structure of Noh as he often alludes to Noh and other classical literature of Japan and China in his work. Gary Snyder, *Mountains and Rivers without End: Poem* (Berkeley: Counterpoint Press, 1996). W. B. Yeats's Noh-inspired *At the Hawk's Well* is often thought of as the earliest English-language play inspired by Noh, but I did not know of it until much later. To the best of my knowledge, unlike Britten and Snyder, Yeats never witnessed an actual performance of Noh. However, *At the Hawk's Well* is greatly admired in Japan, and *Takahime* (The Hawk Princess), its Japanese adaptation by the Noh scholar Yokomichi Mario, is now performed as a New Noh. W. B. Yeats, *At the Hawk's Well* (Overland Park, KS: Digireads, 2011); Yokomichi Mario, "Nō Takahime" (The Hawk Princess, a Noh Play), *Shingeki* 15, no. 1 (January 1968), 124–130.

[11] Ōoka Makoto, *Oriori no uta: Poems for All Seasons*, translated by Janine Beichman (Tokyo: Kodansha International, 2000); Ōoka Makoto, *Taiyaku Oriori no Uta, Poems for All Seasons: An Anthology of Japanese Poetry from Ancient Times to the Present*, translated by Janine Beichman (Tokyo: Kodansha International, 2002); Ōoka Makoto, *A Poet's Anthology: The Range of Japanese Poetry*, translated by Janine Beichman (Santa Fe: Katydid Books, 1994).

[12] Janine Beichman, "Bungaku ni okeru seisabetsu—Yosano Akiko no hyōka wo megutte" (Gender Discrimination in Literature: On the Evaluation of Yosano Akiko), *Kashin* 1, no. 2, (August 1987), 29–35.

20

Confessions of a Biographer

Phyllis Birnbaum

> *I once believed that novelists drew their characters from the endless colors of the imagination—infinite shades of red and blue and green—while a biographer was stuck with only a couple of dented buckets filled with the facts. But now I see that the biographer may add more blue to a subject's portrait if so moved, or leave yellow out entirely. It is surprising how a splatter of red can change the final picture.*

PHYLLIS BIRNBAUM is a writer, translator, and editor. Her translation of Uno Chiyo's *Confessions of Love* (1989) received the Japan-US Friendship Commission Prize for the Translation of Japanese Literature in 1989. Her recent biographies include *Manchu Princess, Japanese Spy: The Story of Kawashima Yoshiko, the Cross-Dressing Spy Who Commanded Her Own Army* (Columbia University Press, 2015), and her recent translations include Takarabe Toriko's autobiographical novel, *Heaven and Hell: A Novel of a Manchukuo Childhood* (2018). She edited the translation of Shiba Ryōtarō's four-volume historical novel *Ryōma! The Life of Sakamoto Ryōma: Japanese Swordsman and Visionary* (2018–2019).

My adventures as a biographer of Japanese women began with journalism assignments, and, looking back, I see those first forays as a time of innocence.

Equipped with the latest in compact Japanese tape recorders and many elaborate introductions to the famous and their associates, I roamed around Tokyo in search of information about my subjects. My problems at the time seemed formidable: Would I be able to arrange the necessary appointments with those I wished to interview? How would I find that critic's camouflaged residence? And why didn't anyone turn on the heat?

But as I nervously checked to make sure that my tape recorder hadn't failed and scanned house numbers in Setagaya, I didn't know yet that I had underestimated my difficulties. I had put too much faith in electronic equipment and the certainties of maps, failing to realize that my journalism projects faced greater obstacles: my work would be hindered by my impatience with the truth. Before I set off, I had read many of the personal essays, fictional works, and autobiographies that my subjects had written. By temperament, I seem to prefer the life of a reader of books rather than the life of a busy reporter, and so I placed much trust in those Japanese volumes. From them, I had formed a very precise picture of the person I was soon to meet, could hear her voice and imagine exactly how she approached a bowl of noodles. If I had been writing a novel, I would have been able to supply this person with dialogue that would bring her quickly and wholly alive.

But journalism is not fiction, and editors tend to take a dim view of reporters who fabricate quotations out of thin air. The subjects of interviews get to speak for themselves.

My subjects did not disappoint me. They were just as extraordinary in real life as their autobiographical writings had promised. I was impressed by their courage, their talent, their tenacity, and also their patience in tolerating my questions. Yet it grieved me to note that their every utterance insisted upon the existence of a woman completely different from the character I had been creating. The discrepancy between the person I had imagined from the writings and the flesh and blood being before me was almost too much to bear. More seasoned reporters have perhaps learned to steel themselves against such daunting developments. Stubbornly, these real live women proclaimed opinions that contradicted the views I had so carefully fashioned for them. Their strong words, their certainties, and, most of all, their solid presences put a dismaying damper on my imagination. So great was my reluctance to part with my inventions that I would not be surprised if stray details of my own creation crept into my written portraits.

Those encounters will make me forever wary of biographers who recreate their subjects only from written materials. I now know too well about the enormous gap between the main figure in one of those long, carefully researched biographies and the person who really dined at home in, say, western Tokyo each evening. Researchers on Murasaki Shikibu base their portraits solely on the memoirs and biographical materials that have survived the centuries. Consider the outcome if a biographer had a chance to interview Murasaki Shikibu in a Kyoto coffee shop. Certainly a totally different portrait would result if the author of *The Tale of Genji* had bawled out the waitress for serving lukewarm tea or confessed to a lifelong battle with stuttering.

Because of these experiences, I changed my approach for my next portraits. When it came time for me to move from journalism to longer biographies of Japanese women, I decided to take the easy way out and not interview anyone. I would write only about the long dead, those who had been immortalized in their own writings and in the works of others, and would then be free to create my subjects' lives from the printed word alone. More importantly, I would not have to be jarred again by the disconcerting reality of the actual person.

With this in mind, I set up my research headquarters in the Tokyo suburbs. By day, I hardly ventured out since I had no interviews scheduled. Instead, I stayed inside with my books and communed with my safely deceased subjects. They were the same kind of figures I had selected for my live subjects—women with an artistic bent and a penchant for drama in their personal lives. It is commonplace that biographers become their subjects, and this seems most true when the author has a choice of whom to write about. By instinct, I chose only those dead people whose lives I could easily inhabit, and perhaps much about me can be deduced from my inability to get inside a Japanese opera star or a literary anarchist, and my contrasting sense of ease in the skin of a hot-tempered actress or a moody artist.

Seeking a smoother journey this time around, I began to acquaint myself with the basic facts about my (dead) subjects' lives. No need to interview anyone, no trips to the other end of town, no anxiety about whether my tape recorder was broken. In choosing these women, I had every intention of presenting their cases fairly, of weighing the evidence and coming forth with an admirably balanced portrait. But I could not restrain my sympathies once I began to read about the hardships they endured. Divorced because he gave her venereal disease? Forcibly married off to an idiot? Ended her days out of her mind? Reading alone there on the floor of my Tokyo apartment, I understood well those moments when my women had stared glumly at the dirty sky or considered desperate strategies to fight off unemployment. I felt stirred to do my utmost to convey these women's efforts to survive in a harsh universe.

It was not only the trouble in my subjects' lives that made my objectivity quiver as the fall days gave way to winter. What swayed me also was a certain kind of secondary material. Since these were my first attempts at research on dead subjects, it was the first time I had ever depended so much on books written by eyewitnesses. Here again I got a great shock. Many times, I put down one of these books and closed my eyes in distress. The first part of the shock was that in certain cases, these chroniclers clearly detested my subjects. They hardly had a good word to say. This did not go well with the admiration I intended to express in my biographies.

The second part of the shock came when I realized that I was tempted to ignore these opinions. I had gone to Tokyo to write about my subjects in peace and quiet. In creating my portraits, I sought the freedom to live within my imagination, to fashion nothing but the truth itself—but at home, where I would commune only with the mist and my muse. Instead, I found myself slogging through the mud, reading page after page of disdainful criticism. One woman sliced up her lover's hat, contemporaries reported; another procured a mistress for her husband; another lacked even a smidgen of talent. In the face of these onslaughts, I could barely make out the glorious women I had envisioned at the outset. They were being overshadowed by those less attractive creatures created by their detractors.

I was surprised at how ready I was to adjust to this setback. I should have incorporated the negative testimony with gratitude, humbly accepting those eyewitnesses' authority and their views. Instead, I found myself prepared to interpret what they said about my women more to my tastes. I looked between the lines of those derogatory biographies and always found my dear girls peeping through. In many cases, the critics were so preposterously prejudiced that I had much leeway to fiddle and mold. In other instances, the charges against my women didn't leave me much room to maneuver. There were times—I admit this with much reluctance—when the critics might have been correct in their damning assessments. Still, I was surprisingly eager to stick to my guns and my views despite these disparaging accounts.

The matter of the commandeered telephone is my most shameful example. The very day after her lover died, one of my women wiped away her tears and strode off to get the rights to his telephone transferred to her own name. To some of her contemporaries, this at the very least amounted to crass scheming during a solemn mourning period; at the most, it constituted theft of a valuable possession. I concede that I saw a certain amount of indelicacy in going down to the telephone office several hours after the love of your life has died and filling out the forms for the phone line. Yet I sought to convince myself that my subject deserved credit for demonstrating practicality and quick thinking in a crisis.

My biographies of women reflect my astonishment at the skewed vision biographers bring to their work. In the end, I made furious attempts to see my subjects from every which way in order to obey the stern commands of accuracy. Having peered at these women upside down and from the right and left, I am left with only the humble feeling that the truth about another person is as hard to grasp as a single autumn leaf rushing down a swollen river. A biographer may not be a novelist, but the methods of both writers are more similar than I had thought. I once believed that novelists drew their characters from the endless colors of the imagination—infinite shades of red and blue and green—while a biographer was stuck with only a couple of dented buckets filled with the facts. But now I see that the biographer may add more blue to a subject's portrait if so moved, or leave yellow out entirely. It is surprising how a splatter of red can change the final picture.

Before the paint hits the biographer's canvas, many things can happen.

A version of this chapter was published in *Modern Girls, Shining Stars, The Skies of Tokyo: Five Japanese Women* (Columbia University Press, 1999). We are grateful to Columbia University Press for the reprint permissions.

21

BACKWARDS AND IN HIGH HEELS

Merry White

> *It was said of Ginger Rogers's dance performances with Fred Astaire that she did everything he did "only backwards and in high heels." Sometimes I think this describes what I have done as a woman in Japanese Studies.... [This is] a story of my own privileged engagement with Japan, a story of making my way, as an American woman, in Japan and in Japanese Studies. I've had my own advantages.*

MERRY WHITE is a professor of anthropology at Boston University, with specialties in Japanese Studies, food, and travel. Her books include *Coffee Life in Japan* (2012); *Perfectly Japanese: Making Families in an Era of Upheaval* (2002); *The Material Child: Coming of Age in Japan and America* (1993); *The Japanese Overseas: Can They Go Home Again?* (1988); and *The Japanese Educational Challenge: A Commitment to Children* (1987). A caterer prior to entering graduate school, she has written two cookbooks, one of which, *Cooking for Crowds*, first published in the mid-1970s, was reissued in 2013.

It was said of Ginger Rogers's dance performances with Fred Astaire that she did everything he did "only backwards and in high heels." Sometimes I think this describes what I have done as a woman in Japanese Studies. Our male counterparts have had some advantages—often a linguistic advantage. So many marry Japanese women and thus have "pillow dictionaries"—as well as having a social advantage in being admitted to the table convened by men. This sounds resentful, but instead it is meant more lightheartedly confident as a preface to a story of my own privileged engagement with Japan, a story of making my way, as an American woman, in Japan and in Japanese Studies. I've had my own advantages.

Remembering Ella (Embree) Lury Wiswell and Robert Smith's 1982 volume, *The Women of Suye Mura*, published long after the 1939 volume written by Wiswell's first husband, John Embree, I think of the advantage of having a woman's view and ear in Japan.[1] The stories of the same village from notes taken at the same time are very different. The first book, a classic rural study, emphasizes the *tatemae*, the ideal, the official version, or the way things ought to be—in this case, the way the village works, the official structures and social politics, or, in other words, the male view as heard by Embree. The second, written almost fifty years later from the notes of his wife who chiefly spoke to the women, is a study of the underlying *honne*, the way things really are on the ground, the messy complexity of people living entangled with each other. It reveals even the drunken, brawling, highly sexualized lives hidden under the "official" version: sometimes the biological father of a child was unknown. And if Ella hadn't kept her notes, we'd have only heard the voices of the men of the village who perhaps had a stake in the "official" version.

This may not represent an absolute advantage—the ability to capture the views of other women—but it is a valuable resource. How many accompanying wives of male scholars of Japan have stories of their own? Perhaps Suzanne Vogel's case is a contemporary example, as she interviewed the women of the families in her husband Ezra Vogel's *Japan's New Middle Class* (1963). Her stories of the women, most of them also included in Ezra's volume, led to her deeper investigation of women's concerns and their sense of themselves in her own publications.[2] But for the most part, her identity as a scholar/writer/observer was folded into Ezra's.

My own story is not that of a helpmate but that of a woman, over several cultural-historical eras, doing it backwards and in high heels, with no Fred Astaire leading. How it all began for me, how I can be included in this estimable group of women studying Japan, goes rather far back.

I was born six months before Pearl Harbor, where one of my uncles narrowly escaped death at Schofield Barracks, which was hit by Japanese fire in the attack, and I was raised in wartime when kids on my rough Chicago street would yell, "Bombs over Tokyo!" as we pummeled each other with randomly gathered missiles from an empty lot. My early toys were stamped "Made in Occupied Japan," and I made up a little song I remember even today, sung in a minor key and rather Orientalized, "Made in Japan, made in Japan, made in Occupied Japan . . ." This might have been an influence, but the real incentive came later, when I attended a very straitlaced, Europhile high school in Boston and became a rebellious youth. My school was an elite girls' school, and, in so many ways, I didn't belong. One of a few Jewish girls there (there were quotas for us in those days), I was a scholarship kid who'd never been skiing in St. Moritz or to London or Vienna on family trips, and I didn't have a blond pageboy, ancestral mansion, or town house and would not make a debut or "come out" to Boston society, though I had had to practice the deep cotillion curtsy in gym class.

Quite good in French, I was told I'd won a year's scholarship to the Sorbonne for what we'd now call a "gap year," but the family who had donated the prize reneged when they found I was Jewish. By then, however, I'd already literally spun the globe in the school library and found my finger pointing to Japan—searching for a place as far away from home as I could get.

Arriving at Harvard that fall for my freshman year, I began to create a new self—one studying Japanese and Russian languages, one who became engaged to be married very early, one who practiced a rather severe avant-garde attitude, wearing a black turtleneck sweater and carrying *The Communist Manifesto* into the coffee shops of Harvard Square. I dropped Russian quickly—much too hard—and found Japanese much easier. I settled on anthropology as my concentration.

That choice was made for me: Harvard then categorized the proper study of a place by how "advanced" its society appeared to be, and Japan then was seen as not modern, a developing (and recovering) society, therefore and hence to be studied in anthropology, the study of premodern societies. John Pelzel, a veteran of the Occupation, was my undergraduate advisor. As I worked my way through my degrees, however, Japan progressed to the point where, in the 1970s when I returned to study Japan in anthropology, I was told that Japan was now a fully modern, economically vibrant society and thus should be studied in sociology, the study of modern societies. I moved accordingly, and, after all, Ezra by then had arrived at Harvard in sociology.

But first, back to June of 1963, when, in a three-day succession, I got married, "commenced," and then boarded a plane, my first, with a passport, my first, to my first foreign country, Japan.

We had a round-the-world ticket and a $5,000 stipend from Harvard. We spent every penny but not one more during those 365 days. This one-year grant demanded that you keep moving and that you prove it by sending postcards from different ports of call every three weeks. We thought ourselves very clever, sending batches of cards signed by us to classmates also on the road all over the world, always to and from American Express offices, so they could send them back to Harvard, proving that we had kept moving rather than "going native" or getting too enamored of one place: the world was meant to attract us but not too much. In fact, of course, we overstayed in Japan considerably. Having arrived on prop planes that refueled in Chicago, Denver, Los Angeles, Honolulu, Midway, Wake Island, and Guam before finally touching down at Haneda, we weren't interested in moving on.

I was a sponge for everything in Japan but mostly for people. My new husband had been to Japan when he was in high school, following his father, a philosopher who'd been brought to Japan in the 1950s to help launch American Studies at the University of Tokyo and other universities. So we landed in the laps of his Japanese colleagues, who were saddled with the obligation to care for us. In my first week in Japan, staying at a cheap hotel, a former residence for Occupation military, I made my "best friend forever," Sachiko Ide. She was also very young at the time, and her work in sociolinguistics, especially on women's language, and her life have always inspired me.[3] Sachiko is my "Japanese sister"—we shared experiences of marriage, childbearing and raising, academic angst, and success in a deep friendship. Her work in linguistics, mine in anthropology, have not been so very far apart, but what especially connects us is our experience of the world as women. Sometimes this has brought us into feminist politics but usually into a grounded sense of shared lives.

Those first weeks were an immersion. It was 1963, the year before the Tokyo Olympics, and, although there were still dirt roads in central Tokyo and empty lots where bombed-out buildings had been and daikon patches here and there, the energy of the run-up to the Olympics was palpable. There were storefront *eikaiwa gakuen* (English language schools) and people coming up to me on the street proudly saying, "This is a pen!"—the first sentence, apparently, in the usual English text. There was construction everywhere, and Kenzō Tange's gigantic swimming pool/gymnasium complex was going up at the edge of Yoyogi Park.

The new friends took us everywhere: seeing Japanese philosophers cavorting on the beach at Enoshima was a treat; eating tempura at Ginza's renowned Hageten restaurant; ringing bells at temples; learning to sit *seiza* (formally, on one's knees, as for the tea ceremony). I don't remember any "culture shock," only culture absorption.

I also don't remember jet lag on that trip; everything was moving too fast to accommodate it anyway, or maybe the long trip to get there mitigated the effect of distance: no jets and no lag? But our hosts thought we would need a rest and booked us into an *onsen ryokan* hot springs inn in Yamanashi, the Fujimisou. And yes, we could see Fuji-san. It was restful, rustic, and we were the exotic elements. In the not-yet-gender-segregated *onsen* bath, nearly all the Japanese guests departed quickly when we entered. One day, dressed in the inn's *yukata* (light cotton robe) and wearing its *geta* (sandals with wood "stilts"), I struck out on a dirt road to see what was out there beyond the hot baths and sweet-smelling tatami and cypress wood. I hadn't gone far toward a modest destination, a wooden shack down the road that held the promise of a chocolate bar, when two older ladies stopped me on the road and engaged me in conversation in Japanese—*"Mushi atsui desu nee"* (It's muggy, isn't it!) and the like. I was happy to respond in kind. But I heard one say to the other, "I bet you didn't know I spoke English!"—after all, she was talking to a *gaijin* (foreigner); she must have been speaking English.

Indeed, it was very hot, and, yes, the shack had a dusty bar of Meiji chocolate, devoured guiltily before another inn dinner of novel substances.

Although we did indeed keep moving that year, everything referred to Japan—Hong Kong was a shock after the warm bath of Japan. Everywhere else felt as though I was "cheating" on Japan—even London, where I had deep roots, even Paris, where I would have been for a year earlier if I had not been Jewish, and even Italy, which much later became a second home away from home.

Hong Kong was, in 1963, crowded, dirty, and squalid unless one escaped up to Victoria Peak, but we, very tightly budgeted, stayed down below, where children were begging and refugees from the mainland were sleeping on sidewalks and scavenging food scraps. We moved on to Bangkok and Delhi, where street encampments seemed chronic, where poverty was endemic. Still in shock over the transition from upbeat, rebuilding, pre-Olympics Japan, I had the impulse to sign over all my American Express traveler's checks, wanting to cash them in for distribution in rupees to palliate my feeling of unhappy, helpless insufficiency, but of course I did not.

I was moved by India's sensory overload, and, still, every time I sniff woodsmoke or a certain kind of petrol, I am back in 1963 Delhi. The initial landing was challenging; arriving at the dark cavernous admission hall at the airport, we showed our passports at a rickety wooden desk, where sat a very large man who was made more imposing by his very tall turban and impressive beard. He ruffled through the pages, making negative noises, and said, "You cannot stay in India, madame, you have no visa." But, we said we'd been told at the Indian Embassy in Tokyo that we didn't need them for our short stay. He responded, complacently, "But now you do, and you will take the next flight out, which is to Taipei." Oh no, I said, we must see India, and I cried, which turned out to be the right strategy for a small young female in this situation, "I must see the Taj Mahal! Sob, sob." The man took our passports and put them in the drawer of his desk. "You may go to Agra but say nothing."

We left the airport in one of the many dilapidated taxis—quite different from those of Tokyo—at the dismal hour of 3:00 a.m. to go to our hotel, quite sure we'd never see our passports again. Hiring a driver the next day to go to Agra, we were stopped by a policeman who traveled with us to the Taj Mahal and back. He kept up a steady conversation with the driver, unintelligible to us. A few days later, quite unbelievably to us, we recovered our passports and flew on to Tashkent and Moscow and the rest of the world.

A year to the day of our departure, we returned to Boston, and I was heavy with child. Already admitted to graduate school in anthropology, I deferred to the spring term. My in-laws were quite dubious about this: "With our grandchild, we don't want you gallivanting around like Margaret Mead! Choose a field you can pursue by the fireside!" And so I did. I switched to literature, received a master's degree, and became ABD in comparative literature in French, Italian, and English because Harvard didn't think Japanese was suitable for the field and because the comparative literature people didn't feel confident in guiding me in it. I pursued the pre-Raphaelites, Dante, Proust, and read Victorian novels voraciously, nursing my baby. We migrated, the three of us, to Oxford, where I read Victorian literature. I became deeply dispirited, lonely, and took to long bicycle rides after dropping my daughter off at nursery school. Rainy days in a "two-up, two-down" row house in a working-class neighborhood with fifteen-watt bulbs in the lamps—well, it all led to seeking "professional help" and a return to Cambridge with my daughter. Eventually, I regrouped, started a career as a professional cook with utterly no experience or skills, managing now as a single mother, and tried to save money to return to graduate school.

It became much more complicated than spinning the globe in my high school library. After all, I'd been to Japan, gotten married and divorced, had a child, been a caterer, journalist, and traveler, and I needed a livelihood. It was not about studying late nights in the dorms with chums or sitting in language lab and breaking out for coffee. After all, I had a young child, and my time was limited. And the meager sustenance from a very well-meaning grant, the Graduate Fellowship for Women from the Danforth Foundation, which was aimed at supporting women like me who'd scrabbled to come back to school with children and slender resources, helped a lot. The language lab was a way of having a quiet time to myself.

The greatest boon of all was a community of scholars, a group of graduate students studying mostly China, although a few engaged with Japan. Ezra assembled us to meet weekly, and soon it was the best thing of all, as we met most often without Ezra, who by now had taken up China and Chinese and was often not around. We met, cooked, ate, and ate, and ate. We also took on a project together, a study of family and social change in China through reading the *Survey of the Chinese Mainland Press* daily, from which we culled at least official renderings of what ought to be the family, the worker, the child, and the woman, stridently declared in the waning years of the Cultural Revolution. We carried the Little Red Book; we read short stories out of China about noble selfless workers, sleepless girl workers who overnight repaired the cloth shoes of their male colleagues. We wanted to believe that workers were revered, that women held up half the sky.

But I was beginning "my own work" at last, landing back in Tokyo in 1975 with just enough Japanese to hold an interview, just enough direction to keep working. My study treated Japanese who had lived and worked or studied overseas and returned to Japan, highlighting and examining a phenomenon of "border crossing," then seen as highly problematic to many. The *kikoku mondai* (return to country problem) became a book, my second on Japan.[4] (The first, a hot seller on Japanese education, was published during the US-Japan trade war and put me occasionally in hot water.)[5] But back to 1975 and my small establishment in Tokyo's Meguro neighborhood—a "2DLK," two tatami rooms, a kitchen-dining area with one table, a bathtub, and a toilet. My daughter was ten and in an international school, our roommate was an American teacher at that school, and we borrowed futon and tatami-appropriate furnishings. Very spare. The unusual aspect of my fieldwork adventure was the presence of my advisor and his family, who lived a ten-minute bus ride away. We were also connected by the fact that our daughters were in the same school and rode the bus together. The good news was that Ezra was available for consultation, and the bad news was that I indulged in *amaeru* behavior, whining at one point that my interviews seemed to be diverging from what I'd expected. Ezra, ever optimistic, said, "Oh good, now you'll listen." His injunction was always to look for "what makes the data sing," and that might be an unexpected song. And after sharing that year, we were friends, with friendly mentoring constant, right to Ezra's death in 2020.

Restless—we'd now call it attention deficit disorder—I found myself needing something else. In Japan I was considered a member of the *nagarazoku*, or "gang of while-ers," needing to do more than one thing at a time. I joined a cooking school founded in the Meiji period in Tokyo's Mejiro neighborhood, the Akabori Ryōri Gakuen, and rather daringly enrolled myself in the *senmon kōsu* (professional course) for four months, preparing *osechi ryōri*, the New Year's foods. I thought, well, this will be relaxing; after all, I've been a professional cook, cookbook writer, and food journalist.[6] But it was so very much harder—so exhausting, so testing of every capacity. Once a week for more than four anxious hours, arriving late at home with whatever sorry version of the day's preparation I had made, I persisted, the only *gaijin* in the class and clearly needing remedial help in every aspect of kitchen work, especially cleaning.

If that weren't enough, tea ceremony lessons were "something else" I had been advised to take because friends saw them as a route to gaining access to my main advisor at the University of Tokyo, a person I thought very austere and a bit frightening. (Instead, I found out later that he was shy, insecure in English, and a retiring sort of scholar.) I was told that his wife just might take me on as the first foreign student in her Omotesenke classes in their beautiful *chashitsu* teahouse in the garden of their house in Tokyo's Ōta ward. He might then hear of my diligence and be more approachable. Another five hours a week, sometimes in full kimono and always on my knees, the only foreigner in the room again, I emulated my teacher's every move. It was almost totally a nonverbal experience, being nudged occasionally, given diagrams for food and hand placement. My teacher was very kind and took me to pottery workshops, tea purveyors, and *chakai* tea gatherings. I received a completely fitted-out tea case on my departure from Japan with every *odōgu* (tea ceremony, tool) I would need and several beautiful old tea bowls. We stayed close for years.

I had no idea back then in the mid-1970s that both of these "extracurricular" activities, possibly by some seen as hedonistic distractions from the drier, more serious work of scholarship, would become part of the then discredited work I would undertake as a food anthropologist. I had already had a hint of the damaging implications of food—particularly cooking and writing about food—on my career in Japanese Studies. One of my advisors (then kindly and appropriately) told me "take those cookbooks off your CV or you'll never have an academic career," and so I did. Another "high heels" and "backwards" moment.

Perhaps my ability to accommodate to cultural norms at different eras might also be an acquired trait among other Japan-based women scholars: we want to fit in, and anthropologists especially hold that as a tenet of methodology, as participant-observers.

From my earliest days in Japan, in the unreconstructed period of the early 1960s, when first-wave feminism had little purchase against the rising middle-class, acquisitive, *sarariman* (salaryman) business culture Ezra described in *Japan's New Middle Class*, I understood what it was I was to assimilate to—insofar as a curly haired *gaijin* woman could. I practiced situational bowing, I worked on *keigo* polite language; I dressed more sedately and neatly than I had in Cambridge where I had a studied louche quality. I was aiming too high to be a good *ojōsama* (proper young woman) and using too much *asobase-kotoba* (feminine vocabulary, particularly of the Kyoto area). I struck some as prissy or laughable. What stays with me from that era is my earnestness, my desire to fit in, to be, in fact, sometimes "*plus japonaise que les japonaises*." My voice goes up when I speak Japanese, especially on the phone or with people I don't know well.

Back home again in America, I seem to have persisted in these habits, the amplification of cultural norms. At a dinner, I would wait to be asked more than once if I would like seconds and often missed my chance at filling up—a story told also in *The Anatomy of Dependence* by Takeo Doi.[7] And I didn't unbutton the top button of my blouses, although all the women around me around me were displaying cleavage.

Am I just good at adjusting my personal culture, or do I have a preexisting condition that makes Japanese norms more attractive to me? That is, did I choose Japan because I was already inclined to be more like those Japanese women, more comfortable in what I imagined their own behavioral comforts to be? My own rebellious manifestations of anger and my reactions to abusive American masculinities found their expression but not in Japan. THOSE men, THAT culture, was not mine, and, however irritating I imagined they would be to Japanese women, I could distance myself from Japanese misogyny and patriarchalism. Was I really, though, just an observer, a member of the audience?

Suzanne Vogel and I engaged with many Japanese women, she more deeply in some cases than I because she worked as a psychiatric social worker in a clinical setting. At the time, we each wrote essays on the Japanese housewife, Sue commemorating women who'd made the hand dealt them a good one by "professionalizing" the housewife role, and I extending that into discussions among American and Japanese feminists on the question, "Is there a universal feminism?"[8] Warring within me were yes and no. Obviously, American women had something to learn; it wasn't just corporate managers who could take lessons from Japan, but we were treading on dangerous ground because the commonly held belief was that women in Japan "walked three steps behind" and had, as Christine Yano points out about Hello Kitty, no mouth. And there was a belief in Japan that American women were liberated, had choices, and were not oppressed.[9]

The pivotal moment in this mutual gazing came in 1978 when I and two Japanese friends—Wakako Hironaka and Sumiko Iwao (the first, a Brandeis graduate, translator, and writer, and senator in the Japanese Diet; the second, professor of social psychology at Keio University and author of many papers and books on women in Japan)—organized the first international women's conference (Kokusai Josei Gakkai) to be held in Saitama in a new women's center.[10] Superstars arrived, like Betty Friedan, and the press swarmed the occasion. Scholars gave papers, activists protested against an academic bias, housewives raised their own movement flags, and some declared the whole event elitist. The rifts drew the attention of the conservative press, such as the *Yomiuri* newspaper, who pointed out that women are by nature petty and contentious. And then I myself became a distraction. I'd just given birth two months earlier to my second child, my son Benjamin, and of course brought him to Japan, neither of us sleeping much. We attracted newspaper attention. The *Yomiuri* newspaper paparazzi stalked me as I tried to hide at the back of the auditorium where the plenary sessions took place so that I could breastfeed my baby discretely. I had a "nursing shawl" that shamefully slipped as a zoom lens captured the primal act. And for three days, the newspaper ran photos of this tiny baby with a cautionary narrative explaining the evils feminism can bring: "She brought a newborn baby halfway around the world, away from her husband's family: is this what women's lib (*ūman ribu*) means? Putting a child at risk?" Ben's stalwart feminism had early roots.

I never had a postdoctoral plan; with two children and a leftover cooking career, I wasn't at all sure I wanted a lengthy academic apprenticeship before security. After a few years of research at the Harvard Graduate School of Education and a rise to the directorship of the project that had hired me, I was hired at Boston University on a Japan Foundation grant to build Japanese Studies there. I made my first bold demand: although I'd never had a tenure-track appointment, I wanted an instant tenure review during my first year, as I had already two books published and a third in press.[11] It worked, and I became an associate professor with tenure after eighteen months. There was grumbling: "She doesn't have any theory," the sociologists said. ("Neither had I," Ezra said, when I complained to him about sociologists). I made the leap back into anthropology, and with the great fortune visited upon me by Christine Yano, who invited me to teach summers at the University of Hawai'i, I made the next leap into food anthropology at Boston University. After all, my old mentor and friend, Julia Child, had helped to establish a gastronomy program there, and my careers began to converge.[12]

My explorations in Japanese food culture took me far—in fact, to Italy, on a Monbushō scholarship in the mid-1990s to study Japanese culinary tourism there. It was the height of the *itameshi* Italian food boom in Japan, and I was riding high, too. The lost and lamented journal *Lingua Franca*, which ceased publication in 2001, wrote that I'd won the "fieldwork scam of the year" award; I must be having rather a good time. And I was. Soon after, I began research on coffee in Japan, having woken up to the fact that I spend much of my time in Japan sitting in *kissaten*, cafes, and coffeehouses, and decided I might find scholarly interest in these urban social spaces. And I did. The book, *Coffee Life in Japan*, is one of the best known of my books, surprising everyone, including my publisher.[13] Now engaged in writing about Japanese food workers, I find myself in factories, cattle enclosures, and domestic kitchens, and trailing after Michelin-starred chefs as they do their marketing. At this writing, I am about to launch a new project, an ethnographic treatment of a whisky distillery and the industry supporting it. This, too, is food. My son Benjamin (Wurgaft) and I have published a book, *Ways of Eating*, an anthropological and historical survey of the world's foods; the dire predictions of the *Yomiuri* newspaper did not become manifest.[14]

After Ezra died in 2020, I have become part of the older generation, and that has been a sobering thought. Do I represent anything that amounts to a generation? The word is like white noise—no meaning, just a soundbite. Are we a coherent entity? And are we women of this "generation" an entity? We've all had our struggles, diverse ones, but here we are, and whatever the "we" might be, I'm glad to be part of it. The next ones coming along may not be wearing high heels and dancing backwards—much more likely, they are wearing running shoes and dashing past their male colleagues. But it's been fun being Ginger Rogers, hasn't it?

Notes

[1] Robert Smith and Ella Embree Wiswell, *The Women of Suye Mura* (Chicago: University of Chicago Press, 1982); John Embree, *Suye Mura: A Japanese Village* (Chicago: University of Chicago Press, 1939).

[2] Ezra Vogel, *Japan's New Middle Class* (Berkeley: University of California Press, 1963); Suzanne Vogel, "The Professional Housewife: The Career of Urban Middle-Class Japanese Women," *Japan Interpreter* 1, no. 12 (1978), 16–43.

[3] Sachiko Ide and Naomi Hanaoka McGoin, *Aspects of Women's Language: Onnakotoba no Sugata* (Tokyo: Kurosio, 1990).

[4] Merry White, *The Japanese Overseas: Can They Go Home Again?* (New York: Free Press, 1988).

[5] Merry White, *The Japanese Educational Challenge: A Commitment to Children* (New York: Free Press, 1985).

[6] Merry White, *Cooking for Crowds* (New York: Basic Books, 1975); *Noodles Galore* (New York: Basic Books, 1976); *Cooking for Crowds*, revised edition (Princeton: Princeton University Press, 2013).

[7] Takeo Doi, *The Anatomy of Dependence*, translated by John Bester (Tokyo: Kodansha International, 1973).

[8] See, for example, Vogel, "The Professional Housewife."

[9] Christine Yano, *Pink Globalization: Hello Kitty's Trek across the Pacific* (Durham: Duke University Press, 2013).

[10] For example, Sumiko Iwao, *The Japanese Woman: Traditional Image and Changing Reality* (New York: Knopf, 1992).

[11] Merry White, *The Material Child: Coming of Age in Japan and America* (Berkeley: University of California Press, 1993).

[12] Julia Child, *Mastering the Art of French Cooking* (New York: Knopf, 1961).

[13] Merry White, *Coffee Life in Japan* (Berkeley: University of California Press, 2012).

[14] Benjamin Aldes Wurgaft and Merry White, *Ways of Eating* (Berkeley: University of California Press, 2023).

22

NIGHT TRAIN TO TOKYO

Susan J. Pharr

Life is filled with the unexpected. I could never have imagined, when I took the night train from Atlanta to the North, that I would end up with Japan at the center of my life.

SUSAN J. PHARR is the Edwin O. Reischauer Research Professor of Japanese Politics at Harvard University. Formerly, she was director of the Program on U.S.-Japan Relations of the Weatherhead Center for International Affairs. Much of her research has explored the social basis for democracy in Japan and East Asia and the origins and development of civil society and its role in social and political change worldwide, particularly in Asia. Her research interests include comparative political behavior, Japanese politics, Japanese foreign policy and the international relations of East Asia, domestic and international NGOs in politics, comparative politics of industrialized nations, democratization and social change in Japan and Asia, political ethics and corruption, environmental politics, the role of the media in politics, women and politics, the role of Japan and the United States in development, and the international political economy of development.

On a warm day in early September 1966, I stepped out onto the platform. New York City at last! But it was a second arrival. An hour or so earlier, groggy from the overnight ride on the gently swaying train from Atlanta, I had awoken to the conductor's roar of "New-Ark." To my Southern ear, that sounded close enough, and, gathering up my suitcases, I had stumbled off the train, helped by one or two kindhearted passengers. The deserted look of the platform alerted me that something was wrong, and, sticking my head back in the train, I mumbled weakly, "This doesn't seem to be New York." A chuckle made its rounds at my end of the compartment, and, soon, the same helpers as before sprang into action. We managed to drag the bags inside just as the train pulled away from the station to leave Newark, New Jersey, for Penn Station.

In those early weeks in Manhattan, my days had a strange, charmed quality, as if the new chapter of my life was being embossed on thick, lustrous paper, not printed on ordinary stock like the chapters before. My arrival set the tone. It never occurred to me to take a taxi, and, somehow, miraculously, I found my way into a crowded subway car headed to Morningside Heights, my luggage pressed against my legs like so many Dobermans. As I caught my breath, I noticed a short, middle-aged man nearby with a newspaper in a foreign language tucked under his arm. In my general state of euphoria at being in the North at long last, I brushed aside my mother's warning to never speak to strange men and caught his eye. Nodding toward his newspaper and groping to steady my wobbling suitcases, I asked, "Is that German?" He was a music critic, he told me, once he had recovered from the shock of being spoken to by a stranger in the New York subway. He had arrived from Hamburg that very day to attend the grand opening of the new Metropolitan Opera House at Lincoln Center the following Saturday night. The famous soprano Leontyne Price would sing, he told me. Now, it happened that even in my limited world up until that time, I had heard of Leontyne Price. As stations rumbled by, we chatted amiably, until at last he said, quite shyly, that the news magazine *Der Spiegel* had given him two tickets for the opening, and would I like to join him? As he gathered himself together to exit at his stop, we made hasty plans to meet at the fountain in front of Lincoln Center the coming Saturday. As soon as I settled in at my destination, I was on the phone with my mother, asking her to ship me my one evening gown and explaining how it was that within an hour of my arrival in New York for graduate study at Columbia, I was headed for a gala at the Metropolitan Opera with a foreign man I had met on the subway.

My actual destination was not the Columbia stop at West 116th Street and Broadway but West 125th and Broadway, from which I would make my way to International House at 500 Riverside Drive. A budding political scientist embarking on the study of the world should live in a community with foreign students, I had reasoned. The only alternative was a women's dorm. Only seven or eight blocks from Columbia, I-House, I soon discovered, might as well have been on another planet. True, a number of Columbia graduate students lived there but few who were in my department. And all around me was a dazzling array of exotic people with all kinds of interests, from fashion to fruit flies. There were dances, art shows, festivals, excursions into Manhattan nightlife or upstate New York, all of which collectively created a hum that seemed wildly out of resonance with what I had come to do—namely, to study for a PhD. Little wonder, then, that the state of elation evoked on the subway persisted.

Magical things continued to happen. Soon after settling in at I-House, I took a wrong turn in the labyrinth of corridors surrounding the dining hall and came upon a sign that said "*Mikado* Tryouts." Drawn by the strains of "Three Little Maids from School Are We," familiar from my days in a choir, I soon was auditioning for an off-Broadway production. To my amazement, I landed a spot, and I blithely signed up for a grueling schedule of rehearsals. Soon, reality set in as I began to tackle the staggeringly long reading assignments that came with my first classes at Columbia, and I dropped out. But the possibilities before me seemed boundless.

The charmed quality to life so far set the stage for an encounter that would change my life forever. Collecting my mail in the I-House lobby one day in early October, my eye strayed to a bulletin board with a small, handwritten sign that said "Judo Instruction Offered on Sundays." Many things went through my mind. One was the appeal of a way to get some exercise. But judo was attractive in another way. I knew little about the sport, but warnings about the dangers of walking the blocks from I-House to the Columbia campus, especially at night, rang in my ears, and it occurred to me that I might feel safer if I had a few defensive skills. What I also felt was the powerful lure of the foreign. My resolve firmed up when I saw a Japanese man, like me in his early to mid-twenties, leaving the I-House gym wearing a white getup with a black sash. When he caught me staring, he bowed. I was intrigued.

On Sunday, I showed up in that same gym at the appointed hour. Into the room filed some twenty Japanese men roughly my age, all of them wearing black belts, and four or five hesitant Americans. Greeting the group in halting English, the instructor warmly welcomed the Americans, urging us not to feel intimidated and assuring us that these sessions would be only for fun and exercise. Several things struck me as I sat on the floor, transfixed. The first was the deep formalism in the meeting. Even in the rough-and-tumble setting of a gym, the Japanese men who had assembled listened with strict attention to what the instructor said and bowed when he was through. The second was the grace of the movements. Clutching instructions on where to secure a judo uniform (*gi*), I hung around with the other Americans to watch some sparring after the session ended. The instructor seized a partner, and, together, they glided over the mat in what almost appeared to be a waltz. But soon the instructor tossed his opponent over his shoulder as if he were no more than a bag of flour or a spare cushion.

The Japanese men in the judo class were all students in programs around the city, many of them in Columbia's ESL (English as a second language) program. One evening a few days later, I came upon the instructor eating alone in the I-House dining hall and asked if I could join him. Predictably, he bowed. After a brief silence, he cleared his throat and spoke.

"How many cigarettes do you smoke a day?" he asked.

"Pardon?"

"How many cigarettes do you smoke a day?"

"None," I replied.

"One?" he said, misunderstanding me.

"I said none. I don't smoke."

I was confused to see his face fall in obvious disappointment. He then explained that in a recent session of his English conversation course at Columbia, the teacher had covered smoking to the point that he could now sustain quite a long conversation if we stuck to that topic, but he couldn't do much else. Thus, I dutifully asked him how many cigarettes *he* smoked a day, and we continued until the topic was exhausted. Silence descended.

"Have you ever been to Japan?" he asked finally.

"No," I replied.

He then produced a thick-nibbed fountain pen and a small, unlined index card. He began to draw with a sure and deliberate hand.

"Japan has four main islands," he said.

The particulars of Japan's geography had never registered with me, and I watched the moving pen with fascination. Soon he was naming the islands and surrounding seas and adding dots for Tokyo, for the city in central Japan where he lived, and then for all the major cities of Japan.

"Can you use chopsticks?" he asked.

"No," I replied.

The events that followed had a logic of their own. Soon the judo class had become a regular, once-a-week feature of my life, and, as the group got to know each other, there were excursions first to Chinese restaurants in the I-House neighborhood and then to sushi restaurants in the West Forties off Fifth Avenue. My classmates marveled, as have so many Japanese since, at my affinity for sea urchin (*uni*), which was instant and deep. While these adventures took place outside the realm of my graduate work, they gradually came to resonate with it. I had come to Columbia to study comparative politics—that is, areas of the world outside the United States. Students in my subfield were required to develop a knowledge of three countries or regions, and so far, I had selected only two: West Africa and the UK. So although I had no clear plan in mind, by late fall, I began to think that in my second semester at Columbia, I would take a course or two on Japan.

In retrospect, I now see that the pull toward Japan was very powerful. Looking back, events in the sphere inhabited by the judo class and my growing circle of Japanese friends play in Technicolor. In the other sphere of the Columbia classroom, they play in grainy black and white. At the outset of the academic year, in a rare meeting held for the entering graduate students by the Department of Public Law and Government (as the political science department was then called), a stern-faced professor told us pointedly that we should not be at Columbia if we expected to be held by the hand. Clutching our schedules, we were then turned loose to fend for ourselves. On the new landscape, nothing looked even remotely familiar. Based on my experience in college back in Atlanta, a "seminar" was five to ten students, all listening in respectful attention to what the instructor and the other students had to say and then raising their hands for chances to have a go themselves. At Columbia, in contrast, seminars were vast free-for-alls in which twenty to thirty combatants vied for the floor, interrupting one another and snorting derisively at the opinions of others while the professor watched in seeming amusement, intervening only to lob in new questions. Or so it seemed to me at the time as a Southern woman who had been taught never to interrupt.

The lecture classes were intimidating in their own way. Master's and doctoral students took basic graduate courses together, so the numbers were shockingly large to my mind. Into the cavernous case-style classrooms of Columbia Law School came one or two hundred students to wait expectantly until the professor appeared at a podium on a platform. Some of these professors were quite brilliant, and I enjoyed many of my courses. But asking a question or offering a comment from the floor required the aplomb of a practiced performer.

Each student had been assigned an advisor, of course, and, early in the semester, I took my place in the seating area outside a famous scholar's office to wait to see his secretary, a forbidding woman before whom there was a large black appointment book. As I began speaking, I watched with a sinking heart as she pored over its densely filled pages.

"September is a bad month," she mused. "Who are you again?"

"I was told that he's my advisor," I replied weakly.

"Oh," she said grudgingly, still turning pages. "Well, I'm afraid it's looking like a bad few months. Do you really need to see him this fall? Things get better in the spring."

I explained apologetically that I needed my advisor to approve the courses I was currently taking, and, finally, we carved out a few minutes the following week. The secretary, kinder now that I was in the book, gently warned me that I should brace myself for disappointment, for he might need to cancel. My sliver of time did, in fact, materialize, and, as these hard-won appointments gradually accumulated, I found the courage to tell my advisor of my growing interest in Japan. But the impression I made had not registered too deeply, it seemed. The following fall, in a rare chance encounter with him on campus, he boomed heartily, "Mrs. Zabonowitz, so how was Turkey?"

From these miseries of Morningside Heights, judo and the world of International House offered respite and a sense of community. By spring of my first year, the distance, initially so great, between my two worlds began to close in important ways. I continued to pursue my course work on Africa, and, in January, I applied for a fellowship to start the study of the Hausa language, a lingua franca in West Africa, the following academic year. But at the same time, I began a gradual academic tilt toward Japan.

Thus, the second half of my first year at Columbia brought me into the classrooms of sociologist Herbert Passin, whose course was on Japanese society, and James William Morley, who taught Japanese politics and foreign policy and Japan's political development. Two people could not have been less alike. With his hooded eyelids and air of decadence, Herbert Passin quietly reeled you into his space, and then he would suddenly nail a point with wit and a crackling intelligence. James William Morley, the child of a Methodist minister, was reserved and a bit aloof, but his lectures awed with their depth and historical reach. Here, for the first time at Columbia, were faculty members with whom I could begin to connect. A few years later, both would serve on my dissertation committee, and James Morley would chair it.

There is another dimension to this story, and it lay in the intellectual realm. In my field, political science, the study of Japan was in no way an esoteric endeavor at the time. In a 1960s world in which a host of former colonies were newly independent, the great puzzle of the day was how traditional societies could make the passage to modern statehood. Modernization theory was in its heyday, and, in the search for successful examples, Meiji Japan stood out. How was it that Japan, emerging from a feudal system in the middle of the nineteenth century, had managed to establish itself as one of the world's leading powers and development success stories by the time of its victory in the Russo-Japanese War in 1905? Questions such as this sparked the interest of a great many political scientists, who eagerly studied the late Tokugawa and early Meiji periods to discover how samurai almost overnight became modern bureaucrats. I saw myself as joining this quest. I remember sitting in the basement of Columbia's Uris Hall, where I often studied, taking meticulous notes on the ranking system for samurai and committing the names of the ranks to memory, not because I was required to know these things but because I was helpless with admiration for a system so intricate that had primed elites to take their place in modern forms of organization.

In my studies, it helped, of course, that over dinner I could talk to my Japanese friends about what I was learning. The disjuncture of those early years at Columbia, when I studied Hausa and West Africa and later did an MA thesis in African Studies but, at the same time, became increasingly engaged with Japan, did not really trouble me. My broader intellectual interest, in both cases, was trying to understand how modern political systems emerged from traditional societies.

Late spring of my first year at Columbia brought an entirely new kind of encounter with Japan. The parents and associates of a judo classmate made their first-ever trip to America, and I agreed to take the group around Manhattan. The father, a high school graduate who had worked as a civilian in Manchuria during the war, was totally unlike the Japanese I had been meeting at I-House and Columbia, who for the most part were Tokyoites, well-traveled and accustomed to the West. A self-made man who headed a successful company, he knew little of life outside a small city in Nagano. Surrounding him were subordinates who fell over themselves to do his bidding. My classmate's diminutive mother floated in her own world. Oblivious to Manhattanites' stares, she wore a kimono, *tabi*, and *geta* everywhere we went. At the Metropolitan Opera, she hopped up on the seat, tucked her feet beneath her, and, except for the intermission, held the position for the entire three hours without moving. I had not yet studied Japanese, and my communication with the visitors was limited, but I watched the dynamics within the group with fascination.

Two years later, I had switched the primary focus of my studies to Japan and had embarked on the study of the Japanese language. And then a chance came my way for a summer homestay in Japan. At Haneda Airport, I got my first look at Japan and the Japanese people. A woman of average height in America at five feet, six inches, I towered over most Japanese women and many men. It was a shock to look so different from the people around me. That first summer, several times in a train station or department store, I would glance at a mirror and catch sight of an anomaly in the crowd, a tall and long-limbed pink woman with yellow curls on her head. Hungry for company, for a moment of sameness, I caught myself turning my head to find her. The story of that remarkable summer is too long to tell here, but by the end of it, the pull of Japanese Studies was irresistible.

Beginnings: Becoming an Internationalist

At the end of the long tunnel that is graduate school, I emerged as a scholar of Japan, and I credit judo and my judo classmates with my launch in the field. But there is a prior question—namely, how was it that I became an international person? In graduate school, I debated *which* part of the world to study, but I had been on track to be an internationalist for a surprising number of years.

I did not arrive by any of the obvious routes. In Japanese Studies, an earlier generation of Japan specialists were products of World War II and its immediate aftermath: James Morley, who was forty-six when I first took a course with him, had been a code breaker in naval intelligence, and Herbert Passin, then fifty-one, had served with the Allied Occupation. Many of my Columbia classmates were ex-military who had been stationed in postwar Japan or were the children of missionaries or businessmen posted there. Others were Japanese nationals or legacy students with family ties to Japan.

My story was entirely different. I was born in Atlanta, Georgia. Until I arrived in Manhattan for graduate school, I had never met a Japanese person. Neither of my parents, and none of my grandparents and other relatives, were college-educated or had ever traveled outside the United States, and rarely had they ventured beyond Georgia. After my father's death many years ago, I found an entire scrapbook filled with photographs from a business trip he once took to San Francisco, the great adventure of his lifetime.

Like many ambitious men of limited means in his day, my father, Marion Taylor Pharr, had gone to night school, and, with the law degree he earned there, he became a claims adjuster for Western Union, a company that in his time dispatched telegrams and shipments. My mother, Gladys Chappelear Pharr, was a housewife, and, later, after my parents divorced when I was five, a secretary. After the divorce, I lived with my mother and circumstances were strapped—unlikely beginnings for an internationalist.

But a series of fortuitous happenings rocked my orbit. Three stand out. The first was an extraordinary opportunity that came my way to tour Europe at age fifteen. The public high school I attended in northeast Atlanta was ordinary in most respects, but it had an ambitious choir director, Mr. Lowrance, who set his sights on taking fifty of his choristers on a tour of Europe. To help cover the costs, the parents sold Christmas trees and light bulbs; we teenagers peddled giant North Fulton Special Choir chocolate bars door-to-door. Parents had to top up, and my mother took out a second mortgage on the house to pay my way. I was the youngest person on the tour.

The year was 1959, and, coming out of World War II, American teenagers got a warm welcome in Europe. The choir sang on a television show in Madrid and in a packed opera house in Bilbao. In Munich, the mayor gave the choir the keys to the city and told us teenagers that it was now our duty to each down a huge stein of beer, a task that we gleefully embraced, hardly believing our good fortune.

Mr. Lowrance was determined that beyond giving concerts, we choristers would have some culture and history packed into our empty skulls. Clutching the mic on the bus, he pointed out the blackened ruins of buildings that had been bombed in the war as we drove past them, and he marched us through museums and cathedrals. When we sang on a military base in Italy, he lectured us on the Cold War. When weary choristers slumped in their bus seats, he hissed in their ears, "Wake up. This is the chance of a lifetime to see the Alps." He had no need to shake me, however. My eyes were as round as saucers. Holding a candle at a world choir festival in Innsbruck, Austria, I joined my voice with those of young people from choirs around the world and felt at one with them.

I describe the trip in such detail because I was not the same person afterward. The more ample spending money of my fellow choir members brought home my meager circumstances. Still, being selected for the tour and reveling in everything I saw gave me the feeling that I had been singled out in some way.

The second happening was more about the push to find a new direction than the pull of new possibilities. Increasingly, by my early high school years, I felt out of step with the world around me. After the divorce, my mother, who had worked only briefly during the war, bought a secondhand typewriter, brushed up her skills, and looked for a job. "If I don't work, we'll lose the house," she told me matter-of-factly, for the alimony and child support she received from my father did not cover expenses. She found a job as a church secretary and thrived until, one day, a newly arrived minister called her in and told her that, alas, he would have to let her go because as a divorcee, she set a bad example in a Christian community. The new minister soon gave the job to the secretary who had worked for him in his former church. Much later, it came out that he was having an affair with her, but the revelation hardly helped my mother, who struggled to recover from the blow to her ego and find work. Times were hard. We lived in a middle-class house in a nice neighborhood, but there were stretches without gas or electricity. And then things took a sharp turn for the better. A minister, indignant over my mother's treatment in her former job, stepped in and helped her land another secretarial post. This time, she worked for a meritorious individual, a kindly intellectual named Paul Rilling, who headed a small civil rights organization that was lending support to Martin Luther King Jr.'s efforts to bring racial integration to Atlanta and the South. My mother often helped out at the registration desk for weekend conferences on fair housing or voting rights at Morehouse or Spelman, Black universities that supported Dr. King's work. I sometimes joined her, and I had the privilege of meeting Dr. King. My mother was never an activist, but she felt pride in being part of a just cause.

At first glance, these activities, aimed at effecting radical change in the South, would appear to bear no relation to my emergence as an international person. But the fact was that I wanted to be like Mr. Rilling, who had studied in the North, and whose special interest was the links between developments in the American South and Africa. His organization, among other things, provided travel funds to African leaders who wanted to meet Dr. King and to see the civil rights movement firsthand. From time to time, Mr. Rilling dispatched my mother, with me in tow, to the Greyhound Bus terminal to meet small delegations from Kenya, Somalia, and other African countries to take them to conferences. As I looked at the South through the eyes of these visitors, I felt ashamed of the segregated world around me. Looking back, I now see how these encounters with African visitors kindled an interest in Africa, and how Mr. Rilling, a man I knew mainly through my mother's admiring accounts, became a role model for the kind of person I wanted to become.

The third step in my opening to the international came in my sophomore year in college. At that stage, the choir trip had been my only experience abroad. A patchwork of scholarships, loans, and summer work had made college possible, and I had won a spot at Emory University, which was close to my home. But I was restless and needed direction. An opportunity that would change my life profoundly soon came my way. That year, I took a history course from a professor, a specialist on the Middle Ages who was known to be demanding and unapproachable. I was told on good authority that the professor had a penchant for fraternity boys who wore penny loafers and had antipathy for women students. But I was dazzled by his course, and, when the term ended, I was emboldened to knock on his door. He seemed to know who I was and told me to sit. I am sure that I must have rambled a bit, but, finally, I asked, simply, "What should I do next?" Retrospectively, it was an odd question. And yet he seemed not at all surprised, and his reply was immediate and urgent, "Get out of here, get out of the South." And then he went back to whatever he had been doing, as if the matter was settled.

I stumbled out of his office, and, almost immediately, my eyes fell on a bulletin board advertising a graduate institute on French-speaking West Africa to be held the coming summer at Georgetown University in Washington, DC, sponsored by the Ford Foundation. I was a college sophomore and not a graduate student, but I had studied three years of French and was taking a course on the peoples of Africa. I saw the notice as something akin to a divine intervention. I headed back to my dorm room and wrote a letter asking for a scholarship—a letter addressed simply to the "Ford Foundation, New York, New York" that began "Dear Sir." And amazingly, a reply came, granting my request. For me at the time, Washington, DC was the far North, and I was soon on my way. I never crossed paths with the professor again, but, years later, I wrote to thank him for his words of advice that set in motion a lifetime of engagement with the world.

Figure 22.1: Susan Pharr and Margi Haas at the Tokyo Symposium on Women, July 1978. Photograph courtesy of the author.

From that point forward, I trod a path toward the international. I eagerly sought out courses on politics and societies in Africa and on Third-World development. The following spring, yet another sign on a bulletin board alerted me to a summer program, this one in Dakar, Senegal. By the time I entered my senior year at Emory, my teachers thought of me as a budding specialist on African politics. With their blessing, I headed to Columbia University on a Woodrow Wilson Fellowship to pursue a PhD in political science, with a focus on West Africa.

None of the three interventions I describe was very personal. I cannot recall a single conversation I ever had with my high school choir director or Mr. Rilling, my mother's boss. And the words of advice from my college professor consisted of only a sentence or two. They are reminders that the smallest kind of boost from an older person, coming at the right time, can reverberate over the lifetime of someone starting out, a truth that I have taken to my life as a teacher and mentor, and that has kept me going when the line at office hours was long.

Intellectual Directions

What is remarkable about a life is how a mosaic of experiences, many of them sheer happenstance, come together and then generate their own logic. Judo and the summer in Japan propelled me toward Japanese Studies. They, coupled with my earlier experiences, also affected what I wanted to know about Japan, the puzzles that intrigued me.

First and foremost, my observations of the world of Japanese women—undoubtedly coupled with my own experiences as a woman—led me to the study of women, status, and gender. Japanese gender roles and expectations erect formidable barriers to women's achievements in the public sphere outside the home, such as politics, and yet some women had found ways around them and managed to succeed. How had they done it? That question led to my choice of a dissertation topic and my first book, *Political Women in Japan: The Search for a Place in Political Life* (1981).[1]

I then took a step back. Clearly, socialization in the home and society constrain women's options in all societies, but changes do occur. I became intrigued with legal changes in Occupied Japan that had opened up new possibilities for women. How had these measures emerged in a military occupation?, I wondered. What had turned soldiers into feminists? This puzzle led to my work on the origins of Articles 14 and 24 in the postwar Constitution of Japan granting equal rights guarantees that, to this day, women do not have in the United States, and on a little-noticed policy alliance made up of women, American and Japanese, that formed during the Occupation years to promote women's rights in Japan.[2]

My interest in women was grounded in a broader fascination with social hierarchy and social organization that dated from my earliest encounters with Japanese people, when I watched Japanese bow and interact in my judo class at International House. All societies mark and maintain status differences in a variety of ways, and I was intrigued by how, in the Japanese context, all this affects relations in the workplace, within political parties, and in many other spheres. Soon I was at work on *Losing Face: Status Politics in Japan* (1990), which dealt with status-based conflicts—the ways in which people locked into power asymmetries based on status differences (younger politicians vis-à-vis their seniors in political parties, women vis-à-vis men in the workplace, *burakumin* vis-à-vis the majority population in a variety of social contexts) express their grievances and struggle to improve their lot.[3]

A common thread in my subsequent work has been how people perceive the social and political institutions within which they operate and respond to them—how they find a voice and push back against the obstacles they face. In any society, the media play a central role in this process: who do the media listen to and side with when social groups go up against the state? My search for an answer led to *Media and Politics in Japan* (edited with Ellis Krauss, 1996).[4] Another project took a broader view and explored the bonds between citizens and government, not only in Japan but in the United States and Western Europe. The project led to *Disaffected Democracies: What's Troubling the Trilateral Countries* (edited with Robert Putnam, 2000), which sought to account for the decline in confidence in leaders and government across the three regions.[5] Written decades ago, the book presaged the pervasive distrust in political institutions found today among large swaths of the public in so many developed democracies.

Increasingly, my interest in the links between citizens and states led me to the study of developments in Asia more broadly. For shaping those links, the key was the state and nature of civil society—voluntary groups that operate outside the state, workplace, and family—in any country. Just as there are varieties of capitalism, there are varieties of civil societies to be found across the globe. With Muthiah Alagappa and Frank Schwartz, I embarked on a project that sought to take the measure of civil societies across Asia, which at the time had been little studied and rarely compared. The first volume (edited with Frank Schwartz, 2003) focused on Japan and sought to explain an anomaly: By virtually every measure—socioeconomic standing, high levels of media consumption, well-established democratic institutions—we would expect Japan to have a vibrant civil society, and, yet, with some prominent exceptions, civil society groups in Japan are characterized by the "four smalls"—small in membership, number of professional staff, budget, and geographic scope. The book explores how political institutions and historical legacies help explain this outcome. The other volume examined a number of civil societies across the region to lay the groundwork for comparison.[6]

My fascination with the nature and role of civil society globally extended to the classroom. It resulted in a graduate seminar, "Civil Society West and East," that I led at Harvard for two decades with Grzegorz Ekiert, a colleague whose work focuses on Eastern Europe, and a parallel course I taught for undergraduates. Around the world, a number of former students from these courses have become leading scholars on civil society, activists in civil society organizations, international human rights lawyers, and reform-minded political leaders. I take great pride in their achievements.

Many of the puzzles that engage me throughout my career have centered on domestic developments in nations, as opposed to their international relations. But I also have a long-standing interest in US-Japan relations and in Japan's search for a place in the world, dating from the country's emergence from a policy of national isolation in the mid-nineteenth century until today.⁷ For me, the US-Japan alliance, forged in the aftermath of a horrific war, is a signal achievement; in a world in which efforts at reconciliation so often fail, its success holds out hope that former adversaries can find a way forward. For thirty-two years, I led the Harvard Program on US-Japan Relations, which had been founded in 1980 by Samuel Huntington, Owada Hisashi, and Ezra Vogel to address issues and challenges that came with Japan's rise in the world. Over my years as director, the program annually brought together some fifteen or sixteen midcareer scholars, journalists, public officials, business leaders, and others to conduct independent research and engage in dialogue at Harvard, and in the broader Boston-Cambridge community, on common problems of the developed democracies, Japan's relations with the rest of the world, and domestic issues that bear on Japan's international role. Over five hundred visitors, including a succession of outstanding postdoctoral fellows, took part and, in many cases, later rose to positions of leadership in a variety of fields. The opportunity to lead the program was one of the high points of my life, intellectually and professionally.

#MeToo

The #MeToo movement has led older generations of women to reconsider their pasts, me included. I now see things that I did not perceive at the time. For example, my early intellectual interests ran in the direction of sociology, but the door to that field effectively closed to me because of a ludicrous experience of sexual harassment. As a college freshman, I attended a concert off campus, and, when a sociology professor from my university offered me a ride home, I accepted, thinking of the professor as a kindly old man. What ensued was a brief tussle that I soon joked about with my friends in the dorm. What I did not see then was how my embarrassment over the incident led me to avoid not only the professor but also the area where he had his office—namely, the sociology department.

Discrimination and harassment take myriad forms, many of which by now are well understood. But there are particular challenges women face in academia, some of them quite subtle. While there can be much camaraderie in a doctoral program, the competition is real. Graduate students, to move ahead, must shine in seminars and engage the interest and support of busy faculty. In fields like political science where men predominate, the obstacles to achieving this, then and now, can be formidable. For the first three years in graduate school, I hardly said a word in seminars or in class. I was there, but the instructor did not see me, did not bob his head in encouragement when I spoke. Harry Potter was not alone in having an invisibility cloak; I wore one for years. Survival required that I find a way to register and expand my presence. So, painfully, I forced myself to speak up, to interrupt, to push my way in. Although I was unconscious of it at the time, my Southern accent, which I felt was an impediment to being taken seriously, largely disappeared in the process. I did find that when I asked for help, I often got it. A turning point came when, summoning my courage, I went to the office of James Morley and asked him to advise my dissertation. He told me, in a not unkindly way, that yes, he would advise my thesis, but he didn't know who I was: where had I been? I pointed out that I had taken three courses with him, with A grades in all of them. Together we puzzled over my invisibility, and we agreed that he would call on me in class if I did not speak up. This he did, and I began to claim space. One trick I learned was priming myself to ask or respond to the first question in a seminar, before the blood pumping through my head drowned out what others were saying. Later on, when I finally became a teacher myself, I served on dozens of committees whose objective was to push faculty to bring all students into the conversation, and I coached countless women students on how to be more efficacious and how to make their presence felt in the classroom and in a variety of professional settings.

Problems of the kind I have described bubbled up from time to time throughout my career. For my first few years on the senior faculty at Harvard, students and visitors to my office often assumed that I was a staff assistant. In meetings with my colleagues and senior administrators, I would make a point, only to have it ignored until Bob or Dick made the same point and got the credit for it. I never need to explain slights of this kind to other professional women. They know. These are small annoyances, but they rankle.

#MeToo, of course, has multiple meanings. It evokes solidarity with other women that has another side: the shared benefits of improvements in women's lot. Stepping back, I now see that, at virtually every stage, my career benefited from the expansion of opportunity that followed the women's movement in America. In the early 1970s, fresh from fieldwork in Japan, I experienced the women's movement firsthand in its epicenter: Manhattan. I was in several women's groups; a picture in *The New York Times* in 1973 shows me in my best pantsuit, perched in a metal chair on the front row of a conference on women and work.[8] I learned from all this. But the world learned, too. In my third year in graduate school, in 1968 or so, my announcement to potential committee members that I wanted to do a dissertation on women in Japan was met with frowns. Four years later, laboring over my manuscript in a carrel at Columbia, I was suddenly getting invitations to appear on panels; and, by 1976, when I gave a job talk at the University of Wisconsin-Madison, the room was packed. In fits and starts, the academic world was opening to women, and to the study of women. Then and in the years that followed, I was a beneficiary of these changes.

When all is said and done, I owe my early career almost entirely to men, because from the time I became a political science major until I gained a foothold in academics, there were hardly any women in my orbit. Earlier, three men, as

I have said, turned me into an internationalist. A prominent exception, late in my graduate student years, was the brilliant sociologist Tsurumi Kazuko at Sophia University, who mentored me during my fieldwork in Japan and gave me introductions that made it possible.[9] But as my career took shape, many women, American and Japanese, became important mentors and role models. I have an especially great debt to Japanese women, and I treasure my ties with so many of them. Like Merry White (chapter 21), I participated in the Tokyo Symposium on Women (Kokusai Josei Gakkai) in July 1978 (figure 22.1).[10] In my career, from the time I met him in 1982, my late husband, Robert Cameron Mitchell, stood beside me, supporting me every step of the way. Standing behind me, of course, was my mother, who took out loans to educate me, sacrificed to give me opportunities, and steadfastly believed in me.

Two Arcs: Conclusion

Life is filled with the unexpected. I could never have imagined, when I took the night train from Atlanta to the North, that I would end up with Japan at the center of my life. I never dreamed that a great many of the graduate students I advised from the earliest days of my career would become colleagues and friends and fully a part of my life decades later. One of them, Christina Davis, became a senior colleague in my department at Harvard and my successor as director of the Harvard Program on US-Japan Relations. I never thought that I would teach at Harvard and be the first woman to chair its Department of Government; or imagined, when I met a clutch of young Japanese women undergraduates at Harvard in the 1980s, that among them would be the future empress of Japan. I would never have dreamed, as a person who loathes cold weather, that I would spend most of my adult life bending to the wintery blasts of Wisconsin and then New England.

All of us bear the marks of the era in which we live. One arc I have already described: Dating from the early 1970s, opportunities for women were expanding exactly at the time that my career was taking shape. But a second arc is equally important: my career perfectly tracked the arc marking Japan's rise and the ebb and flow of American interest in Japan over many decades.

When scholars of my generation embarked in Japanese Studies in the 1960s, Japan was an exotic but minor country rarely in the limelight. In the rarified world of academics, scholars mined the Meiji period for clues on how countries could modernize; still, few students took courses on Japan, and media interest was tepid. But in a way that people, including me, hardly noticed at the time, Japan was quietly emerging from its national income-doubling decade of the 1960s as a country to be reckoned with, a nation that only a few years later was squaring off as a US rival. A job market closed to Japan specialists sprang open, and positions began to appear, including at the University of Wisconsin-Madison, where I launched my academic career. *Shōgun*, a 1975 novel by James Clavell and, later, a television miniseries in 1980, brought undergraduates into classes on Japanese politics in my early teaching days in Wisconsin. Then, in 1979, my future Harvard colleague Ezra Vogel, in *Japan as Number One: Lessons for America*, turned the spotlight on Japan's achievement. The American media struggled to make sense of the rising behemoth, and Japan specialists, even junior ones like me, were suddenly in demand as speakers, explainers. Business schools generated studies of how Japan had done it, and features of the Japanese workplace, such as quality control circles and just-in-time production, gained American business adherents. By the mid to late 1980s, when rapid yen appreciation made Japanese abroad rich overnight, enchantment with the nation's success story had turned to fear and uncertainty. Could we compete? What would we have to sacrifice to go head-to-head with our rival? The Japanese were so work-centric that the Japanese language had a special word (*karōshi*) for death from overwork, the American media reported to worried Western readers.

Japan's rocket-like economic rise during these years swept along all of us, the Japan scholars of our day. It was my good fortune, on a leave from Wisconsin, to spend two years in Washington, DC, as Japan Chair at the Center for Strategic and International Studies (CSIS), at a pivotal time in US-Japan relations. I took a senior position at Harvard in 1987, when Japan's economy and visibility were at their peak, bringing hundreds of students into Harvard classrooms for courses taught by me and my faculty colleagues. During these heady years, I was explaining Japan to Steve Jobs and Bill Clinton. Curiosity about Japan, including their predilections as consumers, knew no bounds. In the discussion following a talk to a business audience at the University of Alaska, someone asked if Japanese would like reindeer sausage, and a governor of Massachusetts once took me aside at a meeting to ask if young Japanese women would drink cranberry juice, a question foremost on the minds of cranberry growers soon to accompany him on a trade mission to Japan.

Then, in 1990, the economic bubble burst, and, gradually, the harsh reality of the so-called "lost decade(s)" set in. The surge of students heading for classrooms receded as compared to five years before. But Japanese Studies in America by that time had sent down long roots, aided by the Japan Foundation, a government-funded agency that has been the mothership for Japanese Studies in the United States. And in the academic world, even if the study of Japan's political economy lost steam, there were new puzzles.

In the great waves of ideas and interests that fuel public discourse and engage the academic world, a new Japan was always emerging. Japan's 1994 landmark electoral reform sparked a whole body of work by political scientists, and the growing appeal of the nation's popular culture, or J-pop, to young people around the world, attracted the interest of political scientists studying "soft power." There have always been Japans to learn from and study. Today, one is Japan as an aging society and the country's role as a bellwether—a canary in the coal mine—for the ever-growing number of nations with shrinking birth rates and populations on the decline. It has been my privilege to be there through these decades of astonishing change and to have moved through them with colleagues whose stories appear in this book, and with many other friends in Japan, the United States, and around the world. For this I am truly grateful.

Notes

[1] Susan J. Pharr, *Political Women in Japan: The Search for a Place in Political Life* (Berkeley: University of California Press, 1981).

[2] Susan J. Pharr, "The Politics of Women's Rights," *Democratizing Japan: The Allied Occupation*, edited by Robert E. Ward and Sakamoto Yoshikazu (Honolulu: University of Hawai'i Press, 1987), 221–252.

[3] Susan J. Pharr, *Losing Face: Status Politics in Japan* (Berkeley: University of California Press, 1990).

[4] Susan J. Pharr and Ellis S. Krauss, eds., *Media and Politics in Japan* (Honolulu: University of Hawai'i Press, 1996).

[5] Susan J. Pharr and Robert D. Putnam, eds., *Disaffected Democracies: What's Troubling the Trilateral Countries?* (Princeton: Princeton University Press, 2000).

[6] Frank J. Schwartz and Susan J. Pharr, eds., *The State of Civil Society in Japan* (Cambridge: Cambridge University Press, 2003); Muthiah Alagappa, ed., *Civil Society and Political Change in Asia* (Stanford: Stanford University Press, 2004).

[7] See, for example, Susan J. Pharr, "Japan's Defensive Foreign Policy and the Politics of Burden Sharing," *Japan's Foreign Policy after the Cold War: Coping with Change*, edited by Gerald L. Curtis (Armonk, NY: M. E. Sharpe, 1993), 235–262.

[8] Lisa Hammel, "Working Women: The Job Ahead," *New York Times*, Sept 19, 1973, 52. Photo credit: Bill Aller.

[9] See Tsurumi Kazuko, *Social Change and the Individual: Japan Before and After Defeat in World War II* (Princeton: Princeton University Press, 1970).

[10] Merry White and Barbara Maloney, eds., *Proceedings of the Tokyo Symposium on Women* (Tokyo: International Group for the Study of Women, 1979).

23

FROM CHŪSHINGURA TO COMMONS

Margaret McKean

*If I think back on how I developed as a scholar, the important
ingredients were settings offering intense conversations.*

MARGARET MCKEAN is a professor emerita at Duke University. She studies political institutions, particularly electoral arrangements and property rights, and is interested in applying theories of cooperation to the management of common-pool goods like environmental resources. One strand of her work analyzes policymaking and elections in Japan; her other work has examined traditional arrangements used in Japan to foster cooperation in limiting use to sustainable levels. She was a member of the National Academy of Sciences Panel on Common Property (1982–1987), where she helped to organize the Annapolis Conference on Common Property (1985) and to build the initial Common Property Network. She cofounded the International Association for the Study of Common Property (IASCP) in 1989. She organized the first global meeting of the IASCP at Duke (1990) and the IASCP global meeting held on the Mount Fuji Commons (2013). She served as fifth president of the IASCP (1995–1996). She has worked with European and Japanese colleagues on several collaborative projects, including a special issue of *The International Journal of the Commons* (vol. 9, no. 2, 2015), "The Commons of Industrialized Developed Countries."

Seeing Kurosawa Akira films during high school is probably what sent me, less than a week after I arrived at UC Berkeley as a first-year student in January 1964, into the administration building to sign up for the new study abroad program in Japan. I was crushed to learn that I had to be a rising junior, so I hurriedly gathered up college credits I'd earned in high school, along with summer school credits (in Japanese literature!), in order to become a junior in three semesters. During the interim, Inagaki Hiroshi's acclaimed film, *Chūshingura* (1962), was shown in Berkeley for a forty-one-week run, and I felt compelled to see it five times during my sophomore year as I waited for my study abroad year to begin.[1] The magnificent color cinematography—along with the wonderful music, attention to detail in costumes and sets, and, of course, the gripping story of the forty-seven *rōnin*—utterly captured me.

The minute I reached Japan in September 1965—traveling first with my UC group to Kyoto and beyond and then attending International Christian University (ICU)—I became even more fascinated. I was also determined to learn Japanese quickly in order to get rid of the profound discomfort of being illiterate. One of the many mistakes I made was buying cheese that could not melt, even when cut into one-eighth-inch cubes, because I could not read the labels identifying the "melty" (*merutii*) cheese that I should have bought. I did not have a host family—although I taught English to the Mimori family, who became my lifelong Japanese family—because we all lived in ICU dorms in rooms of four people each. My roommates thought I was not progressing in the language because I never spoke Japanese to them, but the problem was that I could not say anything worth saying. By this time, ICU had developed an excellent language program, with a textbook that not only offered logical explanations of grammar but also illustrated changes in pitch between syllables. At the end of the year, when we had finally learned to assemble complex sentences, I surprised my roommates by switching to Japanese. Then, in early summer, I traveled to Kyushu with my dorm-mate Dianne Meredith, who had identified from Ted Kidder's courses where several really good archaeological sites should be. Even our rudimentary language skills enabled us to understand warnings in rural Kumamoto that a storm had recently destroyed a bridge we had to cross, and we took off our shoes and waded across the river to get to a cave with wonderful red paintings on the stone walls. One striking image was a boat carrying a horse—showing not the horse-rider armies theorized by archeologist Egami Namio but perhaps a horse-savvy Yayoi migrant from Korea centuries earlier. (The Yayoi period lasted from possibly 300 BCE to 250 CE, with some estimates placing the start date as early as 900 BCE.) Everything I encountered in Japan made me want to learn more.

Although interested in all things Japanese, my deep questions were about political issues. My interest in politics had come from my parents, who both

Figure 23.1: Margaret McKean with Edwin O. Reischauer, US Embassy, April 1966. Photograph courtesy of the author.

fought against Hitler, my father as a P-47 Thunderbolt pilot and my mother in Britain's Royal Ambulance Corps. Political scientist Hans Baerwald directed the UC program at ICU and got us into the Japanese National Diet building and the US Embassy, where I sat on the same couch as Ambassador Reischauer himself (figure 23.1)! I could not imagine then that Reischauer would be my graduate advisor just two years later. Living in Japan only twenty years after the end of World War II made me think about the challenges of building democracy and maintaining it once established. Upon returning to Berkeley, I had so many credits accumulated from the ICU trimester system that I was able to major in both political science (my senior thesis was a long missive on prewar Japanese nationalism written under Arend Lijphart) and an individually created program in Japanese Studies.

I did not originally plan on a career as a scholar and started looking for jobs in my senior year at Berkeley. Like Susan Hanley, I applied to the Foreign Service, but that tedious process ended in rejection (see chapter 9). I thought I had flunked the security clearance because my mother had opted to remain British after emigrating to the United States in 1945, but the Foreign Service told me that I was turned down because I was planning to get married, which marked me as unreliable. I considered other options and discovered the Woodrow Wilson Fellowship. To get one, I would need to go to graduate school, which was fine with me because I had always liked school. I won a full scholarship, including room, board, and tuition in any amount. Then I noticed in the fine print that I could use the scholarship only at a graduate school other than my undergraduate institution, and so I rushed off an application to the most expensive graduate school I could think of, Harvard, and fortunately got into the MA program in East Asian Studies. By happenstance, I was headed for an academic career, although I didn't know it yet.

If I think back on how I developed as a scholar, the important ingredients were settings offering intense conversations: my junior year abroad at ICU, a small liberal arts college, and my one-year MA program, where eight students had a weekly thesis seminar with three illustrious professors—Don Shively, Peter Duus, and Ed Reischauer, who had just returned from his ambassadorship in Japan—who paid close attention to what we were writing. At Peter Duus's suggestion, I wrote an MA thesis on prewar Japanese history textbooks (which suited my reading level nicely), further deepening my fascination with Japanese history.

A National Defense Foreign Language Fellowship in Japanese took me back to Berkeley for my PhD, but, by this time, I had married the man I had met years earlier when assigned by the Student Nonviolent Coordinating Committee (SNCC) to summer work in one of Lyndon Johnson's Great Society projects, meant to end poverty and racial injustice, in Los Angeles. I was lucky that my husband simply accepted that I would go off to Japan for extended periods of time as part of the deal. Married and living off campus, I did not hang around the Department of Political Science and did not realize how much I might be missing. I attended Japanese Studies talks at the faculty club, enjoying the friendly sparring by Chalmers Johnson, Irv Scheiner, Bernie Silberman, and Harry Harootunian with their guest speakers, although I thought Chal went too far when he lambasted Al Craig for noting that Saigō Takamori had a 19.5-inch neck. My husband and I also rushed to campus for every musical and dance performance we could find, for the incredible student price of fifty cents. My research fellowship at Berkeley's Survey Research Center—a program in political behavior that had nearly nothing to do with Japan—allowed me to work for Jack Citrin, who had grown up in Japan and whose wife (a classmate of mine!) had also entered the graduate program to study Japanese politics. Jack's parents, longtime residents of Tokyo and collectors of beautiful *netsuke* miniature sculptures, sponsored me for my research visa to do my dissertation.

The year in Japan for dissertation research (January to December 1972) was an intense experience. I lived with the wonderful Mimori family in Tokyo's Setagaya neighborhood, took tea ceremony lessons with Aunt Tamiko, spent hours discussing Theodore Dreiser with my sister Shigeko, accompanied Taneko Mama upstairs to give Renko Obaachama her 5:00 p.m. cup of sake, and read newspaper clippings that Shigeyoshi Papa cut for me from his seven daily newspapers. I commuted to the Institute of Social Science at the University of

Tokyo, where Ide Yoshinori was my sponsor. I attended Ui Jun's lectures at his famous Citizens' Forum (Jishu-kōza) on pollution and watched in amazement as Japanese environmental movements rose to protest the first major issue in postwar Japan that was not related to unresolved issues connected to World War II. I abandoned my advisor's original recommendation to study interest groups and instead organized interviews with environmental activists all over Japan. I also met Susan Pharr, and we discussed our research plans over *okonomiyaki* (see chapter 22)!

After a year of intense writing back at Berkeley, I started hunting for jobs. My advisor, Bob Scalapino, expected that, as a married woman, I would want to stay in California, but he was happy to support a broader search. I accepted a position in Japanese politics that Duke University had funded with a Japan Foundation expansion grant, and my husband requested a transfer in his job for the federal government to a location near Duke. We had to leave our regular backpacking in the High Sierra, but we built a new life in North Carolina with azaleas, pine trees, and humid summers.

My first years of teaching at Duke were probably the most important for my intellectual development—designing courses, responding to students' questions, chatting with colleagues in hallways and during reading groups, meeting them socially, attending talks, and more. Although there was a coterie of Japan scholars at Duke, I was the only Japan specialist in my department, and I was constantly learning from my colleagues and having to explain what was interesting about this or that feature of Japan in comparison to other societies. This intellectual stimulation that should have occurred in graduate school gradually turned me from a behaviorist into a comparative political economist.

It took me a decade to get used to teaching. I came in knowing about Japan's environmental movement, but this was rice-roots politics, not decision-making, not policy choices for problem-solving. When a colleague from public policy asked me in my first year if I would teach a course on environmental policy, I not only agreed but foolishly decided to make the course comparative. I had to learn a new subject, not just in Japan but also in the United States and the Soviet Union, along with bits and pieces about Britain, Germany, Denmark, and other countries. I must have been out of my mind to take on such arduous work, but it gave me both a theoretical compass and an ambitious research plan for the rest of my career. The first course I taught, "Pollution of the Rich," turned into several spinoff courses on environmental politics in developing countries, international environmental politics, international environmental law, and my keystone course on collective action, property rights, and environmental outcomes. In addition to the affiliations with the Asian/Pacific Studies Institute and with Comparative Area Studies expected for a Japan specialist, I also helped to design a new undergraduate major in Environmental Sciences and Policy, served on the committee that created Duke's Nicholas School of the Environment, and acquired a secondary appointment in Environmental Science and Policy as well.

In search of a unifying rubric for my students, I explained that environmental quality was a desirable but elusive goal everywhere in the world for the same structural reason: individuals want the outcome but are not willing to make the personal sacrifices and contributions necessary to achieve it unless they have assurance that others will do the same. Sacrificing without that assurance risks being a "sucker"; delaying one's own sacrifices and contributions then "free rides" on the sacrifices and contributions of the suckers. ("Free-riders" and "suckers" are technical terms in game theory.) The actual amount of collective goods any given society gets depends on its ratio of suckers and free-riders; the more free-riders there are, the fewer suckers are likely to remain, leaving us all in a suboptimal trap with much lower levels of the collective good than suckers and free-riders had actually desired. The same dynamic, which political economists call a "collective action problem," exists at all levels, from small groups of individuals to nations full of citizens to international organizations full of governments. I used this insight as a cross-cultural tool in teaching and turned my research focus toward solutions: How can humans develop remedies for this life-threatening dilemma? Are we permanently stuck with what Garrett Hardin calls the "Tragedy of the Commons," in which people refuse to band together to produce the collective goods they need and want because they cannot solve their free-rider problems?[2] This focus on political economy and rational choice was both new and not new to me—I was amazed that my work on Japan was taking me back full circle to dinner table comments about free-riders, once repetitive and boring, from my father, a Chicago School public choice economist who called himself a "bleeding-heart conservative" and voted for Adlai Stevenson. I was propelled further along this quest for the next few years by a sequence of accidents, from my leisure reading to an accidental publication to a friendly conversation in a bar.

While reading Japanese economic history for fun, I was surprised to learn from Tom Smith's book, *The Agrarian Origins of Modern Japan*, that Japan had "commons," or shared ownership and use of land. But how could this be? I "knew" from Hardin's "Tragedy of the Commons" that commons suffered inevitable ruin, but I also knew that Japan was largely covered in forest today. So something had to be wrong with this picture: either the tragic theory or the facts in Japan had to be wrong! In actuality, both were wrong. The truth was much more complicated: hundreds of years of experience in Japan (and everywhere else) of both theoretically predicted ruination and surprising recovery cannot be usefully compressed, and the theory itself requires modification. I now had a mission: to learn whether Japanese history and institutions might offer solutions to collective action problems. Was the often-noted, both praised and condemned, Japanese "skill" in cooperation involved here?

I began with a research project that included Japan's "classic" commons in forests and meadows, experience with rationing (cooperation) and the black market (cheating) during and after World War II, and experience with energy conservation after the oil shocks of the 1970s. From January to August 1980, I once again lived with the Mimori family in Tokyo, with help from Uncle Takeya on *komonjo* (old documents) on land disputes. (I also made sure to attend kabuki theater for a full day every month with a Duke student, Deborah Vanis, who was spending her junior year at ICU.) This project introduced me to new groups of colleagues who were not particularly interested in Japan but were eager to consider solutions for environmental problems. I delivered a paper on Japan's common forests at the annual meeting of the American Society of Environmental History (ASEH) in January 1982. My anxiety increased as I realized that Lynn White Jr.—a renowned medieval historian who argued in *Science*, no less, that the root of the West's environmental crisis was probably the Judeo-Christian tradition (and that Zen might be a more suitable philosophy)—was sitting just three yards from me in the front row. Worse, his expression grew grumpier and more skeptical as I proceeded (no Zen, maybe?). I planned to submit the paper to *The Journal of Japanese Studies*, whose readers might find my Japan focus interesting, not heretical. But a few months later, before I could get back to the paper, my colleague John Richards mentioned that he had enjoyed reading the paper I published in *Environmental Review* in the fall of 1982.[3] I was astonished because nobody had written to me about the selection process, to ask me for permission, or to let me revise the paper! John explained that the ASEH had selected what it considered to be the best papers presented at the January meeting and published them in its journal, obviously without the usual legal niceties. I was confused but flattered, and this fortuitous publication led me in new directions.

As I pursued my new interests in commons, I attended workshops at Duke, particularly the Triangle East Asia Colloquium, where I got to know Kristina Troost (chapter 29). Gradually, we realized that we were both interested in traditional communities and resource management. I had studied twentieth-century commons in Yamanashi Prefecture, and she was studying the creation of the social infrastructure and rules for commons managed and claimed by self-governing villages in the medieval period. We became fast friends, not only starting our families at the same time (first children expected on same due date!) and celebrating holidays together but always bouncing ideas off of each other. Life continued to fall into place: in the 1981–1982 academic year, I received tenure; my husband got a promotion and transfer to a nearby federal office that reduced his commute from one hour to fifteen minutes; we bought land and built a solar house on it; and I had our first daughter.

On the academic front, John Richards invited me to join his 1983 conferences at Duke on forest history, and, after one of these meetings, we all retreated to drinks and dinner at Slug's at the Pines in Chapel Hill, where I talked with new acquaintances David Feeny (an economist specializing in property rights and forests in Thailand) and Jamie Thomson (a political scientist studying property rights and land use in West Africa, particularly Niger). They had read my article in *Environmental Review* and suggested that perhaps there were enough people working on common property to attempt an ambitious comparative project on commons. Jamie soon invited me to join a National Research Council panel on "Common Property and Environmental Management."

Thus, in one year's time, an accidental publication and a conversation with new colleagues at Slug's sent me to the National Academy of Sciences. Over several years, our panel organized a worldwide network of 4,200 scholars and organizations concerned with commons as a tool of environmental management and designed a set of preparatory workshops and a major conference in Annapolis in April 1985, bringing together people doing the best work on the commons. We invited Elinor Ostrom (Jamie's dissertation advisor, known to us as "Lin") as a keynote speaker—a task that launched Lin's intense work on commons, cooperation, and collective action, leading to her Nobel Prize in Economics in 2009. Lin brought an early "portable" computer (three clunky sections, in green) to the Annapolis conference, and she was determined to code the findings of the thirty-five researchers presenting work on the commons during the week so that she could fold a robust summary of results into her keynote address on the final day of the conference. She quickly found, of course, that this was an overwhelming task destined to occupy the rest of her career, as she developed major databases on various different resource systems with teams of colleagues from Uganda to Bolivia and Nepal.

Lin was particularly interested in forests and asked me to serve on the committee that designed the International Forest Resources and Institutions (IFRI) database during the 1990s. We wrote together and went together several times to the Beijer Institute at the Royal Swedish Academy of Sciences in Stockholm for meetings on ecological systems and social institutions. While staying there in guest housing, Bob Costanza, leading ecological economist, tried to teach us how to make gnocchi, but Lin and I could not flip them with our thumbs the way he could, and we kept shooting our pathetically misshapen lumps of dough across the kitchen. I sent half a dozen students to do postdoctoral work with Lin at the Ostrom Workshop at Indiana University. Lin and I thought very much in the same way (we were both fusspots about terminology), and, when she was too busy to go to certain events or meetings, she sometimes suggested that I go in her place.

That is how I ended up working with Marilyn Hoskins and Krister Andersson in the Forests, Trees, and People Program at the Food and Agricultural Organization in Rome. Lin expected to live a long time and spoke in 2003 at a panel of senior women in political science about career and retirement, saying she had good genes for longevity.[4] But she died from pancreatic cancer just a few years later in 2012. Like everyone else working on commons, I was shaken at her death. She nurtured legions of graduate students and was one of the most conscientious and decent human beings one could ever know. I will always be grateful for her personal and intellectual friendship.

My children were well-timed. One month after the Annapolis conference, in May 1985, I had my second daughter. Our National Academy panel concluded its work in 1987, but many of us had developed a serious team commitment to promoting the study of common property, and I tried to keep the momentum going by organizing several conferences at Duke in the late 1980s. After a flurry of travel to meetings, I had my third daughter in 1988. A militant breastfeeder, I managed to nurse the babies through (a total of) 6.5 years in spite of a demanding travel schedule that taught me the wonders of dry ice. Meanwhile, our post-Annapolis group decided to stop meeting in stealth and founded the International Association for the Study of Common Property (now the IASC) in 1989, and I organized our first international conference in 1990 at Duke.[5] We have since gone on to have general meetings around the world: Zimbabwe, Mexico, Peru, the Netherlands, and Kenya, as well as regional meetings in many other countries. In 2009—by which time all three daughters had started or even finished college—we acquired a fourth child, our nephew, after my husband's brother died.

Even as I studied Japan's commons, I continued teaching Japanese politics, shifting to political economy's focus on incentives that may explain behavior and outcomes that would otherwise seem perverse or mysterious. A true leader in this approach was Frances McCall Rosenbluth, who showed political scientists who would not have given a second glance to Japan that the Japanese case could modify or refute general propositions that were otherwise widely accepted. She saw Japan as a "normal" country that not only can be but must be compared to other industrial democracies, and she turned comparative political economists who wrote with her—Gary Cox, Matt McCubbins, John Ferejohn, and Torben Iversen—into budding Japan specialists themselves.[6] I was devastated to learn that Frances died of a glioblastoma on November 20, 2021; those who knew her well and coauthored with her are still in shock at her death. Many obituaries are available, but the one by Isaac Yu in *Yale Daily News* describes her extraordinary teaching at Yale and compares her personality to an iron fist in a velvet glove: firm, determined, but always polite and genteel.[7]

I met Frances in June 1989 at a conference organized by Gary Allinson. The conference was particularly memorable because, during an evening walk outdoors, Gary used an early mobile phone to relay to us incoming news from his wife, Pat, about the massacre at Tiananmen as it was taking place. Frances's first book was about Japanese banking, but, during her stay in the UC San Diego political science department (whose senior comparativist, builder of the Lijphart Elections Archive at UCSD, was actually my undergraduate thesis chair, Arend Lijphart), she became fascinated by electoral systems because Japan had a very unusual system that generated perverse incentives and outcomes.[8] As Frances began publishing along these lines, Chalmers Johnson, who by then was also at UCSD, began issuing ad hominem attacks on Frances, her coauthors, and rational choice institutionalism. Frances herself remained silent, simply letting her pathbreaking work speak for itself, but I, along with others, jumped into the fray to defend her work and to explain rational choice institutionalism to confused critics who incorrectly believe that its users are necessarily anti-regulation right-wingers.[9] (Although people who classify themselves as "public choice" folks are often libertarians, virtually all the exponents of rational choice institutionalism whom I know are quite progressive!) Frances was extraordinarily prolific—even while raising three sons—writing on topics ranging from financial regulation to gender inequality, childcare and social policy, war and democracy, and even medieval history. But the dominant stream in her work concerned electoral politics and political parties, and her final book in 2018, with Ian Shapiro, dealt with the way electoral systems and the political party systems they produce can affect the rise of right-wing populism and undermine the very democracy that allows these movements to emerge.[10] Both Japanese Studies and political science have lost a giant.

As I learned about commons around the world, I came to realize that, although the arrangements for shared use and ownership of natural resources are very widespread, only a few long-enduring systems outside of Europe have good historical documentation—most notably, India and Japan—making these cases all the more vital for scholars around the world to learn about. I have long hoped to see Japanese scholars studying Japan's own commons. Japanese scholars in legal sociology and economic history (Hōjō Hiroshi, Watanabe Yōzō, Kamimura Masana, and Hayasaka Keizō, among others) have produced a rich literature on Japanese commons and the landmark legal battles over them, to be sure, but they have studied the commons as a matter of legal rights, not also as experiments in solving collective action problems to generate sustainability in resource use.[11] Thanks to Inoue Makoto and Akimichi Tomoya, there are now many Japanese scholars who study sustainability in commons management in Southeast Asia, as well as in Japanese fisheries.[12] But Japanese researchers were not studying Japan's own commons as environmental management until Murota Takeshi, an environmental economist at Doshisha University, created the Commons Research Group (Commons Kenkyūkai) to mobilize younger scholars in Japan.[13] He invited me to Doshisha in 2003 to give a talk on the Japanese commons at an event where his advanced graduate students presented their work on Japanese commons. All appreciated the theoretical connections via environmental concerns and institutional rational choice among commons anywhere in the world, and all were committed to further studies of Japanese commons. Some are studying new commons, or new uses and new users for preexisting commons. Around half are women. Now researchers and faculty members themselves, they include, among others, Mitsumata Gaku, Yamashita Utako, Saitō Haruo, Tamura Norie, Shimagami Motoko, Ohno Tomohiko, Shimada Daisaku, and Hayashi Masahide.[14] This new generation of scholars became the backbone of the organizing effort behind the IASC's 2013 meeting in Japan, held on the very Kitafuji (northern Mount Fuji) commons I had studied, sponsored by the Kitafuji commoners. It is truly heartwarming to know that these younger scholars will continue to bring Japan's experience with commons to the attention of the international scholarly community.

I "retired" from regular duties at Duke in 2012 in order to organize the 2013 conference, but I have continued to teach—lately, premodern Japanese history, which allows me to indulge in archaeology, medieval economic history, and kabuki. And I am determined to fulfill my promise (to Karen Remmer, who chaired my department when I retired, and to Lin) to complete a full-scale legal and political history of Japan's landed commons, as well as a book on new commons in Japan with my Japanese colleagues.

Notes

[1] In 1965, the Berkeley Cinema Guild learned that the American release of Inagaki's *Chūshingura* would be only half of the film's original length. Disgusted, the Cinema Guild acquired the distribution rights to the full 207-minute version and showed it at the Cinema Theatre in Berkeley for forty-one weeks before distributing the film in New York City. "Landberg Serves Samurai Buffs Full '47 Ronin,'" *Variety* 240, no. 7 (October 6, 1965), 15.

[2] Garrett Hardin, "The Tragedy of the Commons," *Science* 162, no. 3859 (December 1968), 1243–1248.

[3] Margaret McKean, "The Japanese Experience with Scarcity: Management of Traditional Common Lands," *Environmental Review* 6, no. 2 (Fall 1982): 63–88.

[4] Naomi Black, "Staging a Career, Staging a Life: Strategies for Retirement," *PS: Political Science and Politics* 38, no. 2 (April 2005), 277–281.

⁵ More information on IASC can be found at https://iasc-commons.org.

⁶ See, for example, J. Mark Ramseyer and Frances McCall Rosenbluth, *Japan's Political Marketplace* (Cambridge, MA: Harvard University Press, 1993); Gary W. Cox and Frances Rosenbluth, "The Electoral Fortunes of Legislative Factions in Japan," *American Political Science Review* 87, no. 3 (September 1993), 577–589; Gary W. Cox, Frances McCall Rosenbluth, and Michael F. Thies, "Electoral Reform and the Fate of Factions: The Case for Japan's Liberal Democratic Party," *British Journal of Political Science* 29, no. 1 (January 1999), 33–56; John A. Ferejohn and Frances McCall Rosenbluth, eds. *War and State Building in Medieval Japan* (Stanford: Stanford University Press, 2010).

⁷ Isaac Yu, "Frances Rosenbluth, Who Redefined Japanese Comparative Politics, Dies at 63," *Yale Daily News*, November 28, 2021, https://yaledailynews.com/blog/2021/11/28/frances-rosenbluth-who-redefined-japanese-comparative-politics-dies-at-63/.

⁸ Frances McCall Rosenbluth, *Financial Politics in Contemporary Japan* (Ithaca: Cornell University, 1989); J. Mark Ramseyer and Frances McCall Rosenbluth, *The Politics of Oligarchy: Institutional Choice in Imperial Japan* (Cambridge: Cambridge University Press, 1995).

⁹ I posted defenses of Frances and rational choice on the Dead Fukuzawa Society listserv, after which Neil Waters asked me to write a chapter explaining rational choice as a research method for his book. Margaret McKean, "Rational Choice Analysis and Area Studies: Enemies or Partners?," in *Beyond the Area Studies Wars: Toward a New International Studies*, edited by Neil Waters (Hanover, NH: University Press of New England, 2000), 29–63.

¹⁰ Frances McCall Rosenbluth and Ian Shapiro, *Responsible Parties: Saving Democracy from Itself* (New Haven: Yale University Press, 2018).

¹¹ See, for example, Watanabe Yōzō and Hōjō Hiroshi, *Rin'ya iriai to sonraku kōzō: Kitafuji sanroku no jirei kenkyū* (Common Access to Forests and Village Structure: A Case Study from the North Fuji Slope) (Tokyo: University of Tokyo Press, 1975); Hōjō Hiroshi, *Kinsei ni okeru iriai no shokeitai* (The Various Forms of Common Access in the Early Modern Period) (Tokyo: Ochanomizu shobō, 1979); Hōjō Hiroshi, *Mura no iriai no hyakunen shi: Yamanashi-ken sonmin no iriai tōsōshi* (A Hundred Years' History of a Village and Its Common Access: The History of the Common Access Struggle of the Villagers of Yamanashi Prefecture) (Tokyo: Ochanomizu shobō, 1978); Hōjō Hiroshi, *Yamanashi-ken iriai tōsōshi: Kindai 130 nen no iriaiken no unmei* (The History of the Struggle over Iriai in Yamanashi Prefecture: The Fate of 130 Years of Common Access Rights) (Tokyo: Ochanomizu shobō, 1998); Kawashima Takeyoshi, Ushiomi Toshitaka, and Watanabe Yōzō, *Iriaiken no kaitai* (The Dismemberment of Common Access Rights), 2 vols. (Tokyo: Iwanami shoten, 1959 and 1961); Watanabe Yōzō, *Iriai to hō* (Common Access and the Law) (Tokyo: University of Tokyo Press, March 1972); Kamimura Masana, *Sonraku seikatsu no shūzoku, kanshū no shakai kōzō* (The Social Structure of the Folkways and Customs of Village Life) (Tokyo: Ochanomizu shobō, 1979); Hayasaka Keizō, *Kita-kamiyama chi no yamakage kara—Iwate no hitobito* (From the Mountain Shade of North Kamiyama: The People of Iwate) (Tokyo: Sanshōdō, 1984); Hayasaka Keizō, "The Kotsunagi Archives: From Legal Disputes on the Commons to Large-N Analysis of

Commons in Iwate Prefecture, Japan, in the Twentieth Century," paper presented at the International Association for the Study of the Commons, Edmonton, Alberta, May 2015.

[12] See, for example, Inoue Makoto, *Komonzu-ron no chōsen: Aratana shigen kanri wo motomete* (The Challenge of Commons Theory: Seeking New Natural Resource Management) (Tokyo: Shinyōsha, 2008); Utako Yamashita, Kulbhushan Balooni, and Makoto Inoue, "The Effect of Instituting 'Authorized Neighborhood Associations' on Communal (Iriai) Forest Ownership in Japan," *Society and Natural Resources* 22, no. 5 (April 2009), 464–473; Akimichi Tomoya, *Komonzu no chikyūshi: Gurōbaruka jidai no kyōyūron ni mukete* (The Planet's History of Commons: Toward a Theory of Shared Ownership for the Global Age) (Tokyo: Iwanami shoten, 2010); Kenneth Ruddle and Tomoya Akimichi, eds., *Maritime Institutions in the Western Pacific* (Osaka: National Museum of Ethnology, 1984).

[13] Murota Takeshi, ed., *Gurōbaru jidai no rōkaru komonzu* (Local Commons in the Global Age) (Tokyo: Minerva shobō, 2009); Takeshi Murota and Ken Takeshita, eds., *Local Commons and Democratic Environmental Governance* (New York: United Nations University Press, 2013).

[14] See, for example, Murota Takeshi and Mitsumata Gaku, *Iriai rin'ya to komonzu* (Iriai Forests and Commons) (Tokyo: Nihon hyōronsha, 2003); Mitsumata Gaku and Saito Haruo, eds., *Toshi to shinrin* (City and Forest) (Tokyo: Kōyō shobō, 2017); Mitsumata Gaku and Saito Haruo, *Mori no keizaigaku: Mori ga mori rashiku, hito ga hito rashiku aru keizai* (Forest Economics: An Economics in which Forests Are Like Forests and People Are Like People) (Tokyo: Nihon hyōronsha, 2022); Yamashita Utako, *Iriai rin'ya no hen'yō to gendaiteki igi* (Transformations and Contemporary Significance of Common Access Forests) (Tokyo: University of Tokyo Press, 2011); Haruo Saitō and Gaku Mitsumata, "Bidding Customs and Habitat Improvement for Matsutake (*Tricholoma matsutake*) in Japan," *Economic Botany* 52, no. 3 (October 2008), 257–268; Tamura Norie, "Umi o tsukuru, mori wo tsukuru: Gyomin no morizukuri to chiiki kanri (Making Seas and Making Forests: Fisherfolk's Afforestation and Community Management), in *Ekorojii to komonzu: Kankyō gabanansu to chiiki jiritsu no shisō* (Ecology and Commons: Environmental Governance and the Idea of Local Self-Reliance), edited by Mitsumata Gaku (Kyoto: Kōyō shobō, 2014), 129–141; Tamura Norie and Hein Mallee, "Japan's Fishery Forest Movement as a Sustainability Transition," 4th APSAFE (Asia Pacific Society for Agricultural and Food Ethics) Symposium Proceedings, December 2020, 114–118; Reiji Suzuki, et al., "Traditional Skills and Knowledge Inherited from Japanese Swidden Cultivation: Toward Restoration of Degraded Satoyama Forests," *Journal of Agroforestry and Environment* 5 (2011), 71–74; Ohno Tomohiko, "Ryūiki gabanansu no bunseki furēmuwāku" (An Analytical Framework for the Study of Watershed Governance), *Suishigen kankyō kenkyū* (Journal of Water and Environmental Issues) 28, no. 1 (July 2015), 7–15; Daisaku Shimada, "Multi-Level Natural Resources Governance Based on Local Community: A Case Study on Semi-Natural Grassland in Tarōji, Nara, Japan," *International Journal of the Commons* 9, no. 2, (2015), 486–509; Masahide Hayashi, Keizō Hayasaka, and Margaret A. McKean, "Explaining Resource Shortages and Restrictive Rules on the Japanese Commons in the Early 20th Century," paper presented at the International Association for the Study of the Commons, Edmonton, Alberta, May 2015.

24

Encounters

Kate Wildman Nakai

For me, though, the process of arriving at a topic to investigate has largely been amorphous, shaped more by coincidental encounters than by self-direction and a sense of purpose.

KATE WILDMAN NAKAI is a professor emerita at Sophia University, Tokyo, where she taught from 1980 to 2010. She received her BA and MA from Stanford and her PhD from Harvard. Before moving to Japan, she taught at Harvard University and the University of Oregon. From 1997 to 2010, she served as editor of *Monumenta Nipponica*. Her research has focused on Edo-period intellectual, social, and religious developments; she has also worked on issues concerning shrines, education, and church-state relations in the prewar period. Recent publications include *Christian Sorcerers on Trial: Records of the 1827 Osaka Incident* (coedited with Fumiko Miyazaki and Mark Teeuwen, Columbia University Press, 2020), a translation and analysis of judicial records concerning a group of supposed Christians in Osaka and Kyoto brought to light in the early nineteenth century. She is currently working on a history of Sophia University.

We advise students to come up with a well-defined topic for a paper or thesis, and concern for a particular issue undoubtedly drives many research agendas. For me, though, the process of arriving at a topic to investigate has largely been amorphous, shaped more by coincidental encounters than by self-direction and a sense of purpose. The first and most consequential of those encounters was with Japan itself, which occurred in the summer of 1959, between my second and third year of high school, when I spent two months in Japan (in Matsusaka, Mie Prefecture) on the American Field Service (AFS) program. I returned to the United States from that summer experience knowing that I wanted to study Japan and to find a way to study it that would bring me back quickly. This objective led to my entering Stanford University, which I had heard was starting a program in Japan; majoring in Japanese; and returning to Japan in the spring of 1962 to study at the Stanford Center in Tokyo (now the Inter-University Center for Japanese Language Studies in Yokohama). Mine was the center's second entering class.

This far, it is fair to say, a concrete aim guided my path. But the impulse behind it was something visceral, or at most aesthetic, not intellectual. I knew I wanted to study Japan, but I had no real idea of what specifically I wanted to investigate or from what perspective. The answers to those questions would only emerge slowly through the playing out of other encounters.

Before sketching some of the academic side of that development, I would like to make a brief detour to commemorate an interaction of a different sort that also dates back to those two initial engagements with Japan. Barbara Sato, then Barbara Wool, was another member of the contingent of American high school students dispatched by AFS to Japan in the summer of 1959 (see chapter 31). As it happened, we were assigned to the same cabin buried in the third-class quarters of the *Hikawa Maru* for the close to two-week voyage across the Pacific. (Retired from service the following year, the *Hikawa Maru* now lies permanently at anchor in Yokohama Harbor.) Barbara and I immediately formed a bond, which deepened when she too came to study at the Stanford Center. Without her companionship and adventurous spirit, I'm sure I would never have undertaken the exploration of Tokyo in the spring and summer of 1963 that led to other encounters (most notably with my future husband) and shaped my life thereafter. Barbara and I ended up pursuing quite different avenues within Japanese Studies, but the vivid memory of the shared experiences from some sixty years ago was an enduring link.

To revert to the evolution of my academic career, in the 1960s, as now, the study of Japanese language was paired institutionally with the study of literature, and, because I liked to read, I assumed initially that my point of entry into Japanese Studies would be through literature. In the fall of 1963, I went back to Stanford, where Donald Shively and Edward Seidensticker had joined the faculty of the Asian Languages Department (now the Department of East Asian Languages and Cultures). Having obtained extra credits from a summer intensive class in second-year Japanese as well as from the Stanford Center program, I had graduated (a

Figure 24.1: Barbara Sato (left) and Kate Nakai (right), Tokyo, September 1963. Photograph courtesy of the author.

year early) while still in Tokyo and thus was now a graduate student. The Asian Languages Department required a translation as an MA thesis, and, through a sequence of decisions that I no longer clearly remember, I ended up translating the last part of Natsume Sōseki's *The Gate* (*Mon*). Although I did not fully appreciate it at the time, I learned much from Ed Seidensticker, and I am grateful to have had the opportunity to study with him. But in the course of that year, I also realized that liking to read was not the same thing as the academic discipline of literary studies and that probably I was more suited to some other approach. But what? Perhaps history, I thought, without really knowing what history was either. I increasingly felt, too, that I would like to focus on a premodern topic. So when Don Shively, who was moving to Harvard, suggested that its program in the Department of East Asian Languages and Civilizations (then Oriental Languages) might better fit my inclinations, I opted to try that. It was very much a "that is what Tiggers like" series of decisions, and it is owing greatly to the kindness and patience of my mentors that it ultimately worked out.

The next significant encounter was with Albert Craig. As I recall, one day, not too long after I arrived at Harvard in September 1964, he and Don Shively took me to lunch to talk about possible topics for a seminar paper. Al Craig suggested doing something with *Theses on Spirits* (*Kishinron*), a discussion of spirits from a Confucian perspective by the Tokugawa-period scholar Arai Hakuseki (1657–1725). I later learned that Al put substantial effort into identifying a range of topics and sources that students might explore, and I imagine that *Theses on Spirits* was one of these. Quite likely what drew it to his attention was its association with the rise of a rationalist outlook in Tokugawa thought. I adopted the suggestion to take *Theses on Spirits* as the subject for the seminar paper (in which I indeed connected what I learned about the text and Hakuseki with a rationalist worldview) and went on to write my PhD dissertation on Hakuseki as well. In the next decade or so, as I revised (more than once) the dissertation into a book and wrestled with approaches, I came to look at Hakuseki quite differently. Abandoning the issue of rationalism and barely touching on *Theses on Spirits*, I focused on other connections, such as how Hakuseki's reading of Chinese political theory intersected with his view of Tokugawa governance, or how the combination of those elements shaped his distinctive interpretation of the early myths and the course of Japanese history. The book's title, *Shogunal Politics: Arai Hakuseki and the Premises of Tokugawa Rule*, was an attempt to convey the shift in my perspective.[2]

The quest for a seminar paper topic thus had a variety of unforeseen but fortuitous consequences. Without the link through Hakuseki, I would hardly have thought to look into the nature of Tokugawa Confucianism, a theme that became one thread of my academic life. Pursuit of his activities and writings provided glimpses of multiple avenues for further exploration, some of which continue to beckon. The long evolving relationship with Hakuseki also brought a recognition that, important as it is to arrive eventually at a problem around which to structure one's findings, a more productive initial step may be to explore a source and see where it leads. Later experience has only confirmed that realization.

In the remainder of this meandering reminiscence, I'd like to share another chain of encounters across time, one pertinent to some of the research themes that have occupied me recently. During my years at Harvard, I took a course on reading Tokugawa judicial sources taught jointly by Don Shively and Hiramatsu Yoshirō, a professor from Nagoya University and a specialist on Tokugawa legal history, who spent a year at Harvard as a visiting scholar. Other than the fact that one of the cases we read involved a double suicide, I no longer remember the details of the materials introduced in the class, and they did not feed directly into a research agenda in the way the seminar paper on *Theses on Spirits* did. What the class conveyed, even if I was not clearly aware of it at the time, were the many benefits of working with materials like these—the analytical training provided by trying to untangle a case's ins and outs, the more nuanced understanding that comes from seeing how individual cases both bring to life and raise questions about standard interpretations of the Tokugawa historical setting, and the sense of immediacy offered by a view into the exigencies confronted by otherwise obscure people.

Once I began to teach, I wanted to find ways for my students to experience the rewards of grappling with firsthand materials. The need to use sources available in English, rather than documents in Japanese such as those taken up in the Harvard class, inevitably posed a challenge. After some years, though, I discovered a partial solution in John Henry Wigmore's *Law and Justice in Tokugawa Japan*, nineteen volumes of English translations of Tokugawa judicial materials.[3] The story of how this collection came about deserves a more thorough investigation and retelling than the brief mention possible here. Wigmore (1863–1943), its initiator, was a young American jurist who came to Japan in 1889 to assist in the establishment of the law section of the new university division of Keiō Gijuku (the institution that eventually became Keio University). He continued to take an interest in the project after returning to the United States in 1893, where he went on to become dean of the Northwestern University School of Law and a leading authority on jurisprudence and comparative law. Others also promoted the project, and translation and publication of the collection of materials proceeded intermittently over the following decades. Interrupted by World War II and Wigmore's death, publication resumed in the late 1960s, with the last volume to appear coming out in 1986. The collection stands as a true monument of English- and Japanese-language collaboration. Its format and organization can make it forbidding at first sight, but for those who persevere, it offers a treasure trove of firsthand information about Tokugawa society and economy as well as judicial procedures.

Having learned of the existence of *Law and Justice in Tokugawa Japan*, I spent many hours absorbed in perusing its contents, identifying items that could be used in the classroom, and eventually building a course on Edo society around it. I toyed with the idea of trying to organize and present some of the material in the collection in a more accessible manner so that it might find a wider audience, but retirement came and went without any concrete steps in that direction. Happily, though, another set of encounters led to a complementary if smaller-scale venture. A little over a decade ago, several people with a shared interest in Tokugawa society—Mark Teeuwen, Fumiko Miyazaki (Umezawa), Anne Walthall, John Breen, and myself—undertook to translate *An Account of What I Have Seen and Heard* (*Seji kenbunroku*), a well-known late-Tokugawa survey of the ills of the day.[4] After that project was finished, Mark, Fumiko, and I agreed to look for another Tokugawa text to translate. At Fumiko's suggestion, and with her preparing a transcript of the manuscript, we decided on a source she had come across some time previously: the records of a dramatic case from 1827 involving a group of women and men in Kyoto and Osaka accused of being Christian. In contrast to *An Account of What I Have Seen and Heard*, which, although lively and informative, presented a picture of society filtered through the consciousness of a Tokugawa intellectual, here was a source that afforded a more direct view into the ins and outs of people's lives and the government of the time. It was a worthy counterpart to the documents included in *Law and Justice in Tokugawa Japan*.

The materials, which we ultimately published under the title *Christian Sorcerers on Trial: Records of the 1827 Osaka Incident*, led back to another connection as well: Professor Hiramatsu. The judicial documents translated in *Law and Justice in Tokugawa Japan* are basically of a civil character. Being squeamish, I had always avoided the parallel area of criminal law, and, although I had made use of other of Professor Hiramatsu's writings on Tokugawa law, I had never looked at his magnum opus on criminal procedure, a 1,024-page book titled *Studies in Early Modern Criminal Jurisprudence* (*Kinsei keiji soshōhō no kenkyū*).[5] Now, however, I needed a better understanding of just that topic, and so I delved into what proved a truly remarkable work—full of concrete details and extensive quotes from sources about judicial process and norms, lucid in organization and exposition. It was as if the figure who long ago introduced me to the value of Tokugawa judicial materials was now providing pointers for deciphering a notable example. In my mind, *Christian Sorcerers on Trial* carries a silent dedication: "In homage to J. H. Wigmore and Hiramatsu Yoshirō." For these and all the encounters that have marked my journey so far—human and textual, the few mentioned here and the many that are not—I am deeply thankful.

Notes

With special gratitude to Anne Walthall. It was our recent conversations about *Theses on Spirits* and its connection to other mutual interests that led me to think about that long-ago seminar paper and where it had led.

[1] Kate Wildman Nakai, *Shogunal Politics: Arai Hakuseki and the Premises of Tokugawa Rule* (Cambridge, MA: Council on East Asian Studies, Harvard University, 1988).

[2] John Henry Wigmore, ed., *Law and Justice in Tokugawa Japan: Materials for the History of Japanese Law and Justice under the Tokugawa Shogunate 1603–1867*, 19 vols. (Tokyo: University of Tokyo Press, 1967–1986).

[3] Mark Teeuwen and Kate Wildman Nakai, eds., *Lust, Commerce, and Corruption: An Account of What I Have Seen and Heard by an Edo Samurai* (New York: Columbia University Press, 2014).

[4] Fumiko Miyazaki, Kate Wildman Nakai, and Mark Teeuwen, translators, *Christian Sorcerers on Trial: Records of the 1827 Osaka Incident* (New York: Columbia University Press, 2020).

[5] Hiramatsu Yoshirō, *Kinsei keiji soshōhō no kenkyū* (Studies in Early Modern Criminal Jurisprudence) (Tokyo: Sōbunsha, 1960).

25

I OWE MY CAREER TO MEN

Anne Walthall

*I owe my career to men, but much of my career
enrichment has come from women.*

ANNE WALTHALL is a professor emerita of Japanese history at the University of California, Irvine. Her books include *The Weak Body of a Useless Woman: Matsuo Taseko and the Meiji Restoration* (1998); *The Human Tradition in Modern Japan* (2002); *Japan: A Cultural, Social, and Political History* (2005); *East Asia: A Cultural, Social, and Political History* (coauthored with Patricia Ebrey and James Palais, 2008); *Recreating Japanese Men* (coedited with Sabine Frühstück, 2011); and *Politics and Society in Japan's Meiji Restoration: A Brief History with Documents* (coauthored with M. William Steele, 2016).

When I was growing up, most of my teachers in the lower grades and those for high school English were women; men taught languages and the sciences. The man who taught geometry and algebra II made it clear that higher mathematics was beyond the ken of female students, a belief I was only too happy to share. At the University of Wyoming, where my father taught, female professors were few (figure 25.1). I don't remember the first female professor of history there—she had been hired away from Yale before World War II because Yale refused to promote her beyond the rank of instructor. As for my mother, she prepared three nutritious meals a day for her family, a feat that I failed to appreciate, and she had me clean bathrooms, a chore that I hated. My role model was my father. I remember how he would occasionally come home late because he had to attend a faculty meeting. It was decades before I connected his meetings, which I had imagined as important and mysterious, to the ones that I saw as an enormous time suck.

I regret that I never thanked the man who pointed me toward the study of Japan. He was a Japanese American who served as high school librarian during my junior and senior years, and, because I liked libraries, I got to know him. I also liked languages, little realizing that enjoying the steep learning curve in first-year French, German, or Spanish did not mean that my brain was wired for the code-switching necessary to become truly proficient in any foreign language. Carl Abe taught me how to write numbers in Japanese, and I was taken by the idea of a language that didn't use the alphabet. I knew they were Chinese characters, but, in 1965, China didn't exist for me because Americans couldn't go there. Many decades later, when I reflected on how fortunate I had been in my choice of career, I tried to find Mr. Abe to let him know how much I owed to him. He had long since left Wyoming, and my early searches on Google turned up only the fact that Abraham Lincoln's middle name was Carl. The American Association of School Librarians listed a Carl Abe who had worked at a school on an American military base in Okinawa, but, if he was the man whom I had known, he was already dead.

In the meantime, in 1965, I went to the University of Wisconsin because it boasted many language departments, including one for Japanese. I enjoyed my classes, and, when I realized that I had to select a major, I chose Japanese Language and Literature. It was a small program, with seldom more than ten students in a class, much to the disgruntlement of my roommate, whose sociology classes numbered in the hundreds. Alas, my enthusiasm for Japanese did not match my ability to master the language. Again, I was fortunate that one of my language teachers, Akira Komai, told me that I needed time in Japan, where I might learn more, and arranged for me to teach English as a second language at the Kyoto YMCA. I took one course in ESL, thinking perhaps it might make a good career choice, and off I went. My Japanese language skills improved, and I learned that I did not find ESL of sufficient interest to make it my life's work.

While I was in Madison, I had the great good fortune to take a course in Japanese history from Tetsuo Najita. Over fifty years later, I still remember how excited he got while explaining the *shōen* (manorial system) and the different kinds of *shiki* (rights to income) that tied court, temples, warriors, and landholders into a complex system of protection and revenue extraction. It is easy to say that he made history come alive, but what he really did, at least for me, was to make history meaningful. While I was teaching ESL in Kyoto, I studied medieval Japanese history with Professor Uwayokote Masataka and read John Whitney

Figure 25.1 Wilson J. Walthall Jr., PhD, University of Texas, 1947; Anne Walthall, PhD, University of Chicago, 1979. Photograph courtesy of the author.

Hall's *Government and Local Power in Japan, 500 to 1700*.[1] When I decided that I wanted to go to graduate school in Japanese history, I wrote to Professor Najita, who had subsequently moved to the University of Chicago, and asked him for suggestions on where to apply. "Come to Chicago," he replied, and so I did.

Compared to today's applicants to graduate programs in history, I was woefully unprepared. Thanks to the women who had taught high school English, I could write a decent essay, but I had no idea of what to write about. As an undergraduate, I had written papers on topics that grew out of classroom work; I never had to generate a research proposal on my own. For the first few weeks, I floundered, suggesting one topic after another in my meetings with Professor Najita. When I proposed writing on Hōjō Masako (1157–1225), the wife and spokesperson for the first shōgun, he was furious. If I really wanted to pursue women's history, which was nothing but a fad, I'd better go someplace else. He so terrified me that I didn't go near the field for well over a decade. (He later forgot that he had ever said any such thing.) I finally wrote my first seminar paper on village headmen. It was not of publishable quality, but he allowed me to continue into the PhD program.

Harry Harootunian arrived at the beginning of my second year, and, together, the two men built the best graduate program in the country in Japanese history. They practiced intellectual history, which their own advisors had deemed too difficult for them, although they tolerated other methods as well. At the same time, they encouraged their students to study European history in addition to the courses we had to take in Chinese history. They believed, and rightly so, that we would be more likely to get jobs if we could talk to fellow historians across different fields and if we understood the diverse theoretical underpinnings of historical research. Again, I was fortunate that the labor and social historian William Sewell Jr. led me to the work of Marc Bloch on French agrarian history. At the Ida Noyes pool, the noon hour was reserved for women so we wouldn't have to wear a swimsuit. Thrashing through the water one day, I had a eureka moment—I would write my dissertation on peasant uprisings.

In the late seventies and early eighties, the study of peasant uprisings was a hot topic in Japanese and world history. The Ministry of Education, Sciences, Sports, and Culture that provided my dissertation fellowship placed me at the University of Tokyo, its preferred recipient of government funds, and graduate students there introduced me to the research group on peasant uprisings led by Professor Fukaya Katsumi at Waseda University. He later opened the door for me to publish an essay in Japanese in the journal *Rekishi hyōron* (*Critical History*). For the first time, I found myself in a group of scholars as passionate about my topic as I was. We remain friends to this day, even though our interests have diverged over time.

For my last year at the University of Chicago, Professor Najita arranged for me to receive the International Harvester Dissertation Writing Fellowship. The story I heard was that when the emperor of Japan had come to the Midwest in 1975, International Harvester had promised to give the University of Chicago money for graduate students if Najita could help the company get a picture of the emperor on its farm equipment. I never saw any such picture, but that was the name of my fellowship. Professor Najita, or Tetsu as I learned to call him, wrote numerous letters of recommendation for me while I was applying for jobs in the fall of 1978, and, when the University of Utah flew me to Salt Lake City for a job interview, he insisted on writing a "fresh" one. Remember that this was back in the dark ages before word processors, when each letter had to be typed anew. Tetsu and Harry later stepped in when the major university presses balked at publishing my manuscript on peasant uprisings. I never developed a close relationship with either of them, but they were there when I needed them.

The academic year I was on the job market, 1978–1979, was a terrible year for my field. There were several positions open in Asian history, but, to my knowledge, they all went to people who studied China. There was just one tenure-track position in Japanese history, the one at the University of Utah, and another that Brown University had promised the Japan Foundation would eventually become tenure-track. My chief competitors were men from Harvard whose advisor had them write dissertations on a man and an event or a man and an institution, topics that had little resonance beyond scholars of Japan. As it turned out, the men on the search committee for the position at Utah had trained as social historians and liked my work. (The one woman on the committee supported a fellow graduate student at Chicago because she was older.) The position at Brown went to a man who had written his dissertation at Yale on urban history.

Getting a position did not mean I could keep it. The department had fired my predecessor because he refused to publish, and so it monitored my progress more than the usual. For my third- and fifth-year reviews, it solicited outside letters, to the astonishment of some senior men in the field. Peter Duus, William Hauser, and Richard Smethurst all sent me copies of the (overly) glowing letters they wrote on my behalf, and I have been thankful for their support ever since.

While I was at the University of Utah, I lost my fear of women's history. During the 1985–1986 academic year, the History Department turned a position vacated by the retirement of a senior male into one for women's history because the American caucus had decided that the History Department had to have one. I was amazed. I never thought a caucus, or a department, would willingly give up a field that had long been the preserve of men. Perhaps women's history wasn't a fad after all. The woman we hired, Peggy Pascoe, taught me much about the issues that structured the field of women's history. She was so well organized that when I asked her about writing a woman's biography, she pulled out a file folder with a bibliography on precisely that topic. She died young, in 2010, just after publishing her award-winning second book, *What Comes Naturally: Miscegenation Law and the Making of Race in America*.[2]

I enjoyed living in Salt Lake City, learning to ski, and going backpacking in the spectacular scenery of the Mountain West, but friends kept suggesting that I should seek greater academic opportunities. When the History Department in the University of California, Irvine decided to search for a historian of Japan, Ken Pomeranz and R. Bin Wong went to UCLA to ask Herman Ooms for suggestions on whom to approach. At his urging, Bin asked me to apply. For years, Herman and I had our own mutual admiration society, and I knew I could always count on him for support. To him and to Ken and Bin, as well as all the other men I have mentioned above, I owe an enormous debt of gratitude.

I owe my career to men, but much of my career enrichment has come from women. One of the first was Sharon Nolte, who was already working on her dissertation when I arrived at the University of Tokyo in the fall of 1975. We shared stories about other members of our cohort, and she taught me how to navigate the Japanese system of higher learning. So far as I know, she was the only woman to earn her PhD at Yale under James Crowley, and it hadn't been easy. She told me that once, as she was turning the corner heading for his office, she saw him stick his head out the door, glance around, and scurry off in the opposite direction. She received her PhD the same year I did, but, without financial support from Yale, she had been forced to find work before finishing her dissertation. She always had a job, but, for too many years, it was catch-as-catch-can. She taught at Appalachian State University in Boone, North Carolina (1978–1979), the University of Wisconsin–La Crosse (1979), and the University of Iowa (spring of 1980). She thought she had a tenure-track position at Southern Methodist University in Dallas, but the History Department terminated her at her third-year review for specious reasons. Following her last year at SMU as the department pariah, she moved to DePauw University in 1984. There she had already started working in women's history before she published *Liberalism in Modern Japan: Ishibashi Tanzan and His Teachers, 1905–1960* just months before she died of an aneurism in her brain in July 1987.[3] She was thirty-eight years old. Her sudden death shocks me still.

One of the unexpected benefits of moving to Utah in 1979 was getting to know two women already teaching Japanese history in the Mountain West. At that time, the Japan Foundation sponsored regional seminars for scholars whose nearest colleagues might live hundreds of miles away. Thanks to it and the Western Conference of the Association for Asian Studies (WCAAS), I met Joyce C. Lebra (chapter 3) from the University of Colorado and Gail Lee Bernstein from the University of Arizona. At one WCAAS meeting held at Park City, Utah, in 1986, the three of us, plus other scholars, decided to produce an edited volume on women in Japanese history.[4] For many, it was the first time to write on this subject. Unlike my advisor at Chicago who had received SSRC and ACLS grants for a conference, "Conflict in Modern Japanese History," held at a resort at Monterey, California, we made do with more meager funds. But the book that Gail edited, *Recreating Japanese Women, 1600–1945*, has had the greater staying power.

Joyce was the first woman to receive a PhD in Japanese history in the United States, at Radcliffe in 1958 (taking classes and being advised at Harvard), and she was the first woman to teach in the History Department at the University of Colorado, but it didn't come easily. In the 1950s, the hiring process consisted of a department chair calling a professor and asking if he had anyone he could recommend for a job. Most men, who were assumed to have families to support, went straight from graduate school to a tenure-track position. Not Joyce. She spent four years bouncing around from the University of Texas at Austin to Rutgers University before landing at what was then a small regional university overwhelmingly geared toward undergraduates, the University of Colorado Boulder. There she taught for twenty-nine years, leading fights against sexism and misogyny and struggling to get salary equity and fair treatment for women.

As she describes in chapter 3, Joyce was a prolific scholar. Like other women who received their PhD in history from an Ivy League university before 1979, she wrote her dissertation on a man—in her case, Ōkuma Shigenobu—but she did not publish a book on him until after she had already pivoted to military history. Also in the 1970s, she published two books on the Imperial Japanese Army and the Indian National Army in mainland Southeast Asia during World War II and edited a collection of essays on Japan's Greater East Asia Co-Prosperity Sphere.[5] This research led to a teaching field in Indian history and later a study of the Rani of Jhansi.[6] In 1970, she happened to be at the Japan Ground Self-Defense Force Headquarters when the novelist Mishima Yukio arrived to harangue the troops on their lack of Japanese spirit. Her eyewitness account of how they mocked him before he went inside and committed suicide by cutting open his belly appeared in *The New York Times* and the *Mainichi Daily News Tokyo*.[7] While finishing up her military history projects, she started working on women. She led three research teams to Japan, Southeast Asia, and India to study women in the labor force, focusing on women's roles in diverse occupations.[8] She also wrote three historical novels set in Japan and India.[9] In 2021, the Japanese government awarded her the Order of the Rising Sun, Gold Rays with Neck Ribbon for her contributions to promoting academic exchange and mutual understanding between Japan and the United States. *The Japan Times* reported that she was wearing it when she died.[10]

In 1968, Gail was the fourth person and first woman to receive her PhD at Harvard under Al Craig. As she was finishing her dissertation, he called her and fellow student Richard Minear into his office to inform them that both the University of Arizona and The Ohio State University needed professors to teach Japanese history. Gail thought Arizona sounded interesting; Richard wanted Ohio State. Gail thus took a position in the Department of Oriental Studies without ever having visited Tucson and with no money to help her move across the country. Instead, the department chair graciously raised her original salary offer from $7,800 to $8,000, although she did not receive her first paycheck until after she started teaching. To pay for the books that she had shipped COD, she had to borrow money. Perhaps intimidated by her Harvard PhD, the American instructor of Japanese language tried to sabotage her career by soliciting a critical letter for a supposed career review. He was so inept that his ploy was soon discovered. The department chairman protected her but did nothing against her enemy.[11]

Like Sharon and Joyce, Gail did not start out in women's history. With Al Craig as her advisor, she wrote her dissertation on Kawakami Hajime. When she revised it into a book, Al recommended it to the editor for the Harvard East Asia Series. Gail charted the long and twisting path that brought Kawakami to Marxism, incorporating his psychology and personal life into the trajectory of his ideas.[12] The volume proved so engaging that it won the 1977 John K. Fairbank Prize from the American Historical Association. It was translated into Japanese in 1991.[13] Having proven herself as a historian, Gail then ventured into uncharted territory by pursuing the oral history of a farm woman and putting herself in the book, a different approach from what she had learned at Harvard. *Haruko's World: A Japanese Farm Woman and her Community*, first published in 1983, vividly depicts how Haruko, who called her work "helping my husband," had become the mainstay of the family farm. When Gail went back for an updated edition published in 1996, the farm work that had given Haruko's life its meaning had largely disappeared.[14] Gail's intimate portrayal of one woman's life over the course of twenty years thus puts a human face on the large-scale transformation of rural Japan. *Isami's House: Three Centuries of a Japanese Family* grew out of Gail's first homestay while in Tokyo as a graduate student.[15] This personal connection and her access to family stories allowed her to dramatize how the expansion of Japan's colonial empire brought ordinary citizens to Manchuria and Indonesia and how members of the rural elite became urbanites.

The circumstances under which I started my career were not the same as those for Joyce and Gail. For me, the job market was much tighter, search committees were the norm, and men had become accustomed to having women as colleagues. Today, it seems to me, graduate school has become a much narrower gateway for men and women. Jobs are still scarce, but students have more leeway in choosing their dissertation topics. Some even write on women.

Notes

[1] John Whitney Hall, *Government and Local Power in Japan: A Study Based on Bizen Province, 500–1700* (Princeton: Princeton University Press, 1966).

[2] Peggy Pascoe, *What Comes Naturally: Miscegenation Law and the Making of Race in America* (New York: Oxford University Press, 2009).

[3] Sharon H. Nolte, *Liberalism in Modern Japan: Ishibashi Tanzan and His Teachers, 1905–1960* (Berkeley: University of California Press, 1987).

[4] Gail Lee Bernstein, ed., *Recreating Japanese Women, 1600–1945* (Berkeley: University of California Press, 1991).

[5] Joyce Lebra, *Ōkuma Shigenobu: Statesman of Meiji Japan* (Canberra: Australian National University Press, 1973); *Jungle Alliance: Japan and the Indian National Army* (Singapore: Asia Pacific Press, 1971); *Japan-Trained Armies in Southeast Asia: Independence and Volunteer Forces in World War II* (Hong Kong: Heinemann Educational Books, 1977);

Japan's Greater East Asia Co-Prosperity Sphere in World War II: Selected Readings and Documents (London: Oxford University Press, 1975). See chapter 3 for discussion on these books.

[6] Joyce Lebra-Chapman, *The Rani of Jhansi: A Study of Female Heroism in India* (Honolulu: University of Hawaiʻi Press, 1986).

[7] Joyce Lebra, "Eyewitness: Mishima," *New York Times*, November 28, 1970, 26; "Last Speech on Balcony Witnessed," *Mainichi Daily News Tokyo*. November 28, 1970.

[8] Joyce Lebra, Joy Paulson, and Elizabeth Powers, eds., *Women in Changing Japan* (Stanford: Stanford University Press, 1978); Joyce Lebra and Joy Paulson, eds., *Chinese Women in Southeast Asia* (Singapore: Times Books International, 1980); Joyce Lebra, Joy Paulson, and Jana Matson Everett, eds., *Women and Work in India: Continuity and Change* (New Delhi: Promilla, 1984).

[9] Joyce Chapman Lebra, *Durga's Sword* (Mumbai: Indus, 1995) and *Scent of Sake* (New York: Harper Collins, 2009); Napua Chapman, *Sugar and Smoke* (Frederick, MD: PublishAmerica, 2005).

[10] David Cortez, "Joyce Lebra: Trailblazing Scholar and Witness to Japanese History," *The Japan Times*, November 7, 2021, https://www.japantimes.co.jp/community/2021/11/07/our-lives/joyce-lebra-history-obituary/.

[11] This discussion was prepared through personal communication with Gail Bernstein.

[12] Gail Lee Bernstein, *Japanese Marxist: A Portrait of Kawakami Hajime, 1879–1946* (Cambridge, MA: Harvard University Press, 1976).

[13] Gail Lee Bernstein, *Kawakami: Nihon-teki Marukusu-shugisha no shōzō* (Kawakami Hajime: Portrait of a Japanese Marxist) (Kyoto: Minerva shobō, 1991).

[14] Gail Lee Bernstein, *Haruko's World: A Japanese Farm Woman and Her Community: with a 1996 Epilogue* (Stanford: Stanford University Press, 1996).

[15] Gail Lee Bernstein, *Isami's House: Three Centuries of a Japanese Family* (Berkeley: University of California Press, 2005).

26

Embracing the Unexpected and Weaving a Life

Anne E. Imamura

> *I always told my students that while it is good to be focused on a particular goal, they should remain open to opportunity and serendipity.*

ANNE E. IMAMURA was the director of the Area Studies Division at the Foreign Service Institute (US State Department) and an adjunct professor of sociology at Georgetown University. She taught at Sophia University, the University of Malaya, and the University of Maryland. Twice a Fulbright Scholar to Japan and the recipient of a Japan Foundation Dissertation Fellowship, she holds a PhD in sociology from Columbia University and an MA in Asian Studies from the University of Hawaiʻi, where she was twice an East-West Center Fellow. Her publications include *Re-Imaging Japanese Women* (1996), *Urban Japanese Housewives: At Home and in the Community* (1987), and articles and book chapters, including comparative work on foreign wives of Nigerians and Japanese.

It all began in 1966 with a letter telling me that I had been accepted into the Junior Year Program at the East-West Center. I was so excited: a whole year in Hawaiʻi, all expenses paid (no need for a part-time job) and the chance, perhaps, to travel to Japan! Little did I know that this year would launch me on a lifelong journey far from my Eurocentric focus.

The East-West Center expected us to both do well academically and participate in the cross-cultural programs and opportunities the Center offered. In addition, each of us had a roommate from Asia. In my case, she was from Japan. This provided many opportunities and challenges as we tried to learn from one another, communicate in English, and, later in the year, try out my Japanese. She became a lifelong friend. I also had the opportunity to study, travel, live, and interact with people from many countries in Asia and the Pacific Islands. This incredibly expanded my perspective as someone who had grown up in the Midwest with people of very similar values and culture.

Also, I had no idea how difficult Japanese was. The Junior Year Program took us through four academic years of college Japanese in a single calendar year. One of our *sensei* (teachers) lived in the men's dormitory, and evening review sessions and extracurricular activities were the norm. Because my roommate was Japanese, I never felt that I could raise my frustrations with learning the language to her. One night, when she was out and I had worked for hours trying to translate something, I hurled my Japanese-English character dictionary against the cement-block wall of our dorm room and broke its spine. Many years later, I had it rebound in plain red without a title on the spine, and it sits on my bookshelf to this day, an anonymous reminder.

After that year at the East-West Center, I went to Japan for the first time with the Junior Year Program. My experiences there, and living with my host family, cemented my interest in Japan, and I knew I wanted to continue to learn. I was also aware that all the Japanese I had studied in Hawai'i enabled me to only scratch the surface, and I needed to study more.

I received a second East-West Center grant to do an MA in Asian Studies at the University of Hawai'i and a second field study back to Japan in 1969, where I researched the training that Japanese diplomats and businessmen and their families were given before they were posted abroad. I was interested in joining the Foreign Service but changed my mind when I realized that what I really wanted to do was immerse myself in local society and study it.

I also met Yuki, who became my husband, and added the role of the wife of the eldest son, whose family business was a sake store in a small town in Hokkaido. To my (then) great surprise, his family and their neighbors were so understanding of his ambitions to work in international development but also so adamant that it was unfortunate that he was the eldest son and thus would have to shelve those ambitions (which he did not do). Sometimes when I visited, I felt as if everyone had read one of the ethnographies of Japan I had studied and was using it as a script. This experience drew me to focus on social structure and norms and the discipline of sociology.

Having decided on sociology rather than the Foreign Service, I next had to decide what I wanted to do with sociology. My East-West Center grant was over, and I was teaching and editing English as I tried to figure this out. I heard that the international division of Sophia University in Tokyo might have opportunities to teach, so I scheduled an interview. They were looking for someone to teach a course on religion in Japanese history and asked if I could do that. Based entirely on the fact that a TA in Japanese history at the University of Hawai'i had written good things about an exam essay question I answered on this topic, I said that I could teach the course and was hired. I very quickly checked out every book on the subject in the Sophia University Library and laughed at myself as I read many of the books I had returned to the University of Hawai'i Library the previous year, thinking I would never need them again after completing my MA oral exam. I fell in love with teaching undergraduates.

My next journey was to Kuala Lumpur, Malaysia, when Yuki was transferred there to represent the Japan Chamber of Commerce and Industry. Japanese history at the University of Malaya was taught by a professor who came from Japan, and I became the tutor for that course during our first year there. I taught the course during my second year there because there were challenges finding a Japanese professor. This experience both deepened my love for teaching and expanded my perspective as I learned about Malaysia and other Southeast Asian societies. It also prepared me to better understand Islamic societies and laid an indirect foundation for the work I did much later in Nigeria.

Both Yuki and I wanted to do graduate work in the United States. I wanted to do a PhD in sociology, and Yuki wanted to do an MA related to international development. We ended up at Columbia University, where my advisor was Herbert Passin, and, of course, I benefited from the rich faculty and research resources related to Japan and East Asia. If I close my eyes, I can see Professor Carol Gluck enthusiastically challenging us to consider issues in Japanese history, recall discussions with then PhD candidate Susan Pharr about women and political issues in Japan, and remember being in class with then graduate student Barbara Hamill Sato (chapters 22 and 31).

In the mid-1970s, when I was developing my dissertation topic, there were several studies of how the corporation was replacing the residential community as the most significant community for Japanese men. The seminal work of Ronald Dore and Ezra and Suzanne Vogel laid an important foundation for understanding the changes having a salaried breadwinner meant for urban Japanese families, and I was eager to learn more about the impact on Japanese women's lives. I was also interested in the role that housing type played in shaping women's community participation and perspective. With funding from Fulbright and the Japan Foundation, I pursued the research that became my dissertation and provided the basis for *Urban Japanese Housewives: At Home and in the Community* (1987) and related articles.[1]

While working on my dissertation in Tokyo, I met Helen Hardacre, my fellow graduate student (chapter 30), Professors Sumiko Iwao and Hiroko Hara, Merry White (chapter 21), and so many other women whose scholarly contributions are foundational to our study of Japan.[2] Beyond academia, I met and retained both personal and professional connections with Mariko Bando, who was the first director general of the Japanese Cabinet Office's Gender Equality Bureau (Danjo Kyōdō Sankakukyoku, established in 2001) and authored the first white paper on gender inequality in Japan.[3] I also was fortunate to know and consider as a mentor Kazuko Tsurumi (professor, Sophia University), with whom I had the opportunity over several years to have informal discussions about Japan, Malaysia, and gender roles.[4]

Before my dissertation was completed, Sophia University asked me to teach again, and to my surprise, the Japan Foundation approved this exception to their research funding rules. When I reached the stage of writing my first draft, I decided it would be a good time to start a family, and our son was born in Tokyo. One day, while I was at home working on my dissertation, Yuki called to tell me that he had received an offer from the United Nations Development Programme (UNDP) to be posted in Lagos, Nigeria. (Yuki applied to the UNDP after completing his master's in international affairs at Columbia University, but the UNDP had a hiring freeze at that time.) He asked what I wanted to do. Until then, I had been focused on completing my dissertation and possibly obtaining a permanent position at Sophia University. However, I had always wanted to go to Africa and always looked for new opportunities. So how could I turn this down?

Off we went. I completed and defended my dissertation. For many people, successfully defending a dissertation leads to a celebration. In my case, we were staying in an apartment a friend had vacated for us. Yuki was sick with the flu, our son was not a year old, and neither of us was in a position to celebrate. I went to pick up take-out Chinese food and realized that everyone in the restaurant was glued to the television. This was the day the US hostages were taken in Iran (November 4, 1979). So, in one sense, the day I defended my dissertation was indeed unforgettable.

While we were living in Nigeria and I was revising my dissertation for publication, I received an invitation from the Department of Sociology at the University of Maryland to come for an interview. They were looking for a sociologist who did comparative research, and they offered me the opportunity to teach a double course load in one semester and have the other semester off for research and writing. This enabled me to commute between College Park and Lagos, Nigeria, and later, Mogadishu, Somalia. Our daughter had been born in Nigeria, and we traveled to the University of Maryland for me to teach my first semester when she was three months old. Our family had a very interesting period of balancing both Yuki's and my careers. Yuki would take home leave in the middle of the semester I was teaching in Maryland.

In Nigeria, I noticed families in which the wife appeared to be from somewhere other than Nigeria. I became intrigued by this and wondered how their experiences compared with those of their counterparts in Japan and whether they had an organization similar to that in Japan. I explored these questions in a comparative research project with Anne Bamisaiye (University of Lagos) and Janet Shibamoto (University of California, Davis).

This research was funded by my second Fulbright Fellowship in Japan and provided the opportunity to both spend a semester there and to immerse our children in Japanese society. This opportunity also connected me to Patricia Steinhoff (chapter 12) because the house we were renting in Tokyo had previously been rented to her. The cumulative result of this period of my career was a deeper understanding of the importance of social structures and roles in both Japan and Nigeria.[5] In Japan, my academic understanding was enriched by my personal experiences as the mother of Japanese children in day care, where I interacted with Japanese mothers and learned the many rules expected of mothers and how Japanese got around some of them.[6] I also continued my role as the wife of the eldest son in my husband's family, which provided a rather unvarnished glimpse into changes and continuities in gender roles and familial obligations in Japan. After completing the research, I was able to present it to associations of foreign wives in Japan and Nigeria. A very interesting anecdotal result of these presentations was that each group said both groups faced challenges in terms of standard of living and role expectations within their families, but each said that they were able to cope better with the challenges their group faced and that the challenges of the other group were much harder.

After our son reached elementary school age, splitting the academic year between countries became challenging. Yuki decided to pursue other opportunities because I was located in the Washington, DC, area, and there was great interest in bringing Japanese investment into various development projects. Our family was now in the same place.

During my years at the University of Maryland, I was deeply indebted to Marlene Mayo and Eleanor Kerkham (chapters 5 and 28) for their support and advice. I had begun to give guest lectures at the US Department of State's Foreign Service Institute, and when the Chair of Asian Area Studies retired, I applied for and was selected for the position. From 1988 until I retired in 2015, I was first the Chair of Asian Area Studies and then the Director of the Area Studies Division.

This gave me the important responsibility of providing area studies knowledge to our foreign affairs professionals and of expanding my responsibilities beyond Japan to East and Southeast Asia as the supervisor of those programs. Originally, Asian area studies also included South Asia, but as US interests in that region increased, it became a program of its own. In some ways, I felt like the circle had closed, and I, who had decided not to pursue a Foreign Service career, was now providing area studies to foreign affairs professionals.

However, academic research was not one of my responsibilities, and I could no longer apply for grants. I turned my academic focus to some writing based on former research but more importantly to developing and editing the collection *Re-Imaging Japanese Women* (1996), which picked up where Gail Bernstein's edited collection, *Recreating Japanese Women, 1600–1945* (1991) had left off.[7]

I was able to continue teaching undergraduates. In 1989, I taught Japanese society at Georgetown University. However, given that I had a full-time job at the Foreign Service Institute and two young children, I stopped. Once my younger child left for college, I returned to teaching at Georgetown, one course a semester ("Japanese Society" and "Family and Gender in Japan"), first at night and then, after I retired from the Foreign Service Institute, in the daytime. After twenty years, I taught my last class in the spring of 2020, ending with all the challenges that the pandemic shutdown brought.

As I write this and review my professional life, I realize even more how my professional and personal roles and experiences were interwoven to deepen my insights and focus. I also recognize the importance of all the personal and professional connections to which I am indebted. There are so many more beyond those listed in this chapter.

Finally, I would like to close with the advice I gave to my students. I always told them that while it is good to be focused on a particular goal, they should remain open to opportunity and serendipity. To prove my point, I shared with them how my junior year in Hawai'i changed my life.

Notes

[1] See, for example, Anne E. Imamura, *Urban Japanese Housewives: At Home and in the Community*. Honolulu: (University of Hawai'i Press, 1987).

[2] Professors Hara Hiroko (Ochanomizu University and subsequently Josai International University) and Sumiko Iwao (Keio University) were leading scholars of Japanese women. Their numerous publications and academic participation within and outside of Japan were seminal in the development of women's studies. Each carried her work beyond the academy as founders, participants, and advocates in groups such as the International

Group for the Study of Women and the Asia Pacific Women's Watch. They were advisors to the Japanese government and representatives of Japan in international meetings and conferences. They were also role models who took the time to mentor and advise students, scholars, and others and thus contributed to the ongoing study of gender in Japan. See, for example, Hara Hiroko, *Jendā mondai to gakujutsu kenkyū* (Gender Issues in Academic Research) (Tokyo: Dometsu shuppan, 2004); Iwao Sumiko, *The Japanese Woman: Traditional Image and Changing Reality*. New York: Knopf, 1992.

[3] See, for example, Bando Mariko, *Danjo kyōdō sankaku shakai e* (Toward a Gender Equality Society) (Tokyo: Keisō shobō, 2004).

[4] Tsurumi Kazuko, *Social Change and the Individual: Japan Before and After Defeat in World War II* (Princeton: Princeton University Press, 1970).

[5] See Anne E. Imamura, "Ordinary Couples? Mate Selection in International Marriage in Nigeria," *Journal of Comparative Family Studies* 17, no. 1 (Spring 1986), 33–42; "The Loss That Has No Name: Social Womanhood of Foreign Wives," *Gender and Society* 2, no. 3 (September 1988), 291–307; "Strangers in a Strange Land: Coping with Marginality in International Marriage," reprinted in *Journal of Comparative Family Studies* 21, no. 2. (1990), 171–191.

[6] For example, one day, as I walked to the day care center carrying a bag of groceries that I had purchased at the nearby supermarket, I ran into another mother who asked me if I had not been worried about getting caught. I asked what she meant and learned that parents were supposed to go directly from work to pick up their children, and stopping off to get groceries was not allowed. She told me that the other mothers went to a grocery store far from the day care center and put their purchases in their own bags so they would not get caught.

[7] Anne E. Imamura, *Re-Imaging Japanese Women* (Berkeley: University of California Press, 1996); Gail Lee Bernstein, *Recreating Japanese Women* (Berkeley: University of California Press, 1991).

27

MY LIFE IN TRANSLATION

Juliet Winters Carpenter

Learning to translate professionally, not merely to dabble, was invaluable. I learned the importance of observing deadlines; of immersing yourself in books and articles about a topic in order to absorb the vocabulary and thinking of people in the know; of reading between the lines and not translating merely the surface of the Japanese; and of maintaining the highest possible standards, of always doing no less than your very best.

JULIET WINTERS CARPENTER is a professor emerita of Doshisha Women's College and the translator of fiction by Abe Kōbō, Enchi Fumiko, Watanabe Shin'ichi, Miyabe Miyuki, Shiba Ryōtarō, Miura Shion, and Hirano Keiichirō, among other authors, and poetry by Tawara Machi. Her numerous awards include the Japan-US Friendship Commission Prize for the Translation of Japanese Literature in 1980 for Abe Kōbō's *Secret Rendezvous* (1979) and in 2014 for Mizumura Minae's *A True Novel* (2014), which also won the American Translators Association's Lewis Galantière Award.

Since age seventeen, I have known that I wanted to be a Japanese literary translator. I was doing research for a term paper on Japanese literature at the Evanston Township High School (ETHS) library.[1] The topic was suggested by my teacher (whose name I no longer recall); he knew I was studying Japanese and urged me to write about the brilliant new writer Mishima Yukio. I ended up writing about Mishima's *Temple of the Golden Pavilion*, but, along the way, I read all the books of Japanese literature in translation that our school library had—a mere handful. I read *Sound of Waves*, which showed a completely different side of Mishima; *Botchan* and a couple of other works by Natsume Sōseki; and several novels by Tanizaki Junichirō. The name that most stayed with me from that first foray into the world of Japanese literature, however, was the name not of a novel or an author but that of the master translator who would become my inspiration, my mentor, and my friend: Edward Seidensticker.

The translator's crucial role first became clear to me when I read two works by the same author, translated by different people. I had chosen to read a second work by Sōseki because I enjoyed the first one so much, but what a disappointment! It seemed the man could hardly write a good English sentence. Saying those words to myself brought an aha moment—Sōseki, of course, *hadn't* written anything in English (little did I know that his English was actually quite up to the task). It was the skill or clumsiness of the translator that made the words sparkle on the page or fall flat. I then encountered a translation by Seidensticker. I savored the clear beauty of the words, memorized the unfamiliar name of the translator, and thought, "If I could do anything, *this* is what I would want to do." I didn't know if becoming a literary translator was possible, especially considering that I had been studying Japanese for only a year and a half. But I vowed I would give it a shot.

Seidensticker was teaching at the University of Michigan, which seemed like a good omen since I'd been born in Ann Arbor. I applied there early decision and never looked back. Robert H. Brower, my undergraduate advisor, encouraged me to immerse myself in English literature as well as in the study of all things Japanese—excellent advice, as the more one has read in English, the deeper the internal well of language and literature one has to draw on. I was fortunate to study classical Japanese with him in a class of only three or four students; I was the only undergraduate. He introduced me not just to *waka*, *zuihitsu* (literary jottings), *renga* (linked poetry), *monogatari* (extended prose narrative) and more but also to George Sansom's *Japan: A Short Cultural History* (1931), which filled in gaps in my knowledge. The Japanese language teachers I remember the most from intensive classes (Monday through Friday, two hours daily, one after breakfast and one after lunch) are Hiroko Quackenbush and Susumu Nagara.

Although I had gone to U of M expressly to study with Professor Seidensticker, in my junior year, 1968, when I finally could have taken his class in reading modern Japanese literature in the original, he went on sabbatical. That was also the year Kawabata Yasunari was awarded the Nobel Prize in Literature; Seidensticker was his main translator. The following year, Seidensticker returned to Ann Arbor, and

I finally (!) was able to take a class with him: a survey course on Japanese literature in translation. I remember that I wrote a paper for him on Mishima's *Confessions of a Mask*, and he gave it an A. That was one of the most satisfying grades I have ever received in my life. I also remember my amazement when he mentioned to the class that lots of people were more qualified to teach a survey course than him, which I found hard to believe. The class was fun and challenging and over all too soon.

After graduating, I attended the Inter-University Center for Japanese Language Studies in Tokyo, then run by Ken Butler, and to my delight found myself turning into an actual speaker of Japanese, not just a student of the language, over the course of the year. My reading ability also zoomed. For the first time, I started reading Japanese literature not as homework but on my own for pleasure.[2]

Due to a mix-up, my letter accepting an MA fellowship from the U of M didn't reach the department in time, and the fellowship went to someone else. What seemed like a disaster turned out to be the best thing that could have happened to me. I stayed on in Tokyo for another two years, cementing and expanding my Japanese ability, and I got some writing chops working for Thomas Elliott as an assistant editor and translator for the Toyota corporation's quarterly review, *The Wheel Extended* (published 1971–1997). Learning to translate professionally, not merely to dabble, was invaluable. I learned the importance of observing deadlines; of immersing yourself in books and articles about a topic in order to absorb the vocabulary and thinking of people in the know; of reading between the lines and not translating merely the surface of the Japanese; and of maintaining the highest possible standards, of always doing no less than your very best.

As it happened, it was Seidensticker who encouraged me to resume my academic career. I met him for coffee in the lobby of the Imperial Hotel, showed him a book I had been working on, and was delighted to receive his assurance that, despite having taken away my fellowship two years before, the Department of Far Eastern Languages and Literatures would welcome me back. Bob Borgen, a fellow member of the IUC class of 1969, also encouraged me to return—and so I did, blithely thinking, "*Now* I can really delve into Japanese literature."

What awaited me was two years of immersion in Chinese. Passing the French language requirement was easy because I had taken French classes every year of school since fourth grade, but Chinese was terra incognita. I had to learn both modern Mandarin and classical Chinese, while taking Seidensticker's *The Tale of Genji* seminar and classes with Bill Sibley, my thesis advisor, who shepherded me through an annotated translation of selected portions of Higuchi Ichiyō's diary. Those were heady, exciting years.

Figure 27.1: Juliet Winters Carpenter in James-kan at the Imadegawa Campus of Doshisha Women's College, 2019. Photograph by Yamamoto Tetsuji, courtesy of the author.

Why not do my MA under Seidensticker, you ask? It may seem odd, but after all this time, just when I had the chance to work closely with him, I was somehow stricken with shyness. Also, I was genuinely interested in Meiji literature. Nevertheless, I remained on good terms with the great sensei, and, later on in Japan, our paths crossed repeatedly. Over twenty years ago, he recommended me to translate a book on Pure Land Buddhism and the teachings of Shinran, which I did under his general supervision.[3] That was one of many times that the universe has brought me full circle. I am proud of that book by Kentetsu Takamori, Akehashi Daiji, and Itō Kentarō, *You Were Born for a Reason: The Real Purpose in Life*, and grateful for the excuse it provided to spend hours in that lovely man's company, often just drinking beer or telling stories over lunch in his favorite restaurant by Shinobazu Pond.[4]

In 1978, thirteen years after my awakening in the ETHS library, I had the opportunity to make good on that vow to pursue literary translation. My husband Bruce and I had moved to Ikoma in Nara Prefecture, and I was working on a dissertation on Izumi Kyōka when I received a letter from Knopf.[5] Abe Kōbō was looking for a new translator. Sibley, Brower, and Seidensticker had all recommended me. Would I be interested in translating Abe's new novel? Would I ever! I submitted a sample, and it was accepted. Charles Elliot at Knopf gave me six months to finish the translation. I dropped my dissertation and devoted myself to Abe, an author I had always liked. I paced myself by translating four pages of the original every day, practicing *koto* and *shamisen* in between. Bruce read every word I wrote and offered candid, helpful advice and encouragement. To this day, I find it amazing that my first-ever project was a book by a perennial Nobel Prize candidate. On top of that, the Japan-US Friendship Commission Prize for the Translation of Japanese Literature had just been inaugurated, and the 1980 prize went to my debut translation, *Secret Rendezvous*.[6]

I became a mother and a published translator at about the same time. Other babies and other translations quickly followed. *Masks* by Enchi Fumiko was the perfect foil to *Secret Rendezvous*: the latter was absurdist and concerned with male sexuality, the former was a modern story with traditional roots in classical poetry and *The Tale of Genji*, concerned with female sexuality. This time, Charles Elliott, my editor at Knopf, rejected my first draft and invited me to try again. I completely redid the translation while coping with fussy babies, and the revamped version was accepted.[7] Following so closely on the accolades I had received for the Abe book, this humbling experience taught me a great lesson. *Masks* and *Secret Rendezvous* both remain in print and continue to bring in small royalties.[8]

With those two major works to recommend me, when my youngest was three, I became a full-time instructor at Doshisha Women's College of Liberal Arts, where I stayed for over thirty years until my retirement in 2019 as professor emerita. My teaching career was fulfilling, and I have wonderful memories of sharing with students the joys and challenges of translation, which we approached through film subtitles and a variety of other genres. I feel lucky that my three careers—wife and mother, translator, and professor—dovetailed so neatly and that I was able to serve as a role model for my students. Having been inspired and mentored exclusively by men myself, it was wonderful to teach in a women's college and help educate other women to pursue their dreams.

Thirty years after graduating from ETHS, I was invited back to speak to the students studying Japanese about my translation of Tawara Machi's modern tanka collection, *Salad Anniversary*.[9] My life has come full circle.

Notes

[1] My interest in Japan dates from five years earlier; I first visited Japan on a trip with my father in March 1960, just after the birth of Emperor Hirohito's first grandchild, the current emperor. I began studying Japanese in the summer of 1964.

[2] The first work of Japanese literature I ever read in the original purely for pleasure was *No Longer Human* (*Ningen shikkaku*) by Dazai Osamu, in 1970.

[3] Kentetsu Takamori, *Unlocking Tannisho: Shinran's Words on the Pure Land*, translated by Juliet Winters Carpenter (Ashland, OH: Ichimannendo Publishing, 2011).

[4] Kentetsu Takamori, Akehashi Daiji, and Itō Kentarō, *You Were Born for a Reason: The Real Purpose of Life*, translated by Juliet Winters Carpenter (Ashland, OH: Ichimannendo Publishing, 2007).

[5] Decades after working on Izumi Kyōka in graduate school, in 2010, I was given the opportunity to join professional actors onstage in a theatrical reading (*yomishibai*) of his masterpiece, *The Song Lantern* (*Uta Andon*), in Kyoto.

[6] Abe Kōbō, *Secret Rendezvous*, translated by Juliet Winters Carpenter (New York: Alfred A. Knopf, 1980).

[7] Enchi Fumiko, *Masks*, translated by Juliet Winters Carpenter (New York: Alfred A. Knopf, 1983).

[8] Among the most rewarding of the book translations I have done are the four made in close collaboration with author Mizumura Minae (a fifth is underway). It has been a joy and privilege to pick her brain and observe close up how she comes at both languages, Japanese and English, and what the acts of writing and translating mean to her. These books include Mizumura Minae, *A True Novel*, translated by Juliet Winters Carpenter (New York: Other Press, 2013); and *An I-Novel*, translated by Juliet Winters Carpenter (New York: Columbia University Press, 2021).

[9] Tawara Machi, *Salad Anniversary*, translated by Juliet Winters Carpenter (Tokyo: Kodansha International, 1990).

28

STILL ON THE WAY

Eleanor Kerkham

Japan? Well . . . I remembered the garden-enclosed house and the beautiful bowls and said okay.

ELEANOR KERKHAM is associate professor emerita of Japanese literature at the University of Maryland. Her publications include studies on Matsuo Bashō's poetry and travel literature and Tamura Taijirō's stories about war.

Lawton, Oklahoma: Soldiers and Yoga

My first inklings of Japan came at about the age of four, with images of my mother greeting the mailman each day, fearful that my father would be drafted. It turned out that my dad, with three children and a milk business, was not chosen, while his brother, who was also his business partner (no children), went off to the Navy, along with our family doctor across the street. Both returned. Then there were the picture show's frightening newsreels—or were they cartoons?—showing scary Japanese soldiers. And finally, a favorite uncle joined the Marines and came back with stories of fighting in the Philippines—one of hiding under a jeep from a Japanese patrol. Army kids and their families came and went from Fort Sill, the large military base next to my Oklahoma town. Another uncle went to Occupied Japan with General MacArthur's troops. His wife followed soon after, and there were letters describing a beautiful garden-enclosed house in Tokyo, very polite people, and pleas to send my father's winter suits, which she traded for two precious bowls. (Desperate families having to sell their treasures? Or bargains on the black market?)

My actual journey toward Japanese Studies began indirectly one day in high school. We had just moved into a new school building near my home, and I decided on a whim to go home for lunch. There, I found my mother (the daughter of a Methodist preacher) practicing exercises from a little gray book, *An Introduction to Yoga*. I lay down beside her. We eventually read the book together, learning to do its exercises. Curious about the Indian exercise program, I chose to write about philosophical yoga in a term paper for freshman English at Pomona College. My hair stood on end when I started reading; an abiding interest in Asian philosophies and religions had begun. I was a premed major for my first two years and taking, but not enjoying, the required courses. In 1958, there was nothing at Pomona on India, but, sophomore year, I found a course on Chinese thought. My heart leapt as our professor lectured on the Daoist classic, the *Zhuangzi*. He made a gesture I'd never seen a man make before. It was an innocent, spontaneous movement, and it suddenly opened for me a new, unexpected way people could be. That week I asked the professor, Dr. Chen Shou-Yi, and the school office to change my major. There were other equally illogical reasons for abandoning my life's dream of becoming a doctor: the smell of formaldehyde in zoology class and unwanted pressures from my physics lab instructor. The Pomona Asian Studies major was broad and, in addition to Chinese poetry, included history and thought. Students could take courses at the Claremont Graduate University on anything related to Asia. I remember a fascinating class on farming in Bangladesh. I wanted to spend my junior year in India, but, because Dr. Chen could not find a suitable school for me, he recommended International Christian University in Japan. Japan? Well ... I remembered the garden-enclosed house and the beautiful bowls and said okay.

The summer before leaving, I enrolled in a three-credit Japanese conversation course at the University of California, Berkeley. It was presented by a totally uninterested instructor who read the day's conversation. The course was so easy that I thought by the end that I knew pretty much all the Japanese I would need! The ocean voyage from Seattle on the tiny *Hikawa Maru* was an adventure, with high seas at times, and, in the lowest level were students, disapproving missionaries, and a Catholic priest in the bar every night sharing his huge bottle of sake with those who could drink or dance. I had no idea how I was going to find ICU upon landing, but a professor's wife was there in Yokohama to drive three of us to Mitaka.

International Christian University

Because I knew almost nothing about Japan—its people, its history, even World War II, or the thirteen years since 1945—the drive in 1958 seemed both forlorn and wonderous. On one of the first days in the school dining hall (all the new Americans had gathered at one table), an older student, Tom, suggested that we climb Mount Fuji that night. We would arrive at the summit by sunrise. Most of us said yes. I went to my dorm, dressed for the climb, and set out. When I arrived at the meeting place, only Tom was there. Thomas Elliot (see chapter 27)—who later became a translator, poet, owner of a successful translation company connected to Toyota in Tokyo, and a translation professor at the Inter-University Center for Japanese Language Studies—had been a soldier in Japan, had climbed Mount Fuji off season, and knew the train system. The mountain, surrounded that night by gorgeous clouds, thunder, lightning, and rain all around, was truly magnificent. I thought that if I got to the top, I would be able to do anything. Three Japanese workers in the weather station on the summit gave us warm Calpis milk drinks and a lesson on how to slide down the mountain's back side. When I returned to ICU, I was in big trouble for leaving. Fortunately, I had the most understanding dorm mother and student leaders and only received a stern scolding.

The next day, I entered the ICU yearlong intensive Japanese language course. We used *Naganuma's Basic Japanese Course*, an oral learning method by Naganuma Naoe.[1] The instructors, young linguists who were experimenting with their own and other new language-learning materials, were excellent and seemed committed to teaching Japanese to a disparate group of American and Chinese students. We were fortunate, for instance, to have Nobuko and Osamu Mizutani, who later published many Japanese language texts and tools, including the well-known and very useful *The Japan Times* daily column, "Nihongo Notes."[2] Karen Brazell—later Japanese literature professor and specialist on Noh drama at Cornell University (see chapter 10)—was in the class, as well as John David Rockefeller IV, also known as Jay Rockefeller. We all competed furiously—in class and on the football field—and we worked very hard. My plan was to stay just one semester in the Japanese language course and then take content courses in English with archeologist Dr. Edward Kidder and other well-known scholars teaching at ICU at the time. My classmates, however, wouldn't let me leave, and I continued studying language all year. The course was so demanding that I hardly had time to go beyond the campus except to take bike rides in the countryside, participate in the ICU tennis club, and take occasional Sunday trips to Shibuya. My near total ignorance of Japan and Japanese culture at the time was dramatized by the fact that, when Jay asked me if I wanted to play mixed doubles with the Japanese Crown Prince, Akihito, and his fiancé, Michiko, I said, "No, I'm too busy!"

New York City and Columbia University

When I returned to New York City where my mother was living, I realized that I had a year of intensive Japanese language training and nothing to go with it. So I delayed my return to California to enroll in Professor Donald Keene's classical

Japanese language and literature classes at Columbia. Dr. Keene was fascinating. In the English translation course, he lectured without a single note and had us read Arthur Waley's *The Tale of Genji* in a week. He brought goosebumps when he suddenly intoned lines from a comedic *kyōgen* play. I don't believe he ever once mentioned Buddhist or Daoist influences on Japanese literature, but his lectures were thrilling, and I imagined I saw Buddhist teachings in almost everything we read. Ichiro Shirato presented an imaginative advanced language course, allowing students (two) to choose topics for translation and discussion. I found very quickly that I was not ready for my first choice, Zen priest Eihei Dōgen's (1200–1250) masterwork *Shōbōgenzō* (*Treasury of the True Dharma Eye*), and settled instead on Japanese newspaper articles about Daisetsu (D. T.) Suzuki's "Zen boom" in the West.[3] When I returned to Pomona College, I was able to become part of the excitement the night Dr. Suzuki spoke on campus, moving me, my classmates, and our faculty, especially two young philosophy professors who engaged him heatedly on several basic human problems. My experiences at Columbia with Keene, Shirato, and others were pivotal in helping me to consider what to do with my ICU language training. In addition, Professor Shirato introduced me to a small Zen Buddhist temple for meditation practice, which allowed me to survive what was then a seriously polluted and loud New York City.

As it happened, my mother was subletting an apartment next to the well-known East-West Bookstore on Sixty-Second Street. It was there that I spent most of my spare time reading and, when possible, buying everything available on Japanese literature and language (there were not yet many translations or serious monographs). Two women sat in a small office located on a loft overlooking the room of books, attending their store. I tried to think of questions to ask them because one always came down to point me to all sorts of hard-to-find books on Japan. If only I had known that I was speaking with Ethel Weed (1906–1975), who was the Women's Information Officer in the Civil Information and Education Section (CI&E) during the Occupation.[4] I could have learned so much about her significant experiences and the role of Japanese women before and after World War II. Another unique chance missed!

Stanford in Tokyo and Palo Alto

When I returned to Pomona to complete my BA, Dr. Chen informed me of the new fellowships for Japanese language study through the National Defense Education Act and suggested that I apply to Stanford University. I did not have a specific professional ambition at the time but wanted very much to return to Japan. Stanford was initiating a new "Stanford in Japan" program, which later evolved into today's Inter-University Center for Japanese Language Studies. Our group flew to Japan together. After a stint in a YWCA, the women (more than half, I believe) were placed in with different Japanese host families. Our group included Ann (Lardner) Waswo and Byron Marshall, who both became historians of modern Japan. Byron brought his wife and baby. I remember Ann's dry sense of humor, laugh, and elegance.

Our group was told that we were part of an important educational experiment in language and cultural learning. Looking back, I can see that, although the actual language training was not systematically planned, the program offered unique opportunities and an invaluable twenty-month-stay in Tokyo. Well-known Japanese scholars, primarily in arts and humanities, lectured and taught classes. American scholars passing through Tokyo stopped by to speak about their own research and language-learning backgrounds. I only remember two courses: one on *The Tale of Genji*, taught by the brother of the Center's coordinator, Professor Hiroshi Miyaji, and another on author Akutagawa Ryūnosuke, which I was allowed to attend at the University of Tokyo.

While in Japan, I chose to research Noh drama. I lived in a medical doctor's house, which also included his clinic, near Shinjuku. I spent countless hours at a Noh theater located just three streetcar stops away, where several performances, both professional and amateur, were held each week. Professor Miyaji and the Stanford staff found for me a Noh flute master, and, for the short time in Tokyo, I was able to step into the world of Noh performance. Dr. Helen McCullough was my advisor. We seldom met, and I had no classes with her. But even with very little interaction, I was deeply inspired by my first female professor in Japanese literary studies and by the depth of her knowledge of difficult classical Japanese texts. (My previous female teachers all instructed language.) Several weeks before I was to return to Palo Alto for the fall semester, I handed Dr. William McCullough, head of the Center at the time, a draft of my introduction to and translation of one of five Noh plays featuring Heian-period poet Ono no Komachi, to give to his wife. Back at Stanford, I waited for a response, assuming that my work was so inaccurate that she did not know how to respond. Months later, because Dr. Donald Shively, chair of the Stanford program on East Asian Languages and Cultures, was on his way to the Tokyo Center, I asked him to inquire about my paper. It seems that Dr. McCullough had forgotten to hand it to his wife, and it was still deep in his desk drawer! Dr. Shively retrieved my translation and took over as my advisor, providing the critique and help I needed to complete an MA thesis.

Stanford course offerings were dreamlike and privileged: Professor Edward Seidensticker's survey course on Japanese literature in translation provided the detail and breadth I had not needed or wanted in my undergraduate course with Professor Keene, but which proved invaluable for my later teaching career when I had to come up with similar classes. His course on translating modern Japanese fiction was difficult, demanding, and full of practical advice. Dr. Shively's course on research methods stayed with me through years of research and writing.

While I enjoyed my seven years of studying Chinese language and literature—begun in Tokyo at a Confucian cultural center (where public lectures and classes about China were held) and continued as required courses through Stanford and Indiana Universities—I now wonder why Japanese literature majors were required to spend so much time studying Chinese. At the time, it seemed obvious and necessary to me, and I longed for more time with Chinese poetry. In addition, I did not question my own desire to make English literature a third subject area at Pomona, Stanford, and Indiana. The English literature professors and fellow students were always challenging and stimulating, and the classes added a more sophisticated understanding of literature. I marvel now at how quickly Japanese literature graduate students today seem to focus on narrower subject areas and spans of time, even as they dip into the most popular critical theories of the day, sometimes appearing to leave out actual literary texts. I chose to write my PhD dissertation on *renga* and *renku*, "serious and comic" linked verse, respectively. I hadn't previously studied either, but the little I had gleaned suggested that they were the poetic forms that most directly led practitioners (and readers, I thought) toward understanding and living basic Buddhist truths. Dr. Shively suggested that I investigate the life and work of *haikai* (linked verse) poet, Matsuo Bashō (1644–1694). I enjoyed everything I could find on Bashō, and I was especially happy to learn that he, too, had studied Chinese poetry and the *Zhuangzi*!

My years of National Defense Foreign Language Fellowship support ended, and I signed for the last time the required pledge stating that I planned to teach Japanese language in an American institution of higher learning. But I was struck by the fact that I was hardly qualified to do so. At the time, 1963, I assumed that I would marry a Japanese or Chinese Studies scholar and follow his career, quietly holding on to my own interests in the background. No matter what my plans were at that time, I was certain that I needed more training in Japanese language. Dr. Shively had informed me that Dr. Leon Zolbrod, a young, dynamic *haikai* specialist with a PhD from Columbia University, had been hired by Indiana University's Japanese literature program. So, I applied and drove from California to Indiana to work with him. When I arrived, I learned that Professor Zolbrod was on a yearlong leave in Japan. There were many required courses for the PhD, and I happily carried on with excellent Chinese and English literature courses. The visiting professor from Japan replacing Professor Zolbrod startled the only two female students in his graduate seminar with individual invitations to view "genuine Tokugawa woodblock prints" in his apartment. We both fortunately figured him out in time to escape, leaving his *shunga* (erotic prints) behind. We were harassed by him all year, but neither we nor the department administration (hearing only hints from us) knew what to do about the problem. I chose marriage as a path away from the professor, and my colleague left Indiana.

Professor Zolbrod extended his leave in Japan for a second year. This time, his replacement was a brilliant visiting professor from Kyoto University, who taught *The Tale of Genji* and other Heian classics. During my third year, once again, Professor Zolbrod did not appear; he had resigned his position in Indiana to remain in Japan. The third visiting professor's field was comparative literature, and his focus was Lafcadio Hearn and US-Japan literary relations. I dutifully attended his seminars, but I was finally assigned a dissertation advisor: Professor Toyoaki Uehara, head of the Japanese program and language-pedagogy specialist. Together, we read Bashō's *haibun* (poetic prose essays) and *kikōbun* (poetic travel literature). At Indiana, I also benefited from working with the university's Sanskrit and Tibetan specialist, Professor Friedrich Bischoff, and three Chinese literature graduate students on planning, editing, and launching a new Asia-focused literary journal, *The Tea Leaves*. This resulted in my first publication: a translation of Bashō's 1688 travel journal, *Oi no kobumi* (*Notes from a Traveler's Satchel*).[5]

Colby College: Dissertation versus Political Activism

My professors at Indiana were very good at helping their graduate students find jobs, and I didn't have to look long because the Japan Foundation had begun offering its institutional grants for the creation of faculty lines in Japanese Studies. First, I interviewed at the University of Tennessee and was startled to be asked what my husband was going to do. I had no idea what he was going to do in Tennessee and stumbled through the question. Professor Uehara informed me later that Tennessee thought I seemed too immature to handle the teaching job they had in mind and that they would not be able to find a role for Mr. Kerkham! It happens that Colby College was applying for Japan Foundation funds, and they did not ask about a husband. Colby did not receive the grant, but the language department chair and Colby's Japanese history professor, George Elison (known today as Jurgis Elisonas), managed to convince the administration of the importance of a Japanese language and literature position. And so I set out, sans husband, to a very pleasant spot, Waterville, Maine. We were soon able to implement a Japanese Studies major. We sent our majors to Waseda University and a variety of other established study abroad programs. When my now most well-known student, Larry Kominz (who made his career at Portland State University), returned to campus, he taught a group of students the art of Noh mask carving.

Colby students were well prepared for college; they worked hard, were smart, had time to study during the long Maine winters, and were a joy to teach. I learned a great deal from them about popular culture (the Stones, the Beatles, and Janis Joplin), which I had not had time for in graduate school. The teaching load was heavy and broad: I taught Japanese language courses, along with Japanese literature in translation, from the *Man'yōshū* to Mishima Yukio. It required continued wide-ranging reading and thinking about literature (just as in graduate school), and I thought it miraculous to be paid for doing what I wanted to do. I was unsuccessful at convincing a new department chair and the administration that I needed the help of a trained Japanese language instructor, particularly given the semi-intensive credit hours of first- and second-year Japanese. Instead, Colby offered to hire Japanese students who had graduated from Doshisha University with English majors to help drill students in class and to live and converse with them in the student dormitory. This arrangement ended up being more trouble than it was worth.

Because Colby was so geographically isolated, the university provided its faculty with generous professional development and program support that we could use to attend conferences, screen Japanese films, and sponsor speaker series. We were expected to teach a short "January program" every other year on any topic of our choice. For my first January program, I selected Japanese cinema and was given the funds to rent the films I needed. For my second and last program, I chose the second-wave feminist movement, which was flourishing at the time. This January program was followed by a semester-long course on "Women in American Society," which I cotaught with a colleague. We invited well-known, active feminist leaders from around the country to come speak with our students. Becoming politically active at Colby led to participation in demonstrations against a Maine shoe manufacturer for better pay for women workers, two trips to Washington, DC, to join anti-Vietnam War rallies, and calling the US Equal Employment Opportunity Commission (EEOC) to Colby to investigate and address the pay inequality for women workers. I soon found that my friends in the English Department, several of whom were members or "friends" of the Peoples Labor Party (PLP), had more time than I did to fight for such things, and I extracted myself, feeling somewhat guilty.

In the meantime, we had invited Dr. George Wilson, a specialist in Japanese history from Indiana University, to give a talk to students and the campus community. While at Colby, he told me about the new Indiana-Tenri University faculty exchange and development program. I applied and was accepted to spend a year in Tenri City, Nara Prefecture. There, I was able to work with a young *haibun* specialist, Professor Uetani Hajime, and to use the Tenri Library's *haikai* collection. This experience changed my professional life as I was introduced to major scholars, had access to an extensive Bashō bibliography, and began my participation in annual meetings of the Haibun Association (Haibun Gakkai), which were held at historical sites related to Bashō or *renga* and at special library collections. When I returned to Colby, the pressures of a heavy teaching load, the desire to stay involved politically, and the desire to show off in my dissertation all I had discovered about Bashō finally overwhelmed me, and I asked Professor Uehara about leaving Colby and returning to Tenri. He suggested that I was trying to say too much about Bashō's career in my dissertation and that I should not return to Tenri until I had completed my dissertation. I took his advice and spent the summer completing my dissertation, a critical study of Bashō's *Oku no hosomichi* (*Narrow Road to the North*).[6] After I graduated with my PhD, Professor Uehara found a way for me to return to Tenri.

Teaching at Tenri University

And so I left for Japan to teach advanced language and literature in the Tenri University English Department. Perhaps it is inaccurate to say I "taught literature" because, in my two literature courses, we read and discussed only one short novel and several poems by Maya Angelou, along with English translations of Akutagawa's short stories. Tenri students were well trained in English. Many were remarkable, especially the women who dared to speak in class and the men and women who were members of the more radical student clubs: for instance, the anti-emperor institution club (not its real name) or the club that worked with discriminated *burakumin* (historical outcast) groups living in Tenri. I biked early every morning to a Zen temple near Nara for *zazen* (seated Zen meditation) practice and, with two other bikers, made pilgrimages to many Buddhist temples in Nara, Osaka, and Kyoto. Professor Uehara's family was closely connected to the Tenri religion (Tenrikyō). Their churches were in Okayama Prefecture, which I visited several times. He asked me to follow the Tenrikyō tradition of listening to the Founding Lecture ten times and to learn the chants, *tai-chi*-like dances, and other Tenrikyō daily rituals performed by its believers. I reluctantly agreed but ended up enjoying and benefiting from my involvement with this interesting, relatively new religion and becoming inspired by the story of its female founder, Nakayama Miki (1798–1887). The Tenri University English Department's required, smoke-filled, faculty meetings were a revelation. I heard discussions about how Tenri's entrance exam was created and implemented, university faculty gossip, and considerations of student grades, backgrounds, and graduations. I was surprised in the last meeting I attended to hear the faculty discussing the failing grade of one of my students—a young man who was very unhappy, it seems, to have a female instructor. Although the student read nothing, wrote nothing, and said not a word in class, his grade was changed to a pass!

During the summer of 1976, after a year and a half at Tenri, two events propelled me toward a professional choice that I had been avoiding. The first occurred at a Noh performance in Nara. I found myself sitting behind Dr. Karen Brazell, who was carefully taking notes. We had not met since our ICU days (1958–1959), except in passing at the Association for Asian Studies conferences, but it seemed as if we had just said goodbye to one another in Mitaka. Before she even asked what I was doing, she said she had just received a notice from Dr. Marlene Mayo at the University of Maryland that a tenure-track position in

Japanese literature had unexpectedly become available. "You must apply," she said. "It is in the eastern part of the country, which I think you want, and it is a large state university, which, according to Marlene's notice, will probably be expanding its East Asia programs." Days later, again just as unexpectedly, I met Dr. Shively who had received the same notice. He asked, "What are you doing in Tenri? You were trained to teach Japanese literature, not English literature or Japanese literature in translation!" Perhaps karma was at work, or perhaps I knew all along that I shouldn't stay at Tenri, however much I loved living there. I decided to see whether I could find an acceptable replacement for my job. The following day, I met an acquaintance living near Nara who was considering going to an American graduate program in Japanese literature. She was interested in the Tenri position because it would give her time to think. The English Department was happy to hire her. She eventually went to Indiana University and studied with Japanese literature specialist, Dr. Kenneth Yasuda. She earned her degree and wrote on the Noh drama. I applied for the University of Maryland position. Two professors (Chinese history and Japan political science) passing through Tokyo interviewed me. Late in the summer of 1976, I headed to Maryland.

The University of Maryland

I entered an Oriental and Hebrew Program (as it was then called) in considerable turmoil and was told that I would need to reapply for the position. I was stunned but thought, I'm here, so I'll apply. A newly hired professor and chair of the Department of German and Slavic Studies was made our program's interim chair and head of a large search committee. I managed to avoid his advances, as did several secretaries in his own department, and was chosen again for the position. The offending professor moved on to another university. In chapter 5, Marlene discusses many of the struggles we faced in establishing Japanese Studies at the University of Maryland. To summarize, my main tasks included teaching Japanese to a growing number of students and creating a Japanese literature and language major using the university's resources, such as a well-equipped, well-funded language lab and the East Asia library that includes the Gordon W. Prange Collection.

Over the years, our Japanese language and literature faculty, student enrollments, and majors grew (second to Spanish at times), thanks to Japan's rapid economic growth, the large Korean population in the Maryland area, and the popularity of Japanese film and, later, popular culture. I was able to argue first for a language and linguistics tenure line; two full-time language instructors with job security followed. We were fortunate to have Dr. Thomas Rimer as our department chair for five years (1986–1991). But it took over twenty-five years before the university decreased the expected teaching loads for language and literature faculty from four to two and a half courses per semester. From the beginning, I was free to create new literature courses; these included "Japanese Women

Writers," "Buddhism and Japanese Literature," and my favorite, "Postwar Japan through Film and Fiction," cotaught with Marlene. We began teaching this course in the mid-1980s when students were thrilled to watch Japanese-language films on 16 mm projectors or on videocassettes shown with awkward equipment. Along with advanced Japanese and classical Japanese, I taught business Japanese. With help from a professor from the School of Business, I was able to institute a joint business-Japanese major track. Interest in this difficult double major lasted about as long as Japan's economic growth. In addition, I created my most challenging advanced language class, "Translating Diplomatic Japanese," with Professor Hideki Ohata from Waseda University, a visiting professor in the Political Science Department.

Looking back, it seems that certain challenges never really ended at Maryland as administrators and fundraisers came and went, and their interest in East Asia waxed and waned, depending often on whether money could be raised from Japanese sources or from American businesses. Our formal department designations periodically changed, and we collaborated with different programs through the years. Yet Japanese and other languages in the Oriental and Hebrew Program found their own department designations and remain vibrant at the University of Maryland (see chapter 5).

A Japanese Soldier's Fictional Memories

I became more closely involved with the Prange Collection in 1988 when Marlene alerted me to a novel by Tamura Taijirō (1911–1983) titled *Biography of a Prostitute* (*Shunpuden*). The novel had been censored in its entirety in 1947 by SCAP censors in the Press, Publications, and Broadcasting (PPB) unit of the Civil Censorship Detachment (CCD, 1945–1952). Although the reasons given for censoring the story changed several times, it is clear that SCAP did not want the story of young Korean women controlled by the Japanese military during the war to be published. In both the Prange and the National Records Center (Suitland, Maryland, now housed at the National Archives at College Park), I was able to find documentation of the complicated censorship process, a mimeographed copy of a stage play adaptation, copies of all of Tamura's literary works published during the Occupation, and numerous newspaper and journal articles by and about Tamura, calling him the postwar spokesperson for "literature of the flesh" (*nikutai bungaku*). My work on Tamura began before the Imperial Japanese Army's extensive, systematic use of "comfort women" (*ianfu*) gained international media attention in the mid-1990s. *Ianfu* were young women, primarily Korean, who were forced or tricked by procurers, parents, Japanese and Korean officials, brothel owners, and others to sexually service Japanese soldiers, most often in frontline fighting areas. Expanded awareness of the subject was due in large part to the work of women's groups in Korea and Japan who were able to link the subject of *ianfu* to high-level Japanese-Korean political relations.[7] In the original, uncensored *Biography of a Prostitute*, Tamura portrays the lives of three Korean *ianfu*, but, in his many subsequent published versions and in the stage play and two film adaptations— *Escape at Dawn* [*Akatsuki no dassō*], directed by Taniguchi Senkichi, 1950, and *Story of a Prostitute* [*Shunpuden*], directed by Suzuki Seijun, 1965)—the Korean women have been transformed into Japanese women working as prostitutes on the frontlines in northern China.[8]

In preparation for a two-day conference in 1992 at the University of Maryland on "War, Reconstruction, and Creativity, in East Asia, 1920–1960," organized by Marlene and Tom Rimer, I expanded my research on Tamura's career, his historical contexts, and other contemporary artistic depictions of *ianfu* during the Occupation and through the early 1960s. The 1992 conference resulted in the edited book, *War, Occupation, and Creativity: Japan and East Asia, 1920–1960*, and a chance to work more closely with Tom and Marlene.[9] I later translated and analyzed Tamura's novel *Locusts* (*Inago*, 1963, considered his masterpiece) and his short story "The Naked Woman Convoy" (*Rajo no iru tairetsu*, 1954), both set in war-torn China toward the end of the war. In "The Naked Woman Convoy," Tamura exposes the abuse of a Chinese woman and her mother by a Japanese military officer and ultimately by the other soldiers and the storyteller himself. In *Locusts*, Tamura returns to the setting of *Biography of a Prostitute*, dropping, this time, the plot of the love story and clearly identifying the group of now five *ianfu* as Korean women being transported through fighting areas, experiencing multiple gang rapes by Japanese troops and deadly attacks by Chinese village snipers and American planes before finally being delivered into a Japanese battlefront camp where lines of soldiers are waiting for their turns with the two women who survived the journey.

My interest in the war and Occupation was stimulated by other events held at the University of Maryland. The first was the forty-year memorial of Japan's postwar Constitution (1987), which included an exhibit featuring Prange Collection documents and photographs and a symposium featuring a keynote talk by Dr. Carol Gluck and a panel of the surviving authors of the original draft Constitution, including Charles Kades, Beate Sirota Gordon, and Joseph Gordon. I felt I was watching history, a chapter in the making of an important document. Most moving was the sight of the panelists, eight men and one woman, clustered around the exhibit, gesturing, pointing, laughing, and talking to one another about their shared memories. A second two-day conference commemorated the fiftieth anniversary of the end of the Asia-Pacific War (1995) and featured a keynote talk by historian John Dower (Massachusetts Institute of Technology) and a summation by Norma Field (University of Chicago). Talks, interspersed with oral histories, involved many prominent scholars as well as former US military and civilian personnel. We heard, for instance, the stories of a former mayor of College Park who had been an Army lieutenant in early Occupied Japan, a Dutch woman whose family was interned by the Japanese in Indonesia, and a retired Korean librarian who spoke of his love for a Japanese teacher (during the Japanese occupation of Korea) who inspired his lifelong love of Confucianism. I also fondly remember an Okinawan dance performance, at which the audience was asked to come on stage for a final communal folk dance. And finally, there was the screening of the documentary, *Go for Broke!* (Robert Pirosh, director, 1951), to a packed audience, who laughed and cried together while watching the story of Japanese American soldiers during World War II. Events such as these inspire students, scholars, and the surrounding communities; share information; broaden worldviews; and create powerful, long-lasting memories.

The "Bashō Boom"

The friendships and connections I made while working at Tenri University and living in the Kansai area provided many opportunities for research, lecturing, writing, fundraising, and publishing throughout my career. I was fortunate to have been part of a cultural and political phenomenon that Japanese media dubbed the "Bashō Boom," or widespread interest in Bashō's *Narrow Road to the North*. Several scholarly articles and cultural celebrations were planned starting in the mid-1980s for the 300th anniversary of Bashō's 1689 journey through Northern Japan. For example, local officials in towns or villages along Bashō's actual travel route celebrated the anniversary with publishing opportunities, lectures, conferences, symposia, dramatic and musical performances, radio and television presentations, dramas and documentaries, haiku contests, hikes, travel and pilgrimage opportunities, department store exhibits, and more.[10]

My experiences with the Bashō Boom began in October 1989 with an invitation from the Haibun Association to give the keynote address at their annual meeting in Tsuruoka, Yamagata Prefecture.[11] Just before the trip, I was asked to serve as the judge for two English-language haiku contests inspired by Bashō and sponsored by Japan Airlines. In addition, I gave a paper at a symposium in Sōka City, Saitama Prefecture, one of the first stops along Bashō's historical route.[12] There, I found myself onstage with Professor Zolbrod. I was able to finally scold him for causing me to wait in vain for him for three years at Indiana University. He was surprised and amused, and we exchanged many *haikai*-related stories.

The following summer, I was invited back to Yamagata Prefecture, where Bashō and his disciple and travel companion, Kawai Sora (1649–1710), spent the longest time and composed the most poetry. While there, I was asked to speak on my relationship with Bashō's poetic travel account, this time to local audiences in Nishikawa and Haguro cities, the religious centers of the Three Sacred Mountains of Dewa (Mount Haguro, Mount Gassan, and Mount Yudono).[13] I was hosted by Mr. Hoshino Fumihiro, a Tsuruoka City official and Yamabushi priest, and stayed at his home and lodging for his Yamabushi followers, which led to the entrance to Mount Haguro. (Yamabushi are mountain ascetic hermits.)[14] He guided me along the paths of the Three Sacred Mountains of Dewa taken by Bashō and thousands of pilgrims throughout Japanese history. I walked the beautiful cryptomeria-lined steps of Mount Haguro and had audiences with the presiding Shinto priests at the shrines at the peak and foot of the mountain. The climb up Mount Gassan was far more strenuous. The tiny Shinto shrine on top was filled with more rugged, white-unformed pilgrims. Descending Mount Gassan requires use of a steel hanging ladder. After I arrived at Mount Yudono, with its hot springs bubbling over a gigantic rock (which is said to look like a pregnant woman), I was led into a rigorous, purifying waterfall. I had an informal talk with the main priest of the Yudono Shrine about the relationships between Yamabushi and Shinto. I had dinner and drank local sake with the priest and three shrine maidens (*miko*) who, after a day's work, had their hair in curlers. I was told that my tour was a small taste of the Haguro spiritual pilgrimage, or the week-long Yamabushi rebirth or rejuvenation workshop planned as a way to celebrate *Narrow Road to the North* and advertised throughout Japan. In addition, Mr. Hoshino took me on a tour of sites in Yamagata Prefecture, where Bashō composed some of his best-known *hokku* (first verse in linked verses) and participated in linked-verse sessions with local poets. Now major tourist attractions, these include the Ryūshakuji Temple, or Yamadera, where Buddhist nun and novelist, Jakuchō Setōuchi (1922–2021), was given a small home attached to the temple, and the house of the merchant Seifū in Obanazawa. Our tour ended at the so-called border-guard hut (*hōjin no ie*) where Bashō and Sora spent three days waiting for a storm to pass.

Not long after my search for Bashō and Sora in Yamagata, I fundraised to invite Mr. Hoshino to the University of Maryland. His lively demonstrations of Yamabushi rituals, steeped in martial arts and accompanied by the eerie sound of the Yamabushi conch, thrilled a large audience of students and faculty. Mr. Hoshino attracted a large crowd as he walked across Maryland's large campus in his mountain priest clothing, sounding his conch. He had brought for me a white Yamabushi pilgrim outfit, which he insisted I wear as we walked together. Mr. Hoshino and another Yamagata official came to help plan a later scholarly discussion on Yamabushi, including a Yamabushi evening performance and a documentary on Yamabushi history.

I participated in other commemorative activities in Japan that were organized by both local officials and individual citizens. They can be read as a part of a larger effort to glean hints from Bashō's life experiences, literary texts, and way of thought on how to structure one's own life journeys, learn from people whose paths cross our own, and spend one's leisure time more creatively. During my visits, I encountered Professor Matsuda Yoshiyuki of Tsukuba University, who specialized in leisure, travel, and recreation. He advocated the belief that people could take "enlightened travel," capturing the spirit of journeys like Bashō's and applying it to different contexts. He also introduced me to Yamagata-native Mori Atsushi's (1912–1992) 1974 Akutagawa Prize-winning novel, *Moon Mountain* (*Gassan*), and his *And Me Once Again on the Narrow Road to the North* (*Ware mo mata Oku no hosomichi*, 1988). At his suggestion, I presented my analysis of Mori's works at a seminar sponsored by the Leisure Development Center and Tokyo Women's University, held in Tokyo on November 3, 1989.[15] Mr. Hoshino and Professor Matsuda asked me to speak at an international symposium held at the newly opened Edo-Tokyo Museum in Tokyo in July 1993 in honor of the 1,400th anniversary of the founding of the Dewa Sanzan Shugendō (Religious Discipline of the Three Sacred Mountains of Dewa) and of Bashō's relationship to Yamagata. Escalating in 1994, more commemorative events were held to celebrate the 350th anniversary of Bashō's birth (1644) and the 300th anniversary of his death (1694) and of his completion of *Narrow Road to the North*. Most important for me were the scholarly conferences and exhibits and the publication of catalogs of *haikai* collections, reprints of manuscripts and *haiga* (haiku paintings), and new Bashō studies. I fundraised to hold a conference on "Matsuo Bashō, Commemorating the 300th and 350th Anniversaries of Japan's Master Poet," at the University of Maryland (November 4–5, 1994) to discuss with around twenty Japanese and American Bashō and *haikai* scholars some topics that I had not understood or learned enough about during my years of Bashō research. The conference resulted in an edited book of eleven essays.[16]

I seem to have ended as I began, with art from Japan—my mother's beautiful bowl and Bashō's *Narrow Road to the North* and *haikai*—and a Japanese soldier in World War II (Tamura Taijirō). My passion for a way of life influenced by Buddhism and Daoism continues with research and a Korean *tai-chi-kigong*-yoga exercise system, which emphasizes in physical ways something favorite Buddhist and Daoist classics only hinted at—brain and body integration. My advice to people entering the field is simple and is shared with my colleagues who spend time in Japan: go to Japan as often as you can and stay in touch with the friends you meet there and on your other travels.

Notes

[1] Naganuma Naoe, *Naganuma's Basic Japanese Course* (Tokyo: Kaitakusha Publishing, 1950).

[2] See, for example, Osamu Mizutani and Nobuko Mizutani, *Nihongo Notes*, vols. 1–10 (Tokyo: The Japan Times, 1992–1993); *An Introduction to Modern Japanese* (Tokyo: The Japan Times, 1977).

[3] Daisetsu (D. T.) Suzuki (1870-1966) was a Japanese American Buddhist monk, religious scholar, and author of many books on Zen Buddhism. See, for example, D. T. Suzuki, *Zen Buddhism: Selected Writings of D. T. Suzuki* (New York: Doubleday, 1956).

[4] See Malia McAndrew, "Ethel Weed through Her Letters: The Personal Reflections of a Woman in the US Occupation of Japan," *US-Japan Women's Journal* 55/56 (2019): 108-127.

[5] Eleanor Kerkham, "*Notes from the Traveler's Satchel*: An Annotated Translation of Matsuo Bashō's *Oi no kobumi*," *The Tea Leaves* 2 (Autumn 1965) 26-46.

[6] *Narrow Road to the North*, completed in 1694, is Bashō's poetic narrative of a journey he and his disciple, Kawai Sora, made through Northern Japan from spring to late autumn, 1689.

[7] For a detailed chronology of events and publications covering the period from January 1990 to December 1996, see Asian Women's Fund, *Ianfu kankei bunken mokuroku* (Bibliography of Publications on the Comfort Women Issue) (Tokyo: Gyōsei, 1997), 207-227. The bibliography includes Japanese, Korean, and Chinese monographs, articles, reports, and book reviews written on the subject.

[8] See Eleanor Kerkham, "Censoring Tamura Taijirō's *Biography of a Prostitute* (*Shunpuden*)," in *Negotiating Censorship in Modern Japan,* edited by Rachael Hutchinson (London: Routledge, 2013), 153-175.

[9] Eleanor Kerkham, "Pleading for the Body: Tamura Taijirō's 1947 Korean 'Comfort Woman' Novel, *Biography of a Prostitute*," In *War, Occupation, and Creativity: Japan and East Asia, 1920-1960*, edited by Marlene J. Mayo, J. Thomas Rimer with Eleanor Kerkham (Honolulu: University of Hawai'i Press, 2001), 310-359.

[10] Ogata Tsutomu suggests that some events staged in 1988—including the memorial celebration at the Mitsukoshi department store in Sendai; a summit on the *Narrow Road to the North* held in Ōgaki, the final stop on the journey; and the publication of dedicated sections on Bashō in daily newspapers, general interest magazines, and specialized journals—can be viewed as encouraging interest in the Japanese government's official policies on "Revival of Villages" (*mura-okoshi*) and "Revival of Rural Areas" (*chihō-okoshi*). See Ogata Tsutomu, "Oku no hosomichi sanbyakunen" (*Oku no hosomichi*, Three Hundred Years), *Bungaku* 5, no. 56 (May 1988), 1-9.

[11] My talk was published as Eleanor Kerkham, "*Oku no hosomichi* no kozo to sono kuraimakkusu" (*Narrow Road to the North*'s Structural Peaks), in *Dewasanzan to Nihonjin no seishinbunka: Kakō genzai, soshite mirai . . .* (The Three Sacred Mountains of Dewa and Japanese Spiritual Culture: Past, Present, and Future . . .), edited by Matsuda Yoshiyuki (Tokyo: Pelican Press, 1994), 104-110.

[12] Eleanor Kerkham, "Close Encounters with a Classic," *Proceedings for the Second International Symposium on Oku no hosomichi* (Sōka City: Gyosei Press, 1990), 44-50.

[13] Eleanor Kerkham, "*Oku no hosomichi* to watakushi" (*Narrow Road to the North* and Myself), *Loisir* (Leisure Development Center Monthly) March 1989, 30-33.

[14] For information about Yamabushi, see "The Yamabushi: The Holy Men of Shugendō," KCP International, November 28, 2019, https://www.kcpinternational.com/2019/11/yamabushi/.

[15] The symposium was the second of a series of four presented in four different locations sponsored by Yamagata Prefecture, Tsuruoka City, Haguro town, and the Ideha Museum. The overall theme of the series was "The Three Sacred Mountains of Dewa and Japanese Spiritual Culture: Past, Present, and Future." The series resulted in a monograph by the same name. See Eleanor Kerkham, "*Oku no hosomichi* no kozo to sono kuraimakkusu."

[16] Eleanor Kerkham, ed., *Matsuo Bashō's Poetic Spaces: Exploring Haikai Intersections* (New York: Palgrave Macmillan, 2006). The monograph is dedicated to Professors Earl Miner and Leon Zolbrod, two scholars whose work I had hoped to include.

29

Growing Up, or How I Learned to Be a Japanese Studies Librarian

Kristina Kade Troost

Our careers don't necessarily take us where we think they will. I learned how to read critically, ask questions, and make an argument from doing a PhD, skills that served me well in my job as a librarian.

KRISTINA TROOST received her BA from Carleton College and her PhD in history and East Asian Languages from Harvard University. She was the Japanese Studies Librarian and Head of International and Area Studies at Duke University and served as the Director of Graduate Studies for Duke's MA program in East Asian Studies for many years before retiring in 2020. Her professional service includes serving as the Chair of North American Coordinating Council on Japanese Library Resources (NCC, 1998-2000) and President of the Council for East Asian Libraries (CEAL, 2008-2010). She was the inaugural recipient of CEAL's Distinguished Service Award (2020). Her publications include a chapter drawn from her dissertation on medieval common property in *The Origins of Japan's Medieval World: Courtiers, Clerics, Warriors, and Peasants in the Fourteenth Century* (edited by Jeffrey P. Mass, 1998) and a chapter on Duke's East Asian Collection in *Collecting Asia: East Asian Libraries in North America, 1868-2008* (edited by Peter X. Zhou, Association for Asian Studies, 2010). She is a founding member of the Queer Japan Web Archive.

Figure 29.1: Kristina Kade with her host grandfather, Nakatsugawa Naokazu, Hōryūji Temple, October 1970. Photograph courtesy of the author.

They say hindsight is twenty-twenty, so looking back, I should have been able to predict that I would become a Japanese Studies librarian. Not so, I think. So much was happenstance, or at least so it seems to me. I grew up in North America before Japan's economic miracle and the age of Japanese popular culture. I had no courses on world history, let alone Asian history, in high school. When I got to Carleton College in Northfield, Minnesota, I took a class in Chinese history because I thought China was too large a part of the world to know nothing about. Then, because I needed a class to fill an unusual scheduling niche, I took Japanese history. It was a better class, perhaps because it was the professor's own field and perhaps because it was easier to cover Japanese history in fifteen weeks than Chinese history. As a result, I took more classes on East Asia in religion and art history and decided I wanted to study abroad.

In those days, Americans could not go to mainland China, but we could go to Japan, and Carleton College had a long-standing program there. I went to

Japan in the summer and fall of 1970. Most of my time was spent in Kyoto; I lived with a wonderful host family, the Nakatsugawas. My host grandfather (figure 29.1), whose classes in medical school at Kyoto University in the early twentieth century were taught in German, was the most comfortable member of the family in speaking English, and he took me under his wing. He was deeply interested in Japanese art and architecture and shared his knowledge with me, taking me on excursions to numerous temples and shrines every weekend. But it was only after I returned to America, and found adjusting to life in the United States more difficult than adjusting to life in Japan had been, that I realized that Japan had become an important part of who I am and a part that I wanted to maintain and strengthen.

Likewise, studying to be a historian came gradually. I had always done better in the sciences than in the humanities and took "Introduction to Biology" in the fall term of my freshman year. Over the next three years, my intellectual path changed, and I took many classes in sociology and history and realized that I am a historian. While I like to see the big picture, and while sociological theory is useful for framing my argument, I start with the nitty-gritty of history and hunt for patterns to come up with plausible, defensible generalizations rather than starting with theory and finding evidence to test it.

Fast forward to a PhD program at Harvard in Japanese history. While I had no idea about what sort of career I would pursue when I started at Carleton, by the time I entered Harvard, my goal was to teach at a place like Carleton that values teaching. I chose to study a problem in medieval Japanese history because I wanted to avoid World War II and revisiting well-researched topics. My choice was undoubtedly influenced by the fact that I had enjoyed studying rural societies in medieval Europe and early modern China, as well as the fact that my generation pursued social and economic history more than the previous generation.

I learned as much, if not more, from my fellow graduate students as from my professors. Harvard, in those days, struck me as a "sink or swim institution." The resources were there, and one was surrounded by brilliant fellow students, but the faculty did not actively engage with their students' research topics. Patricia Sippel taught me a lot about writing and being broadly curious.[1] Wayne Farris suggested a collection of medieval documents from Suganoura in Ōmi that was famous for laws (*okite*) asserting its status as a self-governing village (*sō*); these documents formed the initial basis for my dissertation.[2] I learned how to read scholarly books and articles critically and quickly. I also learned about cooking, Chinese food, and community building from Alice Valentine, Corky White (chapter 21), Bob Entenmann, Tim Bradstock, and Kent Guy, skills that I took with me when I started at Duke. Both Don Shively and Al Craig supported me through some rough personal times; in other words, the faculty, even if they seemed aloof at times, were there when I needed them. More importantly, for my dissertation,

Figure 29.2: Professor Watanabe Norifumi with Kristina Troost in his office, Hiroshima University, School of Integrated Arts and Sciences, summer of 1980. Photograph courtesy of the author.

through Harvard's multiplicity of connections, I received an introduction to Professor Nagahara Keiji at Hitotsubashi University, an eminent historian of Japan's medieval social and economic history who welcomed foreign students into his seminar.[3]

In 1977, we moved to Raleigh for my husband to take a job at North Carolina State University (NCSU). The move challenged, and ultimately strengthened, my goals. Although I was separated from my graduate student cohort, I joined a community of Japan scholars at Duke, the University of North Carolina-Chapel Hill (UNC-CH), and NCSU through the Triangle East Asia Colloquium. There, I presented the seminar paper I wrote on Suganoura and met Jim White and Meg McKean (chapter 23).[4] I learned that in order to keep people's interest in something as "obscure" as medieval village society, I needed to explain what makes these issues important for understanding the evolution of medieval society and how they are relevant to the problems of the current day.

My husband, Kay, and I went to Japan in March 1980. Kay had a Fulbright Fellowship to teach American society at Hiroshima University and Hiroshima Shūdō University, and I was planning to work on my dissertation. Shortly after our arrival, Professor Watanabe Norifumi (figure 29.2) at the Hiroshima University School of Integrated Arts and Sciences (Sōgō Kagakubu) invited me to join his seminar reading the documents from Yugenoshima no shō, an estate which illustrates the political, social, and economic changes of the Kamakura period.[5] I learned to read documents and walk the land. One of the highlights of his seminar was a trip to the salt-producing estate on Yugenoshima in the Inland Sea. I learned about different methods of making salt, and we worked to place the locations mentioned in documents; in other words, I was learning how to do research in local history.

A year later, Kay returned to the States, and I moved to Tokyo, where Professor Nagahara had invited me to join his seminar reading medieval Japanese documents. The seminar ran all afternoon, and we went out to eat (and drink) after in the nearby Kunitachi neighborhood. In addition to reading the documents of Ota no shō, a large, well-documented, fairly typical medieval estate in Bingo Province (today, the eastern part of Hiroshima Prefecture) managed by the Buddhist temple settlement on Mount Kōya, each of us presented our own research. Nagahara was insightful. His method was to ask presenters provocative questions that helped them to frame arguments and to view their research materials as more than collections of factoids. It was wonderful watching him train his students to be good historians and to benefit from his ability to see the question you were not asking.

Studying with Nagahara was formative for me in several ways: Nagahara assumed I was smart and serious, a new experience that put a different sort of pressure on me than I had experienced at Harvard, which was not nurturing of its graduate students and had created a climate of insecurity. I learned how history was practiced and how reading *Akahata* (*Red Flag*, the newspaper of the Japanese Communist Party), which did penetrating stories on the news of the day, encouraged a critical reading of history. Early on, Nagahara suggested examining the documents of the other well-known, self-governing village community, Imabori, to supplement my work on Suganoura.[6] He also assigned me a tutor, Kuramochi Shigehiro, whose interests overlapped mine and who was a good match in terms of personality.[7] Kuramochi, more than anyone, taught me how to read documents, to query each word for its text and subtext, and to assemble a picture of the community that produced the documents. He and his wife became my lifelong friends (figure 29.3).[8]

After two and a half years in Japan, I returned to the United States. I was seven months pregnant; my child was born in October, and, four years later, I had my second child. I would describe this time as my wandering-in-the-wilderness years. I taught at Duke one year after historian Tom Huber left; I supported my husband in his teaching and writing; I took care of my children and helped with another whose mother had committed suicide; but I did not make much progress on the dissertation. It was always at the back of my mind, percolating, but I did little writing. In the end, it was a more substantive dissertation because

Figure 29.3: Kristina Troost with Kuramochi Shigehiro and Kuramochi Yasuko in Tokyo, June 2019. Photograph courtesy of the author.

I did not write up my research as soon as I returned from Japan. Because of the encounters I had with people in the Triangle, instead of doing three village studies, my dissertation developed a novel argument about why some village communities became self-governing and how they had asserted control, and then ownership, over the resources held in common. These resources were often uncultivated lands or water for irrigation but were also fishing and commercial rights, as the examples of Suganoura and Imabori illustrate.

A few events and encounters made the difference in what the final product looked like. In 1985, I chaired the Triangle East Asia Colloquium. As chair, I got to choose the topics, so I organized an all-day conference on common property to learn what "mountains and fields" (*sanya*) meant in medieval Japanese documents. Did the term refer to a form of medieval common property? Or to the precursor to Tokugawa common property (*iriaichi*)? In preparation for the conference, Meg McKean explained to me the difference between open-access land; common property; private, individually owned property; and state-owned property. Understanding the difference between open-access and common land became fundamental to my dissertation.

I also read documents with Anne Walthall (chapter 25), who taught at Duke for a semester while Andrew Gordon, then the resident Japanese historian, was on leave. She came to my house, where we sat and read the documents together. It was much like what I had done with Kuramochi, except this time I had to translate the Japanese into English instead of modern Japanese. Using English words requires us to fully understand the meaning of the original Japanese words and thereby hone our thinking about them. I benefited from Anne's encouragement to focus and finish, as well as her treating me seriously and my topic as worthwhile. Anne and I became lifelong friends.

Finally, there was Conrad Totman, who was deeply interested in premodern social and economic and environmental history.[9] We became acquainted in 1978 when he was teaching at Northwestern and wrote a review essay in *The Journal of Asian Studies* critiquing several recent monographs in Japanese medieval institutional history.[10] I sent him my seminar paper on Suganoura, and he returned it marked in red ink, together with several typed pages of comments, identifying my contribution (or potential contribution) to the field and what arguments were not worth pursuing. We kept in touch thereafter, and he wrote periodically to nudge me to finish, stressing that my work was important and needed. Together with Professors Nagahara, Kuramochi, and McKean, he had the greatest influence on my work.

In time, I did indeed finish. As I was finishing, I mentioned to everyone I knew in the Triangle that I was looking for a job that would allow me to continue to work on Japan. Andrew Gordon, whom I had known from my Harvard days, said that there was a half-time job in the Duke University Libraries. I thought it would be great to rewrite my dissertation for publication while working in the library. I quickly learned that there is no such thing as a half-time job, just half-time pay. But the job introduced me to librarianship, and I learned that I enjoyed it as a profession. The profession was in the process of changing, and I had a great boss in Deborah Jakubs, who encouraged me to move beyond book selection, the task that traditional bibliographers focused on. Don Shively was supportive of my becoming a librarian at a time when most faculty wanted their students to follow in their footsteps. For the next two years, I taught half-time in the history department and worked half-time in the library; this convinced me that librarianship was my vocation. I enjoyed doing something different each day and always learning something new.

In sum, librarianship was not something I trained for, but it became something I embraced that motivated and satisfied me. My two years of teaching convinced me that librarianship was a better fit and more rewarding for me than becoming a professor would have been. I learned that I could make a bigger difference as a librarian than as a historian. So once again, happenstance played a role in the development of my career. Connections, timing, and the part-time nature of the library position meant that I got a job that I grew into, but it was not what I had planned. The library and the faculty took a risk and hired me despite my lack of training in librarianship and my specialization in medieval Japan. (Duke's program focused on the nineteenth and twentieth centuries.)

My timing was fortunate, and I could use the skills I had gained while researching and writing my dissertation. Libraries were transitioning to greater use of computers, and I was already comfortable using one. I had written my dissertation on a computer and had learned to program it to properly use macrons and to romanize Japanese language. I had been a remote scholar without access to any major research library and relied on interlibrary loan; this influenced my perspective on which materials to buy and which to borrow. I argued for the importance of meeting the needs of remote scholars, while developing services to support scholars based in the Southeast. In other words, East Asian librarianship was less technologically advanced than other areas of librarianship, but my facility with computers, combined with my research experiences, meant that I approached librarianship differently than more experienced bibliographers did and could move the field forward.

Moreover, I was the first Japanese Studies bibliographer hired at Duke. Although Duke already had about thirteen thousand volumes in Japanese, the faculty had no expectations of what a Japanese Studies librarian could do for them.[11] I was not trying to fill someone else's shoes. When the East Asia faculty approached the university and library administration about needing to build up the East Asian Collection before I was hired, they were listened to but not necessarily understood. I understood them; I was experiencing the same frustrations and could explain them to my fellow librarians. The faculty were supportive and appreciative of everything I did.

I was not hired with a charge of creating an East Asian Collection, but, even though I did not know it at the time, it was not happenstance that it was the first major thing I tackled. The faculty had long asked for a separate collection, and the library was thinking about renovations, and a separate East Asian Collection was in their tentative plans. Then Andrew Gordon got an outside offer from the University of California San Diego in the spring of 1991, and part of the agreement he negotiated to stay was the creation of a separate East Asian Collection sooner rather than later. That summer, I pulled all the books from the stacks. I worked with Meg McKean and Andrew Gordon to increase the materials budget that had not grown in a decade. I improved services by sending copies of the tables of contents of the Japanese journals received by Duke to faculty in the Triangle and throughout the Southeast.

Although early in my career, I had the opportunity to participate in the national conference held at the Hoover Institution at Stanford University in 1991 to strategize how to address problems confronting Japanese collections. The problems we discussed ranged from communicating amongst ourselves by email to collection development, retrospective conversion (the conversion of paper records from the card catalog into online, machine-readable records), training new librarians, and improving interlibrary loan. There, I met Amy Heinrich (chapter 15), who became a lifelong friend.[12] The conference led to my involvement with the National Planning Team, the predecessor of the North American Coordinating Council on Japanese Library Resources (NCC), which appointed me to the Subcommittee for Japan Foundation Library Programs.

Serving on the NCC Subcommittee for Japan Foundation Library Programs was the beginning of my active participation in national planning efforts and gave me an opportunity to take a leading role in rethinking old practices. I went to the Japan Foundation offices before our first meeting and reviewed prior grant applications. I read many proposals that had selected noteworthy books by reputable scholars, and I wondered why these libraries needed to collect monographs already widely held by other libraries in the United States. Monographs had become easier to identify and request through interlibrary loan because libraries were putting records for their collections online. As a result, I thought that we needed to look at collection development through new eyes, to see the collection in the United States as a national collection, and to target grant support to either (1) deepen existing collections of note or (2) support the growth of new collections without duplicating the monographic collections held by the major libraries. This recommendation was adopted by the Japan Foundation; a year later, not duplicating materials also became central to the "Multi-Volume Sets" proposal to the Japan-US Friendship Commission. Six years later, at the prodding of Karen Brazell, I served as the third chair of the NCC (1998–2000), organized the second-decade conference, and hired Victoria Bestor as the director, thus helping the NCC to identify its mission and create a structure that ensured its survival.[13] Then, from 2002 to 2008, I served on the American Advisory Committee to the Japan Foundation, before serving as President of the Council on East Asian Libraries (CEAL) from 2008 to 2010. All these activities gave me a chance to help American scholars find the information they needed, whether by training librarians or advocating for change in access to resources. They also benefited me as I worked with and learned from scholars researching Japan, including Beth Berry, Patricia Steinhoff, John Campbell, Steven Snyder, and Laura Hein, to name a few (chapters 11 and 12).

I learned librarianship by listening and doing. Opportunity provided the impetus. When I arrived, there were only the bare bones of a collection: twenty-three thousand volumes in Chinese and Japanese.[14] I was fortunate to meet experienced librarians who were generous with their knowledge. In the summer of 1991, I visited the Library of Congress and met former chief of the Asian division Warren Tsuneishi, who peppered me with questions that helped me to choose which issues to focus on; I learned the importance of listening and how to lead by watching him.

Early in my work as Japanese Studies librarian, I taught a course in research methods at the prompting of Andrew Gordon, as the students had asked him for such a course. The students came from many fields, including art history, cultural anthropology, history, library science, political science, religious studies, and the law school. This was before there were any electronic resources in Japanese, and many tasks that are easy now were challenging then. I covered how to find the correct reading of a name; how to search the print version of *Zasshi kiji sakuin* (the periodical index developed by the National Diet Library); how to learn about the history of a place or find a law; and why statistics might be useful in nonstatistical fields like art history. I also covered resources—journals, dictionaries, yearbooks—for the fields taught at Duke and invited the professors in these fields to join the class on their subject. A couple of them sat in on the whole course. Later, as electronic resources became readily available, I taught how to search them and how the structure of the Japanese written language facilitates Boolean searching. I developed new classes on software like ArcGIS and Simile.

I learned from teaching graduate students and helping them to find materials we did not have at Duke and from building collections to support both faculty and graduate students. While teaching, I discovered many holes in the collection: the collection had been built by the faculty to support their research and so was strong in some specific areas but lacked the scope to support a graduate program and was missing many key reference works. More recently, the emphasis on teaching with original materials has driven collection development and library instruction. Using original resources in instruction requires research to identify materials to purchase as well as to teach with them. Duke now has over 210,000 volumes in Chinese, Japanese, and Korean, plus electronic resources and materials held in Special Collections.[15]

Not long after I arrived, another opportunity presented itself. The Asian/Pacific Studies Institute at Duke decided to develop an MA program in East Asian Studies. I volunteered for the committee that drafted the proposal because I had positive experiences with Harvard's interdisciplinary MA program and thought it was a successful model. Circumstances resulted in my writing the final version that we submitted to the graduate school and, eventually, in my serving as director of graduate studies for eleven years. Once again, a need became an opportunity that shaped my career.

The library field has changed greatly since I began, although our fundamental premise, preserving and making accessible information and helping people to find it, has remained constant. I was hired as the Japanese Studies bibliographer, a title that was common in 1990 but is no longer in use. It has been replaced by Japanese Studies librarian. My two primary responsibilities were the selection of materials in Japanese for Duke, UNC-CH, and NCSU and the provision of reference support for those same faculty and students. My job when I retired continued to prioritize those two tasks.

The term "bibliographer" became dated in part because many people viewed it as only reviewing catalogs and selecting books. That task has become easier, not so much because of the internet but because the vendors for US libraries have gone to great lengths to make it easier, sending new book lists every month, introducing us to publishers of expensive sets to make sure that we do not miss something our users might need. Japanese Studies librarians are aware that our budgets do not allow us to build collections comprehensively; rather we must be selective, targeting our collections to the faculty and students we work with. At the same time, even though many books can travel through interlibrary loan, large sets do not travel easily, and, because not all are well indexed, a user cannot readily identify the volume(s) needed. As a result, the core task of the bibliographer, collection development and book selection, continues to be a crucial part of our job, requiring knowledge of the field and the program and the wisdom to know the difference.

Without question, the internet has made some parts of our tasks easier; no longer do we need to look through paper copies of *Zasshi kiji sakuin* or the print index to the *Asahi* newspaper to find relevant articles. With online catalogs and authority records, we can find how to romanize a name with the correct pronunciation more easily, and information about famous people is often available online. But being fluent in Japanese is not sufficient to make full use of library collections, whether in print or online, for students (and faculty) may not know the best place to search or how to make their searching effective. They do not necessarily know how to evaluate what they find—they cannot place it in context—and they do not know how to sift through and organize the large quantity of materials they unearth. Because many primary sources have not been digitized, print sources remain useful. The internet hides many things; the guides that we create make them easier to find. The materials we collect may have changed, and some of the technology we use to preserve materials is new as we are learning how to do web archiving to preserve online content. People use different strategies to find information—searching is more important and browsing less so, from what I have observed—and student knowledge of Japanese resources is different, but they still need the assistance of subject librarians who remain a fundamental part of the library.

I could not have done anything without the support, encouragement, and mentoring from many people, some in Japanese Studies, some not. I benefited from introductions to scholars, museums, and libraries from colleagues both in the United States and in Japan—it is possible to see much more with an introduction. Izumi Koide has been a friend and colleague from the 1980s; she is an insightful leader who knows both the Japanese and American library worlds and helps us navigate them. She mentored an NCSU librarian in 1981 at the International House Library, and, after I started working at Duke, we combined our resources to bring Izumi to the Triangle. She gave a talk to Duke's Librarians Assembly on the organization of Japanese information, spatially not alphabetically, that has stuck with me.[16] Since then, we have visited multiple libraries together, and, through her introductions, I have been included in special events.

I also learned from many colleagues in the United States. Kären Wigen was a colleague at Duke who became a friend, sharing her own life experiences as well as her scholarship. We started at Duke the same year and gave papers on common property at the first International Association for the Study of Common Property conference in 1990 (see chapter 23). She introduced her paper with a story on the commons shared by households on the hillsides of Berkeley; from her, I learned how to engage an audience and pull them into your argument.[17] Other Triangle faculty have played important roles in educating me and making me feel appreciated. I became a Japanese Studies librarian with a background in history, but I needed to select materials in literature, art history, religion, and political science. They taught me how their fields are structured and what resources are important to own; many have also become my friends.

In addition to Amy Heinrich mentioned above, three librarians have had a major influence on me. Ellen Hammond is a brilliant librarian and friend.[18] I was introduced to her by Laura Hein, I supported her in her move back to the United States, and I worked with her during her years at the University of Iowa and Yale University. We continue to talk about our research and our lives. Haruko Nakamura and I were paired by Vicky Bestor to room together at a workshop organized by the NCC. We stayed up all night talking and have since traveled together. She is a thoughtful librarian, always wanting to learn more and eager to take on new initiatives. Maureen Donovan (chapter 18) had served as a consultant for the Japanese collection at Duke before I was hired, and I contacted her after I read her report. Subsequently, I benefited greatly from picking her brain; she would mention things that took my thoughts in new and more productive directions.

Mentoring and teaching are opportunities for two-way learning. Not only do those I teach learn from me, but I also learn from them. I learned from the library school students who interned under me, most especially Katherine Matsuura, Alison Raab Labonte, Miree Ku, and Yoriko Dixon.[19] And I learned from the people I hired at Duke.[20] Being a boss can be challenging but rewarding, and they made it more rewarding than challenging.

As I look back on my career, I see my most important contributions as having mentored many people and having advocated for change at Duke, nationally and internationally, through groups like the NCC, CEAL, and International and Area Studies Collections in the 21st Century (IASC21). In addition to librarians at Duke and library school students now working elsewhere, I mentored a multitude of graduate and undergraduate students. Some even lived with me. As a result, I learned how to do research in Buddhist Studies and how to use realia in teaching, and I met their friends teaching at other institutions. I maintain ties to many of my former graduate students.

My role as a mentor was not happenstance; rather, it was something I learned at a young age. As early as fourth grade, the teacher would divide the class in two and have me work with half the class. I was the oldest of six children, and my parents traveled and left my siblings under my care. I went from a novice librarian to the head of a department of ten librarians, most of whom I hired. Additionally, my training as a professor and my teaching experience helped me in working with students. I understand the research process and how to ask significant research questions, conduct research both within the United States and internationally, and write a dissertation. While working on my dissertation, I lived in Japan for two and a half years, and I understand the stress involved in studying abroad. All these experiences aided me when I served as director of graduate studies and worked with diverse students.

Our careers don't necessarily take us where we think they will. I learned how to read critically, ask questions, and make an argument from doing a PhD, skills that served me well in my job as a librarian. We may not know what the future will bring. We may not know what new technologies we will need to learn or what will be ephemeral or transitional, but we need to be open to figuring out new ways of seeing and doing things. It is important to examine what we do and to find better ways of doing the tasks that remain important, even as we embrace new tasks that would have been unimaginable ten years ago. I strongly advocate listening to people, especially those who disagree with you: Although you may or may not change your proposal, both you and your proposal will become stronger. Happenstance or not, I have had an enjoyable career, and the people I worked with are a major reason for that.

Notes

[1] Patricia Sippel came from Australia and entered Harvard the same year I did. After completing her dissertation on Tokugawa land administration, she taught at Tōyō Eiwa University until 2020 and wrote about environmental history. For an overview of her

work, listen to "Episode 106–Dr. Patricia Sippel," *The Meiji at 150 Podcast*, April 26, 2019, https://meijiat150.podbean.com/e/episode-106-dr-patricia-sippel-toyo-eiwa/.

² Suganoura (also Sugaura) was a small village dating back to Heian times on the north shore of Lake Biwa opposite Chikubushima. Its inhabitants made their living largely through fishing and shipping and a few agricultural products. The documents were stored in the local shrine (*miyaza*) and were "discovered" by a scholar in 1917; they cover a dispute with a neighboring village, taxes inhabitants paid to their proprietors, and laws they wrote to regulate their own affairs. Shiga Daigaku Keizaigakubu Fuzoku Shiryōkan, eds., *Suganoura monjo* (Suganoura's Documents), 2 vols. (Hakone: Shiga Daigaku Nihon Keizai Bunka Kenkyūjo, 1960–1967).

³ Professor Nagahara was receptive to having foreign students in his seminar and was interested in encouraging debate. Unlike most professors of medieval Japanese history, his interests, like mine, spanned the period from the twelfth to the seventeenth centuries.

⁴ Both are political scientists interested in premodern Japan. James W. White has published widely on mass movements in Tokugawa and modern Japan. Margaret McKean, who has taught at Duke since 1974, was one of the first people I met when I moved to North Carolina. I remember her from the Southeast Conference of the Association of Asian Studies (SEC-AAS) when the annual meeting was held at UNC in 1982; we quickly discovered our overlapping scholarly interests in the management of common property. After I returned to North Carolina later that summer, we learned that we had overlapping due dates for our first children. I appreciate her for her wide-ranging interests and her willingness to help whenever needed.

⁵ The Sōgō Kagakubu was founded in 1974 and is therefore less bound by traditional hiring practices and subjects than more established schools. Because Kay's Fulbright appointment was in it, we met faculty from it.

⁶ These documents had recently been published in an authoritative edition: Nakamura Ken, ed., *Imabori Hiyoshi Jinja monjo shūsei* (Collected Documents of the Imabori Hiyoshi Shrine) (Tokyo: Yūzankaku, 1981). Other self-governing villages include Okujima, also in Ōmi Province, and Kokawadera Higashimura in Kii Province (covering part of present-day Wakayama and Mie Prefectures), but Suganoura and Imabori are the best known and best documented. Okujima's laws covered the management of fishing grounds and disputes over timber from forest land, and Kokawa Higashimura's laws concerned building ponds and the management of irrigation. Lee Butler's examination of Kujō Masamoto's diary about Hineno shō in Izumi Prefecture shows another aspect of village management. Lee Butler, "Four Years in Izumi: Village Japan in the Early Sixteenth Century," unpublished manuscript, April 2022.

⁷ Kuramochi Shigehiro taught medieval social and economic history at Rikkyō University from 1999 until he retired; CiNii lists twenty-nine books and fifty-one articles he either wrote or coauthored, largely on the formation of medieval villages. He once remarked to me that the medieval period is characterized by the right amount of documentary evidence, unlike the preceding period, where there is so little that you have to imagine what happened, and the later period, where there is so much that you cannot read all

of it. See, for example, Kuramochi Shigehiro, *Nihon chūsei sonrakushi no kenkyū* (Study of the History of Medieval Japanese Villages) (Tokyo: Azekura shobō, 1996); *Chūsei sonraku no keisei to mura shakai* (The Formation of Medieval Villages and Village Society) (Yoshikawa kōbunkan, 2007).

[8] Kuramochi Yasuko ran a nursery school (*hoikuen*) until she retired. When I last saw her in 2019, she was volunteering for a helpline for young adults.

[9] Conrad Totman earned his PhD from Harvard; he taught Japanese history at the University of California, Santa Barbara, Northwestern University, and Yale University before retiring in 1997. See, for example, Conrad Totman, *An Environmental History* (London: I. B. Tauris, 2014).

[10] Conrad Totman, "English-Language Studies of Medieval Japan: An Assessment," *Journal of Asian Studies* 38, no. 3 (1979), 541–551.

[11] For the statistics cited in this chapter, see Council on East Asian Libraries Statistics, *CEAL Statistics Database*, https://ceal.ku.edu (accessed June 27, 2022). Duke began to contribute statistics in 1964, when it reported 3,700 volumes in Chinese and 1,600 volumes in Japanese.

[12] Amy became the Head of the C. V. Starr East Asian Library at Columbia shortly thereafter and was asked to lead efforts that led to the establishment of the NCC. As we were both beginning our careers at the same time, we bonded on being outsiders to a close-knit group of Japanese Studies librarians (which we in time became full members of). We have roomed together at AAS annual meetings and have visited each other's homes.

[13] I hired Vicky at Patricia Steinhoff's recommendation, and she served as director from 1999 to 2017 and spearheaded such initiatives as the Junior Japanese Studies Librarians training project and a conference on copyright that resulted in the Image Use Protocol. She wrote grant proposals, provided continuity, and was central to NCC productivity. See North American Coordinating Council on Japanese Library Resources (NCC), "Japanese Library Studies Multimedia History Project: Full Interviews and Other Resources," *NCC Japan*, 2019, https://guides.nccjapan.org/multimediahistory/full_interviews.

[14] Council on East Asian Libraries Statistics.

[15] Ibid.

[16] For example, while states are usually listed alphabetically, from Alabama to Wyoming, in gazetteers, Japan lists its prefectures geographically from Hokkaido to Okinawa.

[17] See, for example, Kären Wigen, "The Geographic Imagination in Early Modern Japanese History: Retrospect and Prospect," *Journal of Asian Studies* 51, no. 1 (1992), 3–29.

[18] Ellen Hammond earned a BA from Oberlin College in 1977 and attended the successor to the Carleton program I attended, the Associated Kyoto Program. She then earned an MA in Japanese history with John Dower and an MLS at the University of Wisconsin-Madison. After living and working in Japan for over a decade, she returned to the United States and worked first at the University of Iowa as a Japanese Studies librarian and then at Yale as the Head of the East Asian Collection and Co-Director of the Department of

Area Studies and Humanities Research Support. After she retired in 2017, she returned to Japan, where she taught library science at Rikkyō University from 2018 to 2021.

[19] Katherine Matsuura works as the Japan Digital Scholarship Librarian in Harvard University's Fung Library, and Alison Raab Labonte works on the Library Infrastructure Team at the Federal Reserve Board. I still use the library guides that they created. Miree Ku has been Duke's Korean Studies librarian since 2007. Yoriko Dixon is an associate academic librarian and Japanese bibliographer at the University of Wisconsin-Madison.

[20] Most especially, Luo Zhou (Chinese Studies librarian), Sean Swanick (Middle East and Islamic Studies librarian), and Rachel Ariel (Jewish Studies librarian).

30

WITH A LOT OF HELP FROM MY FRIENDS

Helen Hardacre

When I first began researching and writing about Japanese religions, I would sometimes imagine the men who had been my graduate school teachers looking over my shoulder. Now, however, I find myself mentally turning to the women who have been my mentors, guides, and friends. Their image strengthens my resolve and determination and helps me preserve a sense of humor.

HELEN HARDACRE is the Reischauer Institute Professor of Japanese Religions and Society. Her research on religion focuses on the manner in which traditional doctrines and rituals are transformed and adapted in contemporary life. Her books include *Lay Buddhism in Contemporary Japan: Reiyūkai Kyōdan* (1984), *The Religion of Japan's Korean Minority: The Preservation of Ethnic Identity* (1984), *Kurozumikyō and the New Religions of Japan* (1986), *Shintō and the State, 1868–1988* (1991), *Marketing the Menacing Fetus in Japan* (1999), and *Shinto: A History* (2016).

The women who have influenced me professionally are the main characters in the story to follow, but it was a man who started me on my path. General William Westmoreland, Chief of Staff of the United States Army from 1968 to 1972, is ultimately responsible for my life in the study of the religions of Japan. Around 1968, when I was an undergraduate at Vanderbilt University, Westmoreland appeared on television news, speaking on the staggering number of both Vietnamese and Americans killed in the Vietnam War. Westmoreland commented that because the Vietnamese believe in Buddhism and hence expect to have future lives beyond the one lost to American weapons, their deaths have a different meaning than the deaths of American soldiers.[1]

I felt a nauseating moral revulsion at the general's words. But what was Buddhism, and why had my compulsory schooling made no mention of it, Vietnam, or any other place beyond Europe and the Americas? Horrified, I had watched a television news film of Buddhist monks immolating themselves on the streets of Saigon to protest the war.[2] Where did they find the courage to do such a thing, and what did Buddhism have to do with their mighty resolve?

Long nights searching for answers followed, sitting cross-legged on the floor of the Divinity Library with books on Buddhism piled around me. When anti-war protests were held, I was there. In the late 1960s and early 1970s, even in Nashville, anti-war sentiment was strong among students, along with civil rights protests and nascent feminist gatherings. The three appeared to me to be intimately connected, and it seemed natural to gravitate toward all three. While Vanderbilt was an oasis for those like myself who were strongly drawn to these three causes, they were tearing the country apart at the time, and Nashville was increasingly inhospitable. Friends who dressed from the army-navy store were accosted by toughs on the street who would razor off any insignia or signs of rank, and just having long hair was enough to provoke taunts about "hippies and yippies."

I decided on religious studies as my major and soon encountered my first academic mentors beyond my parents. Winston King and Charles Hambrick were both teaching at Vanderbilt; King was a Harvard-trained Buddhologist, while Hambrick was an historian of Japanese religions who had studied under Joseph Mitsuo Kitagawa at the University of Chicago. Both nurtured my naive interest in Buddhism, and their strong focus on Japan soon led to courses on the arts of Japan, which sealed my decision to focus on Japanese religions.

My father, Paul Hoswell Hardacre, was a professor in the history department at Vanderbilt, and, during my high school years, my mother, Gracia Manspeaker Hardacre, had taken a master's course in library science.[3] I had grown up watching my father's enactment of the life of a college professor; his field was British history, especially the Puritan Revolution. It was a quiet but demanding life; he spent each weekday in the office he shared with another professor, and, in the evenings, he prepared lectures and marked blue books until bedtime. In Southern universities at the time, people carefully distinguished between faculty who were to be addressed as Doctor so-and-so and those who were called Mister. Publication beyond one's dissertation and the occasional article was considered pushy and ungentlemanly until around 1965, when Vanderbilt transformed itself from a regional college into a research university. I saw my mother assert her independence through her archivist's qualifications and the study of Russian. She took this step in the early 1960s, brushing aside my father's blustering objections at the family dinner table that ended with the cliched but empty threat, "Over my dead body." I cheered her on and was very proud of the fact that she had better things to do than cook; in fact, the less said about her cooking, the better. Degree in hand, she went to work for the Southern Education Reporting Service (SERS), a news agency that documented the civil rights movement from the local newspapers all over the South, accumulating massive clipping files, which she and her colleagues annotated and curated.[4]

In my senior year, I began a series of anthropology courses taught by Joanna Overing on the history of the discipline, with emphasis on the British school of structural functionalism and the study of kinship systems. She was a striking presence, accompanied by two enormous, elegant dogs, an Irish Wolfhound and a Borzoi. Joanna (quite unusually for Vanderbilt at the time, she invited students to address her by her first name) gave riveting lectures. She was a demanding teacher, frequently requiring written essays and regularly conducting in-class tests and final exams. In those days, it was expected that our essays would be written by hand. She would return them to us covered in corrections and further questions. I cherish my image of her sweeping across the campus in a cloak that billowed out behind her as the loping dogs pulled her along. In my second year of study with her (by this time I was in a master's course at Vanderbilt), she addressed the works of Claude Lévi-Strauss and a structuralist analysis of kinship systems. This school had an obnoxious way of describing marriage relations in tribal societies in terms of "exchanging women," taking it for granted that women were chattel for men to trade back and forth. Joanna urged us to question the unapologetic sexism of this rhetoric.

To my everlasting good fortune, Joanna invited me to assist her as she prepared the manuscript that became *The Piaroa: A People of the Orinoco Basin: A Study in Kinship and Marriage*.[5] This work stemmed from her dissertation at Brandeis and was a comprehensive ethnography of Piaroa society. I had no skill as a writer, but I could spot small things like typos and duplications. I worked at her home, also getting to know her husband at that time, Michael Kaplan. After editing sessions, they often invited me to stay to dinner, and I still make an eggplant dish that I learned from her. I loved my time with the two of them. Their interchanges were earthy and hilarious, from which I deduced that a scholar's life need not be as dull and buttoned-up as I imagined my parents' lives to be.

Joanna's descriptions of her time among the Piaroa inspired me to conduct ethnographic research on contemporary Japanese religions. She had made lasting friendships, particularly among Piaroa women, some of whom were fascinated by her physique, especially her waist. Piaroa women did not have an indentation midtorso and thought it very odd that Joanna was formed in this strange way, offering her various speculations on problems of pregnancy, intimate relations with men, and other matters likely to be affected by what seemed to them to be a deformity.

Joanna provided my first entry to a female scholar's workshop and showed me what a life of research was like. Through our discussions, I learned about the countless issues that can arise in scholarly writing and how ideas are honed, clarified, and refined through repeated drafting. Her dedication, determination, and the high standards she set for herself formed my earliest image of what I wanted to become.

Thanks to Charles Hambrick's recommendation, I was able to enter the History of Religions program at the University of Chicago Divinity School in 1972. I found no female mentors there, but my advisor, Joseph Kitagawa, then Dean of the Divinity School, accepted my plan to study a contemporary Japanese religious group called Reiyūkai Kyōdan, which had derived from the Nichiren school of Buddhism and had developed novel doctrines and practices regarding ancestor worship and the family. I researched my dissertation in Japan between 1976 and 1979.

From 1977, I was a visiting student at the Department of Religious Studies at the University of Tokyo. Student life in the department centered on the "research room" (*kenkyūshitsu*), where Nakamura Kyōko was one of two *joshu*, senior staff in charge. Having spent time at Harvard and the University of Chicago in her student days, she was well acquainted with the nature of my training, and she helped me become established in the world of Japanese religious studies. Nakamura became a great friend who advised me at many crucial points. For example, she advised me against getting too close to a particular Buddhist movement that I wanted to research as a comparison to Reiyūkai. She explained that if I accepted favors from the group, I would soon find my photo showing up in its English-language publications, captioned to imply that I was on the payroll or otherwise had become its creature. If I allowed such a thing to happen, it would always be expected that I (and my future students) would be "available" to provide positive publicity. I learned from Nakamura to return presents and to be vigilant in maintaining academic integrity. Back then, I was so "green" in my dealings with Japanese religious associations and so eager to gain experience among them that I needed to be told such things.

Nakamura took me with her to visit a variety of religious associations and introduced me to scholars and research institutes that could help me. Observing how she spoke with religious figures and how she posed questions on sensitive topics, I learned the importance of verbal and physical practices that communicate a sincere desire to learn and that reassure the other that one is open to instruction—honorific language, proper dress, and correct posture when seated on a floor or when offered a cushion. These attributes are crucial to interacting with religious figures, and it was an immense benefit to have Nakamura model them for me.

It was also during my dissertation research that I began to understand just how robust and deep-seated Japanese patriarchy is. For starters, Nakamura's male successor as *joshu* bluntly informed me that women had no job prospects in religious studies. He said that the best positions always went to men, and the best women could hope for was adjunct appointments or positions at women's junior colleges. I pictured a blindfolded figure of Justice, weighing on one end of the scale Nakamura's closely annotated English translation of *Nihon ryōiki* (*Record of Miraculous Events in Japan*), a collection of religious tales dating around 787 and 824, which is still the classic version of this text.[6] On the other end, I pictured a pile of the hastily written books on contemporary religion that many male scholars were publishing at that time. What a waste of talent and ambition, I thought, a tragedy for each of the women scholars relegated to an academic backwater. The vision went a long way toward explaining the large number of female Japanese academics who decided to make their careers outside Japan. It would take another thirty years to make even a dent in the armor of Japanese academic patriarchy.

My dissertation research in Japan was funded by a combination of fellowships from Fulbright and the Social Science Research Council (SSRC), and both were denominated in dollars. In 1977 and 1978, the rate of exchange dropped, causing my grant money to lose about one-quarter of its value. Many foreign students faced the same shortfall, and we all cheerfully began job hunting, thinking that it would be an adventure to experience the Japanese world of work. Nakamura introduced me to faculty at her alma mater, Tsuda College, where I was hired to teach English once a week for about a year. While at Tsuda, I met Nakanishi Tamako, who became another strong presence in my life.

Tsuda prided itself on English education, and its graduates were highly skilled. Nakanishi graduated from Tsuda in 1940 and worked for SCAP in the field of women's labor issues. After the Occupation ended, she worked for the International Labor Organization, a specialized agency of the United Nations. Returning to Japan, she became a director at Tsuda and eventually became the head of its board of directors. She was a feminist powerhouse with a reputation for getting things done, especially when working on women's issues.

In the late 1970s, Nakanishi became the founding director of a specialized language school in central Tokyo affiliated with Tsuda. In that position, she worked with the United Nations University, Tokyo (founded in 1972) to ensure that Japanese people could be competitive applicants for UN positions. Although there was an abundance of talented Japanese professionals whose expertise could be put to use at the UN, many lacked sufficient English abilities. Nakanishi's solution was to create a special set of language courses for prospective UN applicants. She hired me to help her create the program and to be its faculty coordinator.

Working with Nakanishi to build this program from the ground up was a tremendous opportunity for me and one of the most exciting periods of my life. Nakanishi gave me carte blanche to design courses, hire faculty, and manage the program. Most of my hires were foreign graduate students whose stipends had suddenly declined and who lacked credentials in teaching English as a second language. (In my experience, most people teaching English in Japan at that time had no such credentials.) Nevertheless, many of them became career English teachers and remained in Japan for many years.

Nakanishi taught me how to be sufficiently flexible to handle whatever crisis might arise in the classroom, in dealings with the teachers, or in students' relations with the school—in short, how to manage something larger than my own research. Our students were working professionals whose only time for study was in the evenings. Classes ran from late afternoon to 9:00 p.m.

Nakanishi liked to unwind over a glass of whiskey after a long day, and she would sometimes take me with her to a hotel bar she frequented near the Yasukuni Shrine. In that setting, I had a chance to ask her about her remarkable life, the struggles she had experienced, her techniques for dealing with sexist men, and her hopes and ideals for working women. She was adept at working productively with other women and could inspire them to push through whatever obstacles might arise by using their skills, determination, and resolve not to take no for an answer. She succeeded in creating a pipeline for Japanese professionals to gain UN employment, and the program long outlived my tenure.

I remained in contact with Nakanishi for many years after returning to the United States. When the language-course initiative finished, she went into politics and was twice elected to the Upper House of the National Diet, serving from 1983 to 1995. Nakanishi's example was a shining counterpoint to my main research problem at the time, which concerned the gender dynamics of Reiyūkai.

When I worked with Nakanishi, I was within around a year of completing my dissertation, and I was struggling to understand Reiyūkai women. There were many female grassroots leaders, among them some of the strongest women one could ever meet. They counseled other women, and they frequently led regional branches of the religion that included many thousands of people. (The organization at the time had a membership of over two million.) They were highly capable, dedicated, and unshakable in their faith. But their faith involved a variety of ideas of women's inferiority to men, and their solution for all problems between women and men began with having the woman apologize to the man and reaffirm his priority. Later on, the man might be brought to see that he had been in the wrong, but it appeared to me that Reiyūkai's preferred approach inevitably called for deeper entrenchment in an ethic of women's subordination to men. This was the understanding I had reached in two years of observation, interviewing, survey research, and study of written accounts of problems solved.

The religious basis for Reiyūkai's stance on gender was steeped in the history of popular interpretation of *The Lotus Sutra*, the most popular text of the lay Buddhist movements of the time. The text includes the story of a dragon girl who achieves Buddhahood by first changing into a male, based on the belief that Buddhahood is unattainable in female form, given that the historical Buddha was male. In interviews with Reiyūkai women, I tried to understand their interpretation of the story and their reasons for believing that men are superior to women. One interview in particular was particularly depressing. I spoke at some length with the woman at Reiyūkai headquarters who was in charge of day care there. She informed me that women are born female because of offenses in their past lives. What offenses? Well, they menstruate, which is unclean, and they experience childbirth, which is also unclean, and, furthermore, they are preoccupied with childcare, cleaning, and cooking, all of which involve them in further uncleanness. All these things are offensive and generally troublesome to men. Leading a life like this, they can hardly expect to be reborn as men and thus have access to the highest levels of religious attainment. The result is that they are reborn as women again, and the cycle repeats for all eternity.

As we were talking, I could see into the room where the preschool children in this woman's care were playing, and I imagined how she communicated these ideas to them. The thought was sickening. I exchanged several letters with my mother on this theme, which she described as "soul-killing." It appeared to me that the Reiyūkai women whom I otherwise admired had created roles for themselves outside the home precisely through transmitting beliefs that deepened women's subordination to men, justified by religious rationales. This phenomenon among conservative women is of course not limited to Japan, and, at the time, it was playing out in the United States among anti-feminist women like Phyllis Schlafly and her followers who helped defeat the Equal Rights Amendment.

I had not yet planned to leave Japan, but, while on a visit home in 1979, Professor Kitagawa told me that a job had suddenly opened at Princeton and urged me to apply. The Department of Religion had been hoping to persuade

Carmen Blacker, then on a visiting appointment, to become a regular member of the faculty, but she had decided to return to England. The opening arose because of her decision, and, largely because it came suddenly, I was hired. I became friends with Blacker, whom I had admired from a distance.

Blacker, the first woman in England to earn a PhD in Japanese history (University of London, 1957), was a renowned scholar of Japanese religions and was reputed to have climbed every sacred mountain in Japan. During the war, she had been a codebreaker at Bletchley Park, where British intelligence had worked to decode the German military's communication, and after the war, she regularly traveled to Japan.[7] Her book on Japanese shamanism, *The Catalpa Bow*, included a penetrating analysis of shamanic practices among Japanese new religious movements.[8] The book, published shortly before I began my study of Reiyūkai, taught me how central shamanic elements were to an idea I was developing to discuss the commonalities across new religious movements, regardless of their doctrinal origins in Buddhism, Shinto, Christianity, or the revelations experienced by a founder. I began discussing my idea with Carmen, and she encouraged me to develop them further.

During a conference at Cambridge University in honor of her retirement, Blacker took two professors from Japan and me to see a nearby cathedral. Although she married her partner Michael Lowie late in life, she had not been a fan of the institution of marriage. While we were examining the cathedral's sepulchers, a wedding concluded. Regarding the bride with a sidelong glance, she quipped, "Another one bites the dust."

I began teaching at Princeton in the fall of 1979 and remained there for nine years. It was fortunate for me that John Gager was the head of the Department of Religion. He took me aside and told me that three things were most important to gaining tenure: research, teaching, and service. He told me in no uncertain terms that, "Of these, only research really matters," and that whenever I faced a choice among the three, I should prioritize research.

As it happened, research was the only area in which I had any confidence because, at the University of Chicago, there had been no opportunities for graduate students to learn to teach. Thus, I went into my first Princeton classes not understanding much about teaching, and, as one might have predicted, I was a total flop the first year. I was also a blank slate on a number of other basic academic skills and practices, like how to form a group of academic mentors beyond one's graduate school advisors and how to submit a journal article or book manuscript for publication. I therefore vowed that I would never let a graduate student of my own be so defenseless, and I eventually developed a course for graduate students to teach these and other fundamental academic skills that I taught for many years.

During my first year at Princeton, it became apparent that only one of us two junior faculty in East Asian religions would be tenured and that the senior faculty were betting on my colleague. He had been given a titled preceptorship and other perks that made our relative standing clear. After all, I had only been hired because Blacker had turned down the offer. And given how poorly I initially performed as a teacher, it was not unreasonable that the graybeards should bet on the other horse.

At the end of my first year of teaching, I returned to Japan to begin a second monograph, this time on Kurozumikyō, a new religious movement deriving from Shinto. I had made contacts before beginning my job at Princeton, and the Fukumitsu family of the Ōi Church of Kurozumikyō in Okayama City had agreed to host me during my research. By the time I arrived in Okayama, I was somewhat embittered and cynical, believing that the deck was stacked against me at Princeton. Setting that aside as much as possible, I sought to compile a comprehensive account of Kurozumikyō's history, beliefs, and practices, and to document its branch churches across Japan. I hoped to compare my findings with what I had learned about Reiyūkai and to articulate common elements among new religious movements in a more convincing way than the trait lists that were common in the existing scholarship.

My experience with the Fukumitsu family was transformative. At Princeton, I felt so overwhelmed and exhausted with teaching and dealing socially with the university that I sought ways to conserve my energy and reduce my commitments to have enough time for research and to feel sane. From my present vantage point, this sounds tremendously dramatic and silly, but it was my mindset when I arrived in Okayama.

The Fukumitsu family was headed by the Bishop of Kurozumikyō, Fukumitsu Sasuke, and his wife Hiroe. They managed the Ōi Church with their daughter Katsue and her husband Kōichi. While the settlement of Ōi was technically within Okayama City, it was quite rural, and the church's followers were virtually all farmers. I understood almost immediately that the Fukumitsus' attitude toward life was the polar opposite of mine, and I could see that they were much happier than I was. As I became fond of them, I tried to understand their thinking by imitating their way of life. The older couple invited me to address them as Otōsan and Okaasan (father and mother). An informal group of older women came to the church daily to tend to the kitchen garden and to generally "hang out." I came to know them and their families well. Because Hiroe was keen to help me meet as many Kurozumikyō followers as possible, she took me to branch churches all over Western Japan. She was in her sixties, full of energy, and determined that I should write the best study of the group possible. I threw myself into each day, met everyone I could, went to dozens of branch churches, observed countless rituals, and interviewed anyone who would talk with me. After a few months, my cynicism dissipated, and I had become a much happier person. Although I had gone to Okayama to learn *about* Kurozumikyō, I learned *from* the Fukumitsus a new way of living.

Kurozumikyō followers believe that the group's founder, Kurozumi Munetada (1780–1850), received a "heavenly mission" (*tenmei*) to proclaim his teaching and broadly use the concept of a task assigned to a person by heaven. Hiroe told me that I had a heavenly mission to teach and write about Japanese religions. She believed that she and the ministry of Kurozumikyō as a whole had a mission to spread the founder's teachings. Humor was an important touchstone for her, and laughter was fundamental to every sermon or interaction with followers. She enacted her sense of mission joyfully, whether counseling followers who came to her with problems, preaching, conducting ceremonies, acting as a mentor for younger ministers, or playing the group's Kibigaku sacred music using *shō* (musical instrument) and Kurozumikyō's *kagura* (ceremonial dance).

Observing Hiroe and living with her family in their church led me to a major turning point. I could see that they derived tremendous strength from the belief that they had a divinely appointed mission. That belief gave them physical endurance and helped them to bring out the best in themselves. They never spontaneously articulated the belief, but they acted on it and encouraged me to think as they did, urging me to write the best work that I could. Thanks to these experiences, I returned to Princeton with a different frame of mind.

John Gager was right: I was granted tenure in 1986 based on my research. Although my teaching had improved, it was only after I was tenured that I gained confidence in the classroom. By the time of my tenure decision, I had published two books and had a third in press.[9] I believe that these early publications went smoothly because Japanese Studies was growing, contemporary Japanese religions had not yet become a crowded field, and my studies were largely based on fieldwork, the writing of which came easily to me. In addition, my parents helped edit my first book manuscript, and I learned a great deal about academic writing from their corrections and suggestions, as well as from editors at Princeton University Press, including Miriam Brokaw, who had grown up in Japan. After a stint at the University of Tokyo Press, she returned to Princeton, became an editor and associate director, and founded the Princeton Library of Asian Translations.

As I wrote some years ago in an essay published in *Doing Fieldwork in Japan*:

Frequently, the researcher on religion can be unsure how distinctive the religion in question is, how far it departs from patterns recognizable to the rest of society. In such cases, it is very useful to have a friend outside the religion who can act as a sounding board for puzzling data of observation or interaction. While fellow academics can play this role, it is also useful to be in contact with a friend outside the academic world, someone you regard as levelheaded and sympathetic to the goals of your research even if not fully informed on all nuances of your project.[10]

Ever since Anne Walthall (chapter 25) introduced me to her in 1977, Suemoto Yōko has been my "friend in the field" and my best friend in life. Anne, Yōko, and I traveled together around Japan, visiting obscure places. In 1980, Yōko came to Okayama and met the Fukumitsus. She has assisted all my fieldwork projects. For example, she helped me read through huge reams of microfilm for my study of state Shinto and assisted my research on *mizuko kuyō*, the ritualization of aborted fetuses and stillbirths.[11] She traveled with me to field sites, where she helped to conduct interviews and to make sense of them later. After her parents died, leaving vacant the upper floor of their house in Yokohama, Yōko allowed me to set up a base there, where I now reside during each stay in Japan. I even stayed there for a year-long research sabbatical (2004–2005) that led to my history of Shinto.[12] After I returned to the United States, we talked daily by Skype, reviewing data and reading texts relevant to my research. These sessions gave me an opportunity to try out my interpretations on Yōko and to hear hers. She rescued me from misunderstandings of both texts and human interactions countless times.

During her working life, Yōko was a bookkeeper, and she is adept at processing statistical information. These abilities have been a godsend for me in my present project, *The Dignity of Shrines: Shinto and the Public Purse, 1906–1945*. For this project, Yōko and I have traveled to every prefectural library in Japan to collect statistics on how much public funding was spent on shrines at the level of the village, town, prefecture, and nation. After many attempts, we created a way to display this data for all the prefectures; I could not have reached this point without Yōko's help.

The relevant data was originally published in each prefecture's annual statistical yearbooks; thus it is necessary to access the thirty-nine volumes at each prefectural library for the thirty-nine-year period of public funding (1906–1945). Because compiling this data requires a datasheet of about forty rows and eleven columns for each prefecture, a lone researcher could not confidently transcribe the information accurately if working by hand—to say nothing of the subsequent transcription to a digital format—and then ensure accuracy in the needed calculations. Yōko helped with each stage of this work, double- and triple-checking our work.

I feared that this project might be truly onerous for Yōko and me, but we developed a rhythm and pacing so that it never became overwhelming. To complete data collection, I visited Japan twice a year over a period of five years, each time traveling to contiguous prefectures. Interspersing periods of work with off days, visiting shrines and other sites in each prefecture, and occasionally staying at hot springs has made it easier to sustain the focus on detail that the project requires. Yōko has a feel for numbers that I lack, an ability to display them in ways that make them easy to understand, and a determination to get the figures right. Without her many contributions, I could never hope to complete this project.

Yōko and I continue our daily sessions, now on Zoom instead of Skype. For me, they begin at 7:00 a.m. Thanks to Yōko's generosity, I am able to spend at least one hour reading and speaking Japanese each day. Many of our conversations turn to the random, idiosyncratic things that happen to us or that appear in the news. Laughter has proven to be a crucial sustaining force in my research life as I progress into my seventh decade. Yōko's encouragement has helped me to sustain optimism and hope for better days through these last few years, especially when the coronavirus made travel to Japan impossible. Her friendship adds meaning and depth to my efforts to understand Japanese religions and society.

When I first began researching and writing about Japanese religions, I would sometimes imagine the men who had been my graduate school teachers looking over my shoulder. Now, however, I find myself mentally turning to the women who have been my mentors, guides, and friends. Their image strengthens my resolve and determination and helps me preserve a sense of humor. I am deeply grateful to them and proud to acknowledge the debt. My fondest hope for future generations of women scholars of Japan is that they also may be so blessed as I have been.

Notes

[1] He reiterated the point in an interview that appeared in the 1974 documentary film *Hearts and Minds*. Following an excruciating portrayal of Vietnamese families mourning their dead, including an old woman who climbed down into a grave in despair and a little boy crying on his father's coffin, Westmoreland blithely remarked, "The Oriental doesn't put the same high price on life as does a Westerner. Life is plentiful, life is cheap in the Orient. And as the philosophy of the Orient expresses it: life is not important." See Peter Davis, dir., *Hearts and Minds* (Hollywood: BBS Productions, 1974).

[2] Ibid.

[3] See Samuel T. McSeveney, "In Memoriam: Paul H. Hardacre (1915–2010)," *Perspectives on History*, American Historical Association, January 1, 2011, https://www.historians.org/publications-and-directories/perspectives-on-history/january-2011/in-memoriam-paul-h-hardacre.

[4] Gracia Hardacre was a manuscripts librarian at the Huntington Library in California, the Tennessee State Library and Archives, and Fisk University. Her works on the personal papers of civil rights activists, along with other documents amassed by SERS, were later incorporated into the Paul and Gracia Hardacre Collection at Vanderbilt's Jean and Alexander Heard Library, with some of her collection folded into the Amistad Research Center at Tulane University. See, for example, "Paul and Gracia Hardacre Collection,

1894–1969," Amistad Research Center, Tulane University, 2012, http://amistadresearchcenter.tulane.edu/archon/?p=accessions/accession&id=906.

[5] Joanna Overing Kaplan, *The Piaroa: A People of the Orinoco Basin: A Study in Kinship and Marriage* (Oxford: Clarendon Press, 1975).

[6] Kyoko Motomuchi Nakamura, *Miraculous Stories from the Japanese Buddhist Tradition: The Nihon Ryoiki of Monk Kyokai* (London: Routledge, 1996).

[7] For more on the Bletchley Park code breakers, see "Who Were the Codebreakers?," Bletchley Park.org, February 23, 2002, https://bletchleypark.org.uk/our-story/who-were-the-codebreakers/.

[8] Carmen Blacker, *The Catalpa Bow: A Study of Shamanistic Practices in Japan* (London: Allen & Unwin, 1975).

[9] Helen Hardacre, *Lay Buddhism in Contemporary Japan: Reiyūkai Kyōdan* (Princeton: Princeton University Press, 1984); *The Religion of Japan's Korean Minority: The Preservation of Ethnic Identity* (Berkeley: University of California Press, 1984); *Kurozumikyō and the New Religions of Japan* (Princeton: Princeton University Press, 1986).

[10] Helen Hardacre, "Fieldwork with Japanese Religious Groups," in *Doing Fieldwork in Japan*, edited by Theodore Bestor, Patricia G. Steinhoff, and Victoria Lyon Bestor (Honolulu: University of Hawai'i Press, 2003), 87.

[11] Helen Hardacre, *Shintō and the State, 1868–1988* (Princeton: Princeton University Press, 1989); *Marketing the Menacing Fetus in Japan* (Berkeley: University of California Press, 1997); *Religion and Society in Nineteenth-Century Japan: A Study of the Southern Kantō Region, Using Late Edo and Early Meiji Gazetteers* (Ann Arbor: University of Michigan Center for Japanese Studies, 2002).

[12] Helen Hardacre, *Shinto: A History* (New York: Oxford University Press, 2017).

31

BEING AN OUTSIDER-INSIDER

Barbara Sato

Perhaps this was the first sign of a theme I held with me throughout my career: being able to be an outsider-insider who could "manage" in circumstances where others might seem uncomfortable or overly foreign.

BARBARA SATO (1942–2021) was a professor of modern Japanese history, women's history, and media studies at Seikei University (Tokyo). As the first foreign student admitted to the PhD program at the University of Tokyo, Institute of Journalism and Communication Studies, Sociology Department, her focus on the 1920s "modern girl" was a practically unknown entity in Japanese scholarship, and her use of mass women's magazines as research materials was unprecedented. She is the author of *The New Japanese Woman: Modernity, Media, and Women in Interwar Japan* (2003); editor of *Nichijō seikatsu no tanjō: senkanki Nihon no bunka henyō* (*Origins of Everyday Life: Changing Cultural Patterns in Interwar Japan*, 2007); and coeditor of *Gender and Modernity: Rereading Japanese Women's Magazines* (1998) and *Kindai shomin seikatsushi: ren'ai, kekkon, katei 9* (*A People's History of Everyday Life: Love, Marriage, Family*, vol. 9, 1986). She wrote extensively in English and Japanese on ordinary women and the formation of a new reading culture in interwar Japan. Her final research project was on socialist feminist Tanaka Sumiko and the changing family and configurations of domestic space and social relations in postwar Japan.

Discovering the Study of Women and Japan

Because I spent my teaching career in Japan, my contributions to Japanese Studies and women's studies are of a different nature than those of my colleagues. This essay focuses on two things: my research life as a regular graduate student at the University of Tokyo, studying the then unheard-of topic of women's mass magazines, and my experiences as a professor at Seikei University (Tokyo) in the fields of intellectual history and women and media. But the story begins earlier—I first encountered Japan and became interested in the lives of women when I was a high school student in the American Field Service (AFS) in 1959.

From the time I boarded the *Hikawa Maru* in Seattle as a sixteen-year-old representing Vermont, my life changed. My roommate in steerage and closest friend was none other than Kate Nakai (figure 24.1). During my initial interview for AFS in Burlington, I was asked what I would do if I couldn't bathe for several days or if I lived where plumbing was primitive. I answered that I would manage. Later, I learned I was the only person who did not cringe, which may have accounted for my becoming the lucky candidate. Indeed, my host family in Hamamatsu, Shizuoka Prefecture, did not have a flush toilet. Hygiene still being what it was in the aftermath of the war, red water bugs (a species never encountered in Vermont), cockroaches, and large daddy longlegs adorned the walls of our bathroom, located oddly enough between the family room (*chanoma*) and my host parent's four-mat room. I ended up taking it all in and more, and, by the end of my stay with the host family, I vowed to return. Perhaps this was the first sign of a theme I held with me throughout my career: being able to be an outsider-insider who could "manage" in circumstances where others might seem uncomfortable or overly foreign.

My four months in Hamamatsu were pivotal in many ways, but none more than instilling in me that the study of Japanese women would be my calling. It sounds simple, but the fact that my host father and brother took the first baths, while the women of the family waited for their turns, troubled me. My host father, the children, and I enjoyed excursions while my host mother remained at home as "*rusuban*," responsible for watching over the house. Our small refrigerator held only two or three bottles of milk, reserved for my father, ostensibly because a country doctor should be in good health. My conviction that my life's work would be in Japanese women's studies was further solidified by my experience working at a Japanese company in New York after graduating from the University of Vermont. There, I experienced firsthand the persistent discrimination women face in the workplace, despite advancements throughout history.

Becoming a PhD Student at the University of Tokyo

I arrived in Japan in 1979 as a PhD candidate at Columbia. I planned to spend two years in Japan: one year at the Inter-University Center for Japanese Language Studies and one year as a research student under prominent media scholar Uchikawa Yoshimi at the University of Tokyo's Institute of Journalism and Communication Studies (Shimbun kenkyūjo).[1] In the fall, a few months into my studies, Uchikawa-sensei invited me to lunch at the Japan National Press Club, a haunt for journalists and academics. But at this time, women were rarely seen there. During our lunch, Uchikawa-sensei, who offered me endless support, broached the subject of my applying to the University of Tokyo as a regular graduate student. I never forgot my surprise at that moment.

It seems that most American research students met a few times a month with their advisors and spent their days combing the National Diet Library and elsewhere for research materials. Uchikawa-sensei and several other professors who advised these students, however, had reservations about this process. The dissertations that these students completed after their return to the United States either cited many primary sources well known to Japanese researchers or lacked original critical analysis. Uchikawa-sensei and his colleagues believed that this process did not allow for innovative research. Uchikawa-sensei expressed his frustration with me and followed with a life-altering proposal: "It seems like you have acclimated to life in Japan and are enjoying it. How about if you consider taking a bigger step and matriculating in our PhD program and joining us for the next three years to conduct intensive research?" His proposal had instant appeal. I was already leaning heavily on the advice of Kōchi Saburō, a pioneering scholar of print-culture research, and Arase Yutaka, whose unique insights into the modern history of Japanese journalism were encouraging reevaluations of field.[2] The Institute was impressive both in stature and depth. I found myself nodding yes. Uchikawa-sensei continued, "Of course, this invitation is conditional to passing an oral entrance exam for the PhD program."

In February 1980, I sat for the exam interview. Twelve stone-faced male professors grilled me for two hours about my research and source materials. My proposal was still in its rudimentary stages, but I explained that mass women's magazines played a central role in connecting urban middle-class women with consumerism, particularly after the Great Kantō Earthquake of 1923. I was emphatic that these magazines were, in fact, invaluable source materials. My examiners looked horrified. Not only did they criticize my sources (calling them "*kuzu*," or "commercialized trash"), but they also urged me to change to a more conventional topic that utilized materials at the university's Meiji Newspaper and Periodical Archives (Meiji Shimbun Zasshi Bunko). Uchikawa-sensei ended the interview by adding, "Thank you for an afternoon of *uchū banashi*." Not being a part of my Japanese vocabulary, I rushed outside and consulted *Kenkyūsha's New Japanese-English Dictionary*, only to find the definition as "space talk." I went home humiliated. Two days later, Arase-sensei called at 7:00 a.m., congratulating me on my acceptance as the first foreign student admitted to the University of Tokyo PhD program.

Studying Women's Magazines and Modern Mass Culture

Now as an official PhD student, I began frequenting the University of Tokyo's various libraries and quickly realized why my research proposal was deemed "*uchū banashi.*" Women's monthly magazines, which had hundreds of thousands of copies in circulation between the 1920s and 1940s, were nowhere to be found in the libraries. In the 1980s, the main library carried a few back issues of *Fujin kōron* (*Woman's Review*) and *Josei kaizō* (*Women's Reconstruction*), both considered sufficiently "intellectual," but the most widely read magazines—*Shufu no tomo* (*Housewife's Companion*), *Fujokai* (*Woman's Sphere*), and *Fujin sekai* (*Women's World*)—were nowhere to be found. These magazines were considered entertainment "for the masses" and thus not worthy of being in the stacks of university libraries. This was the first hurdle I faced as a newly matriculated student.

There were only a handful of institutions with collections of popular magazines dating back to the 1920s. The National Diet Library had a few issues on microfilm, but accessing any issue there involved a thirty-minute wait for it to come up on the gurney. The inroads I made in my research were through odds and ends. I walked all over Tokyo in search of magazines at used bookstores, and following the leads of fellow researchers, I knocked on the doors of publishing houses.

Shufu no tomo was one exception and was accessible, thanks to the foresight of one of the magazine company's founders, Ishikawa Takeyoshi, who had established a women-only library with all their back issues for his readers in 1947, officially named the Ishikawa Takeyoshi Memorial Library in 2013.[3] I frequented the library and was the first foreign student to use its collection. Uchikawa-sensei was able to procure an introduction to the librarian of the Chuō Kōron-sha publishing company, who was happy to have their collection of *Fujin kōron* recognized for academic purposes; in addition, Inoue Ken, who taught comparative literature, alerted me to Waseda University's *Fujin kōron* collection, which had the added advantage of permitting photocopies of the back issues. I found other early twentieth-century popular magazines at used book fairs with relative ease thanks to their previously high monthly circulation, but each issue cost the equivalent of more than thirty dollars and were prohibitive on a student's budget. The best that I could do was acquire a few issues that I felt were most crucial to my research.

Today, popular magazines are used as critical research materials across academic disciplines—most notably, in modern history, literature, and sociology. One simple reason behind this shift is that many periodicals published in modern Japan are now easily accessible and affordable through digital media and databases.

For example, *Shufu no tomo* was made available on CD-ROM in 1998, and *Fujin kōron* on DVD-ROM in 2006. *Fujokai* could later be accessed through the Ishikawa Takeyoshi Memorial Library database.

In addition, forward-thinking academics' support of the utility of popular magazines as historical documents cannot be understated. I am indebted to Harry Harootunian, who appreciated the significance of the articles in women's magazines cited in my dissertation and whose meticulous comments for further critical analysis helped lead to the publication of my book, *The New Japanese Woman: Modernity, Media, and Women in Interwar Japan*.[4] It was not until 2003, after the publishing of my book and when I was already on the faculty at Seikei, that several well-respected University of Tokyo professors told me that my research led them to reevaluate their stance on women and mass magazines. This was a huge moment in my career.

Participating in the Social Psychology Research Group

A few months after joining the University of Tokyo graduate program, I met Minami Hiroshi, professor emeritus of Hitotsubashi University. Minami-sensei was one of the first scholars to recognize the importance of studying mass culture and was credited with introducing social psychology to Japan. His book, *The Psychology of the Japanese People* (*Nihonjin no shinri*, 1953) became one of the best-selling books of 1950s Japan, a rare feat for an academic monograph.[5] Minami-sensei received his PhD in social psychology from Cornell University in 1943 and continued his studies in the United States, where he became the only Japanese scholar to refuse repatriation during World War II. He eventually returned to Japan in 1947. His determination not to return to Japan during the war won him respect in various intellectual circles, irrespective of ideological leanings.

Until the late 1970s, many scholars in Japan and other parts of the world considered only highbrow culture worthy of academic research. The exception in Japan were a few pioneering historians, such as Irokawa Daikichi, Yasumaru Yoshio, and Amino Yoshihiko, who paved the way for the study of the ideas and culture of the common people.[6] By and large, however, the mass culture that had emerged with the rapid development of mass media from the end of the nineteenth century to the beginning of the twentieth century was still largely considered to be nothing more than a degraded imitation of highbrow culture, and its originality and historical significance were not recognized. Minami-sensei's edited volume, *Taishō Culture* (*Taishō bunka*, 1965), was the only academic book to take popular media seriously.[7] When Minami-sensei heard that I was exploring the possibility of change for urban common women in the context of the development of mass media and consumer culture, he invited me to join his Social Psychology Research Group (Shakai Shinri Kenkyūkai).

At that time, Minami-sensei and his research group were preparing to start a new study on "Japanese *modanizumu*" (Japanese modernism). It is easier to understand "Japanese *modanizumu*" when viewed as a different concept from "modernism" as it is used in art history and literary history. From around the time of the Great Kantō Earthquake to the mid-1930s, Japanese society, especially urban society, was in a period of great change in terms of lifestyles, culture, and thought. Minami-sensei insisted that this period should be considered as the second wave in the fundamental turning point for modern Japan, following the top-down push for "Civilization and Enlightenment" (*bunmei kaika*) after the Meiji Restoration of 1868. A buzzword of the time, "*modanizumu*" denoted this massive social change and regularly appeared in newspapers and magazines.

When I was assigned to work on this new research project's ideological side, I encountered several inspiring articles written about the Japanese "modern girl" (*modan gāru*) by Marxist literary and social critic Hirabayashi Hatsunosuke (1892-1931). More a media concept than a lived reality, the dangerous and seductive modern girl, who moved about the city with ease, embodied the fears of intellectuals, authors, and social critics that Westernization and consumer capitalism had advanced too far in Japan; the modern girl embodied many aspects of "*modanizumu*." Most Japanese socialists and Marxists, including pioneering feminist Yamakawa Kikue (1890-1980), disparaged "*modanizumu*" as a social phenomenon and modern girls as frivolous. "Japanese *modanizumu*," they argued, was influenced by the decadent, hedonistic culture promoted by American advanced capitalism. Americanization, they called it, was only a superficial novelty, announcing no essential changes. Only Hirabayashi focused on the technological and economic developments after the 1923 earthquake and predicted they would directly impact the achievement of women's rights. Minami-sensei encouraged me to turn an oral presentation on Hirabayashi that I gave to the research group into a chapter for a book on *The Study of Japanese Modanizunu: Thought, Society, and Culture* (*Nihon modanizumu no kenkyū: shisō, seikatsu, bunka*). This chapter, "The Idea of Japanese *Modanizumu*: Focusing on Hirabayashi Hatsunosuke" (Nihon teki modanizumu no shisō—Hirabayashi Hatsunosuke o chūshin to shite), was my first published work in Japanese.[8]

Minami-sensei's research group continued to actively pursue collaborative research on Japanese mass culture from the interwar period to the postwar period. In 1987, we published *Shōwa Culture: 1925-1945* (*Shōwa bunka, 1925-1945*), followed three years later, in 1990, by the sequel, *Shōwa Culture, Part 2: 1945-1989* (*Zoku—Shōwa bunka, 1945-1989*).[9] Both studies encouraged discussion about the legitimacy of popular culture as a field of research. My contribution to the first volume, "Women: *Modanizumu* and the Consciousness of Rights" (Josei: Modanizumu to kenri ishiki), focused on the modern girl, the professional working woman, and the housewife—women who generally did not have awareness of women's causes or activist beliefs but whose attitudinal changes should be welcomed as proof that some women wanted to perform challenging tasks.[10] In the second volume, I published "Postwar Women's Dreams and Realities: Focusing on Readers' Roundtable Discussions" (Sengo josei no yume to genjitsu: dokusha zadankai ni miru) and showed that the fight for changes that would alter women's lives in the wake of the Occupation reforms was already underway in the 1920s, both socially and psychologically.[11] Marriage of one's choice, freedom to divorce, and property rights fell within a woman's legal rights, but Japanese women were not reborn as a consequence of World War II. The editors of *Rekishi hyōron* (*Critical History*) approached me shortly thereafter to join a debate on *modanizumu* and intellectuals' responses to it, and I contributed an article titled "The Emergence of the Modern Girl and the Intellectuals" (Modan gāru no tōjō to chishikijin).[12] In 1993, thanks to Carol Gluck and Victoria de Grazzia's advice, I published my first article in English, "Moga Sensation: Perceptions of the Modan Garu in Japanese Intellectual Circles during the 1920s."[13]

Through this research, I was able to change the dominant perception that mass magazines do not accurately reflect society's essential changes and people's views. During the interwar years, women's magazines had circulations of several hundred thousand, sometimes more than a million. In the 1950s and 1960s, they became sites for molding more inclusive gendered identities. Minami-sensei gave me and my colleague, Ueda Yasuo, the opportunity to edit one volume in his twenty-volume collection of primary source materials showing the lives of ordinary people in the modern era. For this volume, we selected magazine articles around the themes of love, marriage, and family and were able to further highlight the significance of popular women's magazines as historical documents.[14]

Teaching at Seikei University

Because I was hired to teach in Japanese, having publications in both Japanese and English boosted my chances for an enduring career at Seikei University, a university nestled in west Tokyo's Kichijōji neighborhood. The vetting process for my hire lasted almost one year, and, despite being a foreigner and a woman, I became the first in the Faculty of Humanities to teach my expertise—modern Japanese intellectual history and women and media—to undergraduate and graduate students. I encountered women who expressed jealousy, even anger, that a foreigner took a job away from someone who is Japanese. This shocked me: as a foreigner and a woman, I was an "outsider," but as a full-time faculty member of a university, I was also an "insider."

Seikei takes pride in requiring undergraduates to take intensive two-year seminars in which they study in small groups with professors. Because many

Japanese undergraduates do not receive much training in verbal communication, this curriculum is challenging for them and their professors. Yet students find the seminars helpful and memorable. Their resulting graduation theses are critiqued by all professors in their major departments. For example, when students from a seminar I held around twenty years ago came to our home for a reunion, they reminisced about reading and discussing Wagatsuma Sakae's research on postwar legal changes to the Japanese family system and the questions I asked about how they would pattern their own lives.[15] My female students wanted different things than women did decades ago. Some of them got married soon after graduation but applied to graduate schools in their early thirties and pursued careers in fields like social work, public health, and finance. They thanked me for encouraging them and spoke of my influence in helping them to redefine themselves and their roles within their own families.

At Seikei, I tried to make a difference for my students and colleagues. For example, based on my experience working as an ombudsperson for Temple University, Japan, I created a committee to tackle issues of sexual harassment and power harassment that my colleagues had swept under the rug for years. As a result, Seikei was one of the first schools in Japan to develop a policy to deal with harassment and discrimination. Although there are many plusses to teaching at a Japanese university, the workload is heavy with time-consuming administrative duties. I taught between six and seven courses (each meeting once a week) per semester, depending on the number of graduate students. I helped write, proctor, and grade university entrance exams. Senior faculty are expected to do more service work than their junior colleagues. Thus, there was limited time to pursue independent research and to engage colleagues in intellectual discussions.

I needed to devote much time to parenting because our son suffered from asthma, and day-care facilities could not provide the supervision that he needed or we were comfortable with. Thus, I did not have time to participate in feminist organizations and study groups early in my career, and this limited my contact with women outside the university. Yet I was fortunate to become friends with sociologist Inoue Teruko, a pioneer of gender studies. At her suggestion, after retiring from Seikei, I began to research socialist feminist Tanaka Sumiko's (1909–1995) writings in commercial women's magazines as a site for molding more inclusive gendered identities in the 1950s and 1960s.[16]

My interest in Tanaka is manifold. While her political activities are well documented, her influence as one of the most popular commentators on everyday issues facing Japanese women and her scholarly impact are practically unknown. Tanaka was elected to the Upper House of the Japan's National Diet on the Japanese Socialist Party (JSP) ticket from 1965 to 1983, where she led efforts to pass the Equal Employment Opportunity Law (1985). She was the first woman to serve as the vice-leader of the JSP, but her qualifications and popularity were not enough to break the social barriers preventing women from becoming party leaders. Tanaka got her political start by working on the staff of her mentor, Yamakawa Kikue, at the Women's and Minor's Bureau of the Ministry of Labor in 1948. By the time Tanaka ran for election, she was popular among women in both urban and rural areas who knew her through the articles she wrote for women's magazines. Tanaka's approach was practical and based on her insights into the changing conditions of common women in Japan. She understood that young women who were still high school age, suburban housewives, and women working full-time jobs all wrestled with injustices in the workplace. Tanaka's articles helped pave the way for the second wave of feminism in the 1970s, and her loyal readership elected her to the Upper House.

The period between the beginning of the twentieth century and the 1960s was a golden era for women's magazines. These magazines lost influence as their readerships began to gradually decline in the 1970s. With a few exceptions, such as *Fujin kōron* and *Fujin gahō* (*Illustrated Women's Gazette*), most women's magazines ceased publication in the twenty-first century. In the 1970s and 1980s, a number of visually oriented "lifestyle magazines" for women were launched; they emphasized fashion, gourmet food, and travel but did not influence views on society or politics like their forbearers did. It remains uncertain whether print media will still have the potential to change the lives of Japanese women. I hope my work has shown that, for media to have a positive impact, they need to convey the core strategic values that Tanaka used to improve the working environment for women in Japan.

Let me close with a few words for young researchers. Oftentimes, it is hard to take criticism. I was not a good writer when I started out. My advisor, Carol Gluck, more often than not put a large X on what I submitted to her. I rewrote and rewrote. Carol's purpose was not to intimidate, and, from her feedback and from my experiences with Minami-sensei and my other mentors, I learned not only to write but also how to guide my students in Japan, most of whom were not prepared for large reading and writing assignments. Most of all, I learned the importance of not being satisfied with the mediocre.

Notes

[1] See, for example, Uchikawa Yoshimi, *Masu mejia hōseisakushi kenkyū* (Research on the History of Mass Media and Legal Policy) (Tokyo: Yūhikaku, 1989).

[2] Kōchi Saburō, *"Dokusha" no tanjō: Katsuji bunka wa dono yō ni shite teichakushita ka* (The Birth of the "Reader": How Was Print Culture Established?) (Tokyo: Shōbunsha, 2004); Arase Yutaka, *Jiyū, rekishi, mejia: Masu komyunikēshon kenkyū no kadai* (Freedom, History, Media: Issues in Mass Communication Studies) (Tokyo: Nihon Hyōronsha, 1988).

[3] For a library guide, see "Ishikawa Takeyoshi Memorial Library," *NCC Japan*, 2017, https://guides.nccjapan.org/researchaccess/ishikawa-takeyoshi/library.

[4] Barbara Sato, *The New Japanese Woman: Modernity, Media, and Women in Interwar Japan* (Durham, NC: Duke University Press, 2003).

[5] Minami Hiroshi, *Nihonjin no shinri* (The Psychology of the Japanese People) (Tokyo: Iwanami shoten, 1953).

[6] See, for example, Irokawa Daikichi, *The Culture of the Meiji Period*, translated by Marius Jansen (Princeton: Princeton University Press, 1988); Yasumaru Yoshio, *Yasumaru Yoshio shū* (Collected Works of Yasumaru Yoshio), 6 vols. (Tokyo: Iwanami shoten, 2016); Amino Yoshihiko, *Rethinking Japanese History*, translated by Alan S. Christy (Ann Arbor: University of Michigan Center for Japanese Studies, 2012).

[7] Minami Hiroshi, *Taishō bunka* (Taishō Culture) (Tokyo: Keisō shobō, 1965).

[8] Barbara Hamill, "Nihon teki modanizumu no shisō—Hirabayashi Hatsunosuke o chūshin to shite" (The Idea of Japanese *Modanizumu*: Focusing on Hirabayashi Hatsunosuke), in *Nihon modanizumu no kenkyū: Shisō, seikatsu, bunka* (The Study of Japanese *Modanizumu*: Thought, Society, Culture), edited by Minami Hiroshi (Tokyo: Burēn shuppan, 1982), 89–114.

[9] Minami Hiroshi, ed., *Shōwa bunka, 1925–1945* (Shōwa Culture: 1925–1945) (Tokyo: Keisō shobō, 1987); *Zoku—Shōwa bunka, 1945–1989* (Shōwa Culture, Part 2: 1945–1989) (Tokyo: Keisō shobō, 1990).

[10] Barbara Hamill, "Josei: Modanizumu to kenri ishiki" (Women: *Modanizumu* and the Consciousness of Rights), in *Shōwa bunka, 1925–1945* (Shōwa Culture: 1925–1945), edited by Minami Hiroshi (Tokyo: Keisō shobō, 1987), 198–231.

[11] Barbara Hamill, "Sengo josei no yume to genjitsu: Dokusha zadankai ni miru" (Postwar Women's Dreams and Realities: Focusing on Readers' Roundtable Discussions), in *Zoku—Shōwa bunka, 1945–1989* (Shōwa Culture, Part 2: 1945–1989), edited by Minami Hiroshi (Tokyo: Keisō shobō, 1990), 84–97.

[12] Barbara Hamill, "Modan gāru no tōjō to chishikijin" (The Emergence of the Modern Girl and the Intellectuals), *Rekishi hyōron* (Critical History) 491 (1991), 18–26.

[13] Barbara Hamill Sato, "Moga Sensation: Perceptions of the *Modan Gāru* in Japanese Intellectual Circles During the 1920s," *Gender & History* 5, no. 3 (1993), 363–381.

[14] Minami Hiroshi, et al., eds., *Kindai shomin seikatushi 9: Ren'ai, kekkon, katei* (The History of Modern People's Lifestyles 9: Love, Marriage, Family) (Tokyo: San'ichi shobō, 1986).

[15] Wagatsuma Sakae, *Kaisei minpō yowa: Atarashii ie no rinri* (Stories of the Revised Civil Code: The Ethics of the New Household) (Tokyo: Gakufū shoin, 1949).

[16] Barbara Sato, "Tanaka Sumiko and Her Struggle to Create a Gender-Equal Society in Postwar Japan," Association for Asian Studies Conference, online, March 2022.

32

JAPANESE LITERATURE AS REFUGE

Esperanza Ramirez-Christensen

It was what she felt she saw as gleams of gold in the shadows of the English text, glimmerings of a different fountainhead and history of the soul, to be grasped only by learning to read the Japanese and to listen to its shifting voices through the layers of time. Those glimpses of buried gold in a strange new land, those intimations of immortality breathing in age-old temple gardens, might also have been flights of fancy, an unconscious desire to escape the forces of historical circumstance in the Philippines of her time.

ESPERANZA RAMIREZ-CHRISTENSEN is a professor emerita at the University of Michigan specializing in classical Japanese literature, especially Heian and medieval poetry, narrative, and criticism. Her research interests include literary hermeneutics and Buddhist intellectual philosophy, as well as feminist readings of Heian women's writing. Her publications include *Heart's Flower: The Life and Poetry of Shinkei* (1994) and *The Father-Daughter Plot: Japanese Literary Women and the Law of the Father* (coedited with Rebecca Copeland, 2001).

Prologue: Kyoto 1967, Manila 1966

Was it an iris leaf? An arrowroot blade? Someone shot it into the air above the still waters of the pond, and, as it hung there trembling for an infinitesimal moment, suddenly the temple before her came into clear focus with the distant hills and hovering white clouds. The moment held her in its grip and seemed to stretch on and on. She never forgot that instant when time stopped and she was taken out of herself, experiencing an epiphany whose source, however, she could not grasp.

I put that experience in the third person because it was so compelling, and yet I could not place it, did not know from what wellspring it had arisen then. It was the spring of 1967, the girl was twenty, an English literature graduate from the Philippines tasting the air and look of a foreign land for the first time. She was in Japan as a simple tourist, seeking mindless rest from the first year of teaching the general humanities courses required of all freshmen in the university where she herself had just graduated the previous year. She needed distance from the academic milieu she was not certain she wished to join permanently. And respite from the immense conflict in her mind, between remaining a mere observer or becoming an active participant in the sociopolitical struggles of her time. Why would Japan, a place that did not even exist in her imagination, exercise such a hold on her sensibilities? Walking through the narrow winding streets of Kyoto, admiring the darkly gleaming floors of Kiyomizudera high up in the hills. Absorbed by the thick green moss in the aged stillness of Kokedera, the islands of rocks in a sea of sand in Ryōanji. The glimmer of wet flagstones in the spring rain, the moist reddish pink of azalea blossoms setting aglow the bushes on the hillslope at dusk. And that moment out of time in—was it Kinkakuji? The whole town was like a secret garden she had not imagined existed.

Even the smells were different. In Tokyo, she remembered standing along some street overlooking the Kabukiza Theater and wondering at the sweetish sea odor wafting in the air, which she would later realize must be from the fish, soy sauce, and sugar so typical of the local cuisine. No doubt Manila also had its smells, but familiarity had dulled them. Unless it was the delicate fragrance of the garlands of small white *sampaguita* flowers in the dimness of the old stone church of her hometown. Each year in the month of May, she and her friends walked in procession, bearing flower offerings to the Virgin Mary. It was one of the many Catholic rituals that marked the annual calendar and cast a religious patina upon the social life of the friends and families of her youth. Later in Japan, she would discover another calendar, even more replete with custom and ritual but sprung from a vastly different foundation.

In Tokyo then, one could still encounter so many women in kimono. How could they walk so gracefully in those silken sheaths with tightly bound sashes around their waists, feet shod in gleaming white socks and open sandals? There was something elegantly incongruous in the traditional costumes worn against the glass and steel of modern skyscrapers. Yet another puzzle that tugged at her mind. It was the same with those men in the train, dressed in informal kimono finished off with a Western suit jacket, and wooden clogs for footwear. The traditional and modern worn together, the odd jostling together of East and West. And the exotic came even closer in the old restaurant at Gion, where their small group was entertained with *samisen* and a gracious dance, and where *maiko* (apprentice geisha) in full elaborate costume and chalk-white makeup helped serve exquisite delicacies with tea and sake. Familiar as she was with the quality of service at people's homes or when dining out, the way these *maiko* put everyone, old and young alike, at ease, was on a different level altogether. They were obviously too grand to be the help. Sitting right on the tatami floor among the guests, their manner of interacting with them was refined and studied yet unobtrusive. It radiated a care, warmth, and charm meant as if for oneself alone. In sum, everything she saw and experienced in Japan that first time was like a delicious feast, engaging her senses, absorbing her mind, exercising a fascination she felt compelled to explore.

And explore she did. On reaching home, she bought all the Japanese works—poetry, fiction, art books—that she could find. There were not many, and how could there be? Japanese was not even taught at her university at the time. She was absolutely ignorant of the country and culture prior to that "cherry blossom tour" with the Japan Travel Bureau (JTB). But there was enough to engage her and raise further questions. Sei Shōnagon in Arthur Waley's voice was one of the first books she read.[1] Being an English major, how could she not feel at home with that arch wit and irony as in Jane Austen, and, familiar with the Elizabethan poets, how could the nature images and lyrical voice of *waka* fail to move? What a discovery. There they were, dressed in those exotic kimono, but their literature was so English and their poetic sensibility so familiar to one schooled in the Romantic poetry of Wordsworth and Keats or the sonnets of Petrarch and Shakespeare. It was Waley's English voice, even in his translation of *The Tale of Genji*, that had rendered them intelligible, of course, and doubtless also left behind the specific color of their accents.[2] Nevertheless, there was enough similarity and—more to the point—difference preserved between the lines of those English translations to compel what would later, as the years passed by, reveal itself as her lifelong engagement with Japanese literature. It was what she felt she saw as gleams of gold in the shadows of the English text, glimmerings of a different fountainhead and history of the soul, to be grasped only by learning to read the Japanese and to listen to its shifting voices through the layers of time.

Those glimpses of buried gold in a strange new land, those intimations of immortality breathing in age-old temple gardens, might also have been flights of fancy, an unconscious desire to escape the forces of historical circumstance in the

Philippines of her time. The Vietnam War was raging. It was impossible to turn away from the television images of thin, poorly nourished Vietnamese soldiers, bare feet in flip-flop sandals, determined to resist the bombs exploding over their villages. In our innocent idealism, we Filipino students could not stomach the sight of the big, powerfully armed American soldiers invading from across the seas in order to kill puny Asians in their own country, their own hamlets and homes. The images were indelible. A naked girl fleeing from the violence, her face a mask of terror and despair. A soldier bracing himself before the gun trained inches from his head, the instant before his brain explodes in the air from its unstoppable force. B-52s flying from Clark Air Base in Pampanga to drop bombs in Vietnam. The Pacific Fleet, with its aircraft carriers berthed in US Naval Base Subic Bay in Olongapo, Zambales: was not our nation in various ways complicit in the murder of tens of thousands of fellow Asians? But also the terrible daily toll of American soldiers dead, young men lacking privilege to dodge the draft, fighting valiantly before the disenchantment set in.

It is difficult now to comprehend the depth of the Filipino youths' commitment to the values of liberty and social justice when they were under blatant repression from the Marcos regime. And it is equally startling to remember our strong opposition to the Vietnam War as a glaring demonstration of US imperialism. We had little fear of the communism that was the justification for the war. We had no inkling that this fear was quite rabid in the hometowns and cities of America, and that whole nations and citizenries—Korea, Vietnam, Laos and Cambodia, Indonesia, the Philippines—would suffer for this stoked-up terror before the communist ideology of the USSR, China, and North Vietnam. On our campuses, in the streets where students and workers demonstrated, the struggle to free the country from interminable foreign domination merged with the anti-war movement. It would join with the resistance to the deployment of the police and military to repress the genuinely democratic forces of freedom and human dignity.

A night in particular remains brightly in her memory. Was it on October 24 or 25 of 1966, when President Lyndon Johnson was in Manila on the invitation of Philippine President Ferdinand Marcos for a summit meeting with the heads of state of South Vietnam, Australia, New Zealand, South Korea, and Thailand? They were staying at the historic Manila Hotel along Manila Bay, where General Douglas MacArthur himself used to reside until 1941, when Philippine history became directly entangled with Japan on the eve of World War II. We marched from campus and gathered in the square in front of the hotel to protest before the visiting dignitaries against the senseless killing of civilians and the defoliation of peasant farms and villages in the Vietnam War. As we sang songs of exhortation and protest, and, as activist leaders delivered speeches, voices were raised in anger, tempers flared, and, suddenly, the riot police, who surrounded the demonstrators, started firing into the crowd. Being in the front line, she quickly raised her arms to protect herself against the policeman who had raised his truncheon, threatening to hit her. The police had never used their guns in these peaceful political demonstrations peopled mostly by students and laborers. This was the first time. She tried to argue with the man, telling him they were protesting for peace for the Vietnamese people and for social justice in the Philippines, and they were wrong to shoot. While she struggled to hold on to the policeman's truncheon, one of her companions, who had instinctively run away at the first sound of gunfire, thankfully noticed her absence and returned to the front line to pull her away to safety. She was greatly shaken and remained in shock for a long, long while. Why had she not fled at once but remained to argue with a policeman? In all her twenty years, she had never been caught in this kind of violence that could end one's life in an instant. All the fire of her idealism screamed against the idea that some mechanical device, a mere machine, could be deployed so powerfully against the absolute rightness of human ideals of freedom, a just society, the solidarity of compatriots, the timeless verity of goodness, and of truth.

It was stunning. She ran away with her friends; on the way, one of them, Cheryl Bocobo Olivar, stopped to dissuade the police from beating the students on their heads, some of whom were already bleeding.[3] But all their fury at the use of force to respond to peaceful protest was ineffectual. The days and weeks that followed did not lessen the shock of experiencing how puny words and ideals were when confronted with firepower. And the fragility of flesh and blood and bone, the helplessness of one human or a thousand, when tyrannical third-world rulers were aided by imperialist nations to oppress their citizens, to treat them as enemies. It was a sign of the relative innocence of some politicians at the time, whose children were no doubt participants in that same demonstration, that Congress called for an investigation of police brutality. She was one of the witnesses called to testify. A news photographer had captured precisely that moment when she was grappling with a policeman's baton, her mouth open in a scream as she strove to convince him to stop. The photo landed on the front page of one of the papers. All she could state during the testimony was that, from the front line where she stood, she heard the order to "Fire!" but could not see where it was coming from. But her identity could not be hidden. Her father sent word, through her sister, that she must stop participating in such public protests. Apart from the danger, she needed to consider his position as president of the nation's foremost teacher-training college. That was another shock. She was a graduate of the largest public university in the country, newly hired there as an instructor. Their professors had taught them to exercise their minds to analyze the sociopolitical condition of the country, to be vigilant in defense of the democratic principles of a free press and free speech, the rights to assembly. They were enjoined to pay attention to the poverty of the people, the rampant graft and corruption, and to reflect on what to do to reform the status quo. How could her own father object to her participation in the momentous social movements of the times? She would only learn years later, when it no longer mattered, that he himself had been questioned by authorities about his daughter's protest activities. Why was it a secret? Was he embarrassed to seem to be controlling the independent mind of his adult child? Could not the source of the inquiries be divulged? Why had he advised her to live abroad for the time being? Because he was no longer certain he could protect her.

Tokyo, 1968-1970

Such then was the tumultuous background, the set of circumstances, the *engi*—the unforeseen and inextricable threads of cause and effect, or fate—that led me back to Tokyo in April 1968, just a year after my first mind-opening visit, equipped with a Monbushō (Ministry of Education) Scholarship, for the first stage in the Japanese language and literature training arranged by the ministry and facilitated by the staff of International Education at Waseda University, where I had been placed. Daily, from 10:00 a.m. to noon, and then again from 1:00 p.m. to 3:00 p.m., I was one of the international scholars undergoing intensive Japanese language training at the university's Gogaku Kyōiku Kenkyūjo (Language Education Research Institute). So effective was the instruction carried out by a team of highly experienced language instructors that after six months, I could hold my own in daily conversation. My facility further improved when I moved out from the Komaba Ryūgakusei Kaikan dormitory that was like a miniature United Nations. My roommate was an Oxford girl who was dating a Thai boy, and our dining room companions hailed anywhere from Spain to Iran and Argentina, from Ceylon and Malaysia to France. Indeed, my initiation to raw fish, barely a week after my arrival, was by a Frenchman, who took me out for beer and sashimi in nearby Shibuya. No doubt he regarded himself a connoisseur and wanted to guide my appreciation. Unable to abide that raw texture in my mouth, however, I quickly swallowed it whole after one bite. I was too embarrassed to mention it was also my first beer—at the time, Filipinas did not know how to drink alcohol. Be that as it may, staying on at the dorm with other foreign scholars was bound to slow down my acquisition of Japanese, so I requested a homestay arrangement with a Japanese family.

The Japanese family I went to live with was chosen by Monbushō. The father was president of an oil company subsidiary of Mitsui located in Nihonbashi, near the Maruzen bookstore and Takashimaya department store. His wife was a kind, gracious lady who took me into her heart and made sure to initiate me in the traditional arts of flower arrangement, calligraphy, and tea. I took lessons in *ikebana* and *shodō* because of her. It was possibly also a consideration that the mother and two daughters were, like my own family, Catholic; one was at the University of the Sacred Heart (Seishin Joshi Daigaku), the other at Shirayuri University (Shirayuri Joshi Daigaku). I lived with them at an old house in Nishi-Ogikubo. It was suggested that the mother and daughters would do well to learn English from me, but there was hardly any pressure to do it. It was rather as if the mental, almost physical efforts required went against the very proper yet easygoing lifestyle of the women of the household. The father was another matter; he was very strict about everyone's conduct. The house had to be spotless, time was only to be used for work or study, and so on. Due to his strict enforcement of discipline, order, and rectitude, the mother called him a *"Meiji no gankona hito,"* a Meiji-period-like inflexible man. But company duties consumed him, so we women were allowed to be "Shōwa modern"—as befitting the times, I gathered—and we went on with our lives, lunching at the Ōkura, the mother's favorite hotel, viewing pottery or painting exhibits at Isetan department store, attending school benefit programs at Shirayuri University. We made time to go sightseeing in Hakone and visit the mother's sister in Kobe, where they had grown up in the Kansai culture but with international overtones due to the presence of consular establishments there. They became like a foster family for me. Whenever any of my Philippine family visited, my host family entertained them. In return, the parents and a daughter traveled to Manila with me and stayed at my house, getting to know my milieu. Everyone marveled at how Mama-san, speaking in Japanese, and my eldest sister, speaking in English, found a way to communicate across this linguistic gap. They seemed to find a magical, instinctive empathy that I thought I understood. Pretty, charming, and gracious, they had both learned how to accommodate themselves unobtrusively to the patriarchal order in which they were born but to which they did not necessarily adhere. Before getting married herself, my eldest sister had been our surrogate mother and my widowed father's hostess during official receptions at home. I found out Mama-san had been married once before and had been left a young war widow after the death of her husband in one of the Pacific Islands. Where exactly they did not seem to know, or the name was withheld; was that out of delicacy, or did they never recover his remains? As long as the parents were living, I was met at the airport whenever I returned to Japan from Manila or, later, from the United States. When my father came on an official visit, he and my host family together beamed with pride that my Japanese was good enough to act as his interpreter. My activist phase was as good as over.

Although I thought myself so grown-up then, remembering Japan now in my mid-seventies, I have to smile to notice how young I really was. True, I already possessed a self-confidence that has remained pretty much unbroken to this day. Still, I have to observe how my personality and outlook acquired an openness owing to living in various foreign cultures, first and foremost Japan. To begin with, residing in Japan in my early twenties reconfigured my mind that had heretofore been so West-oriented. This was inevitable, given my undergraduate major in English literature. And should I mention the more than three centuries of Spanish colonial rule (1565–1898) and nearly fifty years of American occupation

(1898–1946) that had permanently formed my country and its people? We used to have a Philippine literature in Spanish; our national hero, Jose Rizal (1861–1896), executed by Spain for treason, wrote two novels in Spanish that helped spark the 1896 Philippine Revolution, while studying in Madrid and Heidelberg.[4] Even at present, we maintain a written literature in English, side by side with that written in Filipino, the national language. The 1960s of my college years was still the post–World War II period in Asia, and US geopolitical and cultural dominance was unquestioned, including in—or especially in—the Philippines. Consequently, apart from some readings from Confucian texts and Indian epics in my sophomore class on Eastern thought, frankly, I was virtually ignorant of Asian civilizations. Not surprisingly, I had no true knowledge of what reading and writing in the Japanese script entailed. While speaking the language fluently after a year, I was embarrassed by how slowly my reading skills were progressing. After all, in my experience, it took only a couple of years to read French with a dictionary after learning the grammar, not to mention Spanish, which was compulsory in the educational system. But it gradually dawned on me that the 2,100 and more kanji characters needed to learn to read literature, including classical or premodern documents, would take perhaps ten years of spare time from other work, while reading all the literary and critical texts of the field would take more than a lifetime. I was aghast. Moreover, thinking about it now, even the expert teaching staff at the institute did not seem to fully understand the enormous challenge reading posed for foreign students who did not come from a kanji culture like that of Japan and Korea, countries that were historically part of the imperial Chinese sphere of influence, where Chinese literacy constituted the traditional knowledge base. There was absolutely no comparison between the time and effort needed to learn the twenty-six letters of the Roman alphabet and the years necessary to recognize the forms and learn the meanings of 2,136 kanji, to be exact, and the ways to pronounce them, of which there are 4,388 because each character has at least two pronunciations. In effect, learning to read Japanese is like having to revert to the K–12 level of schooling, when students were taught the 2,136 in an orderly sequence from grades one through six, then through middle school and high school—in effect for twelve years—in national language (*kokugo*) classes. For a college graduate like myself, who had even begun to teach college courses back home, it was a painful process to learn to read Japanese. Rote memorization with writing practice was just about the way to do it. It was not an effective method, but rather dull and uninspiring. Particularly in an intensive program aimed at placing the students into regular content classes in three semesters, kanji instruction was bound to be inadequate. I was not sure what our teachers had in mind, and I suspected they realized the difficulty of the problem but had not yet found an effective method to solve it.

A more meaningful and effective way to teach kanji would have been to have the students memorize, first of all, the 214 essential "radicals" (*bushu*) that constitute the basic graphs common to groups of kanji, thus providing them with a foundation for analyzing the semantic and phonetic components of each new kanji they encounter on their path to literacy. Such a method would have rendered learning characters more rational, interesting, and effective. Although numbering 214, the radicals functioned somewhat like the twenty-six letters of the alphabet in that they occur as elements in all the words to be found in the dictionary. As for myself, the pain of learning by rote memorization was healed by attendance at calligraphy classes taught by my foster mother's friend. Learning how to write kanji with brush, ink stone, and white rice paper took my understanding to a new level. It was easier to appreciate the design and various elements of each character when one had to brush it in a bigger scale and in several iterations before taping the final specimen on the wall for the sensei's critical evaluation. Working actively with one's hand, especially the wrist and fingers wielding the brush, helped almost physically to "digest" the graph as an abstract design, both in the shape of the various components of each graph and in the handling of space—which component is at the top, which down, which goes right, left, or all around. There was also the aspect of musicality in the sequence of the strokes—like playing a melody, you have to remember with which note to begin, continue, and end with, from stroke one to as many as twenty-nine, if one was writing the character with the highest stroke number in the official general-use kanji chart (*utsu* 鬱 in the two-character word for "melancholy," *yūutsu* 憂鬱). Understanding kanji in this way, I was eventually able to overcome the difficulty that initially alienated me from the Japanese script before discovering its fascination and beauty.

Waseda, the campus itself, was a rather different milieu from my foster parents' household. Another thing no one had bothered to inform me about during the Monbushō orientation was that, as in Manila, the Japanese students were in revolt. Their cause was heated opposition to the renewal of the US-Japan Security Treaty (Ampo) that they felt violated the country's sovereignty because it allowed US military bases both on the Japanese mainland and on Okinawa, and involved Japan in the military activities of the US globally, especially, needless to say, in the war in Vietnam. This was in violation of the peace constitution, itself promulgated with the help of the occupying American forces after the war. In other words, the sentiments of the Japanese students were not much different from ours in the Philippines. There were frequent demonstrations on campus, sometimes just outside the political science and economics building, where our language classes were held, adjacent to the statue of the university's founder, Ōkuma Shigenobu (see chapters 3 and 13). Occasionally, the building would be occupied by the students, and our classes had to be held at professors' houses or apartments outside campus. That was such a trying *gomeiwaku* (hassle) for our dedicated mentors; they had to accommodate us in their modest apartments in a Tokyo that was little over twenty years away from the city flattened by war. There was even a period when all the literature departments were placed under lockdown by the Kakumaru-ha, one of the Marxist factions of the nation-wide Zengakuren (All Japan Student Federation). Some professors inside were harangued by radicals about their lack of political engagement, their complicity with a university system training their students to be obedient slaves in a soulless capitalistic economy. I was not surprised that leftist thinking was not uncommon among the future humanists and cultural intellectuals of the literature department, although I was not quite certain where the political sentiments of my classmates in the Japanese literature seminars lay, as opposed to, say, French or Chinese.

During my second year at Waseda, I enrolled in seminars on *waka* poetry; on author Tsubouchi Shōyō (1859–1935) and his analysis of fiction, *The Essence of the Novel* (*Shōsetsu shinzui*, 1885–1886), taught by Professor Inagaki Tetsurō; and even kabuki and the Edo-period work on the art of performance, *Actors' Analects* (*Yakusha rongo*), taught by Professor Torigoe Bunzō. Busy keeping up with difficult texts, I was not about to get drawn into such activism that I had already forsworn. But I could not completely avoid it. The danger for some students came right before my eyes when the police came to the house where I was then residing with yet another family. I had left my foster family after a year because they steadily refused to let me pay for my board and lodging. I was accumulating so much debt that I could not easily repay it later. My foster mother complained of my being *girigatai*—that is, unpleasantly meticulous about repaying one's debt of gratitude. She wished I would *amaeru* (presume on her indulgence) more. But young though I was, I was not used to being on the receiving end of a patronage relationship. Also desiring more freedom to come and go as I pleased, I persisted, went to the Waseda International Office for a *geshuku*-like paid housing arrangement, and ended up with a family with two children: a daughter in middle school and a son who went to college at where else but Waseda. That was a pleasant surprise; I had no objections to observing how it was with a son in the family who was enrolled in the political science and economics (*seiji keizaigaku*) track. The house was an old villa with a traditional garden and architecture in the quieter outskirts of Tokyo, in Ōizumi Gakuen. The son was a very nice young man, highly intelligent, serious, and interested in international affairs, including the student movement in the Philippines. Trying to keep up with his conversation was difficult, as he used the technical and specialized vocabulary of sociopolitical and economic theory. It was a shock then to discover how involved he had been with the Kakumaru-ha students, so involved that the police came one day, went up to his room to examine his library, and took him into custody along with some of the books they found, presumably on Marxist thought.

Was he in prison for a few weeks or months? I forget now so many decades later. But during that period, a pall fell over the house. It was always eerily quiet, and the mother walked around with red eyes either from tears, lack of sleep, or both. The intensity of her anxiety, the distress visible in her face and sensible in the very air in the rooms, although she tried to keep it from me at first, was a revelation. Born into a family of only daughters, and motherless (our mother passed away in 1949, when I was only three), I had not realized the depth and intimacy of the emotional bond between a mother and son. The son's incarceration cast a dense shadow over everyone, even myself, but especially the mother. No doubt the sense of social shame (*haji*) and guilt for the transgression of the eldest child and only son of the family, whose father was an upstanding division chief at a well-known company, was uppermost in their minds. It was not so long ago that leftist intellectuals and dissidents were persecuted by the authorities and considered undesirable members of society. So the fear for the son's physical safety must have been great as well. Although the incident was taboo in our conversations, the mother and I became close during those hours when everyone else was away. I felt my unique presence in the household as a non-native Asian girl who nonetheless spoke the language and was familiar with implicit rules of interaction within the family, and who took away some of the strain and stress around the taboo incident while we chatted on random topics of no grave import, affording the mother a degree of distance and liberation. The interior of the Japanese house, with its porous spaces, was such that you heard what happened in the rooms adjacent to yours, and the sense of sharing the same air, sounds, and smells, created an intimacy among its inhabitants that was not easily shared with strangers, whether native or foreign. Happily, the government this time apparently adopted a policy of reforming the students after their release from prison. Unlike the Philippines, where more radical activists lacking high political connections would be punished by torture, in Japan, they were aided to return to ordinary life. That upstanding young man, I would later hear from his cousin who came to New York on a business trip, had married and was appointed to a local government post, despite the earlier trouble with the law. So he did utilize his Waseda degree in political science and economics after all!

On the topic of student activism, I also paid attention when novelist Mishima Yukio visited Waseda and gave at least two speeches at the Ōkuma Auditorium. The auditorium was so packed that I had to stand outside to listen through the loudspeaker. I even bought his book of essays addressed to the students, *For Young Samurai* (*Wakaki samurai no tame ni*, 1969), in order to flesh out where his solidarity with them was coming from.[5] It turned out that he, too, was against the transformation of sovereign Japan into what at the time was called an "economic animal," a nation striving only for vulgar financial gain. He derided the soft-headedness of peaceful times, when death, precisely what gave existence its meaning, had fled from common awareness. He was a patriot advocating for the restoration of the feudal moral values of physical courage, discipline, and pure-hearted loyalty to the nation as symbolized by the emperor. More to the point, he criticized the students' lack of seriousness, sarcastically pointing out their tendency to posturing, the absence of genuine conviction to die for their cause. I would learn still later, when I was planning the general humanities course at the University of Michigan, which I dubbed "Love and Death in Japanese Culture" and chose *Hagakure: Way of the Samurai* by Yamamoto Tsunetomo (1659–1719) as one of the readings, that this book, so widely disseminated all throughout the 1930s and the war years, was one of Mishima's favorites and had influenced the central place of death in his philosophy and fiction.

"The Way of the Samurai is found in death." And "As everything in the world is but a sham, death is the only sincerity."[6] Such lines from *Hagakure* must have been emblazoned in Mishima's mind when he put together his commentary on this classic text in *Introduction to Hagakure* (*Hagakure nyūmon*) in 1967.[7] I was still shocked, nevertheless, later when at Berkeley, where I had moved in August 1970, my Japanese literature reading companion called to tell me with tears in her voice that the famous novelist had committed *seppuku* at the eastern headquarters of the Self-Defense Forces on November 25, 1970 (see chapter 3). He was still exhorting his countrymen to remain loyal to the Japanese spirit as he saw it and gave his life to make a point. My friend, a Japanese literature major herself, did not necessarily agree with his *seppuku*, but she was very moved by his sincerity, the pure-heartedness (*makoto*) of his gesture. "As everything in the world is but a sham, death is the only sincerity." Indeed. We had been reading Kawabata Yasunari's *Snow Country* (*Yukiguni*) together. I knew her love and devotion to the Japanese language and to the spirit animating it in the literary works that she wanted me to grasp. She had taken me with her to Nikkō (famous for the Tōshōgū Shrine of the first Edo-period shōgun Tokugawa Ieyasu) during semester break to show me the big old house and milieu where she had grown up. It consisted of tatami room after tatami room separated by sliding doors, with a veranda running along them. They were of a size so large it made one think of those Edo-period establishments in the *ukiyoe* woodblock prints where people held parties with geisha entertainers. Perhaps it was used as such long ago. The house had an aged and lonely patina already when I stayed there. She also recounted the case of the first major industrial pollution disaster around the Ashio Copper Mines in the mountains above the Watarase River in Nikkō. The mines had been in operation since the Edo period, but it was during Meiji when modern Western technology was adopted that massive environmental damage to the hills and rice fields below the river began to be detected. Deforestation, soil erosion, flooding, and mineral contamination of the wastewater from the toxic smoke of the smelting and refining process poisoned or flooded the farmers' rice fields across several villages. It was striking that the peasants fought back by petitioning the government for redress and help and continued their activism across generations as long as the mines were in operation. That was until 1973, although the refinery operations continued until 1980, as I was to read later. My friend's desire to retell this narrative, motivated no doubt by her ancestors' involvement in it, made me understand that Japanese literature students like her were also sympathetic to the struggles of the peasants. This was manifest in the long-standing student resistance to the construction of the Narita International Airport due, among other factors, to the displacement of the farmers there. In this and many other ways, she, too, became part of my sociopolitical education in Japan, happening at close range, through the eyes of its inhabitants, while living and traveling together with them.

By the summer of 1970, I was ready to move on. My departure was motivated by a need to escape from life as a quasi-Japanese girl acquiring a graduate education before settling down to marriage. Was I going through an identity crisis? Having conformed so naturally to the manners and speech of certain Japanese women of my age, I was sometimes mistaken for one. Except I was not and could not imagine being a Japanese wife. I had closely observed their lives and could not see myself in that role. Looking back, I think I might have preferred, and would easily have found, a boyfriend in order to experience the culture at even closer range, but I was too young and innocent then to know for sure. As a middle-class Filipina, I was inwardly put off by the lower social status of girls in Japan. An educator himself, my father had taken his daughters' studies seriously, taught us to regard education as a means to become independent on our own. A widower for too long, he had no idea how to marry us off. He did try it once, but the result was so disastrous he gave up and allowed us to chart our own matrimonial destinies. This was fine with me. The idea of marrying for wealth and status was quite repellent. I even exulted secretly that, because I was always a scholarship girl, my tuition was paid for through my own efforts, and I need not feel bound to obey my father's establishment-class politics. My sense of self-respect had to be based on financial independence. I thought perhaps the experience of Caucasian girls in Japan would be quite different. While they might have problems smoothly settling into life in a Japanese family, at school, their frank speech and bolder body language were probably accepted as such and not thought unpleasant and strange. In other words, they were not expected to conform as much as I was because of my Asian appearance. No doubt the class hierarchy of nations implicit in global politics was also operative. And while I did not mind for the most part because I was brought up in the same feminine modesty and reserve, in time, I could no longer endure the difference in status between men and women when the latter were serious, as I was, about pursuing a profession. Mine was Japanese literature. But despite the Monbushō sponsorship and attending classes with leading names in the field, I did not find a professor who I felt was serious about guiding me along the path to competence, if not mastery, of some slice of the field. As is well-known but taboo to say among foreign Japanologists, the national literature establishment did not truly believe that foreign scholars could understand their literature; they believed that only natives could have an intuitive feel for the essence of the "Japanese spirit" inhering in Japanese language and literature. True, perhaps, but when you were a woman, and neither Japanese nor white, the skepticism becomes even deeper. But then again, the truth might have been that the distinguished and graying professors, who came to class with their thread-bound first editions still carried in *furoshiki tsuzumi* (cloth-wrapped bundles), were simply at a loss about how to deal with a twenty-two-year-old Filipina girl just starting to read *waka*, not to mention the Meiji-period prose of Tsubouchi Shōyō, who wished to become a *kokubungakusha* (national literature scholar). After all, at the time, I was the only Filipina I knew reading *kokubungaku* at Waseda; the other foreign students, mostly men, were in more gainful fields like engineering and economics, where the faculty was more likely to read and speak some English and thus feel more comfortable with foreign students.

Here, I have no wish to accuse Japanese of racism or misogyny, then or now. Racist they might be, but isn't, in some sense, everyone? In general, we are all more comfortable with people of our own kind. Condemnation or absolution of people for this reason is beside the point. It is their words and actions, and their consequences within specific contexts, that must be judged with clarity and also compassion. The war in the Pacific left a legacy of racist contempt in some of its older citizens, but it also continues to motivate a desire to help the former colonies in the hearts of others. In the late 1960s, the war was still a part of the Japanese psyche, so traumatic had been the ceaseless carpet firebombing of Tokyo, not to mention the dropping of the atomic bombs in Hiroshima and Nagasaki in August 1945. In the late 1960s, survivors and some hooded disfigured victims could still be seen on the streets during memorials and antinuclear demonstrations. People were still smarting from a sense of victimization by white men.

In the Philippines, too, the damage had been great. Manila was a beautiful Spanish colonial city before the war and was graced also with government buildings in classical architecture built after the 1898 US takeover of the country. Dubbed the "pearl of the Orient" by its newest conquerors, it would become the second-most destroyed city in the Pacific battles, pitilessly bombed by the Japanese when they invaded to occupy it and by the Americans when they returned to reclaim their colony at war's end in 1945. I was born in 1946, and, when I graduated from college at twenty, I was not so conscious of the war and the Japanese occupation of the Philippines. Years later, when exchanging memories with my older sisters about the past, this is what I could piece together: When the war broke out, my father was a public school official assigned to Surigao Province. The Japanese invasion of the

Philippines began on December 8, 1941, just ten hours after the devastating attack on Pearl Harbor. It was so sudden, the family was forced to abandon our house and all our possessions except for the most necessary. They hurriedly fled up north to the rice and tobacco farming region of Isabela, my mother's home province. There, in the course of the war, two of my parents' five children perished from malnutrition and disease. My mother took the little rice and tobacco she could hide from their farms and traveled in a truck to sell it on the black market in order to buy eggs and medicine for her children. The accounts of the brutal bayoneting of children as the Japanese defeat became clear in 1945 would be passed on even into my own time. Ghosts sometimes flitting in the classrooms of our elementary school were said to be of Japanese soldiers who had been killed and buried in the schoolyard. But in general, Filipinos of my generation, born after the war, were not educated in the details of the conduct of the war. It was almost as if those who lived through them would rather forget the terrible suffering of those years.

So I was quite startled when one of my language professors, who was also the director of the Gogaku Kyōiku Kenkyūjo, invited me to his office one day to show me an issue of the internal magazine (*dōnin zasshi*) *Sampaguita*, named after my country's national flower, written by and circulated among the soldiers of the company he headed during the occupation. The company was responsible for Japanese language education and information services vis-à-vis the local population. The articles were brief reminiscences of the country, the towns they lived in, the people they met, the natural scenery, and their experiences teaching Japanese. The old professor briefly apologized for the war, and, while repeatedly praising the pristine beauty of the country, referred to his soldiers' nostalgia for the lands and natives among whom they lived until just twenty years earlier. I did not know how to respond to the almost unbearable irony of the delicate, fragrant white flower turned into a symbolic object of a former occupying army's longing. However, I was, of course, moved. How could I not be, to meet with someone who actually lived and worked in Manila until just a year before my birth, and who was now teaching me Japanese, the same way he had done then in Manila? What sort of destiny was playing out through these unimaginable coincidences? More, he revealed that his office had been in the Philippine Normal College on Taft Avenue, the very same college of which my father was president from 1958 to 1970. It had been founded by the Americans, along with my own University of the Philippines. Ironically, it was still receiving some funding from US foundations when my father was questioned about what must have been construed as my anti-American activities in 1966.

The war was not a topic of conversation back home, except for the most sensational events with propagandistic effects, such as the Bataan Death March (April 1942), in which so many American soldiers, and even more Filipino soldiers (thirty thousand in one count), perished, or the victorious return of General Douglas MacArthur on the beach of Leyte at war's end.[8] People were focused on making lives for themselves just a couple of decades after, so much so that the Philippine GDP was at that period the highest in Southeast Asia, which is why there was absolutely no political tension or conflict in my mind in studying Japanese literature in 1968. True, my friends thought it an eccentric and unexpected choice.

The country I had long set my heart on for graduate study, to the point of enrolling in Manila's Alliance Française (an organization to promote knowledge of French language and culture), was France. I had read Montaigne, Pascal, and Rousseau in college, had been enthralled by the meandering, sometimes breathless style of Proust's *Remembrance of Things Past*. Prior to that, I had been utterly absorbed in Dostoyevsky's profoundly soul-gripping dramatization of the questions of good and evil, crime and punishment, and life and death in *The Brothers Karamazov* and his other great novels with their unforgettable characters. But I was drawn back into French literature by Albert Camus. In *The Rebel*, his apparently crystal-clear reflections about how to live when confronted with the death of God, the inhumanity of man to man, the arbitrariness of circumstance, the slaughter of innocents—some of the same questions that tortured the minds of Dostoyevsky's intellectuals—compelled my attention. Camus was almost a contemporary, having just died in 1960. A member of the resistance, he had a heroic aura despite the seeming nihilism of his outlook, plus a lucidity of mind visible in his prose. I felt he had taught me that one must still decide and engage in action in the face of meaninglessness and despair, and that is what existential freedom signifies. In other words, while I was not aware of any political contradiction in choosing to study Japanese (I might as well have felt rebellious about reading American literature because of the US invasion and takeover of the Philippines in 1898), I actually felt strangely at home in the postwar mood of disappointed cynicism in its literary culture; somehow it felt like the *après-guerre* melancholy of French existentialism. Especially after my indelible, traumatic experience of the puniness of ideals before murderous firepower, this sense of melancholy among the ruins of the broken civilizations of Europe resembled the despair at the futility of heroism, and the paradoxical beauty in sadness running through Kawabata, Tanizaki, and Mishima, the triumvirate of postwar Japanese literature, that spoke to me at the time. The sentiment was very much the same—the eruption of modernity in the context of global power conflicts the same—although their historical contexts were different. It was Japan's unique placement in my mind within Western modernity, problematic for a country with a wholly different tradition and history, that made its literature a viable continuation of the comparative literature track I had been pursuing in my mind since graduation. The educated class in the Philippines was so Americanized already, and, despite the US intelligence service's paranoia about communism in the country, I was absolutely certain the Filipinos could not be turned into communists. The communist ideology and history in the USSR and China did not appeal to me either, although, admittedly, the Scandinavian practice, which was based on a socialist ethos, held much appeal. Japan was different. While holding on to its traditional culture, it was obviously determined to succeed in the process of modernization that had been interrupted by the war. Maybe Japan had something to teach someone whose country had been colonized by Western powers the longest in all of Asia.

Berkeley, 1970-1973

There is no need to question why I ended up next at the University of California, Berkeley. The Waseda international division office was encouraging me to stay longer and pursue an MA; I would be the first Filipino to do so. However, fed up with the inadequacy of my academic mentoring in Japan, I decided on the next best thing: to just go quickly for an MA degree at a suitable American university and then return to my old position at the University of the Philippines. In addition to its reputation as one of the three premier institutions (with Columbia and Harvard) for training in Japanese Studies, I chose UC Berkeley because I had an older sister who was a US citizen living in San Francisco. She had done postgraduate studies at the University of Minnesota and later immigrated to San Francisco with her husband.

In August of 1970, I landed in San Francisco to the sight of brown hills and air so dry I had nosebleeds the first few days. The immigration officer looked through my papers and strangely demanded to know if I had come to Berkeley to march. I did not and said so. Although I felt awkward and missed the moist greenness of Japan, living in the Bay Area, so close to the Pacific Ocean just as we did in Manila, was glorious. And as it turned out, the atmosphere at Berkeley was heady and electric with new ideas and attitudes that people were not merely thinking but actively living. Like parts of San Francisco, it was a free, liberated city—all that Tokyo could not then be. Hippies were everywhere. Being "square" was not tolerated; "cool" and "vibes" still had a novel, fresh ring. Occasionally, a naked guy would streak across campus, frolic in the fountain, and disappear among the thick bushes. Hare Krishnas in their colorful costumes sang and danced, and some spectators would join in. Joan Baez sang at Sproul Hall, and Norman Mailer got aggressive while giving a half-drunken talk. Busloads of tourists would get off at Telegraph Avenue across from Sproul Plaza and ogle the weirdos. It was a time when young people all seemed to know how to play the folk guitar. And everyone seemed able to sing those folk songs, many alluding to the youth's resistance to the draft, the Vietnam War, the wasteful death of young men. We could thumb for a ride at passing cars or trucks and no one ever refused. People smiled at you for no reason. Here, strangely, the atrocities of the Vietnam War even seemed to occasionally fade from view, such were the good-natured vibes all around.

I was back to residing in a dorm setting. This time it was the International House at the top of the campus, from where the central artery that went down to Telegraph started. The residents of I-House, as it was nicknamed, were all graduate students: half of them American, the other half international. They worked hard but played hard and made it a practice to have parties at some room or other every weekend, irrigated with cheap jugs of California red wines. No one seemed to notice how crowded it was, so high was the energy level, the intensity of engagement in the conversations. It was the same in the dining hall, where at dinner time, you could find yourself seated with Americans from across the country and foreigners from Europe, Asia, and the Middle East, all carrying on exciting discussions about political or cultural issues, which might continue come the weekend if the group decided to eat pizza with pitchers of beer down along Telegraph. Dinner was not available at I-House on weekends, if I recall correctly. Was it the atmosphere at Berkeley that promoted such intensity of discussion and debate? The mixed racial-geographical origins of the participants? Their ages from their mid to late twenties and early thirties and the fact that they were mostly unmarried? Whatever it was, what is clear was that the sociocultural experiment transpiring in the Bay Area was a significant factor for many who chose to come to Berkeley. Most of all, there was the pleasure of the wit and intelligence of superior minds, old enough to have experienced something of the world and acquire a level of maturity, confidence, and sophistication, to appreciate one another's distinct customs and traditions—that is, the pleasures of diversity. I was, during the year of my residence at I-House, friends with many Asian Americans, but also with a Frenchman, Dane, Turk, and Japanese—all attracted to my Asian ethnicity and friendliness, I guess, and my two and a half years of residence in Tokyo. Japan, site of the 1964 Tokyo Summer Olympics and the Expo '70 in Osaka, had visibly risen to economic power barely twenty-five years after the wartime defeat and was an object of great interest to many at the time regardless of nationality. The openness to diverse cultures was such that there were quite a few interracial marriages just after a year, mine one of them. In December 1971, I married my Danish friend Steen Christensen, who had engaged me in interminably long conversations since our first meeting, managing to outdo other interested parties. Our wedding was held at Newman Chapel just down the street from I-House, a Jesuit church that was known to be sheltering some conscientious objectors. (Coincidentally, the apartment where Patty Hearst, at the time a Berkeley sophomore in art history, was kidnapped by a radical urban left group in February 1974, was also close by.) My friend and classmate in the Japanese Studies MA program, Phyllis Birnbaum of New Rochelle, New York (chapter 20), had tied the knot with her friend, an electrical engineer from Bombay, India, earlier that year. We had immediately formed a bond because of our common undergraduate major in English literature.

It was at the Department of Oriental Languages (as it was then called) at Berkeley that my real education in Japanese literature as a branch of Japanology began. To put the matter succinctly, at the time, the study of Japanese literature was taught as a philological and sociohistorical discipline by the senior professors of the field there, Professors Helen Craig McCullough and William H. McCullough. As the leading experts in the United States—and practically the world—in classical or premodern literature, they taught in the way they had learned to produce the formidably long list of books that had made them famous.[9] We were privileged to be students in the graduate seminars where some of their books had, in a sense, their incubation. My training in *bungo*, the classical language, at Waseda, had consisted of mastery of the grammatical system that would enable one to comprehend the text. One acquired the ability to conjugate the various parts of speech, mainly verbs and adjectives but also, importantly, the suffixes denoting various aspects of modality, whose declension shifted according to the word preceding them. With the instruction and textbook being all in Japanese, learning was relatively simple. One was tested on the grammar and the ability to parse passages into modern Japanese to show one's comprehension. But whereas studying *bungo* in Japan did not necessarily inspire one to delve deeper into the literature, at Berkeley, under the tutelage of the McCulloughs, digging into what lay within and behind the text, so to speak, was a minimum expectation. One had to scrutinize more thoroughly the meaning of words because graduate coursework involved producing English translations of the poems or prose under study, along with annotations of any item in the assigned passage that was not within the common understanding. This could be a placename; the color, style, or part of a particular kimono or samurai armor; the details of a religious ritual; and so on. One had to become an "archeologist" of classical texts, and this involved learning to use all the specialized dictionaries and/or encyclopedias of *waka*, biographies, genealogies, Buddhism, dress and costume, warrior armor and implements, period architecture, courtesan houses, flowers and trees, birds and insects, calendar systems, ranks and offices in various historical periods, and more—the list of bibliographical sources that we had to learn to use in Professor Bill McCullough's bibliography seminar, which was as rigorous as Helen's, was endless. It was a wonder that the Oriental Languages Library had all these sources.

One had to become an "encyclopedist" of all things Japanese in order to write an annotation that met Helen's very high standards. But this wasn't all. Translating the Japanese text into English meant you had to learn to interpret it. This was an extra step that I did not have to take in the *bungo* class I had taken at the institute in Waseda, which was essentially an advanced language class; you just had to learn to read. It was the process of learning to translate *waka* in Helen's seminar on the *Kokinshū* that gradually awakened me to the beauty of the language of classical poetry. In sensing the body of the text, I observed the structure of the lines, the dynamic flow of the syntax, how a line twisted and turned into a metaphor, where the pregnant pauses or ellipses were, whether a question was real or rhetorical, and so on, from line one to five. Of course, I had learned how to analyze poetry in this way as an English major. Generally, my early undergraduate training in the critical reading of literary texts was an indispensable foundation for my development as a Japanese literature specialist. But analyzing poetry in the classical Japanese language, and holding two vastly distinct linguistic cultures together, filtering them against each other, was a different process altogether. Translation is, in this way, a highly interpretive and thus creative endeavor, and that is how it was that at Berkeley I decided to specialize not in modern but premodern literature. Through the tracery of numberless poems on the four seasons and the vicissitudes of love in the *Kokinshū*, or the haiku dotting Bashō's record of his poetic journey cum pilgrimage in *The Narrow Road to the Deep North* (*Oku no hosomichi*), I was also beginning to get an inkling of what lay behind the glimmers of gold I had sensed in the ancient temple gardens of Kyoto. Even more affecting was reading the early chapters of the masterpiece by Japan's greatest woman writer, Murasaki Shikibu (c. 978–1014), *The Tale of Genji* (*Genji monogatari*), with its fascinating texture of lyrical poetry woven into the prose narrative, in another seminar with Bill. All this rich classical heritage was also surely what Kawabata, Tanizaki, and Mishima, each in his own way, were fiercely defending and cherishing amidst the ashes of a dying tradition in the war's aftermath.

Helen became my master's thesis advisor. I made this decision in a kind of fear and trembling. We were all awed by her. Our weekly written assignments for her *Kokinshū* seminar included translating a couple of individually assigned poems from the anthology, accompanied by annotations, and writing two-to-five-page critical commentaries where you had to draw on your native wit to talk up what was distinctive about each poem, its author, style, and so on. We had to write a final ten-to-fifteen-page term paper on a topic of our choice. We were all grateful that there were any number of Japanese critical commentaries on all the poems in the anthology, as well as volumes of modern scholarly research, to draw from. Still, Helen found many parts in our papers to mark with her red ink pen and decorate with a questioning or critical comment, pointing out mistakes, ambiguities, and less than felicitous turns of phrase. Such marginalia could sometimes be too much to take. I have to admit I was a bit prideful then, and I once became so incensed at Helen's comments that I took one of the painted porcelain ashtrays that Steen's mother had sent from Denmark as souvenirs for the guests at our wedding and threw it angrily at the wall of our apartment. It shattered into shards on the floor. In time, I slowly calmed down and accepted Helen's scholarly authority, reflecting that we should in fact be grateful that she took the time to comment so meticulously on our work in the process of training us. What could be better for future professionals in our field? I came to recognize that pride was out of place in

Figure 32.1: Esperanza Ramirez-Christensen with Kaneko Kinjirō, Helen McCullough, William McCullough, Tsurusaki Hiroo, Steven Carter, and Mack Horton, University of California, Berkeley, 1980. Photograph courtesy of the author.

Japanology because the field was so vast and difficult; a PhD easily took ten years to complete, and mastery was achieved only by a few. I, too, came to expect of myself the meticulousness necessary for reliable, competent scholarship. While following this rule, I acquired the more mature scholar's fortitude necessary to satisfy the fierce desire to know everything one could about the question being pursued. I reminded myself that an undergraduate professor, the same who had hired me to teach after graduation, had said, apropos one of my papers, that the analysis was so detailed and thorough that reading it was like encountering a tiger and following him all the way back to his lair. By the time I reached Harvard to do my PhD in 1976, I had learned so much from Helen and Bill—including working as their research assistant for their multivolume translation of *Eiga monogatari* (later, in 1980, published as *A Tale of Flowering Fortunes: Annals of Japanese Aristocratic Life in the Heian Period*)—that I was confident that, given the requisite time, I could read, translate, and analyze any classical text as long as necessary references were available. There was always something new and difficult to excavate in the premodern archive.

Back to Japan, 1979-1980

Japan returned to me after nearly ten years of absence (apart from brief trips) when I went to do research for my PhD dissertation on *renga* linked poetry and the Buddhist poetics of the poet-monk Shinkei (1406-1475).[10] I chose Tōkai

University in Hiratsuka City, Kanagawa, to work with Professor Kaneko Kinjirō, the author of the thick tomes of research constituting the modern archives of a whole new field.[11] I was no longer a young ingenue in the field but a PhD candidate at Harvard's Department of East Asian Languages and Civilizations. Along with my Berkeley MA and intensive Japanese studies at Waseda, I had added two years of teaching premodern language and literature at the Østasiatiske Institut of Copenhagen University, Denmark, where I lived with my husband from 1973 to 1976; there, I encountered several kinds of students interested in Japan, including young Americans who had fled from the draft and found shelter among progressive young Danes. Professor Olof Lidin, director of the Østasiatiske Institut, had been Helen's student at Berkeley. Did the unbidden threads of destiny follow me across the Atlantic as well? At Harvard, I worked mainly with Professor Edwin Cranston on Heian-period literature and with Howard Hibbett on Edo-period texts, particularly Saikaku. I attended cross-disciplinary classes taught by leading authorities in Japanese history, classical Chinese, Mahayana Buddhism, contemporary critical theory, and modernist poetry.

Although I was my old nonchalant self, the gravitas exuded by age and experience must have showed. This time in Japan, the guidance provided by my mentor, Professor Kaneko, was strict and deliberate. He created four seminars mainly for my benefit and invited me to a fifth to broaden my cultural context. The seminars comprised eight graduate students, all male except for myself and Sook Young Wang, a Tōkai PhD student in medieval *waka*.[12] We discussed *Murmured Conversations* (*Sasamegoto*, 1463–1464), the poetic treatise considered the most representative of the medieval period because its conceptual foundation in Buddhist philosophy, particularly Zen, had influenced the development of classical arts like *ikebana,* tea ceremony, and Noh theater. But Kaneko-sensei also wanted me to learn about how Shinkei's life was reflected in his poetry, style, and criticism. I was soon plunged into studying and presenting more than a hundred of Shinkei's *hokku* and *tsukeku* from the second imperial *renga* anthology, *Shinsen tsukubashū* (1495).[13] I was particularly attentive to Shinkei's self-annotations and the commentaries on them by his premier disciples, Sōgi (1421–1502), who had been appointed to compile the *Shinsen tsukubashū*, and Kenzai (1452–1510). A particularly important source was Sōgi's *Solace in Old Age* (*Oi no susami*, 1479), a critical evaluation of verses by the so-called "seven sages of *renga*" (including Shinkei). Through studying *Solace in Old Age*, I learned what linking between one verse and the next, and thus between one poet and another, truly meant in *renga*.

The seminar on *Murmured Conversations* was more challenging. I remember feeling like I was on stage performing for my classmates. Everyone knew that my dissertation was to be an annotated English translation of the treatise and that Kaneko-sensei had offered the seminar and required their attendance for my sake. In my weekly presentations, I read the requisite sections in the original classical

Japanese, full of quotations from Buddhist sutras and Buddhist anecdotal literature, Confucian texts, and anthologies of *waka* and *renga*. I felt particularly proud of my ability to read in *yomikudashi kanbun* (Sino-Japanese) lines by Tang Dynasty poets Du Fu and Bai Juyi and passages from *The Lotus Sutra*. I could sense my male classmates' wordless admiration because *kanbun*, the language of literacy in Japan until the nineteenth century, had historically been reserved for men. Because I had studied classical Chinese at Berkeley and Harvard, I could comprehend the quoted passages directly and spontaneously translate them into the *yomikudashi* style of converting Chinese into Japanese syntactic order. After reading a passage aloud, I translated it into modern Japanese to offer my own interpretation for Kaneko-sensei's evaluation and my classmates' feedback. For instance, if I had failed to point out the connection between Shinkei's main point and the embedded quotation from, say, *The Analects*, Kaneko-sensei would question me on it, and, if my answer was inadequate, he would correct it. Then he would explain to the class how the passage is cited in other medieval texts. Through listening to Kaneko-sensei and my dialogical give-and-take, the class would learn the importance of context and interpretation of the classics. Another of Kaneko-sensei's seminars was a "mad verses reciting group" (*kyōginkai*) in which we read the manuscript precursor of the comical, bawdy *Doggerel Tsukubashū* (*Inu Tsukubashū*, circa 1530). Here, I felt less the center of attention. Because everyone participated in explicating the text, I was able to learn from my classmates and to discover what the pecking order in the classroom was. How discussion was conducted seemed sometimes more pertinent than the content itself; that is, the more senior members of the class were expected to say more. My classmates seemed almost workman-like; each member had a job to do, which they did earnestly and cheerfully. There seemed to be an unspoken rule that one should not say more than was necessary. While in the seminars on Shinkei, my presentations were fulsome; I performed like a docent at a museum, pointing to the distinctive features of a painting. Although I might have been overdoing it, the group listened carefully, finding my mode of exegesis (I thought of it as my old New Criticism mode) novel and interesting. A case could be made that Sōgi's style of analysis in *Solace in Old Age* was close to an early example of *explication du texte*. I was allowed to speak that way because I was a visiting researcher and not expected to know or follow the pecking order.

At the time, Sensei's closest *deshi* (disciple) was a PhD student we called Kaji-san, who was researching *wakan renga*, a hybrid Sino-Japanese linked poetic form. Kaji-san was a consummate bibliophile, ready with the source reference for each citation. He was tasked with coordinating both our weekly seminars and the *kompa* drinking parties after, which were held at local restaurants where Kaneko-sensei treated us to drinks and food and where we could all unwind and learn more about each other. Kaji-san gave me so much advice in both scholarly and practical matters that I thought that Kaneko-sensei had asked him to see to my

Figure 32.2: Esperanza Ramirez-Christensen, PhD graduation, Harvard University, 1983. Photograph courtesy of the author.

every need so that I could comfortably carry out the research and training I had come to do. He probably thought I needed close guidance there because I had only lived with families in Tokyo, never alone in an apartment in the near countryside that Hiratsuka City was at the time. Kaji-san even escorted me on trips to used bookstores in Kanda, Tokyo, a mecca for us bibliophiles. We both smoked in those days—Rothmans for me (for those who know, a strong but smooth English cigarette). We would always enjoy a smoke or two at some nice local coffee shop after our absorbing book-browsing and buying spree, talking shop or gossiping about figures in the field. Kaneko-sensei had mentored many students, many of them already professors; his followers, young and old, surrounded him at literary events, which were like reunions. It gave me a warm and fuzzy feeling to be introduced as one of his *deshi* and accepted as such. Kaneko-sensei's former students invited me to their campuses, offered to help me find old manuscripts in archives and the like. And so it was under Kaneko-sensei's strict but warmhearted tutelage that I finally came to experience the sense of belonging to a professional in-group in Japan. When I returned to Cambridge, I was asked to write a review article on Professor Earl Miner's *Japanese Linked Poetry*, the first volume in English on *renga*, for *The Harvard Journal of Asiatic Studies* (1981), and to submit a paper I had written for Professor Cranston's *The Tale of Genji* seminar for inclusion in one of the earliest collections of English studies of that Heian masterpiece, *Ukifune: Love in The Tale of Genji* (1982).[14] These two texts were, in effect, my first published works, launching my career as a specialist of premodern Japanese literature.

Coda: Japanese Literature as Refuge

I went on to a career that spanned more than three decades, teaching at Smith College (1982–1987) and the University of Michigan (1987–2013). As I look back across the span of time from 1968, when I left Manila, to the present, I am overwhelmed by a deep sense of gratitude at the kindness of strangers—people in Japan, the United States, and Denmark who took me into their homes and their hearts. When I left the Philippines, it felt like my country had betrayed me. The decades from the late sixties through the seventies and the early eighties—unstable, dangerous, lacking decent jobs for the educated but unconnected—had seen a massive brain drain, the enforced exile of disaffected college graduates and professionals mostly into the United States, the very country that had sponsored the Marcos dictatorship under President Lyndon Johnson and President Ronald Reagan. I certainly belonged to the earliest batch of those exiles, although my first destination could not be the United States but Japan. There would be two decades of repression until the successful uprising of the People's Power Revolution of 1986, which would be just the prologue for yet another era of frustration, another abortion of the people's long-cherished desire for democracy and social justice, or just plain human dignity.

That revelatory demonstration in 1966 had led me to a protracted examination of conscience. For years thereafter, through the rigors of working toward two advanced degrees and then working as a Japanologist in a foreign country, I could not cease from feeling guilt about my departure. Did I betray my country by leaving? True, my fellow budding activists had said while we bade goodbye to one another that I need not stay; it would be enough to keep the light burning. Moreover, many of my high school and college classmates, including some of the professors, also emigrated during those years of repression, part of a brain drain that proved fateful for Philippine development, for we constituted a generation whose loss would hold the country back for yet another half-century or more. For some twenty years thereafter, I studied and worked as if on indefinite reprieve from the true project I should be pursuing. Happily, premodern Japan was so challenging that I could never be satisfied until I knew all that I could. The hard work required proved to be a bulwark against melancholy. Even in Japan in 1980, I still needed to reflect on what lay behind the epiphany I had experienced in 1967 beside a pond at a Kyoto temple—that magical moment when a leaf traced a quivering arc before me and time seemed to stop. Perhaps I knew then that studying Shinkei's poetry and Buddhist poetics was the way to go.[15] But I needed to finally accept that I had neither the physical strength nor the ideological conviction to wage guerilla warfare in the hills. Nor could I imagine risking life and limb in political reeducation campaigns in urban streets. Being of a poetic bent, I could not be that kind of fighter. Someone with a sterling commitment to the good, the true, and the beautiful, yes, and firmly adhering to democratic ideals of freedom, equality, and justice. But I had always shunned violence, whether of word or deed. I could imagine marching for an urgent cause, for a lofty ideal, and being shot dead for it. Looking back now, I would have been happy and at peace with myself had I indeed been killed at twenty on that fateful night in October 1966. It turned out to be the most life-changing experience of my life, when acting out of purity of heart, I felt no fear defying police violence in defense of a noble ideal. The gravity of that moment equaled the one in Kyoto in 1967, which would stretch out to be a lifeline, a lamp shining in the darkness of despair, pointing me to a path enabling me to live on. Japanese literature turned out to be a refuge indeed, a way to survive through the kindness of strangers who saw through the brightness to the sadness within.

Notes

[1] Arthur Waley, trans., *The Pillow Book of Sei Shōnagon* (New York: Grove Press, 1960).

[2] Arthur Waley, trans., *The Tale of Genji* (New York: Modern Library, 1960).

[3] Cheryl Bocobo Olivar, a close friend in high school and college, later did graduate studies at the University of Michigan. Her grandfather, Jorge Bocobo (1886–1965), was president of the University of the Philippines in the mid-1930s and translator of Jose Rizal's two novels. Her brother, Gary Olivar, was an activist leader in the 1980s struggle; he was at Harvard when I was there, and so was Senator Benigno Aquino, the opposition leader whose assassination on his return to Manila directly fueled the overthrow of the Marcos dictatorship. The idealism of our generation was surely influenced by educators like Bocobo and his students.

[4] The two novels in Spanish are *Noli me tángere* (*The Social Cancer*, first published in Berlin, 1887) and *El filibusterismo* (*The Reign of Greed* or, alternatively, *The Subversive*, first published in Ghent, 1891). They are realistic depictions of Philippine sociopolitical life under Spanish colonial rule and may be considered the first modern novels in Asia, along with those from Japan and China. Jose Rizal, *The Social Cancer*, translated by Charles Derbyshire (New York: Floating Press, 2009); *The Lost Eden*, translated by Leon Ma. Guerrero (New York: Greenwood Press, 1968); *The Reign of Greed*, translated by Charles Derbyshire (Portland: Mint Editions, 2022); *The Subversive*, translated by Leon Ma. Guerrero (New York: Norton, 1968).

[5] Mishima Yukio, *Wakaki samurai no tame ni* (For Young Samurai) (Tokyo: Kyōbunsha, 1969).

[6] Yamamoto Tsunetomo, *Hagakure, Way of the Samurai*, translated by William Scott Wilson (New York: Kodansha International, 1992), 17, 141.

7 Mishima Yukio, *The Way of the Samurai: Yukio Mishima on Hagakure in Modern Life*, translated by Kathryn Sparling (New York: Perigee Books, 1977).

8 The exact casualty figures for the seventy-six thousand captive soldiers (sixty-six thousand Filipinos, ten thousand Americans) forced to undergo the brutal Bataan Death March of April 1942 are unknown, but researchers have calculated that some 28,500 Filipinos and two thousand Americans died during the march and later while confined at the Camp O'Donnell prison. See, for example, "Bataan Death March," *Encyclopedia Britannica*. 2018. https://www.britannica.com/event/Bataan-Death-March.

9 For a list of Helen and William McCullough's books, see chapter 11, note 20, 180.

10 One of the most popular poetic genres of the medieval period, *renga* was composed in *hyakuin* (hundred-verse) sessions, during which groups of poets took turns writing verses of three lines of five-seven-five syllables and two lines of seven-seven syllables that linked to each other. The opening verse, *hokku*, in three lines, is the predecessor of modern haiku. *Tsukeku* is the lower verse of any two-verse pair from a session. Once a pastime of the court aristocracy, *hyakuin* were held by medieval shōgun and *daimyō* to foster solidarity and by monks and poets as a form of literary meditation practice. The archives of temples and shrines include numerous manuscripts of *renga hyakuin* offered up as prayer, thanksgiving, or memorial.

11 Kaneko Kinjirō's (1907–1999) many publications in Muromachi-period *renga* studies include authoritative modern editions of the second imperial *renga* anthology, *Shinsen Tsukubashū: Sanetaka-bon* (edited with Yokoyama Shigeru, Tokyo: Kadokawa shoten, 1970) and verse collections of the "seven sages of *renga*," *Shichiken jidai renga kushū* (edited with Ōta Takeo, Tokyo: Kadokawa shoten, 1975). He produced collections of important documents for *renga* research, including *Renga kichō bunken shūsei* (Tokyo: Beiseisha, 1978); a collection of *renga* commentaries, *Renga kochūshaku shū* (Tokyo: Kadokawa shoten, 1979); and annotated textbooks of *renga* and *haikai* verses, including *Renga haikai shū* (Tokyo: Shōgakkan, 1974). He published commentaries on Sōgi's famous hundred-verse sequences, *Sōgi meisaku hyakuin chūshaku* (Tokyo: Ōfusha, 1985) and thick tomes on both imperial *renga* anthologies, *Shinsen Tsukubashū no kenkyū* (Tokyo: Kazama shobō, 1969) and *Tsukubashū no kenkyū* (Tokyo: Kazama shobō, 1983); on the history and poetic genealogy of the *renga* commentaries from the Muromachi and Edo periods, *Renga kochūshaku no kenkyū* (Tokyo: Ōfusha, 1974); and on the life and works of Shinkei (*Shinkei no seikatsu to sakuhin*, Tokyo: Ōfusha, 1982) and Sōgi (*Sōgi no seikatsu to sakuhin*, Tokyo: Ōfusha, 1983). He edited volumes of research articles by younger scholars and mentored other international scholars who became professors, notably Steven Carter (Stanford University) and Mack Horton (UC Berkeley). Kaneko-sensei added breadth and depth to the field of Japanese poetry and poetic practice in the United States by introducing this unique collective genre of poetry and poets that had long been overlooked by scholars elsewhere.

12 Sook Young Wang lived in Japan while her father was president of Korean Airlines in Tokyo. She later became professor of Japanese literature at Inha University in Seoul and is a loyal colleague and friend to this day.

[13] Anthologies of *renga* do not typically include Shinkei's hundred-verse *hyakuin* but rather his selected *hokku* and *tsukeku* in order to show the poetic process. The manuscripts of *hyakuin* circulated among a poet's followers and in the archives of temples, shrines, and the private collections of the courtly aristocracy and samurai lords.

[14] Esperanza Ramirez-Christensen, "The Essential Parameters of Linked Poetry," *Harvard Journal of Asiatic Studies* 41, no. 2 (December 1981), 555–595; "The Operation of the Lyrical Mode in the *Genji monogatari*," in *Ukifune: Love in The Tale of Genji*, edited by Andrew Pekarik (New York: Columbia University Press, 1982), 21–61.

[15] Esperanza Ramirez-Christensen, *Heart's Flower: The Life and Poetry of Shinkei* (Stanford: Stanford University Press, 1994); *Emptiness and Temporality: Buddhism and Japanese Poetics* (Stanford: Stanford University Press, 2008); *Murmured Conversations: A Treatise on Poetry and Buddhism by the Poet-Monk Shinkei* (Stanford: Stanford University Press, 2008).

33

Historical Periods and Major Events in Japanese Studies

Major Eras in Japanese History

Japanese coins, calendars, and other media are often dated both by the Japanese reign period and the Gregorian year (for example, Reiwa 5 and 2023). The earliest periods take their names from archeological history. The Asuka, Nara, and Heian periods are named for areas where imperial capitals were located, and the Kamakura, Muromachi, Azuchi-Momoyama, and Edo periods for areas where military capitals were located. Since 1868, periods correspond with the reigns of individual emperors and are assigned salutary names selected by the Prime Minister's Cabinet. (Meiji, for example, means "Enlightened Rule.")

- Jōmon Period: 10,000–300 BCE
- Yayoi Period: 300 BCE–250
- Kofun Period: 250–538
- Asuka Period: 538–710
- Nara Period: 710–784
- Heian Period: 794–1185
- Kamakura Period: 1185–1333
- Muromachi Period: 1336–1568 (also known as the Ashikaga Period, after the ruling clan)
- Azuchi-Momoyama Period: 1568–1600
- Edo Period: 1603–1868 (also known as the Tokugawa Period, after the ruling clan)
- Meiji Period: 1868–1912

Taishō Period: 1912–1926
Shōwa Period: 1926–1989
Heisei Period: 1989–2019
Reiwa Period: 2019–Present

Turning Points in Japanese Studies

Below is an annotated, chronological reference list of major organizations and events described in *Women in Japanese Studies: Memoirs from a Trailblazing Generation*. Definitions are specifically tailored to the book. They are meant to provide context and do not claim to be conclusive analyses or attempts to standardize history. These events represent culminations of historical changes that made it possible to learn about Japan, establish careers in Japanese Studies, and live between Japan and the United States. This appendix offers a capsule history of the field and of its leading institutions, the geopolitical context in which Japanese Studies developed in North America, and the counterculture within it during an eventful eighty years.[1]

Japan Society was founded in 1907 in New York City by American and Japanese philanthropists and business elites, many with ties to Japan's silk trade. It hosted exhibits, dignitary visits, and other activities showcasing Japanese culture, arts, society, and business; and it fostered connections among people interested in Japan.[2] Japan Society provided a chance to see Japanese art and cultural properties in the United States before museums opened galleries devoted to Japan. (For example, the Metropolitan Museum of Art opened their Japanese galleries in 1987.)[3] Barbara Ruch (chapter 4) and Christine Guth (chapter 17) participated in exhibits at Japan Society, and Takako Lento (chapter 7) interpreted for poetry events there. Today, Japan Societies operate in additional global cities, including Boston and London.

Association for Asian Studies (AAS): On **June 6, 1941**, the Far Eastern Association was formed through the collaboration of existing groups of scholars of Asia—including those at the Oriental Division of the Library of Congress, American Oriental Society (1842), and the Harvard-Yenching Institute (1928)—with the support of the American Council of Learned Societies (ACLS, 1919) and the Rockefeller Foundation (1913). A goal was to publish *The Far Eastern Quarterly*, which was established in 1941 and retitled *The Journal of Asian Studies* in 1956 when the organization was renamed the Association for Asian Studies (AAS). The association published *The Bibliography of Asian Studies* as a supplement to the journal (1941–1991). AAS's annual meetings began in 1949 and expanded into regional and international conferences. Four elected councils—Northeast Asia, East and Inner Asia, South Asia, and Southeast Asia—were created in 1970 to give members studying different regions more say in the organizational leadership. Cora Alice Du Bois (1903–1991) was the first woman to preside over the AAS (1969–1970).[4] Ten years later, Eleanor Harz Jorden became the second female president (1980–1981). Book contributor Mary Elizabeth Berry (chapter 11) also served as president (2004–2005). Marlene Mayo (chapter 5) created the Marlene Mayo Graduate Paper Prize given at the Mid-Atlantic Regional Association for Asian Studies Conference (MAR–AAS), and Sumie Jones (chapter 13) established the Sumie Jones Prize for Project Leadership in Japan-Centered Humanities.

Military Intelligence Service and Japanese Language Schools, November 1941–June 1946: On November 1, 1941, around one month before the Japanese attack on Pearl Harbor (December 7, 1941), the US Military Intelligence Service (MIS) opened a school in The Presidio in San Francisco to train interpreters and translators. Because many instructors and students were Japanese Americans, the school closed after President Franklin D. Roosevelt issued Executive Order 9066 (see below). The school reopened in Minnesota, first at Camp Savage (June 1942) and later at Fort Snelling (August 1944) as it grew larger and was renamed the Military Intelligence Service Language School (MISLS). Before closing in June 1946, MISLS graduated more than six thousand intelligence officers proficient in Japanese.[5] Other training facilities included the US Navy Japanese Language School, which first opened at Harvard University and the University of California, Berkeley (1941) and then moved to the University of Colorado Boulder (1942–1946); and the smaller Japanese Language School (1945–1946) at Oklahoma Agricultural and Mechanical College (Oklahoma A&M College, renamed Oklahoma State University–Stillwater in 1957). From 1942, members of the newly established Women's Army Auxiliary Corps (WAAC), renamed the Women's Army Corps (WAC) and made a branch of the army in 1943, and Navy WAVES (Women Accepted for Volunteer Emergency Services) enrolled and received similar training to men. The curriculum included intensive study of Japanese reading, writing, interrogation, translation, document analysis, geography, military structures, politics, and society. Female graduates were not sent to the battlefront but assisted the war and Occupation in other ways, such as intelligence gathering, working in branches of the Supreme Command of the Allied Powers (SCAP), and teaching English at elite Japanese universities. Helen Craig McCullough (chapters 11 and 32), Donald Keene, and Edward Seidensticker, all discussed in the book, are examples of language school graduates who became professors and translated important Japanese writings into English.[6]

Attack on Pearl Harbor, December 7, 1941: The Japanese Imperial Navy Air Service (353 planes launched from four carriers) attacked the US Naval Base at Pearl Harbor, Hawai'i, on Sunday at 7:55 a.m. The attack lasted an hour and fifteen minutes and killed 2,403 US personnel (including sixty-eight civilians) and

129 Japanese soldiers.[7] One Japanese soldier, Sakamaki Kazuo, was captured on a submarine and became the first Japanese prisoner of war.[8] In 1941, the United States was supplying the British forces in their fight against Nazi Germany and pressuring Japan to halt imperialism in Asia. A code message about the Pearl Harbor attack was decrypted on December 6.[9] President Roosevelt declared war on Japan on December 8, famously calling the day "a date which will live in infamy."[10] On December 11, Germany and Italy declared war on the United States. The surprise attack was fodder for racist stereotypes of Japanese men in wartime propaganda as sneaking, sly, cunning, and cruel (chapter 5).

Executive Order 9066 (February 19, 1942) and Japanese American Incarceration: President Roosevelt issued Executive Order 9066, authorizing the Secretary of War to designate military areas from which certain groups could be excluded, leading to the incarceration of persons with Japanese ancestry living on the West Coast in "relocation centers," commonly known as "internment camps," in remote interior regions of the United States.[11] On March 21, 1942, Congress passed Public Law 503, which made violation of Executive Order 9066 punishable by up to one year in prison and a $5,000 fine.[12] Around 122,000 people were confined to ten internment camps; among them, nearly seventy thousand were American citizens.[13] Concurrently, more than thirty thousand Japanese Americans served in the US military in segregated units.[14] For decades after the war, efforts were made to promote awareness of this history and to compensate incarcerated people for property loss. Congressional efforts increased in the 1980s and resulted in the signing of Public Law 100-383 on August 10, 1988, by President Ronald Reagan. The law acknowledged the injustices of incarceration, offered a formal presidential apology, provided funds for public education to prevent such events in the future, and made restitution to people who had been relocated to internment camps.[15]

Similarly, through a series of orders in 1942, approximately twenty-three thousand Japanese Canadians (more than 75 percent of whom were Canadian citizens) were relocated away from the West Coast.[16] Around seven hundred Japanese Canadians were placed in prisoner of war camps, while about four thousand were sent to work on sugar beet farms to fill in labor gaps. The Canadian government confiscated the property of Canadian Japanese and, after the war, pressured around four thousand people to move to Japan or Eastern Canada.[17] In 1988, the War Measures Act of 1914, the legal justification for the internment of Germans, Italians, Japanese, and others, was replaced by the Emergencies Act, and Prime Minister Brian Mulroney formally apologized to Japanese Canadians and their families who had been incarcerated and relocated. He signed a $300 million (CAD) compensation package that included restitution for survivors and funds to establish foundations to promote awareness of this history.[18]

The internment shaped the field of Japanese Studies in North America and Japan in several ways by removing specialists from their jobs, forcing the relocation of Japanese language schools, motivating the founding of scholarships by people who had been incarcerated, and stimulating the publication of magazines, literature, and other materials written at internment camps.[19]

Servicemen's Readjustment Act of 1944, commonly known as the GI Bill: The GI Bill was a force behind the development of universities during the time period covered in the book. Under the GI Bill (signed into law by President Roosevelt on June 22, 1944), returning veterans who had been on active duty for more than ninety days and had been honorably discharged were eligible to receive financial benefits for education, job training, unemployment, and housing. Veterans were offered payments for tuition and fees (up to $500 per year), books, and expenses ($50 per year) to attend high schools, vocational schools, or universities.[20] The GI Bill exemplified the belief that education was a means toward social mobility and access to jobs requiring specialized knowledge. By the time the original bill expired in July 1956, around half of the sixteen million World War II veterans had used the benefits for education, with 2.3 million attending colleges and universities. The number of advanced degree holders more than doubled between 1940 and 1950.[21] The GI bill was also a catalyst for additional education funding. For example, in 1950, the US government provided $300 million in long-term loans for private and public universities to build dormitories to house the growing number of students.[22] Concurrently, schools increased their rates. Both Harvard and the University of Pennsylvania raised yearly tuition to $600 in 1949.[23] (This was equivalent in purchasing power to $7,482.30 in January 2022.)[24] Women (including around 330,000 female World War II veterans) and minorities were entitled to the same benefits as white male veterans but faced systemic discrimination in accessing education, training, and loans for housing.[25] The legacy of the GI Bill endures through subsequent legislation and veterans' programs.

Atomic bombings of Hiroshima and Nagasaki, 1945: The United States began funding the development of nuclear weapons (code-named the "Manhattan Project") in 1940 and conducted the world's first nuclear explosion (code-named "Trinity") in Los Alamos, New Mexico, on July 16, 1945. On **August 6, 1945**, at 8:15 a.m., a B-29 bomber, the *Enola Gay*, dropped the first atomic bomb (code-named "Little Boy") on Hiroshima. A second atomic bomb (code-named "Fat Man") was dropped by the B-29 bomber *Bockscar* on Nagasaki on **August 9, 1945**, at 11:02 a.m. Estimates of how many people died in the bombings have varied: between seventy thousand and 135,000 deaths in Hiroshima and sixty thousand to eighty thousand in Nagasaki.[26] In addition, many suffered from burns, radiation sickness, and other injuries, or went missing. Because victims are still dying from radiation sickness, the death toll continues to mount.

Book contributors, including Phyllis Lyons (chapter 8) and Esperanza Ramirez-Christensen (chapter 32), describe seeing *hibakusha*, survivors of the atomic bombings, and media reports about them, in Japan. Marlene Mayo (chapter 5) mentions American television coverage of the "Hiroshima Maidens," twenty-five women in their twenties who spent one year in the United States (1955–1956) having reconstructive burn surgeries at New York City's Mount Sinai Hospital while living with Quaker families. Two Hiroshima maidens, along with their chaperone and the project leader, Reverend Tanimoto Kiyoshi, and his family, appeared on the American television documentary show *This Is Your Life* on May 11, 1955, filmed live in front of a studio audience. In *This is Your Life* (originally broadcast 1952–1961), creator, producer, and host Ralph Edwards narrated events in the lives of his guests and reunited them with people from their pasts. On this episode, Tanimoto and the Hiroshima Maidens (who remained obscured behind a screen so their identities could be protected and their burns hidden from audiences) were "reunited" with Captain Robert Lewis, the copilot of the *Enola Gay*. While Lewis appears choked with emotion, reporters noted that he may have actually been drunk. The show was also an appeal for donations and raised the huge sum of $55,000.[27]

Japan's surrender, 1945: The United States, the United Kingdom, and China issued the Potsdam Declaration, defining the terms of Japan's unconditional surrender, on **July 26, 1945**. Emperor Hirohito's recorded address (*Gyokuon-hōsō*, literally the "jewel voice broadcast") announced the end of the war on **August 15, 1945**, at 12:00 p.m. in Japan.[28] The "Instrument of Surrender," prepared by the US War Department, was signed by representatives of Japan, Foreign Minster Shigemitsu Mamoru and General Umezu Yoshijirō, and of the Allied powers (including the United States, the Republic of China, the United Kingdom, the Soviet Union, Australia, Canada, France, the Netherlands, and New Zealand) aboard the USS *Missouri* battleship on September 2, 1945.[29] The Potsdam Declaration laid the groundwork for Japan's postwar Constitution (see below); for example, Article 10, stated, "The Japanese government shall remove all obstacles to the revival and strengthening of democratic tendencies among the Japanese people. Freedom of speech, of religion, and of thought, as well as respect for the fundamental human rights, shall be established."[30]

Allied Occupation of Japan: To contextualize book chapters, below is a simplified timeline of some key events, told mainly from the American perspective. The Japanese empire came to an end, and around six million civilians and military were repatriated from Japan's former colonies and the battlefront, an effort that took several years.[31] The Occupation of Japan by the Allied forces began under American leadership, and General Douglas MacArthur arrived on August 30, 1945. President Harry S. Truman appointed General Douglas MacArthur to be the Supreme Commander of the Allied Powers (SCAP) with General Headquarters (GHQ) first in Yokohama and then in Tokyo. In addition, in 1947, MacArthur was made the head of the Far East Command. Truman relieved MacArthur of his duties and replaced him with General Matthew Bunker Ridgway on April 11, 1951. Especially during the first stage of the Occupation (1945–1947), GHQ/SCAP established structures for democracy and pacifism, as exemplified by the postwar Constitution (1946), educational laws (1947), and cultural exchange programs (see below). The emperor became a symbol, and the parliamentary system was given more political control. Land reform was enacted to help end farm tenancy and reduce the power of landowners, and the patriarchal household system (codified under the Civil Code of the 1890s) was abolished. The Japanese military was dismantled, and efforts were made to break up large business conglomerates (*zaibutsu*). War crimes trials for twenty-eight Japanese defendants, including General Tōjō Hideki, were held in Tokyo between May 3, 1946 and November 12, 1948. So-called "Reverse Course" measures (1947–1948) reflected a shift in Occupation priorities toward Cold War containment, alliance building, and the growth of the Japanese export-based economy. Starting in 1950, preparations were made for the Treaty of San Francisco (see below) to end the Occupation and establish a Cold War defense alliance. During the Occupation, the United States ceased to view Japan as a militaristic threat, rather coming to understand the country as a necessary component of defense against communism in Asia.[32] Ellen Conant (chapter 2) provides a firsthand account of Occupation-era Japan.[33]

Treaty of San Francisco (San-Furanshisuko kōwa-jōyaku) was signed by forty-nine Allied nations on behalf of the United Nations on **September 8, 1951**. (The Soviet Union, Poland, and Czechoslovakia did not sign, in part due to opposition to provisions preventing Japan from conducting business with the People's Republic of China. The People's Republic of China and Italy were among the countries not included as signatories.) The treaty officially terminated Japan's role as an imperial power, accepted the judgments of the war crimes trials, provided reparations for people who were harmed by Japan's war crimes, and restored sovereignty to Japan (with the exception of Okinawa).[34] The US-Japan Security Treaty, a bilateral security pact that permitted tens of thousands of US soldiers to remain in Japan on American military bases, came into force at the same time (see "Ampo" below).[35] Japan signed separate treaties and reparations agreements with Taiwan (1952), the Philippines (1956), and Indonesia (1958) (chapter 32). The Treaty of San Francisco went into effect on **April 28, 1952,** and ended the Occupation.

The postwar Japanese Constitution (Nihon-koku Kenpō) was promulgated on **November 3, 1946,** and went into effect on **May 3, 1947,** replacing the Meiji Constitution of 1889. Written in 103 articles, organized under eleven chapters, provisions included the reduction of the emperor's status to a symbolic and ceremonial role (Articles 1 through 8), the renunciation of war and the declaration that no offensive military forces would be maintained (Article 9), and a parliamentary system of government, individual rights, and human rights. Article 81 established the Supreme Court of Japan (Saikō Saibansho). American workers for SCAP played large roles in writing the Constitution. Beate Sirota Gordon (1923–2012, then still in her twenties) authored Article 14 about equality: "All of the people are equal under the law and there shall be no discrimination in political, economic or social relations because of race, creed, sex, social status or family origin." She also wrote Article 24, which gave women choice in marriage and family matters (chapter 22).[36] Constitution Memorial Day (Kenpō Kinenbi), May 3, is a national holiday in Japan. As of 2023, the Japanese Constitution has not been amended.

Japan's Fundamental Law of Education, 1947: Passed on **March 31, 1947,** the Fundamental Law of Education (Kyōiku kihon hō) was one of the most extensive educational reforms during the Occupation. Provisions included guaranteeing academic freedom; adopting the American system of six years of elementary school, three years of junior high, and three years of high school; extending free compulsory education to nine years; establishing coeducation; and elevating the status of colleges and universities. Four years of education became standard at universities.

Imperial universities turned into national universities; for example, Tokyo Imperial University (Tokyo Teikoku Daigaku) became the University of Tokyo (Tokyo Daigaku). The first imperial university to accept women was Tōhoku Imperial University (Tōhoku Teikoku Daigaku, now Tohoku University, Tōhoku Daigaku) in 1913: Kuroda Chika (1884–1968) and Tange Ume (Umeko) (1873–1955) in chemistry and Makita Raku (1888–1977, who married painter Kanayama Heizō) in mathematics. All three earned advanced degrees. Tange entered Tōhoku Imperial University at age forty after working at her alma mater, Japan Women's University (Nihon Joshi Daigaku). After graduation, she spent ten years studying in the United States with funding from the Japanese government. She earned two doctoral degrees, one in chemistry from John Hopkins University (1927) and another in agriculture from the University of Tokyo (1940).[37]

Especially before 1947, the few women's colleges established in the early twentieth century were generally equivalent to vocational schools or junior colleges. Under the new law, Japanese colleges could apply for four-year university status. Decisions were initially made by the University Chartering Steering

Committee in collaboration with SCAP. For example, Gakushuin University and Doshisha Women's University were elevated in 1949. By April 1949, applications by 180 schools (sixty-nine national, nineteen public [prefectural or municipal], and ninety-two private) had been approved.[38] The law was revised in 2006.

Ellen Conant (chapter 2) was a Fulbright research student (see below) at the University of Kyoto while major changes in the Japanese educational system were taking effect. Takako Lento (chapter 7) graduated from Tsuda University, a women's university that had benefited from these reforms, in 1964. Sumie Jones (chapter 13) recounts how lingering cultural attitudes about women who attend coed universities affected her education. All the book's contributors studied or researched at Japanese universities. In 1980, Barbara Sato (chapter 31) became one of the first and only foreigners to be accepted as a regular PhD student at the University of Tokyo. Janine Beichman (chapter 19) reflects on how becoming a regular faculty member at a Japanese university took her career in directions she had not expected.

Commercial transpacific flights began in 1947: On November 8, 1945, SCAP issued a ban on Japanese commercial and civil aviation and dissolved Japanese companies engaged in these businesses. Starting with Northwest Airlines (US) in 1947, seven non-Japanese airlines offered flights out of Haneda Airfield (commonly called Haneda Airport, Haneda Kūkō), which also serviced US military flights.[39] SCAP lifted the ban in 1951, paving the way for Japanese airlines to offer domestic and, beginning in 1953, transpacific flights. Haneda Airport was returned to Japan on July 1, 1952 and renamed Tokyo International Airport (Tokyo Kokusai Kūkō). Japanese passenger traffic increased when international travel was liberalized in 1964. Most international flights were moved to Narita Airport (Narita Kokusai Kūkō) after it opened in 1978, while Haneda remained a hub for domestic flights. Additional runways were completed in the 2010s for international flights. Most of the book's contributors first traveled to Japan by the *Hikawa Maru* (see below) or flights through Haneda Airport and treasure the memories of these trips (see, for example, chapters 9 and 22).

Fulbright Program between Japan and the United States started in 1952: Proposed by and named after Senator J. William Fulbright from Arkansas, the Fulbright Program was created on August 1, 1946, as an amendment to the Surplus Property Act of 1944. It was intended to foster mutual understanding and goodwill between the United States and other countries through educational exchange and interpersonal interactions. Foreign governments could sell American surplus war materials, including daily-use items, medicine, machinery, and weapons left behind after World War II to earn credits to finance American students and specialists to serve as visiting researchers and lecturers and to pay for their students to attend US graduate schools. Because of the nature of these credits, the Fulbright Program paid US recipients' travel, tuition, and living expenses abroad but only covered foreign recipients' travel costs. The first Fulbright agreements were signed in 1947 with China and Burma. The Fulbright Program has been administered by binational committees comprised of representatives from the United States and the recipient countries. It has been managed by the Institute of International Education (IIE, founded in 1919) based in New York City.

The Fulbright Program needed to find new sources of funding as foreign credits were being exhausted. On **January 27, 1948, Congress passed the US Information and Educational Exchange Act**, commonly called the Smith-Mundt Act (named for Congressman Karl Mundt of South Dakota and Senator H. Alexander Smith of New Jersey, Public Law 80-402), to oversee information about the United States disseminated in foreign countries. The act promoted educational exchange as a form of cultural diplomacy and authorized the US Department of State to request Congressional funding outside of the sale of war properties, thus increasing the numbers of countries eligible for Fulbright agreements and the range of acceptable academic fields.[40] In **1961, Congress passed the Mutual Educational and Cultural Exchange Act (Public Law 87-256), commonly called the Fulbright-Hays Act** because it was cosponsored by Congressman Wayne Hays of Ohio. The act amalgamated government-sponsored exchange programs and consolidated payments for them. It emphasized the binational agreement and encouraged contributions from foreign governments and the private sector.[41] In 1963, the Austrian government became the first to co-finance the Fulbright Program, followed in 1964 by Australia, Germany, Norway, and Sweden; ten countries shared costs by 1966.[42]

Twelve days before the signing of the Treaty of San Francisco, Prime Minster Yoshida Shigeru (in office 1946–1947 and 1948–1954) and US Ambassador William J. Sebald signed the Exchange of Notes permitting Japan into the Fulbright Program.[43] In 1953, the first cohort of around thirty Americans lecturers and research scholars (two categories) were sent to Japanese universities. Among them was Ellen Conant, then a graduate student in art history, who describes her experiences in chapter 2.[44] The first Japanese Fulbright cohort included thirty-one research scholars. In chapter 3, Joyce Lebra describes how she spent two years in Japan and India (1955–1957) thanks to Fulbright Fellowships. Marlene Mayo (chapter 5) was one of our many book contributors who had multiple Fulbright Fellowships. She was a Fulbright student in London (1954-1955) and researcher in Tokyo (1967-1968). Beginning in 1955, applications in all fields of study were accepted.[45] American students received stipends in yen while in Japan, but Japanese scholars needed to find money from sources such as grants from their American host universities. Thanks to the Fulbright Program, Sumie Jones attended the University of Washington in 1962 (chapter 13), and Takako Lento (chapter 7) participated in the Iowa Writers' Workshop in 1965. The number of awards plummeted after 1968. Budget cuts in 1969 forced the discontinuation of fellowships in natural science, arts, and teaching. Arts funding restarted in 1972, the year that journalism was added. The Fulbright Program in Japan reached a financial low in 1978 and could only finance thirty-eight Japanese and sixteen American scholars, in part due to the rising costs of attending American universities.[46] The Japanese government began cost-sharing in 1979, and the Japan-United States Educational Commission (JUSEC) replaced the United States Educational Commission in Japan (USEC/J) to reflect this revised bilateral agreement. Contributions from private Japanese interests began in 1981.[47]

Preceding Fulbright in Japan, between 1949 and 1952, the Interchange of Persons Board—a conglomerate of SCAP agencies, including the Civil Information and Education Section (CI&E), the Occupation's propaganda arm—awarded comprehensive one-year scholarships for study at US universities as part of Government Aid and Relief in Occupied Areas (GARIOA) to between 787 and 806 Japanese university graduates, among them between 133 and 182 women.[48] (It is difficult to ascertain the exact number of GARIOA scholarship students because Army and IIE sources give varying counts. GARIOA continued to support students from Okinawa until 1972.) The largest-ever number of Japanese exchange students came to the United States in 1951. The scholarships were intended to foster educated people who could promote US democracy, good will, and know-how in Japan. The primary purpose was to provide firsthand experience of US democracy; earning advanced degrees was secondary.[49] Applicants were chosen by tests that assessed their English skills and abilities to acclimate to American life; successful candidates also needed to pass medical examinations, including one that took place immediately before their departure for the United States. Recipients were not allowed to choose where they were sent and were assigned to schools by IIE, and many were sent to land-grant universities and lived in small towns and rural areas where they were among the only Japanese residents.[50] They received the same tuition payments and monthly allowances that US veterans received under the GI Bill (see above), along with stipends for field trips. GARIOA was a more composite and unilateral program than Fulbright and emphasized learning from "ordinary Americans" as well as from educational elites.

Fulbright is the largest and most representative of the US government's diplomatic use of cultural exchange. The US Department of State administers other programs, including the Peace Corps (1961) and Critical Language Scholarship Program (1974).

Fellowships from philanthropies and the Japanese government: Private organizations, like the Carnegie Foundation (founded in 1905), Rockefeller

Foundation (founded in 1913), and Ford Foundation (founded in 1936), have funded researchers and programs like Fulbright and have given institutional grants to promote cultural and educational exchange (see entries on the Association for Asian Studies and the International House of Japan).[51] For example, Ellen Conant (chapter 2) extended her study of art in Japan thanks to a fellowship from the Rockefeller Foundation. Barbara Ruch (chapter 4) and Marlene Mayo (chapter 5) attended Columbia University graduate school and Susan Pharr (chapter 22) attended a summer institute with funding from the Ford Foundation. Susan Pharr (chapter 22) and Margaret McKean (chapter 23) received Woodrow Wilson Fellowships for graduate study (awarded 1945–early 1970s with support from the Rockefeller, Carnegie, and Ford Foundations). Beginning in 1954, the Japanese government has offered scholarships to foreign scholars through the Ministry of Education, Culture, Sports, Science, and Technology (Monbukagakushō, MEXT; Monbushō before 2001). Christine Guth (chapter 17), Merry White (chapter 21), and Esperanza Ramirez-Christensen (chapter 32) all mention their Monbushō scholarships.

Hikawa Maru **commissioned to transport students, 1949–1960:** Named after the Hikawa Shrine in Saitama Prefecture, this Japanese ocean liner for the Japan Mail Shipping Line (Nippon Yūsen Kabushiki Kaisha) was launched in 1929 for routes among Yokohama, Vancouver, and Seattle.[52] She was used as a hospital ship during World War II (1941), carried repatriated soldiers back to Japan (1945–1946), became a cargo ship (1947–1953), and was finally returned to her former transpacific route until being decommissioned in 1960. The *Hikawa Maru* took Japanese students to the United States and American students to Japan on memorable two-week journeys.[53] Kate Wildman Nakai and Barbara Sato, both members of the American Field Service (see below), met on the *Hikawa Maru* (chapters 24 and 31). The American President Lines was a US company operating ocean liners to Japan in the 1950s and 1960s (chapter 5).[54]

Korean War, 1950–1953: Imperial Japan annexed Korea in 1910 and occupied the country until 1945. In August 1945, the United States and the Soviet Union divided Korea along the Thirty-Eighth Parallel into two north-south occupation zones. Over the years, tensions escalated at the border, and the Northern Korean People's Army invaded South Korea on June 25, 1950.[55] Japan became a principal supplier to the United Nations forces and was a recipient of a large US procurement policy. The war improved Japan's economy and solidified the nation's role as a US ally. Greater numbers of women and Japanese exchange students attended US universities while college-age American men were off fighting the war. Ellen Conant (chapter 2) and Marlene Mayo (chapter 5) describe the impact of the Korean War on cultural exchange and education.

***Rashomon* shown in American movie theaters, 1951:** In 1951, *Rashomon* (1950), which was neither commercially nor critically successful in Japan upon release, won a Golden Lion Award at the Venice Film Festival and became the first Japanese film screened in the United States (released by RKO Pictures) after the war.[56] *Rashomon* and its adaptations were used to attract crowds to Japanese cultural events; for example, Japan Society featured a Broadway play version at a fundraiser for study abroad scholarships on January 18, 1959.[57] Kurosawa's samurai epics were remade as American Westerns: for example, *Rashomon* as *The Outrage* (directed by Martin Ritt, 1964) and *Seven Samurai* (*Shichinin no samurai*, 1954) as *The Magnificent Seven* (directed by John Sturges, 1960). Tōhō Studios sued director Sergio Leone because his *A Fistful of Dollars* (1964) too closely resembled Kurosawa's *Yojimbo*. Book contributors, including Margaret McKean, state that samurai films piqued their interest in Japan (chapter 23).

The "Second Red Scare" and the effects of McCarthyism on education, 1947–1957: Fears that communism was infiltrating American society, schools, and the government increased in the context of such Cold War events as the Berlin Blockade (1948–1949), the end of the Chinese Civil War (1949), the Soviet Union's nuclear weapon test (1949), the Korean War (see above), the trial of Alger Hiss (1948), and the execution of Julius and Ethel Rosenberg (1953). This "Second Red Scare" (the first having taken place after the Russian Revolution of 1917) was stoked by propaganda and fueled by prejudice (including of race and sexual orientation), and it incited moral panic. It was influenced by power struggles within the Central Intelligence Agency (CIA) and the US government. It had a profound effect on many aspects of American life and led to accusations of espionage. The House Committee on Un-American Activities (formed in 1938 and dissolved in 1975, with functions now held by the House Judiciary Committee) and the Senate committee headed by Joseph McCarthy of Wisconsin investigated people in diverse fields and held public hearings (1953–1954); those who did not cooperate or who were suspected to be communist supporters were blacklisted.[58] Loyalty oaths to the United States were required for federal and state employees, including university instructors, under such provisions as Executive Order 9835, "Federal Employees Loyalty Program," signed by President Truman in 1947, and California's Levering Act (1950). The National Council for American Education was founded in 1946 to "eradicate" Marxism and communism from American schools and produced pamphlets and books attacking textbooks and educators. In 1951, they published *Red-ucators*, which listed seventy-six "pro-communist" professors at Harvard, eighty-seven at Columbia, sixty at the University of Chicago, thirty at Yale, and many more at elite women's colleges.[59] Graduate students of the time recall pressures to renounce their views, to accuse colleagues, and to show they did not uphold communist ideologies in order to receive fellowships and job offers.⁶⁰ McCarthy investigated the US military, including war heroes and members of the United States Army Signal Corps (that managed communications and information systems). The Army–McCarthy Hearings, televised between April 22 and June 17, 1954, led to McCarthy's public decline and Senate censure. In chapter 5, Marlene Mayo remembers watching the daytime hearings on the television in her university's cafeteria. She watched journalist Edward R. Murrow's March 9, 1954 evening television exposé of McCarthy's communist name-calling tactics with her family on their new television set.

Eleanor Hadley (see chapter 5) was recruited for the CIA in 1947, the year it was established, only to learn that she could not accept the job because she had been blacklisted by Major General Charles Willoughby, the ultraconservative leader of SCAP's Military Intelligence Section. She finally cleared her name in 1966.⁶¹ In his interview with Marlene Mayo on May 18, 1981, Japan film specialist Donald Richie discusses being interrogated while working as a writer for *The Pacific Stars and Stripes* military newspaper during the Occupation. After he published a negative review of a spy film about the Fifth Column, his mail was stopped, and his friends were questioned. Richie did not recant his review. He was exonerated but fired from his job. A job offer to decode Russian maps for SCAP was rescinded, and Richie returned to the United States.⁶²

On March 1, 1954, the *Lucky Dragon No. 5* (*Daigo Fukuryū-Maru*) tuna fishing boat encountered nuclear fallout from a US H-bomb test at Bikini Atoll near the Marshall Islands (an American nuclear testing site from 1946 to 1958). The twenty-three crew members suffered from radiation sickness, and one died. The boat was one of 846 Japanese fishing vessels impacted by the nuclear weapon tests and was reported to have taken irradiated tuna on board.⁶³ The boat was decommissioned in 1967, abandoned in the garbage dump on Yume no shima (Dream Island) reclaimed land in Tokyo, and later preserved thanks in part to citizens' efforts. The Tokyo Metropolitan government opened the Daigo Fukuryū-Maru Exhibition Hall (Daigo Fukuryū-Maru Tenjikan) in 1976 to publicly display the boat and promote awareness of the destruction wrought by nuclear weapons. Bikini Atoll was designated as a UNESCO World Heritage Site in 2010 (see chapter 5).

American Field Service (AFS) in Japan: Begun as a volunteer ambulance corps in 1915, AFS started international exchange programs and scholarships for high school students in 1946. Kate Nakai (chapter 24) and Barbara Sato (chapter 31) went to Japan on AFS in the summer of 1959.

The Experiment in International Living in the 1950s: As described by Susan Matisoff (chapter 10), the Experiment in International Living is a cultural exchange program for high school and young college students established in 1932.

It currently offers "summer abroad programs on five continents that empower young people to step off the beaten path, experience the world as a classroom, immerse themselves fully in another culture, and build the knowledge and skills needed to confront critical global issues."[64] In the 1950s, its scope was narrower, sending American youths to only a few countries, primarily in Europe.

International House of Japan (Kokusai Bunka Kaikan, I-House), 1955, and International Houses for students: The book's contributors fondly remember staying at the International House of Japan, nicknamed "I-House," and meeting colleagues there. The International House of Japan, Inc. was established in 1952 and moved into its current building on June 11, 1955—a cultural center equipped with a library on Japan (formed in 1953) cultivated by trailblazing librarian Fukuda Naomi, facilities for lectures and meetings, and a residence for visiting scholars.[65] Plans for I-House began with discussions between Matsumoto Shigeharu and John D. Rockefeller III at the Third Conference of the Institute of Pacific Relations held in Kyoto in 1929. Rockefeller was a member of the 1951 delegation led by John Foster Dulles, tasked by President Truman to negotiate a peace treaty between Japan and the United States. The delegation report recommended the construction of a cultural center sponsored by both governmental and private interests. Three Japanese architects—Maekawa Kunio, Sakakura Junzō, and Yoshimura Junzō—collaborated on the building. (Maekawa planned the expansion completed in 1976.) The garden, designed by landscape artist Ogawa Jihei VII in 1929, was part of the residence formerly on the building site. Funding for I-House was secured from the Rockefeller Foundation ($680,000 in 1951), the foreign community in Japan, organizations of writers, and other parties involved in cultural exchange.[66]

The English name is the same as that of the International Houses near urban universities, including those in New York (1924), Berkeley (1930), and Chicago (1932). As described by Susan Pharr (chapter 22) and Esperanza Ramirez-Christensen (chapter 32), these International Houses are dormitories where students from around the world live together and learn about each other's cultures. The idea was formulated by Harry Edmonds, a secretary for the YMCA, and funded by John D. Rockefeller.[67] The International House of Japan was so named to avoid associations with American cultural centers run by CI&E during the Occupation.[68]

Japanese Exhibition House, June 16, 1954–October 15, 1955: An exhibit of a Japanese traditional house designed by Yoshimura Junzō (one of the architects of the International House of Japan) at the Museum of Modern Art in New York, different from the mass, public housing then being constructed in Japan, drew large crowds. In the same year, the museum hosted the large photography show *The Family of Man* (January 24–May 8, 1955), visualizing global solidarity despite national differences.[69] The experience of visiting the Japanese Exhibition House left a deep impression on Janine Beichman (chapter 19).

Commercial translations of modern Japanese literature in the mid-1950s: Harold Strauss, graduate of the Military Intelligence Service Language School and editor at Alfred A. Knopf (1942–1966), spearheaded English translations of literature by living Japanese authors. In 1954, he edited and introduced Osaragi Jirō's *Homecoming* (*Kikyō*, 1948), translated by Brewster Horwitz—the story of an exiled soldier returning to Japan and the first modern Japanese novel to be published in the United States since 1929.[70] In 1955, Strauss edited Seidensticker's translation of Tanizaki's *Some Prefer Nettles* (*Tade kū mushi*, 1929). Knopf's strategy was to publish several works by the same Japanese authors, thereby promoting their names. Seven of Knopf's first nine Japanese literary translations were by Tanizaki Jun'ichirō, Kawabata Yasunari, and Mishima Yukio.[71] Thus, Strauss cultivated a commercial market for and established an English-language canon of Japanese literature. These novels accentuated differences between Japan and the United States.

Other publishers were inspired by Knopf's successes. For example, in 1955, Grove Press published two anthologies edited by Keene: *Anthology of Japanese Literature: From the Earliest Era to the Mid-Nineteenth Century* and *Modern Japanese Literature: An Anthology*. The latter book was one of the first compendiums of nineteenth- and twentieth-century Japanese fiction commercially available in the United States. Translation liberties were taken to help Americans understand unfamiliar Japanese culture. As a result, some cultural context and literary style was lost in favor of readability.[72] Janine Beichman (chapter 19) and Juliet Winters Carpenter (chapter 27) credit Meredith Weatherby's translation of Mishima's *Confessions of a Mask* (*Kamen no kokuhaku*, published by New Directions, 1958) as inspiring their love for Japanese literature. Richard Smethurst (chapter 14) and Sonja Arntzen (chapter 16) consider how postwar translations of classical Japanese literature also reflected their academic and publishing context.

Japanese literature was promoted by newspapers and literary magazines aimed at broad audiences and events held at Japan Society (see above) and other public forums. For example, a supplement to the January 1955 issue of *The Atlantic* offered seventy-eight pages of literary translations. Included were poems by Yosano Akiko and Natsume Sōseki; selections from Kawabata's *The Izu Dancer: A Story* and Tanizaki Jun'ichirō's *In Praise of Shadows: A Prose Elegy*; and essays on Japanese literature, culture, and international relations by rising male academics and political figures (i.e., Yoshida Shigeru's "Japan's Place in Asia").[73] Yet, as contributors to our book explain (for example, chapters 15 and 16), graduate study of Japanese literature before 1980 focused on classics, and methodologies of the field of modern literary studies were still being developed.

Council on East Asian Libraries (CEAL): Originally, the Committee on American Library Resources on the Far East (CALFRE), CEAL was founded in 1958 as an AAS committee to discuss concerns facing libraries and to develop East Asian resources. CEAL has published the *Journal of East Asian Libraries* since 1963. Past presidents of CEAL include Maureen Donovan (1994–1998) and Kristina Troost (2008–2010) (chapters 18 and 29).

National Defense Education Act, Title VI, 1958: The launch of Sputnik 1 on October 4, 1957, which triggered the Space Race between the United States and the Soviet Union, inspired the National Defense Education Act (NDEA). Signed into law on September 2, 1958 by President Dwight D. Eisenhower, the NDEA sought to increase the number of educated Americans to meet national security needs and to outdo the Soviet Union in science and technology. The NDEA provided federal support for developing institutions of higher learning and for establishing student loan programs. The US government bolstered the study of foreign cultures deemed essential to compete with the Soviet Union and, for the first time, offered fellowships for studying "less common" languages like Japanese. Title VI provided funds for nineteen language and area studies centers (later called National Resource Centers, NRCs); modern foreign language fellowships (National Defense Foreign Language [NDFL] Fellowships, precursors of the Foreign Language and Area Studies [FLAS] Fellowships in the 1970s); international research and studies (IRS); and language institutes (LI). Partly thanks to the NDEA, the number of university students in the United States increased from 3.6 million in 1960 to 7.5 million in 1970.[74] Yet the NDEA included affidavits that raised concerns. Until it was repealed by President John F. Kennedy in 1962, a disclaimer prevented the use of the NDEA to desegregate schools.[75] Until it was reauthorized and amended by Congress in 1964, recipients were required to sign a loyalty oath that they would not overthrow the United States government (see chapter 8).[76] The Higher Education Act (HEA) of 1965 (officially expired in 2013) increased federal funding for universities, scholarships, and low-interest student loan programs; created a National Teachers Corps to improve staffing at elementary and secondary schools in low-income areas; and emphasized the value of international studies expertise beyond defense needs, including in education, business, media, and health.

Protests against the US-Japan Security Treaty (Ampo), 1959–1960 and 1970: The Treaty of Mutual Cooperation and Security between the United States and Japan (Nihon-koku to Amerika-gasshūkoku to no aida no sōgo kyōryoku oyobi anzen hoshō jōyaku)—"Ampo jōyaku," shortened to "Ampo" (also written "Anpo")—is the main military alliance between the two countries and one of the longest alliances between two world powers. The first such agreement was signed on September 8, 1951, immediately after the Treaty of San Francisco (see above) and went into effect at the same time. The treaty was renegotiated in

1959 and extended the US military presence and bases in Japan. Prime Minister Kishi Nobusuke's administration (1957–1960) passed Ampo and submitted the revised treaty to the Diet (Japan's legislature), which ratified it in June 1960. Protests against Ampo (Ampo tōsō), involving various groups across the political spectrum, were held around Japan in 1959 and 1960. Sumie Jones and Esperanza Ramirez-Christensen (chapters 13 and 32) observed the student strikes at Waseda University. Kanba Michiko (1937–1960), a University of Tokyo student and member of the Zengakuren (All Japan Student Federation), was killed during clashes between demonstrators and the police at a massive protest at the National Diet Building on June 15, 1960. Her death was widely discussed in the media and may have been one of the reasons for the resignation of Prime Minister Kishi and the cancellation of President Eisenhower's planned visit to Japan.[77] The renewal of Ampo in 1970 again ignited protests.[78]

US-Japan Conference on Cultural and Educational Interchange (CULCON) was established in 1961 as a binational advisory panel to the Japanese and US governments. Plans for CULCON developed through discussions between President Kennedy and Prime Minister Ikeda Hayato (in office 1960–1964) on how the two countries could cooperate to foster educational and cultural exchange.[79] CULCON was restructured in 1991, and permanent Japanese and American secretariats were created. Funding organizations include the US Department of State and the Japan-US Friendship Commission.[80] Members of the advisory council have come from both inside and outside academia (see chapter 15).

Inter-University Center for Japanese Language Studies (IUC) began in 1961 as a campus for Stanford University and became a consortium in 1963. IUC has focused on intensive Japanese language training. Several of the book's contributors attended IUC and fondly remember Dr. Takagi Kiyoko, scholar of Japanese history and religion and tanka poet, who served as the associate director (1961–1981) (see, for example, chapters 10, 11, and 15). Takagi earned her PhD in religious studies from the University of Tokyo in 1991 at age seventy-three (see chapter 19).

Genesis of "affirmative action": Simply defined, "affirmative action" is a "set of procedures designed to eliminate unlawful discrimination among applicants, remedy the results of such prior discrimination, and prevent such discrimination in the future."[81] The term was first used in Executive Order 10925, signed by President Kennedy on March 6, 1961.[82] The order stipulated that government contractors "take affirmative action to ensure that applicants are employed and employees are treated during employment, without regard to their race, creed, color, or national origin."[83] On September 24, 1965, President Lyndon B. Johnson signed Executive Order 11246, prohibiting discrimination based on "race, color, religion, and national origin" by federal contractors and subcontractors. In 1967, Johnson added "sex" to the anti-discrimination list. Executive Order 11246 has been further amended to include religion, sexual orientation, and gender identity.[84] Federal contractors are required to promote the "full realization of equal opportunity for women and minorities."[85] Employers and institutions that contract with the federal government or receive federal funds must document their affirmative action practices and metrics.

Related legislation includes the Civil Rights Act of 1964 (see below), Section 504 of the Rehabilitation Act of 1973 (people with disabilities), Title II of the Americans with Disabilities Act of 1990, and the Age Discrimination Act of 1975. Affirmative action has been applied to university admissions to ensure diversity and equity, but lawsuits have challenged its fairness. On June 29, 2023, the US Supreme Court ruled against "racially-conscious" college admission programs.[86] Marlene Mayo (chapter 5), Susan Hanley (chapter 9), Susan Matisoff (chapter 10), and Mary Elizabeth Berry (chapter 11) discuss how affirmative action practices affected their job searches, salaries, and workplace treatment.

Equal Pay Act of 1963, signed into law by President Kennedy on June 10, 1963, amended the Fair Labor Standards Act of 1938 to prohibit "sex-based wage discrimination between men and women in the same establishment who perform jobs that require substantially equal skill, effort, and responsibility under similar working conditions."[87] According to the US Census Bureau, in 1960, women only earned, on average, sixty-one cents for every dollar earned by men, with variations according to race, location, age, and other identity factors. Subsequent legislation has expanded the law's enforcement, but pay gaps persist. In 2011, around fifty years after the law's passage, women earned, on average, seventy-seven cents for every dollar earned by men, and they comprised the majority of workers in low-wage sectors.[88] In 2022, women earned eighty-three cents for every dollar earned by men, while women of color in general were more disadvantaged.[89] In 2020, tenured female faculty members earned eighty-two cents for every dollar earned by men at the same level.[90] Studies in 2009 showed that female academics were tenured at a lower rate than men and remained at the associate professor rank for a longer period of time.[91] Women still remain underrepresented in many academic disciplines.[92]

Civil Rights Act, July 2, 1964: Signed into law by President Johnson, the Civil Rights Act outlaws discrimination and segregation in businesses, schools, and other public places, as well as voting discrimination. Title VII of the law created the Equal Employment Opportunity Commission (EEOC) to "enforce laws that prohibit discrimination based on race, color, religion, sex, national origin, disability, or age in hiring, promoting, firing, setting wages, testing, training, apprenticeship, and all other terms and conditions of employment."[93] Eleanor Kerkham (see chapter 28) discusses how the EEOC addressed pay inequality based on gender at Colby College.

1964 Tokyo Olympics: The Summer Olympic Games held in Tokyo from October 10 to 24, 1964, were the first Olympic Games hosted in Asia, the first transmitted live by satellites, and the first televised (albeit partially) in color. Japanese government and private interests saw the 1964 Tokyo Olympics as a chance to show the world the nation's postwar recovery and peace. To convey this message, Sakai Yoshinori—born in Hiroshima Prefecture the day the atomic bomb was dropped on Hiroshima City (August 6, 1945) and a first-year student and sprinter at Waseda University in 1964—was chosen to light the Olympic Cauldron. (Sakai did not qualify to compete on Japan's Olympic team.[94]) Marlene Mayo (chapter 5) and Merry White (chapter 21) describe how much Tokyo changed in the years leading up to the Olympic Games. Large urban development projects included the construction of sports venues, hotels, elevated highways, trains and subways, a monorail connecting Haneda Airport with the center of the city (see above), and the new Tōkaidō *shinkansen* bullet train linking Tokyo and Osaka (inaugurated on October 1, 1964).[95] Judo and volleyball became Olympic sports. The Japanese women's volleyball team won the gold medal. Margaret Lock (chapter 6) explains how Olympic judo surprisingly led to her study of Japanese and comparative medical anthropology. Tokyo was chosen to host the Summer Olympic Games three times: 1940 (moved to Helsinki after Japan's invasion of China and later canceled due to the war), 1964, and 2020 (postponed to 2021 due to the COVID-19 pandemic).[96]

Social Science Research Council (SSRC) and American Council of Learned Societies (ACLS) support for research on Japan: The SSRC, with roots in the American Political Science Association, was first convened in 1923 to advance study of the social sciences. Susan Hanley (chapter 9) and Helen Hardacre (chapter 30) both received SSRC grants to research their dissertations in Japan. The SSRC has partnered with other organizations, such as the ACLS (a federation of scholarly groups promoting the humanities) and the Japan Foundation (see below). Marlene Mayo (chapter 5) and Susan Matisoff (chapter 10) were able to convene seminars and conferences thanks to funding from the SSRC-ACLS Japan Committee (1967–1996).

Kawabata Yasunari won the Nobel Prize for Literature in 1968: Kawabata was the first Japanese author and the first Asian since Rabindranath Tagore (1913) to win what has been regarded as the world's most prestigious literary award. Countries nominate candidates for the prize, and the winner is selected by a committee of Swedish judges, who most likely read literature originally written in Japanese and other world languages in English translation. Writers are chosen for their entire oeuvre rather than for one particular work, and for their engagement with humanist themes. Winners attend the prize ceremony in Sweden and deliver Nobel Lectures. Kawabata was chosen based on readings of his fiction steeped in classical Japanese aesthetics, such as works translated by Seidensticker (not for his grittier prewar fiction about modernizing Tokyo). Kawabata's Nobel Lecture, "Japan, the Beautiful, and Myself," (Utsukushii Nihon no watashi), delivered on December 12, 1968, explains how the influence of Zen Buddhism on Japanese literature is a distinguishing quality from literature produced in the so-called West.[97] According to Takako Lento (chapter 7) and Juliet Winters Carpenter (chapter 29), Kawabata's Nobel Prize increased the demand for Japanese literary translations.

Title IX of the Education Amendments of 1972: Signed into law on July 23, 1972, by President Richard M. Nixon, Title IX states, "No person in the United States shall, on the basis of sex, be excluded from participation in, be denied the benefits of, or be subjected to discrimination under any education program or activity receiving federal financial assistance."[98] Title IX updates Title VII of the Civil Rights Act, which prohibited gender discrimination in employment but not in education; another precursor was Executive Order 11246 (see above). Title IX transformed faculty-hiring practices by making job searches more transparent and equitable, and it gave people of all genders equal access to university facilities like sports and faculty clubs that were formerly limited to men (see chapters 4 and 25). In chapter 11, Mary Elizabeth Berry explains how Title IX affected her and many other women working at American universities. Court cases over the years have interpreted Title IX as a means to prevent sexual harassment and violence.[99] Schools are required to adopt and publicize policies for preventing and addressing gender-based discrimination and to offer redress, support, and security for victims.[100] In 2002, Title IX was renamed the Patsy T. Mink Equal Opportunity in Education Act after the congresswoman from Hawai'i who helped to pass it.

Vietnam War: North Vietnam fought against South Vietnam and its main ally, the United States, in a complex war that lasted decades; some turning points are outlined below.[101] The conflict was exacerbated by the Cold War between the United States and the Soviet Union. France (beginning in the nineteenth century) and Japan (1940–1945) occupied Vietnam. In the mid-1940s, a North Vietnamese army, under the leadership of communist Ho Chi Minh (1890–1969), fought against the renewed French occupation. Under the Geneva Accords of 1954, France withdrew from northern Vietnam, and the country was temporarily divided along the Seventeenth Parallel. South Vietnam was led by Emperor Bao Dai (1913–1997) and later by Ngo Dinh Diem (1901–1963), with support from

France and the United States. The North and South fought to unify Vietnam under the respective control of Ho and Diem. Diem was deposed in a coup d'état in 1963, increasing Vietnam's instability.

The United States became actively involved in the military conflicts after 1954: for example, by stationing troops in Vietnam, by heavily bombing neighboring Laos (1964–1973) to cut off supply lines and to prevent the rise of communist forces there, and by spraying herbicide (Agent Orange) in the forests of Vietnam, Laos, and Cambodia between 1961 and 1971. North Vietnamese torpedo boats attacked two US destroyers in the Gulf of Tonkin in August 1964, and President Johnson retaliated by bombing North Vietnamese targets. In March 1965, President Johnson decided to send US combat troops to support South Vietnam. Protests against US involvement in the Vietnam War erupted, especially at American universities, and escalated after North Vietnam's Tet Offensive in 1968 showed that the war was not nearing a resolution. In May 1970, the National Guard shot students at Kent State University who were protesting the US invasion of Cambodia. President Nixon signed the Paris Peace Accords and ordered the withdrawal of American troops in 1973. Communist forces seized control of South Vietnam in 1975. The war claimed the lives of around two million Vietnamese civilians, 1.1 million North Vietnamese soldiers, 200,000 to 250,000 South Vietnamese soldiers, and 58,220 US soldiers.[102]

The Vietnam War, and the demonstrations and riots against it—and against other issues of the era—affected the book's contributors personally and professionally. It was also a time when students protested various policies, injustices, and decisions at their universities. For example, Patricia Steinhoff (chapter 12) outlines the rising tides of student protest at the University of Michigan in the early 1960s; her husband Bill spent time in Vietnam and researched American youths' experiences of the war. Mary Elizabeth Berry (chapter 11) describes feelings of frustration and disillusionment among some Asian Studies scholars at the failure of the discipline to speak out against atrocities. Sonja Arntzen (chapter 16) was advised by American professors who moved to Canadian universities in opposition to the war. Helen Hardacre (chapter 30) was inspired to study Buddhism while watching television footage of the murder of Vietnamese civilians and monks' self-immolation in Saigon (today, Ho Chi Minh City) in protest. Other of the book's contributors discuss their participation in anti-war protests and how the war caused disagreements among their family members and expanded generational divides.

Committee of Concerned Asian Scholars (CCAS) was founded in March 1968 by young professors and graduate students to oppose US foreign policies in Southeast and East Asia, including involvement in the Vietnam War and the containment of the People's Republic of China, and to break the silence of Asian

Studies specialists with regard to these policies (see chapter 11). CCAS expressed the need to reform the field of Asian Studies, which had largely developed according to Cold War, anti-communist mentalities. Many CCAS members had been active in civil rights, feminist, anti-nuclear, and New Left movements, and they sought a more critically engaged Asian Studies. According to Mark Selden, one of the group's founders, CCAS grew from

> an upsurge of anti-war and social movement activity coupled with a political awakening in the years between 1968 and 1979, one targeting American militarism and imperialism and assessing the national liberation and revolutionary movements throughout Asia and Pacific. ... CCAS was part of a broader movement within American society to rethink the role of the citizen and researcher in a time of crisis that was also framed by radical possibilities and hopes. The dimensions of that crisis were etched not only by the Indochina Wars and US-China relations but by race, class, and gender issues.[103]

CCAS published the *Bulletin of Concerned Asian Scholars*, renamed *Critical Asian Studies* in 2001.[104]

Anti-miscegenation laws in the United States became unconstitutional in 1967: In forty-one states, anti-miscegenation laws prohibited interracial marriages, and in some states, interracial sexual relations and cohabitation. (Nine states—Alaska, Connecticut, Hawai'i, Minnesota, New Hampshire, New Jersey, New York, Vermont, and Wisconsin—did not have these laws.) The first such prohibition began in 1661, predating the founding of the United States. Anti-miscegenation laws were passed, amended, and repealed in different states at various times; most explicitly forbade marriage between Blacks and whites. In 1910, twenty-eight states had anti-miscegenation laws, but in only seven (Arizona, California, Mississippi, Montana, Nevada, Oregon, and Utah) did they apply to marriages between whites and Asians. Statutes had different terminologies—for example "Mongolians" (Arizona, California, Mississippi, and Utah), "Chinese" (Nevada and Oregon), or "Chinese and Japanese" (Montana). Between 1910 and 1950, eight states added anti-miscegenation statutes that applied to Asians (Georgia, Idaho, Maryland, Missouri, Nebraska, South Dakota, Virginia, and Wyoming); laws in Georgia and Virginia stated that whites could only marry whites.[105] Under the Expatriation Act of 1907, US-born women who married foreigners took the nationalities of their husbands and thereby lost their American citizenship. Under the Cable Act (1922), women who married men eligible for naturalization could maintain their US citizenship, but women who married "aliens ineligible for citizenship," generally meaning first-generation Asians, could not.[106] In 1967, the US Supreme Court ruled in *Loving v. Virginia* that anti-miscegenation laws were unconstitutional under the Fourteenth Amendment. These laws affected where people in interracial marriages could live and work.

Suicide of Mishima Yukio: As described in chapters 3, 19, 25, 27, and 32, author Mishima Yukio (born in 1925), whose literature sold more in translation than that of any other Japanese writer at the time, committed *seppuku*, ritual disembowelment historically reserved for samurai, on **November 25, 1970**. In his literature, though press interviews, and by cultivating his own militia, the Sword Society (Tate no Kai, 1968–1970), Mishima advocated his interpretation of the *bushidō* samurai code. He dramatized this notion of samurai ethics in his short story *Patriotism* (*Yūkoku*, 1961) and its film adaptation (1966, codirected with Domoto Masaki), in which he starred.[107] Before committing suicide, Mishima and the Sword Society attempted to seize the headquarters of the Japan Ground Self-Defense Force (Jieitai) in Tokyo and gave a speech to rally Japanese soldiers to stage a coup d'état and restore the powers of the emperor as the leader of Japan. International news outlets generally reported Mishima's attempted coup and suicide as acts of extremism rather than as a validation of the samurai ethos.[108] Joyce Lebra (chapter 3) witnessed the event and published news articles about her perspective.[109]

Red Army, hijackings, and hostage taking, 1969–1972: As Patricia Steinhoff explains in chapter 12, the Red Army Faction (Sekigunha) emerged as a faction of a major New Left organization called the Communist League (Kyōsanshugisha Dōmei), nicknamed Bund, at the peak of the protest cycle in the fall of 1968. The Red Army faction was led by Shiomi Takaya, who was in charge of all the student chapters on college campuses. Shiomi advocated the formation of a guerrilla army because street clashes with the police were no longer effective. His group secretly developed improvised explosive devices in the chemistry labs of universities where strikes were being held. The idea of such escalation polarized Bund, which expelled Shiomi and his followers in the summer of 1969. As they began implementing their plans independently under the Red Army Faction name (given to them by their opponents in Bund), many members were arrested, and the remainder were forced underground. Shiomi theorized that they needed to find refuge in international bases to learn guerrilla warfare in order to foment a revolution in Japan.

In March 1970, nine members of the Red Army Faction hijacked a domestic Japanese commercial plane bound for Fukuoka and ordered it to fly to North Korea, where several group members remain to this day. They became known as the Yodogō group, after the name of the hijacked plane. The following year, Red Army members Okudaira Tsuyoshi and Shigenobu Fusako went to Beirut, Lebanon, to volunteer with a faction of the Palestine Liberation Organization (PLO), the Popular Front for the Liberation of Palestine (PFLP), which had an ideology similar to the Red Army Faction. Shigenobu went to work for *Al Hadafu*, the PFLP magazine, while Okudaira joined the section that carried out guerrilla attacks, including airplane hijackings and embassy invasions. They invited others to join them, and, after operating for several years under PFLP, they formed an independent Japanese group that took the name bestowed upon them by the foreign press: the Japanese Red Army (JRA).[110]

The United Red Army was formed in late summer of 1971 by a merger of remnants of the Red Army Faction that had carried out a series of bank and payroll robberies (led by Mori Tsuneo) and another small group known publicly as Keihin-Ampo Kyoto (led then by Nagata Hiroko) that had robbed a gun shop and acquired guns and ammunition. Both groups were wanted by the police, and they retreated into the mountains of Japan in the winter of 1971 and 1972. Police caught up with them in mid-February and arrested Mori and Nagata in a mountain cave. The rest fled on foot over the Japanese Alps with police helicopters searching overhead. They descended in the outskirts of the resort town of Karuizawa, where more were arrested. The final five fled to a corporate mountain lodge called Asama-Sansō, where they took the housekeeper hostage and held off three thousand Japanese riot police for ten days (February 19–28), until the police demolished the front of the building with a construction crane and brought out the five men and their hostage, unhurt. The final siege was watched live on television by around 90 percent of the Japanese viewing audience.[111] While interrogating the group, police discovered that they had carried out an internal purge, in which the survivors had tortured and killed a dozen of their own members. The Asama-Sansō siege and the subsequent revelations of the purge effectively ended the New Left era in Japan.[112]

Expo '70: Japan World Exposition, Osaka, 1970 (Nihon bankoku hakurankai, nicknamed "Osaka banpaku"), was held in Suita, Osaka Prefecture, from **March 15 to September 13, 1970.** It was the first world's fair in Asia and Japan's largest national project since the 1964 Tokyo Olympics. The main theme was "Progress and Harmony for Mankind" (*jinrui no shinpō to chōwa*). The fairgrounds were designed by Tange Kenzō, assisted by twelve additional architects. Expo '70 featured artworks, such as Okamoto Tarō's *Tower of the Sun* (Taiyō no tō), and futuristic exhibits, including a moon rock brought back by US astronauts in 1969 and Canada's IMAX film. Expo '70 staff wore stylish uniforms.[113] Seventy-seven countries participated, and around 64.2 million people attended.[114] Sonja Arntzen (chapter 16) worked at the Canadian Pavilion.

Japan Foundation (Kokusai Kōryū Kikin) was established in **1972** by the Japanese government to promote the study of Japan, first in the United States and later in other countries. The Japan Foundation has provided program grants that can be used to create teaching positions (see, for example, chapters 5, 16,

21, 22, 23, and 28), research fellowships, research collections (chapter 29), and support for educational events. It has documented the growth of the field (for example, through the directory projects described in chapters 11 and 12). In 2003, the Japan Foundation became an Incorporated Administrative Agency under the jurisdiction of the Ministry of Foreign Affairs. A predecessor organization was the Society for International Cultural Relations (Kokusai Bunka Shinkōkai), founded in 1934, that produced a journal, *International Culture* (*Kokusai bunka*, 1939–1972), documentary films about Japan (1930s to 1950s), and books such as *Introduction to Contemporary Literature* (1939).[115]

The book's contributors discuss large-scale projects supported through the Japan Foundation that fostered the growth of Japanese Studies in the 1970s. For example, in 1973, the Japan Foundation distributed one million dollars to ten established programs chosen for their "traditions, past achievements and the present scope of Japanese Studies." They were called the "Tanaka Ten" after Prime Minister Tanaka Kakuei (in office 1972–1974, see chapters 9 and 11).[116] The Japan Foundation's Tanaka Fund was established in Canada in 1974: Canada paid the Japanese government one million dollars to promote Canadian Studies in Japan, and, in exchange, the Japanese government gave Canada three million yen to cultivate Japanese Studies at Canadian universities. These government grants were concurrent with private donations from Japanese corporations. For example, in 1972, Mitsubishi Heavy Industries gave one million dollars to Harvard Law School to establish a chair in Japanese legal studies. Nissan Motor Company, Ltd. gifted one million dollars to Japanese Studies programs at Harvard in 1973.[117] The Sumitomo Group gave two million dollars to Yale and one million dollars to Japan Society in 1973.[118]

Oil Shocks of 1973–1974 and 1979: The Arab countries of the Organization of Petroleum Exporting Countries (OPEC), led by Saudi Arabia, cut oil production and limited exports to nations that had supported Israel in the Yom Kippur War (1973), and later to other countries. The embargo dramatically increased the price of petroleum, causing fears of shortages and drawing attention to the use of energy as a political and economic weapon. During a time of concurrent inflation, slow economic growth, and rising unemployment (stagflation), President Richard Nixon started a petroleum-rationing program, which resulted in long lines at gas stations, public panic, and larger conversations about dependence on oil, alternative energy sources, and environmental issues. A second shock came in the wake of the Iranian Revolution (1979) and the start of the Iran-Iraq War (1980–1988). The shocks had large-scale economic and political ramifications and raised questions about US international influence and Cold War hegemony. Maureen Donovan (chapter 18) writes that it was difficult to find jobs in both the private sector and at public universities due to funding cutbacks and hiring freezes at this time. Japan was reliant on oil imports and suffered economically.[119] Japanese compact cars, less expensive and more fuel-efficient than American sedans and with names like Accord and Celica that were easy for Americans to pronounce and remember, made inroads into the US market and revealed failings in the US automobile industry.

"Japan Bashing" in the 1980s: Encouraged by Japan's economic rise, "Japan Bashing," or anti-Japanese sentiment, arose in the United States, resulting in strong criticism of, and even attacks on, Asian people and products. By the mid-1980s, Japanese radios and televisions were common in the United States, and Japanese brands like Sony were widely known. On September 22, 1985, financial ministers from the United States, Japan, France, the United Kingdom, and West Germany signed the Plaza Accord (at the Plaza Hotel in New York City) to depreciate the US dollar in relation to the yen and Deutsche Mark to make American and European exports more competitive with Japanese products. Although largely ineffective in reducing US trade deficits with Japan, the Plaza Accord made American assets more affordable to Japanese interests. Japanese corporate purchases of famous American cultural industries and landmarks—such as Sony's purchase of the CBS Records Group (including Columbia Records) in 1988 (renamed Sony Music Entertainment in 1991) and Columbia Pictures in 1989, and Mitsubishi Estate Company's 1989 purchase of controlling shares in the Rockefeller Group that owns the Rockefeller Center—led to fears that Japan was "buying up" America. Many of these deals became less profitable in the 1990s.

On June 19, 1982, the night of his bachelor party, Vincent Chin (born in 1955), a Chinese American worker for Chrysler, was severely beaten by Chrysler plant supervisor Ronald Ebens and his stepson, Michael Nitz, a laid-off autoworker, who mistook him for being Japanese American and who blamed Japan for the troubles facing US automakers. Chin died of his injuries on June 23, 1982. Ebens and Nitz were found guilty of second-degree murder but negotiated charges down to manslaughter. They paid fines of three thousand dollars each but did not serve jail time. The brutal murder and lenient sentences ignited movements for Asian American civil rights.[120] On July 2, 1987, nine members of Congress smashed a portable Toshiba radio with sledgehammers on the Capitol steps. Their anger was directed at the Toshiba Machine Company for illegally selling eight computerized, multiaxis milling machines to the Soviet Union for easier production of quieter submarine propellers that could avoid US detection.[121] The context of Japan Bashing affected the perception and funding of Japanese Studies programs (see chapter 22).

Japan-US Friendship Commission (JUSFC), 1975: The Japan-US Friendship Act (Public Law 94-118) was passed by Congress and signed by President Gerald

Ford on October 20, 1975. The timing coincided with Emperor Hirohito and Empress Nagako's visit to the United States (September 30–October 13, 1975). The commission was created to distribute a US trust fund established with the money Japan owed to the United States from the reversion of Okinawa and the remaining balance in the GARIOA account set aside in 1962 for educational and cultural exchange (for information on GARIOA, see the above entry on the Fulbright Program).[122] JUSFC has supported several programs discussed in the book, including Fulbright Fellowships, IUC, SSRC grants, and NCC. In addition, JUSFC has funded American Studies programs in Japan; in its first two decades, JUSFC spent twice as much promoting Japanese Studies in America as it did on American Studies in Japan.[123] JUSFC collaborates with CULCON (described above).

The Japan-US Friendship Commission Prize for the Translation of Japanese Literature began in 1979. A single prize was given annually until 1988. Starting in 1989, prizes were awarded in two categories: classical and modern literature. Our book includes memoirs by winners Juliet Winters Carpenter (1980 and 2014–2015), Phyllis Lyons (1983), Phyllis Birnbaum (1989), Mae Smethurst (2001), Esperanza Ramirez-Christensen (2009), Takako Lento (2014 and 2018–2019), and Janine Beichman (2019–2020) (chapters 27, 8, 20, 14, 32, 7, and 19). Sumie Jones (2018–2019) and Juliet Winters Carpenter (2021–2022) were given the Lindsley and Masao Miyoshi Prize (begun in 2017) for their lifetime achievements (chapters 13 and 27).

Second-wave feminism: Inspired by the civil rights movement, diplomatically represented by the United Nations Decade for Women (1975–1985), and concurrent with the sexual revolution, what became known as "second-wave feminism" disclosed how notions of biological determinism created a binary between men and women, resulting in different norms for the two genders. Second-wave feminism encompassed various groups, including those seeking an end to physical and metaphorical violence against women and those fighting for the inclusion of women in politics and for equal pay for equal work, an acknowledgement of the gendered division of labor at home, an improvement of women's roles in universities, an awareness of how women have been represented in media, reproductive freedoms, and sexual health. Awakening individual women to their own discrimination was a step toward changing patriarchal society. Recording women's stories was a means to amplify silenced voices and to appreciate overlooked work, as demonstrated by Phyllis Birnbaum's biographies (chapter 20) and Anne Imamura's research on housewives (chapter 26). Many second-wave feminists viewed women as a category of people unified by their sex, while also taking into account how experiences of gender have been shaped by race, class, ethnicity, and nation, especially with the influence of poststructuralist theories and the individualism and diversity of "third-wave feminism" in the early 1990s.

The United States exerted a strong influence on Japanese feminism, both as a social and political example and as a source of texts and programs. The Japanese term "*josei gaku*," a literal translation of "women's studies," shows origins in American efforts. The 1979 manifesto of the Women's Studies Association of Japan (Nihon Josei Gakkai) defined the field as the "interdisciplinary study of women and of problems related to women, predicated on a respect for women as human beings and dedicated to a thorough reconsideration of all preexisting academic disciplines from women's points of view."[124] Women's studies proponents also sought to rectify discrepancies in the tenure system and disparities in the academic salaries of men and women.[125] Acknowledging the perceived gender binary between men and women and how institutions have adhered to it were instrumental in this process.

The First Tokyo Symposium on Women (Kokusai Josei Gakkai), July 24–26, 1978: The symposium, conducted in both Japanese and English, was held at the National Women's Education Center of Japan (Kokuritsu Josei Kyōiku Kaikan, established in 1977) and consisted of five panels and a closing discussion (see chapters 21 and 22 and figure 22.1). The event attracted around one hundred participants from eight countries. The symposium originated in a women's study group begun in 1975, with committees in Japan and the United States.[126] A goal was to establish a larger international research organization to promote the study of gender and Japan.

Bubble economy era, 1985–1991, was a time of prosperity accompanied by extravagance. The soaring stock market and rampant speculation in real estate built on cheap credit led to a rapid increase in the paper value of land assets. By 1991, the stock market and real-estate bubble had burst, and Japan entered a deflationary spiral. Chapters 13 and 22 discuss trends associated with the bubble economy era.

North American Coordinating Council on Japanese Library Resources (NCC) was founded in 1991 to collaborate with librarians, faculty, and funding organizations to strengthen Japanese library collections and to promote access to information about Japan. Amy Heinrich served as the first chair and explains the roots of NCC's unusual name (chapters 15 and 29).

"Lost decades" (*ushinawareta jūnen*) **starting in the 1990s** refers to Japan's period of economic stagnation in the 1990s after the bursting of the Japanese stock market and real-estate bubble. Although official unemployment rates were relatively low compared to the United States and Europe and Japan's economy remained the second largest in the world, the country experienced years of deflation, and youth saw diminished job prospects. Companies reduced the hiring of regular workers in order to cut costs. As a result, upon graduating from high school or university, many youths could find only low-paying part-time or temporary jobs. This long deflationary era continued on for more than two decades, which can be described as "lost decades." Some believe that the lost decades is a myth, attributing Japan's economic underperformance to a declining population, as on a per-worker basis, between 1991 and 2012, Japan's output rose respectably.[127] Susan Pharr (chapter 22) discusses changes in Japanese Studies during these lost decades. The generation born between 1971 and 1982, who were university-aged during the bubble economy era and who entered the job market in the 1990s, has been referred to as the "lost generation" (*ushinawareta sedai*).[128]

Notes

[1] I thank an anonymous reviewer for this observation.

[2] Japan Society, "A Short History of Japan Society" (New York: Japan Society, n.d.).

[3] Michael Brenson, "Art: Met's New Japanese Galleries," *New York Times*, April 24, 1987, Section C, 32.

[4] Cora Alice Du Bois (1903–1991), the Samuel Zemurray Jr. and Doris Zemurray Stone-Radcliffe Professor, was the first woman to be tenured at Harvard University's Department of Anthropology (1954) and the second in the Faculty of Arts and Sciences. She conducted research in Southeast Asia, among other places, and served in the Office of Strategic Services (OSS) during World War II.

[5] James C. McNaughton, *Nisei Linguists: Japanese Americans in the Military Intelligence Service during World War II* (Washington, DC: Department of the Army, 2006).

[6] Kelli Y. Nakamura, "Military Intelligence Service Language School," *Densho Encyclopedia*, October 16, 2020, https://encyclopedia.densho.org/Military_Intelligence_Service_Language_School/.

[7] US Census Bureau, "Remembering Pearl Harbor: A Pearl Harbor Fact Sheet," n.d., https://www.census.gov/history/pdf/pearl-harbor-fact-sheet-1.pdf.

[8] "Kazuo Sakamaki, Pacific P.O.W. No. 1," *New York Times*, December 21, 1999, Section C, 23.

[9] Joel Shurkin, "Decrypting the Japanese Cipher Couldn't Prevent Pearl Harbor," *Inside Science*, December 6, 2016, https://www.insidescience.org/news/decrypting-japanese-cipher-couldn%27t-prevent-pearl-harbor.

[10] "FDR's 'Day of Infamy' Speech," *Prologue Magazine* 33, no. 4 (Winter 2001), https://www.archives.gov/publications/prologue/2001/winter/crafting-day-of-infamy-speech.html.

[11] "Executive Order 9066: Resulting in Japanese American Incarceration," *National Archives*, January 24, 2022, https://www.archives.gov/milestone-documents/executive-order-9066.

[12] Brian Nilya, "Public Law 503," *Densho Encyclopedia*, July 15, 2020, https://encyclopedia.densho.org/Public_Law_503/.

[13] "Executive Order 9066."

[14] Ibid.

[15] "Public Law 100-383—August 10, 1988," GovInfo, n.d., https://www.govinfo.gov/content/pkg/STATUTE-102/pdf/STATUTE-102-Pg903.pdf (accessed January 1, 2023).

[16] Matthew McRae, "Japanese Canadian Internment and the Struggle for Redress," *Canadian Museum for Human Rights*, 2022, https://humanrights.ca/story/japanese-canadian-internment-and-the-struggle-for-redress; "British Columbia Wages War against Japanese Canadians," *CBC Learning*, 2001, https://www.cbc.ca/history/EPISCONTENTSE1EP14CH3PA3LE.html.

[17] Ibid.

[18] "Government Apologizes to Japanese Canadians in 1988," *CBC Archives*, September 22, 2018, https://www.cbc.ca/archives/government-apologizes-to-japanese-canadians-in-1988-1.4680546.

[19] See, for example, "Footstep of Japanese American Robert Shiomi (4) Japanese Internment," *Shiomi House*, May 8, 2016, http://shiomihouse.com/en/543/; "The Japanese American Internment Camp Newspapers, 1942–1946," Library of Congress, n.d., https://www.loc.gov/collections/japanese-american-internment-camp-newspapers/about-this-collection/ (accessed January 1, 2023).

[20] "G.I. Bill," *History.com*, June 7, 2019, https://www.history.com/topics/world-war-ii/gi-bill.

[21] For the text of the act and statistics about its use, see "Servicemen's Readjustment Act (1944)," *National Archives*, May 3, 2022, https://www.archives.gov/milestone-documents/servicemens-readjustment-act#:~:text=Within%20the%20following%20seven%20years,on%2Dthe%2Djob%20training.

[22] Leslie Miller-Bernal, "Introduction: Coeducation: An Uneven Progression," in *Going Coed: Women's Experiences in Formerly Men's Colleges and Universities, 1950–2000*, edited by Leslie Miller-Bernal and Susan L. Poulson (Nashville: Vanderbilt University Press, 2004), 9.

[23] Frank Olito, "Here's How the Cost of Harvard Has Changed throughout the Years," *Insider*, June 10, 2019, https://www.businessinsider.com/how-the-cost-of-harvard-has-changed-throughout-the-years2019-6; Mark Frazier Lloyd, "Tuition and Mandated Fees, Room and Board, and Other Educational Costs at Penn," *Penn Libraries*, 2003, https://archives.upenn.edu/exhibits/penn-history/tuition/tuition-1950-1959/.

[24] Ian Webster, "The US Dollar Has Lost 92% of Its Value Since 1949," Official Data Foundation, January 13, 2022, https://www.in2013dollars.com/us/

inflation/1949#:~:text=%24100%20in%201949%20has%20the,power%22%20as%20%241%2C247.05%20in%202023.

[25] See Connor Lennon, "G.I. Jane Goes to College? Female Educational Attainment, Earnings, and the Serviceman's Readjustment Act of 1944," *Journal of Economic History* 81, no. 4 (December 2021): 1223–1253.

[26] See, for example, Alex Wellerstein, "Counting the Dead at Hiroshima and Nagasaki," *Bulletin of the Atomic Scientists,* August 4, 2020, https://thebulletin.org/2020/08/counting-the-dead-at-hiroshima-and-nagasaki/; Jessie Kratz, "Little Boy: The First Atomic Bomb," *National Archives,* August 6, 2020, https://prologue.blogs.archives.gov/2020/08/06/little-boy-the-first-atomic-bomb/.

[27] Robert Jacobs, "Reconstructing the Perpetrator's Soul by Reconstructing the Victim's Body: The Portrayal of the 'Hiroshima Maidens' by the Mainstream Media in the United States," *Intersections* 24 (2010), http://intersections.anu.edu.au/issue24/jacobs.htm.

[28] For an English translation, see "The Jeweled Voice Broadcast," Atomic Heritage Foundation, 2022, https://ahf.nuclearmuseum.org/ahf/key-documents/jewel-voice-broadcast/.

[29] For the text of the "Instrument of Surrender," see "Japanese Instrument of Surrender, 1945," National Archives Foundation, 2022, https://www.archivesfoundation.org/documents/japanese-instrument-surrender-1945/.

[30] For a text of the "Potsdam Declaration," see "Text of the Constitution and Other Important Documents," National Diet Library, 2003–2004, https://www.ndl.go.jp/constitution/e/etc/c06.html.

[31] See, for example, Lori Watt, *When Empire Comes Home: Repatriation and Reintegration in Postwar Japan* (Cambridge, MA: Harvard East Asian Monographs, 2010).

[32] "Occupation and Reconstruction of Japan, 1945–52," Office of the Historian, Foreign Service Institute, 2017, https://history.state.gov/milestones/1945-1952/japan-reconstruction#:~:text=The%20occupation%20of%20Japan%20can,formal%20peace%20treaty%20and%20alliance.

[33] For example perspectives of the occupiers and the occupied, see Eleanor Hadley, *Memoirs of a Trustbuster: A Lifelong Adventure with Japan* (Honolulu: University of Hawaiʻi Press, 2002); John Dower, *Embracing Defeat: Japan in the Wake of World War II* (New York: W. W. Norton and Company, 1999).

[34] For the full text, see "Treaty of Peace with Japan," *Taiwan Documents Project*, n.d., http://www.taiwandocuments.org/sanfrancisco01.htm (accessed November 10, 2022).

[35] "Treaty of Peace with Japan (with Two Declarations)," No. 1832, United Nations, April 28, 1952, efaidnbmnnnibpcajpcglclefindmkaj/https://treaties.un.org/doc/Publication/UNTS/Volume%20136/volume-136-I-1832-English.pdf.

[36] Article 24 reads, "Marriage shall be based only on the mutual consent of both sexes and it shall be maintained through mutual cooperation with the equal rights of husband and wife as a basis. With regard to choice of spouse, property rights, inheritance, choice of domicile, divorce and other matters pertaining to marriage and the family, laws shall be

enacted from the standpoint of individual dignity and the essential equality of the sexes." "The Constitution of Japan," Prime Minister and His Cabinet, n.d., https://japan.kantei.go.jp/constitution_and_government_of_japan/constitution_e.html (accessed January 1, 2023).

[37] "Occupied Japan: Gender, Class, Race," Maryland Institute for Technology in the Humanities, n.d., https://archive.mith.umd.edu/gcr/public/displayTheme.php%3Fid=28.html (accessed January 2, 2023).

[38] "Newly Authorized Universities Now Total 180," *CI&E Bulletin*, June 8, 1949, vol. 3, no. 2, 5.

[39] The other airlines were Pan American Airways, Qantas Empire, British Overseas Airways, Philippine Airlines, Canadian Pacific Airlines, and Civil Air Transport (China). Yoshiko Nakano, "Japan's Postwar International Stewardesses: Embodying Modernity and Exoticism in the Air," *US-Japan Women's Journal* 55/56 (2019), 86–87.

[40] For the text of the law, see "Smith-Mundt Act," US Agency For Global Media, n.d., https://www.usagm.gov/who-we-are/oversight/legislation/smith-mundt/ (accessed January 1, 2023).

[41] Ken Kondo, "The Fulbright Program in Japan: Reappraisal," transcript of speech delivered at the Asia Foundation, San Francisco, September 5, 2001, 3. For a text of the Fulbright-Hays Act, see "United States Code Title 22: Chapter 33," US Department of Education, n.d., https://www2.ed.gov/about/offices/list/ope/iegps/fulbrighthaysact.pdf (accessed January 1, 2023).

[42] Kondo, 9.

[43] Kondo, 6.

[44] Two women were sent as lecturers: Ruth Freegard, a retired professor in home economics, taught at Japan Women's University (Nihon Joshi Daigaku), and Maud Makemson (1891–1977), a professor of astronomy at Vassar College, taught at Ochanomizu Women's College (Ochanomizu Joshi Daigaku). As part of her Fulbright Fellowship, Makemson also taught in Punjab, India.

[45] Robert M. Cullers, *The Japanese Fulbright Returns: What Happens to Him after His Return to Japan?* (Syracuse: Syracuse University, 1961), 3.

[46] Kondo, 9.

[47] Ibid., 9, 12.

[48] Through GARIOA (1946–1967), the United States provided more than $4.5 billion of emergency aid to occupied areas. Germany (1945–1950) and Japan (1945–1952) received the largest shares. See "Government Aid and Relief in Occupied Areas (GARIOA) Payments by the U.S. per Year and Country between 1946 and 1967," *Statistia*, 2018, https://www.statista.com/statistics/1229030/us-garioa-payments-country-year/. Scholarships were not the main expenditures. A smaller number of Japanese students received scholarships from private organizations and universities.

[49] See, for example, J. Michell, "Interview Guide for Obtaining Supplementary Data Concerning Students Selected for Scholarships under the GARIOA Student Program,"

June 23, 1951, declassified E. O. 12065 Section 3-402/NNDG No. 775017; Alisa Freedman, "How I Gained 100 Japanese Grandmothers: Reflections on Intergenerational Conversation Inspired by CSWS," *CSWS Annual Review* (2020), 26–27.

50 Alisa Freedman, "The Forgotten Story of Japanese Women Who Studied in the United States, 1949–1966," *CSWS Annual Review* (2016), 12–14.

51 For official histories, see "Our History," The Rockefeller Foundation, 2023, https://www.rockefellerfoundation.org/about-us/our-history/; "Foundation History," Carnegie Foundation, 2023, https://www.carnegiefoundation.org/about-us/foundation-history/; Rachel Wimpee, "A Brief History of the Ford Foundation's Support for Scholarships and Fellowships," Ford Foundation, September 9, 2016, https://www.fordfoundation.org/news-and-stories/stories/posts/a-brief-history-of-ford-foundations-support-for-scholarships-and-fellowships/; "Past Programs," The Woodrow Wilson National Fellowship Foundation, n.d., https://woodrow.org/about/past-programs/ (accessed July 23, 2023).

52 Hikawa Jinja, "Nippon Yūsen *Hikawa maru* ni tsuite" (About the Japan Mail Shipping Line's *Hikawa Maru*), Hikawa Jinja (Hikawa Shrine), n.d., https://musashiichinomiya-hikawa.or.jp/hikawamaru/ (accessed January 1, 2023).

53 Itō Genjirō, *Hikawa maru monogatari* (Story of the *Hikawa Maru*) (Kamakura: Kamakura Shunjūsha, 2015), 153 and 268–269.

54 "American President Lines," *The Last Ocean Liners*, n.d., https://lastoceanliners.com/line/american-president-lines/?l=APL (accessed July 7, 2023).

55 For a synopsis of the Korean War and related US documents, see "Korean War," Dwight D. Eisenhower Presidential Library, n.d., https://www.eisenhowerlibrary.gov/research/online-documents/korean-war (accessed January 1, 2023).

56 Japanese films were shown in American movie theaters before the war. For example, in 1937, director Naruse Mikio's *Wife! Be Like A Rose!* (*Tsuma yo bara no yō ni*, 1935) became the first Japanese talkie commercially released in the United States (under the title *Kimiko*). *Rashomon* was nominated to the Venice Film Festival by Giuliana Stramigioli, a specialist in Japan and founder (1948) of Italiafilm, which exported Italian films to Japan. Thanks to the popularity of *Rashomon*, the term "Rashomon effect" became an American neologism for an event described or interpreted differently by the people involved. Jasper Sharp, "70 Years of Rashomon—A New Look at Akira Kurosawa's Cinematic Milestone of Post-Truth," *BFI*, August 25, 2020, https://www.bfi.org.uk/features/rashomon-akira-kurosawa.

57 "Theatre Fete to Aid Japanese Students," *New York Times*, January 18, 1959, 91.

58 "McCarthy and Army-McCarthy Hearings," United States Senate, n.d., https://www.senate.gov/about/powers-procedures/investigations/mccarthy-and-army-mccarthy-hearings.htm (accessed January 1, 2023).

59 "Education: Our Enemies," *Time*, July 16, 1951, https://content.time.com/time/subscriber/article/0,33009,889131,00.html. See, for example, National Council for American Education, *Red-ucators at Leading Women's Colleges* (New York: National Council for American Education, 1951). Ben W. Heineman Jr., "The University in the

McCarthy Era," *The Harvard Crimson*, June 17, 1965, https://www.thecrimson.com/article/1965/6/17/the-university-in-the-mccarthy-era/.

[60] For example, Robert N. Bellah, "McCarthyism at Harvard," *The New York Review of Books*, February 10, 2005, https://www.nybooks.com/articles/2005/02/10/mccarthyism-at-harvard/.

[61] Irwin Collier, "Radcliffe/Harvard Economics PhD Alumna Eleanor Martha Hadley, 1949," *Economics in the Rear-View Mirror*, November 24, 2021, https://www.irwincollier.com/radcliffe-harvard-economics-ph-d-alumna-eleanor-martha-hadley-1949/.

[62] "Donald Richie Interview by Marlene Mayo," *Oral History Project on the Allied Occupation of Japan*, May 18, 1981, University of Maryland College Park, 29–32.

[63] "Daigo Fukuryū-Maru," Daigo Fukuryū-Maru Exhibition Hall, 2015, http://d5f.org/en/en-about.

[64] The Experiment in International Living, "History & Mission," https://www.experiment.org/about-history-mission/ (accessed January 11, 2022).

[65] Koide Izumi, "Chronological Biography of Naomi Fukuda," *Journal of East Asian Libraries* 145 (2008), https://scholarsarchive.byu.edu/cgi/viewcontent.cgi?article=2596&context=jeal; *Nichibei kōryū-shi no naka Fukuda Naomi* (Naomi Fukuda and the History of Japan-US Exchange) (Tokyo: Bensei Shuppan, 2022).

[66] International House of Japan, *International House of Japan: Cultural Bridge between East and West* (Tokyo: International House of Japan, 2009), 104–105.

[67] Caroline Donadio, "From the I-House Archives: Happy Birthday, Harry Edmonds!" *International House*, March 11, 2020, https://www.ihouse-nyc.org/news_events/from-the-i-house-archives-happy-birthday-harry-edmonds/.

[68] Takeshi Matsuda, *Soft Power and Its Perils: U.S. Cultural Policy in Early Postwar Japan and Permanent Dependency* (Stanford: Stanford University Press, 2007), 136.

[69] MoMA, "Japanese Exhibition House, June 16, 1954–October 15, 1955," *MoMA*, n.d., www.moma.org/calendar/exhibitions/2711 (April 22, 2022). I thank John Leisure for the insight on "Japanese Exhibition House." Barthes critiques middlebrow "mythologies" of "human community" and the politics they paper over in *The Family of Man*. Roland Barthes, *Mythologies*, translated by Annette Lavers (New York: Hill and Wang, 1972), 100–102.

[70] Peter B. Flint, "Harold Strauss, Editor, Dead; Brought in Japanese Literature," *New York Times*, November 30, 1975, 73.

[71] Edward Fowler, "Rendering Worlds, Traversing Culture: On the Art and Politics of Translating Modern Japanese Fiction," *Journal of Japanese Studies* 18, no. 1 (Winter 1992), 8–11.

[72] For example, as Joan Ericson analyzes, Ivan Morris, renowned scholar and prolific translator of Japanese literature, published a translation of Hayashi Fumiko's short story "Tokyo" (Dauntaun, originally printed in the *Asahi* newspaper in 1948). To help American readers through this story about ordinary people surviving in immediate postwar Tokyo, grounded in the daily life of Occupation-era Japan and steeped in Tokyo mass culture,

Morris changed cultural referents (turning soba noodles into "cold spaghetti"), abridged the protagonist's internal monologue about her life choices, and shortened the names of the characters to be easier to pronounce (i.e., Riyo to Ryo). Joan Ericson, *Be a Woman: Hayashi Fumiko and Modern Japanese Women's Literature* (Honolulu: University of Hawai'i Press, 1997), ix.

[73] Shigeru Yoshida, "Japan's Place in Asia," *The Atlantic* (January 1955), 101–102.

[74] "Sputnik Spurs Passages of the National Defense Educational Act," United States Senate, n.d., https://www2.ed.gov/about/offices/list/ope/iegps/history.html (accessed October 31, 2022). Other reasons include population growth, increases in household resources, and positive images of universities.

[75] For the language of the loyalty oaths and disclaimer, see Sam Walker, "National Defense Education Act Includes Loyalty Oath and Bar to Civil Rights Enforcement," *Today in Civil Liberties History, September 2, 1958*, 2014, http://todayinclh.com/?event=92581958-national-defense-education-act-loyalty-oaths-required-for-students.

[76] "Monro Attacks Disclaimer Affidavit," *The Harvard Crimson*, October 24, 1959, https://www.thecrimson.com/article/1959/10/24/monro-attacks-disclaimer-affidavit-pa-vote/; "Congress Votes to Discontinue NDEA Disclaimer Affidavit," *The Colby Echo*, October 19, 1962, 1.

[77] See, for example, Justin Jesty, "Tokyo 1960: Days of Rage & Grief," *MIT Visualizing Cultures*, 2012, "https://visualizingcultures.mit.edu/tokyo_1960/anp2_essay01.html.

[78] For a text of the "Japan-US Security Treaty," see "Japan-US Security Treaty," Ministry of Foreign Affairs of Japan, n.d., https://www.mofa.go.jp/region/n-america/us/q&a/ref/1.html (accessed January 1, 2023). For more on Ampo history and news images, see Nick Kapur, *Japan at the Crossroads: Conflict and Compromise after Anpo* (Cambridge, MA: Harvard University Press, 2018); Justin Jesty, "Hamaya Hiroshi's Photos of the Anti-Security Treaty Protests," *MIT Visualizing Cultures*, 2012, http://visualizingcultures.mit.edu/tokyo_1960/anp2_essay05.html.

[79] "About CULCON," CULCON, 2018, https://culcon.jusfc.gov/about-us/.

[80] "Japan-United States Joint Communique, June 22, 1961," CULCON, September 2020, https://culcon.jusfc.gov/wp-content/uploads/2020/09/1961-CULCON-Agreement.pdf.

[81] "Affirmative Action," Legal Information Institute, Cornell University, https://www.law.cornell.edu/wex/affirmative_action#:~:text=Affirmative%20action%20is%20defined%20as,or%20looking%20for%20professional%20employment (accessed January 1, 2023).

[82] For the text of the executive order, see "Executive Order 10925—Establishing the President's Committee Equal Employment Opportunity," *The American Presidency Project*, University of California, Santa Barbara, https://www.presidency.ucsb.edu/documents/executive-order-10925-establishing-the-presidents-committee-equal-employment-opportunity (accessed January 1, 2023).

[83] Ibid.

[84] "Executive Order 11246," Office of Federal Contract Compliance Programs. n.d. https://www.dol.gov/agencies/ofccp/executive-order-11246 (accessed January 1, 2023).

[85] "A Brief History of Affirmative Action," Office of Equal Opportunity and Diversity, University of California, Irvine, 2023, https://www.oeod.uci.edu/policies/aa_history.php.

[86] *Students for Fair Admissions, Inc. v. President and Fellows of Harvard College, 20-1199* (2023), https://www.supremecourt.gov/opinions/22pdf/20-1199_hgdj.pdf.

[87] US Equal Employment Opportunity Commission, "The Equal Pay Act of 1963," n.d., https://www.eeoc.gov/statutes/equal-pay-act-1963 (January 2, 2023).

[88] National Equal Pay Task Force, "Fifty Years after the Equal Pay Act: Assessing the Past, Taking Stock of the Future," Obama White House, 2013, https://obamawhitehouse.archives.gov/sites/default/files/equalpay/equal_pay_task_force_progress_report_june_2013_new.pdf.

[89] Greg Iacurci, "Women Are Still Paid 83 Cents for Every Dollar Men Earn," CNBC, May 19, 2022, https://www.cnbc.com/2022/05/19/women-are-still-paid-83-cents-for-every-dollar-men-earn-heres-why.html#:~:text=Women%20are%20still%20paid%2083%20cents%20for%20every%20dollar%20men%20earn.

[90] Colleen Flaherty, "New Analysis of Faculty Pay, Representation," *Inside Higher Ed*, December 10, 2020, https://www.insidehighered.com/quicktakes/2020/12/10/new-analysis-faculty-pay-representation.

[91] Modern Language Association (MLA), "Standing Still: The Associate Professor Survey Report of the Committee on the Status of Women in the Profession," April 27, 2009, https://www.mla.org/About-Us/Governance/Committees/Committee-Listings/Professional-Issues/Committee-on-Women-Gender-and-Sexuality-in-the-Profession/Standing-Still-The-Associate-Professor-Survey.

[92] See, for example, Richard Fry, Brian Kennedy, and Cary Funk, "STEM Jobs See Uneven Progress in Increasing Gender, Racial, and Ethnic Diversity," Pew Research Center, April 1, 2021, https://www.pewresearch.org/science/2021/04/01/stem-jobs-see-uneven-progress-in-increasing-gender-racial-and-ethnic-diversity/.

[93] "Civil Rights Act (1964)," *National Archives*, February 8, 2022, https://www.archives.gov/milestone-documents/civil-rights-act#:~:text=This%20act%2C%20signed%20into%20law,civil%20rights%20legislation%20since%20Reconstruction.

[94] "Boy Born on Day A-Bomb Fell Chosen to Light the Olympic Flame," *New York Times*, August 23, 1964, 8.

[95] "Tokyo 1964 Creates Lasting Legacies," International Olympic Committee, March 30, 2021, https://olympics.com/en/news/tokyo-1964-creates-lasting-legacies.

[96] "Finnish Officials Cancel Olympics," *New York Times*, April 24, 1940, 32.

[97] Yasunari Kawabata, "Nobel Lecture," The Nobel Foundation, 1968, https://www.nobelprize.org/prizes/literature/1968/kawabata/lecture/.

[98] "Title IX of the Educational Amendments of 1972," US Department of Justice, 2015, https://www.justice.gov/crt/title-ix-education-amendments-1972. For resources, see "Title IX of the Educational Amendments of 1972," US Department of Health and Human Services, 2023, https://www.hhs.gov/civil-rights/for-individuals/sex-discrimination/title-ix-education-amendments/index.html#:~:text=Title%20IX%20of%20the%20

Education%20Amendments%20of%201972%20(Title%20IX,activity%20receiving%20 federal%20financial%20assistance.

⁹⁹ "Case Summaries," US Department of Justice, December 21, 2022, https://www.justice.gov/crt/case-summaries; "Title IX: Tracking Sexual Assault Investigations," *Chronicle of Higher Education*, January 16, 2023, http://projects.chronicle.com/titleix/.

¹⁰⁰ "Title IX," RAINN, 2023, https://www.rainn.org/articles/title-ix; Mary Elizabeth Berry, "Mary Elizabeth Berry (1978–2017)," UC Berkeley History Department, 2018, https://history.berkeley.edu/sites/default/files/150w_meb_final.pdf.

¹⁰¹ For a detailed chronology of the war and protests against it, see "Vietnam War: Causes, Facts, and Impact," *History.com*, October 29, 2009, https://www.history.com/topics/vietnam-war/vietnam-war-history.

¹⁰² Death counts vary. See, for example, "Vietnam War US Military Fatal Casualty Statistics," *National Archives*, August 23, 2022, https://www.archives.gov/research/military/vietnam-war/casualty-statistics. The earliest recorded death was in 1956. "How Many People Died in the Vietnam War?," *Britannica*, 2023, https://www.britannica.com/question/How-many-people-died-in-the-Vietnam-War. Soldiers from other countries, including South Korea and Thailand, also died.

¹⁰³ Mark Selden, "Reflections on the Committee of Concerned Asian Scholars at Fifty," *Critical Asian Studies* 50, no. 1 (2018), 3, 13.

¹⁰⁴ "Statement of Purpose," Critical Asian Studies, n.d., https://criticalasianstudies.org/about.

¹⁰⁵ Hrishi Karthikeyan and Gabriel J. Chin, "Anti-Miscegenation Statutes and Asian Americans," *Race, Racism, and the Law*, August 5, 2011, https://racism.org/index.php?option=com_content&view=article&id=306:aspi0201&catid=64:asian-and-pacific-americans&Itemid=235.

¹⁰⁶ For a text of the law, see "Cable Act of 1922," *Immigration History*, 2019, https://immigrationhistory.org/item/cable-act/.

¹⁰⁷ Mishima Yukio, *Patriotism,* translated by Geoffrey W. Sargent (New York: New Directions Publishing, 2010); Mishima Yukio and Domoto Masaki, dirs., *Yūkoku* (Patriotism), 1966 (New York: Criterion Collection, 2008), DVD.

¹⁰⁸ BBC, "Witness History: The Death of Yukio Mishima," *BBC*, November 25, 2014, podcast, MP3 audio, 9:00, https://www.bbc.co.uk/sounds/play/p02c6s3r; Jonathan Watts, "Dead Writer's Knife Is in Japan's Heart," *Guardian*, November 24, 2000, https://www.theguardian.com/world/2000/nov/25/books.booksnews.

¹⁰⁹ For example, Joyce Lebra, "Eyewitness: Mishima," *The New York Times*, November 28, 1970, 26.

¹¹⁰ See Patricia Steinhoff, *Nihon Sekigunha: Sono shakaigakuteki monogatari* (Japan Red Army Faction: A Sociological Tale) (Tokyo: Kawade shobō shinsha, 1991); "Kidnapped Japanese in North Korea: The New Left Connection," *Journal of Japanese Studies* 30, no. 1 (2004), 123–142; "Three Myths about the Japanese Red Army: What You Think You Know Is Probably Wrong," Podcast, *DIJ Tokyo*, May 29, 2014, https://www.dijtokyo.org/

event/three-myths-about-the-japanese-red-army-what-you-think-you-know-is-probably-wrong/.

[111] "Asama-Sansō Incident," *50 Years of NHK Television*, n.d. https://www.nhk.or.jp/digitalmuseum/nhk50years_en/history/p16/#top (accessed January 2, 2023).

[112] See Steinhoff, *Nihon Sekigunha;* "Death by Defeatism and Other Fables: The Social Dynamics of the Rengo Sekigun Purge," in *Japanese Social Organization*, edited by Takie Sugiyama Lebra (Honolulu: University of Hawai'i Press, 1992), 195–224.

[113] Nikkei Asia, "Blast from the Past," *Unlock the Real Japan*, March 2022, https://ps.nikkei.com/unlock/202203/blastfromthepast.html.

[114] Takashi Oka, "Expo '70 Ended after 183 Days," *New York Times*, September 14, 1970, https://www.nytimes.com/1970/09/14/archives/expo-70-is-ended-after-183-days-attendance-was-64-million-sato.html; Jim Ogul, "Expo 2025 Will Build on Osaka's World's Fair Legacy," *InPark Magazine*, March 1, 2022, https://www.inparkmagazine.com/expo-2025-will-build-on-osakas-worlds-fair-legacy.

[115] Japan Foundation, "Collection: Kokusai Bunka Shinkōkai (KBS) Archives," n.d., https://www.jpf.go.jp/e/about/jfic/lib/collection/kbs.html (accessed January 1, 2023); Kokusai Bunka Shinkōkai, *Introduction to Contemporary Literature* (Tokyo: Kokusai Bunka Shinkōkai, 1939).

[116] "Japan Names 10 US Colleges to Share Equally in $10-Million," *New York Times*, August 8, 1973, 14.

[117] Fran Schumer, "Japanese Give $1 Million to Harvard," *The Harvard Crimson*, October 13, 1973, https://www.thecrimson.com/article/1973/10/13/japanese-give-1-million-to-harvard.

[118] "Japan Names 10 US Colleges to Share Equally in $10-Million," 14.

[119] Richard Halloran, "Japan Braces for a Full-Scale Oil Crisis," *New York Times*, December 8, 1973, 1.

[120] Becky Little, "How the 1982 Murder of Vincent Chin Ignited a Push for Asian American Rights," *History.com*, May 5, 2020, https://www.history.com/news/vincent-chin-murder-asian-american-rights.

[121] George R. Packard, "The Coming US-Japan Crisis," *Foreign Affairs* (Winter 1987/88), https://www.foreignaffairs.com/articles/asia/1987-12-01/coming-us-japan-crisis. For information about the context of and popular culture responses to Japan Bashing, see Alisa Freedman, *Japan on American TV: Screaming Samurai Join Anime Clubs in the Land of the Lost* (New York: Columbia University Press, 2021), 53–71.

[122] "Public Law 94-118," Congress.gov, n.d., https://www.congress.gov/94/statute/STATUTE-89/STATUTE-89-Pg603.pdf (accessed January 1, 2023); Francis B. Tenny, "History of the Commission" (Japan-US Friendship Commission, Washington, DC. 1995), n.p.

[123] Tenny, n.p.

124 Inauguration Committee, "The Women's Studies Association of Japan Statement of Purpose," Nihon Josei Gakkai (Women's Studies Association of Japan), January 18, 1979, https://joseigakkai-jp.org/english-home/.

125 Mizuta Noriko, *Josei gaku to no deai* (My Encounter with Women's Studies) (Tokyo: Shueisha, 2004), 40.

126 Merry I. White and Barbara Malony, "Preface," *Proceedings of the Tokyo Symposium on Women*, edited by Merry I. White and Barbara Malony (Tokyo: International Group for the Study of Women, 1979), n.p.

127 Eamonn Fingleton, "Now They Tell Us: The Story of Japan's 'Lost Decades' Was Just One Big Hoax," *Forbes,* August 11, 2013, https://www.forbes.com/sites/eamonnfingleton/2013/08/11/now-for-the-truth-the-story-of-japans-lost-decades-is-the-worlds-most-absurd-media-myth/#2809dd2a3fe4.

128 See "Japanese Generations: Boom, Bubble, and Ice Age," *Nippon.com*, May 12, 2022, https://www.nippon.com/en/japan-data/h00535/japanese-generations-boom-bubble-and-ice-age.html.

Bibliography

Abe Kōbō. *Secret Rendezvous*. Translated by Juliet Winters Carpenter. New York: Alfred A. Knopf, 1980.

"About CULCON." CULCON. 2018. https://culcon.jusfc.gov/about-us.

"About StoryCorps." StoryCorps. n.d. https://storycorps.org/about/ (accessed January 5, 2023).

Abrams, M. H. and Geoffrey Galt Harpham. *A Glossary of Literary Terms, 11th edition*. Belmont, CA: Thomson Wadsworth, 2014.

The Actors' Analects. Edited and translated by Charles J. Dunn and Bunzō Torigoe. New York: Columbia University Press, 1969.

Adichie, Chimamanda Ngozi. "The Danger of a Single Story." TEDGlobal. October 7, 2009. https://www.ted.com/talks/chimamanda_ngozi_adichie_the_danger_of_a_single_story?language=en.

"Affirmative Action." Legal Information Institute. Cornell University. https://www.law.cornell.edu/wex/affirmative_action#:~:text=Affirmative%20action%20is%20defined%20as,or%20looking%20for%20professional%20employment (accessed January 1, 2023).

Akai Tatsurō. *Etoki no keifu* (A Genealogy of Etoki). Tokyo: Kyōikusha, 1989.

Akimichi Tomoya. *Komonzu no chikyūshi: Gurōbaruka jidai no kyōyūron ni muketa* (The Planet's History of Commons: Toward a Theory of Shared Ownership for the Global Age). Tokyo: Iwanami shoten, 2010.

Alagappa, Muthiah, ed. *Civil Society and Political Change in Asia*. Stanford: Stanford University Press, 2004.

"American President Lines." *The Last Ocean Liners*. n.d. https://lastoceanliners.com/line/american-president-lines/?l=APL (accessed July 7, 2023).

Amino, Yoshihiko. *Rethinking Japanese History*. Translated by Alan S. Christy. Ann Arbor: University of Michigan Center for Japanese Studies, 2012.

Arase Yutaka. *Jiyū, rekishi, mejia: Masu komyunikēshon kenkyū no kadai* (Freedom, History, Media: Issues in Mass Communication Studies). Tokyo: Nihon Hyōronsha, 1988.

Ariga, Chieko M. "Dephallicizing Women in Ryūkyō Shinshi: A Critique of Gender Ideology in Japanese Literature." *Journal of Asian Studies* 51, no. 5 (August 1992): 565–586.

Arita, Eriko. "Donald Keene: A Life Lived True to the Words." *The Japan Times*. September 6, 2009. https://www.japantimes.co.jp/life/2009/09/06/people/donald-keene-a-life-lived-true-to-the-words/.

Arnold, Matthew. *Culture and Anarchy: An Essay in Political and Social Criticism*. New Haven: Yale University Press, 1994.

Arntzen, Sonja. "Chinese Community of the Imagination for the Japanese Zen Monk Ikkyū Sōjun." In *Rethinking the Sinosphere: Poetics, Aesthetics, and Identity Formation*, edited by Nanxiu Qian, Richard Smith, and Bowei Zhang, 67–94. Amherst: Cambria Press, 2020.

———. "Differing Demands of 'High' and 'Low' Narratives from the Heian Period for the Translator." In *Narratological Perspectives on Premodern Japanese Literature*, edited by Sebastian Balmes. BmE Special Issue 7. https://ojs.uni-oldenburg.de/ojs/index.php/bme/article/view/109.

———. *Ikkyū and the Crazy Cloud Anthology: A Zen Monk of Medieval Japan*. Tokyo: University of Tokyo Press, 1986.

———. *Ikkyū and the Crazy Cloud Anthology: A Zen Monk of Medieval Japan*. Revised and expanded edition. Basel, Switzerland, Quirin Press, 2022.

———. "In Defense of Kokoro: The Study of Classical Japanese Literature in North America within the Context of the Debate over a World System of Anthropology." *Ritsumeikan Journal of Asia Pacific Studies* 6 (December 2000): 81–83.

———. *The Kagerō Diary: A Woman's Autobiographical Text from Tenth-Century Japan*. Ann Arbor: University of Michigan Center for Japanese Studies, 1997.

———. "Katō Shūichi no nihon koten bungaku kenkyū—sono kokusaiteki eikyō no kansuru shiken" (Katō Shūichi's Research on Classical Japanese Literature: A Personal View of Its International Influence). In *Katō Shūichi o nijūisseki ni hikitsugu tame ni* (To Have Katō Shūichi Carry On into the Twenty-First Century), edited by Miura Nobutaka and Washizu Tsutomu, 111–126. Tokyo: Suiseisha, 2020.

Arntzen, Sonja and Janice Brown. "Old Pond, Students Leap In, Sound of Laughter: Creative Projects in the Teaching of Classical Japanese." *Japanese Language and Literature* 35, no. 1 (April 2001): 17–36.

———, eds. *Across Time and Genre: Reading and Writing Japanese Women's Texts, Conference Proceedings*. Edmonton: University of Alberta, 2002.

Arntzen, Sonja and Itō Moriyuki. *The Sarashina Diary: A Woman's Life in Eleventh-Century Japan: A Reader's Edition*. New York: Columbia University Press, 2018.

"Asama-Sansō Incident." *50 Years of NHK Television*. n.d. https://www.nhk.or.jp/digitalmuseum/nhk50years_en/history/p16/#top (accessed January 2, 2023).

Asian Women's Fund. *Ianfu kankei bunken mokuroku* (Bibliography of Publications on the "Comfort Women" Issue). Tokyo: Gyōsei, 1997.

Baldwin, James and Nikki Giovanni. *Wareware no kakei* (A Dialogue). Translated by Takako Lento. Tokyo: Shōbunsha, 1977.

Bando, Mariko. *Danjo kyōdō sankaku shakai e* (Toward a Gender Equality Society). Tokyo: Keisō shobō, 2004.

Barnstone, Aliki and Willis Barnstone, eds. *A Book of Women Poets from Antiquity to Now*. New York: Schocken, 1980.

Barthes, Roland. *Empire of Signs*. Translated by Richard Howard. New York: Hill and Wang, 1983.

———. *Mythologies*. Translated by Annette Lavers. New York: Hill and Wang, 1972.

Barzun, Jacques. *Teacher in America*. Boston: Little, Brown, and Company, 1945.

"Bataan Death March." *Encyclopedia Britannica*. 2018. https://www.britannica.com/event/Bataan-Death-March.

BBC. "Witness History: The Death of Yukio Mishima." *BBC*. November 25, 2014. Podcast. MP3 audio. 9:00. https://www.bbc.co.uk/sounds/play/p02c6s3r.

Beasley, William. *Great Britain and the Opening of Japan, 1834–1858*. London: Luzac and Company, 1951.

Beichman, Janine. "Bungaku ni okeru seisabetsu—Yosano Akiko no hyōka o megutte" (Gender Discrimination in Literature: On the Evaluation of Yosano Akiko). *Kashin* 1, no. 2 (August 1987): 29–35.

———. "*Drifting Fires*: An American Nō." *Asian Theatre Journal* 3, no. 2 (Autumn 1986): 233–260.

———. "Eigo no shinsaku Nō hyōen: 27 nen no kaiko" (The English New Noh *Drifting Fires*: 27 Years Later). *Hikaku Nihongaku kenkyū sentā kenkyū nenpō* (Comparative Japanese Studies Annual Bulletin) 9 (2013): 45–67.

———. *Embracing the Firebird: Yosano Akiko and the Rebirth of the Female Voice in Modern Japanese Poetry*. Honolulu: University of Hawai'i Press, 2002.

———. *Masaoka Shiki*. Woodbridge, CT: Twayne Publishers, 1982.

———. *Masaoka Shiki*. New York: Kodansha International, 1986.

———. *Masaoka Shiki: His Life and Works*. Boston: Cheng & Tsui, 2002.

———. "New Noh and Noh-influenced Theatre in the Twentieth Century." In *Proceedings of the Nitobe-Ohira Memorial Conference on Japanese Studies*, edited by Leon Zolbrod, 39–82. Vancouver: University of British Columbia, 1988.

———. "Nō wa doko made saigi ka" (To What Extent is Noh Ritual?). *Bungaku* 51, no. 7 (September 1983): 233–260.

———. "Noh in English: Encounters Near and Far." *Japan Quarterly* 33, no. 1 (January–March 1986): 88–92.

———. "Ritual and Theatre in Noh." *Research Report of University of Library and Information Science* (Toshokan Jōhō Daigaku Kenkyū Hōkoku) 2, no. 1 (July 1984): 55–71.

———, trans. "The Priest and the Willow." *20 Plays of the Nō Theatre*, edited by Donald Keene and Royall Tyler, 219–236. New York: Columbia University Press, 1970.

Bellah, Robert N. "McCarthyism at Harvard." *The New York Review of Books*. February 10, 2005. https://www.nybooks.com/articles/2005/02/10/mccarthyism-at-harvard/.

Bellah, Robert, McGeorge Bundy, Clark Kerr, Marshall Cohen, and John Convway, et al. "'Veritas' at Harvard: Another Exchange." *The New York Review of Books*. July 14, 1977. https://www.nybooks.com/articles/1977/07/14/veritas-at-harvard-another-exchange/.

Benedict, Ruth. *The Chrysanthemum and the Sword*. London: Secker and Warburg, 1947.

Bernoff, Josh. "The 11 Qualities of Highly Paid, Ultra-Valuable Editors." *Without Bullshit*. April 12, 2017. https://withoutbullshit.com/blog/11-qualities-wickedly-valuable-editors.

Bernstein, Gail Lee. *Haruko's World: A Japanese Farm Woman and Her Community: with a 1996 Epilogue*. Stanford: Stanford University Press, 1996.

———. *Isami's House: Three Centuries of a Japanese Family*. Berkeley: University of California Press, 2005.

———. *Japanese Marxist: A Portrait of Kawakami Hajime, 1879–1946*. Cambridge, MA: Harvard University Press, 1976.

———. *Kawakami: Nihon-teki Marukusu-shugisha no shōzō* (Kawakami Hajime: Portrait of a Japanese Marxist). Kyoto: Minerva shobō, 1991.

———, ed. *Recreating Japanese Women, 1600–1945*. Berkeley: University of California Press, 1991.

Berry, Mary Elizabeth. *The Culture of Civil War in Kyoto*. Berkeley: University of California Press, 1994.

———, et al. "Helen Craig McCullough, East Asian Languages: Berkeley." *Online Archives of California*. 1998. https://oac.cdlib.org/view?docId=hb1p30039g;NAAN=13030&doc.view=frames&chunk.id=div00035&toc.depth=1&toc.id=&brand=oac4.

———. *Hideyoshi*. Cambridge, MA: Harvard University Asia Center, 1982.

———. "Hideyoshi in Kyoto: The Arts of Peace." PhD Diss. Harvard University, 1975.

———. "Mary Elizabeth Berry." Department of History, University of California Berkeley. 2020 and 2021. https://wayback.archive-it.org/16283/20211216050814/https://history.berkeley.edu/sites/default/files/150w_meb_final.pdf.

———. "Mary Elizabeth Berry (1978–2017)." UC Berkeley History Department. 2018. https://history.berkeley.edu/sites/default/files/150w_meb_final.pdf.

———. "Women in the Department of History." Department of History. University of California, Berkeley. 2020 and 2021. https://wayback.archive-it.org/16283/20210913182815/https://history.berkeley.edu/women-department-history.

Bestor, Theodore, Patricia G. Steinhoff, and Victoria Lyon Bestor. *Doing Fieldwork in Japan*. Honolulu: University of Hawai'i Press, 2003.

Bestor, Victoria Lyon. "A Brief History of NCC." "Curated Archives: NCC Background." August 10, 2022. https://guides.nccjapan.org/archive.

Birnbaum, Phyllis. *Modern Girls, Shining Stars, the Skies of Tokyo: Five Japanese Women*. New York: Columbia University Press, 1999.

Black, Naomi. "Staging a Career, Staging a Life: Strategies for Retirement." *PS: Political Science and Politics* 38, no. 2 (April 2005): 277–281.

Blacker, Carmen. *The Catalpa Bow: A Study of Shamanistic Practices in Japan.* London: Allen & Unwin, 1975.

Bloch, Bernard and Eleanor Harz Jorden. *Spoken Japanese: Book One.* New York: Henry Holt and Company, 1945.

Bollinger, Lee. "Our Accelerated Faculty Diversity Efforts." Office of the President. October 29, 2021. https://president.columbia.edu/news/our-accelerated-faculty-diversity-efforts.

"Boy Born on Day A-Bomb Fell Chosen to Light the Olympic Flame." *New York Times.* August 23, 1964: 8.

Brazell, Karen. *The Confessions of Lady Nijō.* New York: Doubleday, 1973.

Brazell, Karen and Monica Bethe. *Nō as Performance: An Analysis of the Kuse Scene of Yamamba.* Ithaca: Cornell East Asia Series, 1978.

Brecht, Bertolt. *Saint Joan of the Stockyards.* Translated by Frank W. Jones. Bloomington: Indiana University Press, 1970.

Brenson, Michael. "Art: Met's New Japanese Galleries." *New York Times.* April 24, 1987: Section C, 32.

Bridges, Will, Nitasha Tamar Sharma, and Marvin D. Sterling, eds. *Who Is the Asianist?: The Politics of Representation in Asian Studies.* New York: Columbia University Press, 2022.

"A Brief History of Affirmative Action." Office of Equal Opportunity and Diversity. University of California, Irvine. 2023. https://www.oeod.uci.edu/policies/aa_history.php.

"British Columbia Wages War against Japanese Canadians." *CBC Learning.* 2001. https://www.cbc.ca/history/EPISCONTENTSE1EP14CH3PA3LE.html.

Britten, Benjamin, composer, and William Plomer, librettist. *Curlew River.* New York: London Records (A 4156), 1966.

Bromley, Daniel, David Feeny, Jere Gilles, Margaret McKean, Ronald Oakerson, Pauline Peters, C. Ford Runge, and James Thomson, eds. *Proceedings of the Conference on Common Property Resource Management, April 21–26, 1985.* Washington, DC: National Academy of Sciences, 1986.

———, eds. *Making the Commons Work: Theory, Practice, and Policy.* San Francisco: Institute of Contemporary Studies, 1992.

Brown, Philip C. *Cultivating Commons: Joint Ownership of Arable Land in Early Modern Japan.* Honolulu: University of Hawai'i Press, 2011.

Bunkazai Hōgo Iinkai (Japan's Cultural Properties Commission). *Kokuhō* (National Treasures). 6 vols. Tokyo: Mainichi Shimbunsha, 1963–1967.

Burnshaw, Stanley. *The Poem Itself.* New York: Holt, Rinehart, and Winston, 1960.

Butler, Lee. "Four Years in Izumi: Village Japan in the Early Sixteenth Century." Unpublished manuscript. April 2022.

"Cable Act of 1922." *Immigration History.* 2019. https://immigrationhistory.org/item/cable-act/.

Campbell, Robert, ed. *Yomu koto no chikara* (The Power of Reading). Tokyo: Kōdansha, 2004.

———, ed. *Nihon koten to kansenshō* (Japanese Classics and Epidemics). Tokyo: Kadokawa shoten, 2021.

Camus, Albert. *The Rebel.* Translated by Anthony Bower. New York: Vintage, 1991.

Carlton, Genevieve. "A History of Affirmative Action in College Admissions." *Best Colleges,* December 7, 2022. https://www.bestcolleges.com/news/analysis/2020/08/10/history-affirmative-action-college/.

"Case Summaries." US Department of Justice. December 21, 2022. https://www.justice.gov/crt/case-summaries.

Chapman, Napua. *Sugar and Smoke.* Frederick, MD: PublishAmerica, 2005.

Chevray, Keiko Uesawa and Tomiko Kuwahira. *Schaum's Outline of Japanese Grammar.* New York: McGraw-Hill, 2000.

Chiba Tokuji. *Hageyama no bunka* (The Culture of Bald Mountains). Tokyo: Gakuseisha, 1973.

———. *Hageyama no kenkyū* (Research on Bald Mountains). Tokyo: Nōrin kyōkai, 1956.

Child, Julia. *Mastering the Art of French Cooking.* New York: Alfred A. Knopf, 1961.

Childs, Margaret Helen. *Rethinking Sorrow: Revelatory Tales of Late Medieval Japan.* Ann Arbor: University of Michigan Center for Japanese Studies, 1996.

Choi, Kyeong-Hee. "When the Colonized Mother Speaks: Post-Colonial and Maternal Narratives of Toni Morrison, Park Wanso, and Buchi Emecheta." PhD Diss. Indiana University Bloomington, 1996.

Chung, Moojeong. "Korean Art Represented in the United States in the 1950s." *Korean Modern & Contemporary Art History* 14 (2005): 7–41.

Civil Affairs Training School Records." Online Archive of California. n.d. https://oac.cdlib.org/findaid/ark:/13030/tf8t1nb33h/ (accessed July 7, 2023).

"Civil Rights Act (1964)." *National Archives*. February 8, 2022. https://www.archives.gov/milestone-documents/civil-rights-act#:~:text=This%20act%2C%20signed%20into%20law,civil%20rights%20legislation%20since%20Reconstruction.

Clavell, James. *Shōgun*. New York: Delacorte Press, 1975.

"Coeducation at Columbia." Columbia University Libraries. n.d. https://library.columbia.edu/libraries/cuarchives/resources/coeducation.html (accessed January 1, 2023).

Collier, Irwin. "Radcliffe/Harvard Economics PhD Alumna Eleanor Martha Hadley, 1949." *Economics in the Rear-View Mirror*. November 24, 2021. https://www.irwincollier.com/radcliffe-harvard-economics-ph-d-alumna-eleanor-martha-hadley-1949/.

Conant, Ellen P. "Bernard Leach, Frank Brangwyn, and Japan." *Studio Potter* 27, no. 2 (June 1999): 15–20.

———. "'Cut from Kyoto Cloth': Takeuchi Seihō and His Artistic Milieu." *Impressions* 33 (Spring 2012): 71–93.

———. "Leach, Hamada, Yanagi: Myth and Reality." *Studio Potter* 21, no. 1 (December 1992): 6–9.

———. "Preserving the Past, Patronizing the Present: Hosokawa Moritatsu and Eisei Bunko." *Lords of the Samurai: Legacy of a Daimyo Family, from the Eisei Bunko, Hosokawa Collection, Tokyo*. Exhibition Symposium. Asian Art Museum, San Francisco. June 14, 2009.

———. Unpublished manuscript. Submitted to the Rockefeller Foundation, 1957.

"Congress Votes to Discontinue NDEA Disclaimer Affidavit." *The Colby Echo*. October 19, 1962: 1.

"The Constitution of Japan." Prime Minister and His Cabinet. n.d. japan.kantei.go.jp/constitution_and_government_of_japan/constitution_e.html (accessed January 1, 2023).

Cook, Haruko Taya and Theodore Cook. *Japan at War: An Oral History*. New York: New Press, 1993.

Cort, Louise. *Shigaraki, Potter's Valley*. Tokyo: Kodansha, 1979.

Cortez, David. "Joyce Lebra: Trailblazing Scholar and Witness to Japanese History." *The Japan Times*. November 7, 2021. https://www.japantimes.co.jp/community/2021/11/07/our-lives/joyce-lebra-history-obituary/.

Cotter, Holland. "The Art of the Book, the Book of the Art." *New York Times.* November 27, 2009. https://archive.nytimes.com/query.nytimes.com/gst/fullpage-9C0CE1DF163EF934A15752C1A96F9C8B63.html.

Council on East Asian Libraries Statistics. *CEAL Statistics Database.* n.d. https://ceal.ku.edu (accessed June 27, 2022).

Cox, Gary W. and Frances Rosenbluth. "The Electoral Fortunes of Legislative Factions in Japan." *American Political Science Review* 87, no. 3 (September 1993): 577–589.

Cox, Gary W., Frances McCall Rosenbluth, and Michael F. Thies. "Electoral Reform and the Fate of Factions: The Case for Japan's Liberal Democratic Party." *British Journal of Political Science* 29, no. 1 (January 1999): 33–56.

Crockett, Lucy Herndon. *Popcorn on the Ginza: An Informal Portrait of Postwar Japan.* New York: W. Sloane Associates, 1949.

Cullers, Robert M. *The Japanese Fulbright Returns: What Happens to Him after His Return to Japan?.* Syracuse: Syracuse University, 1961.

Curtis, Paula R. "East Asia-Related Job Market Report (2021–2022)." Paula R. Curtis. July 31, 2022. http://prcurtis.com/projects/jobs2022/.

"Daigo Fukuryū-Maru." Daigo Fukuryū-Maru Exhibition Hall. 2015. http://d5f.org/en/en-about.

Davis, Peter, dir. *Hearts and Minds.* Hollywood: BBS Productions, 1974.

Davis, Sandra T. W. *Intellectual Change and Political Development in Early Modern Japan: Ono Azusa, A Case Study.* Cranbury, NJ: Associated University Press, 1980.

Dazai Osamu. "Kamome" (The Seagull). In *Dazai Osamu zenshū* (Collected Works of Dazai Osamu). Vol. 3, 84–99. Tokyo: Chikuma shobō, 1967.

———. *Ningen shikkaku* (No Longer Human). Tokyo: Shinchōsha, 2006.

Deleuze, Giles. *The Deleuze Reader.* Translated by Constantin Boundas. New York: Columbia University Press, 1993.

Deleuze, Gilles and Félix Guattari. *Anti-Oedipus: Capitalism and Schizophrenia.* Translated by Robert Hurley. New York: Penguin Classics, 2009.

Dibble, Lewis. "Crimes of Meaning: Kurosawa and Allegory." In *The Force of Vision 6: Inter-Asian Comparative Literature,* edited by Kawamoto Kōji, Heh-Hsiang Yuan, and Ohsawa Yoshihiro, 501–507. Tokyo: International Comparative Literature Association, 1995.

Dobbins, James C. *Letters of the Nun Eshinni: Images of Pure Land Buddhism in Medieval Japan.* Honolulu: University of Hawai'i Press, 2004.

Doi, Takeo. *The Anatomy of Dependence*. Translated by John Bester. Tokyo: Kodansha International, 1973.

Doi, Tsugiyoshi. *Momoyama Decorative Painting*. Translated by Edna B. Crawford. New York: Weatherhill, 1977.

"Dōmyōji CD-ROM." *IMJS Reports* 13 (December 2003): 37. https://www.imjs-jchi.org/vol-13-december-2003/.

Donadio, Caroline. "From the I-House Archives: Happy Birthday, Harry Edmonds!" *International House*. March 11, 2020. https://www.ihouse-nyc.org/news_events/from-the-i-house-archives-happy-birthday-harry-edmonds/.

"Donald Richie Interview by Marlene Mayo." *Oral History Project on the Allied Occupation of* Japan. May 18, 1981. University of Maryland College Park: 1–57.

Donovan, Maureen. "Analyzing the Appeal of Manga: Teaching Information Literacy Skills Through Japanese Popular Culture." *Education About Asia* 13, no. 3. (December 2008): 62–66.

———. "Challenges of Collecting Research Materials on Japanese Popular Culture: A Report on Ohio State's Manga Collection." In *In Praise of Film Studies: Essays in Honor of Mamoru Makino*, edited by Aaron Gerow and Abé Mark Nornes, 225–232. Yokohama: Kinema Club and Trafford Publishing, 2001.

———. "East Asian Libraries Cooperative World Wide Web: An Experiment in Collaboration to Build Interdependence." *New Review of Information Networking*, 2, no. 1 (1996): 219–228.

———. "Framing Knowledge: Global Youth Culture as Knowledge Society." In *The Open Knowledge Society: First World Summit on the Knowledge Society*. Proceedings of the World Summit on the Knowledge Society, Athens, Greece. September 24–26, 2008. *Communications in Computer and Information Science* 19, edited by Miltiadis Lytras. 618–623. New York: Springer, 2008.

———. "A Legacy of Values to Sustain and Uphold: The East Asian Collection at The Ohio State University." In *Collecting Asia: East Asian Libraries in North America, 1868–2008*, edited by Peter X. Zhou, 266–279. Ann Arbor: Association for Asian Studies, 2010.

———. "Those Were the Days! A Short History of the East Asian Libraries Cooperative World Wide Web." *Journal of East Asian Libraries* 124 (2001): 19–22.

Dore, Ronald P. *City Life in Japan: A Study of a Tokyo Ward*. Berkeley: University of California Press, 1958.

Dostoyevsky, Fyodor. *The Brothers Karamazov*. Translated by David Magarshack. New York: Penguin Classics, 1982.

Dower, John. *Embracing Defeat: Japan in the Wake of World War II*. New York: W. W. Norton and Company, 1999.

Dukes, Jessica. "What Is a Memoir?" Celadon Books. n.d. https://celadonbooks.com/what-is-a-memoir/ (accessed December 1, 2022).

Eco, Umberto. *The Role of the Reader: Explorations in the Semiotics of Texts*. Bloomington, Indiana University Press, 1979.

Education Amendments Act of 1972, 20 U.S.C. §§1681–1688 (2018).

"Education: Our Enemies." *Time*. July 16, 1951. https://content.time.com/time/subscriber/article/0,33009,889131,00.html.

Egami Toshinori. *Hondana no naka no Nippon: Kaigai no Nihon toshokan to Nihon kenkyū*. (Japan on the Shelf: Overseas Japanese Libraries and Japanese Studies). Tokyo: Kasama Shoin, 2012.

Elam, Diane and Robyn Wiegman. *Feminism beside Itself*. London: Routledge, 1993.

"Eleven Books Reach Book Stalls." *CI&E Bulletin*. GARIOA. National Diet Library. January 19, 1949.

Elisséeff, Serge, Edwin O. Reischauer, and Takehiko Yoshihashi. *Elementary Japanese for College Students*. Cambridge, MA: Harvard-Yenching Institute, 1944.

Ellmann, Richard and Robert O'Clair, eds. *The Norton Anthology of Modern Poetry*. New York: W. W. Norton & Company, 1973.

Embree, John. *Suye Mura: A Japanese Village*. Chicago: University of Chicago Press, 1939.

Emmerich, Michael. *The Tale of Genji: Translation, Canonization, and World Literature*. New York: Columbia University Press, 2013.

———. "*A Tokyo Anthology: Literature from Japan's Modern Metropolis, 1850–1920*, edited by Sumie Jones and Charles Shirō Inouye." *Journal of Japanese Studies* 44, no. 2 (2018): 445–450.

Enchi, Fumiko. *Masks*. Translated by Juliet Winters Carpenter. New York: Alfred A. Knopf, 1983.

"Episode 106—Dr. Patricia Sippel." *The Meiji at 150 Podcast*. April 26, 2019. https://meijiat150.podbean.com/e/episode-106-dr-patricia-sippel-toyo-eiwa/.

Ericson, Joan. *Be a Woman: Hayashi Fumiko and Modern Japanese Women's Literature*. Honolulu: University of Hawai'i Press, 1997.

"Executive Order 9066: Resulting in Japanese American Incarceration." *National Archives*. January 24, 2022. https://www.archives.gov/milestone-documents/executive-order-9066.

"Executive Order 10925—Establishing the President's Committee Equal Employment Opportunity." *The American Presidency Project*. University of California, Santa Barbara. https://www.presidency.ucsb.edu/documents/executive-order-10925-establishing-the-presidents-committee-equal-employment-opportunity (accessed January 1, 2023).

"Executive Order 11246." Office of Federal Contract Compliance Programs. n.d. https://www.dol.gov/agencies/ofccp/executive-order-11246 (accessed January 1, 2023).

The Experiment in International Living. "History & Mission." https://www.experiment.org/about-history-mission/ (accessed January 11, 2022).

Fairbank, John K., Edwin O. Reischauer, and Albert M. Craig. *East Asia: The Modern Transformation*. Boston: Houghton Mifflin Company, 1965.

Farge, William J. *A Christian Samurai: The Trials of Baba Bunko*. Washington, DC: The Catholic University of America Press, 2016.

———. *The Japanese Translations of the Jesuit Mission Press, 1590–1614: De Imitatione Christi and Guia De Pecadores*. Lewiston, NY: Edwin Mellen Press, 2003.

Farrell, Robert. "Bacon Quits Post: To Remain Dean during Semester." *The Michigan Daily*. September 30, 1961: 1, 2.

"FDR's 'Day of Infamy' Speech." *Prologue Magazine* 33, no. 4 (Winter 2001). https://www.archives.gov/publications/prologue/2001/winter/crafting-day-of-infamy-speech.html.

Ferejohn, John A. and Frances McCall Rosenbluth, eds. *War and State Building in Medieval Japan*. Stanford: Stanford University Press, 2010.

Fingleton, Eamonn. "Now They Tell Us: The Story of Japan's 'Lost Decades' Was Just One Big Hoax." *Forbes*. August 11, 2013. https://www.forbes.com/sites/eamonnfingleton/2013/08/11/now-for-the-truth-the-story-of-japans-lost-decades-is-the-worlds-most-absurd-media-myth/#2809dd2a3fe4.

Finn, Dallas. *Meiji Revised: The Sites of Victorian Japan*. New York: Weatherhill, 1995.

Finn, Richard. *Winners in Peace: MacArthur, Yoshida, and Postwar Japan*. Berkeley: University of California Press, 1995.

"Finnish Officials Cancel Olympics." *New York Times*. April 24, 1940: 32.

Flaherty, Colleen. "New Analysis of Faculty Pay, Representation." *Inside Higher Ed*. December 10, 2020. https://www.insidehighered.com/quicktakes/2020/12/10/new-analysis-faculty-pay-representation.

Flint, Peter B. "Harold Strauss, Editor, Dead; Brought in Japanese Literature." *New York Times*. November 30, 1975: 73.

"Footstep of Japanese American Robert Shiomi (4) Japanese Internment." *Shiomi House*. May 8, 2016. http://shiomihouse.com/en/543/.

Foucault, Michel. *The Foucault Reader*. Edited by Paul Rabinow. New York: Pantheon, 1984.

"Foundation History." Carnegie Foundation. 2023. https://www.carnegiefoundation.org/about-us/foundation-history/.

Fowler, Edward. "Rendering Worlds, Traversing Culture: On the Art and Politics of Translating Modern Japanese Fiction." *Journal of Japanese Studies* 18, no. 1 (winter 1992): 1–44.

Franklin, Cynthia G. *Academic Lives: Memoir, Cultural Theory, and the University Today*. Athens: University of Georgia Press, 2009.

Freedman, Alisa. "The Forgotten Story of Japanese Women Who Studied in the United States, 1949–1966." *CSWS Annual Review* (2016): 12–14.

———. "How I Gained 100 Japanese Grandmothers: Reflections on Intergenerational Conversation Inspired by CSWS." *CSWS Annual Review* (2020): 26–27 and 29.

———. *Japan on American TV: Screaming Samurai Join Anime Clubs in the Land of the Lost*. New York: Columbia University Press, 2021.

———. "Noriko Mizuta: Biocritical Essay of a Literary Feminist and Global Scholar." *Review of Japanese Culture and Society* 30 (2018): 11–51.

Friedan, Betty. *The Feminine Mystique*. New York: W. W. Norton, 1963.

Friendly, Fred W. and Edward R. Murrow. *See It Now*. New York City: CBS, 1951–1958.

"From Carnal Literature to Carnal Politics." Translated by Barbara Ruch. In Masao Maruyama. *Thought and Behavior in Japanese Politics*, edited by Ivan Morris, 245–267. New York: Oxford University Press, 1963.

Fry, Richard, Brian Kennedy, and Cary Funk. "STEM Jobs See Uneven Progress in Increasing Gender, Racial, and Ethnic Diversity." Pew Research Center. April 1, 2021. https://www.pewresearch.org/science/2021/04/01/stem-jobs-see-uneven-progress-in-increasing-gender-racial-and-ethnic-diversity/.

Fujioka, Ryōichi. *Tea Ceremony Utensils*. Translated by Louise Allison Cort. Tokyo: Weatherhill, 1973.

Fujiwara, Iwaichi. *F. Kikan: Japanese Army Intelligence Operations in Southeast Asia during World War II*. Translated by Akashi Yoji. Hong Kong: Heinemann Asia, 1983.

Fukuda, Naomi. *A Guide to Japanese Reference Books*. Chicago: American Library Association, 1966.

———. *Nihon no sankō tosho* (A Guide to Japanese Reference Books). Tokyo: Nihon no Sankō Tosho Henshū Iinkai, 1962.

Gallant, Aprile. "Remembering Iwami Reika (1927–2020)." Smith College Museum of Art. July 1, 2020. https://scma.smith.edu/blog/remembering-iwami-reika-1927-2020.

"G.I. Bill." *History.com*. June 7, 2019. https://www.history.com/topics/world-war-ii/gi-bill.

Giovanni, Nikki. *Futagoza no on'na* (Gemini). Translated by Takako Lento. Tokyo: Shōbunsha, 1978.

Glassman, Hank. *The Face of Jizō: Image and Cult in Medieval Japanese Buddhism*. Honolulu: University of Hawai'i Press, 2012.

"Government Aid and Relief in Occupied Areas (GARIOA) Payments by the U.S. per Year and Country between 1946 and 1967." *Statistia*. 2018. https://www.statista.com/statistics/1229030/us-garioa-payments-country-year/.

"Government Apologizes to Japanese Canadians in 1988." *CBC Archives*. September 22, 2018. https://www.cbc.ca/archives/government-apologizes-to-japanese-canadians-in-1988-1.4680546.

Grilli, Elise. *The Art of the Japanese Screen*. New York: Weatherhill, 1970.

Grilli, Peter and David Westphal, dirs. *Shinto Arts: Nature, Gods, and Man in Japan*. Cambridge, MA: Fogg Fine Arts Films, 1978.

Gunji Masakatsu. *Odori no bigaku* (Aesthetic of Dance). Tokyo: Engeki Shuppansha, 1957.

Guth, Christine M. E. *Art, Tea, and Industry: Masuda Takashi and the Mitsui Circle*. Princeton: Princeton University Press, 1993.

——. *Craft Culture in Early Modern Japan: Materials, Makers, and Mastery.* Berkeley: University of California Press, 2021.

——. *Longfellow's Tattoos: Tourism, Collecting, and Japan.* Seattle: University of Washington Press, 2004.

——. "Theorizing the *Hari Kuyō*: The Ritual Disposal of Needles in Early Modern Japan." In *Encountering Things: Design and Theories of Things*, edited by Leslie Atzmon and Prasad Boradkar, 65–80. London: Bloomsbury, 2017.

——. "Towards a Global History of Shagreen." In *The Global Lives of Things: The Material Culture of Connections in the Early Modern World*, edited by Anne Gerritsen and Giorgio Riello, 62–80. London: Routledge, 2016.

Guth-Kanda, Christine. "Shinzō: Hachiman Imagery and Its Development." PhD Diss. Harvard University, 1976.

——. *Shinzō: Hachiman Imagery and Its Development.* Cambridge, MA: Harvard University Press, 1985.

Habu Junko. "Rekishi kōkogaku to senshi kōkogaku: Kita Amerika no rei o chūshin to shite" (Historical Archeology and Prehistorical Archeology: Surrounding Examples from America). In *Kinsei kingendai kōkogaku nyūmon* (Introduction to Early Modern and Modern Archeology), edited by Suzuki Kimio, 264–271. Tokyo: Keio University Press, 2007.

Hadley, Eleanor. *Memoirs of a Trustbuster: A Lifelong Adventure with Japan.* Honolulu: University of Hawaiʻi Press, 2002.

Haga Tōru. *Hiraga Gennai.* Tokyo: Asahi Shimbunsha, 1981.

——. *Kaiga no ryōbun: Kindai Nihon hikakubunkashi kenkyū* (The Realm of Painting: A Study in Comparative Cultural History of Modern Japan). Tokyo: Asahi Shimbunsha, 1990.

——. *Tōgen no suimyaku: Higashi Ajia shiga no hikaku bunkashi* (Water Current from the Peach Blossom Spring: A Comparative History of East Asian Poetry and Painting). Nagoya: Nagoya University Press, 2019.

Hall, Ivan P. "Academic Apartheid at Japan's National Universities." *JPRI Working Paper No. 3.* Japan Policy Research Institute. October 1994: 6–10. https://jpri.org/wp-content/uploads/1994/10/Working-Paper-03.pdf.

Hall, John Whitney. *Government and Local Power in Japan: A Study Based on Bizen Province, 500–1700.* Princeton: Princeton University Press, 1966.

Halloran, Richard. "Japan Braces for a Full-Scale Oil Crisis." *New York Times.* December 8, 1973: 1.

Hamill, Barbara. "Josei: Modanizumu to kenri ishiki" (Women: *Modanizumu* and the Consciousness of Rights). In *Shōwa bunka, 1925-1945* (Shōwa Culture: 1925-1945), edited by Minami Hiroshi, 198-231. Tokyo: Keisō shobō, 1987.

———. "Modan gāru no tōjō to chishikijin" (The Emergence of the Modern Girl and the Intellectuals). *Rekishi hyōron* (Critical History) 491 (1991): 18-26.

———. "Nihon teki modanizumu no shisō—Hirabayashi Hatsunosuke o chūshin to shite" (The Idea of Japanese *Modanizumu*: Focusing on Hirabayashi Hatsunosuke). In *Nihon modanizumu no kenkyū: Shisō, seikatsu, bunka* (The Study of Japanese *Modanizumu*: Thought, Society, Culture), edited by Minami Hiroshi, 89-114. Tokyo: Burēn shuppan, 1982.

———. "Sengo josei no yume to genjitsu: Dokusha zadankai ni miru" (Postwar Women's Dreams and Realities: Focusing on Readers' Roundtable Discussions). In *Zoku—Shōwa bunka, 1945-1989* (Shōwa Culture, Part 2: 1945-1989), edited by Minami Hiroshi, 84-97. Tokyo: Keisō shobō, 1990.

Hammel, Lisa. "Working Women: The Job Ahead." *New York Times*. Sept 19, 1973: 52.

Hanawalt, Leslie. *A Place of Light: The History of Wayne State University*. Detroit: Wayne State University, 1968.

Hanley, Susan B. *Edo jidai no isan* (The Legacy of the Tokugawa Period). Tokyo: Chūō Kōronsha, 1990.

———. *Everyday Things in Premodern Japan: The Hidden Legacy of Material Culture*. Berkeley: University of California Press, 1997.

Hanley, Susan B. and Arthur P. Wolf, eds. *Family and Population in East Asian History*. Stanford: Stanford University Press, 1985.

Hanley, Susan B. and Kozo Yamamura. *Economic and Demographic Change in Preindustrial Japan, 1600-1868*. Princeton: Princeton University Press, 1977.

Hara Hiroko. *Jendā mondai to gakujutsu kenkyū* (Gender Issues in Academic Research). Tokyo: Dometsu shuppan, 2004.

Harada, Minoru. *Meiji Western Painting* (Meiji no yōga). Translated by Bonnie F. Abiko. Tokyo: Weatherhill, 1974.

Hardacre, Helen, ed. "Fieldwork with Japanese Religious Groups." In *Doing Fieldwork in Japan*, edited by Theodore Bestor, Patricia Steinhoff, and Vicky Lyon Bestor, 71-88. Honolulu: University of Hawai'i Press, 2003.

———. "Introduction." In *The Postwar Developments of Japanese Studies in the United States*, edited by Helen Hardacre, vii-xxviii. Leiden: Brill, 1998.

———. "Japanese Studies in the United States: Present Stuation and Future Prospects." *Asia Journal* 1, no. 1 (1994): 17–36.

———. *Kurozumikyō and the New Religions of Japan*. Princeton: Princeton University Press, 1986.

———. *Lay Buddhism in Contemporary Japan: Reiyūkai Kyōdan*. Princeton: Princeton University Press, 1984.

———. *Marketing the Menacing Fetus in Japan*. Berkeley: University of California Press, 1997.

———, ed. *The Postwar Developments of Japanese Studies in the United States*. Leiden: Brill, 1998.

———. *Religion and Society in Nineteenth-Century Japan: A Study of the Southern Kantō Region, Using Late Edo and Early Meiji Gazetteers*. Ann Arbor: University of Michigan Center for Japanese Studies, 2002.

———. *The Religion of Japan's Korean Minority: The Preservation of Ethnic Identity*. Berkeley: University of California Press, 1984.

———. *Shinto: A History*. New York: Oxford University Press, 2017.

———. *Shintō and the State, 1868–1988*. Princeton: Princeton University Press, 1989.

Hardin, Garrett. "The Tragedy of the Commons." *Science* 162, no. 3859 (December 13, 1968): 1243–1248.

Harootunian, Harry D. *Things Seen and Unseen: Discourse and Ideology in Tokugawa Nativism*. Chicago: University of Chicago Press, 1988.

Harootunian, Harry and Naoki Sakai. "Dialogue: Japanese Studies and Cultural Studies." *positions* 7, no. 2 (1999): 593–647.

Harvard University Archives. "Who Was the First Woman to Earn a Doctoral Degree at Harvard University?" Harvard University Library. December 14, 2021. https://askarc.hul.harvard.edu/faq/326845#:~:text=In%20 1963%2C%20more%20than%20twenty,women%20candidates%20for%20 the%20Ph.

Hatakeyama Yoshio. *Kaisha wa naze tsubureru ka*. (Why Do Companies Fail?). Tokyo, Manajimento raiburarī, 1958.

———. *Manager Revolution!: A Guide to Survival in Today's Changing Workplace*. Stanford, CT: Productivity Press, 1985.

Hayakawa, Monta. *Shunga: Japanese Erotic Art*. Tokyo: PIE books, 2010.

Hayakawa, S. I. *Language in Action*. Madison: College Typing Company, 1939.

———. *Language in Thought and Action.* New York: Houghton Mifflin, 1949.

Hayasaka Keizō. *Kita-kamiyama chi no yamakage kara—Iwate no hitobito* (From the Mountain Shade of North Kamiyama: The People of Iwate). Tokyo: Sanshōdō, 1984.

———. "The Kotsunagi Archives: From Legal Disputes on the Commons to Large-N Analysis of Commons in Iwate Prefecture, Japan, in the Twentieth Century." Paper presented at the International Association for the Study of the Commons. Edmonton, Alberta, May 2015.

Hayashi, Masahide, Keizō Hayasaka, and Margaret A. McKean. "Explaining Resource Shortages and Restrictive Rules on the Japanese Commons in the Early 20th Century." Paper presented at the International Association for the Study of the Commons. Edmonton, Alberta, May 2015.

Hayden, Tom. *Reunion: A Memoir.* New York: Macmillan Publishing Company, 1988.

Heineman Jr., Ben W. "The University in the McCarthy Era." *The Harvard Crimson.* June 17, 1965. https://www.thecrimson.com/article/1965/6/17/the-university-in-the-mccarthy-era/.

Heinrich, Amy Vladeck, ed. *Currents in Japanese Culture: Translations and Transformations.* New York: Columbia University Press, 1997.

———. *Fragments of Rainbows: The Life and Poetry of Saitō Mokichi, 1882–1953.* New York: Columbia University Press, 1983.

———. "'My Mother is Dying': Saitō Mokichi's *Shinitamau haha.*" *Monumenta Nipponica* 33, no. 4 (Winter 1978): 407–439.

Heyns, Barbara and Joyce Adair Bird. "Recent Trends in the Higher Education of Women." In *The Undergraduate Woman: Issues in Educational Equity*, edited by Pamela Perun, 43–70. Lexington, MA: Lexington Books, 1982.

Hibbett, Howard. *The Chrysanthemum and the Fish: Japanese Humor since the Age of the Shoguns.* Tokyo: Kodansha International, 2002.

———. *The Floating World in Japanese Fiction.* London: Oxford University Press, 1959.

Higonnet, Margaret R. and Sumie Jones, eds. *The Force of Vision 2: Proceedings of the XIIIth Congress of the International Comparative Literature Association.* Tokyo: ICLA Executive Committee, 1995.

Hikawa Jinja. "Nippon Yūsen Hikawa maru ni tsuite" (About the Japan Mail Shipping Line's *Hikawa Maru*). Hikawa Jinja (Hikawa Shrine). n.d. https://musashiichinomiya-hikawa.or.jp/hikawamaru/ (accessed January 1, 2023).

Hiraga, Gennai. "A Lousy Journey of Love: Two Sweethearts Won't Back Down." Translated by Timon Screech. In *An Edo Anthology: Literature from Japan's Mega-City, 1750–1850*, edited by Sumie Jones, 60–64. Honolulu: University of Hawai'i Press, 2013.

Hiramatsu Yoshirō. *Kinsei keiji soshōhō no kenkyū* (Studies in Early Modern Criminal Jurisprudence). Tokyo: Sōbunsha, 1960.

Hirsch, E. D. Jr. *Cultural Literacy: What Every American Needs to Know*. New York: Vintage, 1988.

"Historical Note: World House Galleries Records, 1927–1991, Bulk 1953–1980." Archives of American Art, Smithsonian Institution. https://www.aaa.si.edu/collections/world-house-galleries-records-6036/historical-note (accessed March 2, 2022).

"History of Asian American Studies." Princeton University, n.d. https://asamatprinceton.wordpress.com/history-of-asian-american-studies/ (accessed January 2, 2023).

"History of Women at Princeton University." Princeton University Library. June 14, 2022. https://libguides.princeton.edu/c.php?g=84581&p=543232.

Hoesterey, Ingeborg. *Pastiche: Cultural Memory in Art, Film, Literature*. Bloomington: Indiana University Press, 2001.

Hoff, Frank and Willi Flindt. *The Life Structure of Noh: An English Version of Yokomichi Mario's Analysis of the Structure of Nō*. Concerned Theatre Japan 2, nos. 3 and 4 (Spring 1973): 209–256.

———. *The Life Structure of Noh: An English Version of Yokomichi Mario's Analysis of the Structure of Nō*. Tokyo: Concerned Theatre Japan, 1973.

Hōjō Hiroshi. *Kinsei ni okeru iriai no shokeitai* (The Various Forms of Common Access in the Early Modern Period). Tokyo: Ochanomizu shobō, 1979.

———. *Mura no iriai no hyakunen shi: Yamanashi-ken sonmin no iriai tōsōshi* (A Hundred Years' History of a Village and Its Common Access: The History of the Common Access Struggle of the Villagers of Yamanashi Prefecture). Tokyo: Ochanomizu shobō, 1978.

———. *Yamanashi-ken iriai tōsōshi: Kindai 130 nen no iriaiken no unmei* (The History of the Struggle over Iriai in Yamanashi Prefecture: The Fate of 130 Years of Common Access Rights). Tokyo: Ochanomizu shobō, 1998.

"How Many People Died in the Vietnam War?" *Britannica*. 2023. https://www.britannica.com/question/How-many-people-died-in-the-Vietnam-War.

Hurston, Zora Neale. *Their Eyes Were Watching God*. New York: Chelsea House Publishers, 1998.

Iacurci, Greg. "Women Are Still Paid 83 Cents for Every Dollar Men Earn." CNBC. May 19, 2022. https://www.cnbc.com/2022/05/19/women-are-still-paid-83-cents-for-every-dollar-men-earn-heres-why.html#:~:text=Women%20are%20still%20paid%2083%20cents%20for%20every%20dollar%20men%20earn.

"IASC's 14th Global Conference, 3–7 June 2013, Mount Fuji, Japan." IASC. 2013. https://c-linkage.com/for/iasc2013/en/pdf/IASC2013_Brochure_A4.pdf.

Ide, Sachiko and Naomi Hanaoka McGoin. *Aspects of Women's Language: Onnakotoba no Sugata*. Tokyo: Kurosio, 1990.

Ikumi Kaminishi. *Explaining Pictures: Buddhist Propaganda and Etoki Storytelling in Japan*. Honolulu: University of Hawai'i Press, 2006.

Imamura, Anne E. "The Loss That Has No Name: Social Womanhood of Foreign Wives." *Gender and Society* 2, no. 3 (September 1988): 291–307.

———. "Ordinary Couples? Mate Selection in International Marriage in Nigeria." *Journal of Comparative Family Studies* 17, no. 1 (Spring 1986): 33–42.

———. *Re-Imaging Japanese Women*. Berkeley: University of California Press, 1996.

———. "Strangers in a Strange Land: Coping with Marginality in International Marriage." Reprinted in *Journal of Comparative Family Studies* 21, no. 2. (1990): 171–191.

———. *Urban Japanese Housewives: At Home and in the Community*. Honolulu: University of Hawai'i Press, 1987.

Inaga Shigemi. *Kaiga no Tōhō: Orientarizumu kara postomodanizumu e* (The East in Painting: From Orientalism to Postmodernism). Nagoya: Nagoya University Press, 1999.

Inagaki Hiroshi, dir. *Chūshingura*. Tōhō. 1962; Los Angeles: Image Entertainment, 2001. DVD.

Inauguration Committee. "The Women's Studies Association of Japan Statement of Purpose." Nihon Josei Gakkai (Women's Studies Association of Japan). January 18, 1979. https://joseigakkai-jp.org/english-home/.

Inoue Makoto. *Komonzu-ron no chōsen: Aratana shigen kanri o motomete* (The Challenge of Commons Theory: Seeking New Natural Resource Management). Tokyo: Shinyōsha, 2008.

Inoue Shōichi. *Tsukurareta Katsura-Rikyū* (The Myth of Katsura Princely Villa). Tokyo: Kobundo, 1986.

Inouye, Charles Shirō. *Evanescence and Form: An Introduction to Japanese Culture*. New York: Palgrave Macmillan, 2008.

———. "Pictocentrism." *Yearbook of Comparative and General Literature* 40 (1992): 23–39.

Insider Staff. "What Makes a Great Editor? Part 1." *Times Insider*. June 16, 2014. https://archive.nytimes.com/www.nytimes.com/times-insider/2014/06/16/what-makes-a-great-editor-part-i/#:~:text=A%20good%20editor%20is%20the,rare%2C%20but%20can%20produce%20treasure.

International Association for the Study of the Commons. "History of the IASC." n.d. https://iasc-commons.org/history/ (accessed October 16, 2022).

International House of Japan. *International House of Japan: Cultural Bridge between East and West*. Tokyo: International House of Japan, 2009.

Irokawa Daikichi. *The Culture of the Meiji Period*. Translated by Marius Jansen. Princeton: Princeton University Press, 1988.

Iser, Wolfgang. *The Implied Reader: Patterns of Communication in Prose Fiction from Bunyan to Beckett*. Baltimore: Johns Hopkins University Press, 1974.

Ishigaki Rin. *This Overflowing Light: Rin Ishigaki, Selected Poems*. Translated with an introduction by Janine Beichman. Tokyo and London: Isobar Press, 2022.

Ishikawa Eisuke. *Ōedo risaikuru jijō* (The State of Recycling in Great Edo). Tokyo: Kodansha, 1994.

"Ishikawa Takeyoshi Memorial Library." *NCC Japan*. 2017. https://guides.nccjapan.org/researchaccess/ishikawa-takeyoshi/library.

Itō Genjirō. *Hikawa maru monogatari* (Story of the *Hikawa Maru*). Kamakura: Kamakura Shunjūsha, 2015.

Itō Moriyuki, *Sarashina nikki kenkyū* (Research on the Sarashina Diary). Tokyo: Shintensha, 1995.

———. "*Sarashina nikki* no 'asamidori': Ei ni kansuru kōsatsu—shikisai hyōgen no imi to Genji monogatari no eikyō no chūshin ni" (*The Sarashina Diary*'s "Asamidori" Poem: A Study of Its Poetic Effect, Centering on Its Meaning as an Expression of Color and Influence on It from *The Tale of Genji*). In *Genji monogatari kara, Genji monogatari e* (From *The Tale of Genji* to *The Tale of Genji*), edited by Nagai Kazuko, 346–366. Tokyo: Kasama shoin, 2007.

Iwao, Sumiko. *The Japanese Woman: Traditional Image and Changing Reality*. New York: Alfred A. Knopf, 1992.

Iwasaki, Haruko. "The World of Gesaku: Playful Writers of Late Eighteenth-Century Japan." PhD Diss. Harvard University, 1987.

Izumi Etsuko, dir. *Shinrigakusha Tsuruko Haruguchi no seishun* (The Young Days of Pyschologist Haruguchi Tsuruko). Tokyo: Tess Planning, 2007.

"Izutsu." In *The Noh Drama: Ten Plays from the Japanese*, edited by Nippon Gakujutsu Shinkōkai, 91–105. Rutland, VT: Charles E. Tuttle Company, 1960.

Jacobs, Robert. "Reconstructing the Perpetrator's Soul by Reconstructing the Victim's Body: The Portrayal of the 'Hiroshima Maidens' by the Mainstream Media in the United States." *Intersections* 24 (2010). http://intersections.anu.edu.au/issue24/jacobs.htm.

Jansen, Marius B., ed. *Changing Japanese Attitudes toward Modernization*. Princeton: Princeton University Press, 1965.

———. "History: General Survey." *Japanese Studies in the United States: Part 1, History and Present Condition*, 7–26. Tokyo: Japan Foundation, 1988.

———. "Stages of Growth." *Japanese Studies in the United States: Part 1, History and Present Condition*, 27–68. Tokyo: Japan Foundation, 1988.

Japan Foundation. "Collection: Kokusai Bunka Shinkōkai (KBS) Archives." n.d. https://www.jpf.go.jp/e/about/jfic/lib/collection/kbs.html (accessed January 1, 2023).

"Japan Names 10 U.S. Colleges to Share Equally in $10-Million." *New York Times*. August 8, 1973: 14.

Japan Society. "A Short History of Japan Society." New York: Japan Society. n.d.

"Japan-United States Joint Communique, June 22, 1961." CULCON. September 2020. https://culcon.jusfc.gov/wp-content/uploads/2020/09/1961-CULCON-Agreement.pdf.

"Japan-US Friendship Commission Prize for the Translation of Japanese Literature and the Lindsley and Masao Miyoshi Prizes." Donald Keene Center of Japanese Culture. 2022. https://www.keenecenter.org/translation_prize.html.

"Japan-US Security Treaty." Ministry of Foreign Affairs of Japan. n.d. https://www.mofa.go.jp/region/n-america/us/q&a/ref/1.html (accessed January 1, 2023).

"The Japanese American Internment Camp Newspapers, 1942–1946." Library of Congress. n.d. https://www.loc.gov/collections/japanese-american-internment-camp-newspapers/about-this-collection/ (accessed January 1, 2023).

"Japanese Generations: Boom, Bubble, and Ice Age." *Nippon.com*. May 12, 2022. https://www.nippon.com/en/japan-data/h00535/japanese-generations-boom-bubble-and-ice-age.html.

"Japanese Instrument of Surrender, 1945." National Archives Foundation. 2022. https://www.archivesfoundation.org/documents/japanese-instrument-surrender-1945/.

Jesty, Justin. "Hamaya Hiroshi's Photos of the Anti-Security Treaty Protests." *MIT Visualizing Cultures*. 2012. http://visualizingcultures.mit.edu/tokyo_1960/anp2_essay05.html.

———. "Tokyo 1960: Days of Rage & Grief." *MIT Visualizing Cultures*. 2012. https://visualizingcultures.mit.edu/tokyo_1960/anp2_essay01.html.

"The Jeweled Voice Broadcast." Atomic Heritage Foundation. 2022. https://ahf.nuclearmuseum.org/ahf/key-documents/jewel-voice-broadcast/.

Johnson, Barbara. *A World of Difference*. Baltimore: Johns Hopkins University Press, 1988.

Jones, Hazel J. *Live Machines: Hired Foreigners and Meiji Japan*. Vancouver: University of British Columbia Press, 1980.

Jones, Sumie. "Comic Fiction in Japan during the Later Edo Period." PhD Diss. University of Washington, 1979.

———. "Edo bungaku no ōvā tekusuto: *gesaku*-shinron ni mukete" (Overtext in Edo Literature: Toward a New Theory of Playful Writing). *Edo Bungaku* 20, 98–114. Tokyo: Perikansha, 1999.

———, ed. *Imagining/Reading Eros: Proceedings for the Conference, Sexuality and Edo Culture, 1750–1850*. Bloomington: Indiana University East Asian Studies Center, 1996.

———. "Overtext: A Theory of Reading and Writing in Early Modern Literature and Arts." *Poetica* 52 (1999): 19–36.

———. "Samayoeru bungaku: Amerika no eibungakkai no jijō" (Literature in Exile: The Status of Literature in US Academia). *Bungaku* 1, no. 3 (2000): 33–39.

———. *The Shirokoya Scandal: Two Ways of Looking at the Case Judged by Magistrate Ōoka Tadasuke*. In *An Episodic Festschrift for Howard Hibbett*, edited by John Solt. Vol. 23. Los Angeles: highmoonoon, 2010.

———. "Translation as Overtextual Reading: or, How to Compose a Japanese Rap in English." *Translation Review* 93 (2015): 99–116.

———. "Vanishing Boundaries: Translation in a Multilingual World." *Yearbook of Comparative and General Literature* 54 (2008): 121–134.

———. "William Hogarth and Kitao Masanobu: Reading Eighteenth-Century Pictorial Narratives." *Yearbook of Comparative and General Literature* 34 (1985): 37–73.

Jones, Sumie and Charles Inouye, eds. *A Tokyo Anthology: Literature from Japan's Modern Metropolis, 1850–1920*. Honolulu: University of Hawai'i Press, 2017.

Jones, Sumie, Adam L. Kern, and Kenji Watanabe. *A Kamigata Anthology: Literature from Japan's Metropolitan Centers, 1600–1750*. Honolulu: University of Hawai'i Press, 2020.

Jones, Sumie, ed., with Kenji Watanabe. *An Edo Anthology: Literature from Japan's Mega-City, 1750–1850*. Honolulu: University of Hawai'i Press, 2013.

JPRI Staff. "Foreign Teachers in Japanese Universities: An Update." *JPRI Working Paper No. 24*. Japan Policy Research Institute. September 1996. https://jpri.org/wp-content/uploads/2022/01/Working-Paper-24.pdf.

Kadia, Miriam Kingsberg. *Into the Field: Human Scientists of Transwar Japan*. Stanford: Stanford University Press, 2020.

Kageyama Haruki. *The Arts of Shinto* (*Shinto no bijutsu*). Translated and adapted by Christine Guth-Kanda. Tokyo: Weatherhill, 1973.

Kageyama Haruki and Christine Guth-Kanda. *Shinto Arts: Nature, Gods, and Man in Japan*. New York: Japan House Gallery, 1976.

Kainō Michitaka. *Kotsunagi jiken: Sandai ni wataru iriai ken funsō* (The Kotsunagi Incident: A Struggle over Common Access Rights Extending across Three Generations). Tokyo: Iwanami shoten, 1964.

Kamimura Masana. *Sonraku seikatsu no shūzoku, kanshū no shakai kōzō* (The Social Structure of the Folkways and Customs of Village Life). Tokyo: Ochanomizu shobō, 1979.

Kaneko Kinjirō, ed. *Renga kichō bunken shūsei* (Collection of Important Works of *Renga*). Tokyo: Benseisha, 1978.

———. *Renga kochūshaku no kenkyū* (Research on Medieval *Renga* Commentaries). Tokyo: Ōfusha, 1974.

———, ed. *Renga kochūshaku shū* (Collection of Medieval *Renga* Commentaries). Tokyo: Kadokawa shoten, 1979.

———. *Rengaron no kenkyū* (Research on *Renga* Treatises). Tokyo: Ōfusha, 1984.

———. *Shinkei no seikatsu to sakuhin* (The Life and Work of Shinkei). Tokyo: Ōfusha, 1982.

———. *Shinsen Tsukubashū no kenkyū* (Research on the *Shinsen Tsukubashū*). Tokyo: Kazama shobō, 1969.

———. *Sōgi meisaku hyakuin chūshaku* (Commentaries on Sōgi's Famous Hundred-Verse Sequences). Tokyo: Ōfusha, 1985.

———. *Sōgi no seikatsu to sakuhin* (The Life and Work of Sōgi). Tokyo: Ōfusha, 1983.

———. *Tsukubashū no kenkyū* (Research on the *Tsukubashū*). Tokyo: Kazama shobō, 1983.

Kaneko Kinjirō, et al., eds. *Renga haikai shū* (Collection of *Renga Haikai*). Tokyo: Shōgakkan, 1974.

Kaneko Kinjirō and Ōta Takeo, eds. *Shichiken jidai renga kushū* (Anthology of the Seven Sages of *Renga*). Tokyo: Kadokawa shoten, 1975.

Kaneko Kinjirō and Yokoyama Shigeru, eds. *Shinsen Tsukubashū: Sanetaka-bon*. Tokyo: Kadokawa shoten, 1970.

Kaplan, Joanna Overing. *The Piaroa: A People of the Orinoco Basin: A Study in Kinship and Marriage*. Oxford: Clarendon Press, 1975.

Kapur, Nick. *Japan at the Crossroads: Conflict and Compromise after Anpo*. Cambridge, MA: Harvard University Press, 2018.

Karthikeyan, Hrishi and Gabriel J. Chin. "Anti-Miscegenation Statutes and Asian Americans." *Race, Racism, and the Law*. August 5, 2011. https://racism.org/index.php?option=com_content&view=article&id=306:aspi0201&catid=64:asian-and-pacific-americans&Itemid=235.

Kasamatsu Hiroshi, Satō Shin'ichi, and Momose Kesao, eds. *Nihon shisō taikei 22, Chūsei seiji shakai shisō ge* (Survey of Japanese Thought, Volume 22: Medieval Political and Social Thought, Volume 2). Tokyo: Iwanami 1981.

Kashiwagi, Mari. *Butterfly*. Translated by Takako Lento. Tokyo: Shichōsha, 2020.

Kataoka, Shikō. *Linked Lines: Japanese Women's Texts through Time*. Exhibition Catalog. University of Alberta. Edmonton. August 16–September 7, 2021.

Katō, Shūichi. *A History of Japanese Literature, Volume 1: The First Thousand Years*. Translated by David Chibbett. London: Macmillian Press, 1979.

———. *Nihon bungakushi josetsu* (An Introduction to the History of Japanese Literature). Tokyo: Chikuma shobō, 1975.

Kaverman, Ellie. "Ingeborg Schmidt: 'The First Lady of Visual Science.'" *Voices from the IU Bicentenial*. May 19, 2020. https://blogs.iu.edu/bicentennialblogs/2020/05/19/ingeborg-schmidt-the-first-lady-of-visual-science/#:~:text=Once%20such%20story%20is%20that,the%20IU%20School%20of%20Optometry.&text=Ingeborg%20Schmidt%20was%20born%20on,%2C%201899%20near%20Tartu%2C%20Estonia.

Kawabata, Yasunari. *The Izu Dancer: A Story*. Translated by Edward Seidensticker. *The Atlantic* (January 1955).

———. "Nobel Lecture." The Nobel Foundation. 1968. https://www.nobelprize.org/prizes/literature/1968/kawabata/lecture/.

———. *Yukiguni* (Snow Country). Tokyo: Iwanami shoten, 1952.

Kawahara, Hattie Masuko. "Diplomatic Relations between the United States and Japan from 1931 to 1941." PhD Diss. University of Minnesota, 1949.

———. "I Am an American." *Mademoiselle* 19 (1944): 258, 276, 301.

Kawashima Takeyoshi, Ushiomi Toshitaka, and Watanabe Yōzō. *Iriaiken no kaitai* (The Dismemberment of Common Access Rights). 2 vols. Tokyo: Iwanami shoten, 1959 and 1961.

"Kazuo Sakamaki, Pacific P.O.W. No. 1." *New York Times*. December 21, 1999: Section C: 23.

Keehn, Barry and Chalmers Johnson. "A Disaster in the Making: Rational Choice and Asian Studies." *The National Interest*, no. 36 (Summer 1994): 14–22.

Keene, Donald, ed. *Anthology of Japanese Literature: From the Earliest Era to the Mid-Nineteenth Century*. New York: Grove Press, 1955.

———. *Dawn to the West, Volume 2: Japanese Literature of the Modern Era*. New York: Columbia University Press, 1999.

———, ed. *Modern Japanese Literature: An Anthology*. New York: Grove Press, 1955.

———. *World within Walls: Japanese Literature of the Premodern Era, 1600–1867*. New York: Columbia University Press, 1976.

Keene, Donald and Royall Tyler, eds. *20 Plays of the Nō Theatre*. New York: Columbia University Press, 1970.

Kentetsu Takamori. *Unlocking Tannisho: Shinran's Words on the Pure Land*. Translated by Juliet Winters Carpenter. Ashland, OH: Ichimannendo Publishing, 2011.

Kentetsu Takamori, Akehashi Daiji, and Itō Kentarō. *You Were Born for a Reason: The Real Purpose of Life.* Translated by Juliet Winters Carpenter. Ashland, OH: Ichimannendo Publishing, 2007.

Kerkham, Eleanor. "And Us Too Enclosed in Mori Atsushi's *Oku no hosomichi*." In *Matsuo Bashō's Poetic Spaces: Exploring Haikai Intersections,* edited by Eleanor Kerkham, 173–198. New York: Palgrave Macmillan, 2006.

———. "Censoring Tamura Taijirō's *Biography of a Prostitute* (Shunpuden)." In *Negotiating Censorship in Modern Japan,* edited by Rachael Hutchinson, 153–175. London: Routledge, 2013.

———. "Close Encounters with a Classic." *Proceedings for the Second International Symposium on Oku no hosomichi.* Sōka City: Gyosei Press, 1990: 44–50.

———. "Intersections." In *Matsuo Bashō's Poetic Spaces: Exploring Haikai Intersections,* edited by Eleanor Kerkham, 1–19. New York: Palgrave Macmillan, 2006.

———, ed. *Matsuo Bashō's Poetic Spaces: Exploring Haikai Intersections.* New York: Palgrave Macmillan, 2006.

———. "*Notes from the Traveler's Satchel*: An Annotated Translation of Matsuo Bashō's *Oi no kobumi*." *The Tea Leaves* 2 (Autumn 1965): 26–46.

———. "*Oku no hosomichi* no kozo to sono kuraimakkusu" (*Narrow Road to the North*'s Structural Peaks). In *Dewasanzan to Nihonjin no seishinbunka: Kakō genzai, soshite mirai* . . . (The Three Sacred Mountains of Dewa and Japanese Spiritual Culture: Past, Present, and Future . . .), edited by Matsuda Yoshiyuki, 104–110. Tokyo: Pelican Press, 1994.

———. "*Oku no hosomichi* to watakushi" (*Narrow Road to the North* and Myself). *Loisir* (Leisure Development Center Monthly). March 1989: 30–33.

———. "Pleading for the Body: Tamura Taijirō's 1947 Korean 'Comfort Woman' Novel, *Biography of a Prostitute*." In *War, Occupation, and Creativity: Japan and East Asia, 1920–1960,* edited by Marlene J. Mayo, J. Thomas Rimer with Eleanor Kerkham, 310–359. Honolulu, University of Hawai'i Press, 2001.

Kern, Adam L. *Manga from the Floating World: Comicbook Culture and the Kibyōshi of Edo Japan.* Cambridge, MA: Harvard East Asian Monographs, 2006.

———. *The Penguin Book of Haiku.* New York: Penguin Classics, 2018.

Key, Margaret. *Truth from a Lie: Documentary, Detection, and Reflexivity in Abe Kobo's Realist Project.* Lanham, MD: Lexington Books, 2011.

Kida, Takuya, Meghen Jones, and Trevor Menders. *Vessel Explored / Vessel Transformed: Tomimoto Kenkichi and His Enduring Legacy*. New York: Joan B. Mirviss, Ltd., 2019.

Kikuchi, Yuko. "Hybridity and the Oriental Orientalism of *Mingei* Theory." *Journal of Design History* 10, no. 4: 343–354.

Kimbrough, Keller and Haruo Shirane, eds. *Monsters, Animals, and Other Worlds: A Collection of Short Medieval Japanese Tales*. New York: Columbia University Press, 2018.

Kinney, Ann Rasmussen. *Japanese Investment in Manchurian Manufacturing, Mining, Transportation, and Communications, 1931–1945*. New York: Garland Publishing, 1982.

Kinney, Ann R., Lydia Kieven, and Marijke J. Klokke. *Worshipping Siva and the Buddha: The Temple Art of East Java*. Honolulu: University of Hawai'i Press, 2003.

Kōchi Saburō. *"Dokusha" no tanjō: Katsuji bunka wa dono yō ni shite teichakushita ka* (The Birth of the "Reader": How Was Print Culture Established?). Tokyo: Shōbunsha, 2004.

Koide, Izumi. "Chronological Biography of Naomi Fukuda." *Journal of East Asian Libraries* 145 (2008). https://scholarsarchive.byu.edu/cgi/viewcontent.cgi?article=2596&context=jeal.

———. *Nichibei kōryū-shi no naka Fukuda Naomi* (Naomi Fukuda and the History of Japan-US Exchange). Tokyo: Bensei Shuppan, 2022.

Kokusai Bunka Shinkōkai. *Introduction to Contemporary Literature*. Tokyo: Kokusai Bunka Shinkōkai, 1939.

Komatsu, Kazuhiko. *An Introduction to Yōkai Culture: Monsters, Ghosts, and Outsiders in Japanese History*. Translated by Hiroko Yoda. Tokyo: Japan Publishing Industry Foundation for Culture, 2018.

Kondo, Ken. "The Fulbright Program in Japan: Reappraisal." Transcript of speech delivered at the Asia Foundation, San Francisco, September 5, 2001, 1–14.

"Korean War." Dwight D. Eisenhower Presidential Library. n.d. https://www.eisenhowerlibrary.gov/research/online-documents/korean-war (accessed January 1, 2023).

Koyama, Michael S. *The Boy Who Defied His Karma*. Honolulu: Mutual Publishing, 2011.

Kratz, Jessie. "Little Boy: The First Atomic Bomb." *National Archives*. August 6, 2020. https://prologue.blogs.archives.gov/2020/08/06/little-boy-the-first-atomic-bomb/.

Krauss, Ellis S., Thomas P. Rohlen, and Patricia G. Steinhoff, eds. *Conflict in Japan*. Honolulu: University of Hawai'i Press, 1984.

Kristeva, Julia. *Desire in Language: A Semiotic Approach to Literature and Art*. Translated by Thomas Gora, Alice Jardine, and Leon S. Roudiez. New York: Columbia University Press, 1980.

Kumamoto Kenjirō. "Ōyatoi gaikokujin" (Foreign Employees of the Meiji Government). *Bijutsu* (Art) 16. Tokyo: Kajima kenkyūjo shuppankai, 1976.

Kume Kunitake. *Tokumei zenkan taishi Beiō kairan jikki* (A True Account of the Ambassador Extraordinary and Plenipotentiary's Journey to America and Europe). 5 vols. Tokyo: Hakubunsha, 1878.

———. *The Iwakura Embassy, 1871–73: A True Account of the Ambassador Extraordinary and Plenipotentiary's Journey of Observation through the United States of America and Europe*, edited by Chūshichi Tsuzuki and Graham Healey. 5 vols. Chiba, Japan: Japan Documents, 2002.

Kunikida Doppo. "Meat and Potatoes." In *River Mist and Other Stories*. Translated by David Chibbett, 136–151. New York: Kodansha International, 1983.

Kuramochi Shigehiro. *Chūsei sonraku no keisei to mura shakai* (The Formation of Medieval Villages and Village Society). Tokyo: Yoshikawa kōbunkan, 2007.

———. *Nihon chūsei sonrakushi no kenkyū* (Study of the History of Medieval Japanese Villages). Tokyo: Azekura shobō, 1996.

Kurata Bunsaku. *Hōryūji: Temple of the Exalted Law: Early Buddhist Art from Japan*. Translated by W. Chie Ishibashi. New York: Japan Society, 1981.

Kurosawa Akira, dir. *Rashomon*. Tokyo: Daiei Film, 1950.

———. *Shichinin no samurai* (Seven Samurai). Tokyo: Tōhō, 1954.

———. *Yojimbo*. Tokyo: Tōhō, 1961.

Kyaw, Arrman. "Report: All Faculty Types Suffer Job Losses in 2020–2021 Academic Year." April 8, 2021. *Diverse: Issues in Higher Education*. www.diverseeducation.com/faculty-staff/article/15108970/report-all-faculty-types-suffer-job-losses-in-2020-2021-academic-year.

Lacan, Jacques, Alan Sheridan, and Malcolm Bowie. *Écrits: A Selection*. London: Routledge, 1977.

LaCure, Jon W. *Rhetorical Devices of the Kokinshū: A Structural Analysis of Japanese Waka Poetry*. Lewiston, NY: Edwin Mellen Press, 1997.

"Landberg Serves Samurai Buffs Full '47 Ronin.'" *Variety* 240, no. 7 (October 6, 1965): 15.

Latourette, Kenneth Scott. *A Short History of the Far East*. Revised Edition. New York: Macmillan, 1951.

Lau, D. C., trans. *Lao Tzu: Tao Te Ching*. New York: Penguin Books, 1963.

Leach, Bernard. *Hamada: Potter*. Tokyo: Kodansha International, 1976.

Lebra, Joyce Chapman. *Chandora Bōse to Nihon* (Chandra Bose and Japan). Tokyo: Hara shobō, 1968.

———. *Durga's Sword*. Mumbai: Indus, 1995.

———. "Eyewitness: Mishima." *New York Times*. November 28, 1970: 26.

———. *The Indian National Army and Japan*. Singapore: ISEAS, 2008.

———, ed. *Japan's Greater East Asia Co-Prosperity Sphere in World War II: Selected Readings and Documents*. London: Oxford University Press, 1975.

———. *Japanese-Trained Armies in Southeast Asia: Independence and Volunteer Forces in World War II*. Hong Kong: Heinemann Educational Books, 1977.

———. *Jungle Alliance: Japan and the Indian National Army*. Singapore: Asia Pacific Press, 1971.

———. "Last Speech on Balcony Witnessed." *Mainichi Daily News Tokyo*. November 28, 1970.

———. *Ōkuma Shigenobu: Statesman of Meiji Japan*. Canberra: Australian National University Press, 1973.

———. *Scent of Sake*. New York: Harper Collins, 2009.

Lebra, Joyce and Joy Paulson, eds. *Chinese Women in Southeast Asia*. Singapore: Times Books International, 1980.

Lebra, Joyce, Joy Paulson, and Jena Matson Everett, eds. *Women and Work in India: Continuity and Change*. New Delhi: Promilla, 1984.

Lebra, Joyce, Joy Paulson, and Elizabeth Powers, eds. *Women in Changing Japan*. Stanford: Stanford University Press, 1978.

Lebra-Chapman, Joyce. *The Rani of Jhansi: A Study of Female Heroism in India*. Honolulu: University of Hawai'i Press, 1986.

Lennon, Connor. "G.I. Jane Goes to College? Female Educational Attainment, Earnings, and the Serviceman's Readjustment Act of 1944." *Journal of Economic History* 81, no. 4 (December 2021): 1223–1253.

Lento Takako. *Chigai ga wakaru, Amerika eigo renshū-chō* (Learn the Differences: American Usage). Tokyo: DHC, 2002.

———. *Dame! Sono eigo. Bijinesu hen*. (No, That Does Not Work in English: For Business Situations). Tokyo: Kodansha International, 1999.

———. *Dame! Sono eigo. Nichijō seikatsu hen* (No, That Does Not Work in English: For Everyday Life). Tokyo: Kodansha International, 2002.

———, ed. and trans. *Pioneers of Modern Japanese Poetry*. Ithaca: Cornell East Asia Series, 2019.

Lento, Takako and Wayne Miller, eds. *Tamura Ryūichi: On the Life and Work of a 20th Century Master*. Warrensburg, MO: Pleiades Press, 2011.

Leone, Sergio, dir. *A Fistful of Dollars*. Munich: Constantin Films, 1964.

Lifton, Robert Jay. "Youth and History: Individual Change in Postwar Japan." In *The Challenge of Youth*, edited by Erik H. Erikson, 260–290. New York: Doubleday, 1961.

Little, Becky. "How the 1982 Murder of Vincent Chin Ignited a Push for Asian American Rights." *History.com*. May 5, 2020. https://www.history.com/news/vincent-chin-murder-asian-american-rights.

Lloyd, Mark Frazier. "Tuition and Mandated Fees, Room and Board, and Other Educational Costs at Penn." *Penn Libraries*. 2003. https://archives.upenn.edu/exhibits/penn-history/tuition/tuition-1950-1959/.

Lock, Margaret. *East Asian Medicine in Urban Japan: Varieties of Medical Experience*. Berkeley: University of California Press, 1980.

———. *Encounters with Aging: Mythologies of Menopause in Japan and North America*. Berkeley: University of California Press, 1995.

———. *Twice Dead: Organ Transplants and the Reinvention of Death*. Berkeley: University of California Press, 2001.

London, Jerry, dir. *Shōgun*. Hollywood: Paramount Television, September 15–19, 1980. 5 episodes.

Lynn, Richard John, trans. *The Classic of the Way and Virtue: A New Translation of the Tao-Te Ching of Laozi as Interpreted by Wang Bi*. New York: Columbia University Press, 1999.

———. *Zhuangzi: A New Translation of the Sayings of Master Zhuang as Interpreted by Guo Xiang*. New York: Columbia University Press, 2022.

Lyons, Phyllis. *The Saga of Dazai Osamu: A Critical Study with Translations*. Stanford: Stanford University Press, 1985.

MacDonald, Keiko. "In Search of the Orient: W. B. Yeats and Japanese Tradition." PhD Diss. University of Oregon, 1974.

Makino, Yasuko. "Eulogy of Ms. Naomi Fukuda." *Journal of East Asian Libraries* 145 (2008). https://scholarsarchive.byu.edu/cgi/viewcontent.cgi?article=2588&context=jeal.

Martin, Samuel. *Essential Japanese: An Introduction to the Standard Colloquial Language*. Rutland, VT: Charles E. Tuttle Company, 1954.

Masaoka Shiki. *Masaoka Shiki zenshū* (Collected Works of Masaoka Shiki). Tokyo: Arusu, 1924–1927.

Massey, Elizabeth and Joseph Massey. *CULCON Report on Japanese Studies at Colleges and Universities in the United States in the Mid-70s*. New York: Japan Society, 1977.

Matisoff, Susan. "Images of Exile and Pilgrimage, Zeami's *Kintōsho*." *Monumenta Nipponica* 34, no. 4 (Winter 1979): 449–465.

———. "*Kintōsho*, Zeami's Song of Exile." *Monumenta Nipponica* 32, no. 4 (Winter 1977): 441–458.

———. *The Legend of Semimaru, Blind Musician of Japan*. New York: Columbia University Press, 1978.

Matsuda Koh, ed. *Kenkyūsha's New Japanese-English Dictionary*. Tokyo: Kodansha International, 1974.

Matsuda, Takeshi. *Soft Power and Its Perils: U.S. Cultural Policy in Early Postwar Japan and Permanent Dependency*. Stanford: Stanford University Press, 2007.

Matsuda Yoshiyuki. *Rejaasangyō o kangaeru* (Thinking about the Leisure Industry). Tokyo: Jikkyō Books, 1993.

Matsumoto Takeshi. "Edo no Bosei: Haka ni komerareta mibun chitsujo" (Burial Rules in Edo: Social Class Order Hidden in Tombs). In *Kinsei kingendai kōkogaku nyūmon* (Introduction to Early Modern and Modern Archeology), edited by Suzuki Kimio, 179–193. Tokyo: Keio University Press, 2007.

Matsuo Bashō. *The Narrow Road to the Deep North and Other Travel Sketches*. Translated by Yuasa Nobuyuki. New York: Penguin Classics, 1967.

Matsushita, Takaaki. *Ink Painting*. Translated and adapted by Martin Collcutt. Tokyo: Weatherhill, 1974.

Matsuura Rieko. *The Apprenticeship of Big Toe P*. Translated by Michael Emmerich. New York: Kodansha International, 2010.

———. "For a Gentle Castration." Translated by Amanda Seaman. In *Woman Critiqued: Translated Essays on Japanese Women's Writing*, edited by Rebecca Copeland, 194–205. Honolulu: University of Hawai'i Press, 2006.

———. *Nachuraru ūman* (Natural Woman). Tokyo: Chikuma shobō, 2000.

———. *Oyayubi P no shugyōjidai* (*The Apprenticeship of Big Toe P.*). Tokyo: Kawade shobō Shinsha, 1992.

———. *Ura vājon* (The Reverse Version). Tokyo: Chikuma shobō, 2000.

———. *Yasashii kyosei no tame ni* (For a Gentle Castration). Tokyo: Chikuma shobō, 1994.

Mayo, Marlene J. "American Planning for Occupied Japan: The Role of the Experts." *Americans as Proconsuls: United States Military Government in Germany and Japan, 1944–1952*, edited by Robert Wolfe, 263–320 and 498–515. Carbondale, IL: Southern Illinois University Press, 1984.

———. "Attitudes toward Asia and the Beginnings of Japanese Empire." *Occasional Papers of the East Asian Institute*, 16–31. New York: Columbia University, 1967.

———. "Bakumatsu-Early Meiji Japan." *An Introduction to Japanese Civilization*, edited by Arthur Tiedemann, 132–180. New York: Columbia University Press, 1974.

———. "A Catechism of Western Diplomacy." *Journal of Asian Studies* 26, no. 3 (1967): 389–410.

———. "Civil Censorship and Media Control in Early Occupied Japan: From Minimum to Stringent Surveillance." *Americans as Proconsuls: United States Military Government in Germany and Japan, 1945–1952*, edited by Robert Wolfe, 263–320 and 498–515. Carbondale, IL: University of Illinois Press, 1984.

———. "The Korean Crisis of 1873 and Early Meiji Foreign Policy." *Journal of Asian Studies* 31, no. 4 (1972): 793–818.

———. "Kume Kunitake no *Bei-Ō kairan jikki* o tōshite" (On Kume Kunitake's True Record of Travels in America and Europe). In *Iwakura shisetsu no kenkyū* (Research on the Iwakura Mission), edited by Ōkubo Toshiaki, 263–326. Tokyo: Munetaka shobō, 1976.

———. "Literary Reorientation in Occupied Japan: Incidents of Civil Censorship." *Legacies and Ambiguities: Postwar Fiction and Culture in West Germany and Japan*, edited by Ernestine Schlant and J. Thomas Rimer, 135–161. Washington, DC: Woodrow Wilson Center Press and Baltimore: Johns Hopkins University Press, 1991.

———. "Philadelphia Monogatari: Hida Hamagorō no kōjō shisatusu" (The Philadelphia Story: Hida Hamagorō's Factory Tour, 1872). *Iwakura shisetsudan no hikaku bunka shiteki kenkyū* (Comparative Cultural Studies on the Iwakura Embassy), edited by Haga Tōru, 47–89. Kyoto: Shibunkaku Publishing Company, 2003.

———. "Rationality in the Meiji Restoration: The Iwakura Mission." *Modern Japanese Leadership: Transition and Change*, edited by Bernard Silberman and Harry Harutoonian, 323–369. Tucson: University of Arizona Press, 1966.

———. "To Be or Not To Be: Kabuki and Cultural Politics in Occupied Japan." *War, Occupation, and Creativity: Japan and East Asia, 1920–1960*, edited by Marlene J. Mayo and J. Thomas Rimer with Eleanor Kerkham, 269–309. Honolulu: University of Hawai'i, 2001.

———. "The Western Education of Kume Kunitake, 1871–1876." *Monumenta Nippponica*, 28, no. 1 (1973): 3–67.

Mayo, Marlene J., J. Thomas Rimer with H. Eleanor Kerkham, eds. *War, Occupation, and Creativity: Japan and East Asia, 1920–1960*. Honolulu: University of Hawai'i Press, 2001.

McAndrew, Malia. "Ethel Weed through Her Letters: The Personal Reflections of a Woman in the US Occupation of Japan." *US–Japan Women's Journal* 55/56 (2019): 108–127.

"McCarthy and Army-McCarthy Hearings." United States Senate. n.d. https://www.senate.gov/about/powers-procedures/investigations/mccarthy-and-army-mccarthy-hearings.htm (accessed January 1, 2023).

McClain, Yoko. "My Personal Journey across the Pacific." *Modern Girls on the Go: Gender, Labor, and Mobility in Japan*, edited by Alisa Freedman, Laura Miller, and Christine Yano, 209–225. Stanford: Stanford University Press, 2013.

McCormick, Melissa. "On the Scholarship of Chino Kaori." *Review of Japanese Culture and Society* XV (December 2003): 1–24.

McCullough, Helen Craig, ed. and trans. *Brocade by Night: "Kokin Wakashū" and the Court Style in Japanese Classical Poetry*. Stanford: Stanford University Press, 1985.

———, ed. and trans. *Classical Japanese Prose: An Anthology*. Stanford: Stanford University Press, 1990.

———, trans. *Genji and Heike: Selections from* The Tale of Genji *and* The Tale of the Heike. Stanford: Stanford University Press, 1994.

———, trans. *Kokin Wakashū: The First Imperial Anthology of Japanese Poetry*. Stanford: Stanford University Press, 1985.

———, trans. *Okagami, The Great Mirror: Fujiwara Michinaga (966–1027) and His Times.* Princeton: Princeton University Press, 1980.

———, trans. *Taiheiki: A Chronicle of Medieval Japan.* New York: Columbia University Press, 1956.

———, trans. *The Tale of the Heike.* Stanford: Stanford University Press, 1988.

———, trans. *The Tales of Ise: Lyrical Episodes from Tenth-Century Japan.* Stanford: Stanford University Press, 1968.

———, trans. *Yoshitsune: A Fifteenth Century Japanese Chronicle.* Stanford: Stanford University Press, 1966.

McCullough, William and Helen. *A Tale of Flowering Fortunes: Annals of Japanese Aristocratic Life in the Heian Period.* Vols. 1 and 2. Stanford: Stanford University Press, 1980.

McGurk, Caitlin. "Maureen Donovan and the Manga Collection at The Ohio State University Library: An Interview with Maureen Donovan." *Journal of East Asian Libraries* 162 (2016).

McKean, Margaret. *Environmental Protest and Citizen Politics in Japan.* Berkeley: University of California Press, 1981.

———. "The Japanese Experience with Scarcity: Management of Traditional Common Lands." *Environmental Review* 6, no. 2 (Fall 1982): 63–88.

———. "Rational Choice Analysis and Area Studies: Enemies or Partners?" In *Beyond the Area Studies Wars: Toward a New International Studies,* edited by Neil Waters, 29–63. Hanover, NH: University Press of New England, 2000.

———. "State Strength and the Public Interest." In *Political Dynamics in Contemporary Japan,* edited by Gary Allinson and Yasunori Sone, 72–104. Ithaca: Cornell University Press, 1993.

———. "Success on the Commons: A Comparative Examination of Institutions for Common Property Resource Management." *Journal of Theoretical Politics* 4, no. 3 (July 1992): 247–281.

McKinnon, Richard. *Selected Plays of Kyōgen.* Tokyo: Uniprint, 1968.

McLelland, Mark. "Introduction: The End of 'Cool Japan'?" In *End of Cool Japan: Ethical, Legal, and Cultural Challenges to Japanese Popular Culture,* edited by Mark McLelland, 1–31. Oxford: Routledge, 2017.

McNaughton, James C. *Nisei Linguists: Japanese Americans in the Military Intelligence Service during World War II.* Washington, DC: Department of the Army, 2006.

McRae, Matthew. "Japanese Canadian Internment and the Struggle for Redress." *Canadian Museum for Human Rights*. 2022. https://humanrights.ca/story/japanese-canadian-internment-and-the-struggle-for-redress.

McSeveney, Samuel T. "In Memoriam: Paul H. Hardacre (1915–201)." *Perspectives on History*. American Historical Association. January 1, 2011. https://www.historians.org/publications-and-directories/perspectives-on-history/january-2011/in-memoriam-paul-h-hardacre.

Medine, David. "Law and Kurosawa's *Rashomon*." In *The Force of Vision 6: Inter-Asian Comparative Literature*, edited by Kawamoto Kōji, Heh-Hsiang Yuan, and Ohsawa Yoshihiro, 470–476. Tokyo: International Comparative Literature Association, 1995.

Meech, Julia. *Frank Lloyd Wright and the Art of Japan: The Architect's Other Passion*. New York: Harry N. Abrams, 2001.

Meech-Pekarik, Julia. *The World of the Meiji Print: Impressions of a New Civilization*. Tokyo: Weatherhill, 1986.

"Memoir." *Oxford English Dictionary*. Oxford University Press. 2022. https://www-oed-com.libproxy.uoregon.edu/view/Entry/116334?redirectedFrom=memoir#eid.

Menand, Louis. "A Friend of the Devil." *The New Yorker*, March 16, 2015. https://www.newyorker.com/magazine/2015/03/23/a-friend-of-the-devil.

Merwin, W. S. *W. S. Merwin senshishū* (W. S. Merwin Poems). Translated by Takako Lento. Tokyo: Shichōsha, 2022.

Michell, J. "Interview Guide for Obtaining Supplementary Data Concerning Students Selected for Scholarships under the GARIOA Student Program." June 23, 1951. Declassified E.O. 12065 Section 3-402/NNDG No. 775017.

Michener, James A. *The Floating World: The Story of Japanese Prints*. New York: Random House, 1954.

———. *Japanese Prints: From the Early Masters to the Modern*. Rutland, VT: Charles E. Tuttle Company, 1959.

Middlebrook, Diane. *Anne Sexton: A Biography*. New York: Vintage, 1991.

Miki Fumio. *Haniwa*. Translated and adapted by Gina Lee Barnes. Tokyo: Weatherhill, 1974.

Miller-Bernal, Leslie. "Introduction: Coeducation: An Uneven Progression." In *Going Coed: Women's Experiences in Formerly Men's Colleges and Universities, 1950–2000*, edited by Leslie Miller-Bernal and Susan L. Poulson, 3–21. Nashville: Vanderbilt University Press, 2004.

Minami Hiroshi, et al., eds. *Kindai shomin seikatushi 9: Ren'ai, kekkon, katei* (The History of Modern People's Lifestyles 9: Love, Marriage, Family). Tokyo: San'ichi shobō, 1986.

———. *Nihonjin no shinri* (The Psychology of the Japanese People). Tokyo: Iwanami shoten, 1953.

———, ed. *Shōwa bunka, 1925–1945* (Shōwa Culture: 1925–1945). Tokyo: Keisō shobō, 1987.

———, ed. *Taishō bunka* (Taishō Culture). Tokyo: Keisō shobō, 1965.

———, ed. *Zoku—Shōwa bunka, 1945–1989* (Shōwa Culture, Part 2: 1945–1989). Tokyo: Keisō shobō, 1990.

Miner, Earl. *Japanese Linked Poetry: An Account with Translations of Renga and Haikai Sequences*. Princeton: Princeton University Press, 1979.

———, ed. *The Works of John Dryden*, Volume III: *Poems 1685-1692*. Berkeley: University of California Press, 1969.

———, ed. *The Works of John Dryden*, Volume XV: *Plays*. Berkeley: University of California Press, 1976.

Miner, Earl and Hiroko Odagiri. *The Monkey's Straw Raincoat and Other Poetry of the Bashō School*. Princeton: Princeton University Press, 1981.

Minichiello, Sharon. *Retreat from Reform: Patterns of Political Behavior in Interwar Japan*. Honolulu: University of Hawai'i Press, 1984.

Mishima, Yukio. *Confessions of a Mask*. Translated by Meredith Weatherby. New York: New Directions Publishing, 1958.

———. *Confessions of a Mask*. Translated by Meredith Weatherby. In *Modern Japanese Literature: An Anthology*, edited by Donald Keene, 429–438. New York: Grove Press, 1960.

———. *Patriotism*. Translated by Geoffrey W. Sargent. New York: New Directions Publishing, 2010.

———. *Sound of Waves*. Translated by Meredith Weatherby. New York: Alfred A. Knopf, 1980.

———. *Sun and Steel*. Translated by John Bester. New York: Grove Press, 1970.

———. *Temple of the Golden Pavilion*. Translated by Ivan Morris. New York: Alfred A. Knopf, 1980.

———. *Wakaki samurai no tame ni* (For Young Samurai). Tokyo: Kyōbunsha, 1969.

———. *The Way of the Samurai: Yukio Mishima on Hagakure in Modern Life.* Translated by Kathryn Sparling. New York: Perigee Books, 1977.

Mishima Yukio and Domoto Masaki, dirs. *Yūkoku* (Patriotism). 1966. New York: Criterion Collection, 2008. DVD.

Mitamura Engyo. *Mitamura Engyo zenshū* (Collected Works of Mitamura Engyo). 28 vols. Tokyo: Chūō kōronsha, 1975–1977.

Mitsumata Gaku and Saito Haruo, eds. *Toshi to shinrin* (City and Forest). Tokyo: Kosovo, 2017.

———. *Mori no keizaigaku: Mori ga mori rashiku, hito ga hito rashiku aru keizai* (Forest Economics: An Economics in which Forests are Like Forests and People Are Like People). Tokyo: Nihon hyōronsha, 2022.

Miyazaki, Fumiko, Kate Wildman Nakai, and Mark Teeuwen, trans. *Christian Sorcerers on Trial: Records of the 1827 Osaka Incident.* New York: Columbia University Press, 2020.

Miyoshi, Masao. *Accomplices of Silence: The Modern Japanese Novel.* Berkeley: University of California Press, 1975.

———. *As We Saw Them: The First Japanese Embassy to the United States (1860).* Berkeley: University of California Press, 1979.

Mizoguchi, Saburo. *Design Motifs* (*Monyō*). Translated and adapted by Louise Allison Cort. Tokyo: Weatherhill, 1973.

Mizumura, Minae. *An I-Novel.* Translated by Juliet Winters Carpenter. New York: Columbia University Press, 2021.

———. *A True Novel.* Translated by Juliet Winters Carpenter. New York: Other Press, 2013.

Mizuta Noriko. *Josei gaku to no deai* (My Encounter with Women's Studies). Tokyo: Shueisha, 2004.

Mizutani Osamu and Nobuko Mizutani. *An Introduction to Modern Japanese.* Tokyo: The Japan Times, 1977.

———. *Nihongo Notes.* Vols. 1–10. Tokyo: The Japan Times, 1992–1993.

Modern Language Association (MLA). "Standing Still: The Associate Professor Survey Report of the Committee on the Status of Women in the Profession." April 27, 2009. https://www.mla.org/About-Us/Governance/Committees/Committee-Listings/Professional-Issues/Committee-on-Women-Gender-and-Sexuality-in-the-Profession/Standing-Still-The-Associate-Professor-Survey.

MoMA. "Japanese Exhibition House, June 16, 1954–October 15, 1955." *MoMA*. n.d. www. moma.org/calendar/exhibitions/2711 (April 22, 2022).

Monaghan, Conor. "What Exactly Is a Memoir?" *One Minute English*. 2022. https://oneminuteenglish.org/en/memoir-meaning/.

"Monro Attacks Disclaimer Affidavit." *Harvard Crimson*. October 24, 1959. https://www.thecrimson.com/article/1959/10/24/monro-attacks-disclaimer-affidavit-pa-vote/.

Moretti, Laura. *Pleasure in Profit: Popular Prose in Seventeenth-Century Japan*. New York: Columbia University Press, 2020.

Mori Atsushi. *Gassan* (Moon Mountain). Tokyo: Kawade shobō, 1974.

———. *Ware mo mata Oku no hosomichi* (And Me Once Again on *The Narrow Road to the North*). Tokyo: Nihon Hōsō Shuppan Kyōkai, 1988.

Morris, Ivan. *As I Crossed a Bridge of Dreams*. New York: Penguin Classics, 1989.

Morse, Anne Nishimura, ed. *Drama and Desire: Japanese Paintings from the Floating World*. Boston: Boston Museum of Fine Arts, 2007.

Munsterberg, Hugo. "Art Study in Japan." *College Art Journal* 13, no. 2 (Winter 1954): 132–134.

Murasaki Shikibu. *The Tale of Genji: The Arthur Waley Translation of Lady Murasaki's Masterpiece*. Translated by Arthur Waley with a new foreword by Dennis Washburn. Rutland, VT: Tuttle Classics, 2010.

Murota Takeshi, ed. *Gurōbaru jidai no rōkaru komonzu* (Local Commons in the Global Age). Tokyo: Minerva shobō, 2009.

Murota Takeshi and Mitsumata Gaku. *Iriai rin'ya to komonzu* (Iriai Forests and Commons). Tokyo: Nihon hyōronsha, 2003.

Murota Takeshi and Ken Takeshita, eds. *Local Commons and Democratic Environmental Governance*. New York: United Nations University Press, 2013.

Museum Rietberg. *Love, Fight, Feast: The World of Japanese Narrative Art*. Zurich: Scheidegger and Spiess, 2021.

Naganuma Naoe. *Naganuma's Basic Japanese Course*. Tokyo: Kaitakusha Publishing, 1950.

Najita, Tetsuo and J. Victor Koschmann, eds. *Conflict in Modern Japanese History: The Neglected Tradition*. Princeton: Princeton University Press, 1982.

Nakahara Jun'ichi. *Inokku Āden Tenisun* (Enoch Arden, Tennyson). *Himawari* (Sunflower) 4, no. 5 (June 1950): n.p.

Nakai, Kate Wildman. *Shogunal Politics: Arai Hakuseki and the Premises of Tokugawa Rule*. Cambridge, MA: Council on East Asian Studies, Harvard University, 1988.

Nakai Yoshiyuki. *Ōgai ryūgaku shimatsu* (Circumstances of Ōgai's Study Abroad). Tokyo: Iwanami shoten, 1999.

Nakamura, Kelli Y. "Military Intelligence Service Language School." *Densho Encyclopedia*. October 16, 2020. https://encyclopedia.densho.org/Military_Intelligence_Service_Language_School/.

Nakamura Ken, ed. *Imabori Hiyoshi Jinja monjo shūsei* (Collected Documents of the Imabori Hiyoshi Shrine). Tokyo: Yūzankaku, 1981.

Nakamura, Kyoko Motomuchi. *Miraculous Stories from the Japanese Buddhist Tradition: The Nihon Ryoiki of Monk Kyokai*. London: Routledge, 1996.

Nakano Sanbin. *Kinsei shin kijinden* (New Biographies of Eccentrics of Early Modern Japan). Tokyo: Iwanami shoten, 2004.

Nakano, Yoshiko. "Japan's Postwar International Stewardesses: Embodying Modernity and Exoticism in the Air." *US–Japan Women's Journal* 55/56 (2019): 80–107.

Naruse Mikio, dir. *Tsuma yo bara no yō ni* (Wife! Be Like A Rose!). Tokyo: P.C.L, 1935.

National Council for American Education. *Red-ucators at Leading Women's Colleges*. New York: National Council for American Education, 1951.

National Equal Pay Task Force. "Fifty Years after the Equal Pay Act: Assessing the Past, Taking Stock of the Future." Obama White House. 2013. https://obamawhitehouse.archives.gov/sites/default/files/equalpay/equal_pay_task_force_progress_report_june_2013_new.pdf.

Natsume, Soseki. *Botchan*. Translated by Umeji Sasaki. Rutland, VT: Charles E. Tuttle Company, 1968.

———. *Bungakuron* (Literature Theory). Tokyo: Iwanami bunko, 2007.

———. *Mon* (The Gate). Tokyo: Shueisha bunko, 2013.

———. *Unhuman Tour*. Translated by Takahashi Kazutomo. Tokyo: *The Japan Times*, 1927.

"New Criticism." *Glossary of Poetic Terms*. Poetry Foundation. 2022. https://www.poetryfoundation.org/learn/glossary-terms/new-criticism.

"New Historicism." *Glossary of Poetic Terms*. Poetry Foundation. 2022. https://www.poetryfoundation.org/learn/glossary-terms/new-historicism.

"Newly Authorized Universities Now Total 180." *CI&E Bulletin* 3, no. 2 (June 8, 1949): 5.

Nihon koten bungaku taikei (Anthology of Japanese Classical Literature). 102 vols. Tokyo: Iwanami shoten, 1983–1985.

"Nihon shōkokumin bunko." *The Showa Bookshelf*. November 5, 2009. https://theshowabookshelf.wordpress.com/2009/11/05/nihon-shokokumin-bunko-library-of-books-for-the-younger-generation/.

Nikkei Asia. "Blast from the Past." *Unlock the Real Japan*. March 2022. https://ps.nikkei.com/unlock/202203/blastfromthepast.html.

Nilya, Brian. "Public Law 503." *Densho Encyclopedia*. July 15, 2020. https://encyclopedia.densho.org/Public_Law_503/.

Nippon Gakujutsu Shinkōkai. *The Manyōshū: The Nippon Gakujutsu Shinkōkai Translation of One Thousand Poems*. New York: Columbia University Press, 1969.

Niwa Tamako. "Nakatsukasa naishi nikki" (The Diary of Nakatsukasa naishi). PhD Diss. Radcliffe, 1955.

Nochlin, Linda. "Why Have There Been No Great Women Artists?" *ARTnews* (January 1971): 22–39, 67–71.

Nogami Teruyo. *Tenkimachi: Kantoku Kurosawa Akira to tomoni* (Waiting for the Weather to Turn: Working with Director Kurosawa Akira). Tokyo: Bungei Shunju, 2001.

Noguchi Takehiko. *Ansei Edo jishin* (The Ansei Earthquake of Edo). Tokyo: Chikuma shobō, 1997.

"Noh Terminology." *The Noh.com*. 2022. https://db2.the-noh.com/edic/2010/05/hosho_school.html.

Nolte, Sharon H. *Liberalism in Modern Japan: Ishibashi Tanzan and His Teachers, 1905–1960*. Berkeley: University of California Press, 1987.

Nordyke, Eleanor C. and Y. Scott Matsumoto. "The Japanese in Hawai'i: A Historical and Demographic Perspective." *Hawaiian Journal of History* 11 (1977): 162–174.

North American Coordinating Council on Japanese Library Resources (NCC). "Curated Archives: NCC Background." August 10, 2022. https://guides.nccjapan.org/archive.

———. "Japanese Library Studies Multimedia History Project: Full Interviews and Other Resources." *NCC Japan*. 2019. https://guides.nccjapan.org/multimediahistory/full_interviews.

———. "Japanese Studies Multimedia History Project: Overview." January 16, 2022. https://guides.nccjapan.org/multimediahistory.

"Obituaries: Hattie Masuko Kawahara Colton '43." *Reed Magazine*, May 2009. https://www.reed.edu/reed-magazine/in-memoriam/obituaries/may2009/hattie-masuko-kawahara-colton-1943.html.

"Occupation and Reconstruction of Japan, 1945–52." Office of the Historian, Foreign Service Institute. 2017. https://history.state.gov/milestones/1945-1952/japan-reconstruction#:~:text=The%20occupation%20of%20Japan%20can,formal%20peace%20treaty%20and%20alliance.

"Occupied Japan: Gender, Class, Race." Maryland Institute for Technology in the Humanities. n.d. https://archive.mith.umd.edu/gcr/public/displayTheme.php%3Fid=28.html (accessed January 2, 2023).

Ogata, Sadako N. *Defiance in Manchuria: The Making of Japanese Foreign Policy, 1931–1932*. Berkeley: University of California Press, 1964.

Ogata Tsutomu. "*Oku no hosomichi* sanbyakunen" (*Narrow Road to the Deep North*, Three Hundred Years). *Bungaku* 5, no. 56 (May 1988): 1–9.

O'Grady, Megan. "These Literary Memoirs Take a Different Tack." *New York Times Style Magazine*. September 29, 2021. https://www.nytimes.com/2021/09/29/t-magazine/memoirs-books-nonfiction-identity.html.

Ogul, Jim. "Expo 2025 Will Build on Osaka's World's Fair Legacy." *InPark Magazine*. March 1, 2022. https://www.inparkmagazine.com/expo-2025-will-build-on-osakas-worlds-fair-legacy/.

Ohno Tomohiko. "Ryūiki gabanansu no bunseki furēmuwāku" (An Analytical Framework for the Study of Watershed Governance). *Suishigen kankyō kenkyū* (Journal of Water and Environmental Issues) 28, no. 1 (July 2015): 7–15.

Oka, Takashi. "Expo '70 Ended after 183 Days." *New York Times*. September 14, 1970. https://www.nytimes.com/1970/09/14/archives/expo-70-is-ended-after-183-days-attendance-was-64-million-sato.html.

Okano, Hirohiko. "Bagdad is Burning." Translated by Amy V. Heinrich. *The Tanka Journal* 30 (2007): 1.

Okazaki, Jōji. *Pure Land Buddhist Painting*. Translated and adapted by Elizabeth ten Grotenhuis. Tokyo: Kodansha, 1977.

Okudaira, Hideo. *Narrative Picture Scrolls*. Translated and adapted by Elizabeth ten Grotenhuis. Tokyo: Weatherhill, 1973.

Olito, Frank. "Here's How the Cost of Harvard Has Changed throughout the Years." *Insider*. June 10, 2019. https://www.businessinsider.com/how-the-cost-of-harvard-has-changed-throughout-the-years2019-6.

Omote Akira and Yokomichi Mario, eds. "Kaisetsu" (Commentary). In *Yōkyokushū, Nihon koten bungaku taikei* (Texts of Noh Plays, Treasury of Japanese Classical Literature) 40, edited by Omote Akira and Yokomichi Mario, 5–28. Tokyo: Iwanami shoten, 1960.

Ōoka Makoto. *Beneath the Sleepless Tossing of the Planets: Selected Poems by Makoto Ōoka*. Translated by Janine Beichman. Kumamoto: Kurodahan Press, 2019.

———. *The Colors of Poetry: Essays on Classic Japanese Verse*. Translated by Takako U. Lento and Thomas V. Lento. Rochester, MI: Katydid Books, 1991.

———. *Oriori no uta: Poems for All Seasons*. Translated by Janine Beichman. Tokyo: Kodansha International, 2000.

———. *A Poet's Anthology: The Range of Japanese Poetry*. Translated by Janine Beichman. Santa Fe: Katydid Books, 1994.

———. *Taiyaku Oriori no Uta, Poems for All Seasons: An Anthology of Japanese Poetry from Ancient Times to the Present*. Translated by Janine Beichman. Tokyo: Kodansha International, 2002.

Ōoka, Makoto and Thomas Fitzsimmons, eds. *A Play of Mirrors: Eight Major Poets of Modern Japan*. Rochester, MI: Katydid Books, 1987.

"Oriental Institute Changes Name to the Institute for the Study of Ancient Cultures, West Asia & North Africa." *UChicago News*, April 4, 2023. https://news.uchicago.edu/story/oriental-institute-changes-name-institute-study-ancient-cultures-west-asia-north-africa.

Osada, Hiroshi and Tamura Ryūichi. "Poems." *TriQuarterly 31: Contemporary Asian Literature*. Translated by Takako Uchino Lento. Evanston: Northwestern University, 1974: 86–89, 199.

Osaragi, Jirō. *Homecoming*. Translated by Brewster Horwitz. New York: Alfred A. Knopf, 1954.

Osborne, John. *Look Back in Anger*. New York: Penguin Books, 1982.

Ostrom, Elinor. *Governing the Commons: The Evolution of Institutions for Collective Action*. New York: Cambridge University Press, 1990.

"Our History." The Rockefeller Foundation. 2023. https://www.rockefellerfoundation.org/about-us/our-history/.

Ozawa, Minoru. *Well-Versed: Exploring Modern Japanese Haiku*. Translated by Janine Beichman. Tokyo: Japan Publishing Industry Foundation for Culture, 2021.

Packard, George R. "The Coming U.S.-Japan Crisis." *Foreign Affairs* (Winter 1987/88). https://www.foreignaffairs.com/articles/asia/1987-12-01/coming-us-japan-crisis.

Paglia, Camille. *Sexual Personae: Art and Decadence from Nefertiti to Emily Dickinson*. New York: Vintage, 1991.

Pascoe, Peggy. *What Comes Naturally: Miscegenation Law and the Making of Race in America*. New York: Oxford University Press, 2009.

"Past Programs." The Woodrow Wilson National Fellowship Foundation. n.d. https://woodrow.org/about/past-programs/ (accessed July 23, 2023).

"Paul and Gracia Hardacre Collection, 1894–1969." Amistad Research Center. Tulane University. 2012. http://amistadresearchcenter.tulane.edu/archon/?p=accessions/accession&id=906.

Pelzel, John. "Japanese Ethnological and Sociological Research." *American Anthropologist* 50, no. 1 (1948): 54–72.

Perun, Pamela J. "The Undergraduate Woman: Theme and Variations." In *The Undergraduate Woman: Issues in Educational Equity*, edited by Pamela J. Perun, 3–144. Lexington, MA: Lexington Books, 1982.

Pharr, Susan J. "Japan's Defensive Foreign Policy and the Politics of Burden Sharing." In *Japan's Foreign Policy After the Cold War: Coping with Change*, edited by Gerald L. Curtis, 235–262. Armonk, NY: M. E. Sharpe, 1993.

———. *Losing Face: Status Politics in Japan*. Berkeley: University of California Press, 1990.

———. *Political Women in Japan: The Search for a Place in Political Life*. Berkeley: University of California Press, 1981.

———. "The Politics of Women's Rights." In *Democratizing Japan: The Allied Occupation*, edited by Robert E. Ward and Sakamoto Yoshikazu, 221–252. Honolulu: University of Hawai'i Press, 1987.

Pharr, Susan J. and Ellis S. Krauss, eds. *Media and Politics in Japan*. Honolulu: University of Hawai'i Press, 1996.

Pharr, Susan J. and Robert D. Putnam, eds. *Disaffected Democracies: What's Troubling the Trilateral Countries?* Princeton: Princeton University Press, 2000.

Pirosh, Robert, dir. *Go for Broke!*. Beverly Hills: MGM Studios, 1951.

Poole, Otis Manchester. *The Death of Old Yokohama in the Great Japanese Earthquake of September 1, 1923.* New South Wales, Australia: Allen & Unwin, 1968.

"Profile of Tsunoda Ryūsaku." Global Japanese Studies, Waseda University. n.d. https://www.waseda.jp/flas/gjs/en/research/profile (accessed January 1, 2023).

Proust, Marcel. *Remembrance of Things Past.* Vols. 1 and 2. New York: Vintage, 1982.

Psaty, Ellen D. "Takeuchi Seihō, A Kyoto Painter." *Japan Quarterly* 3, no. 1 (January–March 1956): 42–53.

"Public Law 94-118." Congress.gov. n.d. https://www.congress.gov/94/statute/STATUTE-89/STATUTE-89-Pg603.pdf (accessed January 1, 2023).

"Public Law 100-383—August 10, 1988." GovInfo. n.d. https://www.govinfo.gov/content/pkg/STATUTE-102/pdf/STATUTE-102-Pg903.pdf (accessed January 1, 2023).

Quimby, Joanne. "Performative Citation and Allusion in Matsuura Rieko's *Oyayubi P no shugyōjidai.*" *Publications of the Association for Japanese Literary Studies* 20 (2019): 87–95.

Quinn, Shelley Fenno. "The Back Side of Noh Chant." In *A Kamigata Anthology: Literature from Japan's Metropolitan Centers, 1600–1750,* edited by Sumie Jones, Adam L. Kern, and Kenji Watanabe, 392–398. Honolulu: University of Hawai'i Press, 2020.

———. "The Back Side of Noh Chant: A Yatsushi 'Takasago.'" In *Imaging/Reading Eros: Proceedings for the Conference, Sexuality and Edo Culture, 1750–1850,* edited by Sumie Jones, 135–138. Bloomington: Indiana University East Asian Studies Center, 1996.

———. *Developing Zeami: The Noh Actor's Attunement in Practice.* Honolulu: University of Hawai'i Press, 2005.

Ramirez-Christensen, Esperanza. *Emptiness and Temporality: Buddhism and Japanese Poetics.* Stanford: Stanford University Press, 2008.

———. "The Essential Parameters of Linked Poetry." *Harvard Journal of Asiatic Studies* 41, no. 2 (December 1981): 555–595.

———. *Heart's Flower: The Life and Poetry of Shinkei*. Stanford: Stanford University Press, 1994.

———. *Murmured Conversations: A Treatise on Poetry and Buddhism by the Poet-Monk Shinkei*. Stanford: Stanford University Press, 2008.

———. "The Operation of the Lyrical Mode in the *Genji monogatari*." In *Ukifune: Love in The Tale of Genji*, edited by Andrew Pekarik, 21–61. New York: Columbia University Press, 1982.

Ramseyer, J. Mark and Frances McCall Rosenbluth. *Japan's Political Marketplace*. Cambridge, MA: Harvard University Press, 1993.

———. *The Politics of Oligarchy: Institutional Choice in Imperial Japan*. Cambridge: Cambridge University Press, 1995.

"A Record of Your Life." *The Memoir Network*. 2019. https://thememoirnetwork.com/category/professional-memoir/.

"Record High Number of Female University Students and Faculty Members in Japan." Nippon.com. September 12, 2022. https://www.nippon.com/en/japan-data/h01427/.

Reis, Irving, dir. *The Bachelor and the Bobby-Soxer*. Hollywood: RKO Pictures, 1947.

Reischauer, Edwin O. "Serge Elisséeff." *Harvard Journal of Asiatic Studies* 20, no. 1/2 (June 1957): 1–25.

———. *The United States and Japan*. Cambridge, MA: Harvard University Press, 1950.

Reischauer, Edwin O. and Serge Elisséeff. *Elementary Japanese for University Students: Vocabularies, Grammars, and Notes*. Cambridge, MA: Harvard University Press, 1942.

Reischauer, Edwin O. and John K. Fairbank. *East Asia: The Great Tradition*. Boston: Houghton Mifflin Company, 1960.

———. *East Asia: Tradition and Transformation*. Boston: Houghton Mifflin Company, 1973.

"Remembering Betty Crocker Homemakers of Tomorrow." General Mills. April 9, 2013. https://www.generalmills.com/news/stories/remembering-betty-crocker-homemakers-of-tomorrow.

"Remembering the Strike." *SF State Magazine* (Fall/Winter 2008). https://magazine.sfsu.edu/archive/archive/fall_08/strike.html.

"Resistance and Revolution: The Anti-Vietnam War Movement at the University of Michigan, 1965–1972." *Michigan in the World*. College of

Literature, Science, and the Arts, University of Michigan. 2015. www.michiganintheworld.history.lsa.umich.edu/antivietnamwar/.

Rexroth, Kenneth. "No Action, No Climax, But Realization." *The New York Times Review of Books*. January 10, 1971: Section BR, 8.

Richie, Donald. *A Lateral View: Essays on Culture and Style in Contemporary Japan*. Berkeley: Stone Bridge Press, 1992.

Ricoeur, Paul. *Freud and Philosophy: An Essay on Interpretation*. Translated by Denis Savage. New Haven: Yale University Press, 1970.

Riesman, David. "Letters to the Editor: The Daily and the Nation." *The Michigan Daily*, May 10, 1961: 1.

Riesman, David, Nathan Glazer, and Reuel Denney. *The Lonely Crowd: A Study of the Changing American Character*. New Haven: Yale University Press, 1961.

Ritt, Martin, dir. *The Outrage*. Beverly Hills: MGM Studios, 1964.

Rizal, Jose. *The Lost Eden*. Translated by Leon Ma. Guerrero. New York: Greenwood Press, 1968.

———. *The Reign of Greed*. Translated by Charles Derbyshire. Berkeley: Mint Editions, 2022.

———. *The Social Cancer*. Translated by Charles Derbyshire. New York: Floating Press, 2009.

———. *The Subversive*. Translated by Leon Ma. Guerrero. New York: Norton, 1968.

Rodd, Laurel Rasplica. *Shinkokinshū: A New Collection of Poems Ancient and Modern*. Leiden: Brill, 2015.

Rodd, Laurel Rasplica with Mary Catherine Henkenius. *Kokinshū: A Collection of Poems Ancient and Modern*. Princeton: Princeton University Press, 1984.

Rosenbluth, Frances McCall. *Financial Politics in Contemporary Japan*. Ithaca: Cornell University, 1989.

Rosenbluth, Frances McCall and Ian Shapiro. *Responsible Parties: Saving Democracy from Itself*. New Haven: Yale University Press, 2018.

Rosenfield, John M. "Japanese Art Studies in America since 1945." In *The Postwar Development of Japanese Studies in the United States*, edited by Helen Hardacre, 161–194. Leiden: Brill, 1998.

———. "Yanagisawa Taka (1926–2003)." *Archives of Asian Art* 54 (2004): 99–100.

Ross, Martha J. "Clio at College Park: The Teaching of History at the University of Maryland, 1859–1968." MA Thesis. University of Maryland, 1978.

Ruch, Barbara. "Chūsei no yūgyō geinin to kokumin bungaku no keisei." In *Muromachi jidai: Sono shakai to bunka* (The Muromachi Period: Its Society and Culture), edited by Toyoda Takeshi and John W. Hall, 325–335. Tokyo: Yoshikawa kōbunkan, 1976.

———, ed. *Engendering Faith: Women and Buddhism in Premodern Japan*. Ann Arbor: University of Michigan Center for Japanese Studies, 2002.

———. "Medieval Jongleurs and the Making of a National Literature." In *Japan in the Muromachi Age*, edited by John W. Hall and Toyoda Takeshi, 279–309. Berkeley: University of California Press, 1977.

———. *Mō hitotsu no chūsei zō* (Another Perspective on Medieval Japan). Kyoto: Shibunkaku Publishers, 1991.

———. "Prologue." In *Women, Rites, and Ritual Objects in Premodern Japan*, edited by Karen M. Gerhart, vii-xvii. Leiden: Brill, 2018.

———. "Transformations of a Heroine: Yokobue in Literature and History." In *Currents in Japanese Literature: Translations and Transformations*, edited by Amy Vladeck Heinrich, 99–116. New York: Columbia University Press, 1997.

———. "A Wreath of Memories." In *In Iris Fields*, edited by Barbara Ruch and Michiyo Katsura, 14–18. Kyoto: Tankōsha, 2009.

———, ed. *Zaigai Nara ehon—chūsei kinsei emaki ezōshi* (Nara Ehon Abroad: Illustrated Literature from Medieval and Early-Modern Japan). Tokyo: Kadokawa shoten, 1981.

Ruddle, Kenneth and Tomoya Akimichi, eds. *Maritime Institutions in the Western Pacific*. Osaka: National Museum of Ethnology, 1984.

Russell, John. "Art Treasures of Shinto." *New York Times*. September 10, 1976: 62.

Ryan, Marleigh Grayer. *Development of Realism in the Fiction of Tsubouchi Shōyō*. Seattle: University of Washington Press, 1975.

———. *Japan's First Modern Novel: Ukigumo by Futabatei Shimei*. New York: Columbia University Press, 1972.

Said, Edward. *Orientalism*. New York: Vintage Books, 1978.

Saitō, Haruo and Gaku Mitsumata. "Bidding Customs and Habitat Improvement for Matsutake (*Tricholoma matsutake*) in Japan." *Economic Botany* 52, no. 3 (October 2008): 257–268.

Sansom, G. B. *Japan: A Short Cultural History.* New York: D. Appleton, 1931.

Sarra, Edith. *Unreal Houses: Character, Gender, and Genealogy in The Tale of Genji.* Cambridge, MA: Harvard East Asian Monographs, 2020.

Sato, Barbara. *The New Japanese Woman: Modernity, Media, and Women in Interwar Japan.* Durham, NC: Duke University Press, 2003.

———. "Tanaka Sumiko and Her Struggle to Create a Gender-Equal Society in Postwar Japan." Association for Asian Studies Conference. Online. March 2022.

Sato, Barbara Hamill. "Moga Sensation: Perceptions of the *Modan Gāru* in Japanese Intellectual Circles during the 1920s." *Gender & History* 5, no. 3 (1993): 363–381.

Sato, Masahiko. *Kyoto Ceramics.* Translated and adapted by Anne Ono Towle and Usher P. Coolidge. Tokyo: Weatherhill, 1973.

Schulman, Frank Joseph. *Japan and Korea: An Annotated Bibliography of Doctoral Dissertations in Western Languages, 1877–1969.* Ann Arbor: University of Michigan Center for Japanese Studies, 1970.

Schumer, Fran. "Japanese Give $1 Million to Harvard." *The Harvard Crimson.* October 13, 1973. https://www.thecrimson.com/article/1973/10/13/japanese-give-1-million-to-harvard/.

Schwartz, Frank J. and Susan J. Pharr, eds. *The State of Civil Society in Japan.* Cambridge: Cambridge University Press, 2003.

Seidensticker, Edward. *Gossamer Years: The Diary of a Noblewoman of Heian Japan.* Rutland, VT: Tuttle Publishing, 1989.

Seki Chiyo. "Kōkyo sugido-e ni tsuite" (Cedar Door Paintings of the Meiji Palace). *Bijutsu Kenkyū* (Art Research) 264 (July 1969): 1–32.

Sekine, Eiji. *"Tasha" no syōkyo: Yoshiyuki Jun'nosuke to kindai bungaku* (Erasure of the "Other": Yoshiyuki Junnosuke and Modern Literature). Tokyo: Keiso shobō, 1993.

Selden, Mark. "Reflections on the Committee of Concerned Asian Scholars at Fifty." *Critical Asian Studies* 50, no. 1 (2018): 3–15.

Senior Editors 1960–61, 1961–62. "An Editorial . . ." *The Michigan Daily.* May 30, 1961. Bentley Historical Library, University of Michigan.

Senior Editors. "An Editorial . . ." *The Michigan Daily* (Ann Arbor, Michigan), September 30, 1961. Bentley Historical Library, University of Michigan.

"Servicemen's Readjustment Act (1944)." *National Archives*. May 3, 2022. https://www.archives.gov/milestone-documents/servicemens-readjustment-act#:~:text=Within%20the%20following%20seven%20years,on%2Dthe%2Djob%20training.

Sharp, Jasper. "70 Years of Rashomon—A New Look at Akira Kurosawa's Cinematic Milestone of Post-Truth." *BFI*. August 25, 2020. https://www.bfi.org.uk/features/rashomon-akira-kurosawa.

Shibusawa, Naoko. *America's Geisha Ally: Reimagining the Japanese Enemy*. Cambridge: Harvard University Press, 2010.

Shiga Daigaku Keizaigakubu Fuzoku Shiryōkan, eds. *Suganoura monjo* (Suganoura's Documents). 2 vols. Hakone: Shiga Daigaku Nihon Keizai Bunka Kenkyūjo, 1960–1967.

Shimada, Daisaku. "Multi-Level Natural Resources Governance Based on Local Community: A Case Study on Semi-Natural Grassland in Tarōji, Nara, Japan." *International Journal of the Commons* 9, no. 2 (September 2015): 486–509.

Shimizu, Yoshiaki. "Shūjirō Shimada (1907–1994)." *Archives of Asian Art* 48 (1995): 99–100.

Shimizu, Yoshiaki and Carolyn Wheelwright. *Japanese Ink Paintings from American Collections, the Muromachi Period. An Exhibition in Honor of Shūjirō Shimada*. Princeton: Princeton University Art Museum, 1976.

Shinji Nobuhiro. *Rakugo wa ikanishite keisei saretaka* (How Did *Rakugo* Originate?). Tokyo: Heibonsha, 1987.

Shinkawa, Kazue. *Selected Poems of Shinkawa Kazue*. Translated and edited by Takako Lento and Yotsumoto Yasuhiro. Sydney: Vagabond Press, 2021.

Shinkei. *Murmured Conversations: A Treatise on Poetry and Buddhism by the Poet-Monk Shinkei*. Translated with annotation and commentary by Esperanza Ramirez-Christensen. Stanford: Stanford University Press, 2008.

———. *Sasamegoto* (Murmured Conversations), edited by Kidō Saizō. In *Nihon koten bungaku taikei* (Japanese Classic Literature Compendium) 66: 119–204. Tokyo: Iwanami shoten, 1961.

Shinozuka Sumiko. *Kagerō nikki no kokoro to hyōgen* (*The Kagerō Diary*: Heart-Mind and Expressions). Tokyo: Benseisha 1995.

Shirane, Haruo, ed. *Early Modern Japanese Literature: An Anthology, 1600–1900*. New York: Columbia University Press, 2002.

Shisō no Kagaku Kenkyūkai. *Tenkō*. 3 vols. Tokyo: Heibonsha, 1959–1962.

Shively, Donald H. "Elizabeth Huff and the East Asiatic Library at the University of California, Berkeley." *Journal of East Asian Libraries* 79 (1986). https://scholarsarchive.byu.edu/cgi/viewcontent.cgi?article=1373&context=jeal.

———. *The Love Suicide at Amijima (Shinjū ten no Amijima): A Study of Japanese Domestic Tragedy*. Harvard: Harvard-Yenching Institute, 1953.

———, ed. *Tradition and Modernization in Japanese Culture*. Princeton: Princeton University Press, 1971.

Shurkin, Joel. "Decrypting the Japanese Cipher Couldn't Prevent Pearl Harbor." *Inside Science*. December 6, 2016. https://www.insidescience.org/news/decrypting-japanese-cipher-couldn%27t-prevent-pearl-harbor.

Silberman, Bernard. *Ministers of Modernization: Elite Mobility in the Meiji Restoration, 1868–1873*. Tucson: University of Arizona Press, 1964.

Slater, David H. and Patricia. G. Steinhoff, eds. *Alternative Politics in Contemporary Japan: New Directions in Social Movements*. Honolulu: University of Hawai'i Press, forthcoming in 2024.

Smethurst, Mae. "Aisukyurosu to Zeami no doramatourugi—Girisha higeki to nō no hikaku kenkyū" (Aeschylus and Zeami's Dramatology: A Comparative Study of Greek Tragedy and Noh). Translated by Kiso Akiko. *Geinōshi kenkyū* (Research on the History of Performing Arts) 127 (1994): 57–60.

———. *Aisukyurosu to Zeami no doramatourugi—Girisha higeki to nō no hikaku kenkyū* (Aeschylus and Zeami's Dramatology: A Comparative Study of Greek Tragedy and Noh). Translated by Kiso Akiko. Tokyo: Hosei daigaku shippankai, 1994.

———. *The Artistry of Aeschylus and Zeami: A Comparative Study of Greek Tragedy and Nō*. Princeton: Princeton University Press, 1989.

———. *Dramatic Action in Greek Tragedy and Noh: Reading with and beyond Aristotle*. Washington, DC: Lexington Books, 2013.

———. *Dramatic Representations of Filial Piety: Five Noh in Translation*. Ithaca: Cornell East Asia Series, 1998.

———. "Euripides in Japan." *Brill's Companion to Euripides*. Vol. 2, edited by Andreas Markantonatos, 1088–1108. Brill: Leiden, 2020.

———. *Girishia higeki to nō ni okeru 'geki tenkai': Arisutoterēsu o tebiki ni, soshite kare o koete* ("Theatrical Development" in Greek Tragedy and Noh: From Aristotle and Beyond). Translated by Watanabe Kōji and Kiso Akiko. Tokyo: Nogami kinen Hōsei daigaku nōgaku kenkyūjo: 2014.

———. "Interview with Miyagi Satoshi." *PMLA* 129, no. 4 (2014): 843–846.

———. "Ninagawa's Production of Euripides' Medea." *American Journal of Philology* 123, no. 1 (2002): 1–34.

Smethurst, Mae and Christina Laffin, eds. *The Noh Ominameshi: A Flower Viewed from Many Directions*. Ithaca: Cornell East Asia Series, 2010.

Smethurst, Richard. *Agricultural Development and Tenancy Disputes in Japan, 1870–1940*. Princeton: Princeton University Press, 1986.

"Smith-Mundt Act." U.S. Agency For Global Media. n.d. https://www.usagm.gov/who-we-are/oversight/legislation/smith-mundt/ (accessed January 1, 2023).

Smith, Robert and Ella Embree Wiswell. *The Women of Suye Mura*. Chicago: University of Chicago Press, 1982.

Smith, Roy, Patricia G. Steinhoff, James A. Palmore, and Milton Diamond. "Abortion in Hawaii, 1970–71." *Hawaii Medical Journal* 32, no. 4 (1973): 213–220.

Smith, Thomas C. *The Agrarian Origins of Modern Japan*. Stanford: Stanford University Press, 1959.

Snyder, Gary. *Mountains and Rivers without End: Poem*. Berkeley: Counterpoint Press, 1996.

Sōgi. *Oi no susami* (Solace in Old Age), edited by Kidō Saizō, 137–186. In *Rengaron shū* (Collection of Renga Treatises) 2. Tokyo: Miya'i shoten, 1982.

Solt, John, ed. *An Episodic Festschrift for Howard Hibbett*. 26 vols. Los Angeles: highmoonoon, 2000–2010.

"Sputnik Spurs Passages of the National Defense Educational Act." United States Senate. n.d. https://www2.ed.gov/about/offices/list/ope/iegps/history.html (accessed October 31, 2022).

SSRC-ACLS Joint Committee on Japanese Studies. *Japanese Studies in the United States: A Report on the State of the Field, Current Resources, and Future Needs*. New York: SSRC-ACLS, 1970.

Stanislavski, Konstantin. *An Actor Prepares*. New York: Theatre Arts, Inc., 1936.

———. *Stanislavsky on the Art of the Stage*. Translated by David Magarshack. London: Faber, 2002.

"Statement of Purpose." Critical Asian Studies. n.d. https://criticalasianstudies.org/about (accessed October 31, 2022).

Statler, Oliver. *Modern Japanese Prints: An Art Reborn*. Rutland, VT.: Charles E. Tuttle Company, 1956.

Steibel, Warren, dir. *Firing Line*. First-Run Syndication and PBS. 34 Seasons. 1966–present.

Steinhoff, Patricia G. "Abortion Data from the Soviet Union" (Summary Report of "Statistical Analysis of Outcomes of Pregnancies," by N. S. Sokolova). *Abortion Research Notes* 1, no. 3 (1972).

———. "Death by Defeatism and Other Fables: The Social Dynamics of the Rengo Sekigun Purge." In *Japanese Social Organization*, edited by Takie Sugiyama Lebra, 195–224. Honolulu: University of Hawai'i Press, 1992.

———, ed. *Directory of Japan Specialists and Japanese Studies Institutions in the United States and Canada, Fourth Edition*. 3 vols. Honolulu: University of Hawai'i Press, 2013.

———, ed. *Directory of Japan Specialists and Japanese Studies Institutions in the United States and Canada, Fourth Edition 2016 Update*. 3 vols. Honolulu: University of Hawai'i Press, 2016.

———, ed. *Directory of Japan Specialists and Japanese Studies Institutions in the United States and Canada, Second Edition*. 3 vols. Ann Arbor: Association for Asian Studies, 1995.

———, ed. *Directory of Japan Specialists and Japanese Studies Institutions in the United States and Canada, Third Edition*. 3 vols. Honolulu: University of Hawai'i Press, 2006.

———. "Doing the Defendant's Laundry: Support Groups as Social Movement Organizations in Contemporary Japan." *Japanstudien* (1999): 55–78.

———. "Finding Happiness in Japan's Invisible Civil Society." *VOLUNTAS: International Journal of Voluntary and Nonprofit Organizations* 26, no. 1 (2015): 98–120.

———, ed. *Going to Court to Change Japan: Social Movements and Law in Contemporary Japan*. Ann Arbor: University of Michigan Center for Japanese Studies, 2014.

———. "Hijackers, Bombers and Bank Robbers: Managerial Style in the Japanese Red Army." *Journal of Asian Studies* 48, no. 4 (1989): 724–740.

———. "Japan: Student Activism in an Emerging Democracy." In *Between Protest and Passivity: Understanding Student Activism in Asia*, edited by Meredith Weiss and Edward Aspinall, 77–105. Minneapolis: University of Minnesota Press, 2012.

———, ed. *Japanese Studies in the United States and Canada: Continuities and Opportunities*. Honolulu: University of Hawai'i Press, 2007.

———, ed. *Japanese Studies in the United States in the 1990s*. Ann Arbor: Association for Asian Studies, 1996.

———, ed. *Japanese Studies in the United States: The View from 2012*. Honolulu: University of Hawai'i Press, 2013.

———, ed. *Japanese Studies in the United States: Directory of Japan Specialists and Japanese Studies Institutions in the United States and Canada*. 2 vols. Ann Arbor: Association for Asian Studies, 1989.

———, ed. *Japanese Studies in the United States and Canada: Continuities and Opportunities*. Honolulu: University of Hawai'i Press, 2007.

———. "Kidnapped Japanese in North Korea: The New Left Connection." *Journal of Japanese Studies* 30, no. 1 (2004): 123–142.

———, ed. *The Kōji Takazawa Collection of Japanese Social Movement Materials at the University of Hawai'i*. 2 vols. Honolulu: University of Hawai'i, 2014.

———. "Makers and Doers: Using Actor-Network Theory to Explore Happiness in Japan's Invisible Civil Society." In *Happiness and the Good Life in Japan*, edited by Wolfram Manzenreiter and Barbara Holthus, 127–145. London: Routledge, 2017.

———. "Mass Arrests, Sensational Crimes, and Stranded Children: Three Crises for Japanese New Left Activists' Families." In *Imagined Families, Lived Families: Culture and Kinship in Contemporary Japan*, edited by Akiko Hashimoto and John Traphagan, 77–110. Albany, NY: State University of New York Press, 2008.

———. "Memories of New Left Protest." *Contemporary Japan, Journal of the German Institute for Japanese Studies* 25, no. 2 (2013): 127–165.

———. "New Notes from the Underground: Doing Fieldwork without a Site." In *Doing Fieldwork in Japan*, edited by Theodore Bestor, Patricia G. Steinhoff, and Victoria Lyon-Bestor, 36–54. Honolulu: University of Hawai'i Press, 2003.

———. *Nihon Sekigunha: Sono shakaigakuteki monogatari* (Japan Red Army Faction: A Sociological Tale). Tokyo: Kawade shobō shinsha, 1991.

———. "No Helmets in Court, No T Shirts on Death Row: New Left Trial Support Groups." In *Going to Court to Change Japan: Social Movements and the Law in Contemporary Japan*, edited by Patricia G. Steinhoff, 17–44. Ann Arbor: University of Michigan Center for Japanese Studies, 2014.

———. "Pregnancy Decisions: Locating the Psychological Factors." *Pacific Health* 4 (1971): 11–15.

———. "Premarital Pregnancy and the First Birth." In *The First Child and Family Formation*, edited by Warren B. Miller and Lucile F. Newman, 180–208. Chapel Hill: Carolina Population Center, 1977.

———. *Shi eno ideologi: Nihon Sekigunha* (Deadly Ideology: The Japanese Red Army Factions). Tokyo: Iwanami bunko, 2003.

———. "Shifting Boundaries in Japan's Criminal Justice System." In *Decoding Boundaries in Postwar Japan: The Koizumi Administration and Beyond*, edited by Glenn D. Hook and Hiroko Takeda, 206–233. London: Routledge, 2010.

———. *Tenkō: Ideology and Societal Integration in Prewar Japan*. New York: Garland Publishing Company, 1991.

———. "Three Myths about the Japanese Red Army: What You Think You Know Is Probably Wrong." Podcast. *DIJ Tokyo*. May 29, 2014. https://www.dijtokyo.org/event/three-myths-about-the-japanese-red-army-what-you-think-you-know-is-probably-wrong/.

———. "Three Women Who Loved the Left: Radical Women Leaders in the Japanese Red Army Movement." In *Re-Imaging Japanese Women*, edited by Anne Imamura, 301–223. Berkeley: University of California Press, 1996.

———. "Transnational Ties of the Japanese Armed Left: Shared Revolutionary Ideas and Direct Personal Contacts." In *Revolutionary Violence and the New Left: Transnational Perspectives*, edited by Alberto Martin Alvarez and Eduardo Rey Tristan, 163–181. London: Routledge, 2016.

———. "The Uneven Path of Social Movements in Japan." In *Activism in Contemporary Japan: New Ideas, Players, and Arenas*, edited by Julia Obinger and David Chiavacci, 27–50. London: Routledge, 2018.

Steinhoff, Patricia G. and Milton Diamond. *Abortion Politics: The Hawaii Experience*. Honolulu: University of Hawai'i Press, 1977.

Steinhoff, Patricia G., James A. Palmore, Roy G. Smith, Donald E. Morisky, and Ronald Pion. "Pregnancy Planning in Hawaii." *Family Planning Perspectives* 7, no. 3 (1975): 138–142.

Steinhoff, Patricia G., Roy G. Smith, and Milton Diamond. "The Characteristics and Motivations of Women Receiving Abortions." *Sociological Symposium*, no. 8 (1972): 83–89.

Sterne, Laurence. *The Life and Opinions of Tristram Shandy, Gentleman*. Edited by Judith Hawley. New York: W. W. Norton, 2018.

Students for Fair Admissions, Inc. v. President and Fellows of Harvard College. 20-1199 (2023). https://www.supremecourt.gov/opinions/22pdf/20-1199_hgdj.pdf.

Sturges, John, dir. *The Magnificent Seven*. Hollywood: United Artists, 1960.

Sugawara no Takasue no Musume. *The Sarashina Diary*. Translated with an introduction by Sonja Arntzen and Itō Moriyuki. New York: Columbia University Press, 2014.

Suzuki, D. T. *Zen Buddhism: Selected Writings of D. T. Suzuki*. New York: Doubleday, 1956.

Suzuki, Michiko. "Reading and Writing Material: Kōda Aya's Kimono and Its Afterlife." *The Journal of Asian Studies* 76, no. 2 (2017): 333–361.

Suzuki, Reiji, Suehisa Kuroda, Kazuya Masuda, Tetsuya Imakita, Motoko Shimagami, Naohiko Noma, and Kazuo Ando. "Traditional Skills and Knowledge Inherited from Japanese Swidden Cultivation: Toward Restoration of Degraded Satoyama Forests." *Journal of Agroforestry and Environment* 5 (2011): 71–74.

Suzuki, Satoko and Junko Mori, eds. "Our Challenges and Triumphs: Female Asian Faculty in Leadership Positions in US Colleges and Universities." *Japanese Language and Literature* 56, no. 1 (April 2022): 209–285.

———. "Our Stories as Female Asian Leaders: Introduction." *Japanese Language and Literature* 56, no. 1 (April 2022): 211–217.

Suzuki Seijin, dir. *Shunpuden* (Story of a Prostitute). Tokyo: Nikkatsu, 1965.

Synnott, Marcia. "A Friendly Rivalry: Yale and Princeton Universities Pursue Parallel Paths to Coeducation." In *Going Coed: Women's Experiences in Formerly Men's Colleges and Universities, 1950-2000*, edited by Leslie Miller-Bernal and Susan L. Poulson, 111–150. Nashville: Vanderbilt University Press, 2004.

Takagi, Kiyoko. *Hachinin no jotei* (The Eight Female Emperors of Japan). Tokyo: Taimeidō, 2002.

———. *Hana akari* (The Light of the Cherry Blossoms). Tokyo: Tanka Shimbunsha, 1978.

———. "Last Chance: Tanka by Takagi Kiyoko." Translated and introduced by Amy V. Heinrich. In *IUC Gold: Celebrating Fifty Years of Excellence*, edited by Indra A. Levy, 84. Yokohama: Inter-University Center for Japanese Language Studies, 2013.

———. *Ōkashō* (Selections on Blossoms). Tokyo: Tanka Shimbunsha, 1984.

———. "Religion in the Life of Higuchi Ichiyō." *Japanese Journal of Religious Studies*. 10/2–3 (1983): 123–147.

———. *Sakura futatabi* (Cherry Blossoms Once Again). Tokyo: Tanka Shimbunsha, 1990.

———. *Sakura no shizuku* (Cherry Tree Droplets). Tokyo: Tanka Shimbunsha, 2006.

———. *Sakura: Sono sei to zoku* (Cherry Blossoms: Sacred and Profane). Tokyo: Chūō Kōronsha, 1996.

———. *Yūzakura* (Evening Cherry Blossoms). Tokyo: Tanka Shimbunsha, 1998.

Takazawa, Kōji. *Destiny: The Secret Operations of the Yodogō Exiles*. Edited and translated by Patricia G. Steinhoff, et al. Honolulu: University of Hawai'i Press, 2017.

———. *Frēmu appu* (Frame-Up). Tokyo: Shinchōsha, 1983.

———. *Heishitachi no yami* (The Soldiers' Darkness). Tokyo: Marujusha, 1982.

———. *Shukumei*. Tokyo: Shinchōsha, 1998.

———, ed. *Zenkyoto Graffiti*. Tokyo: Shinchōsha, 1984.

Takazawa, Kōji and Kazunari Kurata, eds. *Shinsayoku riron zenshi, 1957–1975* (The Complete History of New Left Theory, 1957–1975). Tokyo: Shinchōsha, 1984.

Takazawa, Kōji, Masayuki Takagi, and Kazunari Kurata. *Shinsayoku Nijūnenshi* (Twenty-Year History of the New Left). Tokyo: Shinchōsha, 1981.

Takazawa, Kōji, Shiro Sanaga, and Yoichi Matsumura, eds. *Sengō kakumei undō jiten* (Dictionary of the Postwar Revolutionary Movement). Tokyo: Shinchōsha, 1985.

Takeuchi, Melinda. *Taiga's True Views: The Language of Landscape Painting in Eighteenth-Century Japan*. Stanford: Stanford University Press, 1992.

Tamura Norie. "Umi o tsukuru, mori o tsukuru: Gyomin no morizukuri to chiiki kanri" (Making Seas and Making Forests: Fisherfolk's Afforestation and Community Management). In *Ekorojii to komonzu: Kankyō gabanansu to chiiki jiritsu no shisō* (Ecology and Commons: Environmental Governance and the Idea of Local Self-Reliance), edited by Mitsumata Gaku, 129–141. Kyoto: Kōyō shobō, 2014.

Tamura, Norie and Hein Mallee. "Japan's Fishery Forest Movement as a Sustainability Transition." 4th APSAFE (Asia Pacific Society for Agricultural and Food Ethics) Symposium Proceedings. December 2020: 114–118.

Tamura, Ryūichi. *World without Words*. Translated and edited by Takako Uchino Lento. Champaign, IL: Ceres Press, 1971.

Tamura Taijirō. *Shunpuden* (Biography of a Prostitute). Tokyo: Tōhōsha, 1966.

———. *Tamura Taijirō senhū*. Vols. 1–4. Tokyo: Nihon toshokan sentā, 2005.

Tanabe, Willa. *Paintings of the Lotus Sutra*. Tokyo: Weatherhill, 1988.

Taniguchi Senkichi, dir. *Akatsuki no dassō* (Escape at Dawn). Tokyo: Tōhō, 1950.

Tanikawa, Shuntarō. *The Art of Being Alone: Poems 1952–2009*. Translated and edited by Takako Lento. Ithaca: Cornell East Asia Series, 2011.

———. *Ordinary People*. Translated by Takako Lento. Sydney: Vagabond Press, 2021.

Tanizaki Jun'ichirō. "The Bridge of Dreams." In *Seven Japanese Tales*. Translated by Howard Hibbett, 67–106. New York: Berkley Publishing Group, 1965.

———. *Byōjoku no gensō* (Sickbed Fantasies). In *Tanizaki Jun'ichirō zenshū* (Collected Works of Tanizaki Jun'ichirō). Vol. 4, 155–183. Tokyo: Chūō kōronsha, 1983.

———. *In Black and White: A Novel*. Translated by Phyllis I. Lyons. New York: Columbia University Press, 2018.

———. *In Praise of Shadows: A Prose Elegy*. English adaption by Edward Seidensticker. *The Atlantic* (January 1955).

———. *Memoir of Forgetting the Capital*. Translated by Amy V. Heinrich. New York: Yushodo and Columbia University Press, 2010.

———. "Sickbed Fantasies." *Byōjoku no gensō*. Translated by Phyllis Lyons. Unpublished manuscript. n.d.

———. *Some Prefer Nettles*. Translated by Edward Seidensticker. New York: Alfred A. Knopf, 1955.

Tawara Machi. *Salad Anniversary*. Translated by Juliet Winters Carpenter. Tokyo: Kodansha International, 1990.

Teeuwen, Mark and Kate Wildman Nakai, eds. *Lust, Commerce, and Corruption: An Account of What I Have Seen and Heard by an Edo Samurai*. New York: Columbia University Press, 2014.

ten Grotenhuis, Elizabeth. *Japanese Mandalas: Representations of Sacred Geography*. Honolulu: University of Hawai'i, 1999.

Tenny, Francis B. "History of the Commission." Japan-US Friendship Commission. Washington, DC. 1995.

Terayama Shūji. *The Crimson Thread of Abandon: Stories.* Translated by Elizabeth L. Armstrong. Honolulu: University of Hawai'i Press, 2014.

———. *When I Was a Wolf.* Translated by Elizabeth L. Armstrong. Kumamoto: Kurodahan Press, 2018.

Teters, Barbara J. "Press Freedom and the 26th-Century Affair in Meiji Japan." *Modern Asian Studies* 6, no. 3 (1972): 337–351.

"Text of the Constitution and Other Important Documents." National Diet Library. 2003–2004. https://www.ndl.go.jp/constitution/e/etc/c06.html.

"Theatre Fete to Aid Japanese Students." *New York Times.* January 18, 1959: 91.

Thomas, Roger K. *Counting Dreams: The Life and Writings of the Loyalist Nun Nomura Bōtō.* Ithaca: Cornell East Asia Series, 2021.

———. *The Way of Shikishima: Waka Theory and Practice in Early Modern Japan.* Lenham, MD: University Press of America, 2007.

"The Three Priests." Translated by Donald Keene. In *Anthology of Japanese Literature: From the Earliest Era to the Mid-Nineteenth Century*, edited by Donald Keene, 322–333. New York: Grove Press, 1955.

"A Timeline of Women at Yale." Office of Public Affairs and Communications. Yale University. 2023. https://celebratewomen.yale.edu/history/timeline-women-yale#:~:text=November%201968,November%204th%2C%20Coeducation%20week%20commences.

"Title IX." RAINN. 2023. https://www.rainn.org/articles/title-ix.

"Title IX of the Educational Amendments of 1972." US Department of Justice. 2015. https://www.justice.gov/crt/title-ix-education-amendments-1972.

"Title IX of the Educational Amendments of 1972." US Department of Health and Human Services. 2023. https://www.hhs.gov/civil-rights/for-individuals/sex-discrimination/title-ix-education-amendments/index.html#:~:text=Title%20IX%20of%20the%20Education%20Amendments%20of%201972%20(Title%20IX,activity%20receiving%20federal%20financial%20assistance.

"Title IX: Tracking Sexual Assault Investigations." *Chronicle of Higher Education.* January 16, 2023. http://projects.chronicle.com/titleix/.

"Tojo's Daughter in U.S. to Study." *New York Times.* June 16, 1959: 26.

"Tokyo 1964 Creates Lasting Legacies." International Olympic Committee. March 30, 2021. https://olympics.com/en/news/tokyo-1964-creates-lasting-legacies.

Tokyo University of Arts University Art Museum. *Amamonzeki: A Hidden Heritage: Treasures of the Japanese Imperial Convents*. Tokyo: The Sankei Shimbun, 2009.

Totman, Conrad. "English-Language Studies of Medieval Japan: An Assessment." *Journal of Asian Studies* 38, no. 3 (May 1979): 541–551.

———. *The Green Archipelago: Forestry in Preindustrial Japan*. Berkeley: University of California Press, 1989.

———. *An Environmental History*. London: I. B. Tauris, 2014.

Toyomune, Minamoto. *Illustrated History of Japanese Art*. Translated by Harold G. Henderson. Kyoto: K. Hoshino, 1935.

Treat, John Whittier. "Japan Is Interesting: Modern Japanese Literary Studies Today." *Japan Forum* 30, no. 3 (2018): 421–440.

"Treaty of Peace with Japan." *Taiwan Documents Project*. n.d. http://www.taiwandocuments.org/sanfrancisco01.htm (accessed November 10, 2022).

"Treaty of Peace with Japan (with Two Declarations)." No. 1832. United Nations, April 28, 1952. https://treaties.un.org/doc/Publication/UNTS/Volume%20136/volume-136-I-1832-English.pdf.

Tregaskis, Richard. *Guadalcanal Diary*. New York: Random House, 1943.

Troost, Kristina Kade. "Common Property and Community Formation: Self-Governing Villages in Late Medieval Japan, 1300–1600." PhD Diss. Harvard University, 1990.

———. "Peasants, Elites, and Villages in the Fourteenth Century." In *The Origins of Japan's Medieval World: Courtiers, Clerics, Warriors, and Peasants in the Fourteenth Century*, edited by Jeffrey P. Mass, 91–109. Stanford: Stanford University Press, 1997.

Tsubouchi Shōyō. *Shōsetsu shinzui* (The Essence of the Novel). Tokyo: Nihon Kindai Bungakkan, 1968.

Tsujimoto Isao, ed. *Kawaranai sora: Nakinagara warainagara* (The Sky Unchanged: Tears and Smiles). Tokyo: Kōdansha, 2014.

Tsukioka Kōgyo, the Art of Noh, 1869–1927. University of Pittsburgh. 2011–2022. https://exhibit.library.pitt.edu/kogyo/.

Tsunoda Ryūsaku, Wm. Theodore deBary, and Donald Keene. *Sources of Japanese Tradition*. Vol. I. New York: Columbia University Press, 1958.

———. *Sources of Japanese Tradition*. Vol. II. New York: Columbia University Press, 1964.

Tsurumi Kazuko. *Social Change and the Individual: Japan Before and After Defeat in World War II*. Princeton: Princeton University Press, 1970.

Tsutsumi Harue. "Kanadehon Hamlet." Translated by Faubian Bowers with David W. Griffith and Hori Mariko. *Asian Theatre Journal* 15, no. 2 (1998): 181-229.

———. *Kanadehon Hamuretto* (Hamlet without Tears). Tokyo: Bungei Shunjusha, 1993.

Tyler, Royall. *Japanese No Drama*. New York: Penguin Classics, 1993.

Uchida, Yoshiko. *We Do Not Work Alone: The Thoughts of Kanjiro Kawai*. Kyoto: Folk Art Society, 1953.

Uchikawa Yoshimi. *Masu mejia hōseisakushi kenkyū* (Research on the History of Mass Media and Legal Policy). Tokyo: Yūhikaku, 1989.

Uchino, Takako. "Western Influence on Modern Japanese Poetry." *Texas Quarterly* (spring 1968): 128–138.

"United States Code Title 22: Chapter 33." US Department of Education. n.d. https://www2.ed.gov/about/offices/list/ope/iegps/fulbrighthaysact.pdf (accessed January 1, 2023).

University of Hawai'i. "The Takazawa Collection of Social Movement Materials at the University of Hawai'i." June 14, 2001. http://www.takazawa.hawaii.edu.

University of Minnesota. "Commencement Program, 1949." University of Minnesota Digital Conservancy. n.d. https://hdl.handle.net/11299/57572 (accessed January 2, 2023).

US Census Bureau. "Remembering Pearl Harbor: A Pearl Harbor Fact Sheet." n.d. https://www.census.gov/history/pdf/pearl-harbor-fact-sheet-1.pdf (accessed June 27, 2023).

US Equal Employment Opportunity Commission. "The Equal Pay Act of 1963." n.d. https://www.eeoc.gov/statutes/equal-pay-act-1963 (January 2, 2023).

"Vietnam War: Causes, Facts, and Impact." *History.com*. October 29, 2009. https://www.history.com/topics/vietnam-war/vietnam-war-history.

"Vietnam War US Military Fatal Casualty Statistics." *National Archives*. August 23, 2022. https://www.archives.gov/research/military/vietnam-war/casualty-statistic.

Vogel, Ezra. *Japan as Number One: Lessons for America*. Cambridge, MA: Harvard University Press, 1979.

———. *Japan's New Middle Class*. Berkeley: University of California Press, 1963.

Vogel, Suzanne. "The Professional Housewife: The Career of Urban Middle Class Japanese Women." *Japan Interpreter* 1, no. 12 (1978): 16–43.

Wada Atsuhiko. *Ekkyōsuru shomotsu: hen'yōsuru dokusho kankyō no naka de*. (Books Across Borders: The Past and Present of Readers' Circumstances). Tokyo: Shin'yōsha, 2011.

Wagatsuma Sakae. *Kaisei minpō yowa: Atarashii ie no rinri* (Stories of the Revised Civil Code: The Ethics of the New Household). Tokyo: Gakufū shoin, 1949.

Waley, Arthur, trans. *Japanese Poetry: 'The Uta.'* London: Percy Lund, Humphries, and Co., 1965.

———, trans. *The Pillow Book of Sei Shōnagon*. New York: Grove Press, 1960.

———, trans. *The Tale of Genji*. New York: Modern Library, 1960.

Walker, Linda Robinson. "The Last Dean of Women." *Michigan Today.* Summer 2002: 6–9.

Walker, Sam. "National Defense Education Act Includes Loyalty Oath and Bar to Civil Rights Enforcement." *Today in Civil Liberties History, September 2, 1958*. 2014. http://todayinclh.com/?event=92581958-national-defense-education-act-loyalty-oaths-required-for-students.

Walthall, Anne. *The Human Tradition in Modern Japan*. Lanham, MD: Rowman & Littlefield, 2002.

———. "Hyakushō ikki monogatari no shiteki bunseki" (An Historical Analysis of Peasant Uprising Narratives). *Rekishi hyōron* (Critical History) no. 394 (February 1983): 2–19.

———. The Life Cycle of Farm Women in Tokugawa Japan." In *Recreating Japanese Women, 1600–1945*, edited by Gail Lee Bernstein, 42–70. Berkeley: University of California Press, 1991.

———. *Peasant Uprisings in Japan: A Critical Anthology of Peasant Histories*. Chicago: University of Chicago Press, 1991.

———. *Social Protest and Popular Culture in Eighteenth Century Japan*. Tuscon: University of Arizona Press, 1986.

———. *The Weak Body of a Useless Woman: Matsuo Taseko and the Meiji Restoration*. Chicago: University of Chicago Press, 1998.

Walton, Andrea. *Women at Indiana University: 150 Years of Experiences and Contributions*. Bloomington, Indiana: Indiana University Press, 2022.

Wang, Ching-hsien. *The Bell and the Drum: Shih Ching as Formulaic Poetry in an Oral Tradition.* Berkeley: University of California Press, 1974.

Ward, Robert, ed. *Political Development in Modern Japan.* Princeton: Princeton University Press, 1968.

Watanabe Yōzō. *Iriai to hō* (Common Access and the Law). Tokyo: University of Tokyo Press, 1972.

Watanabe Yōzō and Hōjō Hiroshi. *Rin'ya iriai to sonraku kōzō: Kitafuji sanroku no jirei kenkyū* (Common Access to Forests and Village Structure: A Case Study from the North Fuji Slope). Tokyo: University of Tokyo Press, 1975.

Watt, Lori. *When Empire Comes Home: Repatriation and Reintegration in Postwar Japan.* Cambridge, MA: Harvard East Asian Monographs, 2010.

Watts, Jonathan. "Dead Writer's Knife Is in Japan's Heart." *The Guardian.* November 24, 2000. https://www.theguardian.com/world/2000/nov/25/books.booksnews.

Webb, Herschel. *Research in Japanese Sources: A Guide.* New York: Columbia University Press, 1965.

Webster, Ian. "The U.S. Dollar Has Lost 92% of Its Value Since 1949." Official Data Foundation. January 13, 2022. https://www.in2013dollars.com/us/inflation/1949#:~:text=%24100%20in%201949%20has%20the,power%22%20as%20%241%2C247.05%20in%202023.

Weigle, Edith. "Pottery Made by Japanese Is Fascinating." *Chicago Daily Tribune.* September 8, 1956: 23.

Wellek, René. *A History of Modern Criticism: 1750–1950: American Criticism: 1900–1950.* New Haven: Yale University Press, 1986.

Wellek, René and Austen Warren. *Theory of Literature.* New York: Harcourt, Brace, and Company, 1948.

Wellerstein, Alex. "Counting the Dead at Hiroshima and Nagasaki." *Bulletin of the Atomic Scientists.* August 4, 2020. https://thebulletin.org/2020/08/counting-the-dead-at-hiroshima-and-nagasaki/.

White, James W. *IKKI: Social Conflict and Political Protest in Early Modern Japan.* Ithaca: Cornell University Press, 1995.

White, Lynn Jr. "The Historical Roots of Our Ecologic Crisis." *Science* 155, no. 3767 (March 1967): 1203–1207.

White, Merry. *Coffee Life in Japan.* Berkeley: University of California Press, 2012.

———. *Cooking for Crowds.* New York: Basic Books, 1975.

———. *Cooking for Crowds*. Revised Edition. Princeton: Princeton University Press, 2013.

———. *The Japanese Educational Challenge: A Commitment to Children*. New York: Free Press, 1985.

———. *The Japanese Overseas: Can They Go Home Again?*. New York: Free Press, 1988.

———. *The Material Child: Coming of Age in Japan and America*. Berkeley: University of California Press, 1993.

———. *Noodles Galore*. New York: Basic Books, 1976.

———. *Perfectly Japanese: Making Families in an Ear of Upheaval*. Berkeley: University of California Press, 2003.

White, Merry I. and Barbara Malony. "Preface." *Proceedings of the Tokyo Symposium on Women*, edited by Merry White and Barbara Malony, n.p. Tokyo: International Group for the Study of Women, 1979.

———, eds. *Proceedings of the Tokyo Symposium on Women*. Tokyo: International Group for the Study of Women, 1979.

White, Morton and Lucia Perry White. *Journeys to the Japanese, 1952–1979*. Vancouver: University of British Columbia Press, 1986.

Whitehouse, Winfred and Eizo Yanagisawa, trans. *Tale of Lady Ochikubo: A Tenth Century Novel*. New York: Anchor Doubleday, 1971.

"Who Were the Codebreakers?" Bletchley Park.org. February 23, 2002. https://bletchleypark.org.uk/our-story/who-were-the-codebreakers/.

Wigen, Kären. "Common Losses: Transformations of Common Land and Peasant Livelihood in Tokugawa Japan, 1603–1868." MA Thesis. University of California, Berkeley, 1985.

———. "The Geographic Imagination in Early Modern Japanese History: Retrospect and Prospect." *Journal of Asian Studies* 51, no. 1 (1992): 3–29.

Wigmore, John Henry, ed. *Law and Justice in Tokugawa Japan: Materials for the History of Japanese Law and Justice under the Tokugawa Shogunate 1603–1867*. 19 vols. Tokyo: University of Tokyo Press, 1967–1986.

Wimpee, Rachel. "A Brief History of the Ford Foundation's Support for Scholarships and Fellowships." Ford Foundation. September 9, 2016. https://www.fordfoundation.org/news-and-stories/stories/posts/a-brief-history-of-ford-foundations-support-for-scholarships-and-fellowships/.

"Women at Harvard." Harvard University Archives. October 7, 2022. https://guides.library.harvard.edu/c.php?g=1108872&p=8085578.

Woolf, Virginia. *A Room of One's Own*. New York: Penguin Classics, 2014.

Wurgaft, Benjamin Aldes and Merry White. *Ways of Eating*. Berkeley: University of California Press, 2023.

"The Yamabushi: The Holy Men of Shugendō." KCP International. November 28, 2019. https://www.kcpinternational.com/2019/11/yamabushi/.

Yamashita Utako. *Iriai rin'ya no hen'yō to gendaiteki igi* (Transformations and Contemporary Significance of Common Access Forests). Tokyo: University of Tokyo Press, 2011.

Yamashita, Utako, Kulbhushan Balooni, and Makoto Inoue. "The Effect of Instituting 'Authorized Neighborhood Associations' on Communal (Iriai) Forest Ownership in Japan." *Society and Natural Resources* 22, no. 5 (April 2009): 464–473.

Yamamoto, Tsunetomo. *Hagakure: Way of the Samurai*. Translated by William Scott Wilson. New York: Kodansha International, 1992.

Yamamoto Yūzō, ed. *Nihon shōkokumin bunko* (An Anthology for Young Citizens of Japan). Tokyo: Shinchōsha,1935–1937.

Yano, Christine. *Pink Globalization: Hello Kitty's Trek across the Pacific*. Durham, NC: Duke University Press, 2013.

Yasumaru Yoshio. *Yasumaru Yoshio shū* (Collected Works of Yasumaru Yoshio). 6 vols. Tokyo: Iwanami shoten, 2016.

Yeats, W. B. *At the Hawk's Well*. Overland Park, KS: Digireads, 2011.

Yiengpruksawan, Mimi. "Japanese Art History 2001: The State and Stakes of Research." *The Art Bulletin* 83, no. 1 (March 2001): 105–122.

Yim Tse, ed. *Karma of the Brush 1995*. Vancouver: Chinese and Japanese Calligraphy Exhibition Committee, 1995.

———, ed. *Karma of the Brush: An Exhibition of Contemporary Chinese and Japanese Calligraphy*. Vancouver: Chinese and Japanese Calligraphy Exhibition Committee, 1985.

Yokomichi Mario. "Nō *Takahime*" (The Hawk Princess, a Noh Play). *Shingeki* 15, no. 1 (January 1968): 124–130.

Yosa Buson. *Collected Haiku of Yosa Buson*. Translated by W. S. Merwin and Takako Lento. Port Washington: Copper Canyon Press, 2013.

Yosano Akiko. *Midaregami* (Tangled Hair). Tokyo: Shufu no tomo sha, 1973.

Yoshida, Shigeru. "Japan's Place in Asia." *The Atlantic* (January 1955): 101–102.

Yoshihara, Mari, ed. *Unpredictable Agents: The Making of Japan's Americanists during the Cold War and Beyond*. Honolulu: University of Hawai'i Press, 2021.

Yu, Isaac. "Frances Rosenbluth, Who Redefined Japanese Comparative Politics, Dies at 63." *Yale Daily News*. November 28, 2021. https://yaledailynews.com/blog/2021/11/28/frances-rosenbluth-who-redefined-japanese-comparative-politics-dies-at-63/.

Zhou, Peter, ed. *Collecting Asia: East Asian Libraries in North America, 1868–2008*. Ann Arbor: Association for Asian Studies, 2010.

Zwerman, Gilda and Patricia G. Steinhoff. "The Remains of the Movement: The Role of Legal Support Networks in Leaving Violence while Sustaining Movement Identity." *Mobilization: An International Journal* 17, no. 1 (2012): 67–84.

———. "When Activists Ask for Trouble: State-Dissident Interactions and the New Left Cycle of Resistance in the United States and Japan." In *Repression and Mobilization*, edited by Christian Davenport, Hank Johnston, and Carol Mueller, 85–107. Minneapolis: University of Minnesota Press, 2005.

Zwerman, Gilda, Patricia G. Steinhoff, and Donatella della Porta. "Disappearing Social Movements: Clandestinity in the Cycle of New Left Protest in the United States, Japan, Germany, and Italy." *Mobilization* 5, no. 1 (2000): 85–104.

Index

#MeToo 16-17, 334-335
20th Century Japan Research Awards 107

Abbess Kasanoin Jikun 75-78
Abbess Mugai Nyodai 74-79
Abe, Carl 359-360
Abe Kōbō 73, 216, 381
Abe Yūji 38
Abington Friends School 63
abortion 189-191, 427
academic memoirs 17
An Account of What I Have Seen and Heard (Seji kenbunroku) 357-358
Actors' Analects (Yakusha rongo) 450
Adichie, Chimamanda Ngozi 5
affirmative action 7, 26 n. 24, 14-15, 161, 171-172, 175, 486-487
Africa 329-331
Age Discrimination Act of 1975 487
Agency for Cultural Affairs (Bunkachō) 274
Agent Orange 490
Akabori Ryōri Gakuen 315
Akahata (Red Flag) 405
Akehashi Daiji 380
Akimichi Tomoya 348
Akiyama Ken 261
Akutagawa Ryūnosuke 387, 391
Albee, Edward 122
Algren, Nelson 118

Allen, Judith 212
Allied powers 474
Allinson, Gary 348
American Association of University Professors 15
American Council of Learned Societies (ACLS) 21-23 n. 5, 480, 488; see Social Science Research Council
American Field Service (AFS) 354, 432, 480, 482
American Friends Service Committee (AFSC) 6, 62, 64
American Oriental Society 470
American President Lines 93, 480
American Society of Environmental History (ASEH) 345
Americans with Disabilities Act of 1990 487
Amino Yoshihiko 435
Amlin, Vince 208
Ampo protests 18, 140, 184, 187, 209, 449-450, 475, 485-486
Andersson, Krister 347
Angelou, Maya 391
Anthology of Japanese Literature: From Earliest Era to the Mid-Nineteenth Century 65, 244, 290-292, 484
An Anthology for Young Citizens of Japan (Nihon shōkokumin bunko) 205

anti-miscegenation laws 491-492
antisemitism 26, 311, 313; see Judaism
Aquino, Benigno 466 n. 3
Arai Haruseki 356
Arakawa Toyozō 39
Arase Yutaka 433-434
Ariga Chieko 215
Arimitsu Kyōichi 36, 46 n. 12
Armstrong, Elizabeth 207-208
Army Specialized Training Program 51
Arnold, Matthew 168, 173
Arntzen, Sonja 3, 18, 253-266, 484, 490
art history, field of 269, 273
Art Institute of Chicago 39, 227
Asama-Sansō siege 200-201 n. 18, 493
Ashio Copper Mine 452-453
Asian American civil rights 495
Asian American studies 11
Association of Teachers of Japanese (ATJ) 95
Association for Asian Studies (AAS) 8, 87, 167, 179 n. 11, 194, 470-471; conferences 20-21 n. 2, 246, 286, 364, 391; directories 179-180 n. 12, 194-195; presidents 167, 171
The Atlantic 484
atomic bombings 86, 138, 454, 473-374, 488; see Hiroshima, "Fat Man," "Little Boy," Nagasaki
autobiographies 16, 150, 215, 254

baby boom generation 7; see *dankai no sedai*
The Bachelor and the Bobby-Soxer 238
Baerwald, Hans 341
Baez, Joan 457
Bai Juyi 463
Baldwin, James 122
Bamisaiye, Anne 373
Bandō Kunio 200-201 n. 18
Bando Mariko 372

Bao Dai 459, 489-490
Barbour Scholarships 93
Barnard College 26 n. 24, 91, 243, 293
Barthes, Roland 220, 503 n. 69
Bartholomew, Jim 283-284
"Bashō Boom" 395-397
Bassuk, Ellen 212
Bataan Death March 455-456, 467 n. 8
Bazzell, Tokiko 286
Beardsley, Richard 172
Beasley, William 89
Beichman, Janine 10, 159, 289-302, 477, 484, 496
Beijer Institute 346
Bell, Marvin 117
Bellah, Robert 187, 199 n. 9
Benedict, Ruth 13, 145, 155, 168; see *Chrysanthemum and the Sword*
Berry, Father Thomas 167
Berry, Margaret 167
Berry, Mary Elizabeth 1, 9, 15, 22, 165-180, 220, 409
Bernstein, Gail 59, 364-366, 374
Beruit 492-493
Bestor, Vicky Lyon 409, 412, 415 n. 13
Bethe, Monica 76, 160
Betty Crocker Homemaker of Tomorrow 183, 198 n. 1
bibliographer 303-307
Bibliography of Asian Studies 470
Bien, David 171
Billy Ireland Cartoon Library and Museum (The Ohio State University) 280, 284
Bingo Province 405
biographies 44, 172, 211, 284, 294, 296, 300, 303-307, 363, 393-394, 496
Birnbaum, Phyllis 303-308, 458, 496
Bischoff, Friedrich 389
Black Lives Matter 16
Blacker, Carmen 94, 424-425

blacklist 481-482
Bloch, Marc 362
Bockscar 473
Bocobo, Jorge 446 n. 3
A Book of Women Poets from Antiquity to Now 124
Borgen, Robert 172, 379
Borton, Hugh 91-92, 104
Boston University 318
Boxer, Charles 172
Bradstock, Tim 403
Brazell, Karen 5, 159-161, 170-171, 239, 246, 252 n. 6, 385, 391, 409
Breen, John 357
Briggs, Ellis O. 38-39
Briggs, Lucy 38
British Museum 227
Britt, Elizabeth 168
Brokaw, Miriam 426
Brown, Delmer 171
Brown, Janice 263
Bryn Mawr College 11, 34
bubble economy 123, 221, 337, 497
Buckley Jr., William F. 220
Bucknell University 96
Buddhism 380, 418, 420; monks 418; nuns 78, 83; women's impact on 76-77
Buddhist art 269-270
Bund 492
bungo 459
Burnshaw, Stanley 222
Butler, Ken 379

C. V. Starr East Asian Library 247-251, 279-280
Cable Act 491
calligraphy 54-55, 71, 83, 255, 259-260, 263, 446, 449
Cambodia 44, 444, 490
Campbell, John 409

Campbell, Robert 218, 228
Camus, Albert 456
Canada 3, 8, 11, 13, 20 n. 2, 44, 112-114, 194, 255-260, 262-263, 472, 474, 493-494
Carleton College 402-403
Carnegie Foundation 41, 45, 479-480
Carpenter, Juliet Winters 377-382, 484, 489, 496
Carter, Stephen 461, 467 n. 11
Castile, Rand 267, 274
Caswell, Lucy Shelton 284; *see Billy Ireland Cartoon Library and Museum*
Cathedral of Saint John the Divine in New York 250
Catholic University of Louvain 268
chawan 3
Chen, Shou-Yi 384
Chester Beatty Library 71
Chevray, Keiko 117, 127 n. 3
Chevray, René 117
Child, Julia 318
childbirth 268, 272, 276, 423
Childs, Maggie 66
Chin, Vincent 495
China 8, 9, 32, 35, 38, 42, 86, 88, 91, 92, 97, 99, 118, 127, 161, 171, 176-177, 197, 257, 259-261, 269, 302, 314-315, 360, 363, 388, 394, 402-403, 444, 448, 457, 474, 475, 478, 488, 490-491; Cultural Revolution 255
Chinatown 254
Chinese language 254-255, 280-281, 379, 388, 448
Chino Kaori 270
Choi, Kyeong-Hee 210
Chomsky, Noam 69
Christ, Carol 174
Christensen, Steen 458

Christofides, Constantine 217
The Chrysanthemum and the Sword 13-14, 145, 155, 168; *see Benedict, Ruth*
Chrysler Corporation 495
Chūō Kōron-sha publishing company 434
Chūshingura 340, 349 n. 1
CIA 93, 199 n. 4, 481-482,
Citrin, Jack 342
Civil Affairs Training Schools (CATS) 8
Civil Censorship Detachment (CCD, 1945–1952) 393
civil code of the 1890s 475
Civil Information and Education Section (CI&E) 386, 479
Civil Rights Act 170-171, 487, 489
civil rights laws 7, 14, 170, 487-488, 489
civil rights movement 7, 18, 95, 183-184, 329-330, 418-419, 491, 496
civil society 333-334
"Civilization and Enlightenment" (*bunmei kaika*) 436
Clapp, Frederick Mortimer 241
Claremont Graduate University 41, 384
Clark Air Force Base 444
Clark, General Mark W. 38
Clark, Timothy 227
Clemens, Diane 173
close reading 204-205
coeducation 10, 25-26 n. 24, 26 n. 25
Colby College 389-390
Cold War 6, 7, 9, 18, 169, 280, 329, 475, 481, 489, 491, 494
Cole, Robert 172
Cole, Susan 239
collaboration 19, 20-21 n. 3, 226-228, 263-264

Collcutt, Martin 282
"collective active problem" 344
College Art Association 41-42
colonialism 443-444, 447-448, 454-457
Colorado College 250
Colton, Hattie Masuko Kawahara 6, 88
Colton, Kenneth 6, 88
Columbia University 8, 10, 14, 23 n. 8, 25-26 n. 24, 65, 66, 72-75, 80-81, 83, 90-92, 158-159, 162, 244, 246-247, 280-282, 291-293, 323, 325-327, 335, 371, 385-386, 432
Committee of Concerned Asian Scholars 169, 490-491; *Bulletin of Concerned Asian Scholar* 491
commons 344-345, 347-349, 406
Commons Research Group (Japan) 349
communism 7, 88, 183, 187-188, 204, 444, 456-457
The Communist Manifesto 311
comparative literature 213-214, 220
Conant, Ellen P. 9, 11, 29-46, 475, 477, 478, 480
Conant, Theodore R. 44
"Conference on Modern Japan" 169, 179 n. 5
Constitution, Japanese 105, 189, 332, 394, 449, 474-476; Article 9 476; Article 14 332, 476; Article 24 332; memorial day 476
Consulate-General of Japan in Chicago 119
Cook, Walter W. S. 30
cooking 315-316
Cooper, Michael 176
Cornell University 125, 160, 240, 385, 435
Cort, Louise 268, 271
Cosmos Club 239

INDEX : 579

Costanza, Bob 346
Council on East Asian Librarians (CEAL) 282, 287, 409, 413, 485
COVID-19 15, 20-21 n. 3
Cox, Gary 347
Craig, Albert M. 168-169, 342, 345-346, 355-356, 365-366, 403
Cranston, Edward 170, 462, 465
Creeley, Robert 122
Critical Language Scholarship Program 479
Crockett, Lucy Herndon 45, n. 1
Crowley, James 364
cultural exchange programs 475
"cultural literacy" 27 n. 35
cultural studies 220
Curlew River 297
Curtis, Paula 22-23 n. 5

Daitō Bunka University (DBU) 298
Dakota Wesleyan University 121
D'Alesandro Jr., Thomas 238
Danforth Graduate Fellowship for Women 269, 314
dankai no sedai 7
Davidson, LeRoy 41-42
Davis, Christina 336
Davis, Natalie 171, 173
Davis, Sandra 106
Dawn to the West 244
day care (in Japan) 373, 375 n. 6, 423, 438
Dazai Osamu 18, 129, 136, 141 n. 3, 382 n.2
de Bary, Wm Theodore 63, 166
de Grazzia, Victoria 437
Deleuze, Gilles 216
Denmark 462, 465
DePauw University 364
Detroit 86, 182

Diamond, Mickey 190
Dibble, Lewis 223
Dickinson College 237
Didijer, Vlado 172
Dien, Albert 161
Dilworth, David 167
Dixon, Yoriko 412, 416 n. 19
Dobbins, James 82
Doggerel Tsukubashū (*Inu Tsukubashū*) 463
Doi Takeo 316
Doing Fieldwork in Japan 426-427
Domier, Sharon 266 n. 5
Donald Keene Center of Japanese Culture 72-74, 225, 229, 240
Donovan, Maureen 10, 18, 21-23 n. 5, 167, 279-288, 412, 485, 494
Dore, Robert 371
Doshisha University 35, 349, 380, 381, 390, 477
Douglass, Frederick 95
Dove, Kay 106
Dower, John 394
Drifting Fires 296-299; *see Noh*
Du Bois, Cora Alice 158, 471
Du Fu 463
Dudden, Arthur 88, 108 n. 9
Duke University 220, 340, 343-349, 404, 405, 412-413
Duke University Libraries 407-411
Dulles, John Foster 483
Dumbarton Oaks 239
Durt, Hurbert 273
Duus, Peter 342, 363
dyslexia 49

Earhart, Amelia 50
Earlham College 63
earthquakes 136-137, 140
East Asian librarianship 247-248, 279-287, 408-411

East Asian Libraries Cooperative World Wide Web 286
East-West Bookstore 386
East-West Center 147, 190-191, 369-371, 374
Eco, Umberto 216
Edgerton, Winifred 26 n. 24
Edmonds, Harry 483
Edo (city) 226, 236 n. 80
An Edo Anthology: Literature from Japan's Mega-City, 1750–1850 226
Egami Namio 340
Eihei Dōgen 386
Eisenhower, Dwight D. 90, 209, 485, 486
Eisenstein, Elizabeth 171
Elam, Diane 212
Elementary Japanese for College Students 23 n. 8, 91, 133-134
Elementary Japanese for University Students 157
Elison, George (Jurgis Elisonas) 223, 389
Elisséeff, Serge 6, 23 n. 8, 91, 133, 157
Elliot, Charles 381
Elliot, Thomas 379, 385
Else, Gerald 238
Emergencies Act 472
Emmerich, Michael 213, 226
Emory University 330
emperor 362, 452, 470, 475-476, 492, 496; anti-emperor protests 194, 391; female 178
Emperor Daigo 162
Emperor Emeritus Akihito 64, 184, 385
Emperor Meiji 54
Empress Emerita Michiko 78, 184
Empress Nagako 476
Enchi Fumiko 381
Engle, Paul 116-118, 120

Enoch Arden 206
Enola Gay 473-474
Enoshima 312
Entenmann, Bob 403
Eoyang, Eugene Chen 227
Equal Employment Opportunity Commission (EEOC) 390, 487-488
Equal Employment Opportunity Law (Japan) 438
Equal Pay Act 170-171, 487
Ericson, Joan 250, 252 n. 10
Erlanger, Margaret 208
Eshin-ni 82
etoki (the telling of pictures) 69-70
European Consortium for Political Research (ECPR) 196
Evert, Walter 238
Executive Order 9835 481
Executive Order 9066 471-472; see internment
Executive Order 10925 486-487
Executive Order 11246 487, 489
existentialism 456
Expatriation Act of 1907 491
Experiment in International Living 154-155, 482-483
explication de texte 205
Expo '70 257, 458, 493
Expo '85 298

faculty clubs 10, 68, 69, 92, 151, 165, 342, 489
Fahs, (Charles) Burton 40
Fairbank, John K. 9, 144, 156, 171, 366
The Family of Man 483-484
Far Eastern Association 8, 480; see Association for Asian Studies
The Far Eastern Quarterly 8, 470; see *Journal of Asian Studies*
Farge, William 235 n. 72
Farris, Wayne 403

Fass, Paula 173
"Fat Man" 474
Feeny, David 346
Feldhaus, Anne 167
feminism 5-6, 95, 210, 211-213, 258, 260-263, 317, 335, 418; second-wave feminism 190-191, 300, 391, 496-497; third-wave feminism 497
Ferejohn, John 347
Field, Norma 394
First Tokyo Symposium on Women (Kokusai Josei Gakkai) 11, 317-318, 331, 336, 497
Fischer, Felice 295
Fiske, Mother Adele 167
Fister, Patricia 76
Fitzsimmons, Thomas 116, 124, 127 n. 2, 299
Flanigan, Clifford 222-223
Flindt, Willi 297-298
Fong, Wen 276
food anthropology 318
Ford, Barbara Brennan 167
Ford Foundation 6, 9, 11, 44, 65, 88, 90, 92, 179 n. 5, 330, 479-480
Ford, Gerald 495-496
Foreign Service 106, 144, 341, 370
Foreign Service Institute 6, 88, 373-374
foreign wives (study of) 373
Fort Bragg 168
Fort Sill 383
Foucault, Michel 220
France 48, 150, 167, 172, 297, 456, 474, 489-490
Franklin, Cynthia G. 18
Freedman, Alisa 1-2; role in the project 20-21 n. 3
Freegard, Ruth 501 n. 44
French, Cal 172
Frick, Helen Clay 241
Friedan, Betty 96

Fujikawa Fumiko 166, 291
Fujin gahō (*Women's Pictorial*) 439
Fujin kōron (*Woman's Review*) 90, 434-435, 439
Fujin sekai (*Women's World*) 434
Fujokai (*Women's Sphere*) 434-435
Fukaya Katsumi 362
Fukuda Naomi 12, 93, 100, 177, 483
Fukumitsu Sasuke and Hiroe 425-426; see *Kurozumikyō*
Fulbright Program 9, 11-12, 13, 33-35, 38, 40-41, 52-54, 56, 88-91, 98-99, 108 n. 4, 117-119, 192, 194, 245, 284, 372-373, 404, 421, 477-480, 496
Fulbright, J. William 477
Fulbright-Hays 11, 293, 478
Fundamental Law of Education 475-476

Gabriola Island 262
Gaddis, William 122
gagaku 80-81
Gager, John 424-425
Gakushuin University 263, 477
Gangloff, Eric 247
geisha 135, 136, 452
gender 2, 4-6, 45, 65-66, 68-69, 73-75, 82-83, 123, 150-152, 171, 173, 174-175, 191-192, 206, 210, 211, 238-239, 254, 257-258, 273, 312, 316, 332, 334-336, 421, 423, 428, 432, 453-454, 473, 486-488, 491, 496-497; conventions 175, 300; discrimination 269, 334-335, 423; harassment 334, 388, 391, 438; violence 175
General Headquarters (GHQ) 475
generations 7-8, 24 n. 13, 318
Geneva Accord of 1954 489
Gentles, Margaret (Peggy) 39-40, 46 n. 13

Georgetown University 105, 330, 374
Gerow, Aaron 286
gesaku 218, 228, 233 n. 48
Gill, Mary-Louise 240
Ginza Crossing 30-31
Ginza Hageten 312
Gion 443
Giovanni, Nikki 122
Girisha Higeki Kenkyūkai 240
Glassman, Hank 83
Gluck, Carol 19, 102, 105, 107, 282, 371, 394, 437, 439
Go for Broke! 395
Godshall, (Wilson) Leon 34-35, 45 n. 3
Gogaku Kyōiku Kenkyūjo at Waseda University 446, 455
Good, Hiroyuki 285
Gordon, Andrew 407-408, 410
Gordon, Beate Sirota 394
Gordon, Joseph 394
Gordon W. Prange Collection 97, 104, 106-107, 392, 394
The Gossamer Years 261
Gōtō Ryūki 219
Gotoh Museum 227
Government Aid and Relief in Occupied Areas (GARIOA) 479, 496
Gōzō Yoshimasu 120-121, 126
Grayer Ryan, Marleigh 91-92, 94-95, 158, 291
Great Depression 88
Great Kantō Earthquake 137, 138, 140, 433, 436
Great Society Project 342
Greek tragedy in Japan 240
Grilli, Elise 37
Grilli, Peter 156, 275-276
Grove Press 484
Guadalcanal Diary 86
Gunji Masakatsu 208
gunki (battle tales) 69

Guth, Christine M. E. 267-278, 470, 480
Guy, Kent 403
Gyokuonhōsō 474

Habu Junko 221
Habun Association 390, 395
Hadley, Eleanor 105, 482
Haga Tōru 94, 219
Hagakure 452
haibun 389-390
Haibun Association 390, 395
haiku 122, 125-126, 222, 248, 293-296, 395, 397, 460
Hall, Ivan 296
Hall, John Whitney 70, 106, 145, 360-361
Hamada Shōji 39
Hamamatsu 432
Hambrick, Charles 418, 420
Hamlet 206
Hammond, Ellen 412, 415 n. 18
Hanazono University 257
Haneda Airport 145, 154, 312, 327, 477, 488
Hanley, Susan B. 9, 14, 143-152, 176, 221, 341, 487, 488
Hansen, Arthur 238
Hara Hiroko 372, 374-375 n. 2
Harada Takashi 284
Haraguchi Arai Tsuru 26 n. 24
Hardacre, Gracia Manspeaker 418-419, 428-429 n. 4
Hardacre, Helen 8, 13, 21-23 n. 5, 372, 417-429, 488, 490
Hardacre, Paul Hoswell 418-419
Hardin, Garrett 344
Hare Krishnas 457
Harootunian, Harry 87, 132, 137, 216, 342, 362, 435
Hatakeyama Yoshio 199 n. 5

Hatfield, Glenn 217
Harvard University 8, 10, 24 n. 17, 25 n. 24, 54, 60 n. 5, 67-68, 144, 156-157, 168-170, 186-187, 268-269, 311, 314, 318, 321, 334, 336-337, 342, 355, 403-404, 461, 470, 471, 473, 481, 494, 498 n. 4
Harvard-Yenching Institute 470
Hausa language 326
Hauser, William 363
Hawai'i 26 n. 27, 35, 48-51, 156, 189-193, 471-472, 489, 491
Hawai'i Agricultural Experiment Station 50
Hayakawa Monta 219
Hayakawa S. I. 87
Hayami Akira 146
Hayasaka Keizō 348
Hayashi Masahide 349
Hayashi Razan 170
Hayden, Tom 184, 198 n. 2
Hearst, Patty 458
hegemony 2
Heian period women writers 18, 261, 387, 465
Hein, Laura 409, 412
Heinrich, Amy V. 11, 18, 21-23 n. 5, 243-252, 254, 409, 412, 415 n. 12, 497
Hello Kitty 317
hibakusha 454, 474
Hibbett, Howard 157, 170, 217-219, 222, 224, 225, 227, 462
hibutsu 273
Hideyoshi 170, 172, 173
high-growth era 336-337
Higher Education Act 24 n. 12, 485
Highland Park 182
Higuchi Ichiyō 178, 300, 379
Hikawa Maru 12, 34, 52, 354, 384, 432, 477, 480

Hikawa Shrine 480
The Himang, Weekly News Magazine 42
hippies 457
Hirabayashi Hatsunosuke 436
Hiraga Gennai 218
Hiramatsu Yoshirō 356, 358
Hirano Sōjō 257-258
Hirohito 86, 194, 474; visit to the United States 496
Hiromi Arisawa Memorial Award 239
Hironaka, Wakako 317
Hiroshima 138, 404-405, 454, 473-474, 488
Hiroshima Maidens 90, 474
Hiroshima University, School of Integrated Arts and Sciences (Sōgō Kagakubu) 404, 414 n. 5
history, field of 172
Hitomaro Collection 244
Hitotsubashi University 404, 435
Ho Chi Minh 489
Ho, Franklin 91
Hochstedler, Carol 295
Hoesterey, Ingeborg 215
Hoff, Frank 297-298
Hogarth, William 212
Hōjō Hiroshi 348
Hōjō Masako 11, 361
hokku 462
homestay 12, 35-36, 44, 53, 145, 154-155, 185, 210, 370, 386-387, 403, 432, 446-447, 450-451
Honda 283, 285
Hong Kong 44, 259, 313
honne 310
Honolulu 48-50, 147, 174, 188, 194
Hoover Institution, Stanford 100-101, 409
Horton, Mack 461, 467 n. 11
Horwitz, Brewster 484
Hoshino Fumihiro 396-397

Hōshō School 208, 230 n. 9; see Noh
Hoskins, Marilyn 347
Hosokawa Moritatsu 32, 33
Hotta Mitsuo 249-250
House Committee on Un-American Activities 481
housewives 258, 317, 372-373
Hsia, C. T. 281
Huang Zunxian 263-264
Huff, Elizabeth 177
Hughes, H. Stuart 172
Hunt, Herold C. 44
Hunt, Lynn 173
Hunter College 95-96
Huntington, John C. 283
Hurston, Zora Neale 211
Hurvitz, Leon 257
hyakuin 467 n. 10, 468 n. 12

Ianfu ("comfort women") 393-394
Ide Sachiko 312
Ide Yoshinori 343
Ihara Saikaku 462
Iida Shotaro 257
Ijima Tsutomu 36
Ikeda Hayato 486
Ikkyū Sōjun 256-257, 260, 263, 264
Imamura, Anne E. 369-376, 496
Imamura Yuki 370-373
imperial convents 78-79
Imperial Hotel 51, 379
imperial universities 476
Important Cultural Properties (jūyō bunkazai) 274-275, 470
Inaga Shigemi 219
Inagaki Tetsurō 450
India 35, 52, 56-57, 59, 87, 101, 268, 313-314, 348, 365, 384, 458, 478
Indian art 41
Indian National Army 52, 56-57, 365

Indiana University 96-97, 207-208, 211, 215, 218-221, 223-224, 226-227, 229, 284, 346, 388-390, 392, 395
Indonesia 43-44, 366, 395, 475, 494
Information and Education Act (Smith-Mundt Act) 478
Inoue Ken 434
Inoue Makoto 348
Inoue Shōichi 219
Inoue Teruko 438
Inouye, Charles 225, 228
Institute of Journalism and Communication Studies (Shimbun kenkyūjo), University of Tokyo 433
Inter-University Center for Japanese Language Studies (IUC, Stanford Center) 13, 113, 134, 145-146, 162, 170, 177, 185, 197, 251 n. 3, 294-295, 354, 379, 386-387, 432-433, 486; see also Stanford Center
Interchange of Persons Board 478
interdisciplinary study 71, 79
International Association for the Study of Common Property (IASC) 347, 349, 413
International Christian University (ICU) 101, 144-145, 157, 185-186, 340-342, 384-386, 390
International Comparative Literature Association 219
International Harvester Dissertation Writing Fellowship 362
International House of Japan (I-House) 11, 58, 98; library 58, 93, 101, 177, 412
International Houses 322-327, 458-459
International Labor Organization (United Nations) 421
International Research Center for Japanese Studies (Nichibunken) 219, 284

INDEX : 585

International School of the Sacred Heart in Tokyo 166, 168
International Writing Program 117-118, 120-121; see University of Iowa
internment 6, 472-473; United States 472, Canada 472-473
interpreting 121-124
intertext 216; see overtext
Institute for International Education (IIE) 478
Institute for Medieval Japanese Studies (IMJS) 69
"Instrument of Surrender" 474
Iowa Writer's Workshop 11, 116-118, 193, 478
Iran-Iraq War 494
Iranian Revolution 494
Irokawa Daikichi 435
Iser, Wolfgang 216
Ishida Takeshi 187, 192
Ishigaki Rin 299
Ishijima Takako 250
Ishikawa Eisuke 221
Ishikawa Takeyoshi 435
Ishikawa Takeyoshi Memorial Library 434-435
Israel 191, 494
Issei 6
Itagaki Nenjirō 40
Itasaka Gen 157, 170
Itō Kentarō 380
Itō Moriyuki 262-263
Itō Sei 118, 128 n. 4
Iversen, Torben 347
Iwakura Mission 89, 94, 127 n. 1
Iwami Reika 19-20; see Song of the Sea C
Iwao Sumiko 317, 372, 374-375 n. 2
Iwasaki Haruko 217
Izumi Kyōka 381, 382 n. 5
Izutsu (*The Well-Curb*) 292

Jakubs, Deborah 407
Jansen, Marius 106, 167, 276, 282
Japan-America Student Conference 87
Japan as Number One: Lessons for America 123, 337; see Vogel, Ezra
"Japan Bashing" 495
Japan boom in the 1980s 259-260
Japan Business Federation 71
Japan Economic Seminar 146-147
Japan English Teaching (JET) Program 132
Japan Foundation (Kokusai Kōryū Kikin) 10, 11, 21-22 n. 5, 101, 106, 126, 176, 194, 247, 248, 250, 257, 258, 261, 283-284, 286, 318, 337, 343, 363, 364, 372, 383-284, 389, 409, 488, 493-494
Japan Ground Self-Defense Force 12, 56, 492
Japan House Gallery 267
Japan Library Association (Nihon Toshokan Kyōkai) 286
Japan National Press Club 433
Japan Society 8, 71-72, 122, 156, 274-276, 470, 481, 484, 494
Japan Travel Bureau (JTB) 69-70, 443
Japan-US Friendship Act (1975) 10, 495-496
Japan-US Friendship Commission (JUSFC) 104, 247, 284, 286, 409, 486, 495-496
Japan-US Friendship Commission Prize for the Translation of Japanese Literature 10-11, 125, 126, 240, 299, 381, 496
Japan Women's University (Nihon Joshi Daigaku) 476, 501 n. 44
Japan's Cultural Properties Commission (Bunkazai Hōgo Iinkai) 270

586 : WOMEN IN JAPANESE STUDIES

Japan's New Middle Class 310; see Vogel, Ezra
Japan's surrender 474
Japanese company histories 285
Japanese Exhibition House at the Museum of Modern Art 12, 90, 290, 483-484
Japanese language 133-134, 370, 448-449, 455
Japanese popular culture 259, 337-338, 436
Japanese Socialist Party 438-439
Japanese Studies 7-16, 21-23 n.5, 79, 82-83, 129-133, 137, 150-152, 161, 168-169, 183, 192, 194, 217-219, 291, 309-310, 328, 336-339
Jenkins, Kana 106
Johnson, Barbara 211
Johnson, Chalmers 342, 348
Johnson, David G. 281
Johnson, Lyndon B. 342, 444, 465, 486-487, 488, 490
Joint Committee for Japanese Studies, American Council of Learned Societies and the Social Science Research Council (ACLS-SSRC) 9-10, 160, 488
Jones, Frank W. 224
Jones, Hazel 98, 259
Jones, Sumie 5, 11-12, 82, 203-236, 471, 477, 478-479, 486, 498
Jordan Schnitzer Museum of Art 20
Jorden, Eleanor Harz 91, 104, 177, 471
jōruri 162-163, 208
Josei kaizō (*Women's Reconstruction*) 434
Journal of Asian Studies 8, 470
Journal of Japanese Studies 14, 148-149, 176, 226
Judaism 11, 31; see antisemitism
judo 12, 112, 323-328, 332, 488

Junior Scholastic Magazine 86
Justice, Donald 117

kabuki 99, 119, 208, 224, 227, 345, 450
Kabukiza Theater 442, 450
Kades, Charles 394
Kagerō Diary (*Kagerō nikki*) 261-262
Kageyama Haruki 267, 271, 274
Kaiser, Anafu 123
Kakinomoto no Hitomaro 244
Kakumaru-ha 450-451
Kamakura (city) 37, 248
Kamakura period, 74-75, 405, 469
Kamigata 226, 236 n. 79, 236 n. 80
Kamigata Anthology: Literature from Japan's Metropolitan Centers, 1600-1750 226
Kamimura Masana 348
Kanadehon Hamlet 208
Kanashige Toyo 40
Kanba, Michiko 486
kanbun 463
Kaneko Hideo 97-98
Kaneko Kinjirō 462-465, 467 n. 11
kanji 132, 159, 448-449
kanshi 256, 260
Kanze Kojirō Nobumitsu 293
Kanze Motomasa Jurō 297
Kanze School 209, 230 n. 9; see Noh
Kaplan, Michael 419-420
Karukaya 163
Karukaya Dōshin 70
Karukayasan Saikōji 163
Kashiwaki Mari 126-127
Katagiri Yuzuru 120
Kataoka Shikō 260, 263-264
Katō Shūichi 256-257
Katō Tōkurō 40
Kaufman, Laura 269
Kawabata Yasunari 12, 456; Nobel Prize 12, 120, 378, 484, 488-489

Kawai Sora 395
Kawakami Hajime 366
Kawamoto Kōji 219
Keene, Donald 6, 65, 67, 91, 118, 126, 135, 158-160, 162-163, 218, 224, 244-246, 249-250, 291-296, 385-386, 484; Noh seminar 162, 293, 296, 296
Keihin-Ampo Kyoto 493
Keio University 113, 114, 146, 284, 317, 357
Kelleher, Theresa 167
Kelly, Colin P. 86
Kennedy, John F. 485, 486, 487; assassination 96
Kent State University 490
Kenzai 462
Keogh, Bridget 168
Kerkham, Eleanor 102, 107, 373, 383-401, 488
Kern, Adam 228
Key, Margaret 216-217
Kibei 6
kibyōshi 228, 233 n. 48
Kida Shrine 2, 13
Kidder Jr., Edward 35, 340, 385
Kikōbun 389
Kim, Jaewon 39, 46 n. 12
Kimball, Fiske 30
Kimbrough, Keller 66
kimono 221, 316, 327, 442-443
Kinema Club 286
King Jr., Martin Luther 98, 329-330
Kinkakuji 442
Kishi Nobusuke 209, 486
Kishi Tetsuo 222
Kiso Akiko 239-240
Kitagawa, Joseph Mitsuo 418, 420, 423
Kitao Masanobu 212; *see Santō Kyōden*
Kiyomizudera 442
Knopf, Alfred A. 90, 381, 484

Knox, Bernard 239
King, Winston 418
Kishi Tetsuo 222
Kobayashi Tadashi 227
Koch, Adrienne 173
Kōchi Saburō 433
Kōda Aya 221
Kogishi (Yamaguchi) Noriko 93
Koide Izumi 285-286, 412
Kokedera 442
Kokinshū 256, 459-460
Kokubungaku 454
Komaba Ryūgakusei Kaikan dormitory 446
Komai Akira 360
Komatsu Kazuhiko 219
Kominz, Larry 389
Kondō Yūzō 40
Korea 38-40, 42-44, 340; women 394
Korean War 42, 88, 93, 99, 480-481
Korean Contemporary Paintings 43
Koyama, Michael 150
Krakusin, Alfred R. 42
Kristeva, Julia 216
Krokodil 280
Ku, Miree 412, 416 n. 19
Kubota Fuyuhiko 170
Kumamoto Kenjirō 41
Kume Kunitake 94
Kurahashi Ken 210
Kuramochi Shigehiro 405-406, 407, 414-415 n. 7
Kuramochi Yasuko 405-406, 414 n. 8
Kurata Bunsaku 273
Kuroda Chika 476
Kurosawa Akira 98, 222-224, 340
Kurozumi Munetada 426
Kurozumikyō 425-426
Kwok, Michiko 177
kyōgen 69, 217, 386

Kyoto 19, 31-32, 35-39, 44, 52, 66, 70, 72, 76, 78, 93, 113, 170, 221, 226, 236 n. 79, 236 n. 80, 258, 271, 273, 275, 276, 284, 292, 305, 316, 340, 357, 360, 391, 403, 442-446, 460, 465-466, 483
Kyoto Folk Art Movement 36-40, 45 n. 11
Kyoto University 66
Kyoto University's Jinbun Kagaku Kenkyūjo (Institute for Research in the Humanities) 257
Kyūen Renraku Sentā (Support Contact Center) 192
Kyushu Institute of Technology 121
Kyushu University 117, 122

Labonte, Alison Raab 412, 416 n. 19
Lacan, Jacques 215
LaCure, Jon 235 n. 72
Ladurie, Emmanuel Le Roy 172
Lamotte, Étienne 268
land reform 475
Lao Tzu: Tao Te Ching 255
Laos 444, 490
Law and Justice in Tokugawa Japan 357-358
Leach, Bernard 46 n. 11
Lebra, Joyce Chapman 2, 9, 12, 13, 94, 47-60, 364-365, 478, 492
Lebra, William 51-52
Ledyard, Gari 247
Lee Hyung Pyo (Hyeong-pyo Lee) 44
Lento, Takako 1, 5, 11-12, 13, 21-22 n. 3, 115-128, 470, 477, 479, 489, 496
Levering Act 481
Lévi-Strauss, Claude 214, 419
Levinson, Joseph 171
Lewis, Robert 474
Liberal Democratic Party 90, 228

Library of Congress 92, 95, 281, 410, 470
Lidin, Olof 462
The Life and Opinions of Tristram Shandy, Gentleman 209
Lifton, Robert Jay 187
Lijphart, Arend 348
Linden, Allen 88, 91
Lindsley and Masao Miyoshi Prize 225, 229
literary theory 214-216
literary studies 220-221
"Little Boy" 474
Link, Arthur 257
Lock, Margaret 14, 111-114, 488
Lod Airport 191
London 88-90, 112
lost decades, lost generation 337, 497-498
The Lotus Sutra 423, 463
The Love Suicides at Jordan River 208
Loving v. Virginia 491
Lowie, Michael 424
Lucky Dragon No. 5 (*Daigo Fukuryū-Maru*) 90, 482
Lynn, Richard John 263
Lyons, Phyllis I. 10, 18, 129-142, 474, 496

MacArthur, Douglas 97, 134, 240, 383, 444, 456, 475
MacArthur, Douglas II 155
MacDonald, Keiko 238-239
Madama Butterfly 53, 126
Madame Chrysanthéme 53
Maekawa Kunio 483
Maher, Catherine 168
Maier, Victor 68
maiko 93, 443
Mailer, Norman 457

INDEX : 589

Makemson, Maud 501 n. 44
Makino Mamoru 286
Makita Raku 476
Manabe Shunshō 273
manga 280, 283, 284, 286
Manhattan Project 473
Manhattanville College 10, 166-167, 280
Manila 442, 444, 447, 449, 454-456, 457, 465, 466
Manila Hotel 444
Manila's Alliance Française 456
Maples (Dunn), Mary 89
Marcos, Ferdinand 444, 465, 466 n. 3
Marlene Mayo Graduate Paper Prize 471
Marlene J. Mayo Oral Histories Collection 106
Marshall, Byron 387
Martin, Samuel 155
Maruyama Masao 66
Mary Ingraham Bunting Institute 211
Masaoka Shiki 293-294
Masataka Uwayokote 360
mass culture 434-436
mass magazines 434-437, 439
Matisoff, Jim 157-158
Matisoff, Susan 9, 15, 23 n. 8, 165-180, 246, 252 n. 6, 295, 482, 487, 488
Matsuda Shizue 284, 287 n. 2
Matsuda Yoshiyuki 397
Matsudaira Chiaki 239
Matsukaze 293
Matsumoto Shigeharu 483
Matsumoto Takeshi 221
Matsuo Bashō 388- 391, 395-397, 460; celebrations for 395-397; see *"Bashō Boom"*
Matsuura, Katherine 412-413, 415 n. 19
Matsuura Reiko 213

Matsuya Department Store 30, 31
Mayer-Oakes, Thomas Frank 87, 89
Mayo, Marlene J. 9, 20, 23 n. 8, 85-110, 373, 391, 471, 474, 478, 480, 482, 487, 488; *see Marlene Mayo Graduate Paper Prize, Marlene J. Mayo Oral Histories Collection*
McBride, Katherine 41
McCarthy, Joseph 88, 481-482; Army-McCarthy Hearings 88
McClain, Yoko Matsuoka 20
McCormack, Elizabeth 168
McCubbins, Matt 347
McCullough, Helen Craig 6, 178, 180 n. 20, 224, 387, 459-461, 471; seminars 459-461
McCullough, William 6, 178, 224, 387, 459-461; seminar 459
McDermott, Robert A. 167
McKean, Margaret 14, 339-352, 404, 406-408, 414 n. 4, 480, 481
McKinnon, Richard 217
medieval village society 404-405
Medine, David 223
Medlicott, William N. 89
Meech, Julia 268
Mei, Y. P. 118
Meier, Golda 191
Meiji art 40-41, 270
Meiji Newspaper and Periodical Archives (Meiji Shimbun Zasshi Bunko) 433
Meiji Restoration 89, 98, 167, 436
memoir 16; difference with autobiographies 16; *see academic memoirs, professional memoirs, scholarly memoirs*
menopause 113
mentorship 413
Meredith, Dianne 340
Merwin, W. S. 124-127

Meservey, Sabra Follett 25-26 n. 24
Metropolitan Museum of Art 167, 268, 274, 470
Metropolitan Opera 322, 327
The Michigan Daily 183-184, 186
Michener, James A. 38
Middlebrook, Diane 211
Middlebury College 280
Mihara Toko 251
Mikado 323
Military Intelligence Service Language School (MISLS) 471, 484
Miller, Arthur 118
Miller, Roy Andrew 134, 145
Miller, Rush 241
Minami Hiroshi 435-437
Minato Ward Museum of Folk Materials 221
Miner, Earl 214, 464
Minichiello, Sharon 99
Minidoka War Relocation Center 6
Ministry of Education, Culture, Sports, Science, and Technology 15; *see* Monbushō scholarships
Misawa Air Force Base 166
Mishima Yukio 12, 120, 211, 290, 365, 378-379, 389, 456, 460, 484; suicide 57-58, 395, 452, 492; visit to Waseda University 451-452; *For Young Samurai* (*Wakaki samurai no tame ni*) 451-452; *Patriotism* 491; Sword Society (Tate no kai) 492
Mitamura Engyo 221
Mitchell, Breon 224
Mitchell, Robert Cameron 336
Mitsubishi Heavy Industries 494
Mitsui Bunko 177
Mitsumata Gaku 349
Miwa Kai 67, 91, 247
Miyagi Satoshi 240
Miyaji Hiroshi 387

Miyakawa Tetsuo 35
Miyakawa Yukie 259
Miyako 92
Miyazaki, Fumiko 357
Miyoshi, Masao 214
Mizumura Minae 382 n. 8
Mizutani Nobuko and Osamu 385
modanizumu 436
"modern girl"(*modan gāru*) 436
Modern Japanese Literature: An Anthology 290, 484
"modernization theory" 9, 14, 179 n. 5, 326-327
Moffitt, Emiko 100-101
Monbushō scholarships (MEXT) 271, 362, 446; *see* Ministry of Education, Culture, Sports, Science, and Technology
Monumenta Nipponica 14, 94, 176
Moretti, Laura 66
Mori Atsushi 397
Mori Sumio 122
Mori Tsuneo 493
Morita Kan'ya XII 208; *see* kabuki
Morley, James 96-97, 326, 328, 335
Morris, Ivan 66, 118, 262
Morse, Anne Nishimura 273
Mosakusha 193
Mostow, Joshua 72
Mother and Child 37; *see* Onchi Kōshirō
motherhood 257-258, 268-269, 294, 317-318, 347, 373, 381, 405, 438
Mount Fuji 385
Mount Kōya 65, 70, 405
Mount Holyoke College 6, 41, 45, 88
Mulroney, Brian 272
Multi-Volume Sets Project 248, 409
Munakata Shikō 290
Murahashi Katsuko 286
Murasaki Shikibu 64, 304-305, 460, 465

Murase, Miyeko 158, 268
Murmured Conversations (*Sasamegoto*) 462
Muromachi period 70-71, 270, 467 n. 11, 469
Murota Takeshi 349
Murrow, Edward R. 88, 482
music 80-81

Nagahara Keiji 404-405, 414 n. 3
Nagai Michio 73, 185, 191
Naganuma Naoe 170, 385
Nagara Susumu 378
Nagasaki 53-54, 454, 473-474
Nagata Hiroko 200-201, 493
Najita Tetsuo 360-361
Nakahara Jun'ichi 206
Nakai, Kate Wildman 12, 14, 176, 215, 353-358, 432, 480, 482
Nakai Yoshiyuki 214-215
Nakamura Kakujō 80
Nakamura Kyōko 420-421
Nakanishi Tamako 421-422
Nakano Sanbin 218
Nakayama Miki 391
names 19
nanshoku 219
Nara 12, 69-70, 77-78, 102, 169, 270, 273, 381, 390-391, 469
Nara ehon 71-72
Nara National Museum 273
Narita Airport 453, 477
National Academy of Sciences 346
National Council for American Education 481
National Defense Education Act (NDEA), 9, 166, 170, 291, 386-387, 485; Title VI 485; *see National Defense Foreign Language Fellowships*

National Defense Foreign Language Fellowships (NDFL) 9-10, 11, 132-3, 146, 183, 185, 280, 291, 342, 388, 485; FLAS 291; *see National Defense Education Act*
National Diet 57, 88, 184, 209, 422, 438
National Diet Building 209, 341, 486
National Diet Library 93, 99, 184, 410, 433, 434
National Institute for Defense Studies, Military Archival Library 54
National Museum of Scotland 227
National Records Center 393
National Treasures (*kokuhō*) 270, 273-274
Natsume Sōseki 157, 206, 217-218, 355, 378, 484
Neumeyer, David 223
New College of Florida 298
New Criticism 205, 211, 229 n. 2, 463
New Historicism 216, 220-221
New Left 11, 18, 191-197
New York 91-93, 118, 158, 246, 322-323, 386
New York University 30, 33
Ngo Dinh Diem 489-490
Ngo Dinh Nhu 96
Nigeria 371, 372-373
Nihon Josei Gakkai 497
Nihonga 42
nikki (poetic diaries) 18, 261, 262
Nikkō 452
nikutai bungaku 393
Ninagawa Yukio 240
Nisei 6
Nishikawa Kyōtarō 75
Nissan Motor Company 11, 494
Niwa Tamako 68
Nixon, Richard M. 489-490, 494
Nobel Prize in Economic Sciences 346
Nobel Prize for Literature 488-489

Nochlin, Linda 270
Nogami Teruyo 223
Nogi Maresuke 54
Noguchi Isamu 290
Noguchi Takehiko 228
Noh 69, 81, 99, 105, 119, 159, 162, 205-206, 208-209, 217, 230 n. 9, 238-241, 260, 292-298, 302 n. 10, 387, 391, 462; New Noh 296-297
Nolan, Vanessa 208
Nolte, Sharon 364
Nornes, Markus 286
North American Coordinating Council on Japanese Library Recourses (NCC) 11, 21-23 n. 5, 101, 247-248, 409, 497
North Carolina State University 404
North Korea 195, 196, 492
The Norton Anthology of Modern Poetry 122, 127
Nosei Chosa Iinkai 145-146
Novograd, Paul 295

Obama, Barack 49, 66
Occupation of Japan 18, 31, 53, 97, 134, 138-140, 310, 332, 383, 386, 393, 471, 474-476, 479, 482, 483; "Reverse Course" 475
Ochanomizu University 178, 251-252 n. 3, 374 n. 2, 501 n. 44
Oda Yori 170, 177
Odagiri Mineko 31-32, 38; *see* Hosokawa Moritatsu 32, 33
Ogata Sadako 94
O'Grady, Megan 17
Ogawa Jihei VII 483
Ogyū Sorai 169
The Ohio State University 167, 281, 283-287
Ohno Tomohiko 349
oil shocks 281, 345, 494-495

Okamoto Kōzō 191
Okano Hirohiko 249
Okinawa 10, 52, 210, 360, 395, 449, 476, 479, 496
Oklahoma 383-384
Oku Mumeo 107
Okudaira Tsuyoshi 492-493
Ōkuma Shigenobu 52-53, 365, 449
Olivar, Cheryl Bocobo 444, 466 n. 3
Olivar, Gary 466 n. 3
Ōmori Shell Mounds 221
Onchi Kōshirō 36-37
Online Computer Library Center 287
Ōoka Makoto 124, 290, 295, 298-300
Ooms, Herman 363
Order of the Precious Crown, with Butterfly Crest 61
Order of the Precious Crown, Wistaria 177
Order of the Rising Sun, Gold Rays with Neck Ribbon 59, 365
Order of the Rising Sun, Gold Rays with Rosette 129
Oresteia 238
Oriental 9, 133
Orientalism 25 n. 19, 219, 244, 310
Osaka 137, 257, 260, 357, 391, 458, 488, 493
Osaragi Jirō 484
Osborne, John 207
Østasiatiske Institut 462
Ostrom, Elinor 346-347: Nobel Prize in Economics 346
Ota no shō 405
Overing, Joanna 418-420
overtext 216-217
Owada Hisashi 334
Oxford University 89, 214
Ozawa Minoru 295

The Pacific Stars and Stripes 482

Paglia, Camille 212-213
Palestine Liberation Organization 492
Palmore, Jay 190
Paris Peace Accords 490
Parsons, Talcott 186-187
Pasco, Peggy 363
Passin, Herbert 6, 326, 328, 371
Patrick, Hugh T. 145-146
Patsy T. Mink Equal Opportunity in Education Act 489; *see* Title IX of the Educational Amendments of 1972
Paulson, Joy 59
Payne-Gaposchkin, Celia 158
Peace Corps 479
Pearl Harbor 50; attack on 8, 13, 50-51, 62, 86, 97, 182, 310, 455, 470, 471-472; Pearl Harbor Day 121
Pelosi, Nancy 238
Pelzel, John 311
PEN Congress 118-119
PEN Translation Prize 126
People's Power Revolution 465
Peterson, Joannah 208
Pharr, Susan J. 11, 15, 104, 321-338, 343, 371, 480, 483, 498
Philippine Normal College 455
Philippines 18, 118, 383, 442, 444-445, 448-451, 454-456, 465, 475; American occupation 447-448; GDP 456; Japanese occupation 455; revolution 448; United States takeover 456; World War II 454-456
Pian, Rulan Chao 67, 174
The Pillow Book 443
Pimsleur, Meira G. 281
Plaza Accord 495
Poetry International Web 124
police brutality 444-446
Pomeranz, Ken 363
Pomona College 384, 386
Poole, Otis Manchester 140

Port Huron Statement 198 n. 2
Portrait of Chin Jung 32; see Yasui Sōtarō
poststructuralism 216, 496-497
Potsdam Declaration 474-475
pregnancy 44, 158, 175, 244, 246, 257-258, 267-272, 276, 277, 295, 314, 347, 405; childbirth 272
President Lines 93, 480
Price, Leontyne 322
Princeton Festival 126
Princeton University 25-26 n. 24, 34, 159-160, 214, 246, 268, 276-277, 281-283, 286-287, 423-426
Pritchard, Earl 87
professional memoirs 17
pronouns 175
"public choice" 348
Public Law 100-383 472
Public Law 503 472
Punahou School 49

Quackenbush, Hiroko 378
Quakers 62-64, 81, 91, 474: Nobel Peace Prize 64; *see American Friends Service Committee (AFSC)*
Quigley, Harold 51
Quimby, Joanne 213
Quinn, Shelley Fenno 209

race 473
racism 210, 454
Radcliffe College 11, 60 n. 5, 68, 90, 144, 156, 212, 364
rakugo 207-208
Rakuhoku Kōkō-mae Kokenchiku Kenkyū-kai 170
Ramirez-Christensen, Esperanza 12, 441-468, 474, 480, 483, 486, 496
Ramseyer, Mark 172
rape 175

Rashomon 481, 502 n. 56
Rasmussen, Ann 91-92
rational choice institutionalism 348, 349 n. 9
Reagan, Ronald 465, 472
Red Army Faction 192-197, 200-201 n. 18, 492-493; hijackings 492-493
Red Cross 30-31
Rediker, Marcus 240
Reed College 6
Rehabilitation Act of 1973 487
Reischauer, Ann 144
Reischauer, Edwin O. 6, 9, 52, 54-55, 91, 144-145, 155, 156-157, 168, 169, 170, 341, 342
Reischauer, Haru 145
Reischauer, Joan 133
Reischauer, Robert K. 177
Reiyūkai Kyōdan 420, 423-425
Rekishi hyōron (*Critical History*) 362, 437
Remak, Henry 219
Remmer, Karen 349
renga 69, 259, 378, 388, 390, 461-464, 467 n. 10
renku 388
Rexroth, Kenneth 293
Rhee, Syngman 38
Rhoads, Esther 62, 64, 107
"Rice Paddies" 9, 68, 84 n. 4, 144, 152 n. 1, 156, 164 n. 1, 168, 179 n. 4, 449
Richards, John 345-346
Richardson, Bradley 285
Richie, Donald 482
Ricoeur, Paul 216
Riesman, David 185-186, 199 n. 7
Rikkyō University 219
Rilling, Paul 319-320
Rimer, Thomas 392
Rizal, Jose 448, 466 n. 3, 466-467 n. 4
Rockefeller, John D. 40, 483

Rockefeller, John D. III 483
Rockefeller, John D. IV (Jay) 385
Rockefeller Center 495
Rockefeller Foundation 9, 11, 40, 43-44, 470, 479-480, 483
Rockefeller Group 495
Rodd, Laurel Rasplica 250, 252 n. 10
Rogers, Ginger 309, 318-319
Rohlen, Tom 188-189
Roman Catholic Church 168, 442, 446
Roosevelt, Eleanor 103, 107
Roosevelt, Franklin D. 86, 240, 471-473
Rosenbluth, Frances McCall 347-348
Rosenfield, John 70, 157, 268-270, 271, 273, 275-276
Rosovsky, Henry 146
Ross, Martha 106
Ruch, Barbara 1, 7-8, 9, 10, 16-17, 61-84, 470, 480
Russian language 144, 197, 280, 311, 419
Rutgers University 55
Ryōanji 442
ryokan 135, 154, 312

Said, Edward 25 n. 19
Saigō Takamori 342
Saigyō 83, 84 n. 13
Saitō Haruo 349
Saitō Mokichi 244-245
Sakaguchi Eiko 106
Sakaguchi Hiroshi 200-201 n. 18
Sakai Yoshinori 488
Sakaiya Taichi 7
Sakakura Junzō 483
Sakamoto Tatsuki 38
salaryman 316
Sale, Roger 211
Salmony, Alfred 34
Samizdat 197

sampaguita (flowers) 442, 455
Sampaguita (magazine) 455
samurai 12, 211, 218, 226, 326-327, 459, 481, 492
Sansom, George 34, 91, 168, 378
Santō Kyōden 219; *see Kitao Masanobu*
Sarashina Diary (*Sarashina nikki*) 262
Sarra, Edith 213
Sato, Barbara 12, 13, 14, 20, 354-355, 371, 431-440, 477, 480, 482
Scalapino, Bob 343
Scandinavia 457
Scheiner, Irv 342
Schlafly, Phyllis 423
Schliemann, Heinrich 254
scholarly generation 8
scholarly memoirs 16-19
Schulman, Frank Joseph 21-23 n. 5, 100
Schwartz, Benjamin 68, 171
Sebald, William J. 478
Second Red Scare 93, 183, 481
Sei Shōnagon 443
Seidensticker, Edward 6, 63, 104, 172, 224, 261, 354-355, 378-381, 387, 471, 484, 489
Seikei University 437-438
Sekine Eiji 215
Sekino Jun'ichirō 37
sekkyō-bushi 163
Semal, Maryell 267
Semimaru 162-163
semiotics 211-212, 219
Senegal 330-331
Seppuku 12, 58, 492
Servicemen's Readjustment Act of 1944 (GI Bill) 9, 473, 479
Setōuchi Jakuchō 396
Sewell Jr., William 362
Sexton, Anne 211
"sexual revolution" 175, 496

Shakespeare, William 206-208, 443
Shapiro, Ian 348
Shaw, George Bernard 205
Shiba Ryōtarō 73
Shibamoto, Janet 373
Shibusawa, Naoko 24 n. 11
Shigemitsu Mamoru 474
Shigenobu Fusako 492-493
shiki (rights to income) 360
Shimada Daisaku 349
Shimada Shūjirō 268, 276
Shimagami Motoko 349
Shimazaki Chifumi 239
Shimizu Yoshiaki 268
Shinchō Chair for Japanese Literature 74
Shinji Nobuhiro 227-228
shinkansen (bullet train) 488
Shinkei 461-463, 465, 468 n. 13
Shinkokinshū 262
Shinozuka Sumiko 261
Shinsen tsukubashū 462
Shinto 78, 424, 425, 427; arts 271-276; shrines 112, 396; talisman 272
Shinto Arts: Nature, Gods, and Man in Japan 267, 274-276
Shiomi Takaya 194, 492
Shirane, Haruo 225-226
Shirato Ichiro 65, 91, 386
Shirayuri University (Shirayuri Joshi Daigaku) 446-447
shite 209, 230 n. 230, 298
Shively, Donald 6, 158, 168, 170, 224, 342, 354-355, 356, 387-388, 392, 403, 407
shōen (manorial system) 360
Shōgun 337
Shohara, Hide 92, 191
Shufu no tomo (*Housewife's Companion*) 434-435
shunga 219, 388

Sibley, Bill 156, 172, 379, 381
Siggins, Jack 100
Silberman, Bernard 87-88, 342
Silent Generation 7
Sippel, Patricia 403, 413-414 n. 1
Smethurst, Mae 98-99, 237-242, 496
Smethurst, Richard 16, 237-242, 363, 484
Smith College 41, 89, 465
Smith, Henry 170, 227
Smith, Joanna Handlin, 176
Smith, Robert 310
Smith, Roy 190
Smith, Thomas Carlyle 165-166, 173-174
Smith, Tom 344
Snyder, Gary 298, 302 n. 10
Snyder, Stephen 409
social hierarchy 332-333
Social Psychology Research Group (Shakai Shinri Kenkyūkai) 435-437: *see Minami Hiroshi*
Social Science Research Council (SSRC) 21-23 n. 5, 146, 160, 421, 488; *see American Council of Learned Societies*
Social Sciences and Humanities Research Council of Canada (SSHRC) 263
Society for International Cultural Relations 494
sociology 311, 334
soft power 269, 337
Sōgi 214, 462-463
Solt, John 225
Somalia 373
Song of the Sea C 20; *see Iwami Reika*
Sony 124, 495
Soper, Alexander C. 34, 41
Sophia University 150, 296, 336, 371-372

Sōsaku-hanga 40, 269
South (USA) 329-330, 419
Southern Education Reporting Service (SERS) 419
Southern Methodist University 364
Soviet Union 9, 144, 197, 280, 291, 343, 474, 475, 480, 481, 485, 490, 495
Spanish colonial rule 447-448
Sputnik I 9, 144, 280, 291, 485
Stanford Center 185, 197, 354-355, 386-387,486; *see also Inter-University Center for Japanese Language Studies*
Stanford University 100-101, 161-162, 178, 185-186, 197, 354, 386-388, 486; Hoover Institute 100, 409
Stanislavski, Konstantin 207
Starbuck, George 117
Steinhoff, Bill 185, 189, 191, 193, 197, 490
Steinhoff, Patricia G. 22, 176, 179-180 n. 12, 181-202, 373, 409, 490, 492
Stoepel, Anne 168
The Story of Yokobue (*Yokobue no sōshi*) 65
StoryCorps 16
Strauss, Harold 90, 484
structuralism 214
Student Nonviolent Coordinating Committee 198 n. 2, 342
Students for a Democratic Society 198 n. 2
The Subjection of Women 172
Suemoto Yōko 427-428
Suganoura in Ōmi 403-405, 414 n. 2
Sugawara no Takasue no Musume 262-263
Sugiyama Yukari 286
Sukiya style 35
The Sumida River 297
Sumitomo Group 11, 494
Sun and Steel 58

INDEX : 597

Supreme Command of the Allied Powers (SCAP) 30-31, 177, 471, 475
Supreme Court of Japan (Saikō Saibansho) 476
Supreme Court of the United States 487
Surplus Property Act 477-478
Survey Research Center (UC Berkeley)
Suzuki Daisetsu (D. T.) 90, 155, 386, 398 n. 3
Suzuki, Michiko 221
Suzuki Seijin 394
Suzuki Tadashi 240
Suzuki Yukio 209
Sweden 489

Tagore, Rabindranath 488
Takagi Kazuko 286
Takagi Kiyoko 5, 13, 162-163, 170, 177-178, 245-246, 249, 252 n. 3, 294-295, 486
Takagi Toshiro 286
Takahashi Tōru 221
Takamori Kentetsu 380
Takazawa Collection 195-196
Takazawa Kōji 192-196
Takeuchi Itsuzo 35
Takeuchi, Melinda 269
Takeuchi Seihō 35
Taki Kazuo 40
The Tale of Genji 64, 66, 104, 183, 205, 213, 218, 226, 227, 261, 291, 305, 381, 386, 387, 389, 443, 460, 465, 466
The Tale of Lady Ochikubo 264-265
Tales of the Heike (Heike monogatari) 80
Tamura Norie 349
Tamura Ryūichi 120-122, 125
Tamura Taijirō 393-394
Tanabe, Willa 269
Tanaka Fund 494

Tanaka Kakuei 494
Tanaka Sumiko 438-439
"Tanaka Ten" 148, 176, 180 n. 13, 494; see Japan Foundation
Taniguchi Senkichi 394
Tanikawa Shuntarō 120-121, 124-125, 127
Tange Kenzō 312, 493
Tange Ume 476
Tanimoto Kiyoshi 474
Tanizaki, Jun'ichirō 136-138, 140, 214, 249-251, 378, 456, 460, 484
tanka 18, 244-246, 249-250, 254, 262, 294-295, 381
Tan-o Yasunori 219
tatemae 310
Tateno Nobuyuki 118
Tawara Machi 381
tea ceremony 315-316
Teeuwen, Mark 357
Temple University, Japan 438
ten Grotenhuis, Elizabeth 271, 273
tenkō 187-189, 196, 197, 198
Tennyson, Alfred Lord Tennyson 206
Tenri University 390-392
Tenrikyō 291
"terminal uniqueness" 265
terrorism 191-195, 492-493
Tet Offensive 490
Teters, Barbara 98-99
Thailand 44, 158, 346, 444
theater 206-209
Theses on Spirits 355-356
"third-culture kids" 132, 137
This Is Your Life 474
Thomas, Roger 235 n. 72
Thomson, Jamie 346
Thought Section in the Criminal Affairs Bureau of the Ministry of Justice (Shihōsho Keijikyoku Shisōbu) 188

"The Three Priests"(Sannin hōshi) 65-66
Three Sacred Mountains of Dewa 395-397
Thrupp, Sylvia 171
Tiedemann, Arthur 96-97
Tilly, Charles 172
Tilly, Louise 171
Title IX of the Educational Amendments of 1972 7, 15, 170-171, 173, 174, 178, 489; see Patsy T. Mink Equal Opportunity in Education Act
Tōhoku Imperial University 476
Tōjō Hideki 475
Tōjō Kimie 156
Tōkai University 461-462
Tokugawa Ieyasu 236 n. 80, 452
Tokuriki Tomikichirō 36
Tokyo 19, 30-31, 37-38, 41, 52, 93, 98, 138-140, 145-146, 155, 184-185, 219, 221, 226, 236 n. 81, 312, 315, 442-443, 446-457, 464, 488
Tokyo Anthology: Literature from Japan's Modern Metropolis, 1850–1920 226
Tokyo Detention House 193, 200-201 n. 18
Tokyo Olympics (1964) 98, 152, 312, 458, 488, 493
Tokyo University of the Arts 53, 78-79
Tokyo Women's Christian University (Tokyo Joshi Daigaku) 206, 261
Tokugawa Art Museum 227
Tolman Collection 20
Tomimoto Kenkichi 40, 45 n. 2
Torigoe Bunzō 450
Torrance, Richard 283
Toshiba International Foundation 238-239, 241
Totman, Conrad 407, 415 n. 9
trailblazer 6

trailblazing generation 7
translation 120, 122, 124-127, 222-227, 249-250, 264-265, 271, 459-460, 484
transpacific flights 477
Treaty of San Francisco 34, 475, 485
Triangle East Asia Colloquium 345, 404, 406
triple disaster of earthquake, tsunami, and nuclear meltdown (March 11, 2011) 137, 250
Troost, Kristina Kade 12, 18, 345, 401-418, 485
Truman, Harry S. 475, 481, 483
Tsubouchi Memorial Theatre Museum 207
Tsubouchi Shōyō 207, 450, 454
Tsuda College 116, 421
Tsuda Umeko 116, 127 n. 1
Tsujimoto Isao 248, 250
tsukeku 462, 467 n. 10
Tsukuba University 296, 302 n. 8, 397
Tsuneishi, Warren 410
Tsunoda Ryūsaku 6, 23 n. 8, 65
Tsurumi Kazuko 282, 287 n. 1, 336, 372
Tsurusaki Hiro'o 461
Tsutsumi Harue 208
Tung, James S. K. 281-282
Tylbor, Henry 289-290
Tyler, Royall 209

Uchikawa Yoshimi 433
Uchūfū 245, 246, 249, 251, 294
Ueda Yasuo 437
Uegaki, Yasuhiro 200-201 n. 18
Uehara Toyoaki 389-392
Ui Jun 343
Ulak, James 227
Umewaka Naohiko 297-298
Umezu Yoshijirō 474
UNESCO World Heritage Site 482

INDEX : 599

United Nations 44, 104, 118, 280, 372, 421, 446, 475, 480
United Nations Decade for Women 496
United Nations Development Programme (UNDP) 372
United Nations Korean Reconstruction Agency (UNKRA) 44
United Nations Relief and Rehabilitation Administration (UNRRA) 32-33
United Nations University 422
United Red Army 123, 193-194, 200-201 n. 18, 493
University of Alberta 258, 260, 262
University of Arizona 59, 156, 365
University of British Columbia 255-260
University of Calgary 260
University of California, Berkeley 6, 8, 22, 24 n. 17, 94, 113, 157, 161-162, 165-166, 171, 173-174, 178, 340-343, 384, 452, 457-460
University of California, Irvine 363
University of Chicago 11, 24 n. 17, 87, 100, 156, 361, 362, 394, 418, 420, 424, 481
University of Colorado Boulder 55-56, 101, 364-365, 471
University of Georgia 41-42, 44
University of Hawai'i 49, 170, 188-198, 258, 318, 369-371, 374; *see* East-West Center
University of Iowa 30, 117-118, 119-121
University of Kansas 276
University of Kyoto 35-36, 477
University of Library and Information Science (Tsukuba University) 296
University of Malaya 371
University of Maryland 24 n. 17, 97-105, 372-373, 391-394
University of Michigan 8, 35, 67, 156, 159, 170-173, 177, 181-184, 238, 465
University of Minnesota 6, 48, 50-51, 88, 457
University of Pennsylvania 64-65, 68-69, 106, 473
University of the Philippines 455
University of Pittsburgh 99, 238-241, 285
University of the Sacred Heart (Seishin Joshi Daigaku) 446
University of Tennessee 389
University of Texas 55, 342, 361, 365
University of Tokyo 14, 23 n. 8, 53, 93, 177, 187, 192, 195, 206, 219, 227, 240, 271, 284, 293, 294, 312, 315, 362, 364, 387, 420, 432-435, 476, 477, 486
University of Tokyo, Institute of Social Science 187-188, 192, 195, 342-343
University of Toronto 262-263
University of Utah 362-363
University of Vermont 432
University of Washington 8, 12, 24 n. 17, 147-148, 151, 211, 257, 478-479
University of Wisconsin 336-337, 360, 364
University of Wyoming 359
US Air Force 166, 168
US Department of State 6, 88, 117, 373-374, 478, 480, 486
US Department of War 8, 474
US-Japan Conference on Cultural and Education Interchange (CULCON) 248, 486, 496
US-Japan relations 334
US-Japan Security Treaty 140, 209, 485-486, 449, 475

US National Student Association 184-185, 199 n. 4
US Naval Base Subic Bay 444
US Navy Japanese Language School 6, 87, 106, 178, 471
US Office of War Information 13
USS Missouri 474
uta-awase 259

Valentine, Alice 403
Vanderbilt University 418-420
Vanis, Deborah 345
Varley, Paul 166
Victoria and Albert Museum 227, 274
Violet, Andrew 13, 48
Vietnam War 12, 18, 96, 98, 100, 133, 164 n. 11, 168, 169, 184, 186, 193, 257, 280, 390, 418, 428 n. 1, 444-445, 449, 457, 489-491
Vining, Elizabeth 64
Vogel, Ezra 68, 123, 187-188, 197, 200 n. 14, 310, 314-315, 318, 334, 337, 371; see *Japan as Number One: Lessons for America*, *Japan's New Middle Class*
Vogel, Suzanne, 310, 317, 371
Vonnegut, Kurt 118

Wagatsuma Sakae 438
waka 222, 256, 262, 378, 443, 450, 454, 459, 462, 463
Wakayama University English Speaking Society 185
Waley, Arthur 64, 66, 291; translation of *The Pillow Book* 443; translation of *The Tale of Genji* 64, 386
Walsh, Martha Lane 176
Walthall, Anne 11, 357, 359-368, 407, 427
Walthall, Wilson 360-361
Wang, Ching-hsien 217

Wang, Sook Young 462, 467 n. 12
war crimes trials 475
War History Library 56-57
War Measures Act of 1914
Warnke, Frank J. 217
Warren, Elizabeth 198 n. 1
Waseda University 25-26 n. 24, 52-53, 206-210, 211, 219, 362, 389, 434, 446, 449-451, 457, 488; student protests 12, 209-211, 228, 449-450
Washington and Southeast Regional Seminar on Japan 105-106
Wasserstrom, Amy 106
Waswo, Ann 387
Watanabe Kenji 219, 228
Watanabe Norifumi 404-405
Watanabe Yōzō 348
Wayne State University 87
Weatherby, Meredith 290, 484
Webb, Herschel 92, 95, 247
Weed, Ethel 386
Weinstein, Michael 188-189
Weis, Anne 241
Wellek, René 214, 231 n. 27
Wellesley College 44-45
West Africa 325-327, 330, 331, 346
Westmoreland, General William 418, 428 n. 1
Wheelwright, Carolyn 268-269
White, Hayden 88, 108 n. 5, 137
White, James 404, 414 n. 4
White, Merry 11, 309-320, 336, 372, 403, 480, 488
White, Lynn Jr. 345
Wiegman, Robyn 212
Wigen, Kären 412
Wigmore, John Henry 357-358
Wilbur, C. Martin 91-93, 95
Wilde, Oscar 205
Willoughby, General Charles 482
Wilson, George 390

Wiswell, Ella (Embree) Lury 310
Women Accepted for Volunteer
  Emergency Service (WAVES) 6, 471
The Women of Suye Mura 310
Women's Army Corps (WAC) 6, 471
women's colleges, Japan 476-477
women's history 361-362, 363-364
"women's lib" 211, 258, 300, 318
women's magazines 434-437, 439
women's studies 11, 18, 79, 103, 191,
  362, 363, 432; in Japan 11, 432, 497
Wong, R. Min 363
Woodrow Wilson Fellowship 331, 341-
  342, 480
Woolf, Virginia 191, 211, 261
World House Galleries 42, 43, 44, 45
  n. 20
World Monuments Fund 77-78
  World War II 8, 88, 120-121, 204-
  205, 383, 444, 471-475, 477
Wu, K. T. 281-282
Wurgaft, Benjamin 318

Yale University 8, 10, 11, 25-26 n. 24,
  41, 63, 91, 98, 100, 145-146, 160,
  188, 211, 220, 269, 286, 347, 348,
  359, 363, 364, 481, 494
Yamabushi 396-397
Yamakawa Kikue 436, 439
Yamamoto Kenkichi 122
Yamamoto Miyabi (Abbie) 293
Yamamoto Takeo 293
Yamamoto Tsunetomo 452
Yamamura Kozo 146-152
Yamamura Yoichi 251
Yamanaka Reiko 240
Yamashita Utako 349
Yanagi Sōetsu 40, 46 n. 11
Yanagida Seizan 257-258
Yanagisawa Taki 273
Yano, Christine 317, 318

Yasuda, Kenneth 392
Yasui Sōtarō 31, 32
Yasumaru Yoshio 435
Yayoi period 340
Yeats, William Butler 239, 302 n. 10
Yim, Kwan Ha 166
Yim Tse 259-260
Yodogō group 192, 194-196, 492
yoga 384
Yokohama 140-141
Yokohama Harbor 29, 62
Yokomichi Mario 297
yomikudashi kanbun (Sino-Japanese
  readings) 463
Yomiuri newspaper 317, 318
Yoneyama Toshinao 113
Yosa Buson 125-126, 295
Yosano Akiko 296, 300-301, 484
Yoshida Shigeru 478, 484
Yoshimura Junzō 483
Yoshiwara 234 n. 60
Yotsumoto Yasuhiro 124-125
Yu, Issac 347
Yugenoshima no shō 404-405
Yuriko Doi's Theatre 298

Zasshi kiji sakuin 410, 411
"Zen boom" 386
Zen Buddhism 12, 83, 257, 269, 345,
  386, 391, 462, 489; Zen abbesses 74-
  75, 83; Zen monks
  256, 260; *see Buddhism*
Zengakuren 209, 450, 486
Zhuangzi 263, 384, 388
Zōjōji Temple 297-298
Zolbrod, Leon 388-389, 395
Zwerman, Gilda 196

Discussion Questions

1. Why is it important to record personal stories? What can they teach us?
2. What do these personal stories by trailblazing women teach us about the construction of the field of Japanese Studies? About gender and inclusion in the academy?
3. What did you learn about Japanese Studies between 1950 and 1980? How is the field then different and similar to how it is today?
4. How do these trailblazing women's careers represent changes in Japan-US relations?
5. How are the formation of academic fields affected by both global politics and personal choices?
6. How have women faced different challenges than people of other genders?
7. Which chapters in particular did you find more compelling, educational, or instructive? Why?
8. What are memorable pieces of advice you have learned from this book? How will you use this advice in your life and career?
9. What generation are you a part of? How do your historical times affect your development?
10. What can we learn by writing and reading memoirs? How do they differ from other kinds of writing?
11. If you could write your own scholarly memoir, what events, encounters, and people would you feature? How would you write the account? Would it be straightforward? Poetic? Funny? Serious? Who would you like to read it?
12. Please think about a person, book, or event that changed your life or career. How did it change you? How would you write about it?
13. Please find a photograph of an important moment in your personal development. Would you include it in your memoir? How would you write about it?
14. What is your favorite quote from the book? Why is this quote so impactful?

GPSR Authorized Representative: Easy Access System Europe, Mustamäe tee 50, 10621 Tallinn, Estonia, gpsr.requests@easproject.com